A Theology of Compassion

'This long-awaited book is theology of a high order. Oliver Davies interweaves many texts, periods and disciplines with a sure sense of the heart of Christian truth and life. The book pivots around a profound insight into the nature of divine and human compassion, tracing its implications through rich conversations and culminating in a constructive systematic theology.'

David F. Ford, Regius Professor of Divinity, University of Cambridge

'In *A Theology of Compassion*, being is back. With gratitude to postmodernism for dethroning those who sought to displace her (substance or *ousia*, *totum*, *simul* and the like), Oliver Davies reaches back long before modernity to retrieve the one who merits the throne: for him, this is being as image of the triune God and as medium of the relation of self to other. To retrieve being is to regenerate the conditions of robust selfhood: not the narcissist self of modernity, but the self-dispossessing creature of a kenotic, compassionate God. Davies' book is a subtle, discerning, and loving reformation of the history of European metaphysics and theology.'

Peter Ochs, Edgar M. Bronfman Professor of Modern Judaic Studies, University of Virginia

A Theology of Compassion

Metaphysics of Difference and the Renewal of Tradition

Oliver Davies

scm press

© Oliver Davies 2001

British Library Cataloguing in Publication data

A catalogue record for this book is available
from the British Library

0 334 02833 7

First published in 2001 by SCM Press
9–17 St Albans Place, London N1 0NX

SCM Press is a division of
SCM-Canterbury Press Ltd

Typset by Regent Typesetting, London
and printed in Great Britain by
Biddles Ltd, Guildford and King's Lynn

For Denys, in the spirit of conversation

אמר לו : לפי מעשי אני נקרא. פעמים שאני נקרא אל שדי, צבאות, אלהים, ה׳
כשאני דן את הבריות
אני נקרא אלהים, וכשאני תולה על חטאיו של אדם אני נקרא אל שדי,
וכשאני עושה מלחמה ברשעים
אני נקרא צבאות, וכשאני מרחם על עולמי אני נקרא ה׳

Rabbi Abba bar Mammel said: God said to Moses: I am called according to
my acts. At times I am called El Shaddai, Seba'ot, Elohim and Yahweh.
When I judge creatures, I am called Elohim; when I forgive sins, I am called
El Shaddai; when I wage war against the wicked, I am called Seba'ot, and
when I show compassion for my world, I am called Yahweh.

Rabbah on Ex. 3.14

Contents

I
THE METAPHYSICS OF COMPASSION

II
A THEOLOGY OF COMPASSION

Preface

Some books are long in the gestation. This is such a book. The central idea of 'kenotic ontology' came to me, quite suddenly, over ten years ago when in conversation (about something quite different, as I recall) with Rowan Williams, who was then Professor of Divinity at the University of Oxford. I still remember the sense for a period of days afterwards of 'something having happened', but it has taken me all these years to work out what it was in such a way that it can be communicated to the reader, for whom, presumably, it was given in the first place. The writing of this book then has been a journeying with others, in unfolding conversations. In many ways it has been constructed out of conversations, and the multiple debts that I have built up are to those who have shared their time with me over the years, their wisdom, experience and enthusiasm for ideas which are difficult in their realizations. I owe a particular debt of gratitude to Denys Turner and David Ford, of the University of Cambridge. From both I have learned different things in different ways. But I do not think the book could have reached its present form without their active support.

My own theological history began when as a secular liberal, growing up in a generation for whom secular liberalism was a religious way of life, I began inadvertently to read the work of Meister Eckhart. Inchoately I read in those texts the sense that transfigured life has something to do with the nature of text itself, and that therefore certain kinds of texts can at times have an immense capacity to transform us from within, opening out new horizons of existence and meaning. Perhaps a similar instinct prompted me to choose to do doctoral work at Oxford on Paul Celan, a German-speaking Jewish poet, whose poems or 'fragments' are counted among the most powerfully expressive works of art to come out of the Holocaust. Celan confronted me not only with the deepest issues of the post-Holocaust world, but also, once again, with the redemptive power of text. When conversion came for me, one wet afternoon in Oxford, it was bound up with the sudden sense that secular liberalism and existentialism are nothing more than moderated forms of egotism, and that meaning which is hidden (and which is textual meaning) is so much more complex, and therefore interesting, than non-meaning. I knew that I needed to live in and through metaphors of depth rather than surface. And I felt that texts and questions regarding the nature of text would be at the heart of my theological journey.

A book with a lengthy gestation also entails the nomadic wanderings of its author. In my case, this was bound up with the discovery over years that a book on the nature of the self inevitably becomes, or should become, an unfolding of the self who is writing the book. For me this was the gathering realization that I was myself inescapably implicated both in the very thing that I was reflecting upon and in the act of writing about those reflections. The dialogues, textually mediated, with Etty Hillesum, Edith Stein and an unnamed saintly woman, became crucial foci for the deepening sense of myself as author as one teased apart, fractured, pummelled in the very process of producing the book of which I was supposedly in command. There is a certain instability of the authorial self at the very centre of this book therefore (which can perhaps be glimpsed in an occasional tension between the use of an authorial 'I' and 'we'). In the preface to a recent work, Stanley Hauerwas has spoken of his own authorial voice as an 'agonized I', and looks forward to the day when authors will come forward who are free of such a 'transitional' self. My experience has been both cognate and different. Increasingly the 'agonized' self has seemed to me to be the sole site in which radically creative, free-flowing dispossession – as ethical agent and as author – is possible. My discovery has been in writing this book that 'transition' is integral to selfhood as such, and that the struggle with transition, painful and liberating at once, is the self's – that is, my own – struggle with what it is to be a human being, hovering between narratives both human and divine. The discovery that the self is paradoxically most realized in its radical self-dispossession, and that this condition is an essential part of what it is to be a *creature* of the triune God, is the unifying theme of this book.

Amongst those whose conversations have been integral to this project are Paul Fiddes and Rowan Williams, from both of whom I gained immensely, as is Julius Lipner, who carefully read and critiqued the text with kind perspicacity. Catrin Williams, a friend and former colleague at University of Wales Bangor, generously read through the scriptural sections of the book and greatly helped me with the esoteric skills of exegetical style and referencing. I am indebted to her also for much detailed help with rabbinic sources. Any remaining infelicities are of course my own. My former colleague Gavin Flood has been a constant companion and interlocutor, always at hand to help with the finer points of theory and to suggest, dubiously, that a ten-mile run will clear the mind. My thanks go too to colleagues at Lampeter, especially Rosemary Wright, David Cockburn and David Walford. I am grateful also to Anna Hardman of SCM Press, and especially to Alex Wright, its director, whose visionary editorial engagement with modern theology has been a constant and invaluable support. I owe a debt of thanks also to Philip Hillyer and to Kathryn Wolfendale for their fine editorial work. I would also like to thank Wyn Thomas for compiling the indexes, and for valuable comments on the project from an early stage.

I owe thanks to the Principal and Fellows of Regent's Park College, Oxford, for awarding me a visiting fellowship at the Centre for the Study of Christianity and Culture in 1998 and for electing me as a continuing fellow of the Centre. I am in the debt also of the President and Fellows of Clare Hall, Cambridge, for electing me as visiting fellow in 1999. These periods of residence in Oxford and Cambridge gave me valuable access to superb research facilities and to the equally valuable fellowship of many scholarly companions, especially David Moss, Lucy Gardner, Larry Kreitzer, Dan Hardy, Ben Quash and Nick Adams. My thanks go also to Laurence Hemming and Susan Parsons for their comments and concern. I am also deeply in the debt of Peter Ochs, whose invitation to the University of Virginia gave me the opportunity to discuss the central ideas of the book with Robert Gibbs, Martin Kavka, John Milbank and Jamie Ferreira. It was Peter who pointed out that I was in effect producing a pragmatic repairing of the ontological tradition, which was a most timely and creative insight.

Last but not least my thanks go to my wife, Fiona Bowie, and to my sons Isaac and Rory, for lightening the burden and for reminding me of what life is really about.

Oliver Davies
2001

Introduction

La salamandre surprise s'immobilise
Et feint la mort.
Tel est le premier pas de la conscience dans les pierres,
Le mythe le plus pur,
Un grand feu traversé, qui est esprit.

The startled salamander freezes
And feigns death.
This is the first step of consciousness among the stones,
The purest myth,
A great fire passed through, which is spirit.

Yves Bonnefoy

For Christians, the question of what it means to be human has been intimately linked with the question of what it means to be. Christianity speaks of the loss of self for the sake of others, of death and eternal life, and has a necessary commitment to the language of being and to an understanding of the self as self-possessing to the extent that it can knowingly put itself at risk for the sake of the other. In every intellectual age that intimate conversation between selfhood and the philosophy of existence has been taken up anew. But we have today the sense that the multiple social and cultural forces of modernity, and the diverse deconstructionist critiques which they have engendered, have gone far in dismantling all the major forms of Christian metaphysics. The Thomist philosophy of *differentiae* has continually offered new possibilities of renewal, but these have in general been confined to Catholic circles and have stood in tension with Kantian and post-Kantian thought alike. Cartesianism, on the other hand, has exercised a profound and widespread influence on the European mind, positing substantialism and the idea that human existence is a kind of fixed rational substance, set in opposition to the world. On this account, God too exists as substance, though of an infinite kind, and his existence is the guarantee of our own. But the Christian God is in retreat, and the very notion of substance and the substantial has given way to an understanding of reality based upon process and the play of forces. The human self gathers and is dispersed in a dramatic interplay of genetic, social, economic and psychological determinations, which govern us from within and from without. The various advances in our understanding of the causalities that make us what we are have served both to liberate and to illumine. But they have also called the subject into question, obscuring the boundaries between self and other, in such a way that dethroning of the self has become 'the rite of passage through which we proclaim our postmodernism'.[1] In the modern world our encounter with otherness, with the alien or strange, begins not at the borders of the self, but rather *within the self*, at the very core of our identity, and in a way that challenges the self-possession of the subject. Lacking an uncontested centre, the self comes to its own self-awareness through its acquisitive demands: we exist unequivocally as consumers. Our appetite for goods defines our existence, and is reflected in the enticements of the commercial cosmos of advertising and sales. We know ourselves too as the bearers of claims and rights, enjoying an identity in law and real but limited participation in the political life of our communities. But who is it that exercises those rights? Who is it that consumes?

In the realm of religion we encounter this loss of the self as the 'death of the soul'. The language of Christian selfhood as God's *creature* seems curiously out of date to many today, somehow suggestive of cosmologies long since repudiated. In the Bible and in church tradition we inherit an integrated covenantal cosmology, with humanity as its privileged focus. By and large, such a creation is a place in which we find ourselves deeply at home. But such convictions for the modern Christian necessarily coexist with a range of beliefs of another provenance with an entirely different trajectory. These convey the sense of a world in which the emergence of the human race is the arbitrary product of natural selection, and the cosmos itself a theatre of energies which is wholly indifferent to the fate of human kind. We may indeed lack the genetic parameters for survival as a technologically advanced species. Our thinking may be problem-solving and essentially short-term, so that we are destined as a species to play a brief 'walk-on' part in the cosmic drama of life. Being uncertain as to who we are, we are equally disorientated as to our destiny.

It is the purpose of the present book to contribute to the establishing of a new narrative and philosophical space that is hospitable to the human self, in all its creative potentialities, through the renewal of the language of being. This is a task that is undertaken in the belief that contemporary Christianity demands an ontology, which encloses and unifies, if the self is not to be shipwrecked in a sea of incommensurability, fragmentation and the impersonal play of forces, and if Christianity itself is not to be put at risk as a religion of personalist and existential commitments. Also, although the ontology developed in this volume is primarily viewed under the aspect of human subjectivity, it does of itself contain possibilities for more cosmological readings concerning the nature of the world in which we live, and thus for refiguring the createdness of the world as well as the creatureliness of the self. The thematization of 'being', in variations upon the *analogia entis*, held a central place in patristic and medieval accounts of the world as divine creation, as it does still in Catholic theological tradition.[2] To cast this aside would be to step outside the order of Catholic thinking. But at the same time the ontological project stands in need of radical renewal. The thinking of 'difference', in opposition to the unity of being, is far too deeply rooted in modern thought to be a mere secular fashion. The multiple critiques of ontology by the many philosophers of difference who govern critical thinking today have highlighted the extent to which ontologies presuppose identity, thus prioritizing system and order over singularity and difference so that the self is constrained into pre-ordained formations and subtly made subject to an orchestration of social and cultural power.[3] The spontaneity, creativity and freedom of the self rebels against such a prior scripting of our destiny. Being is the medium of relation between self and other, and the language of being is the thinking of that relation. But this tendency of ontology to impose a prior order and system of the most intimate kind on both self and other can rapidly become the 'ontological violence' of which Levinas speaks and to which he has opposed his own concept of pure ethical relation.

Twentieth-century philosophical theologians such as Erich Przawara, Karl Rahner and Hans Urs von Balthasar developed subtle and powerful syntheses and transformations of the traditional concepts of being. But there is a sense that the metaphysics they represent, which was formulated in the main in the early twentieth century, perpetuates in some degree what Paul Ricoeur has called 'the self-positing *cogito*'. It fails in some degree to be truly adequate to the contemporary experience of the self, which is disjunctively distributed through the multiple alterities of biological, psycho-analytical, linguistic and socio-economic deconstructions. A metaphysics for today must in the first place accommodate the specifically *dialectical* encounter with the other, not only in terms of the various narratives that serve to dissolve the boundaries of the self, exposing it to the *Unheimlichkeit* of its own indeterminacy, but also the encounter with the other in demonic guise, which in the form of dispossession and systemic violence, is also part of our historical situatedness. Dispossession in the form of 'the camp', in all its many variations, has a particular resonance in the modern world, with its apparatus of statehood and arbitrary realizations of 'sovereign power'.[4] Amongst these, the Shoah has posed a particular challenge to the values, beliefs and forms of traditional European civilization. Levinas was right to insist that the Shoah calls for a radical turn to ethics in the contemporary project of reasoning. My disagreement with Levinas lies principally in his opposition between ethics and the language of being.

Metaphysics must be thought today in a way that is not an act of retrieval, courting the danger of falling back into retrenchment. We should heed the warning that the simple repetition of frozen speculative systems from the past will fail to convince (Paul Ricoeur).[5] We should avoid 'the imitation substantiality of a metaphysics renewed one more time' (Jürgen

Habermas).[6] Above all, it is necessary to reject the tendency which is inherent in the tradition of *Subjektphilosophie* to assume the referential validity of philosophy of consciousness so that each system is set up in opposition to others with respect to a perceived givenness of the order of things. This is a competitive alignment in which access to reality is disputed and the linguistic, or model-like, characteristics of language about 'being' are left out of view. The method applied in this book is not one predicated upon reference in this sense but rather upon interpretation, and is therefore pragmatic in shape. This means that I read existence itself as the Ur-Text, or the foundation of what is, in reliance upon Judaeo-Christian accounts of creation in and through divine utterance. Human texts and textualities stand in a participative relation to the Ur-Text therefore, but can gain no definitive purchase upon it, since it exceeds any one interpretation or any one set of interpretations predicated upon it. Existence itself is a primal – and divine – bestowal which remains unknown in itself but becomes variously encoded at the point where it precipitates in the formations of culture and speech. Formal ontology, or language about being, is more properly a way of speaking about 'being' therefore which is an existential performativity of the self, as it participates in the primal bestowal unknowable in itself.[7] Ontology is a fundamental or essential narrative of the self which allows us to performatively grasp and enact the shape of existence as it comes to us in the codings of a particular language of 'being'. The principle that existence yields itself into the formations of culture and language and is not itself a point of reference external to the patterns of ontological thought and language against which they are to be competitively measured, allows us to locate our own 'kenotic ontology' as a corrective reading within a continuing sequence of interpretative ontologies which are themselves interpretations at work upon earlier sequencings. It will itself rightly become subject to yet further interpretations. It is this pragmatic method which grounds the corrective redeployment of interpretative strategies from the philosophy of consciousness tradition which characterizes the 'kenotic ontology' found in these pages, seeking to potentiate the unknowability of the primal bestowal in a manner which is congruent with some of the deepest histories of the contemporary world.

Amongst these, primacy belongs to the principle of *difference*. In kenotic ontology, 'being' is thought not beyond or above difference, but rather within difference: indeed, precisely as *ontology of difference*. The Shoah, which is the most acute historical encounter with difference in its demonic guise, is an extreme manifestation of the potentiality towards violence which is still part of our human condition. Indeed, the lesson of the Shoah is that far from making violence a thing of the past, the very sophistication of the social, scientific and administrative systems of our modern world makes an even more annihilating violence possible. Any metaphysics for today needs to be articulated in the memory of the victims of such violence, and in mindfulness of the propensity for violence which remains within us. But difference can be directly perceived too within the domain of the self. If intersubjectivity is the interweaving of self and other, then its most intensive form is compassion. In compassion the self experiences the other primordially, not as a 'second subject' whose own experiences are to be exploited for our own pleasures ('sharing another's joys') but as another who suffers and whose sufferings – against any perceivable self-interest or motivation of the self – become not our own, since they are always recognized as being the suffering of another, but become the cause of our action *as if they were our own*. It is natural for us to seek to escape from pain, but in compassionate acts we expose ourselves to the possibility of suffering by acting on behalf of another whose suffering nevertheless remains their suffering and not ours. In the compassionate moment we acknowledge – as I shall argue – the deep sociality of consciousness in the embrace of a dialectical mutuality of self and other.

The learning of a new language of being, pragmatically construed, entails an attentiveness both to the annihilating encounter with difference within history, as exemplified by the Shoah, and a prioritization of compassion as the most intense encounter with the other within the normative experience of the self. These two domains come together in three narratives of radical, compassionate resistance to the violence of difference within history, which serve as the ground of this analysis. Etty Hillesum and Edith Stein were caught up in the deportations of the Shoah, while an unnamed woman experienced the trauma of ethnic cleansing in Bosnia. The actuality of these historical occurrences eludes final representation, but I have come as close as possible to them through the use of first person accounts and the narratives of eyewitnesses. These texts mediate to us compassionate agency from the past, and are ways of making present to us the dynamic form of compassionate consciousness. In other words, the analysis contained in the following chapter is, to paraphrase Edith Wyschogrod, a 'thinking in the presence of the saints'.[8] As analytical subject, I am not myself a free-standing autonomous self therefore, but rather an individual who is held under the sway of compassion as mediated in these texts. The reading of these texts is itself a form of compassionate engagement with the compassionate actions which they narrate, and is itself an embrace of the dialectical structure of my own consciousness which finds in the compassionate act its own fulfilling realization. Indeed, the project as a whole can be seen to be an unfolding, both dialogical and reflexive, of the *bonum diffusivum sui*: the conviction that goodness of itself communicates across space and time and founds an ethical community. In the language of kenotic ontology developed in the following chapters, this is understood to be the intrinsic attraction of compassion as the site of intensified or enriched existence. The phenomenological reduction which forms the first part of our argument seeks to lay bare the intentional structure of the compassionate act. The subject who emerges is one who is most intimately and constitutively determined by otherness, who comes to itself *negatively* and *dialectically*, precisely in the self-emptying, de-centring processes of dispossession which are the internal form of compassion. This generates a performative language of self-realization as compassionate and joyful personhood that discovers itself to be fundamentally ecstatic, ethical and playful. I shall argue that compassion assumes the self-possession and self-knowing of the subject, without which the subject cannot put itself at risk for another but can only be put at risk by forces alien to itself.[9] If compassion is *knowingly* to put oneself at risk for the sake of the other, then self-dispossessive virtue is predicated upon a prior state of self-possession. Within this 'knowingly' then, we can begin to discern the possibility of a language of being, which can enable the self performatively to articulate its own sense of existing, precisely as a subject who comes to itself *in and through the other*.

The second stage of the argument is what I have termed a theological reduction of compassion. The dispossessive moment – in the argument given in Chapter Two – is so structured that infinite and finite combine in the affirmation of the suffering other. This compassionate affirmation entails both an act of affirming the world, or existence itself, along an infinite trajectory and an act of affirming the concrete other along a finite trajectory. This complex structure of compassion means that it contains an openness to the possibility of the affirmation of an infinite, personal other which, for the Christian, is realized in faith. The theological reduction of compassion then is the discovery that in Jesus Christ, as 'the compassion of God' (cf. Luke 1.78), God has already preceded us. The dialectical truth of our own nature, which is enacted in compassion, finds its centre in the dialectical truth of the divine nature, as divine self-emptying and self-dispossession for the sake of the creation. Just as the God of Genesis creates through divine speech, God renews and refigures the creation through an intensification of the speech act in an incarnational movement which is a divine 'speaking-with'. This is a calling of the creation and of humanity as the speaking image of God to an equality of conversation. Thus the compassion of God is enacted in terms of the originary language of creation: compassion itself is a modality of the divine creativity. And the entry of the compassion of God into the world is the institution of a new form of communication and thus of relation with human kind predicated upon an equality between God and humanity realized in the person of Jesus Christ. A further stage of our theological reduction of compassion is reached with an analysis of the triadic speech of the Trinity which is mediated to us in and through the Incarnate Word. This self-communication of God is interpreted in terms of Bakhtinian readings of speech, stressing the plurality and sociality of language and its world-donating properties. Trinitarian speech itself is understood to be a form of 'envoicing', whereby the voice of one inhabits another, and Jesus Christ is the one in whom a plurality of voices, both human and divine, are united within a single hypostasis. Through him, and the multiple ways of speaking which he embodies, the alien otherness of the creation is taken back into the divine fecundity of the originary trinitarian speech. I shall be attentive in particular to the silence of the Father on the cross, as an eschatological moment in which the very condition of speech as social interaction and as the reality-forming principle is regenerated and restored. Jesus, as the compassion of God, is the way in which God allows human speaking to enter the triadic speech of the divine, and – through the power of a renewed manifestation of the Spirit – allows a divine speaking redemptively to enter the disordered discourses of the creation.

Reflection upon Jesus as the compassion of God, within a framework which understands the self-dispossession of compassion to be a radicalization or intensification of being, sets up an alignment between divinity and existence which recalls the paranomastic self-description of God as *ehyeh ašer ehyeh* ('I am that I am', 'I will be who I will be', or 'I am He that is') recorded at Ex. 3.14. This text has exercised a long fascination upon the Greek and Christian mind and, from earliest times, has been understood to express the sovereign self-containment of the divine being as *necessary* and independent of the changeability and passions of the world. But the emphasis upon divine compassion and creativity as modalities of ontology developed in this book is a contestation of the received 'Athenian' reading of Ex. 3.14. The identification of the divine being implicit in the Tetragrammaton with the compassionate acts of God and with the originary divine creativity for which this book argues looks back to early rabbinic readings of Ex. 3.14 in which an implicit divine 'ontology' of a very different structure from that of Greek tradition was proposed. It is possible therefore to read this book as a reflection upon the phenomenological moment of compassion as a radical modality of goodness, the *bonum diffusivum sui*, revealing a self who, in contrast with the 'grey' self of many postmodern texts, is exuberantly self-possessing in its own existence, foundationally reciprocal, and inhabiting a space which is co-gifted by and with the other. Knowing itself to be self-in-relation, self-through-relation, it discovers too, in the theological reduction, that it is already in relation with the ecstatic personhood of Christ, who – as the compassion of God – speaks *with* us, through the combining of past and future in the unfolding of a eucharistic present which is at once eschatological and anamnetic. But it is possible to read it too as a corrective, pragmatic reorientation of the classical Western metaphysical tradition in the light of early Jewish modes of theological and 'metaphysical' reasoning in which the 'existence' of God is known at the centre of God's creation, as boundless creativity and compassion. To this extent it is a kind of Christian midrash (interpretative commentary) of the passage at Ex. 3.14, in which God reveals Godself as YHWH, whose continuing presence with Israel manifests as God's saving and compassionate acts. This argues for a new kind of 'being' which derives not only from postmodern scepticism about the contemporary authenticity of traditional metaphysics, but also from a new attentiveness to the Jewish voice at the heart of Christian origins. As speech about compassion, compassion which is itself divine speech recreating and regenerating the world, this book seeks to learn a new way of speaking about 'being', in the belief that the metaphysical impulse which has played such a central role across the centuries in the Christian imaging of self and world as signs of God's creativity, can be renewed by a reintegration into its scriptural and liturgical sources and can become once again a powerfully expressive medium for the communication of the good.

A.
Kenotic Ontology

1

Towards a New Metaphysics

Le primat de l'identité, de quelque manière que celle-ci soit conçue, définit le monde de la représentation. Mais la pensée moderne naît de la faillite de la représentation, comme de la perte des identités, et de la découverte de toutes les forces qui agissent sous la représentation de l'identique. Le monde moderne est celui des simulacres. L'homme n'y survit pas à Dieu, l'identité du sujet ne survit pas à celle de la substance.

The primacy of identity, however conceived, defines the world of representation. But modern thought is born of the failure of representation, of the loss of identities, and of the discovery of all the forces that act under the representation of the identical. The modern world is one of simulacra. Man did not survive God, nor did the identity of the subject survive that of substance.

Gilles Deleuze, *Différence et Répétition*

The notion of being has never been so contested as it is today; once again, metaphysics has become, like Hecuba, an exile and an indigent.[1] But Christianity, as a religion of death and resurrection and eternal life, is implicitly metaphysical, and has throughout its history had an intimate alliance with the languages of ontology. Christians, or at least those with a mindfulness of their intellectual tradition, cannot easily unlearn the thinking of being. The broad programme of philosophical opposition to the rule of metaphysics reflects an ambivalence with respect to all questions 'directed to the totality of (hu)man and world', or Lyotard's 'grand narratives', on the grounds that such systems inhibit the possibilities of the self and enclose it within particular rationalist agendas that are in the service of powerful social forces.[2] The very concept of system as order has become problematic, and the rationalism that grounds such systems has come increasingly to be seen as another form of – generally unthematized – subjectivity. Amongst such systems, ontology holds a special place, since the very concept of being as that which is the medium of relation between self and other suggests a governance of self and other through the *thinking* of that relation. Whoever understands being, knows the parameters of both self and other. Ontology therefore is particularly subject to *political* appropriation, however subtle, which instrumentalizes the self within a particular ideology. It is this insight which stands at the heart of Nietzsche's far-reaching and highly influential critique of ontology, in which he equated 'being' with reification of the self and its subordination to a totalitarian, life-denying 'God' on the one hand and to the illusions of reason on the other. Presence implies a kind of unity which is persistence of the same across time. But modernity – and postmodernity – is marked by the rise of *difference*, contesting the totalizing discourses of being, and leading to a new emphasis upon dispersal and fragmentation. It is this which is summarized in Foucault's imperative to 'prefer what is positive and multiple, difference over uniformity, flows over unities, mobile arrangements over systems. Believe that what is productive is not sedentary but nomadic.'[3]

Difference, as 'alterity', 'negation', 'absence', or 'the o/Other', pervades the formations of the modern mind, and is deeply embedded in modern life, consciousness and society. Fracture and individualization, within the specifically modern cosmos of commercialized globalization, are the norms of our Western societies. The deterritorialization and 'schizophrenia' of global capitalism endlessly and orgiastically repeat the alienations of individual desire. Consensus can be little more than pragmatism, and commonality the shared values of nationalism and organized self-defence. The lived parallels to the philosophies of difference are many and have both positive and negative effects in society. The withdrawal of language from the world, or what Paul Ricoeur has called 'the epoché of descriptive reference', is intimately bound up with the revaluing of the stable realm of essences as one which is more fluidly constructed of language and interpretations, and whose nature is thus more fully subject to negotiation and critique.[4] This in turn has created a social environment in which we have become more sceptical of the rhetorics of the sciences, and of those who claim specialized knowledge in the public domain. The information consumer of today knows more than ever before that the world is constructed to us through media, with different levels of discernible interpretation and presentation. In modern society, the relation between theory and data has become more complex, and the appeal to objectivity (whose objectivity?) is less easily maintained. Human thinking has tended to float free of its anchorage in the multiple presences of a world waiting to be known and thought, and, as Jürgen Habermas has noted, 'situating reason' and 'reversing the primacy of theory over practice' are foundational for 'postmetaphysical thinking'.[5] In de Certeau's phrase, 'reason is placed in question by its own history'.[6] The modern world is thus defined by a plurality of knowledges, which are the result not only of an exponential growth in the production of information, but also of a multiplication in the ways of knowing. This 'aestheticization' of knowledge flows from the disabling of common and objective points of reference, and it marks the discovery of knowledge as subjectivity, governed as much by taste and style as by a world perceived.[7] In its more positive aspects, this pragmatic relativism can be humane, cultivated and responsible, expressive of liberal individualistic values, while indebted to a community that is committed to education, pluralism and mutual tolerance. More negatively, however, it can be consumerist in orientation, superficial in its rhetorical blandishments, and untouched by the problematics of responsibility and conscience. In short, cosmetic. It is valuable to recall that postmodernism is itself the product of late capitalism, with its dynamic energy, free and rapid exchange of goods and ideas, enjoyed by a 'salaried official intelligentsia' who as privileged individuals exercise an '*un*conditioned access to goods'.[8]

The various intellectual and cultural expressions of philosophies of difference come together in 'the death of the subject', which for philosopher and social theorist alike has become the defining characteristic of modernity. This is the dissolution of the sovereign self as self-positing *cogito*, exercising an autonomous agency and – potentially at least – regency over all it knows. As noted above, the contemporary situation is marked by the intrusion into the self of multiple forms of alterity, patternings of causality and conditioning which script the self in terms that are alien to it, and disrupt its borders. The function of being as the medium of relation between self and other, and thus of ontology, or the language of being, as the thinking of that relation, have come to be seen as exercising a totalizing tendency which does violence to the particularity of the self and to the innumerable, open-ended negotiations which constitute its de facto relation with the other. In the simplest terms, reality, and that reality which we call the self, have come to be experienced and thought as an excess which transcends any ontological containment.

The creative and liberating preference amongst many leading contemporary figures for the principle of difference has generally been set up in opposition to traditional religious belief, but it is nevertheless a movement from which Christians too can learn. In the first place, Christianity itself contains a body of texts – 'as a memory, an institution, a history, a discipline' – which represents a supreme engagement with alterity, in which otherness as the 'nameable beyond the name', in Jacques Derrida's phrase, is experienced at the very root of human cognition and sensibility.[9] These texts are not extraneous to mainstream Christianity, but are a central, if neglected or at times misunderstood, part of Christian dogmatic and liturgical tradition.[10] As ancient texts they embody epistemologies which are alien to the modern world, but they speak nevertheless in their own terms of radical and personal encounter with otherness and, in the space opened up between the passivity of the created soul and the activity of the Creator God, they play richly and abundantly on the thematic of difference. The Christian apophatic tradition is intrinsic to Christianity itself in its primordiality; and so the opposition between an ecstatic freedom and Christian belief influentially instituted by Nietzsche should not lure us into repetitions of his own rhetoric.

Nietzsche's insight, and the insight of modernity, has been the understanding that radical freedom is caught up with the affirmation not of sameness, conveyed by being, but rather of difference, which is, or which seems to be, at odds with the metaphysical enclosure of ontology in most if not all its traditional forms. In truth however, sameness and difference are ordered one to the other, and the lesson of history is that the thinking of difference is itself subject to and implicated in the thinking of sameness. In short, difference cannot be thought except in the context of identity, over and against which it stands – positively – as a critical and liberating or – negatively – as a disintegrating force. In our task of reimaging metaphysics, we shall have to eschew the affirmation of any language of being then which threatens to efface or coerce difference, and with it, the free particularity of the self in its unscripted and joyful relation with otherness. But at the same time, we shall have to steer a path away from some contemporary affirmations of pure difference, which refuse ontology and issue in a surface play of signification that is as alien to the possibilities of the self as it is to the true radicalism of the creative imagination.

Refiguring metaphysics

It can be objected that difference is already secured by identity in the Christian theological systems of the twentieth century, especially in those which are most influenced by a Thomist philosophy of analogy and *differentiae*. Here a framework of being, the being of Creation, grounds and sustains difference as the principle of the created world. Indeed, the very notion of a creation ordered to God in chaos summoned to system, in diversity called to symphonic harmony, proclaims both the reality and the necessity of difference. There is a concern however, that the prioritization of ontology as a way of thinking the relation between self and other necessarily presupposes the priority of unity against which difference appears; this may itself reflect an historical tendency to prioritize the unity of subjectivity in God over and above the trinitarian differentiations.[11] Order and system are themselves realizations of the unity of being through the diversity that it subtends. This is therefore as much a way of controlling difference as it is of affirming it. But the world of today is characterized more by the experience of what we might call in Deleuze's terms 'the crowned anarchy' and 'nomadic distribution' of difference, where the rule of otherness is subject neither to constraint nor prediction and where, above all, it undermines the very stability which we associate with being, even the harmonious and ordered being of the self. Modern human existence is characterized by the extensive use of technologies, for instance, which destabilize the limits and boundaries of the human body.[12] Globalized economic forces and the powers of the nation state, the primacy of which is one of the defining elements of the modern, operate within the domain of the personal. As Anthony Giddens has argued, the modern nation state represents a radical discontinuity with the past. It functions by 'distanciating' or 'bracketing' local or organic time and space, re-assembling them in new spatial and temporal zones which serve to form a new translocational present at a higher level of organization.[13] This 'dis-embedding' of local activity is at the same time the introduction of a degree of systemic alienation. It is in those periods of history when tyranny has combined with the higher levels of social organization of modernity that we have witnessed another uniquely modern phenomenon which can aptly be termed *demonic* otherness. In the 'camp' of the Shoah and its ana-logues, human beings have been stripped of their legal, civil and cultural identity and have been rescripted in an annihilating play of alien and demonic forces. The very construction of modern civil identity, with all its administrative and legal complexity, which can so extensively serve the interests of its citizens, also allows the meticulous and annihilating dismantling of civil identity as such, in which the eradication of culture and the remembrance of culture becomes part of the oppression and even extirpation of minorities. Although the catastrophic events of the Shoah and, more recently, the wars in the Balkans are not the commonplace of human experience, images of extreme violence are rarely absent from our television screens and form part of the landscape of modernity.

Contemporary thinking of difference is indebted to the confluence of three streams therefore. In addition to the historical trauma of the Shoah, we can cite, secondly, the replication of the self under alienation through the successive deconstructive narratives of modern science. The self contemplates itself distributively as the self of psychology, sociology, linguistics. In addition, the science of genetics brings alterity to the heart of human identity in the phenomenon of biopolitics, or complex medical technologies which offer control over the elements of life. Although fundamentally illumining and enriching in terms of the self-understanding of the human person, these and other mappings of the self can easily become totalizing in their trajectory, a trend which is relativized only by their multiplication. And thirdly, there are the liberating and creative possibilities of thinking the self in a way that is not controlled by a meta-physics of unity. This has no necessary incompatibility with religious thought and belief. It is not only a reaction to a Cartesian reification of the self and the world, but is more generally a way of deconstructing the inevitable tendency of metaphysics towards some kind of instrumentality, where the language of being enters the service of controlling agents of power. These three dimensions do not argue for the jettisoning of meta-physics *tout court*. But they do call for a radical revaluing of Christian meta-physics in a way that rethinks ontology in the light of difference to a degree that significantly exceeds the thinking of difference as we find it in the different kinds of traditional metaphysics. The historical ontologies of the church, which find their centre in received readings of 'I am who I am' from Ex. 3.14, have come under careful and sustained attack in recent years.[14] Since the early church appropriated Greek Septuagint renderings of Ex. 3.14, richly interpreted for the Latin tradition by St Augustine, this passage has been central to the way in which Christians have articulated their experience as human beings and as children of God. However stale this way of speaking about God and being may have become for many, who see here the imposition of Greek philosophical 'attributes' upon the living flesh of the gospel, part of Christian experience is the knowledge that Christian truth is ultimately a statement about loss of self and its transfigured regaining, about death and newness of life. Unless there is a self to be lost, this dynamic, which grounds Christian meaning, will falter, and prove untenable. Existence cannot be assumed without residue into some pure play of signs, or re-employment of significations. There must be a point precisely at which we know that our existence is imperilled through sin and alienation of life, that our existence is wagered through faith in the death and resurrection of Christ, and that we are finally renewed, refigured and transfigured, through our own rising with Christ from the tomb. This would be to reduce the existential dynamic of Christianity to a formal inscription within language rather than opening out into the free, personal space of the one who uses language and who, to paraphrase Vattimo, forever confronts in the infinite mirroring of language the certainty of their own finitude.[15]

But the language of being secures the consciousness of the church as creature of the triune God in further ways. In the first place, as noted in the Introduction, it is only through implicit self-possession that we can ground the possibility of kenotic goodness. If a virtuous act is to put ourselves at risk for the sake of another, then some degree of self-possession as self-awareness is intrinsic to that act. Unless we put ourselves at risk *knowingly*, with the self-awareness of a unified subject who is a responsible agent of their actions, then we do not put ourselves at risk at all. Rather we are put at risk by forces external to the self. Such an awareness of the self as that which is self-possessing and thus capable of self-abandonment can be performatively enhanced through the language of being. What comes into view here then is some innate connectedness, as early tradition affirmed, between being and the good: our self-possession as self-knowing yields the possibility of a free dispossession of self for the sake of the other.

Furthermore, our self-knowing is simultaneously a recognition or condition of our unity. We do not mean by this some sense of self which is transcendentally located outside history and the multiple narratives which constitute our social and historical identity. It is not the purpose of this book to reinforce the notion of such an autonomous and 'observer' self. But we do wish to argue for a self who *comes to itself* precisely within such narratives, and within its relation with multiple forms of otherness. This is to affirm the self in its unity, as that which enables us to identify all the narratives of experience as existence that is 'mine'. Such a sense of unity is the ground of the narrative structure of experience as such, and also entails the recognition that something remains over from the dispersal of the self through the multiplication of its narrativities, which is the 'metanarrativity' or 'essential narrativity' of the self. The historical thematization of this transcendence is as inwardness and interiority, which – whether imaged as the 'heart', the 'inner chamber', the 'ground of the soul' – signifies the sphere of pure self-possession transcendentally given within experience and resistant to reduction to history. This is the site of our self-knowing as *creature*, and is the simultaneous recognition of our dependence on God in sinfulness, finitude and pride. A Christianity which has lost sight of interiority and the implied, though forever deferred, unity of the self, has lost sight also of our *creatureliness* before God. This transcendence manifests not only as contemplation and prayer, in which we are confronted in the midst of our lives with the recognition of our own ultimate ends, but also as the innate availability of the self for refiguring and regeneration by God: a transformation which takes place not over and against the narrative structures of our life, but precisely within them, as the promise of an ultimate disclosure of their final meaning.

And finally, we must consider what is perhaps the ultimate necessity to think being and the person in a way that is consistent with the commitments of Christian tradition. The Christian affirmation that God has taken flesh and that he still lives among us is one which also has implications for a Christian understanding of personhood and existence. Personhood, like presence itself, is rooted in duration of the same across time. In contrast with human personhood, the dwelling of Jesus across time, within his community and, for Catholic Christians, in the real presence of the eucharist, is a presence that is both historical in its origins and eternal in its outcomes. Unless we have some way of articulating God's presence to us in Christ in terms that are both personal and existential, the door is open to purely semantic understandings of Christian revelation, as fortuitous figurings of language. The tendency to assimilate the person of Christ into culture is strong today, and only an account of human personhood and presence which stresses the potential agency of the self as speaker and co-maker of culture can serve as a ground for reflection upon the divine personhood and presence that we encounter in an unparalleled way in the eucharist. Only in this way can we reaffirm the traditional Christian belief that in the incarnation God has not only entered human language and culture but has himself become an agent who speaks with us, who creatively acts upon our culture, and forms our human destiny.

The historical Christian commitment to an implicit metaphysics is such therefore that the wholesale renunciation of an explicit metaphysics would be the significant loss of a higher language by which the Christian and perhaps other religious communities can offer a controlling resource for the shaping of the implicit self who lives and acts in a world of God's making. The purification and radicalization of the language of being which is attempted here, in a pragmatic reordering with reference to the theme of compassion, is based ultimately on the divine self-communication of Ex. 3.14. But I choose to read this text, which has been the ground of so much Christian ontology over the centuries, in the light of rabbinic commentators who see in the revelatory communication of God's presence with us a play upon the themes of creation, compassion and the speech of God. This is the deep logic of the expressivity of God as this is brought before us in the Hebrew scriptural narrative. Somehow, in some sense, at Ex. 3.14, these three are one: in an act of divine presencing which is a boundless and unending being-with. It is this nexus, at the heart of God's self-communication with us, pointing forward already in significant ways to the incarnation, which must guide the articulation of a new language of what it is to be, and to be a Christian.

The ontology of compassion

Classical ontology is shot through with the realization that the location of being is problematic; it comes into view precisely through the emergence of that which is other than being, namely the existent. The Greeks knew the problem that pure or infinite being is unknowable; actualized being is always finite, and therefore falls below the true or highest being. In the terminology of the *Republic*, it manifests rather as 'becoming', as that being which is conditioned by its own negation, in its finitude and contingency. In the platonic universe, being as such is hidden behind its own mimetic representations. For Thomas the *actus essendi* (or 'act of being') is mysterious by virtue of its analogical character, while, for Heidegger, 'being as such' or 'being as a totality' (*das Seiende im Ganzen als ein solches*) is always veiled, since it is concealed behind those entities which exercise its function. We must begin then with a search for the place where being seems most hidden; where it is disguised, even overwhelmed, by difference. If being is the good, then we must look for it in a place of evil.

The indelible image of evil as we advance into the new millennium is that of Auschwitz or the 'camp', which we have already portrayed as an historical event of such magnitude and resonance that it stands as a point of ethical orientation for the religious-intellectual culture of our own day. The origins of this phenomenon lie in measures taken by the Spanish during the colonization of Cuba and by the British against the Boers.[16] But since emerging as part of the colonization process, the camp has played a central, even defining role in the extreme oppressive apparatus of totalitarian states. At its heart is the radical subjection of a community to demonic difference: the reinscription of a whole community in a language alien to itself, entailing the eradication of an identity and a world. By the term 'Auschwitz' therefore, we understand atrocities committed in the European world in which the great strengths of that culture are so disconcertingly implicated, including the achievements of science, technology, social organization, law, culture and religion. Unlike the crazed, atavistic slaughter of Rwanda or the crude political motivations of genocide in Cambodia, Auschwitz was a technological event, in which sophisticated gas-poisoning took the place of killing by shooting. It was a scientific event, in that early genetics played a role in the conceptualization of race which underlay anti-Semitism, and scientific or quasi-scientific motivations lay behind some of the 'experiments' which took place regarding survival in extreme physical conditions and the treatment of diseases.[17] It was also a bureaucratic event in that the organization required to gather together so many victims for transportation could only have been undertaken by the administrative apparatus of a highly sophisticated modern society. It was a juridical event in the sense that the legal passage to the camp can be precisely mapped in German law as the normalization of the 'law of exception'. And it was an event with painful religious associations in that the anti-Semitism of National Socialism evidently owed something to the historical anti-Semitism of many Christians, who liked to recall that the Jewish people would bear the guilt for the death of Christ, 'from generation to generation'.[18] We are left therefore with a sense that Auschwitz is not an alien phenomenon imposed upon European history by a rogue state at an exceptional historical time but is rather, as Philippe Lacoue-Labarthe has argued, the 'apocalypse' of tendencies that are concealed in the very nature of modern European civilization, with its science, technology, Christian inheritance and advanced administrative and legal systems.[19]

In his analysis of 'the camp', Giorgio Agamben has set the phenomenon within the context of a general theory of political power which identifies sovereign power precisely as the 'state of exception' that stands outside the operation of the law.[20] As the power which establishes the rule of law, or *nomos*, with its interiority and exteriority (being within the law and outside it), sovereignty can dissolve the law as well as institute it. Thus in a crucial sense it can itself be said to exist outside the law. Sovereign power establishes the law in order to overcome what Agamben terms 'bare life' (adopting a phrase first used by Walter Benjamin) or *zoê*. 'Bare life' is naked human existence contrasting with *bios*, which is the cultural and social existence of a regulated human community preserved and ordered by *nomos*. As unmediated human existence therefore, *zoê* also exists outside the rule of law which alone makes *bios* possible. Thus Agamben wants to draw our attention to the affinity between sovereign power and the very bare life which it expels, and holds that the actual convergence of sovereign power and 'bare life', as principles which are outside the law, represents one of the most fundamental characteristics of modern society. The figure of the refugee, as an outcast or waste-product of the nation state, also emerges as an example of 'bare life', or what Agamben calls *homo sacer*. The camp reappears therefore in those places, such as border controls and asylum centres, where human beings are in a state of material and civil dispossession, and thus, as *homo sacer*, are precariously outside the rule of law.

Understood in this sense, Auschwitz becomes the place of a uniquely modern form of evil, an encounter with demonic difference, and thus is the site of a distinctively modern form of the concealedness of being. To say that we should seek the regeneration of the language of being here is to acknowledge that goodness is not an abstract concept – any more than evil is – but one which only authentically comes into view within the concrete situations of a lived reality. The turmoil and horror of the 'camp' bred a particular way of being good, just as it manifested a particular way of being evil. It is in resistance to the Shoah then, and in the affirmations of existence in the face of the annihilating forces of the 'camp', that we should seek the peculiarly modern understanding of goodness which shall serve as ground for a new model of what it means to be, for a new language of being which understands, and is equal to, the full force of difference. We are not thinking here of resistance of a military kind, in allied armies and partisan groups, nor of the spirit of resistance which led some to shield those threatened with deportation, nor the affirmation of Jewish prayer and practice in the face of the destruction of the Jewish people, at times evidenced in the praying of the *kadesh* during executions.[21] Our focus is upon that type of resistance which found expression as a voluntary sharing of the fate of others in order to be present with them in the time of trial; and it is the resistance of compassion.

In line with the historical orientation of this project, the analysis is grounded on actual historically observed instances of compassionate resistance to violence, two of which are taken from the Holocaust period. Etty (Esther) Hillesum was born in Middelburg in the Netherlands in 1914.[22] Her parents and two brothers were well-educated; her father, a classical scholar, became headmaster of the grammar school at Deventer. Etty's mother, Rebecca, was a Russian who had come to the Netherlands to flee persecution. Etty first studied law, and then Slavonic languages, finally turning to psychology. From the time of the German occupation in 1940, life became increasingly difficult for the Jewish community in the Netherlands. Large-scale transportations began in the spring of 1942. In July 1942, through the influence of some friends, Etty gained a job as a typist at the Jewish Council, an organization of Jews who enjoyed a degree of protection but who played an important role in the administration of the anti-Semitic policies of the National Socialists. After fourteen days Etty left this work and travelled as a volunteer with transported Jews to Westerbork, the transit camp on the German border which fed Auschwitz. She remained there for over a year, working in the hospital, despite attempts by her friends to persuade her to go into hiding. Finally, she was herself transported to Auschwitz with her mother and two brothers where, according to a Red Cross report, she died on 30 November 1943. From March 1941 to October 1942, Etty Hillesum kept a diary (complemented by letters she wrote from Westerbork) in eight exercise books in which she recorded the events of her life, of the Jewish community in Amsterdam, and her own inner growth and struggle with what she increasingly felt was her destiny. These very remarkable diaries were only made available to the broader public in Dutch in 1981 and to the English-speaking world in 1985.

Edith Stein, born in Breslau in 1891, was a generation older than Etty Hillesum. Like Etty, she came from a well-educated Jewish family, but there was a stronger strain of religious piety in her background. She records that she lost her faith in her teens however, and returned to religion only in her early twenties.[23] Edith Stein studied first psychology in Breslau, before moving on to Göttingen, where she studied philosophy with Edmund Husserl. At Göttingen, she showed an outstanding aptitude for philosophy, and became an active member of the circle around Husserl, which included also the leading philosopher and Jewish convert to Catholicism Max Scheler. It was under Scheler's influence that she became attracted to Catholicism, a trend which gradually took her away from Husserlian phenomenology to the more personalist and value-laden phenomenology of the Schelerian school. In 1916, Edith Stein followed Husserl to Freiburg as his assistant, and submitted her doctoral dissertation *The Problem of Empathy*, which again shows her concern with inter-personal knowledge and with the role of the other in the constitution of personhood.

In 1922, Edith Stein was baptized, and took up a teaching position in a school run by Dominican sisters at Speyer. She published a good deal of material during this time in which she argued for fuller recognition of the role of women in German professional life. Again, her perspective was marked by a sense of the unity and integrity of the human person. In 1932, she was appointed to a lectureship at Münster, where she was called to specialize in the development of a new Catholic pedagogical theory. After only a year she was dismissed from this post as a result of an anti-Semitic employment law introduced by the National Socialists in 1933. In 1934, Edith Stein was clothed in the Carmelite Convent at Cologne, as Teresia Benedicta a Cruce. Here she continued work on her major study *Finite and Eternal Being*, in which she attempted a synthesis of Thomism and phenomenology. In 1938, following the violence of *Kristallnacht*, she moved to the Carmel at Echt in Holland. In 1942, Edith Stein turned down the opportunity to transfer to La Paquier in Switzerland on the grounds that a place could not be found for her sister Rosa, who had also converted to Catholicism. At the beginning of August 1942, Edith Stein was arrested and deported from Holland to Auschwitz, together with her sister. According to Red Cross records, she died there on 9 August. She was beatified by the Catholic Church in 1987, and canonized in 1998.

In different ways, the imperatives of compassion came to dominate the lives of Etty Hillesum and Edith Stein. For Etty, the realization that her own destiny lay with that of her people, despite her very real opportunities to escape or go into hiding, grew deeper with time. At first, in March 1941, it was an inchoate sense that she was on a journey into maturity:

Everything will have to become more straightforward, until in the end I
shall, perhaps, finish up as an adult, capable of helping other souls who
are in trouble, and of creating some sort of clarity through my work for
others, for that's what it's really all about.[24]

But by September of 1942, she has a sense of universal suffering, of being
present in the suffering of all as a redemptive witness and presence,
affirming life itself in its wholeness:

I once thought, 'I would like to feel the contours of these times with my
fingertips.' I was sitting at my desk with no idea what to make of life.
That was because I had not yet arrived at the life in myself, was still
sitting at this desk. And then I was suddenly flung into one of the many
flashpoints of human suffering. And there, in the faces of people, in a
thousand gestures, small changes of expression, life stories, I was
suddenly able to read our age – and much more than our age alone. And
then it suddenly happened: I was able to feel the contours of these times
with my fingertips. How is it that this stretch of heathland surrounded
by barbed wire, through which so much human misery has flooded,
nevertheless remains inscribed in my memory as something almost
lovely?[25]

Although she too was a prolific writer, our access to the thoughts of
Edith Stein is more indirect. In general, the writings of Edith Stein either
reflect her advanced philosophical education, in technical academic
writings and penetrating addresses on the place of women in the modern
age, or are expressive of an almost formulaic Carmelite piety. But her autobiographical work, *Life in a Jewish Family*, was written explicitly to correct
the 'horrendous caricature' of Jews and to counteract 'the attack on
Judaism in Germany'.[26] As an attempt to evoke the reality of Jewish family
existence for the gentile reader, it served as an invitation to empathy, and
can be regarded as an example of Edith Stein's own philosophy of intersubjectivity in action.[27] Her commitment to and continuing identification
with the Jewish community from which she was divided by faith is clear in
a comment she made in 1933: 'God's hand lay heavy on his people, and the
destiny of this people was my own'.[28] She understood her own role to be
like that of Esther, interceding for her people, and increasingly came to see
her own solidarity with her people as a calling to share in the sufferings of
Christ. She expressed herself in these terms when she wrote to Mother
Petra in December 1938, a month following *Kristallnacht*:

One thing I should tell you: when I entered, I had already chosen the
religious name I wanted, and I received it exactly as I had asked for it.
'Of the Cross' I saw as referring to the fate of the people of God, which
even then was beginning to reveal itself. As I understood it, anyone who

recognized that this was the Cross of Christ had a responsibility to bear. it in the name of all. I know a little more now than I did then what it means to be betrothed to the Lord in the sign of the Cross. But it's not something that can ever be understood. It is a mystery.[29]

In a prayer given to the Prioress on Passion Sunday in 1939, Edith Stein again expressed her wish to offer her own suffering as expiation for the impending destruction:

Dear Reverend Mother:
Please permit me to offer myself to the Heart of Jesus as a sacrifice of atonement for true peace, that if possible the reign of the Antichrist might be broken without another world war and a new social order may be established. I would like to do it today, if I could, since it is already the final hour. I know I myself am nothing, but Jesus desires it, and I am sure he is asking it of many others in these days.[30]

Etty Hillesum and Edith Stein were different in age, temperament and belief, but – for all that sets them apart – their two lives converged in what – adapting a concept from von Balthasar – we might call the 'form' of compassion. In the context of the events of 1942 and 1943, they both developed within themselves an understanding of the absolute moral necessity of a radical and self-sacrificial solidarity with their people. Moreover, they both reached a profound understanding of the process at work in them, although variously articulated. Etty seems to have come to this comprehension through hours of introspection and intense reflection (phenomenologically), while for Edith Stein, the phenomenologist, it appeared almost naively, in the unfolding logic of the cross. But on account of this understanding, both are able to give particular witness to the power of compassion, as radical resistance to the life-denying and all-destroying horror, to the dehumanizing reduction to 'bare life' that was taking place about them.

If sanctity has any meaning in the twentieth century, then Edith Stein and Etty Hillesum are both modern saints. In each case however, this claim is not without its difficulties. Etty in particular was headstrong and sensitive and, as a woman of the twentieth century, freely experimented with her sexuality in a number of close relationships. Nor was she conventional in her beliefs. Among the deeply religious influences upon her we must count Dostoevsky and Rilke, as well as Judaism and Christianity. But these seem to be filtered through an extraordinary native gift for an understanding of the redemptive nature of consciousness, as witness, which is reminiscent both of the first of Rilke's *Duino Elegies*, and of the philosophy of consciousness which proved so attractive to Edith Stein. A wholehearted reception and affirmation of life, organically linked with the creativity of the poetic gift, exercised in what Charles de Foucauld called the sacrament of the present moment, is perhaps the most fundamental spirituality that we discern in the pages of Etty's diary. If we dub her a saint, therefore, as indeed we must, then it is in the knowledge that, like so many of her contemporaries, Etty shunned the conventional practice of religion, whether Judaism or Christianity, and experienced life in many respects as an open-ended voyage of self-discovery. And yet, within the concrete historical situation which became for her 'the contours' and 'the signs of the times', she retrieved the very heart of religious existence, and lived a life that pointed radically beyond itself.

Sanctity is no less a complex issue in the case of Edith Stein, canonized as a saint of the Catholic Church in 1998. In this instance, it is not that Edith Stein stands outside formal religious traditions, but rather that she combines them. If Etty represents the modern tendency to separate religiosity from the traditional forms of the religious life, finding it more vitally in literature and her own life experience, then Edith Stein is representative of those many people in the modern world who freely change, or choose, their religion. That too is a consequence of secularism and religious pluralism. But the canonization of a Christian who died because she was a Jew has not been uncontroversial.[31] Indeed, the issue of supersessionism, which so easily attaches to Jewish conversions to Christianity, has a particular sensitivity when the Christian who is killed because she is a Jew, is killed by those whose historical debt to Christian anti-Semitism is plain to see.[32] In the case of Edith Stein then, we may agree with Pope John Paul II that her canonization creates the opportunity for the memory of the Holocaust to enter the heart of Catholic piety and prayer life, and to become part of the remembrance of the church, but we should do so in the knowledge that the Jewish claim upon her as victim and martyr is no less real.[33]

The priority of compassion

We have seen in the above sections an historical context for radical evil in the forced dispossession and destruction of a large number of human beings in the camps, and we have compared this with the resistance of voluntary self-dispossession on the part of the compassionate individual who places herself at risk for the sake of the other. The alignment between the two is not coincidental. Both involve a fundamental displacement of the self, in the one case enacted through force, meaningless in the empty motivations of self-consuming power, while in the other the displacement is undergone voluntarily, specifically for the sake of the other, and in fullness of meaning. The structure that comes into view here then is the redemptive recapitulation of evil in and by the good. The radical goodness to which both Etty Hillesum and Edith Stein felt themselves called, as a driving sense of destiny, was the compassionate re-enactment of destructive and enforced dispossession suffered by their fellow Jews. This was in part the sharing in the physical fate of the Jewish victims of the Shoah, but it was also the very process of dispossession which is itself integral to the phenomenon of compassion. The assumption of another's suffering as one's own entails a radical decentring of the self, and a putting at risk of the self, in the free re-enactment of the dispossessed state of those who suffer. Compassion is the recognition of the otherness of the other, as an otherness which stands beyond our own world, beyond our own constructions of otherness even. But it is also the discovery of our own nature, as a horizon of subjectivity which is foundationally ordered to the world of another's experience, in what Paul Ricoeur has called 'the paradox of the exchange at the very place of the irreplaceable'.[34] It is here then, in the dispossessive act whereby the self assumes the burdens of the other, and thus accepts the surplus of its own identity, that we should recognize the veiled presence of being.

The argument that is presented in the following chapter is a phenomenological analysis of compassion. Compassion itself can be ordered within the broader category of love, but there are significant reasons why we have chosen not to analyse the dispossessive intentionality, or kenosis, of consciousness in terms of 'love'. As Paul Ricoeur has written, '[T]alking about love may be too easy or rather too difficult'.[35] 'Love' embraces concepts and phenomena that are both wholly distinct and easily confused. Thus we need to distinguish with Nygren and others between an eros-love which can be glossed as an 'appetite' or 'need' love and an agape-love which is self-dispossessive. In the complexity of human relations however, eros-love may be characterized by both appetite and need, in equal or differing degree, at different times (we may have an appetite for that which we do not need, and no appetite at all for what we do need). These relations may also be elective or imposed, and again differentially, in a varying degree at different times (we may come to need a partner freely chosen, and may come to have appetite for, or delight in, what was initially a purely need relation). But it is precisely such bonding relations of spouse or partner, family and friends that we commonly describe as 'love' relations, which form the primary structures of our personal world (although the extent to which we say that we 'love' our friends may depend on the language we are speaking). Inevitably therefore, it is in the close relations we share with others on the basis of either appetite or need that we are summoned to an agape-love, of self-dispossessive affirmation for the sake of the specific other. The expression of agape from within eros however, defined in this sense, is not easily divided from its matrix, and it can mask manipulative love, even to the degree of deceiving the one who gives. It is the interpenetration in real life of eros and agape, together with their entirely different volitional structure, which renders any formal typology of love deeply unsatisfactory at the level of human existence, with its unfathomable mix of motivations and understandings.[36]

Compassion, on the other hand, presents a complex but more easily identifiable structure, which in Martha Nussbaum's analysis entails a combination of cognitive, affective and volitional elements.[37] In compassion we see another's distress (cognition), we feel moved by it (affectivity) and we actively seek to remedy it (volition). Compassion differs from *Schadenfreude*, or gloating at another's misfortune, on account of its affective and volitional aspects therefore, as it does also from cruelty, as the intentional inflicting of pain (although compassion shares with cruelty the cognition of another's state). Nor is that person compassionate who understands the suffering of another and is affected by it, but chooses not to act on their behalf (on account of fear, perhaps). The lack of the volitional element identifies this as 'simple pity' in which, for Ricoeur, 'the self is secretly pleased to know it has been spared'.[38] But that man or woman who understands another's suffering and is affected by it, while recognizing that action on behalf of that person is simply not possible (as in the case of terminal illness for instance), can be said to be compassionate, since here it is simply practical constraints which prevent the expression of the will to alleviate suffering. Unlike love then, compassion does present a psychological and cognitive profile that is specific and identifiable. But with love, it shares a foundational character so that it is not so much a particular virtue as a self-dispossessive attitude of mind which makes the particular virtues possible.

The first two of our examples given in the following chapter, those of Edith Stein and Etty Hillesum, can be described as the particular virtues of *solidarity* and of a concrete desire to be at hand in order to comfort others in their distress, while our third example, from the Balkans, is an event of *forgiveness*. Almsgiving, taking care of the sick, visiting those in prison, bringing comfort to the distressed, releasing others from their debts to us, protecting the vulnerable, are all visible acts of altruism in the world. But they can be judged to be truly virtuous and altruistic only on the grounds of the intentionality at work in them. After all, we may come to others in their need, even accepting a degree of self-risk, simply because we perceive it to be in our own interests to do so. Such acts would then count as expressions of calculated self-interest. The defining content of virtue is an other-centred intentionality which manifests in cognition, affectivity and will. Compassion then, rather like 'love', is not in itself a virtue (such as almsgiving or forgiveness), but is rather a kenotic or agapic state of mind which precipitates in virtuous acts. It is a clearly identifiable structure which forms the common ground of those actions in the world in which the self shows itself ready to put itself concretely at risk for the sake of the other.[39]

Dispossessive intentionality is a modality of consciousness and, as such, is accessible to analysis through the phenomenological method. Historically, phenomenology lays claim to being a scientific and objective exploration of the givenness of things.[40] But in fact, as I argue here, the various phenomenologies can be seen to be different interpretative and narrative traditions, in which the mind itself is an actor in the drama. The thought experiments of Descartes, Fichte or Husserl each in their own way configure the nature of the given according to a set of human, cultural priorities, which communicate a certain view of the self. This does not invalidate the phenomenological method however, for this remains the best way to compose a narrative shaping of consciousness *in its own terms*.

The following chapter begins with three first-hand narrative accounts of compassion as resistance to violence, in full acknowledgment of the historical character of virtue as an enactment of the good. We then proceed to a phenomenological reduction which lays bare the intentional structure of compassion as a modality of consciousness. Although deeply indebted to the philosophy of consciousness, the method presented here can be distinguished from the classical forms of this tradition in a number of key ways. In the first place, I disagree with Descartes with respect to the self-positing of the self, and argue that the self is rather mediated in and through the other. There is nothing here that is calculated to give support to the Cartesian observer-self located outside the processes of history. From the perspective of phenomenology, our model is closer to that of Spinoza and Kant, for whom the *cogito* is coposited with the experience of otherness and world.[41] Where I do seemingly follow a Cartesian line is in a linkage of consciousness with the language of being. This is not undertaken in the face of what Marion has referred to as Descartes' 'hyperbolic doubt' however, but springs rather from the Aristotelian insight that self-knowledge entails unity and that unity is the principle of existence.[42] In Heideggerian terms, 'presence' is the persistence of the same across time.[43] The unity that inheres in the reflexivity and self-possession of the conscious subject grounds a sense of existing as subject which finds its legitimate expression in an ontology or language of being.

In contrast with Descartes, that language of being expresses the subject's sense that it has come to itself in and through the other, and not in opposition to the other. I therefore contest the assumption that is widespread in contemporary philosophical texts that the philosophy of consciousness is of necessity to be equated with a sovereign and isolated self, who is resistant to process and whose substantial nature is set up over and against a frozen world of essences. I likewise contest the supposition, again widespread today, that there is a necessary opposition between language and consciousness. While it is the case that the historical tradition of philosophy of consciousness has shown little interest in language, and that the rise of hermeneutics has frequently been in overt opposition to *Subjektphilosophie*, I strongly affirm the principle that language is foundational to the self's knowledge and possession of itself.

Following Mikhail Bakhtin and Emmanuel Levinas, I take the view that language is intrinsically dialogical and that the self comes to its own self-realizations only in and through the relationality of language, primarily language as *conversation* with the human other. Where I differ from these two thinkers, is in an insistence on implicit self-presence and self-possession as an expression of the Kantian ground of unity within the multiple narrative identities of the self as mediated in language. It is this implicitly reflexive self-possession alone which makes self-dispossessive acts of compassion possible, and which lends itself to the development of a formal and in some sense regulative language of ontology.

Amongst phenomenologists, the method presented here most approximates to the work of Husserl's religiously-minded disciples Max Scheler, Edith Stein and Maurice Merleau-Ponty, for whom other selves were intrinsically present to the *cogito* in a way that could not be compromised by any form of the phenomenological reduction. My attempt to put together a philosophy of consciousness with an ethics of dispossessive compassion entails a further indebtedness, to the thought of the German Idealist philosopher J. G. Fichte, whose terminology of 'I' (self) and 'Not-I' (non-self, or other) I have adopted (though adding the further term 'Other-I' to denote other selves). I emphatically depart from Idealist phenomenology however, to the extent that the opposition between self and other, or I and Not-I, is not to be resolved into a further and deeper level of reflexivity. There is, in my view, no power within the self which can overcome the irreducible otherness of Not-I, so that I and Not-I belong to each other in an inexhaustible and unending relation of mutual grounding. I reject the Idealist view therefore that the self must vanquish the other if freedom is not to be extinguished by materialism, or what Fichte termed 'dogmatism'. As René Girard has noted, the destiny of the self lies entirely in its relation with the other and not despite or beyond it.[44]

Before proceeding to the formal exposition of the argument however, it is necessary finally to give some justification as to why it is that an analysis of the intentionality of *compassion* gives access to the very structure of consciousness itself, and thus provides a resource for articulating a new language of being. We have already presented an historical argument, pointing to the centrality of Auschwitz in our cultural and social history as an apogee of dispossession as evil, calling forth a commensurate goodness in the resistance of compassion. This has force in the Western cultural situation. But as an historical argument, it cannot serve as a basis for an analysis of consciousness as such, which should have no pretension to a privileged relation with the Western world or with a particular point in time. The claim that consciousness, as a universal phenomenon, can be accessed in a particular way by an analysis of compassion requires different kinds of arguments, of more general validity.

The first presented here is a sociological argument which turns on the fact that it is not altruism itself which sets radical compassion apart from ordinary experience, but rather the extreme degree of altruism which it exemplifies. Compassion stands at the far end of a continuum of altruistic actions, which begins in the domain of everyday experience. Indeed, a good deal of human behaviour can only be explained by reference to an altruism which is not the refined calculation of self-interest. The principle of self-denying or kenotic love, of which compassion is a particularly radical manifestation, appears to touch all levels of human existence and, indeed, to make harmonious social existence possible. Without such a principle of self-emptying for the sake of the other, enacted in some degree by a myriad people in countless different ways, most human societies could not keep at bay the violent and selfish tendencies of the human spirit. Despite all the ambiguities of human socialization and motivation, the fact that a multitude of ordinary individuals do repeatedly subordinate their own interests to those of another in everyday situations of life can be construed as the very principle of civilization. Compassion, by this account, is 'the basic social emotion', in Martha Nussbaum's phrase.[45] Indeed, there may be some inchoate recognition of this in the extent to which radical acts of self-risking love, motivated by compassion for another individual, constitute for many a point of unsurpassable meaning. Despite all the ambiguities of human motivation and understanding, and the social, cultural and psychological complexities of human interaction, such acts of exceptional self-giving love appear to many to represent a moral ideal and to reflect in radical form a principle of altruism without which social civilization as such would founder.[46] It is also significant in this respect that the major world religions combine in laying a particular stress upon the place of compassion in the hierarchy of spiritual values.[47]

Our second argument is a psychological one and points to the essential *sociality* of the human person, drawing out the extent to which the very notion of personhood is relational in kind. The very earliest contact of a child with the 'world' or non-self is in the form of the mother, or principal carer, who embraces the child in the field of an all-encompassing relation. Although the individuation of the self into personhood may also entail distinguishing oneself, competitively or defensively, from other selves, an open I–Thou relation of self to self provides the existential condition for the emergence of personhood.[48] A child is constantly treated by adults as an adult human being in the making, with all the rights and privileges of adult personhood, and so an existential space is created into which the child can grow as a process of self-determination in personhood. The essence of self, as person, originates in the mutuality of persons therefore, a relation which is animated and quickened by the creative recognition of personhood by one self of another.

Compassion is predicated upon the mutuality of self and other and an interpenetration of the self and other which reflects the very constitution of personhood. Indeed, we would argue that compassion itself represents an epiphany of the sociality of the self, and its relatedness to other human beings. Most forms of human empathy involve the understanding of another's state of mind which is either neutral or even positive. It is easy to understand why we should enter into the feelings of another where these are jubilant, joyful, peaceful, pleasurable, or perhaps merely interesting.

But it is more difficult to see why we should enter into another's sufferings, when we ourselves would normally seek to avoid the experience of suffering. And yet, this is precisely what takes place in compassionate acts. Indeed, we may find ourselves in relation with another specifically on account of their sufferings, when less intense or less negative experiences on their part may not set us in any relation with them at all. In this way compassion can appear to be an epiphany of the sociality of the self, which creeps up upon a person despite his or her sense of a discriminating and individuated distance from others. It is this which will prompt us to speak of an additional, *ontological* dimension to the cognitive, affective and volitional structure of compassion, since in the phenomenon of compassion we not only encounter the other in a new and more intense way, but we also encounter ourselves, in our openness and answerability to the other. Thus, by the argument presented in the following chapter, we are made aware of the fundamental determination of our own existence as a self that is grounded in its relation to the finite other, in which relation it discovers the further horizon of possibility as the encounter with an Other both infinite and personal.

Conclusion

In this chapter we have seen the fundamental critiques of metaphysics in the modern period which have prioritized the principle of difference in opposition to the unifying and enclosing functions of the language of being. While acknowledging the importance of this realignment, the need for metaphysics has nevertheless been stressed, and thus for a regeneration of metaphysics, in the way that Christians speak with themselves and with the world. Holding – with ontological tradition – that being is always concealed, we began our search for a new language of being in the phenomenon of the 'camp', in Auschwitz, where being seems most hidden in the modern world, and where 'difference', as encounter with otherness, is most radically felt. There, in difference, survives the possibility of a new kind of being. In the resistance to evil, through compassion on the part of Etty Hillesum and Edith Stein, we found the outline of a dispossessive and decentred model of the self which redemptively recapitulates the dispossession of evil and, accordingly, manifests both a new radicality of goodness and the possibility of a new – and truly contemporary – understanding of being.

But in addition to the historical premises regarding the cultural and historical priority of compassion for the Western world at this point in its history, and the sociological and psychological arguments for the priority of compassion as such, there is a further theological premise as to why we should apply a phenomenological reduction of compassion in order to lay bare the ontological structure of consciousness as such, pointing to the transformation of 'existence' into the heightened state of 'being'. As I shall argue later in this work, the phenomenological reduction itself leads to the opening of a horizon which constitutes a further stage: a *theological* reduction of compassion. Here at the extreme of human truth, we encounter Jesus Christ – the Compassion of God – as the one who goes before and who is already present to us, if unfathomably, in the compassionate act. In the second half of this book it will be our task to establish the compassionate self as the image of God, and to map out the relation between the ontology of compassion and the trinitarian being of the Divine Persons, in and through a theology of revelation. For if – as I shall argue – the compassionate self is defined by the convergence of being and love, then the life of the Trinity represents their full and total unity, with neither constraint nor residue, holding the created order in dramatic tension with itself, in a compassionate dynamic of difference and identity.

2

The Compassionate Self

Deus enim quoniam pius est, animal nos voluit esse sociale:
itaque in aliis hominibus nos ipsos cogitare debemus.

Since God is kind, he wished us to be a social animal:
and so we should think ourselves in other people.

Lactantius, *Institutes Divinae*

I. *Deconstructing the phenomenological subject*

We begin the following section of this chapter with first-hand accounts of the compassionate actions of three women: Edith Stein, Etty Hillesum and an unnamed woman from Bosnia. These texts are traces which make present to myself and to the reader the historical subjectivity of these women in the most direct way possible. In the third section I shall present an argument for the intersubjectivity of personal existence, made manifest in the compassionate moment which lays bare the foundationally other-orientated character of consciousness itself. And in the fourth and final section I shall conduct a series of conversations with other thinkers whose work has also taken issue with questions of consciousness, transcendence and existence.

At this point then, the act of recognition which precedes this analysis – my own recognition of the compassionate actions of these women – comes into play. It is important that my own analytical perspective not be mistaken for an attempt to take up a position outside the cycle of relationality and answerability for which I am myself arguing. My own phenomenological analysis needs to be preceded therefore by an act of self-reflection and self-appropriation as one who is challenged by the compassionate acts of these women, as communicated in these texts, and who is drawn towards them. Simply stated, I am myself moved by compassion by their acts of compassion. Moreover I understand – or have come to understand – that 'being moved by compassion' is itself a feature of the structure of consciousness itself. I see it to be the 'infectious' or self-communicating nature of being. I have understood that consciousness is dialectical in that it is constituted by self (I) and other (Not-I) in a relation of mutual grounding. Within that relation the self experiences a certain transcendence both with respect to itself before the other and with respect to the other. We can choose to affirm ourselves within the order of things, or the wholeness of our world, in a movement which is known in religious terminology as 'recollection', 'resignation' or 'prayer'. This is the handing over of the self and all its possibilities to God, and it is close to what is meant by the 'contemplative life'. Likewise, we can choose to affirm the specific other precisely as that which is other to ourselves, in an act which approximates to the 'active life' of tradition, or we can 'occlude' the other as that which is neglected, denied or subordinated to our own perceived interests. I have understood that in so far as the self affirms Not-I, it also affirms the dialectical cycle which gives itself existence. Thus the affirmation of what is not itself, at times entailing risk to itself, paradoxically leads to the enhanced or heightened existence of the self. I have called this 'being'. I have also understood that in so far as we ourselves lack fullness of being, we are drawn by that very emptiness towards the greater existential density of those whose lives exemplify the values and performance of radical self-sacrifice. The subjectivity conducting this analysis – myself writing these words – is itself drawn to make this analysis on the basis of a prior election of the good, where election both expresses my wish to prioritize the good in phenomenological reflection and is the recognition of the other people whose compassionate energy has fashioned my existence and whose multiple presences continue to inhabit and to enrich my inner self.

II. *Three narratives*

A.

(The following passages are taken from the diary and letters of Etty Hillesum, written between 1941 and 1943. The 'barracks' referred to are Westerbork, a camp where Dutch Jews were gathered on their way to Auschwitz. In 1942 Etty voluntarily accompanied the first large group to be taken to Westerbork and stayed there, working in the hospital for over a year. Finally she was herself transported to Auschwitz where, on 30 November 1943, she died.)

8 OCTOBER, THURSDAY AFTERNOON. I am still sick. I can do nothing about it. I shall have to wait a little longer to gather up all their tears and fears. Though I can really do it here just as well, here in bed. Perhaps that's why I feel so giddy and hot. I don't want to become a chronicler of horrors. Or of sensations. This morning I said to Jopie, 'It still all comes down to the same thing: life is beautiful. And I believe in God. And I want to be there, right in the thick of what people call 'horror' and still be able to say: life is beautiful.' And now here I lie in some corner, dizzy and feverish and unable to do a thing. When I woke up just now I was parched, reached for my glass of water and, grateful for that one sip, thought to myself, 'If I could only be there to give some of those packed thousands just one sip of water.' And all the time I keep telling myself, 'Don't worry, not everything is that bad.' Whenever yet another poor woman broke down at one of our registration tables, or a hungry child started crying, I would go over to them and stand beside them protec-

tively, arms folded across my chest, force a smile for those huddled, shattered scraps of humanity and tell myself, 'Really, not everything is that bad'. And all I did was just stand there, for what else could one do? (*Etty: A Diary 1941–43*, London: Grafton Books 1985, pp. 246–7)

22 SEPTEMBER. How is it that this stretch of heathland surrounded by barbed wire, through which so much human misery has flooded, nevertheless remains inscribed in my memory as something almost lovely? How is it that my spirit, far from being oppressed, seemed to grow lighter and brighter there? It is because I read the signs of the times and they did not seem meaningless to me. Surrounded by my writers and poets and the flowers on my desk, I loved life. And there among the barracks, full of hunted and persecuted people, I found confirmation of my love of life. Life in those draughty barracks was no other than life in this protected, peaceful room. Not for one moment was I cut off from the life I was said to have left behind. There was simply one great, meaningful whole. Will I be able to describe all that one day? So that others can feel too how lovely and worth living and just – yes, just – life really is? Perhaps one day God will give me the few simple words I need. And bright and fervent and serious words as well. But above all simple words. How can I draw this small village of barracks between heath and sky with a few rapid, delicate and yet powerful, strokes of the pen? And how can I let others see the many inmates, who have to be deciphered like hieroglyphs, stroke by stroke, until they finally form one great readable and comprehensible whole?

One thing I know for certain: I shall never be able to put down in writing what life has spelled out for me in living letters. I have read it all, with my own eyes, and felt it with many senses.
(*Etty: A Diary*, p. 229)

SATURDAY MORNING. Of course, it is our complete destruction that they want! But let us bear it with grace.

There is no hidden poet in me, just a little piece of God that might grow into poetry.

And a camp needs a poet, one who experiences life there, even there, as a bard and is able to sing about it.

At night, as I lay in the camp on my plank bed, surrounded by women and girls gently snoring, dreaming aloud, quietly sobbing and tossing and turning, women and girls who often told me during the day, 'We don't want to think, we don't want to feel, otherwise we are sure to go out of our minds,' I was sometimes filled with an infinite tenderness, and lay awake for hours letting all the many, too many impressions of far too long a day wash over me, and I prayed, 'Let me be the thinking heart of these barracks.' And that is what I want to be again. The thinking heart of a whole concentration camp. I lie here so patiently and now

so calmly again, that I feel quite a bit better already. I feel my strength returning to me; I have stopped making plans and worrying about risks. Happen what may, it is bound to be for the good.
(*Etty: A Diary*, p. 245)

B.
(For the last days of Edith Stein's life we are dependent upon a number of eye-witnesses who either visited her at the transit camp Westerbork or survived the deportation. These accounts are therefore subjective, the first describing Edith Stein among the Jewish inmates and the second among her Catholic sisters. There were ten Jewish Catholic sisters imprisoned in Westerbork at this time. They had all been allocated to the same barracks, but were able to move among the other prisoners at certain times of the day. Edith Stein was transported with many others to Auschwitz on 7 August and died at Auschwitz on 9 August 1942).

It was Edith Stein's complete calm and self-possession that marked her out from the rest of the prisoners. There was a spirit of indescribable misery in the camp; the new prisoners, especially, suffered from extreme anxiety. Edith Stein went among the women like an angel, comforting, helping, and consoling them. Many of the mothers were on the brink of insanity and had sat moaning for days, without giving any thought to their children. Edith Stein immediately set about taking care of these little ones. She washed them, combed their hair, and tried to make sure they were fed and cared for.
(Julius Marcan, in Waltraud Herbstrith, *Edith Stein: A Biography*, trans. Bernard Bonowitz, San Francisco: Ignatius Press 1985, p. 183)

What distinguished Edith Stein from the rest of the sisters was her silence. Rather than seeming fearful, to me she appeared deeply oppressed. Maybe the best way I can explain it is to say that she carried so much pain that it hurt to see her smile. She hardly ever spoke; but often she would look at her sister Rosa with a sorrow beyond words. As I write, it occurs to me that she probably understood what was awaiting them. She was, after all, the only one who had escaped from Germany as a refugee, and this would have given her a much better idea of the situation than the Loebs had, who were still talking about going to work on the missions. As I say, in my opinion, she was thinking about the suffering that lay ahead. Not her own suffering – she was far too resigned for that – but the suffering that was in store for the others. Every time I think of her sitting in the barracks, the same picture comes to mind: a Pietà without the Christ.
(Mrs Bromberg, *Edith Stein: A Biography*, pp. 182–3)

Once it became apparent that in a matter of hours she was going to be transported with the rest of the baptized Jews, I tried to find out whom I should notify. I wanted to know if there was some way I could be of service. Would it help, I asked, if I had a reliable policeman telephone Utrecht? With a smile, she asked me not to do anything. Why should there be an exception made in the case of a particular group? Wasn't it fair that baptism not be allowed to become an advantage? If somebody intervened at this point and took away her chance to share in the fate of her brothers and sisters, that would be utter annihilation. But not what was going to happen now.

(Mr Wielek, *Edith Stein: A Biography*, p. 187)

C.

(The following passage is an informal communication of the Focolare Movement which dates from the year 1993 and the war in Bosnia-Hercegovina.)

I am Ivica Jurilj from Bosanski Brod in Bosnia . . .

In my town the different ethnic groups always lived in peace together; most were Croats, then Serbs, Czechs and Hungarians. The relations between us were very good, we lived happily together, went to the same schools, helped each other out, played together, solved our problems together . . . I have five brothers in my family, and our parents always taught us to help others regardless of their nationality or religion which belongs to it. We had many fields which we had worked for generations, and agriculture was the family tradition.

After the war broke out, the relations between the nationalities began to worsen, under the influence of the mass media. The situation started to become dangerous, many had chosen to leave their homes and to find more secure places, while the goods they left were at the mercy of thieves, who little by little took away everything they could find.

My parents, who had devoted themselves to farming all their lives and had acquired tractors and other kinds of machinery, could not bring themselves to leave everything. Also, they had no idea at all that the situation would worsen so very quickly. The older brothers, including myself, left while the younger ones remained. But then they too were forced to flee, taking refuge with some relatives in Slavone Brod. For months we heard nothing about our parents since all communications were down . . .

We knew nothing about the fate of our parents and used every way to try to get information about them. After a few days, a Serb radio ham who was risking his life told us that they were alive and well. But then the counter attack happened and the occupiers destroyed everything as they left.

During those days they killed my father too, while my mother managed to escape to a nearby wood. After spending two days there in great fear, with the body of my father at her side, she saw the arrival of the Croat army and decided to return to the village. She met the soldiers who asked her for information about the events that had happened, since she was the only survivor left in the village. They showed her a soldier who they had captured. He was a neighbour. They wanted her to accuse him, but she said: 'For me he is a just a person, a friend from childhood of my children.' She did not want to condemn him even at a moment of such tragedy . . .

Soon after hearing of the death of our father, we left for the town where we grew up, and where we knew every corner, every tree and house . . . When we arrived we were terrified to see everything in such a state of ruin . . .

Mother in her grief did not at first recognize us, especially since she thought that we were all dead.

It has been difficult for us all to face reality, but what our mother did has helped us since in these terrible moments she managed not to condemn someone else.

. . . Her example has been a point of light in all this darkness.

(Presentation given at the Family-Fest in Rome, 5 June 1993)

III. *A transcendental analytic of compassion*

The argument

The dialectic of consciousness

The world begins for me when I perceive something which is not myself. The sphere of consciousness, which is my world, is thus constituted by self, or I, and other, or Not-I. Both I and Not-I are thematized in language. In the instant that the self knows another, it comes into possession of itself as knowing act and knows itself as knowing subject. The self-knowing of I is dependent therefore upon the prior existence of Not-I, as that which is known. But Not-I forms part of consciousness only because it is already known by I. Thus the existence of the other within consciousness depends in turn upon the prior existence of the self, as knowing subject. The existence of self and other is determined therefore by a relation of mutual grounding. Neither I nor Not-I can exist without the other. In the realm of consciousness, or existence, which is the medium of the relation of the self and other, the self knows that it is.

Within the relation of mutual grounding, which is the foundation of consciousness, I and Not-I are dialectically structured one to the other. Not-I is defined as that which the self knows to be other than itself, while I is defined as that which knows itself to be other than Not-I. Not-I and I are irreducibly contrary terms. The dialectical structure of their relation is given by their mutual grounding: the existence of I, as knowing act, is founded upon the simultaneous existence of Not-I. We can say that I exists where Not-I exists therefore; and where Not-I does not exist, I also does not exist. Thus I is founded upon Not-I, and the existence of I is determined by what is not itself. In other words, the existence of I is founded dialectically upon its own non-existence: the presence of I is granted by its own absence.

Body, world and language

Body is the *ground* of relation between self and other. As ground, it is both construct and foundation: simultaneously a field of meanings and the pre-semiological base of existence. As ground of the relation between self and other, the semiological construction of the body bears the same dialectical character as the relation between I and Not-I. This is expressed in the fact that I knows the body to be simultaneously itself and Not-I. Under the aspect of self, the body is experienced in an active and a passive mode. In the former it is known as the extension of self, the expression and implementation of the will, while in the latter it is experienced as sentience and encounter, the site of my pleasure and my pain. But under the aspect of the other, the body manifests to the self as the alien and unfathomable, or merely as object. This is particularly the case when suffering illness, or physical distress, or when the body ceases to express the will and falls into uncontrollability. Then the body is experienced as alien otherness, under the aspect of Not-I. As ground of the relation between I and Not-I, body is finite.

The world that begins for me when I perceive something which is not myself is the *unfolding* of the relation between I and Not-I. The dialectical character of that relation is shown in the fact that world is simultaneously mine and not-mine. World marks the encounter and interplay between the self and other, differentiated as other people and objects, other landscapes and relations. As that which is mine, world is familiar and stable and has visible horizons. There I am at home. But as that which is not mine, the horizons of world are open and unpredictable. I am not at home in the world that is strange. As unfolding of the relation between I and Not-I, world is infinite.

Language is the *sphere of expression* of the self–other relation. The other is made thematically present to the self through language and naming. The self calls by name, while the other is named. But the self recognizes other selves (Other-I) as both named and namer, and receives them as presence. Presence is an opening out into the possibility of a realized mutuality. Each language is a distinctive idiom for ordering world, communicating and negotiating it with others, and thus represents a community of presence. Language, too, is dialectically mine and not-mine. It is simultaneously my utterance and the utterance of others: the naming community of which I am a part. I am at home in language where it is ordered as authentic meaning and communication with others and is mine, but where communication fails, by deceit or by accident, language becomes alien and strange.

Each name is the central point of a narrative, structured temporally and spatially towards other names. But the self's own name is the nodal point of a unitive narrative which is personal and constitutive of self, constructed by multiple narratives of time and space. The I knows itself precisely through the ordering of narratives of self-reference, and it knows Not-I by narratives of reference-to-another. But I also recognizes other persons as namers, as self-referential names, and the nodal points of their own respective unified narratives. This creates the possibility of conversation, which is the mutual recognition of persons and narratives, and the interweaving of personal narratives in the negotiated process of creating a third, shared narrative. Conversation as *responsibility* and *answerability* of speech to the other, is a dialectics of presence. As regent of its own narrative, the self must remain observant and alert to the other, and always prepared to correct its own narratives with respect to the other. The self must allow other selves to inscribe themselves in narrative presences to the self, in the fullness of alterity. Indeed, the openness of the self to the horizon of possibility of the emergence of the other in presence to it, mediated through language, is a condition of authenticity of world, as a co-positing of self and other. For the self to refuse emergence to the other is for world, as the unfolding of that relation, to fall into inauthenticity, suffering a diminution of its fullness and its richness.

Freedom and transcendence

The modes of existence of I and Not-I, which together constitute the sphere of consciousness, are distinct. The manner of existence of the other within the habitable space of consciousness is emergence as substance, or being known. The manner of existence of I within consciousness is emergence as act, or knowing and self-knowing. As knower, the self contains the other as known. Thus I is transcendent with respect to Not-I, since I knows Not-I but is not known by Not-I. The self is transcendent with respect to the other also, because the other presents itself thematically to the self through language and is named, while the self is namer. I contains Not-I through knowing and through language, and is not contained by it.

The self knows other selves as body, which is not my body but the body of another. It knows Other-I as both substance and act, as both body, which is known, and as mind which is its own self-possession as knowing. Other-I belongs to the self's own world, as object within it, but also transcends the self's world, as the centre of its own respective world. Thus other selves represent an incalculable centre of meaning.

The mode of existence of I as act, which is reflexivity and self-naming, constitutes two forms of freedom, both of which are to be understood as modes of transcendence exercised within a relation. The first is grounded in the self-reflexive knowing of I whereby I contains itself and thus finds itself in a transcendental relation with respect to itself in the unity of self and other as world. This transcendence before itself means that I is necessarily free with respect to itself. As self-knowing within the unity of self and other, I is free either to creatively affirm or to deny itself, where itself implies the entire relation between I and Not-I, the ground of which is the body, the expression of which is language and the unfolding of which is the world. Thus we can further state that this freedom is one which is ultimately exercised before existence itself, and it forms the basis of an *inner* transcendence.

The second form of freedom or transcendence is the relation of I to Not-I, or self to other. This is the transcendence of act over substance. The self is free therefore either to creatively affirm or occlude the other, whose own freedom constitutes an unsurpassable centre of meaning. We call this *outer* transcendence. Affirmation here implies a positive and creative movement of the will in service of the other. Thus we creatively nourish the object in its determining particularity and distinction from ourselves.

The freedom implied by both forms of transcendence is a necessary one, and inheres in the very existence of I. Thus we can say that the existence of the self is intrinsically ethical. The common ground of this twofold transcendence or freedom is the intrinsic tendency of existence to go beyond itself, to transgress its own limits in a creative surplus of existence. Both forms of transcendence can be understood to be modalities of a primary and originary excess of existence and can be said to partake of the nature of creativity. Within both modalities, this creativity manifests as the exercise of power with respect either to the self-in-relation-to-the-other or to the other. The affirming use of this power is an assisting in the creation of the other or of self-in-relation-to-the-other.

The affirmation of the self in relation to the other, or affirmation of the other, involves the giving over of the self to the creative surplus of existence, in which it partakes. Where this assent to existence entails a degree of self-giving or self-opening in such a way that the self allows itself to be put at risk for the sake of the other, it can be described as *kenotic*. This occurs in inner transcendence where the affirming acceptance of existence requires that we come to terms with something which causes us pain or puts our own life in question, and takes place in outer transcendence when we affirm another by actively engaging ourselves for them at risk to ourselves. The highest expression of this cognitive, affective and volitional displacement of the self for the sake of the other is compassion.

Within the field of consciousness, the existence of the self is founded dialectically upon the existence of the other; I and Not-I exist in a mutually grounding relation. Where the self chooses to affirm the other therefore, it *embraces* its own dialectical relation to the other. In so far as this affirmation includes kenosis, or self-emptying and self-giving, the existence of I is dialectically intensified. The affirmation of the other, and the embrace by I of its own dialectical relation with it, leads to the bestowal of enriched or intensified existence therefore, which we call *being*. In the case of inner transcendence, likewise, the self affirms the other, not specifically as Not-I, but rather as the otherness which is intrinsic to the relation of self and other. The affirmation of this relation, and release of the self into the flow of creativity that grounds existence, may well include a degree of kenosis, or a riskful giving and an opening of the self before existence. To this extent therefore the existence of the self will be dialectically enhanced, and again the self will receive the bestowal of intensified existence, or being. In being, the self becomes alien or strange to itself since the dialectic of consciousness, which is the mutually grounding relation of self and other, is reinscribed in the transformed self as a new simultaneity of self and other. This is not a unity between separate entities, but the inhabiting of a new intensity of self–other relation. As being, we are both self and other.

Inner transcendence: affirmation of existence

If the self is constructed to itself and is rendered transparent to itself as a name, a name which is embedded within multiple narratives (Who am I?, Where do I come from?, What do I want?, What do others want from me?), then affirmation of the name is acceptance by oneself of who one is and has been. Affirmation of the self in its relation to the other presupposes reconciliation with and acceptance of the world, and all its constituent narratives. Forms of past self-alienation are residually present therefore, and the full affirmation of the self implies the appropriation of the 'blank spots' of suppressed narratives which inhere in the self as dead areas. Affirmation of the self thus implies healing, forgiveness, resignation and acceptance of the existential condition which the self finds itself in. The failure to affirm the self, or the occlusion of self, leads to psychological disorders, to chronic absence of self-confidence, to a false self-image and the inability to judge situations. With respect to the body, self-affirmation implies appropriate moderation, hygiene, sensible diet and healthy living. Where the self occludes itself, we see poor styles of living. Extreme cases of alienation from self lead to self-mutilation and suicide. From the perspective of specific contexts of action within the world, affirmation will take diverse forms. In the face of threats it will be courage or fortitude; in the face of obstacles it will be initiative and energy; in the face of insurmountable opposition and tribulation it will be resignation and serenity of mind, whereas occlusion in such contexts will result in cowardice, inertia and fatalism. But the deepest affirmation of the self with respect to the world is that which springs from the creative excess of existence itself, its propensity to become what we have called 'enriched' or 'intensified existence', or *being*. This is the capacity of existence always to transcend itself in the embrace of the other, whether as the specific or generalized other. This inner motion of existence is the primary creative excess which leads to being and to the flow of love and hope which, in displacing the self, create it anew.

Affirmation of the totality which is the self in relation to the other, as world, generates the fundamental attitude of hope; and in the pulsation of self and other, which is the intimate play of existence, it bestows the fundamental attitude of joy. But the affirmation by I of its own world, or existence, as a totality, must include the embrace of that otherness which manifests as death. Affirmation of existence is nowhere tested so rigorously as in the knowledge of our own mortality. The certainty of our finitude calls into question the meaning of the whole of our existence. It challenges us in our entirety. But the affirmation of self before this reality, which constitutes a profound act of self-emptying before existence, is a participation, through freedom and the power which flows from freedom, in the primal creativity of existence itself. It is a sharing in the surplus of existence, its own self-transcending, in the excess we call being. By virtue of this primal creativity therefore, the self is created anew in its own most originary possibilities. Death need no longer be the end of possibility, but can be transformed by this creative force into yet another possibility of existence, however unfathomable and beyond our present comprehension.

Outer transcendence: affirmation of the other

Not-I exists in three modes, as inanimate objects, animate objects, and persons, who are identified as Other-I. Just as the affirmation of the self by the self requires the transparency to self of the name and all its personal narratives, so too the affirmation of the other in all three modes is preceded by the hermeneutical exercise which is the constructed and thematized presence to the self of the other in language.

Both non-organic and organic forms of inanimate objects are identified according to their type, or species, and are categorized as non-sentient. Animate objects, or animals, are sentient creatures, and may sometimes constitute a form of presence to the self which is designated by (personal) name, suggestive of a degree of individuality. But they are not identified as namers. In the case of inanimate objects, affirmation of the other, by which is meant the nourishing of the existence of the other in such a way that its constitution as Not-I is respected and maintained, implies maintenance and preservation; and where inanimate objects are part of an eco-system, conservation. The occlusion of the inanimate other is vandalism or wilful destruction, and, at times, environmental degradation. The affirmation of animals on the other hand requires the recognition that animals are sentient, and that animal species are an integral part of our world. Affirmation takes the form of conservation and husbandry, and of the maintenance of bio-diversity. The occlusion of animate Not-I manifests as neglect and cruelty, as well as environmental degradation.

In the case of other selves, we identify the other as narratively constructed and as the centre of their own world. Getting to know the other is gaining some sympathetic insight into the character of that world. In recognizing the other, the world-narrative of the other is woven into the world-narrative of the self, as we build points of affinity, symmetry and likeness between our world and that of the other. As the centre of its own world, Other-I likewise finds itself in a transcendental relation to its own Not-I. Thus the self's recognition of the other implies a recognition also of the freedom of Other-I, which is embodied in its transcendentality with respect to the world thematized to it in language.

Therefore, in the case of Other-I, affirmation of the other requires recognition of the other precisely and specifically in terms of their own world. Affirmation of the personal other is thus simultaneously affirmation of them as centre of their own world and of the structures, logic and meanings of that world. The imaging of the other, and of the desired and deferred goods of their world, will necessarily be an act of construction in which there is an interplay between extrapolation from one's own experience and attentiveness to the world-centredness of the other. An ethical affirmation of the other is not free of guiding hermeneutical principles however. A balance must necessarily be struck between three factors. The first is the other person's own perception of their good, as free world-centre. The second is our judgment as to the effect of their action upon further persons as legitimate centres of their own respective worlds. The third factor in an ethics based on kenotic ontology is the foundational belief that affirmation of their own other is an intrinsic good also for them. In other words, we must include the belief that it is in their own interest that their actions should also reflect the principle of the affirmation of their Not-I as animate or inanimate object, and as Other-I. This interest can be defined as the reception of enhanced existence or being through kenosis. We can thus speak of an ethical community who seek to propagate in others the intrinsic good of the affirmation of the other. Occlusion is a term which indicates the opposite of affirmation, being the suppression of the other precisely as a free world-centre and the appropriation of the other as object into the parameters and goods of our own world.

The concept of an ethical community functions also in a complementary way. Since the affirmation of the other is a process which precipitates an enhanced or heightened degree of existence, or being, in the self, we can observe that those in whom this dynamic occurs stand in a subtly different relation to other selves than those in whom this dynamic does not occur. Since heightened existence represents a higher degree of ontological density, we can speak of an ontological deficit which emerges between those in whom this process has occurred and those whose existence is not enhanced in this way. The consequences of this deficit is that others are drawn towards them, compelled by the weight of their own existential emptiness. This force of existential gravity, the ontological deficit between one individual and another, shows that kenotic existence is in principle contagious and self-propagating, summoning us to riskful affirmation of the other, precisely where the being of the other possesses a higher degree of actualization than our own. In such cases we are drawn by our own emptiness into a space of possibility.

Affirmation of Other-I may take many forms, from teaching to healing, from forgiveness to encouragement. Caring-for is affirmation through securing the physical and emotional well-being of the other. Forgiveness is affirmation through the restoration of relation and community to someone who has wronged us. Teaching is affirmation of the other through increase of understanding and facility. But its highest expression is compassion, where I enters into the suffering of Other-I, offering companionship by acknowledging the encroachments of alien suffering into the self and seeking to alleviate the suffering of the other. It is here that the kenotic structure of consciousness attains its fullest expression. To the cognitional, volitional and affective dimensions of compassion then we must add the fourth category of compassion as an epiphany of being, or site of the dialectical disclosure of the fullest ontological possibilities of the self.

All forms of affirmation of other selves are predicated on the recognition of the freedom of other selves as their own world-centres. Therefore the occlusion of Other-I, as oppression, is necessarily linked with a failure in the hermeneutical process of reconstructing Other-I precisely as free centre of its own world. Those who become the objects of hatred to others are deprived of their right to recognition as Other-I. Where racial stereotypes prevail, as in anti-Semitism, they may be designated as being outside humanity, legality or the norms of human society. Aspects of common humanity are suppressed, as are the constituent elements of the alien world. Where gender stereotypes obtain, as may happen in particular with male attitudes to women, the expectations that inform male judgments about women may reflect an inherited male perspective rather than women's own contemporary experience. Recognition of Other-I therefore is simultaneously recognition of the world-centredness of Other-I and is affirmation of Other-I's world.

Being and love

Affirmation of the self in relation with the other (inner transcendence) and affirmation of the other (outer transcendence) together constitute the transcendental analytic of the self as the self of compassion. The two types of transcendence relate closely to each other in that the inner transcendence can be said to anticipate outer transcendence. Where we are accepting of ourselves and of our own existence as world, with all its unpredictable openness, we can also say that we tend to be open to the compassionate affirmation of others who we encounter in the world and with whom we experience the unfolding of world. Thus the authentic embrace of our own existence as such opens out into the compassionate affirmation of the concrete other. The affirmation of outer transcendence on the other hand can be said to enact or complete inner transcendence. Where the self puts itself at risk for the sake of the other, the kenotic embrace of existence itself is implicitly performed. In other words, when we affirm the concrete other in compassion, we simultaneously affirm our own existence as such, which is to say our own experience of the unfolding of world.

Inner and outer transcendence together form a unity therefore, which is the transcendental analytic of the self as the self of compassion. Internal to that unity is the possibility of its own intensification. This manifests as an expectation or hope for, or an opening towards the possibility of an encounter with a personal other who is both finite – as persons are finite – but also infinite. This is not just to point to the way in which outer transcendence enacts inner transcendence, entailing the affirmation of existence as such. But it is rather to hold out the possibility of an encounter with existence as such in personal form. This is a possibility so immense and so strange that it stands at the very limit of the horizon of human expectation; and yet nevertheless it is implied as a logical progression in the intensification of the unity of inner and outer transcendence which is the structure of our transcendental analytic of the self. The affirmation of such a personal finite-infinite other would represent the highest kind of affirmation and the supreme form of the dialectical enhancement of existence which we have called being.

IV. *Excursus*

Consciousness

Our analysis of compassion begins with *awareness*, or consciousness, in which self and non-self coexist. Consciousness is constituted by the unity of the self who is aware and the other of which (or of whom) it is aware. Anything which falls outside the sphere of consciousness cannot be said to be immediately present to the self, although we assume of course that it may be so for others and may be again for ourselves. In other words, an analysis of consciousness is concerned only with the subject–object relation as it occurs *within the field of awareness itself*. That field of awareness is for the self simultaneously the field of existence, in which alone objects can be said to be *present* to us.[1] Our identification of consciousness with existence sets our analysis in opposition to the phenomenological method of Edmund Husserl to the extent that Husserl advocated the epoché, or bracketing out of the question of existence, arguing that it is solely the contents of consciousness which constitute the pure given, quite apart from the question as to whether they actually exist or not.[2] Against this we would argue that the *existence* of what we perceive in consciousness is more originary than any act of bracketing, which is an a posteriori strategy of the intellect. Indeed, we assume that what we perceive actually exists, unless we receive evidence to the contrary. At this point we follow Spinoza against Descartes therefore, on the unity of will and knowledge and the grounding of the mind in the ontological order.[3]

The self and other 'exist in a relation of mutual grounding', by which we mean that the one cannot be without the other. The self requires the other to be self. But the other can only exist within the sphere of consciousness-existence if there is a self who is aware of it. Neither self nor other is prior therefore, but they are simultaneous and interdependent. It is in this point that we distance ourselves from Idealist descriptions of consciousness which have tended to assimilate the other into the self. For J. G. Fichte, for instance, the self must vanquish the other if materialism is to be overcome and human freedom is to be preserved.[4] For Fichte, and indeed Hegel, the self–other relation which constitutes ordinary consciousness must be resolved into an ultimate unity of self and other, which underlies both the empirical self and the empirical other. Fichte understands this unity, which is a radicalization of Kant's 'transcendental unity of apperception', to be a higher subjectivity, or a more dynamic consciousness, whose need to attain realization grounds the ordinary self and other of everyday consciousness. Although we use Fichte's basic terminology of I and Not-I, we reject his dissolution of the self–other relation of ordinary consciousness into a deeper principle of unity, and wish to maintain the irreducible and dialectical opposition of self and other within consciousness. Transcendence, as we shall summarize below, takes place *within* the mutuality of self and other, and not beyond it.

Language

We further distinguish ourselves from the Idealist and Husserlian philosophies of consciousness with respect to the role of language in cognition. The non-self is known to us precisely as a complex diversity of entities in the world which can be named. The name, with all its dynamic associations, is integral to the existence of non-self for us within the sphere of consciousness. It is only in so far as objects are named that they have meaning for us and constitute part of our world. This means that our world is necessarily culturally specific, embodying a field of resonances which may not be reproducible, or fully reproducible, outside the community of those who speak the same language as ourselves. But we contest Derrida's view that the sign as foundation of cognition grounds a 'metaphysics' of absence.[5] Signs rather are 'filled' by those things they signify, and the interacting semantic fields which together constitute our world, body forth the multiple presences to us of objects and persons. Language realizes existence, rather than undermining it. In the excess of its expressivity, language not only reveals to us presences in the world, but it also manifests the speech agent: that is, other speakers who like ourselves stand at the centre of their own respective worlds.[6] When we speak, we engage in a complex enterprise of shared meanings and common usages. As P. F. Strawson has written, we are unable to make use of personal terms such as 'I', 'me' and 'you' (so called 'shifters') unless we understand what it is for someone else to make use of these terms.[7] Otherness, in the form of other speakers, is written into the language we speak, whereby we make sense of ourselves and the world. Therefore, if language is the medium in which the self becomes thematically present to itself as a name that stands at the centre of interweaving narratives which together construct 'world', the self can only become a self by participating in the self–other relation through and in language. This is the *expression* of that relation or what Merleau-Ponty called an 'element' of that world.[8] Indeed, it is only within the commonality and exchange of narratives with others that the self is present to itself: as a specific person who is 'me' with a particular history, a particular memory, and a particular participation in the world.

This view of language is presented particularly well by Paul Ricoeur in his study *Oneself as Another*.[9] Ricoeur's own work can be understood to be a reaction against the Husserlian tradition, of which he was himself once a student, and specifically against the notion of the 'self-positing *cogito*', which understands the self to be autonomous and self-contained, without the mediations of language, culture and action. For Ricoeur, the *cogito* of Husserlian–Cartesian tradition is 'as abstract and empty as it is invincible'.[10] He has sought therefore to trace the emplotments of the self in the 'objectifying mediations of language, action, narrative, and the ethical and moral predicates of action'.[11] Although Ricoeur employs the term 'ontology', he argues that ontology today must be radically rethought, and he proposes an adaptation of the Aristotelian notion of being as *analogy*, or the 'polysemy of being', whereby the self comes into view in its diverse manifestations.[12] These include reference, speech-acts, the semantics of action, agency, narrative, ethics, morality and 'practical wisdom'. These manifestations of the self, or 'arduous detours' as Ricoeur calls them, enable us to glimpse the self through a dynamic of *attestation*, which finally yields *trust*, which is 'trust in the power to say, in the power to do, in the power to recognize oneself as a character in a narrative', so that 'attestation can be defined as the *assurance of being oneself acting and suffering*'.[13] Ricoeur's opposition to the Husserlian–Cartesian project of self-transparency is apparent likewise in his commitment to developing an understanding of the self which takes otherness not as something 'added on to selfhood from outside, as though to prevent its solipsistic drift', but as part of 'the ontological constitution of selfhood'.[14] He seeks to establish that 'selfhood of oneself implies otherness to such an intimate degree that one cannot be thought of without the other, that instead one passes into the other, as we might say in Hegelian terms'.[15] In *Oneself as Another* Ricoeur argues for three modes of passivity which establish '*the* attestation of otherness'. These are the passivity of the body in perception, passivity in interpersonal relations and that form of passivity which is conscience. Aristotelian analogy plays its part here too, as Ricoeur stresses the differentiation of passivity, in order to prevent the reconstitution of any foundational theory of the *cogito*. In opposition to the 'broken' or 'shattered ego' of Nietzsche he offers *'an attestation which is itself broken*, in the sense that the otherness joined to selfhood is attested to only in a wide range of dissimilar experiences, following a diversity of centres of otherness'.[16]

Our disagreement with Ricoeur then (for all our indebtedness to him) lies in his identification of the self-possessing *'cogito'* with a monolithic view of the self which excludes the role of otherness in the constitution of the self. The model of philosophy of consciousness which we propose here maps a self that is self-aware and self-possessing: a self that knows that it *is*. But if Ricoeur's argument is – quite correctly – that the self is determined at all levels by its *passivity*, which is its own answerability to the other, then there is no reason why the self-possessing and self-knowing self cannot know that it comes to itself precisely via and in the other. The self-consciousness of the philosophy of consciousness tradition can itself be constituted by the other, specifically at the level of self-awareness, and thus itself be a form of passivity. In other words, there is no intrinsic reason why the *cogito* should be set in opposition to alternative philosophies of the self which seek to place otherness at the heart of the self, even though it is historically the case that *Subjektphilosophie* has either neglected or had extreme difficulty with the notion of the other and specifically with understanding the relation with other selves. This results however not from the nature of self-consciousness as such but rather from the particular narratives of consciousness which Descartes and Husserl, for instance, chose to promote. In Kantian tradition, on the other hand, the *cogito* is not free-standing but is co-posited with every act of perception, without which 'something would be represented in me which could not be thought at all'.[17] Here the *cogito* is the unity of consciousness since 'only in so far as I can grasp the manifold of representations in one consciousness, do I call them one and all *mine*. For otherwise I should have as many-coloured and diverse a self as I have representations of which I am conscious to myself.'[18] Kant's affirmation of the 'transcendental unity of apperception' is not advocacy of a sovereign, wholly self-possessing and unified self however, since 'that self-consciousness which, while generating the representation *"I think"* (a representation which must be capable of accompanying all other representations, and which in all consciousness is one and the same), cannot itself be accompanied by any further representation'.[19] Nor can the *cogito* of perception and the *cogito* of introspection, which is itself a representation, be said to be identical, and so 'the consciousness of self is very far from being a knowledge of the self'.[20] Self-awareness need not be identified with the free-standing and self-luminous substance-*cogito* of Cartesian tradition therefore, but as Kant has argued, some degree of unified self-awareness expressed in the *cogito*, or what P. F. Strawson has called 'the *possibility* of the self-ascription of experiences on the part of the subject of those experiences', is a precondition for the synthesis of experience as such.[21]

The Kantian – and indeed Spinozan – traditions hold the possibility of a reading of consciousness which is significantly at variance with that of Descartes and Husserl to the extent that otherness – and other selves – are seen to be a condition of it. The work of Max Scheler and Edith Stein, who like Ricoeur, Levinas and Derrida were students of Husserl, reflects an attempt to articulate otherness from within consciousness which contrasts with the hermeneutical and anti-ontological philosophies of their more illustrious contemporaries. This can be seen, for instance, in Edith Stein's distinction between the primordial and non-primordial experience of the self. The former is our own and 'issues live from my "I"',[22] whereas non-primordial experience is that of either our own feelings and sensations, alienated in memory or fantasy, or our experience of the feelings and sensations of others. But where the latter entails real empathy, or *Einfühlung*, it becomes an act 'which is primordial as present experience, though non-primordial in content'.[23] Thus the non-primordiality of our empathetic experience of the feelings and sensations of others 'is not simple but is a non-primordiality in which foreign (*fremd*) primordiality becomes apparent'.[24] In other words, our own recognition of the experiences of others, though part of our own world (non-primordial), reveal another human subject to us. According to Stein, this other is known to us, as subject of the alien feelings and sensations that impinge non-primordially upon our world, with all the primordial immediacy that we know our own feelings and sensations. This comes close to our own argument that other selves are recognized as 'Other-I', that is, as the centres of their own respective worlds. Language presents a horizon for the emergence of the other as someone who is 'like ourselves', and who is known with a primordial immediacy which is distinct from the way in which we know objects in our world. Compassion, as we have argued, is the epiphany of the self's own answerability to the other, and thus of the extent to which otherness stands at the heart of the self's own self-possession as knowing subject.[25]

Transcendence

In our phenomenological analysis of compassion we have argued that the self is essentially free with respect to the non-self, and able to act upon it or with respect to it. The freedom of the self is crucial to the argument for the ethical nature of the self in its relation of mutual grounding with the other. Amongst philosophers of consciousness, it is Fichte and Blondel who have laid a particular stress upon the freedom of the self. Fichte recognized that it is the presence of the human other which allows the self to attain moral and even ontological self-realization as freedom before the other, and that the exercise of this freedom itself entails the recognition of the freedom of the other.[26] The other thus constitutes 'a summoning of the subject to a free activity', and is 'the material of action'.[27] Fichte's interest here lies largely in the desire to establish the ground for a community of free individuals, whose sociality is the restriction of their own freedom for the sake of the freedom of others. This is a civilizing process which is guaranteed by the Enlightenment principle of *Bildung* and this paradigm of community as a whole provides the only possible sphere of action for the self-realization of a free and rational self-consciousness: 'human beings only become human amongst other human beings'.[28] For Blondel, likewise, freedom is 'necessarily produced before consciousness', and 'is necessarily exercised'.[29] In the abyss of transcendence, the self knows itself to be confronted with the freedom of its own power, or what Maurice Blondel calls 'a kind of creative sovereignty'.[30] Blondel rightly maintains that acting is a fundamental determinative condition of consciousness. It is intrinsic to the self-realization of consciousness and of the dialectical flow from the outer world to the inner world and back again.[31] It is also the giving over of the agent into an alien power, which is the merging of the will with a motive. Blondel memorably likens acting to the leap of a grasshopper: 'In giving ourselves to action, do we ever know where we shall come down?'.[32] It is part of our fallen state that we cannot know the consequences of what we do, and action involves us in a kind of involuntary culpability: 'that which I had the strength to do, I lack the strength to undo'.[33] Action is finally an act of trust therefore: 'To act is in a way to entrust oneself to the universe', for it is taken *sub specie totius*.[34]

There are a number of real affinities between Blondel's metaphysics of action and our own kenotic ontology, particularly where Blondel speaks of the interconnectedness of action and being, as in his statement that 'the role of action is to develop being and to constitute it', or 'action sees being no longer from the outside; it has grasped it, it possesses it, it finds it within itself'.[35] For kenotic ontology too action is risk, and it is our actions that determine whether our being is enhanced or diminished. Here the enhancement of being derives from the structure of consciousness itself however, while, for Blondel, it follows from the extent to which human action participates in divine action: 'in voluntary action a secret nuptial takes place between the human will and the divine will'.[36] This is a Thomist metaphysics of action therefore which is linked more with a theology of creation than one of compassion, which – as we have argued – radicalizes dispossessive action which is self-risk for the sake of the other.

The model we have proposed, which is that of self and other in a relation of mutual grounding, in which the self finds itself necessarily free before the other, is a dialectical structure, since we have defined the self as 'I' and the other as 'Not-I' and have made these contraries interdependent. It is this dialectical orientation which marks our divergence from philosophy of consciousness tradition as represented by Spinoza and Kant, Scheler and Stein, and shows our indebtedness to the dialectical thinking of J. G. Fichte. Where we differ from the early German Idealist school however, is in our refusal of a transcendentalist account of I and Not-I which would resolve their contrariety into a higher level of unity. The model of transcendence which we advocate here is a transformation of the self *within* its relation with the other and not a passing of the self *beyond* its relation with the other, which is implied in the Idealist synthesis. The appropriate term for transcendence in our sense then is *transfiguration*, which retains the irreducible mutuality of self and other, albeit as unity in opposition.

It is perhaps useful further to contrast kenotic ontology with the transcendental anthropology of Karl Rahner, which has exercised such a powerful and positive influence upon Catholic philosophical theology. Rahner's notion of 'transcendental experience' also arises from the reflexive knowledge of the I in its encounter with the other. For Rahner, transcendence is an aspect of knowing in itself, in a pure movement of epistemological reflexivity, which is triggered by the knowing of any object. It is the 'self-presence of the subject in knowledge' since '[i]n knowledge not only is something known, but the subject's knowing is also co-known'.[37] This is not merely an awareness which follows from the secondary act of knowing a primary act of knowing, which is to say the self knowing that it knows, but is a transcendental determination of consciousness and a feature of all knowing. It is in fact an a priori condition of all knowledge and becomes, for Rahner, the unthematic knowledge of God as the infinite term of that knowledge: the perpetual presence of the self before the givenness of mystery. According to our argument however, the reflexive knowing of the self is foundationally determined by *its otherness from the object of knowledge*, and thus it knows itself precisely as otherness from the object (non-self), that is, as self. Transparency to self in our argument is already thematically constructed as 'I', that is, through language and the dialogical relation imparted by it. While we agree with Rahner therefore, that the 'original self-presence of the subject' escapes reiteration at the level of reflexion and always remains a surplus, we differ from him in that transcendence – as transfiguration – emerges from *within the dialectic* of the subject–object relation and remains within it. For Rahner, transcendence is the ground of all cognition and is ultimately the radical and unconditioned openness of the self to God. For kenotic ontology, reflexive transcendence is rather the self's own innate awareness that it is dialectically structured towards the other in freedom, which relation grounds the possibility of a kenotic ethics and the self's own excess or overcoming. We differ from Rahner then to the extent that knowledge of the other is determined by the object in its particularity and thus in the ethical particularity of the relation of the self to the other, and that transcendence is a possibility which awakens *from within* that relation and not from an a priori ground of all knowing which encompasses it.

The christological dimensions of kenotic ontology are expressed differently from those of Rahner's transcendental anthropology therefore. In the model of the transcendence of compassion, I have argued for a double transcendence, firstly by the self with regard to itself in relation with the other (inner transcendence) and secondly by the self with regard to the other (outer transcendence). The former, which is primarily the sphere of Rahner's 'transcendental experience', opens towards an affirmation in which we trustingly put ourselves at the disposal of reality as a whole. In traditional religious language, this is the love of God, entrusting ourselves to the will of God, and to a journeying towards him which is open-ended, since God is the infinite term of reality and existence. This passivity before the entirety of existence is performed in prayer and in the resigned accept-ance of what befalls us as a condition of our existence. It is exercised most fully before the reality of our own death, which is the most radical expres-sion of our passivity before God. Given the infinity of reality as a whole, this kind of affirmation, which has reality as the unity of self and other as its object, therefore entails the sense of the possibility of an infinite kenosis. Outer transcendence however, which is compassion for a concrete other, has a subtly different structure. The opening horizon of infinite kenosis which likewise characterizes outer transcendence is not grounded in the possibility of our own death as final and inevitable closure within the infinite order of existence and reality however, but rather as the ultimate possible consequence of self-risk undertaken for the sake of a particular other. This is the giving of our own life for that of a friend (cf. John 15.13). Of course, this does not mean that all acts of compassion entail this degree of self-risk, but even small acts of compassion imply a life-orientation which, if consistently carried through in accordance with the extent of the risk to the other, might indeed lead to the offering of the life of the self for the sake of the other. The ultimate compassionate love of Etty Hillesum and Edith Stein for their suffering neighbours is but the most radical example of a self-risking life-orientation which for all its extra-ordinary character is generally expressed in a multitude of quite ordinary ways.

The affirmation of inner and outer transcendence show a thorough-going complementarity. Affirmation of the infinite other opens the self to affirmation of the particular other, while the latter as outer transcendence can itself be seen to be *the enactment* of the former as inner transcendence. When we affirm the concrete other, putting ourselves at risk, we are also already enacting the affirmation of the whole, and affirm both ourselves and existence itself, in trust, openness and hope. If this is lacking in us, then it is restored by compassionate acts. Where outer transcendence again differs from inner transcendence however, is in the extent that it is not grounded in the affirmation of an indeterminate object, such as God or the whole of existence, but is ordered rather to the concrete other, who – as part of our own world – is finite and – as centre of their own unfolding world – is infinite. The concrete other thus bears the marks of both infinity and finitude. The combination of both forms of transcendence in the affirmation of the concrete other means that in the act of compassionate love there is mediated to us a sense of the possibility of an infinite kenosis which is the affirmation of an other who is both infinite and particular. In other words, the act of compassion opens to us an horizon of encounter with God in personal form. It is this realization that brings us to the brink of the subject of the second half of this book, which is a further, theological reduction of compassion. In self-dispossession for the sake of the other, we embrace the dialectical nature of our own consciousness and thus stand in the immediacy of our own most radical truth. This self-apprehension is simultaneously the acknowledgment that we are addressed, even in our dispossessive movement, by another, who is himself an infinite personal other. This is the Word of God who, as the compassionate self-dispossession of God, is the one who has gone before. In the immediacy of our own truth, we begin to apprehend the prior immediacy of divine truth, and it is this 'recognition in dispossession' which forms the ground of our further theological reflections.

Conclusion

Although our analysis stands within the tradition of the philosophy of consciousness, I have been at pains to stress the distance between this project and Cartesianism. My argument proposes that the self is not prior to the other but exists rather in a relation of mutual grounding with it. I argue also that the full realization of the self is only possible via the other, and so the other is implicated at the very core of the self. It is evident however that the perspective of the analysis of compassion given here is centred upon the self. As Paul Ricoeur has argued, in the (Levinasian) system of a 'summons to responsibility', the initiative comes from the other, whereas in a system of 'sympathy for the suffering other', the initiative comes from the self.[38] In the former, the 'I' is object: 'as the initiative of the injunction comes from the other, it is in the *accusative* mode alone that the self is enjoined'.[39] Against this I have argued for a philosophy of the self which is based on the 'I' in the nominative case, but an 'I' which knows itself to have undergone and to still undergo inflection as 'me'. This 'me' therefore constitutes the manner of the 'I''s self-possession, and mediates to it the presences of other 'I's. It is only possible to combine the nominative 'I' with the radical mutuality of other selves because of the place of kenosis, or self-emptying of the 'I' as 'me', which, in the argument given here, actually defines the self as a particularity which is not only open to but also radically determined by its dynamic relation to the other. I have further argued that the self undergoes a transformation through embracing its own kenotic nature and affirming the other. This change has been designated as a movement from 'existence' to 'being', which is a heightened or intensified state of existence. This transformation is essentially a transfiguration, since the transformed self remains within its relation to the other, and does not leave it behind. What we observe in the transformation therefore is an intensification of the mutuality of self and other, so that the other always remains as the final goal and challenge of the transfigured self, and is the site of an ultimate, divine address.

B.
Narratives of Existence

Introduction:
The Grammar of Ontology

Τὸ δὲ ὄν λέγεται μὲν πολλαχῶς

Being is said in many ways.

Aristotle, *Metaphysics*

If existence or 'being' is the medium of relation between self and other, then ontology can be defined as the thinking of that relation. It has consequences therefore both for our description of the world, as the ultimate contextualization for the unfolding of the self–other relation, and for language, as the field of its expression. The following studies in historical ontology seek to draw out the essential narrativity of ontology, tracing the diverse ways in which the philosophy of being implicitly and explicitly determines the potentialities of the self. In the following four chapters we will meet being as the angelically sublime figure of platonic texts, and as the gift from nothingness which sets the Jewish and Christian communities a task of living. We shall observe it intrude as the stubborn limit of thought in the transcendental speculations of idealists and phenomenologists. We shall see it also as the electric charge of authenticity in existentialist texts, and finally as the semi-mythical beast against which valiant deconstructionists time and again ride boldly forth. We shall discern here also a grammar of ontology, according to whether being is thought under aspect (as being or becoming), substantival form (essence or substance), verbal form (as act), participle (analogical mode), mood (the proximity of the indicative and the displacement of the subjunctive) and person (as subjective or objective being).

But the primary typology we employ here is determined by the different points of access into the thinking of being. If being is the medium of relation between the self and other, then one kind of ontology focuses upon the medium itself, to the relative exclusion of self and other, while a second type accesses being through both self and other, and a third through the self alone. A fourth conceivable type of ontology views the self–other relation from the perspective of the other, generally in the form of materialism. We call the first of these types 'Being and Oneness', since an emphasis upon the medium itself tends to stress being as a unity or a totality. From an historical point of view, this is an ontology which begins with Parmenides and concludes, in the modern period, with Heidegger. In the following chapter we shall also survey the work of Plotinus, Eckhart and Spinoza. Although each of these thinkers represents a case apart, we shall argue that their respective philosophical systems presuppose the totality or unity of being in such a way that the central issue for the self becomes its relation to being, rather than to the other. Whether being is directly identified with oneness or distinguished from it, the self is situated in a dialectic of unity and distinction with respect to the medium of its relation with the other, which may be developed in terms of a cosmological model of hierarchy and participation (Plotinus and Eckhart), or of what we have termed a 'cult' of being. This characterizes being as an elusive and all-embracing principle, the 'contemplation' of which is the final goal of the self (Spinoza and Heidegger).

Our second paradigm is entitled 'Being and Nothingness', and it is linked in particular with Judaeo-Christian metaphysics which characteristically understands the fate of the self, and the nature of the self, to be inextricably bound up with the other. This tradition effectively links being and the good, in the form of agapic love. Each of our Christian thinkers, Augustine, Aquinas and Kierkegaard, can be shown to be reacting to non-Christian ontologies, refiguring them in the light of a theology of creation and covenant. For Augustine, it is Plato who forms the backdrop, whose metaphysics of desire and community is an important prelude to an ontology of Christian agapic love and a theology of the church. Aquinas, on the other hand, adapts Aristotle, again in the light of a theology of creation, which stresses the extent to which being is a gift granted by the Creator within specific parameters of responsibility and answerability. Against Hegel, Kierkegaard asserts the claims of a new existence given to the Christian through faith in the entry into existence, or history, of the Infinite God. Incarnation here bestows a new possibility of being which is both temporal and eternal. The ontology of 'Being and Nothingness' reflects the perspective of *both* self and other, and understands the self to be determined by a relation of mutuality and inescapable ethical responsibility with respect to the other. Being, in this context, becomes a challenge and a possibility, since the gift of being is sufficient for the self to desire more, but only in the knowledge that being can also be taken away in perpetual alienation of the self from God. The principle of *creatio ex nihilo* implies both a personal Creator God and the oscillation of created being between its infinite intensification in accord with the will of the Creator and its collapse back into the nothingness from which it came.

Our third paradigm, under the heading 'Being and Consciousness', prioritizes the self to the extent that the other is subordinated to or even assumed into the subjectivity of the self. In Chapter Four, we reflect upon the prioritization of the self in the work of Descartes and Kant, followed by studies of Fichte and Hegel. Idealism in its different forms is born of the sense that the other implicitly constitutes a threat to the self, and yet the very privileging of consciousness above its objects can dissolve the empirical self into disembodied processes of reflexivity, lacking content and will. Rather than safeguarding the irreducible mutuality of self and other, Idealist ontology tends to reduce being to thought, and thus initiates a new crisis for the self, for whom the self–other relation now becomes the modality of a subjectivity that is no longer its own. As the 'limit' of freedom, posited by a grand subjectivity in the process of its own self-realization, being can and must be transcended. Otherwise that ultimate freedom will itself be constrained and governed by materiality, the ascendency of which, for the Idealist mind, would mark the end of philosophy. The final possible paradigm is that of an ontology which proceeds from the other, whereby the self is fragmented and dissolved in the forces of materialism. If for the Idealist, being is seen as a limit that needs to be overcome in the advance of freedom, then for a Marxist such as Theodor Adorno, the language of being appears as 'a jargon of authenticity', which masks the pretensions of a social class in pursuit of power, and is required to be measured against the materialist forces of history.[1]

In this section we have not included a study of the materialist models on the grounds that the issue at stake is precisely the articulation of the self in a distinctive and explicitly ontological register. The active debate among analytical philosophers concerning 'existential predicates' is a related theme but not one which is germane to the discussion here. It may be the case that the statement that an object 'is' (without a predicate) requires a sense of what Maritain understood to be 'the ontological mystery' if it is to be other than an incomplete sentence, or what D. F. Pears calls 'a referential tautology'.[2] Such an intuition underlies the scholastic tradition as it appears in Thomas Aquinas' definition of *ens* as the *quasi-notissimum,* or in Duns Scotus' view that it is the *simpliciter simplex*, defying all definition or reduction to other more fundamental terms.[3] Some sense of existence without predicate is implied also in Leibniz's famous inquiry 'Why is there something rather than nothing?', which Heidegger took to be the central metaphysical question.[4] It may be in fact that our many non-Greek philosophers of being are in the main indebted to a 'strong' ontology, which is grounded in a Judaeo-Christian metaphysics of creation. This introduced into Greek thinking what Charles Kahn has called the 'notion of *radical contingency*', which reflects upon being not only from the perspective that what is might have been different but also that what is might not have existed at all.[5] Kahn takes the view that 'existence in the modern sense becomes a central concept in philosophy only in the period when Greek ontology is radically revised in the light of a metaphysics of creation: that is to say, under the influence of Biblical religion'.[6]

Although there is an influential school of thought which – since Kant – has advocated a return to the purely veridical meaning of the copula, which was characteristic of the Greeks (whereby the use of the copula serves only to affirm the truth or otherwise of a statement, as in 'It is a cat' – 'It is not a cat'), Western thought in its Idealist, Existentialist and

Christian forms has by and large been committed to an understanding of being as that which finds its opposite in nothingness.[7] It is for this reason that we have maintained the use of the terms 'being' and 'existence' throughout this book, which are most naturally opposed to 'nothingness', rather than 'reality', for instance, which is more naturally opposed to 'illusion', the 'unreal', or even 'falsity'. But from the perspective of the present study, we need only be able to maintain that the words 'I am' (without a predicate) or 'I exist' can meaningfully be said by an ordinary speaker of English in order to argue that the question as to the *content* of these words is a key metaphysical problem. We need not progress along the Leibnizean and Heideggerian path of asking what is the meaning of being as such, which would inevitably be to replace our preferred paradigm, which is concerned specifically with the self in relation to the other, with the model we have called 'Being and Oneness', which focuses upon the medium of being itself, to the relative exclusion of the concrete other.

Our intention here then is to engage with the meaning of being for the human subject ('What does being mean for me?' – 'What is it for me to be?') and to resolve it primarily with reference to the other, rather than to explore the nature of existence as such. From one perspective therefore, the present project stands broadly within the tradition of *analogia entis*, as this was developed in personalist and existentialist ways by such figures as Gustav Siewerth, Eric Przawara, Karl Rahner and Hans Urs von Balthasar. 'Kenotic ontology' is analogical to the extent that we shall argue in the second part of this volume for the status of the compassionate self as created analogue to the Trinity itself. It is important to refuse the temptation of drawing comparisons between intersubjectivity and aspects of contemporary scientific accounts of the world however, such as relativity and quantum theory, as others have done.[8] Scientific theory appears to be in a particularly fluid state at present, and, as Colin Gunton has argued, it is unclear what is to be gained from the comparison of specific theological models with specific scientific models beyond a certain cultural synchrony.[9] But in the Conclusion to the present volume, we shall propose the outline of a model of objective existence as such which grows from the phenomenological and theological reductions of compassion, in what is a kind of 'cosmological reduction'. Once again however, our concern will be with the relationality of being with respect to the human subject.

As noted in Chapter One, the language of being can be thought of as articulating the 'metanarrativity' or 'essential narrativity' of the self, which is implicated in all other narratives of the self and its identity, and yet which can also exist apart from other narratives as its own distinct discourse. The language of being guarantees a kind of self-transparency which is not exhausted by the multiplicity of stories of the self; its transcendence is manifest precisely in the repeated narratability of the self and in the resistance of the self to reduction to any one or to any one combination of narratives. Furthermore, the advocacy of ontology stands as a challenge to the postmodernist tendency to model the self as a splintered and fractured reality which is denied any unity. To this extent we are affirming the Kantian principle that it is only the unity of the self which makes possible the manifold of experience, as 'my' existence and 'my' world. Without the unity of the *cogito*, experience as such cannot be, and yet – with Kant – we acknowledge that the *cogito* itself cannot ever know that unity directly or completely, but only discursively, as it is distributed through the range of perceptions, both external and internal. If schizophrenia is the condition of the modern world, as Deleuze and Guattari have suggested, then the language of being offers an important resource for articulating and drawing forth the intrinsic unity of the self which, albeit deferred, is the ground for the knowledge of the world as such.

The unity of the self is the persistence of the same across time which, for Heidegger, grounds presence.[10] As Aristotle argued in the *Metaphysics*, unity, or sameness, is intrinsic to the constitution of an entity.[11] Only by remaining fundamentally consistent with itself across the changing narratives which constitute historical existence, can the self truly be said *to be*. Furthermore, the fact that the self knows itself as existing as the same self within the diverse narrative spaces of identity, character and history, signals the *creatureliness* of the self. If, on the one hand, the existence of the self is its very narratability and capacity to lend itself to ever more narrative formations, without being exhausted by any, then – from a Christian point of view – we can say that the language of being safeguards the capacity or availability of the self to be re-scripted or re-authored within a divine narrative of ultimate meanings, in a revaluation of the traditional concept of the soul. The unity of consciousness then, expressed in the language of existence, is the mark of our creatureliness, without which we can never know what it is to fall into alienation from being, nor to be called back to being, and which in its incomplete state serves as a pledge in this life for the fullness of existence and knowledge in the life to come.

The model of kenotic ontology which is proposed here then is an attempt to make a new kind of language of being available, as existential performance, in which we can articulate ourselves as a kind of being which has encountered radical *difference*: as ontology *of* difference. This ontology understands the self to come into deeper existence through processes of self-giving and self-emptying, where our own innermost self-determination is excess, as we enter a place where we are as much other as self. This is to understand human being as journeying in hope, and the self as embrace of paradox and possibility, within the enveloping context of the good. But it is not the creation of a new esoteric jargon of existence, for existence itself is performed at every moment in the structures of ordinary speech, and, as thinking beings, it is natural that we should have an innate interest in thinking about being.[12] Since we know that we are, it is inevitable that we should be interested in what it means to be. As Karl

Rahner has observed, 'There is in the human person an inescapable *unity in difference between one's original self-possession and reflection*'.[13] And reflexivity, according to Anthony Giddens, is a particularly significant condition of high modernity.[14] Whether we think of being at all then, and in what ways if we do, must affect the kind of beings we are, and so the kind of people we can become. From this ethical perspective therefore, we can locate the ontology presented here not only within the long history of the *analogia entis* in Catholic tradition, but also as an *aggiornamento* which is a return to the deep structures of ontological thinking as we find them in the Hebrew Scriptures and most specifically at Ex. 3.14. There God declares Godself to be *ehyeh ašer ehyeh* ('I am that I am', 'I will be who I will be', or 'I am He that is'). This most complex utterance has exercised both Jewish and Christian exegetes in ways which mark the estrangement between Jerusalem and Athens on the question of divine metaphysics. 'Athenians' (both Christian and Jewish) have read this enigmatic state-ment as pointing to the necessary existence of God, whose being is eternal. The Jerusalem camp, on the other hand, have taken these words as referring to the continuing and saving presence of God for his people in history, understanding divine presence to be coterminous with divine saving acts. The identification of 'being' and 'love' which informs this project as a whole, is an attempt to articulate a deep connectedness between presence and compassion, between being and the good, which is marked by what Hermann Cohen termed 'a correlation' between human and divine actions in such a way that the human goodness of compassion for 'the stranger' and the 'widow or orphan' becomes the expression and indeed even enactment of the divine creativity. Through our compassion, the God of compassion creates the world anew, or, better, God deepens and intensifies God's primary act of creation.[15]

In the previous two chapters we have traced a philosophical outline of the self through a phenomenological reduction of compassion. In Chapters Three to Six we shall survey ontologies of the past and present and argue for a new ontology of difference (the reader whose interests are less histori-cal can proceed directly from this introduction to Chapter Seven where modern reconstructions of the self are surveyed and the self of kenotic ontology is developed). In Chapters Eight to Thirteen, in a theological reduction, we shall seek to explore a Christian appropriation and intensifi-cation of that model, by rethinking it in the light of the incarnation, the theology of difference which is manifested in the passion, and the continu-ing presence among us of God made flesh. The Afterword begins to point to a kind of cosmological reduction which is predicated on the essential textuality of existence as such, which enters the world in the Word made flesh, made present to us in the repeated celebration of the divine eucharist. In this way, we shall argue, the divine speech reaches into the heart of human culture, transforming it from within. Thus the current project is a pragmatic rereading of the Western metaphysical tradition in the light of rabbinic exegesis of Ex. 3.14, taken together with a post-Holocaust emphasis upon a dispossessive ethics which is supremely manifest in compassion as the embrace of difference. As such it seeks to set up a new alignment between human and divine compassion, renewing and regrounding an *analogia entis* which is rooted in tradition on the one hand and is authentically contemporary on the other.

3

Being and Oneness: Hierarchy and Cult

οὕτως οὖν ἀίδιόν ἐστι καὶ ἄπειρον καὶ ἓν καὶ ὅμοιον πᾶν.

In this way, then, it is eternal and infinite and one and wholly homogeneous.

Melissus of Samos

The origins of the story of being in the European tradition lie in the cosmological reflections of the Presocratic philosophers. It is chiefly in Parmenides and the Eleatic school that we see the emergence of what is to become the ontological tradition, although the form which it takes is – perhaps inevitably – that of our first paradigm, which appropriates being (as the medium of relation of self and other) not from the perspective of either the self or the other, but from being itself. Here the stress lies upon the *unity* of being, to the exclusion of the self and other, and being itself, as Being-One, easily becomes the object of cultic devotion. The term 'cultic' here designates a way of relating to being which does not pass through the other, but draws the gaze directly to itself. Unity was a key principle in Presocratic thought, since from its inception, their thinking was governed by a need to establish the unifying principle of what is. For Thales of Miletus, whom Aristotle called 'the founder of natural philosophy', water was the universal substance, or that 'from which the other things come into being, it being preserved'.[1] It was Anaximander, Thales' pupil, however, who first used the key terms *archê* and *to apeiron* for the 'indefinite origins of the universe' and 'the limitless', from which the contrasting and opposed properties of the world were separated.[2] Anaximenes, another Milesian philosopher, linked the neuter *apeiron* with the notion of 'infinite air', while Heraclitus, looking back to Anaximander's principle of contrasts, identified fire as the element which governs the cycles of change and the perpetual mobility of the world.

Parmenides

Milesian cosmology formed an important background to the thought of Parmenides of Elea, but an entirely new stage was reached with his suggestion in the *Way of Truth* that it is 'being' (εἶναι) which is the universal element. Whereas water, air and fire offer themselves to the senses, being as being does not. It is the appropriate object, not of sense perception but rather of *thought*. Whatever the exact meaning of the important and much disputed line τὸ γὰρ αὐτὸ νοεῖν ἔστιν τε καὶ εἶναι may be (perhaps 'for the same thing can be thought as can be' or 'whatever it is that can be thought, can be'), a new kind of symmetry between being and thought is clearly posited here, which represents a level of abstraction and is at a remove from ordinary experience.[3] Most particularly, we find in Parmenides the belief that what is not cannot be thought, with the consequence that the phenomenon of generation and substantial change (from previous non-existence) must be dismissed out of hand, as unthinkable. This inaugurates a new emphasis upon being as unity (or Being-One), according to which everything that is, is united, and what is not cannot be thought. This was infinite, irreducible into parts, eternal and unchanging:

> Only one story, one road, now is left: that it is. And on this there are signs in plenty that, being, it is ungenerated and indestructible, whole, of one kind and unwavering, and complete. Nor was it, nor will it be, since now it is, all together, one continuous. For what generation will you seek for it? How, whence, did it grow? That it came from what is not I shall not allow you to say or think – for it is not sayable or thinkable that it is not.[4]

The abstraction of being and its removal to another sphere, beyond that of sense experience, set up a metaphysics of displacement that was to be powerfully influential in Greek thought. Oneness itself lies outside the sphere of the senses and ordinary experience, and presents itself (teasingly) to thought. As Augustine was to remark many centuries later: 'whoever thinks with exactitude of unity will certainly discover that it cannot be perceived by the senses. Whatever comes into contact with a bodily sense is proved to be not one but many, for it is corporeal and therefore has innumerable parts.'[5] Thus, as a unity that is thought, Being-One also marked an early stage in the evolution of a new kind of philosophy of the self. After all, if all being is one, who is it that is *thinking* being in this way? Being-One immediately opens up a new, dialectical structure which is imposed by thought itself, for the self comes into view again as the subject who thinks being as oneness: who is both one with the being that is thought and other than it by virtue of the act of thinking. This points strongly in the direction of a cult of being therefore, whose high-priestly caste are those individuals most equipped intellectually and psychologically to reflect upon abstracted and universal existence as the principle of all that is. Indeed, we can find cultic elements already in Parmenides' discussion of the nature of truth, since his *Way of Truth* and *Way of Opinion* are preceded by a proemium in which Parmenides describes how he is transported in a chariot drawn by mares and guided by the daughters of Helios. Like the sun itself, the chariot moves from east to west to where double gates mark the meeting point of day and night. The daughters of the sun persuade the goddess Dike or 'Justice' to open the gates to them, and the young man is finally greeted by another goddess (who may be Dike), who tells him that he must 'learn all things, both the unwavering heart of persuasive truth and the opinions of mortals in which there is no true trust'.[6] The metaphorical content of the journey, which is a movement from darkness into light, suggests both the passage from ignorance to knowledge and a journey to the realm of the dead, with the promise of renewed life. Whether the remote religious origins of this passage lie in Pythagoreanism, Orphism, oracular or inspirational literature, it is suggestive of some kind of privileged and exceptional experience, entailing uncommon illumination.[7]

Plotinus

From the Eleatics Plato inherited the view that being is linked with knowledge, that it is unified and is located in some critical sense beyond the sphere of sense perception.[8] But Plato's concern with being derives from his reflections upon problematics of knowledge and experience within the world, and we shall consider him in Chapter Five under a different heading. In certain respects it is in the philosophy of Plotinus that we can see most clearly the development of Eleatic thought. In Porphyry's account of his life, we see a man with an exceptional philosophical mind and an austere and committed religiosity, who exercised a powerful influence upon his small band of disciples. He was born in Lycopolis, in Egypt, in AD 205, and may have been from a Greek or a hellenized Egyptian family.[9] In Alexandria Plotinus came under the influence of the Neoplatonist philosopher Ammonius, but he subsequently moved to Rome, in 245, where he died in 270 or 271. We find little trace in his work of the political and social turmoil of the period, though the existence of so many distinct influences in his philosophy is a reminder of the syncretism and exuberant religious culture of late hellenic civilization.[10]

Whereas Plato offered no more than an outline of absolute unity in Books Six and Seven of the *Republic*, where he proposed the Good as the highest of the ideal forms and the ultimate expression of the Real, for Plotinus the One becomes the supreme metaphysical principle which sustains the universe.[11] Plotinus is a more systematic thinker than Plato, as we see for instance in his careful demarcation of the distinction between the Good or the One (for Plotinus the two terms are interchangeable[12]) as an absolutely prior and transcendent principle with respect to the other ideal realities. This is evident, too, in his reflection upon the mechanisms whereby the architecture of the universe, with its distinct levels of being, can be supported and sustained by that same principle of unity which by its very nature can experience no lack and can maintain no contact or concern with the multiple and interconnected realities which are ranged beneath it. The pivotal element within the plotinian universe is his notion of the 'image', which indicates that each level of the universe is an imperfect copy of the preceding and higher level, though one which includes a genuine participation or sharing in its principle:

> there is from the first principle to the final one an outgoing in which unfailingly each principle retains its own seat while its offshoot takes another rank, a lower, though on the other hand every being is in identity with its prior as long as it holds that contact.[13]

Plotinus envisages a double function for each principle or level of being, one which is internal to it and another which represents its action upon the lower levels of being, though both functions are essential to the principle and do not imply its reduction or change.[14] In consequence of his theory of the image, the plotinian universe is one which is filled with beauty, as a reflection of the highest principles: 'the Universe is a life, organized, effective, complex, all-comprehensive, displaying an unfathomable wisdom. How, then, can anyone deny that it is a clear image, beautifully formed, of the Intellectual Divinities?' Though only a copy, nothing has been omitted from the visible world 'which a beautiful representation within the physical order could include'.[15] In line with Plato's asceticism however, Plotinus points to the illusory condition of the physical order and the extent to which the physical entrapment of the soul bars it from the realm of authentic being. He warns against those who 'identify body with real being and find assurance of truth in the phantasms that reach us through the senses, those, in a word, who, like dreamers, take for actualities the figments of their sleeping vision'.[16]

To the physical domain with its ghosts and fictions, Plotinus opposes a transcendental realm consisting of the One, Intellect and Soul. Soul, the lowest of the triad, both serves to mediate between the transcendental and the physical realm and itself constitutes the animating life of the universe. The true site of being however, lies in Intellect, the second term, which contains the essence of all that is in pure, self-sufficient and unchanging being:

> Here is rest unbroken: for how can that seek change, in which all is well; what need reach that, which holds all within itself . . . its knowing is not by search but by possession, its blessedness inherent, not acquired; for all belongs to it eternally . . . this is pure being in eternal actuality.[17]

Intellect represents a divine reality in which the knower and the known exist in a unity, and it is here that being is formed.[18] The pluriform character of both being and intellection are mutually implicating therefore.

The notion that being belongs irreducibly to the realm of multiplicity, as does knowledge, and that both are opposed to their own origin and source in the One, or absolute unicity, marks Plotinus' chief development of the parmenidean and platonic inheritance. Being now ceases to function as the highest expression of unity, and becomes ultimately a form of *deficiency* since the One itself 'has no need of being . . . we use the term the Good to assert identity without the affirmation of being'.[19] It is the One that now stands as the object of cultic contemplation, and with it, Plotinus introduces an intensification of the dialectical structure that has already been prefigured in Plato and Aristotle. But in contrast to the dramatic and mythic dialectic of Plato, based upon the ambiguities of the human condition in contest and moral struggle, longing and unrest, we find in Plotinus a more dominant concern with the logical problematics of the relation between the One and the many.[20] The One is 'all things and no one of them; the source of all things is not all things; and yet it is all things in a transcendental sense'.[21] Similarly, the One is both 'everywhere and yet nowhere' and 'from none is that Principle absent yet from all'.[22] This dialectic becomes acute with respect to the end of humanity, since we, like all other beings, seek ultimately to return to our source. That source however, is utterly transcendent in kind. The One or the Good is even beyond all self-knowing, since 'if we assume within it the distinction of knowing and known, we make it a manifold; and if we allow intellection in it, we make it at that point indigent'.[23] Plotinus affirms that the One is beyond our knowing, since it is 'in truth beyond all statement'.[24] Indeed, to clothe it in any name or image is to reduce it and to make of it a thing amongst other things.[25] Even the term 'the Good' is only used since 'sheer negation does not signify'.[26]

And yet, dialectically, even if the Good escapes thought and language, it is nevertheless powerfully present in the plotinian universe and our gaze is drawn constantly towards it. At times Plotinus is optimistic that we can indeed come to know it in a way. He affirms: 'Cleared of all evil in our intention towards the Good, we must ascend to the Principle within ourselves; from many we must become one; only so do we attain to knowledge of that which is Principle and Unity'.[27] Elsewhere however, he is more cautious about the possibilities of knowledge, though he stresses that even if we cannot know or state it in itself, we can paradoxically possess it by reflecting upon its effects:

> We do not, it is true, grasp it by knowledge, but that does not mean that we are utterly devoid of it; we hold it not so as to state it, but so as to be able to speak about it. And we can and do state what it is not, while we are silent as to what it is: we are, in fact, speaking of it in the light of its sequels; unable to state it, we may still possess it.[28]

The root of the problem which underlies these passages is the nature of knowledge itself, as Plotinus repeatedly admits, for knowledge presupposes the manifold, a unity composed of the knower and the known.[29] Apprehension of the One, on the other hand, must simultaneously be access to a point beyond duality, and here lies the difficulty, since knowledge implies subjectivity and subjectivity difference, while unity, the supposed object of this transcendental knowledge, can admit of no duality or distinction. Thus in knowing Unity, the mind 'is prevented by that very unification from recognising what it has found; it cannot distinguish itself from the object of the intuition'.[30]

Plotinus is the first Western philosopher whose thought is dominated by the irresistible, though impossible, need to attain union with the source of existence itself. As J. M. Rist has argued, he differs from Plato in that he is more concerned with *union* with the divine than *likeness* to it.[31] Here he anticipates a significant element in the Christian mystical tradition, although there it is union through the will – or intellect powerfully informed by will – that is generally paramount. For Plotinus however, the dialectic is worked out in terms of cognition. He repeatedly seeks to find a way around the problematic which his own absolute prioritization of the One has set him, ingeniously suggesting that in our vision of the One the object of knowledge is the possibility of knowledge itself, or that the knowledge by which we know the One is not a knowledge at all, since 'awareness of this Principle comes neither by knowing nor by the Intellection that discovers the Intellectual Beings but by a presence overpassing all knowledge'.[32] It is something we know by a 'direct intuition'.[33] Pierre Hadot has well captured this predicament of the self, who is both one with the One and by virtue of consciousness is other than the One, in a passage on the problematic of personal union with the One: 'here we have the whole paradox of the human self: we only *are* that of which we are aware, and yet we are aware of being more fully *ourselves* precisely in those moments when, raising ourselves to a higher level of inner simplicity, we lose our self-awareness'.[34] Plotinus appears to follow Plato in advocating the role of love in the return of the many to the One, and he points also to the important mediatory role of beauty.[35] But once again the differences between Plato and Plotinus are instructive. Plotinian beauty is altogether more diffuse and inclusive (embracing also artistic beauty) than its platonic counterpart; nor does it focus in particular upon the beauty of the human body, leading to erotic love.[36] Indeed, Plotinus is deeply sceptical of the 'gadfly' *erôs*, which he believes to belong irremediably to the realm of 'pathos and craving'.[37] If beauty offers access to the realm of the truly Real, then it does so in a way that suggests easeful contemplation, or what Hadot calls 'the oscillatory movement' between disjunctive modes of consciousness, rather than divine inspiration and the moral conflict of the self torn between a carnal and a spiritual mode of self-propagation.[38] Moreover, in plotinian thought the platonic link between being and immutability has been lost, and being is defined by its own deficiency. Nor does the One, unlike platonic being, become for Plotinus a world-transforming programme of ethical and aesthetic practice.[39] For the One can be made present on earth only fitfully, in rare and solitary ecstasy, and is the flight of the alone to the alone.[40]

Meister Eckhart

During the later Middle Ages, the metaphysics of the One appeared under a new guise and in a Christian context in the thought of the German Dominican school. The chief sources were Proclus and Maimonides, and the highly platonized Aristotelianism which penetrated the learned circles around Albert the Great.[41] The philosophical theology of Meister Eckhart (1260–1327/8) was close to that of Dietrich von Freiberg, Ulrich von Strasburg and Bertold von Moosberg, and it shows the same focus upon a theory of intellect which embodies a significant radicalization of traditional Augustinian illuminationism.[42] Eckhart himself, who from 1302–3 and 1311–13 served as *magister regens* at the University of Paris, was the chief spokesman of this school. Although the German Dominican movement was effectively stopped in its tracks by the bull *In agro dominico* of 1329, in which 28 propositions extracted from Eckhart's work were described as 'heretical as they stand' or 'evil-sounding, rash and suspect of heresy', it represented in its own time an important alternative to the influence of Thomism in the Dominican Order.[43]

Like Thomas, the German Dominicans were engaged in a task of assimilating ancient thought, though their sources were not so much the new translations of Aristotle himself as the earlier work of commentators on Aristotle and the Neoplatonists. Where Eckhart differs from Thomas again is that he is not concerned with marking out limits between distinctively philosophical and theological positions, but sees ancient philosophy, the ethical commands of the Pentateuch and Christianity as representing a comprehensive unity: 'all that is true, whether in knowledge, in Scripture or in nature, flows from a single fount, a single root', so that 'the teachings of the holy Christian faith, and the writings of both Testaments are to be understood with the help of the natural reasonings of the philosophers'.[44] A persistent emphasis throughout his work is on understanding a metaphysics of the One and Christian doctrine in terms of each other, as expressive of what he perceived to be the unity of truth.

The platonic notions of 'participation' and of the 'image', which were of such central importance in Plotinus' description of the hierarchical structure of the universe, are revalued by Eckhart in the light of a Christian theology of creation. In an important passage from his *Commentary on John*, Eckhart argues that if the Son is of one essence with the Father, though different in person, then the just man is the 'offspring' (*proles*) of justice, and is one essence with justice, though different in person. This is to apply the dynamics of the inner-Trinitarian relations to the Creation itself, and it serves to emphasize the extent to which the transcendentals, for Eckhart, remain *within* God. He explicitly rejects a Thomist understanding of analogy therefore, whereby the creation is related to the Creator as an effect to a cause, and is ranked below the Creator, advocating instead a form of analogy which maintains that the property of the first analogate does not properly belong to the second analogate but inheres in it only by imputation. This applies to every perfection, including existence.[45] Thus, as Joseph Koch has argued, if for Thomas Aquinas the being of a creature is a gift given by God which God might at any point take back, then, for Eckhart, being is *on loan* to the creature, and never properly comes into its possession.[46] By mapping the relation between the transcendentals and God in terms of the identity-distinction which obtains between the Father and the Son, Eckhart offers a radically unified view of the universe.

In particular, he employs the motif of the Word in order to structure the realm of existent things around the principle of unity. In a German sermon, Eckhart points to the word as creation, intellect and the Second Person:

> There is one uttered word: that is the angel, man and all creatures. There is another word, thought but unuttered, through which it can come that I imagine something. There is yet another word, unuttered and unthought, which never comes forth but is rather eternally in him who speaks it.[47]

It is the second form of the Word here, the quality of being intellect, which exemplifies that unity. Eckhart departs significantly from Thomas Aquinas' reflections on the unity or simplicity of God when he identifies Oneness supremely with intellect, of which alone it is 'the distinguishing characteristic', since all material things are compound.[48] God therefore is himself 'all intellect', and 'intellect is the one God'.[49] But Eckhart does not confine intellect to God alone:

> The intellect is properly of God, and God is one. Something possesses God, the One and oneness with God therefore to the extent that it possesses intellect or the intellectual. For the one God is intellect, and intellect is the one God. Therefore God is never and nowhere God except in intellect.[50]

Like the divine intellect, the human intellect is 'detached from here and now', and is 'like nothing', which means to say – according to Eckhartian metaphysics – that it is 'like God'. It is like the divine nature in that it is both 'pure and uncompounded' and is reflexive 'or ever inwardly seeking'.[51] Essentially, then, human intellect is the 'image' of the divine, since the quality of being an image, for Eckhart, is that the image and the source of the image are one, as the Father and the Son are one.[52] For an analogy of what constitutes an 'image', Eckhart points to a reflection of oneself in a mirror: 'The image is not of the mirror, and it is not of itself, but this image is most of all *in* him from whom it takes its being and its nature' (my italics).[53] Thus the human intellect and the divine nature exist one in the other, and show a dynamic symmetry which becomes a programme for the mystical knowledge of God:

> Intellect peeps in and ransacks every corner of the Godhead, and seizes on the Son in the Father's heart and in the ground, and sets him in its

own ground. Intellect forces its way in, dissatisfied with goodness or wisdom or truth or God himself . . . It bursts into the ground whence goodness and truth proceed, and seizes it *in principio,* in the beginning where goodness and truth are just coming out, before it has any name, before it burgeons forth, in a much higher ground than goodness and wisdom.[54]

Eckhart differs from Plotinus in his exploration of the metaphysics of the One primarily in his debt to a theology of incarnation. The Christian profession of the birth of God amongst us in Jesus Christ places God, who is the One, at the centre of the created world. When combined with a metaphysics of unicity therefore, the logic of incarnation imposes upon Christian theology a greater continuity between the divine and created order than is the case certainly in Plotinus.[55] Eckhart's understanding of participation, which is more dynamic and comprehensive than that of Plotinus, finds its fullest expression at the level of the 'word' and the 'image', which represent the self-reproduction or generation of God within the created order. The concept of 'the birth of God in the soul' through the intellect becomes the unitive metaphor for the state of *abegescheidenheit,* or 'detachment', in which the ethical soul, freed from particularity, no longer pursues its own ends against those of others but treats all without distinction. The Oneness therefore, which we possess in our intellectual nature and which constitutes our dynamic connaturality with God, frees us from the constraints and particularities of 'being', which are the root of all our selfishness and desire. In so far as the potential of 'divine' intellect is realized within ourselves, which comes about through the 'birth of God' in us, we become like God and are reformed cognitively and ethically as his 'image' in the world.[56]

Benedict de Spinoza

If Plotinus and Eckhart both operate with an important distinction between unlimited oneness on the one hand and finite being on the other, then for Spinoza the two become identical again. The particular terms in which this was accomplished however, belong specifically to the metaphysical reasoning of the seventeenth century. Substance, both finite and infinite, already dominated the thought of Descartes, whom Spinoza studied and commented upon in depth, and came to the fore in the thought of Leibniz. Where Spinoza differs from both Descartes and Leibniz however, is in his view that substance is necessarily infinite and therefore single and indivisible.[57] This he calls 'God or nature'. The plurality of the world is explained on the grounds of the 'attributes' of this substance, which are themselves infinite in number and in each of which the one substance is infinitely expressed.[58] From the outset Spinoza shows a particular concern with modes of cognition in his metaphysical definitions. Substance itself is conceived only through itself, and its 'concept does not require the concept of another thing through which it must be formed'.[59] The attributes are 'what the intellect perceives of a substance, as constituting its essence', while the 'modes' and 'affects' of substance both imply 'another' through which they are conceived.[60] As with Descartes therefore, there is a sense that Spinoza's method is governed by the perspective of human cognition, with an emphasis upon the primacy of substance which requires nothing other than itself for its intellectual realization. The single divine substance is set apart from all other metaphysical categories on account of its unity and indivisibility, and the cognition which is most adequate to that substance is itself singular and unified.

Spinoza's belief that the most perfect reality represents total and indivisible unity becomes the foundation for a penetrating and systematic philosophy of the self and for a practical programme of liberation of the self from its bondage in multiplicity, contingency and the passions. The diverse operations of the human mind are ordered to the unity of the divine substance, and are more fully realized the more they are able to reflect the unity that underlies all things. Thus Spinoza insists that mind and extension, which are the primary attributes of God, ultimately form a unity: for every idea there necessarily exists its corresponding object. Human ideas are 'true' therefore, where human thinking has penetrated to the underlying metaphysical unity of the world, conceived as both subjectivity and objectivity within an encompassing system of divine substance. Where human thought fails to reflect this unity, it is erroneous and random and is itself caught up in contingency. Spinoza attributes this inadequate form of knowledge to the operations of the 'imagination', which is based upon 'singular things which have been represented to us through the senses in a way which is mutilated, confused and without order for the intellect', constituting 'knowledge from random experience'.[61] Above all, the imagination presents to us 'fictions' or ideas for which there is no corresponding reality. The 'intellect' or 'reason', on the other hand, shows 'the common notions and adequate ideas of the properties of things'.[62] Above all, if the imagination shows 'quantity' as 'finite, divisible and composed of parts', then 'intellect' conceives it as 'substance' which 'will be found to be infinite, unique and indivisible'.[63] If the imagination presents things as random, then 'reason' perceives things 'as they are in themselves, that is not as contingent but necessary'.[64] The third and highest stage of intellection is represented by the 'intuition', which combines the capacity of the imagination to attend to the particular and the capacity of the intellect to see the general. Intuitive knowledge appears to spring from the hidden unity of idea and object, and like the knowledge of the intellect, it is necessarily true.[65]

The intensely cognitive character of Spinoza's thought can mislead us into thinking that his rationalist philosophy lacks the personalist and religious dimensions of Plotinus and Eckhart. That this is not the case is evident however, from his twofold critique of Descartes. Firstly, he does not separate intellect and will, but rather assumes the act of the will into cognition in a way that recalls Eckhart's fusion of the essence of the self and understanding. Against Descartes' concept of the suspension of judgment in intellectual perceptions (whereby we can have an idea of something – such as a winged horse – without committing ourselves to a belief in it), Spinoza vigorously argues that ideas are commitments and that to think of a winged horse is to believe in the wings of the horse, unless we have other perceptions that persuade us of the non-existence of the horse's wings and help us to attribute this particular idea to the activity of the imagination rather than the intellect.[66] Thus, if for Descartes error is the result of free will, Spinoza 'presents the belief in free will as a paradigm illustration of his account of error as fragmentation'.[67] In an important sense, for Spinoza, we are what we know, and it is ultimately the knowledge of God that will provide our greatest tranquillity and bliss. A second way in which Spinoza differs from Descartes is in his belief that the human mind and body are ordered one to the other. It is the body itself which is the object of the idea which initially constitutes the human mind.[68] Human cognition and bodily existence are therefore linked to an extraordinary degree for Spinoza. What he calls the *conatus*, or striving, which is the essence of any thing and which drives it to maintain itself in existence, against whatever might destroy it from without, finds its lower expression in the human person at the level of the passions.[69] Where the striving only touches upon the mind, it is called 'will', and where it involves both mind and body, it is called 'appetite'.[70] The ideas of the mind are governed by the need to 'increase or aid the body's power of acting', and to 'recollect things which exclude the existence' of what might harm the body.[71] Spinoza thus places intentionality at the heart of human cognition. The passions, or 'affects', which lead to love and to hate, to joy and sorrow, to fear and to hope, are 'inadequate' or 'confused ideas' by which the mind seeks to affirm the body and thus to attain to what it perceives to be a greater degree of reality, or 'persistence in being'.[72]

It is in his analysis of the relation between mind and body that Spinoza constructs the ontology of unicity in a new way. In Plotinus and Eckhart we have seen a tendency to oppose unicity and plurality on metaphysical grounds, and to hold up the possibility of cognition based on oneness as a transcendent overcoming of pluralistic knowledge (of the material world). Spinoza, on the other hand, roots the fragmentation of material cognition not directly in the world order but rather in the capacity of the body to undergo diverse and repeated experiences. From one perspective the body forms a single idea which then constitutes the human mind, but from another that single idea can be shown to conceal a whole range of ideas in proportion to the capacity of the body to be acted upon in many different ways.[73] These experiences are caused by the impact of other material entities upon the 'fluid' or 'soft parts' of one's own body, and with each 'affect' or impact there comes the associative idea of that external body, so that the mind knows both its own body and the idea of the body which impacts upon it.[74] Thus human consciousness itself is called into existence by the encounter in the body with the world, but it is also necessarily determined as a form of cognition which is subject to multiplicity and fragmentation. Furthermore, the mind retains the associations between the experiences undergone by the body and the ideas of the material entities which initially caused them, despite the fact that these same bodies do not remain the consistent causes of sensations. And so the ideas which constitute the mind are not only multiple and diverse but also often illusory, since the remembered objects and passions, which may be feared or anticipated, are no longer present. Ordinary human consciousness is governed by indeterminate or 'confused' ideas therefore which, as projections of the imagination, lack the truth which comes from an adequate and rational correspondence between the idea and its object.[75] The *conatus*, which is the 'striving' or 'desire' to remain in existence and which constitutes human essence, is fatally linked therefore with false, inadequate and affective notions concerning ourselves and the world.

The ordinary human state is marked by confused ideas, passions, and – above all – by the condition of being acted upon rather than oneself acting.[76] Imaginings and affects induce in us a state of passivity. It is reason which leads to liberation from this morass of illusion and desire since it alone gives understanding and adequate ideas, and grounds action. The *conatus* which is ennobled by reason then becomes virtue, which is synonymous with 'power', or the ability to act.[77] Reason moreover corresponds to human essence or nature, and is native to us as human beings.[78] In so far as we pursue our own advantage, or persistence in being, through reason therefore, we shall come into agreement with other people, who share our rational nature, and shall contribute to the construction of a rational and harmonious community.[79] In so far as it permits us to act, reason also counters the subjection to contingency and passivity which is necessarily part of the human condition. Although Spinoza acknowledges that we shall always remain in the power of unpredictable external causes, reason and understanding can allow us to:

> bear calmly those things which happen contrary to what the principle of our advantage demands, if we are conscious that we have done our duty, that the power we have could not have extended itself to the point where we could have avoided those things, and that we are a part of the whole of Nature, whose order we follow.[80]

The climax of Spinoza's cognitive philosophy comes in Book Five of the *Ethics* where he treats of 'the power of reason, showing what it can do against the affects, and what freedom of mind, or blessedness, is'.[81] Here he advocates a process of thinking which detaches the 'affects' or 'passions' from the objects that induce them. This allows us to form a clear and distinct idea of the passions, and thus to be liberated from them: 'the more an affect is known to us, then the more it is in our power, and the less the mind is acted on by it'.[82] From the very beginning of his work Spinoza stressed that the concept of God is implied in every perception of a discrete object, since 'each idea of each body, or of each singular thing which actually exists, necessarily involves an eternal and infinite essence of God'.[83] The highest form of cognition entails the greatest degree of understanding ourselves and the world in terms of the unified substance which is God or nature. Grasping that God is the cause of all that is, releases us from the affects of sadness and hate, and from the passions as such, as we increasingly come to be like God himself who is beyond every 'passion' and 'affect'.[84] Spinoza articulates this within his scheme of embodied cognition by seeking to focus on 'the mind's duration without relation to the body'. This is a different kind of thought-experiment from that which Descartes undertakes in Part Four of his *Discourse on Method*. There Descartes simply 'thinks away' the body. Spinoza, on the other hand, urges his reader to conceive of the essence of the body which is in God and is thus eternal. This allows the self to consider itself as it exists *sub specie aeternitatis*. Only by conceiving of the body in this way, under the aspect of eternity, is it possible to understand objects in the world from the same perspective.[85] This perception of the underlying unity of things represents the same kind of knowledge as 'intuition', which Spinoza opposed to both 'imagination' and 'intellect' in his discussion of the three ways of knowing discussed above. According to that knowledge, we infer the divine substance from the essence of each particular thing. By aligning ourselves with God in this way, we come to experience the 'intellectual love of God', attended by joy, which is a form of participation in the love God has for himself.[86]

The theistic philosophy of Spinoza contains much that recalls other systems, both medieval (scholastic) and contemporary (rationalist). But it remains a highly individual philosophy with a deeply religious slant. In a virulent attack against conventional theism, Spinoza advocates a God who has neither will nor intellect in any recognizable sense and who is the efficient and not final cause of all that is. He is equally dismissive of conventions such as good and evil, which he reinterprets in utilitarian terms as signifying the usefulness to us or otherwise of individual things.[87] But despite his dismissal of important aspects of conventional religion, the passivity of the self before the divine substance and the advocacy of *apatheia* rooted in the knowledge and love of God which are fundamental to his work are equally devout. And like Plotinus and Eckhart, Spinoza understands unity to be a quality that is uniquely linked with divinity, and that our own passage from 'bondage' to 'freedom' is a journey from multiplicity to oneness. Unlike his predecessors however, Spinoza does not image that journey as an ascent through the spheres to a higher realm or a withdrawal into the inner recesses of the soul, but understands it rather to be a reordering of our cognition, mediated through the body, giving expression to the unity of mind and object which is the prior truth of the world.

Martin Heidegger

In Heidegger's work, the unity of being comes into view in a new and quite distinct way. According to his critique of the history of philosophy, being was caught sight of by the Presocratics and was then lost from view in the tradition that stretches from Plato to Nietzsche: 'Anaximander, Parmenides and Heraclitus are the only primordial thinkers'.[88] The history of metaphysics shows a fourfold opposition between being and becoming, appearance, thinking, and the 'ought', in which being itself is judged to be limited by the parameters of its partner concept.[89] Against this Heidegger argues that each of the delimiting concepts is itself to be understood as an aspect of being, and thus the enquiry into the essence of being is itself obscured by the metaphysical projects of the past. His own linkage of being and time is to be seen not as an attempt to think being in the light of another concept that is intrinsically alien to it, but rather as an elucidation of the temporal character of being itself.

Heidegger stands within that same tradition which we have seen in Parmenides, Plotinus, Eckhart and Spinoza, which focuses not upon the self or the other but rather upon the medium of their relation. Whereas to an extent the earlier thinkers assume the infinite unity of being and seek to address cosmological, epistemological and ethical themes which derive from it, Heidegger is concerned with the problematics which are specific to thinking being in this way. He is more keenly aware of the parameters within which the self, as an existent among existents, can grasp or come to some intuition of the very principle of being itself, which grounds both self and world. In other words, he asks the question: how can we know the unity of being when we ourselves are differentiated from it? There is much in Heidegger's writings therefore which is metaphorical and allusive, and at times his method appears to approximate to that of the apophatic tradition which seeks to represent the transcendent through a subversion, or a negation, of the representational.[90]

The key to Heidegger's approach to the understanding of being lies in his analytic of *Dasein*. This German term, which has the literal meaning of 'being-there', ordinarily has the sense of 'existence'. For Heidegger however, it has the very particular meaning of that aspect of being which itself relates reflexively to being.[91] In other words, it is natural to human beings to inquire into the nature of being. But *Dasein* is not to be identified with human consciousness, which would open the door to Idealism, nor does it signify human subjectivity as such. Rather, Heidegger conceives the human self fundamentally as a space, or 'clearing', in which being reveals itself in a particular, self-reflexive way. Being itself is in an important sense the true subject of *Dasein*. The notion of subject and object, or self and other, which is intrinsic to most ontological narratives, is systematically transcended here since the being that comes into view at this point (in Heidegger's terminology *das Sein* as distinct from *Seiendes* or *das Seiende*:

being as being which is distinct from the being of things that exist) is the ground of the possibility of all that is. It is this 'being as such' or 'the total-ity of being' which is Heidegger's central concern, and his work is finally an attempt to awaken his readers to a mindfulness, or what he calls *das andenkende Denken* ('thinking that recalls'), of being in this most primary sense.[92]

From one perspective human beings exist in the world like any other entity, within the subject–object relation, but from another, human beings are unique in their relation to being itself. Heidegger reserves the terms *Existenz* and *existieren* specifically for that mode of reflexive being which distinguishes *Dasein*, and he plays upon their evocation of the notion of 'standing out' ('ek-sistence').[93] The essence of *Dasein* itself is precisely 'standing out' or 'projection' into the world and into the 'openness of being'. This is a paradoxical notion which Heidegger seeks to express by phrases such as 'ecstatic inherence in the truth of being' and 'ecstatic in-standing within the clearing'.[94] What he means is that we are as human beings uniquely defined as beings by our reflexive consciousness, which is our belonging to the openness of being. We come to ourselves only in the world where we are in a sense placed out of ourselves, ecstatically, and discover ourselves as 'being-in-the-world', grounded in an intimate engagement with the world which Heidegger calls 'solicitude' or 'care'. For Heidegger therefore, the ordinary human condition is one in which we are 'thrown' by being into the world and 'into care', as involvement with individual entities. And yet it is only in the thinking of being as being that the self can realize its true essence, since 'the human being essentially occurs in his essence only where he is summoned or claimed by being'.[95] We can experience the world therefore, not just as 'any realm of beings' but rather as 'the openness of being' itself.[96] This is to recognize and embrace the truth of our own existence, which is the truth that 'of all beings, only the human being, called upon by the voice of being, experiences the wonder of all wonders: *that* beings *are*'.[97]

We can state Heidegger's position in slightly different terms, specifically recalling elements in Spinoza, if we say that, for him, the human self is that part of the whole which is defined in its own essence by its relation with the whole. Inevitably the self will engage with other 'parts of the whole' rather than the whole itself, but the self can and must be brought back to a mindfulness of the whole since, in this alone, its own nature can be fulfilled. But what distinguishes Heidegger's position, and terminology, from this more accessible way of articulating his problematic is that he conceives the whole specifically as *being as such* and the engagement of the self with the whole to be specifically an act of *thought* or *understanding*. For him, the self – or *Dasein* – is called not simply to relate to the whole in its actions or beliefs but rather to *think* and to *understand* the unity of the whole, which is being. But the kind of thinking which is required, and which Heidegger calls 'recollective thought' (*Andenken*), is markedly different from the representational thought of metaphysics as the 'science of beings'. The latter is a technological rationality which seeks to understand entities in relation to each other. *Andenken*, on the other hand, is primary and originary thinking which understands that 'beings as being appear in the light of being': it is only because there is being as such, as the openness which we call the totality of being, that there can be individual entities.[98] But this being as such does not reveal itself, except as something other than that which emerges in the individual being:

> that which is never and nowhere a being unveils itself as that which distinguishes itself from all beings, as that which we call being. No matter where or to what extent all research investigates beings, it nowhere finds being. It only ever encounters beings, because from the outset it remains intent on explaining beings. Being, however, is not an existing quality found in beings. Unlike beings, being cannot be represented or brought forth in the manner of an object. As that which is altogether other than all beings, being is that which is not.[99]

The notion of negation or nothingness (*das Nichts*) is fundamental to Heidegger's reflections upon being as such therefore. It is the apprehension of nothingness within beings (which is in fact the way in which being as such announces its presence – as that which is always distinct from individual beings and yet without which they cannot be) that grounds the human mood of anxiety. Anxiety is the inchoate experience of nothingness; it is the mood that 'makes manifest the nothing'.[100] But the emergence of the nothing also makes possible a new way of understanding the being of beings, since 'only on the ground of the original manifestness of the nothing can *Dasein* approach and penetrate beings'; indeed, 'for the human *Dasein*, the nothing makes possible the manifestness of being as such'.[101] With the intimation of nothingness, communicated through the mood of anxiety and 'the total strangeness of beings', *Dasein* begins to gain some sense of the mystery of being and of the primal question, which – for Heidegger – is the ultimate and truest question *Dasein* can ask: 'Why is there something rather than nothing?'. Only with this Leibnizean question does *Dasein* arrive at philosophical maturity and enter into the wonder '*that* things *are*'. This heralds a new kind of thinking as we pass from 'the thinking that is set in place by beings as such, and is therefore representational and illuminating in that way' to 'a thinking that is brought to pass by being itself and is therefore in thrall to being'.[102]

The ideal object of thought for Heidegger is, therefore, not the other within the subject–object relation, but is rather the medium of relation itself. Heidegger states this unequivocally when he says: 'The distinction of the two as subject and object . . . becomes absolute and banishes thinking into a dead end. Any positing of "being" that would seek to name "being" from the perspective of the subject–object relation fails to ponder something worthy of question that is left unthought.'[103] Being as such, which is the final object of thought, is of course both other than the self, in so far as it represents a totality, and is identical with it, in so far as the self is part of that totality. This is what we have termed the 'Parmenidean dialectic', whereby reflection progresses through the totality and finally returns to that which thinks the totality, namely the self. Heidegger is quite clear that *Dasein* is not a subject in any final sense: 'the essence of *Dasein* is nothing human'.[104]

But at the same time there is apparent in his work a strong rhetorical current which serves to privilege the role of the philosopher in the elucidation of being. This can be seen in his discussion of the metaphysical question 'Why is there something rather than nothing?' in the *Introduction to Metaphysics*. Here he makes the important point that this question can only be asked in part *from outside* being: 'The question "why" may be said to confront the essent (*das Seiende*) as a whole, to break out of it, though never completely.'[105] Heidegger describes this act of questioning as 'not just any occurrence', within the fold of being, but rather as 'a privileged happening that we call an *event* (*ein Geschehnis*)'.[106] This is the most fundamental of all questions, which constitutes 'a leap' (*ein Sprung*) which – as it opens up the ground of being – becomes itself a 'source' or 'origin' (*Ursprung*). Philosophy is 'a daring attempt to fathom this unfathomable question by disclosing what it summons us to ask, to push our questioning to the very end'.[107] But this is a task which can be undertaken only by 'the few', who are called to 'a thinking that breaks the paths and opens the perspectives of the knowledge that sets the norms and hierarchies, of the knowledge in and by which a people fulfils itself historically and culturally . . .'.[108] It is the philosophers then who guide the people towards the destiny of their thought.

Heidegger refers specifically to Europe as his own cultural milieu here, which is 'squeezed between Russia on one side and America on the other'.[109] But he appears to have Germany specifically in mind which, as 'the most metaphysical of nations', has the task of moving 'the history of the West beyond the centre of their future "happening" and into the primordial realm of the powers of being'.[110] In the primary metaphysical question, *Dasein* is 'summoned to its history in the full sense of the word, called to history and to decision in history'.[111] That history is inextricably bound up with *Geist* and the inheritance of German Idealism, and it finds its fullest expression in 'the destiny of language', which is 'grounded in a nation's relation to being'.[112] From the argument that the 'why-question' is posed ambiguously from the edge of being itself, from which perspective alone being in its totality can be glimpsed, Heidegger has moved to a privileging of a particular social group at work within a particular linguistic and cultural tradition. To that extent the universality of the 'why-question', which is always 'untimely', 'out of order', and 'based wholly and uniquely on the mystery of freedom', has seemingly become the outline for a nationalistic programme of cultural positivism.[113]

Conclusion

All talk of being implies a degree of unity and duration. Presence is persistence across time of the same. In most ontological thinking however, a variety of entities are held to exercise presence in this way, and so the concept of the unity of being is tempered with or balanced by the plurality and differentiation of things. In the case of the thinkers we have discussed in this section however, there is an emphasis upon being *as a totality*. This is the case even for Plotinus and Eckhart, although they operate with a distinction between being and the One, since by 'being' they mean 'finite existence' and by the One, they mean the totality of all that is.[114] But such a focus upon the unity which is intrinsic to the notion of being as such can easily lead to the occlusion of the differentiation which is simultaneously part of the world as we ordinarily experience it, as a sphere of *presences*. Furthermore, the privileging of the relation of the self with the absolute other of originary being as the totality of all that is, can undermine the relation of the self with the concrete other, coposited with ourselves within the realm of being as unity and differentiation. In other words, by prioritizing the relation of the self to the totality above any other relation, philosophers in this tradition will inevitably determine the ethical possibilities of the self primarily with respect to the whole and not, as we have advocated, with respect to the concrete other. Even though Eckhart and Spinoza – in accordance with their respective religions – promoted an altruistic ethics more than either Plotinus and Heidegger, altruism was still grounded for them in a *cognitive* state which reflects or enacts the primal unity of all that is. Thus the absolute primacy of the ethical relation with respect to the concrete other which is the linchpin of kenotic ontology is superseded in this, our first ontological paradigm, by the claims of being as a whole upon the destiny of the self.

Furthermore, the prioritization of the absolute other as all-encompassing being inevitably leads to what we have described as the 'Parmenidean dialectic', whereby the self is returned to itself as the subject who contemplates the Oneness that is being. In effect, this removes the human subject from the whole, as the one who becomes aware of the dialectic of unity and distinction and is thus separated from the whole by that act of thinking. This will tend to stress the cognitive properties of the human self at the cost of the affective and imaginative faculties, but it will also tend to lend a certain status to the philosopher, as one set apart from the rest of humanity.[115] Thinking from the margins of society, from the margins of being itself, the philosopher of the One may easily become prey to various forms of social elitism, and to the *agôn* of a mind in conflict with itself, which is the subtlest form of narcissism.

4

Being and Nothingness: Creation and Community

Il semble que nous possèdions assez d'être pour ne pouvoir nous passer d'en avoir; trop, pour nous en détacher; trop peu, pour nous en contenter; plus ou moins que nous ne souhaiterions, puisque nous n'en avons que pour sentir que nous n'en avons pas.

It seems that we possess enough being not to be able to get along without some; too much, to be detached from it; too little, to be content with it; more or less than we would hope, since we have it only to sense that we do not have it.

Maurice Blondel, *L'action*

Our second ontological paradigm is one which approaches the question of being not from the perspective of being itself, nor from the perspective of either self or other, but from the perspective of self and other in relation. It is in general the paradigm which has been developed by Christian thinkers, working within a model of existence which is controlled by the scriptural accounts of creation. Fundamental to this perspective therefore is the concept of *creatio ex nihilo*, and the belief that being is opposed to nothingness. In the previous chapter, we have already noted this as a sub-division within the tradition of thinking being as oneness, especially in the case of Martin Heidegger. But in this, as in other respects, Heidegger is himself inheritor of a distinctively Christian ontological tradition; where he differs decisively from Christian thinkers is in his rejection of God as creator of being, and his insistence that the question of the existence of God must be subordinated to the question of being.[1] For the Christians, on the other hand, the notion that being is radically contingent is tied in with belief that it is the gift of the Creator God who reveals himself to us in the person of Christ. Karl Barth perhaps overstates the case, but there is a real sense for Christians in every age whereby the incarnation reveals the creation and 'faith in Jesus Christ is a life in the presence of the Creator'.[2] That awareness itself has ethical entailments. The Christian self is placed in a relation with the other, since the gift of being is one which describes the space between self and other specifically in ethical terms. In other words, the understanding through faith that being is the gift of the Creator God, who has also revealed himself to us in Jesus Christ, is simultaneously the recognition that the end of humanity is an active discipleship of love for God and our neighbour.

In this chapter we shall be primarily concerned with Christian theologians therefore, although with one necessary reservation. Ontology is not the primary concern of Christian theology, which has to engage with questions of faith and revelation. And so Christian languages of being have been in the main *reactive*, as theologians in different periods have responded to significant developments in the sphere of ontology whose provenance has been pre-Christian (Plato, Aristotle), quasi-Christian (Hegel) or post-Christian (Nietzsche, Heidegger, Derrida). The claim of faith that what is, is because of the creative act of the Father, and that the Word, through whom all things were made (cf. John 1.3), was born among us in order that we should not fall back through sin into the non-existence from which we came, as Athanasius maintained, together constitute a criterion against which secular ontologies are to be measured and within which they are to be finally realized and fulfilled.[3]

Augustine and the Platonists

In his *Commentary on the Epistle to the Galatians* Jerome wrote that no one had heard of Plato but a handful of 'idle old men', and yet platonic thought was mediated to the early Christian world through a whole range of texts, and its influence was immense.[4] Plato himself was born at a time when the Athenian community was confronting a time of crisis and change. The homeric inheritance, which was still an active force in the realm of Athenian art, education and entertainment, presented an ethical landscape of fixed points, according to which the moral character of men and women was closely associated – if not coincident – with their social roles, as kinship and contractual friendship. In the world of sophoclean drama, however, those roles, and the moral codes underpinning them, came more visibly into conflict with each other and were shown finally to be at odds in a way that imperilled the individual. But in neither the homeric nor the sophoclean world could the individual escape his or her fate through reflexivity; the conflict between social moralities could not be resolved by relativism or by a meta-morality, but could only be endured, and the human self, defined precisely by its social role, was brought to destruction.[5] In this environment, Plato stood out as a great moral reformer, who was concerned to meet the new crisis in moral thinking with a penetrating analysis of the relation between polity, individual responsibility and ethical reasoning. He can be said to combine the critical acumen and enquiry of the Presocratic philosophers with the moral concern of the tragedians in a new synthesis whose locus was the Greek city-state of Athens, where questions of personal morality and public polity merged as one.[6]

A second major element which contributed to the formation of platonic metaphysics and which also lent it a particular communicative quality was that of narrative and myth. Myth has 'founding significance' in the *Timaeus* (which narrates Plato's understanding of the 'creation' by the Demiurge), and in the *Phaedrus* (which gives his understanding of love), and represents also 'unseen places' in the reflection on 'the true heaven and the true light and the true earth' which closes the *Phaedo*.[7] So pervasive is the influence of myth in Plato's thought that, as John Sallis has stressed, *logos*, as something akin to 'rational discourse', and *mythos*, as 'something spoken', have common boundaries.[8] Plato's use of the terms darkness and light (as well as those of height and depth) to describe them, principally in the allegory of the cave from the *Republic*, might seem to suggest that they are set in irreducible opposition, but the employment of this kind of imagistic language ensures that the very difference between *mythos* and *logos* is expounded in terms ultimately of mythic structures.[9]

One of the most influential examples of this form of philosophical narrativity was the platonic theme of 'recollection', which recounted how the soul is born into the world with some memory of a previous existence in which it gained direct access to the realm of truth and existence. The notion of a displaced realm of true being began to emerge in the *Phaedo*, a dialogue from the middle period, where the *Begriffsphilosophie* of the earlier dialogues (to use Friedländer's phrase), which was concerned primarily with the definition of terms, gives way to an objectification of concepts and thus to the postulation of a transcendent realm where they can be said to subsist.[10] In the *Phaedo*, Plato's Socrates uses the objective existence of 'beauty and goodness and all such reality' (*ousia*) to support his argument for the pre-existence of the soul.[11] Human cognition is natively subject to flux, deception and unpredictable variation, and true judgment exists as a possibility only on account of the beneficial influence of the Forms as cognitive principles. These intelligible entities and the realm of their existence differ from empirical realities on account of their invariability. In contrast, the concrete expressions of these same principles in the empirical world, which constitute ordinary human knowing, 'are never free from variation'.[12] In the *Republic* they are described as standing between being and non-being.[13] Human beings, then, are caught in the tension between *doxa*, which is 'opinion' or 'uncertain knowledge', predicated upon the imperfect existence of the objects known, and *epistêmê* which is truth founded upon the invariable, unchanging reality of the transcendent Forms.[14]

But the displacement of being, which has the consequence of casting the human race adrift in a world of partial knowledge and dimly perceived virtues, also sets up cosmic structures of mediation. The original knowledge of the real is retrieved in the *Republic* through education, through memory in the *Phaedo* and through love in the *Symposium* and the *Phaedrus*. According to the account in the *Phaedrus*, some trace of the primal vision is retained in the empirical world, where *ousia*, as 'being' or 'reality', is visible to us through the manifestation of beauty, which lies open to the gaze.[15] The appreciation of beauty is not free from that essential ambiguity within the human person however, since this same moment may excite the passions, especially when we perceive Beauty in the form of another human being, leading to entanglements rather than the pure, intellectual apprehension of universal or absolute beauty. But where the passions are controlled, the vision of the beloved gives access to the pure contemplation of beauty itself and of the real.[16] It is in the earlier *Symposium* however, that we find the classic affirmations of platonic love. There Socrates' teacher Diotima links love with the desire or longing for personal immortality, for freedom from the realm of constant change, and declares that the nature of 'love is a longing for immortality'.[17] The object of love, then, is not so much 'a longing for the beautiful itself, but for the conception and generation that the beautiful effects': it is 'to bring forth upon the beautiful, both in body and soul' as an act of self-propagation.[18] The sexual union of man and woman leads to procreation, and thus to a form of personal immortality, in a physical sense.[19] But fame too is a significant form of immortality, and glory is commensurate with a 'love of the eternal'.[20] The generation which is of the spirit produces 'wisdom and her sister virtues' and, Diotima adds, 'it is the office of every poet to beget them, and of every artist whom we may call creative'.[21] Justice or a system of law are one form of spiritual progeny, which bring their author undying fame and blessing, but a further, and fundamental, form of self-propagation is through a particular form of companionship, or what A. W. Price calls 'educative pederasty',[22] which is a shared and intimate search for the ultimate vision of beauty.[23] A key passage from Diotima's speech draws out the principle of community and of mutuality between the love and his beloved

> who will help each other rear the issue of their friendship – and so the bond between them will be more binding, and their communion even more complete, than that which comes of bringing children up, because they have created something lovelier and less mortal than human seed.[24]

As the embodiment of platonic *erôs*, it is Socrates himself who founds that community of friends or lovers, whose *philia* is their common love of beauty and truth, and adherence to the good.[25] In sum then we can say that as a 'passion for immortality', love represents an attempt to re-enact on the temporal plane the immutability of the divine realm: it is an attempt to accomplish on earth the divine *ousia*.[26]

In Book Seven of the *Confessions*, Augustine (354–430) tells us that he was greatly influenced by reading certain *libri platonicorum*.[27] We do not know which particular platonist texts Augustine had in mind, although the influence of Plotinus is apparent. It is not the metaphysical philosophy of the plotinian One which emerges however so much as the general platonic philosophy of what later tradition called the *transcendentalia*, or 'transcendental properties'. This affirmed the ultimate identity of Being, Goodness, Truth and Beauty, which, conceived together, constitute the platonic realm of sublime reality.

The trajectory of Augustine's early thinking is indebted in many ways to the platonic tradition, but a particular and enduring area of influence is the belief that being represents a state of unchangingness, for 'that which truly exists is that which remains without changing'.[28] In his exegesis of Ex. 3.14, St Augustine 'baptizes' platonic metaphysics by advancing the view that God can uniquely be said to exist:

> He is without doubt a substance, or essence, which the Greeks know as *ousia*, for as wisdom derives from being wise and knowledge from the act of knowing, so what we know as essence comes from being. And who can be said to exist more than he who said to his servant Moses 'I am that I am' and 'thus shall you say to the children of Israel, He who is has sent me to you'. But other things which are called essences or substances admit of accidents, whereby they undergo a change, whether great or small. But there can be no accident of this kind with regard to God, and so he who is God is the only unchangeable substance or essence, to whom being itself, from which the name of essence derives, most truly belongs. For that which is changed does not retain its own being, and that which can undergo change, although it may not actually do so, can be that which it has not been. Therefore it is solely that which not only does not undergo change but also cannot do so which truly falls under the category of being.[29]

But Augustine's rapprochement of Plato's *ousia* with the Christian Creator God has the consequence that God-Being (to use Emilie zum Brunn's phrase) now stands in a relation with ourselves which is *dynamically ontological*.[30] It is this new thematic which is expressed in Augustine's gloss on a line from Vulgate Ps. 101: *mutabis ea et mutabuntur; tu autem idem ipse es* ('you shall change them, and they shall be changed; but you are always the same').[31] The focus of Augustine's interest here falls substantially on the contrast between God's perfect and unchanging being and our own flawed, limited and unstable existence, so that the immutable being of God creates the existential horizons of our own being: it determines our own moral state and the degree to which we can attain happiness both in this world and the next.

In *On the Good Life* Augustine adds a specifically moral dimension to the veridical associations of Plato's reflections upon being as unchanging reality, explicating good and evil in terms of 'being' and 'nothingness'. *Sapientia*, or Wisdom, is defined as 'plenitude', while its opposite, *stultitia*, the state of ignorance and folly, is given as 'need'. The metaphors of nourishment and health, and the vices which are implicit in the state of ignorance and need, are now explicated as *nothingness* through an extended etymological analysis:

> The body which lacks nourishment most frequently falls victim to ailments of all sorts, which weaknesses reveal the hunger in it, and the

mind is full of illnesses which hunger reveals. In fact, the ancients claimed that depravity (*nequitia*) was the mother of all vices, since it is nothing (*nequiquam*), because it is nothingness (*nihil*). The opposite virtue for this vice is called 'fruitfulness' (*frugalitas*), a word which comes from *frux* (harvest) and includes the notion of fruit (*fructus*), for this virtue leads to a certain fecundity of the soul. On the other hand, depravity (*nequitia*) takes its name from the sterility it causes, that is to say, from nothingness (*a nihilo*). For all that passes, that dissolves and melts away and continually perishes is nothingness (*nihil*); and so we say that those who are depraved are 'lost'.[32]

It is the identification of goodness with being and evil with non-being that becomes the cornerstone of Augustine's dynamic ontologism, or ethical metaphysics, reflecting his sense that the human soul, as creature of the Creator God, is suspended between being (as redemption) and nothingness (as sin).[33] In a further key insight of Christian metaphysics, Augustine argues that the soul is caught between two levels of existence: the one guaranteed eternally by the creative power of God and the other represented by the ethical choices of the soul, according to whether it loves the things of God or the passing things of the world.[34] Our very existence therefore, as part of God's creation, causes us to desire an enriched state of being. This can only be realized by focusing our desire upon that which endures:

> The more you will love being, the more you will yearn for eternal life and the more also you will desire the transformation that will allow you not to tie yourself any more to temporal possessions, the love of which scars you and burns you . . . Build on this foundation in you, which is the very fact that you want to be; increase it by always being more: you will rise and you will be edified in that which exists supremely. Thus you will prevent the inferior things from dragging you down in their fall toward nothingness.[35]

Augustine's early discussions of being assume a structure of *erôs* as yearning and need, which is a second aspect of his debt to platonic tradition. The notion that love is an appetitive power and that we finally become what we desire, substantially underlies the distinction which Augustine makes between *caritas*, which is 'the love of God' and *cupiditas*, which is 'the love of the world, the love of this life'.[36] It is the daily and uncompromising struggle between these two kinds of love, the latter leading to our descent into nothingness and the former finally to our deification, which forms the basis of his moral thinking.[37]

But increasingly superimposed upon the appetitive theory of love is another, which derives specifically from the ethical imperatives of biblical passages such as Matt. 22.39 and John 13.34. This affirms the primacy of

Christian love as self-emptying love of the neighbour. Tension between the two paradigms is resolved in *The Life-Style of the Catholic Church*, where the love of God implies also an appropriate form of self-love and indeed of mutual love, since 'our love of our neighbour is a sort of cradle of our love of God'.[38] The two loves 'rise together to fullness and perfection' for 'the love of our neighbour is first in coming to perfection' and 'we reach perfection more easily in lower things'.[39] But in *On True Religion*, which was written only some two years later in 390, love of God and love of our neighbour have come into conflict again: 'If we are ablaze with love for eternity, we shall hate temporal relationships'.[40] We are enjoined not to love the specific individual, with whom we may stand in a particular familial relationship, but rather to love only the 'real self' and 'human nature'.[41] Augustine also argues against any intrusion of grief on account of another into the serenity of the mind fixed on God.[42]

A higher level of synthesis is achieved in the early books of *On Christian Doctrine* however, dating from around 396. The initial discussion is set in the context of a distinction between 'enjoyment' (*frui*) and 'use' (*usus*), which correspond to the earlier vocabulary of *caritas* and *cupiditas*: 'to enjoy something is to hold fast to it in love for its own sake. To use something is to apply whatever it may be to the purpose of obtaining what you love – if indeed it is something that ought to be loved'.[43] More specifically, 'the things which are to be enjoyed then are the Father, the Son, and the Holy Spirit, and the Trinity that consists of them, which is a kind of single, supreme thing shared by all who enjoy it'.[44] Augustine continues, 'only those things are to be enjoyed which we have described as being eternal and immutable; others are to be used so that we may be able to enjoy those', and he answers the question whether we 'enjoy' or 'use' (in this sense) ourselves and others with the view that humankind is to be loved for the sake of something else and is thus not to be 'enjoyed'.[45] We love both God and our fellow human beings therefore, but our love for our neighbour is 'for the sake of' our love for God and serves this end.[46]

In the text *On John's Epistle*, which belongs to the year 407, a more deeply ecclesial and soteriological matrix for Augustine's reflections on the nature of love appears.[47] Love, and benevolence towards others, is the ground of all virtue: 'Let the root of love be within, nothing can spring from this root but what is good.'[48] Love is 'discipline', based upon concern for our neighbour's true happiness, and is to be opposed to the 'feebleness' which betrays a lack of concern.[49] We should seek 'equality' for others under God, so that all will be equally provided for.[50] But Augustine now writes with passion about love for our enemies: 'wish for him that he might have with you eternal life; wish for him that he might be your brother; when you love him, you love a brother; for you love in him not what he is, but what you wish that he may be.'[51] Now love clearly has a kenotic dimension, for 'how should we love, if he had not loved us first?'[52] Christ died for us in the flesh, 'because by that he taught us much of love'.[53] In a series of powerful passages Augustine argues that God loved us through the kenosis of the incarnation in order to teach and improve us.[54] Our love of God, in this context, is a reflection of God's love for us and is a transforming power which makes us conform to the beauty of the divine nature.[55] By loving our neighbour we show that we love God.[56] Now love is no longer the appetitive power that defines our moral struggle, but, reconceived through the incarnation, it has now become identified with God himself:

> He says: 'Love is of God; and all who love are born of God and know God. He who does not love, does not know God.' Why? 'For love is God.' What more could be said, brothers? If nothing were said in praise of love throughout the pages of this epistle, if nothing whatever throughout the other pages of the Scriptures, and this one thing were all we were told by the voice of the Spirit of God, 'For love is God', nothing more ought we to require.[57]

Over the course of his long life, Augustine moved from a strongly platonized world-view, governed by the displacement of being and the appetitive *erôs* of longing, to a more kenotic and incarnational understanding of love, modelled upon Christ's love for us. Substantially, this was to exchange a platonic paradigm, with its account of being as immutability and source of truth, for a Christian ecclesiology, as an account of the ethical realm between self and other, opened up by the creator God. What we do not find in Augustine however, is a specifically ontological account of his mature view of love, since the language of being which he uses extensively in his earlier work derives not from the New Testament insights of christocentric and ethical existence, but from the divine theophany narrated in Exodus, understood in the light of a Greek metaphysics of the displaced real. His reaction to platonic metaphysics therefore is not in itself specifically metaphysical, but is rather to be seen as the superseding of platonic understandings of being and love, as the *erôs* of longing and desire, by a Christian emphasis upon love as self-abandonment for the sake of the other. This constitutes a new kind of community, formed not by the like-minded companionship of friends, united in their common pursuit of goodness and truth, nor by the corporal mediations of the beautiful, but a community of those whose own relationships with God and with one another have been refigured through participation in the total, self-giving love of God for humankind.

Thomas Aquinas and Aristotle

The second great Christian reaction to classical metaphysics came in the thirteenth century with the work of Thomas Aquinas (1224/5–74). Latin translations of Aristotle's works on logic had been known from the early Middle Ages, but from the mid twelfth century his major philosophical texts began to circulate and, in 1255, the University of Paris approved their extensive use in the programme of advanced study. Aquinas wrote numerous commentaries on Aristotle's works, mainly during his second teaching period in Paris (1268–72), including an extended commentary on *Metaphysics*. On internal evidence, the work is likely to have been begun in the university year 1270–71, although it is conceivable that it dates in its earliest version from Thomas' years at Rome, between 1265 and 1268.[58] Thomas is a thinker who is deeply indebted to Aristotle for a range of ideas and themes, and for a supple and sophisticated vocabulary which in his own work and that of others became the characteristic building-blocks of scholastic metaphysics.

At eighteen years of age, Aristotle (384–322 BCE) arrived as a student at the Academy of Plato. He remained there until Plato's death in 348 BCE, when he departed for another branch of the academy directed by Hermeias at Assos in Asia Minor. Aristotle was interested in many of the same questions which concerned Plato, including the nature of justice and of the good, issues to do with the nature of the body politic and questions concerning the fundamental structure of human knowledge. But he was deeply critical of Plato's theory of the forms, as self-subsisting principles independent of material manifestations. Whether or not he moved away from an initial platonist position following the death of Plato, this far-reaching critique of Plato's idealism is evident from the text *On Ideas*, and from the extensive discussion of the platonic Forms in the *Metaphysics*.[59] Aristotle argues against any notion of forms that exist outside the realm of matter, preferring the concept of form as the principle of actuality which combines with the potentiality of matter in the formation of an entity in the world. The *Metaphysics*, in which he presents his ideas, is a complex and fragmentary text however, which 'has no consecutive story to narrate'.[60] The order of the books appears generally arbitrary, and is likely to have been the work of Andronicus, the ancient editor of Aristotle's texts. The title simply indicates its position after the *Physics* in the Aristotelian corpus.[61] The method employed in the *Metaphysics* is also one that is heuristic rather than demonstrative, and, in the judgment of W. D. Ross, represents 'the adventures of a mind in its search for truth'.[62] The thrust of the argument is characterized not by the application of accepted axioms but rather by an attempt to establish such fundamental principles in the field of metaphysical enquiry. Jonathan Barnes has argued that there are four distinct problematics in the *Metaphysics*: the science of first principles, the study of being qua being, theology and the investigation into substance.[63] Even if we recall that the Greek term *to on* ('being') is more visibly connected with *ousia* ('substance') than is the case in most English translations, it is evident that Aristotle's attempt to bring the being of individual entities under a single universal concept is fraught with difficulties, not least the fundamental one that the universal is the object of knowledge and of definition, while substance or *ousia* is the principle of separate individual entities.[64]

In Book Alpha, Aristotle sets out the need for a science that 'investigates the first principles and causes' of all things, that is of reality as a whole, noting that such a concern is rooted in the 'wonder' which first impelled humankind to philosophize.[65] In Book Gamma, this is the 'science which investigates being as being', in contrast with the special sciences – such as mathematics – which only 'cut off a part of being and investigate the attributes of this part'. A science which seeks to 'grasp the first causes' must take as its object 'being as being' (*to on hê on*).[66] But 'there are many senses in which a thing may be said to be', Aristotle tells us, and if we are to reflect upon 'being as being', then we must investigate the 'one central point, the one definite kind of thing' to which being in all its senses can be seen to relate. As a parallel, Aristotle cites 'health', which has what modern scholars have termed a 'focal meaning': '[e]verything which is healthy is related to health, one thing in the sense that it preserves health, another in the sense that it produces it, another in the sense that it is a symptom of health, another because it is capable of it'. In the case of 'being as being' the focal term, to which all its usages relate, is 'substance' (*ousia*) and 'substances' (*ousiai*) and it is of these that 'the philosopher must grasp the principles and causes'.[67]

Aristotle offers a threefold typology of substance. In the first place there exists 'sensible' substance, which is either 'eternal' or 'perishable', while a second type is 'immovable' and can exist apart from matter. Platonists assert that the latter includes the forms, but Aristotle prefers to include only the principles of mathematics in this category. These imply movement and are thus 'the subject of natural science'. The third type however, 'belongs to another science, since there is no principle common to it and to the other kinds'.[68] In Book Epsilon, the third type is characterized as that which is 'eternal and immovable and inseparable', and it is 'theology' which – as the 'highest science' of the 'highest genus' – reflects upon it.[69] It is the study of this 'immovable substance' which is prior and universal and which therefore constitutes 'first philosophy'.[70] The need to postulate and reflect upon 'immovable' substance is grounded in the nature of those substances which constitute the objects of our ordinary experience. These are compound entities, of form and matter, and their distinguishing characteristic is change (or 'movement'), understood as generation, through art, nature or spontaneity. In the *Physics* Aristotle specifies four different kinds of change, brought about through material, formal, efficient or final causality.[71] Aristotle envisages a world in which every substance comes from another of the same kind, in a self-perpetuating chain of causality. If every entity is composed of an actual and potential dimension as form and matter, where the former represents the capacity of an entity itself to initiate change and the latter is the entity's own capacity to undergo change, then Aristotle allots priority to actuality as the cause of change.[72] Aristotle's argument at this point is that actuality is existence and that if an entity proceeds not from actuality but from potentiality, then it could be said to have come from non-being, which is impossible.[73] Aristotle uses the same argument in Book Lambda, where he is discussing the Prime Mover as the ultimate principle of substance.[74] This principle is itself 'pure actuality', for its very substance is actuality, and lacking all possibility of change, it is 'eternal', 'immaterial', 'indivisible', 'good' and 'necessary'.[75] The *noêsis noêseôs* of Book Lambda is pure thought, actuality, duration and life:

> And life also belongs to God; for the actuality of thought is life, and God is that actuality; and God's essential actuality is life most good and eternal. We say therefore that God is a living being, eternal, most good, so that life and duration continuous and eternal belong to God; for this *is* God.[76]

Above all, it is this principle which initiates change in the universe, while remaining itself wholly unmoved, and the character of its causality is that of a final cause. All things look to it as perfection; it is both 'the object of desire and the object of thought', which 'move without being moved'.[77] Desire and thought find their unity in the good, and so the Unmoved Mover is itself the good, which moves the universe by prompting love: 'Thus it produces motion by being loved, and it moves the other moving things.'[78]

In Thomas Aquinas we find Aristotelian distinctions between 'actuality' and 'potentiality', 'form' and 'matter', as well as the fourfold scheme of causality, the prioritization of intellectual contemplation, and an emphasis upon the sensible concrete entity as the first object of knowledge. There are however, deep differences in the metaphysical schemes of both men which go back in the main to Thomas' understanding of the origin of things not as a Prime Mover, sovereign and aloof, who acts impersonally as an ultimate and final cause upon the changing world, but rather as the Creator God of Judaeo-Christian tradition, who is intimately engaged with his creation at every level, through covenant and incarnation. It is in *Quaestio* 45 of the *Summa Theologiae* that Thomas reflects upon the act of 'creation' as such and asks 'whether to create is to make something from nothing?'. He determines that nothing can be held to have preceded that creation which is 'the emanation of all being from the universal cause, which is God': '*Nothing*' is the same as '*non-being*', and so 'as the generation of a man presupposes the *non-being* which is *non-man*, so creation, which is the emanation of all being, presupposes the *non-being* which is *nothing*'.[79] Creation, therefore, is always a creation from nothing, and the being which comes into existence as a result of the creative act demands to be understood in opposition to non-being or nothingness. As such, the power to create is specifically a property of God. The craftsman, for instance, produces his works from pre-existing material, as do the generative processes of nature.[80] Our own ability to initiate change depends again upon the pre-existence of the material upon which we act, and the 'secondary instrumental cause' cannot be said to 'share in the action of the superior cause'.[81]

The principle of *creatio ex nihilo* both serves to radicalize being by opposing it to nothingness and to unify being by referring all that is to a single point: the Creator. The unity of being is expressed in Thomas' notion of the *ens commune* ('being that is held in common' or 'being as a whole'), which suggests the totality of all created things.[82] It is the *ens commune* which in the prologue to his commentary on Aristotle's *Metaphysics* constitutes the subject of metaphysics.[83] A second consequence of Thomas' creationism is the distinction he draws between what something is and the fact that it is: between its 'essence' (*essentia*) and 'existence' (*esse*).[84] Aristotle made no distinction on this point, arguing that '*one man* and *a man* that is and a *man* are the same'.[85] For Thomas however, if 'a being' (*ens*) is a real existent, or 'something positive in reality', then 'essence' (*essentia*) is the composite of matter and form and 'is used because through it, and in it, that which is has being (*esse*)'.[86] In the words of Gerald Phelan:

> The selfsame thing which is and which is known is a composite of elements, the one essential, the other existential, neither of which can *be* or be intelligible without reference to the other but both of which are co-existent and co-intelligible in the unity of the thing . . . *Things* are known (not natures or acts of being) and they are known *to be* through their *esse* and to be what they are through their essence.[87]

Importantly, Thomas argues that the essence and the existence of a thing are known through two distinct types of cognition, the former being grasped through 'simple apprehension' and the latter through what he calls 'judgment'.[88]

The way from his early sketch of the 'real distinction' in *On Being and Essence* to the fully mature theory of the *actus essendi*, the understanding of being as pure act which is the fulcrum of Thomas' creationist metaphysics, was not immediate however.[89] In *On Truth* he put forward the view that the relation between creature and Creator was only an analogy of proportionality, arguing that there can be no *proportion* as such between a finite and an infinite being.[90] But in his *Commentary on the De Trinitate of Boethius* he proposed an analogy of participation, based upon what Thibault has called 'creative causality', maintaining that the relation between creature and Creator is the real relation which obtains between an effect and its cause.[91] In the *Summa Theologiae* this position is further developed in that God, who is defined as 'self-subsisting' (*esse per se subsistens*) or 'pure being' (*esse tantum*), creates being from himself *se toto*, from the pure act of being that he himself is.[92] The being that comes from him, and in which all entities participate,[93] 'is the actuality of every form or nature'[94] and is 'the most perfect of all things'[95] since '[a]ll the perfections of all things pertain to the perfection of being; for things are perfect precisely so far as they have being after some fashion'.[96] The very quality of existing makes us like God: 'all created things, so far as they are beings, are like God as the first and universal principle of all being'.[97]

The created order participates in divine life therefore to the extent that it possesses being. But the analogy of participation serves to divide creatures from the Creator as much as to unite them. For 'it is of the essence of a thing caused to be in some way composite',[98] and, as we have seen, every being or entity (*ens*) is a compound of essence (*essentia*) on the one hand and of existence or being (*esse*) on the other. No caused entity can generate its being from its own essence, but is rather dependent upon its own prior cause.[99] In the case of God however, who as the First Mover is himself unmoved and uncaused, being and essence are one, for God's own nature is utterly simple. In him there are neither division nor body, nor potentiality nor accidents.[100] Since the divine being is not participated with respect to some prior cause, it follows that 'God is his own being and not merely his own essence'.[101] God is separated from his creatures by an infinite gulf therefore, as well as being united with them through his creative causality, for the being of creatures is determined by their essence, with which it combines in the compound state that is the condition of creaturely existence. Thus being, and the actuality which it constitutes, is necessarily limited and finite, and contingent upon God's will.

Thomas Aquinas' achievement was to adapt sophisticated Aristotelian terminology for the articulation of a Christian creationist metaphysics. The key to that change was the understanding that existence falls outside the range of this vocabulary, and cannot be accommodated within it. Whereas for Aristotle actuality is a property of 'form' in its conjunction with 'matter', Thomas understood the compound of form and matter which grounds an individual entity to itself participate in a prior ontological cause, the ultimate origin of which is God. This is to give much clearer shape to the notion of being as actual existence, separated from *what* a thing is. But this new and more dynamic understanding of being, for which the notion of participation in God as the ultimate origin of being is central, does not establish a dominant relation between the self and being as we find in the thinkers of Chapter Three. Thomas' emphasis upon God as creator of a differentiated world breaks down any narcissistic gazing of the self upon being as the unified medium of relation with the other. Only in the *ens commune* does the unity of being come into view, and the status of this rarely used term is ambiguous in Thomas' thought.[102] Far more significant is the concept of the *differentiae* of being and of their coherence within the logic of analogy.[103] In *On Truth* Thomas states that while nothing can add to being as such, since being is not a genus, there are nevertheless distinct *modes* of being, which serve to differentiate it:

> There are different grades of being insofar as different modes of being are grasped. The different genera of being are based on these modes. Substance does not add some difference to being which would designate

some nature superadded to being; rather a certain special mode of being is expressed by the term substance, namely, *per se* being, and so it is with the other genera.[104]

His interest is not in the unity of being as a whole as grasped by the intellect, but rather in the rich interactions that inhere in the created order. A further mode of being occurs 'insofar as it follows on one being in its relation to another'. This stems firstly from the differentiation of being, which is the division of one thing from another: 'just as a being is called one insofar as it is undivided in itself, so it is called something insofar as it is divided from others'. It derives secondly from 'one being's harmony with another', which can only be the case if there is something 'whose nature it is to be in harmony with every being'. This is the human soul, through which, Thomas argues, the transcendentals, which are convertible with respect to being itself, come into view. Thus truth is the 'harmony of being with intellect', and goodness is the 'harmony of being with appetite'.[105] For Thomas then the human self holds a central position in a differentiated universe. The transcendentals of truth and goodness are implied within being itself, and do not 'add' to it, but are manifest in the operations of the human mind, which can perceive other beings in truth and can desire them appropriately, through grace, in goodness.

The harmony between beings of which Thomas speaks finds its highest expression in his theory of love. The Greek *philia*, denoting 'positive interaction between human beings', embraced a variety of relationships and feelings which extend beyond the range denoted by the category of 'friendship' in modern European languages.[106] But it would also be true to say that the classical notion of *philia* generally denoted an elective relationship with other persons of like mind. Aristotle clearly identified the unity of friends in the Good, and understood the unity of friendship to be an extension of the unity and friendship that a good man enjoys with himself.[107] He was fascinated by the way in which adherence to the Good, with its implied unity of intention and perspective, informs our relations with others who also pursue the Good in such a way that a close friend becomes 'another self', and we seek what is good for them for their own sake, since they are good, and not for our own.[108] Thomas took up and adapted these Aristotelian ideas within a Christian context. He identified love (*caritas*) as 'friendship with God', based upon a certain 'fellowship', or *communicatio*, between ourselves and God, resulting from processes of grace and predicated upon equality.[109] Love is 'not based on human virtue' but is 'a certain participation in the Holy Spirit'. The divine essence itself is love, and we share in the divine love through our likeness to God as his creatures.[110] Christian love primarily has God as its object, but intrinsic to its dynamic is a universal love of our fellow human beings:

> Now the light in which we must love our neighbour is God, for what we ought to love in him is that he be in God. Hence it is clear that it is

specifically the same act which loves God and loves neighbour. And on this account charity extends not merely to the love of God, but also to the love of neighbour.[111]

Thomas has exchanged Aristotelian friendship therefore, with its social particularity, for a universal concept of love which extends even to our enemies as those whom we must love in the light of our love for God, which is itself a participation in the divine love which God has for himself. The moral imperative to love even those who hate us is rooted in the recognition of the sovereignty of God as Creator, who has made all that is for himself. Thomas' ethical vision then is one which is itself predicated upon a particular way of understanding the ordering of the world. It is the analogical metaphysics of differentiated being, whereby all things relate through participation to God as the cause of being and thus to each other as co-creatures of the Creator God, which animates and sustains Thomas' ethics of universal love.

Søren Kierkegaard and the Hegelians

Kierkegaard (1813–55) grew up in pious Danish Lutheran circles much influenced by the philosophy of Hegel and his Danish theological advocates. His writings reflect a penetrating Christian critique of idealism, in its Hegelian form, both in an analytical medium and from the perspective of human reality as depicted in literary works. He lived as an alien within his own society and died as an implacable opponent of the established Danish Lutheran Church. Whereas Augustine and Thomas Aquinas can be said to have appropriated classical models of metaphysics, adapting them in the light of a Christian doctrine of creation, Kierkegaard offered a substantial critique of Hegelian metaphysics, arguing that it clashed irreconcilably with the true meaning of Christianity. His debt to secular metaphysics is polemically reactive therefore, and the understanding of existence with which 'the father of existentialism' has been associated is one which essentially grew out of a milieu in which Hegel's philosophy of Spirit was judged to be the definitive intellectual system which grounded all human knowledge.

Hegel's philosophy, like many of the most influential conceptual systems, was predicated upon a single, magisterial thought.[112] This was the idea that in encountering the world the mind does not engage with something extra-mental and definitively other than itself but rather encounters itself under the guise of otherness. This led to two, not unrelated consequences. The first was a destabilizing of the everyday human mind with respect to universal mind, or Spirit (*Geist*), and the second was that the human self and the world itself, in all their rich diversity, become susceptible to a rational analysis, where rational implies that particular understanding which derives from the mind's reflections upon its own constitution, leading to a comprehension of itself as modality of Spirit. The Hegelian system entails the argument that mind is constituted precisely by its encounter with otherness, and that that otherness is necessarily posited by itself, in a cycle of affirmation, negation and synthesis. Mind is essentially dynamic and is only realized where it encounters an object, but the mind that thinks and the object that is thought are for Hegel ultimately one, even though that is a unity which can only come into view precisely within the differentiation which is a condition of the subject's knowing. Hegelian knowing is a pendulum swing as the unity which underlies all things, which most essentially constitutes all things, finds realization in the ongoing dialectic of affirmation, negation and synthesis, which is the structure of Spirit or mind. Human consciousness is not itself to be identified with mind as such, since it is necessarily finite and contingent. But the human self can realize for itself the nature of Spirit (or universal mind) where it conforms in its thinking with the structure of Spirit itself. This is precisely to comprehend the world and to look upon it in the understanding that it is the sphere of dialectical manifestation of universal mind, which can only come to its own self-realization through assuming guises of otherness which it then overcomes and assumes to itself in an eternal process of self-positing and self-realization. Understanding the true identity of Spirit within the multiplicity of distinctions in the world, the self and history, is our human destiny and the highest expression of our rationality.

There were two areas of expression of Hegel's philosophy of Spirit which were of particular interest to Kierkegaard. The first was his theory of ethics, which affirmed the ethical ground to be the free identification of the self in others (*beisichselbstsein in einem Anderen*). The primary realization of this, for Hegel, lay in the sphere of society, its mores and institutions. The self could only attain to its own free self-realization through reason by and with other people, with whose interests one identified. The term Hegel used for this was *Sittlichkeit*, which suggested the 'customs' or 'mores' of civil society (*die Sitten*), in contrast with the individual subjectivity and responsibility of 'morality' (*Moralität*). Conformity to the moral law as realized within the rational community of civil society with its norms and institutions was the fulcrum of Hegel's ethical thinking.

The second aspect of Hegel's system which especially concerned Kierkegaard was his understanding of the relation between philosophy and religion. Hegel's prioritization of the communal and social dimensions of ethics led to an emphasis upon the historical role of Protestantism as the mediation of such a – Christian – communitarian ethics within modern societies.[113] The link between philosophy and ethics, through rationalism, was explicit, but the intimate connection between traditional Christianity and Hegel's speculative philosophy was more complex and – in his own day – very much more controversial. Hegel lived at a time and place where contrasts between the intellectual and affective aspects of Christian life were the cause of real social and political conflict. In Frederick IV's Prussia, an anti-intellectualist 'dogmatic' trend found expression in the politically influential pietist circles, which rejected his own speculative philosophy as being outrightly 'atheist'. Intellectualist theology was branded as 'dry' and 'dead'. It is against this background that we must see the work of Schleiermacher, and his appeal to 'feeling', as well as the theologies of those who willingly embraced Hegel's philosophy as a scientific advance in Christian thought. In the prefaces to the second editions of both his *Encyclopaedia* and *Logic*, written towards the end of his life, Hegel himself sought to represent his philosophy as an intellectualist version of Christian truths, to be distinguished from traditional belief only on the grounds of its mode of cognition. He thus wished to maintain that his philosophy did not break with Christian tradition as faith, but only sought to capture it within a different medium, as knowledge. That new and scientific medium was suited to the rationalism of the age, and offered important new means for the propagation of the gospel and the instilling of a Christian spirit among the populace, although Hegel knew that it was always likely to appeal to a minority, and he praised the capacity of traditional Christianity to present the same truths in a way that was accessible for the less educated.[114]

It was in the text *Fear and Trembling*, published in 1843, that Kierkegaard began to articulate his attack upon the Hegelian version of the Christian faith which exercised such influence in Danish ecclesiastical and scholarly circles during the mid nineteenth century. His critique is framed as a series of extended reflections upon the Abraham and Isaac story, focusing in particular on the nature of faith and its relation to ethics. The ethical system in question is recognizably that of Hegel himself, who stressed the universality of ethics in the *Philosophy of Right*. Kierkegaard reads into this a rationalist agenda, since he equates ethics in this sense with language and the power of explanation. According to this view, the agent of an ethical act must be able to give a good account in terms shared with the community of what constitutes the good, and of the specific reasons they have for acting in the way they do. Abraham, on the other hand, remains silent and does not give an account of his actions to either Eleazar, Sarah or Isaac, who are the people most involved in his actions.[115] It is not that Abraham does not wish to speak, but rather that he *cannot* speak, except in the ambiguity of irony which, for Kierkegaard, is itself a kind of silence.[116] For Abraham to be able to speak would be for him to inhabit the universal, with its ground in rationalism, since 'the relief of speech is that it transfers me into the universal'.[117] Abraham stands outside the sphere of reason and the universal, and by virtue of his faith, 'now exists as the particular in opposition to the universal'.[118] His preparedness to sacrifice Isaac, whom he loves, must be seen as this 'suspension of the ethical', in which love does not cease but its expression might be 'opposite . . . to that which, ethically speaking, is required by duty'.[119]

For Kierkegaard, Abraham represents the condition of faith, which stands in stark contrast to Hegelian rationalism. Faith is founded on paradox, and is described as 'the highest passion in a person' which is akin to the 'divine madness' of the Greeks.[120] Abrahamic faith has two elements to it. The first is the power of infinite resignation, which has its source in human agency, while the second is miraculous and is 'believing by virtue of the absurd'.[121] It is the second which shows a distinctively historical character, so that Abraham 'did not believe that someday he would be blessed in the beyond, but that he would be happy here in the world'.[122] Resignation, which represents the 'last stage prior to faith', had to be followed by an act whereby 'he grasped everything again by virtue of the absurd'.[123] That act of belief in the absurd establishes the self as a sphere of subjectivity which is 'incommensurable with reality' and of inwardness which is 'higher than [Hegelian] outwardness'.[124]

The theme of the paradox and of faith appears again in the two associated texts, *Philosophical Fragments* (1844) and *Concluding Unscientific Postscript to Philosophical Fragments* (1846), both works being attributed to the historical figure John Climacus as author and S. Kierkegaard as editor. Here the paradox is explicitly defined as 'the coming into existence of the eternal God', or incarnation, and Kierkegaard's primary engagement is with the character of faith. He is concerned to argue against the notion of objective historical truth on the one hand and of objective, systematic thought encompassing faith on the other. The former is a problematic raised by the influential writings of Gottfried Ephraim Lessing, who – in the memorable image of the 'broad ugly ditch' – stressed the chronological gulf between the earliest Christian sources and the contemporary believer, while the latter marks a return to Kierkegaard's critique of the Hegelians.[125] Against Lessing, Kierkegaard advances the sceptical argument that the immediacy of the senses and the 'historical' is illusory and that all 'historical' knowledge is constructed. In the case of faith, that construction has the consequence that the modern believer is no more cut off from the sources than was the earliest Christian, for the faith of both is equally founded in the subjective appropriation of the paradox.[126] Kierkegaard is clear however, that the paradox itself is not a purely subjective phenomenon. The paradox comes about in the relation between the finite human mind and the entry of the infinite God, as 'eternal truth', into finite, spatio-temporal existence.[127] His point is that the paradox, which is the substance of faith, is not mediated to the mind through objective historical knowledge or objective rational thinking, but comes about through the collision of God (or 'the god', as he prefers to call him) who enters into history, with our human awareness: 'when the eternal truth relates itself to an existing person, it becomes the paradox'.[128] Indeed, it is this collision, or 'the passion of faith', which brings about the fulfilment or realization of the subjectivity which is intrinsic to our nature. If 'existence yields passion', then 'existence accented paradoxically yields the maximum of passion'.[129] Against the advocates of scientific historicism therefore, Kierkegaard argues that faith is the resolve to think the unthinkable, in an act of inwardness which grounds our subjectivity. Human nature is not constrained by the possession of conclusive historical data, or of comprehensive systems of thought, but the locus of truth is within subjectivity itself, and human existence is shown to be a progressive realization of that truth, as a perpetual becoming.

The new understanding of existence which Kierkegaard develops in *Concluding Unscientific Postscript* marks a significant departure in the history of ontology. Existence becomes for him virtually synonymous with 'inwardness', 'subjectivity' and even 'individuality'. Kierkegaard argues that in their enthusiasm for thought the Hegelians have forgotten the one who thinks: 'Hegelian philosophy confuses existence by not defining its relation to an existing person . . .'.[130] For Hegelians, the 'existing subject' remains concealed. For Kierkegaard however, existence is manifest not in intellectual systems but in the passion of the paradox, which is founded not on logic but on the coming-into-existence of God in time and space. This is never known as an historical datum, but only as the paradox that meets the human mind and which grounds the subjectivity of faith. In other words, the existence of faith is commensurate with and ordered to the coming-into-existence of God in the incarnation.

Kierkegaard offers a powerful restatement of the language of existence therefore by drawing our attention to the extent that Hegelian thought obscures the subject who thinks: 'the systematic idea is subject–object, is the unity of thinking and being; existence, on the other hand, is precisely the separation. From this it by no means follows that existence is thoughtless, but existence has spaced and does space subject from object, thought from being.'[131] In particular, he contests the proposition which Hegel advances in the *Encyclopaedia* that 'being' constitutes 'immediacy', which is then resolved into a dialectic of nothingness, transition and thought. In a crucial passage from *Concluding Unscientific Postscript*, Kierkegaard argues that 'the beginning of the system that begins with the immediate *is then itself achieved through reflection*'.[132] Therefore 'the immediate must mean something different from what it usually does'.[133] Against this beginning in reflection, Kierkegaard argues for a beginning in faith, or what he calls – borrowing Lessing's term – 'the leap'. It is only the 'leap' that can counter the circularities and tautologies of beginning with reflection.[134] It is only in faith, as the point of departure, that existence in its immediacy can be truly found. Here Kierkegaard shows his indebtedness to the Lutheran tradition and to Luther's own development of the Pauline notion that faith constitutes a new creation.

Against the primacy of historical data and logical thought, Kierkegaard asserts the values of existence that come into view in human subjectivity and will. These attain their fullest realization in the passionate appropriation of the paradox of God made flesh. It is the Christian testimony not to doctrine, but to 'the fact that the god has existed', which represents the dynamic fulfilment of human nature.[135] And in line with earlier tradition, Kierkegaard is keen to affirm that existence as he has defined it stands in an intimate relation with the transcendentals of truth, goodness and beauty. Faith represents the culmination of the aesthetic to the extent that the passion that 'overwhelms' the self is the most radical form of beauty, which is only hinted at in the experience of the lover. Truth, for Kierkegaard, is withdrawn from the realm of the objective to subjectivity itself, as it is formed and deepened in the appropriation of the paradox, which is the self's own becoming or existence. It is not the 'what' but the 'how' that constitutes truth: the existential depth of its appropriation. But subjectivity can be identified with ethics also, since existence represents the fullest form of self-realization, yielding an ethics of authenticity. This is strongly reminiscent of the expressivist theory of ethics which was favoured by Romantic and Idealist thinkers, and at this point Kierkegaard shows the same difficulty with the notion of intersubjectivity that characterizes the thinking of his opponents. Ethics is determined purely in terms of our relation with God, and there is little sense of the centrality of the love for our neighbour. In *Concluding Unscientific Postscript*, the *bonum diffusivum sui* is expressed by the need to communicate existence–truth–goodness indirectly through artistic writing, which is the only way of communicating the actuality of subjectivity, as a possibility to be appropriated by other selves.[136]

In *Works of Love* however, Kierkegaard revises his understanding of love, and richly develops a thematic of Christian love as a participation in divine kenosis. Love for the neighbour now moves to a central position in his thought, and takes on some of the qualities previously ascribed to faith. It is thus 'hidden' and 'inward' and linked with 'actuality' and 'truth'.[137] In particular, the distinctive mark of Christian love is its tendency or preparedness to find expression as both paradox and passion, since it may be exercised in the face of total rejection:

> Christianly to descend from heaven means limitlessly to love the person just as you see him. If, then, you will become perfect in love, strive to fulfil this duty, in loving to love the person one sees, to love him just as you see him, with all his imperfections and weaknesses, love him as you see him when he is utterly changed, when he no longer loves you, when he perhaps turns indifferent away or turns to love someone else, love him as you see him when he betrays and denies you.[138]

There are resonances too with faith in that love is the result of the absolute command of duty and persists independently of the historical contingencies that surround its object. Christian love is love which has been submitted to the infinite and has 'undergone the transformation of the eternal'.[139]

Conclusion

The three Christian thinkers we have studied in this section have each responded in a particular way to the challenge of a secular metaphysics. In the case of Augustine, that challenge took the form of a platonic displacement of being, which he initially identified with the Christian God, but which increasingly became redundant as the *appetitive* theory of love which it supported gave way in his theology to a deepening exploration of the theme of a *participative*, kenotic and ecclesiological love modelled on the love of Christ. Augustine came to platonic being before his conversion to Christianity, and so his assimilation of it and finally loss of interest in it, may have been dictated by the progression of his own life's journey. As a consequence of this development, we do not find in Augustine an explicit integration of the metaphysics of his earlier works with the ecclesiology of his later thinking. In the case of Thomas Aquinas however, Aristotelian metaphysics is assimilated into a prior Christian theology; it is thus rigorously subjected to and refigured within the parameters of Christian thought and faith. By employing Aristotelian language and concepts, Thomas is able to develop a distinctively Christian metaphysics which is ordered to the primary given of the Christian Creator God. Here love of God and love of the neighbour are intertwined in a comprehensive, cosmic vision of the interchangeability of the transcendentals, as Being grounds Truth and Goodness. Kierkegaard's metaphysical project however, is one which was a reaction against the secular metaphysics represented by Hegelian logic. The Idealist programme threatened the existential commitments of the Christian tradition through an assimilation into rationalism, and Kierkegaard's response was to intensify reflection upon the immediacy of existence as a condition of Christian faith. It was thus to impose upon the metaphysical speculation of Idealist philosophers the absolute imperatives given by the incarnation, engendering new insights into the meaning of Christian existence.

In all three of our thinkers the imaginative and conceptual possibilities of secular metaphysics are refigured in the light of the Christian doctrines of creation and incarnation. It is these that give Christian metaphysics, of whatever kind, a distinctively personalist and existential edge. The Judaeo-Christian belief in a strong theology of Creation places being firmly within the context of a relation: that of the Creator to his creation. Human existence, which is part of the creation, therefore becomes answerable in its depths to God, as the creative Other. But this answerability is expressed not only in terms of a God–self relation but also crucially in terms of a self–other relation. The love of God is matched by love for the neighbour, who is central to the dynamic of the ethical cycle. In the Christian metaphysical conceptuality represented in this chapter, love for the concrete other is not just a sign of the presence of a love for God in us, but is the very energy of that love, without which love itself is called into question.

The recognition that all being comes from the Creator is the simultaneous recognition that our relation with God is co-posited with the relation of his other creatures with him and of them with us. This is a programme not for narcissism but for community. But just as this theology establishes a new and more dynamic understanding of being as divine gift, so too it inaugurates a dramatically new concept of nothingness; since what is given, can also be taken away. It is this that represents the other side of Christian metaphysics: an awareness of the precariousness of existence, of the possibility of its loss as damnation as well as its consummation as eternal life. The sense of existence as both gift and risk, exercised before the face of the Creator, is well conveyed in a line from the Vulgate Ps. 38 (v. 6) in which the psalmist declares that his 'substance is like nothingness' before God: *ecce mensurabiles posuisti dies meos et substantia mea tamquam nihilum ante te verumtamen universa vanitas omnis homo vivens diapsalma*.[140] The contingency of being, so keenly felt by Christian thinkers, is further expressed in the conviction that the ultimate home of the human spirit is not this earth but rather the next world, or the world to come. Socrates spoke of the next world as *apodêmia*, meaning 'foreign land'.[141] But for Augustine, it is this world that is the *regio dissimilitudinis*, a 'place of strangeness', while our true home is in heaven, with God and all his saints.[142]

5

Being and Consciousness: Freedom and Limit

Das einzige positive ist dem Idealisten die Freiheit: Seyn ist ihm blosse Negation der ersteren.

For the Idealist nothing is positive but freedom, and, for him, being is nothing but a negation of freedom.

J. G. Fichte, *Zweite Einleitung in die Wissenschaftslehre*

The beginnings of a philosophy of consciousness and an early kind of idealism are already apparent in the Middle Ages, where mind as *mens* is seen as being hierarchically situated 'above' the material world. The Christian tradition understood the human self to be the creature of the Creator God, and thus to be in a most intimate sense in the image of God. For Augustinianism in particular it was frequently mind itself that was designated as the divine image in us. But the tendency towards idealism, in the sense of emphasizing the priority or transcendentalism of consciousness and its relative independence with respect to the material world, is balanced in Christian tradition by the parallel belief that God is Creator of both human selves and the material reality of which we are a part and which is the site of our moral vocation. Christian metaphysics understands the world to be as real as ourselves, and that its reality is guaranteed by its status – equal to our own – as God's creation.

But in the period between the end of the Middle Ages and the seventeenth century, enormous developments in the conceptualization of reality took place. The emergence of a 'univocal' view of nature undermined the 'analogical' character of the creationist metaphysics of the Middle Ages, with its symbolic structures.[1] Foucault has described this process in terms of an exchange of 'similitudes' for 'sameness and difference'.[2] For Thomas Aquinas, God was at the heart of his creation 'through essence, power and presence', but for the Nominalists of the fourteenth century the universe was already one which was radically exposed to the sovereign and unfathomable 'power' of his creative will, to the relative exclusion of 'essence' and 'presence'.[3] Secondly, we can note the replacement of a metaphysics of forms by one of forces, and the development of mathematics as a language in which to speak of entities in terms of their quantitative characteristics. This new language reflected the material in its own terms, that is, in ways which were subject to empirical verification, and did not serve merely as an ideal image of how the world should be. In a justifiably celebrated passage, Galileo plays upon the contrasts between the 'book of nature' of classical metaphysics and the legibility of nature to the modern scientist:

> Philosophy is written in this great book which constantly opens before our eyes (I mean the universe), but it cannot be understood unless one first learns the language and the characters in which it is composed. It is written in the language of mathematics, and its characters are triangles, circles, and other geometrical figures without which it is impossible to understand a single word of it; without these we wander vainly in a dark labyrinth.[4]

The *mathesis universalis* ('the universal science'), based upon an epistemology of measurement and quantification, also proved to be a different kind of knowledge of the world from its medieval counterpart. Funkenstein calls the former 'ergetic' and contrasts it with the 'contemplative' knowledge of the Middle Ages. There was now a sense that to understand something was to be able to reproduce it; it was to know 'not only how things are structured, but also how they are made'.[5] The old Aristotelian notion of final causes gave way to efficient causality, and science began to feed, through mechanics, into technology.[6] In the changed world of the seventeenth and eighteenth centuries, the human self, too, seemed subject to the inexorable logic of the same causal forces which natural science had discovered. The freedom of the self, and the unity of the self, were vigorously contested by Hobbes and Hume alike, whose scepticism had its origins in the new empiricism. Materialism in its various forms, down to the present day, offers a deterministic view of the self which reflects a mechanical view of the world itself: as a compilation of entities which are grasped solely as the product of a quantifiable though arbitrary play of causes.

It was in this environment that the philosophy of consciousness was born. Characteristically, philosophers in this tradition appealed to human freedom as the principle at stake, in which the idealists showed the extent to which they were in reaction to the determinism of materialist arguments. But at the same time philosophers of consciousness have habitually claimed that critical introspection which seeks to engage with reality as it presents itself to us in its immediacy is itself grounded in the principles of natural science. From the perspective of our guiding formula, that being is the medium of relation between self and other, materialism collapses the self into the other, conceived as a field of forces and determinants. Idealists, on the other hand, understand matter to be a modality of mind, or at least to be fundamentally at the disposal of mind. In both cases, it is the *relation* between self and other which is rendered problematic and intrinsically polemical, and so both materialists and idealists look awry at the classical notion of being as that which unites self and other, the former choosing generally to dispense with it altogether and the latter reformulating it as the boundary or limit posited by mind in the act of its own self-realization.

René Descartes

Descartes (1596–1650) stands at the cusp of the new thinking. He was trained by the Jesuits at La Flèche in Anjou, where he received a substantial education in philosophy, which included mathematics. After leaving college, he embarked first on a military career and took up the study of mechanics and medicine. Despite the anti-Aristotelianism of his philosophy, it is important to see his thought against the background of a number of late scholastic thinkers.[7] In 1619, Descartes had a series of dreams in which he glimpsed the possibility of a method that unified all the sciences. Some early indications of it are given in his *Rules for the Direction of our Native Intelligence* (1628), where he begins to reflect on the nature of knowledge. Here he sets out the different categories of substance which construct the world that we know. But his discussion is informed throughout by the notion of an 'idea' or 'concept' as that by which the world becomes accessible to us.

So strong is the sense in the mature Descartes that the universe is ordered to the cognitive principles of the human mind that Jean-Luc Marion has described Cartesianism as 'an ontology by denial'.[8] It replicates the method of Aristotelian ontology but banishes its sense of *ousia*, so that the world no longer offers itself to us in its irreducible otherness. Here 'la chose' has become 'un objet', since this 'presents an entity more tractable to consciousness than *ousia*'.[9] Marion dubs this an 'ontologie grise', since 'it does not declare itself and hides beneath an epistemological discourse. But above all because it focuses on *the thing* as it causes it to depart from its irreducible *ousia*, so that it takes on the face of *an object*, being entirely subsumed into the exigencies of cognition.'[10] This is a world which only comes into view in a way that is already preordained by the cognitive structures of the human mind, and a metaphysics of ends and means is close at hand. The *hypokeimenon* of Aristotelian tradition, which is the substantial substrate of entities as such, has now become the *subiectum* which is the *cogito* itself.[11] Within this world it is the *cogito* which alone enjoys an immediate relation to being and thus, as a kind of universal subject, inherits *ousia*. Only God cannot be accommodated to this new understanding, for although God too is 'substance' (and therefore self-subsisting), he is 'infinite substance' which necessarily defies any measurement and thus lies beyond the reach of all cognitive appropriations.[12]

The relation between the human mind and existence is explored most dramatically in the *Discourse On Method* (1637) and *Meditations on First Philosophy* (1641). In the *Discourse*, which was written in French, Descartes tells us that he has been prompted to undertake his philosophical task in part on account of the great diversity of opinion and custom which he had observed among different peoples, and declares: 'I learned not to believe too firmly anything that I had been convinced of only by example and custom.'[13] He resolves to strip away all his beliefs, which may be fraught with error, in order to rebuild them on more secure foundations, preserving only fidelity to the laws of his country and to his Christian faith.[14] His chosen method was to proceed from what presented itself so clearly and immediately to his mind as to preclude all doubt, and thereby to build up a line of argument which was akin to 'those long chains of perfectly simple and easy reasonings by means of which geometers are accustomed to carry out their most difficult demonstrations'.[15] Having decided that all knowledge from the senses was open to doubt, since in dreams we perceive things that do not exist in a waking state, Descartes concluded that only the thinking subject who doubts can truly be known to exist, and that this is the first principle of philosophy which he has been seeking.[16] Swiftly following on from this conclusion, and in accord with his first maxim of philosophizing, Descartes argued from his innate knowledge of the imperfection of his own doubting state, which arises from the thought of something more perfect than himself, to the real existence of a perfect being who must have implanted this notion in his mind. This he identifies with God.[17]

The *Meditations,* which were written in Latin for a clerical audience, presents essentially the same argument, though with some interesting additions.[18] Descartes now places much more weight upon the possibility that we are deceived in our normal perceptions, not only evoking more strongly the parallel with dreams but also rhetorically conjuring forth 'an evil spirit', who is 'supremely powerful and intelligent' and who does his utmost to deceive him.[19] Having set the scene with an exercise in what Marion calls 'hyperbolic doubt',[20] Descartes is then able to argue that the deceiver could never bring it about that 'at the time of thinking that I am something, I am in fact nothing', so that 'this proposition "I am", "I exist", whenever I utter it or conceive it in my mind, is necessarily true'.[21] This marks an interesting clarification of the position adopted in the Fourth *Discourse*, quoted above, where the link between consciousness and existence is more generally stated. In the earlier passage the principle is enunciated that the subject who doubts is itself beyond doubt: 'in order to think I must exist'.[22] Descartes is proposing here that if thought, or the *cogito*, engages with an object, then the thinker, or *res cogitans*, must be said to exist. The position outlined in the *Meditations* is subtly different however, in that it proposes that when the *cogito* makes its own existence the object of cognition by affirming that it does itself exist, then that statement has a truth value which is beyond doubt. In other words, while the former is to *infer* the existence of the *cogito* regardless of its object, the latter is to *affirm* the existence of the *cogito* by taking itself as its own object, and hence is a form of transcendental knowledge.[23] If the former is a reflexivity which is given with all perception, then the latter is a heightened or transcendental form of reflexivity where thought engages with its own activity in order to ground an affirmation (i.e. that I am) which resists all possible doubt. Indeed, it is probably the case that the proposition of the Fourth Discourse is itself not inferential but 'performative', as the term *cogito* has what Hintikka calls 'existential presuppositions' in that it appears to presuppose the existence of the one who thinks.[24] Thus the relation of *cogito* to *sum* in Descartes' proposition may not be that of 'a premise to a conclusion', but rather that of 'a process to its product'.[25]

We find diverse elements in the work of Descartes therefore, which set the scene for important developments in the philosophical traditions of the nineteenth and early twentieth centuries. He places the *cogito* at the centre of the world, and constructs the world in such a way as to be most tractable to the cognitions of the human mind. God is to be thought principally not as one who has given himself in mystery, but as one who resists the scales or grids of human knowing. It is not in the sphere of metaphysics that God gives himself to the world, but through causality, exercised in the perfection and omnipotence of his will.[26] At the foundation of this world-view is the human mind itself, which, in performative reflexivity, becomes the truest *evidence* of existence, that which is most immediately known. Heidegger referred to this as exchanging the *verum* for the *certum*.[27] Although not in itself idealism, but rather for Descartes the foundation of a transcendental realism, the project of Cartesian doubt does anticipate idealism in important respects. The immediacy of consciousness lends it a kind of priority with respect to the material world. This is evident firstly in the performative character of the *cogito*, whereby a mental act itself grounds the most secure kind of knowledge. But it can be seen also in Descartes' argument that the independence of consciousness from both body and world can be shown by the fact that the subject can think away both body and world but not his own *cogito* (Descartes may have had the experience of being deceived about the real existence of objects in the world, but he could not meaningfully know what it would be like to be without body or world, since, we may assume, he had never been without either).[28] Both these kinds of strategies will be used again by later idealist philosophers in the explicit pursuit of idealist ends.

Immanuel Kant

The dissolution of the classical model of existence led on the one hand to a Cartesian emphasis upon consciousness as the primary form of immediacy and, on the other, to a reduction of consciousness to the materialist determination of sense experience. For Hume, for instance, the self is 'but a bundle or collection of different perceptions, which succeed each other

with an inconceivable rapidity, and are in a perpetual flux and movement'.[29] Immanuel Kant reacted against both thinkers. In his dismissal of
Descartes' defence of the Ontological Argument, Kant showed that he was
opposed to the strong ontology of the classical Judaeo-Christian tradition,
since for him

> *'Being'* is not a real predicate; that is, it is not a concept of something that
> could be added to the concept of a thing. It is merely the positing of a
> thing, or of certain determinations, as existing in themselves. Logically,
> it is merely the copula of a judgement. The proposition, 'God is omni-
> potent', contains two concepts, each of which has its object – God and
> omnipotence. The small word 'is' adds no new predicate, but only
> serves to posit the predicate in its relation to the subject.

In addition to the 'is' of predicates, Kant also dismisses the absolute 'there
is', since if we say 'God is' or 'There is a God',

> we attach no new predicate to the concept of God, but only posit the
> subject in itself with all its predicates, and indeed posit as being an *object*
> that stands in relation to my *concept*. . . . Otherwise stated, the real
> contains no more than the merely possible. A hundred real thalers do
> not contain the least coin more than a hundred possible thalers.[30]

In his argument against Hume, Kant developed a position that was
also to prove very influential. The *cogito* is co-posited with every act of
perception, without which 'something would be represented in me which
could not be thought at all'.[31] This reflects the unity of consciousness, since
'only in so far as I can grasp the manifold of representations in one
consciousness, do I call them one and all *mine*. For otherwise I should have
as many-coloured and diverse a self as I have representations of which I
am conscious to myself.'[32] Kant calls this 'pure' or 'original apperception',
which is 'the transcendental unity of self-consciousness'.[33] The *cogito* is
grounded in this 'unity of apperception', and without it

> the thoroughgoing identity of self-consciousness cannot be thought. For
> through the 'I', as simple representation, nothing manifold is given; only
> in intuition, which is distinct from the 'I', can a manifold be given; and
> only through *combination* in one consciousness can it be thought.[34]

The *cogito* then is a reflex of the unity which grounds consciousness, and
makes it *my* consciousness. But this unity in itself escapes representation;
it is 'that self-consciousness which, while generating the representation
"I think" (a representation which must be capable of accompanying all
other representations, and which in all consciousness is one and the same),
cannot itself be accompanied by any further representation.'[35] It can neither
be identified with the *cogito* as such therefore, nor with the self of

introspection, which is itself a representation, though one which lacks all trace of intuition.[36] Kant affirms therefore that 'I have no *knowledge* of myself as I am but merely as I appear to myself. The consciousness of self is thus very far from being a knowledge of the self.'[37] Here Kant is laying bare the illusion of the Cartesian subject which, in Strawson's phrase, 'confuses the unity of experiences with the experience of unity'.[38] But in his notion of the unity of consciousness which, though foundational to human understanding and identity, escapes human knowing, Kant bequeathed to posterity an enduring problematic.[39]

Another is the dichotomy between the phenomenal and noumenal spheres, which flowed from his basic insight that the human understanding constructs what we perceive through a combination of intuition, or direct sense-perception that is prior to thought, and the concept. This left a disjunction between the thing in itself and the mind that perceives, a gulf created by the very process of knowledge and thus, seemingly, an irreducible part of human experience. But Kant is keenly aware of the risk that this will open the door to idealism, a position to which he is adamantly opposed. In a change he made in the second edition of the *Critique of Pure Reason* (1787), Kant argues that self-consciousness is always a consciousness in time and that this awareness of the passage of time itself implies an experience of something permanent: 'all determination in time presupposes something *permanent* in perception'.[40] In a correction which he inserted in the Preface to the second edition, Kant argues:

> But this permanent cannot be an intuition in me. For all grounds of determination of my existence which are to be met with in me are representations; and as representations themselves require a permanent distinct from them, in relation to which their change, and so my existence in the time wherein they change, may be determined.[41]

Since nothing permanent can be known in ourselves, through direct 'intellectual intuition', this permanence must be a property of objects external to the self, to which external representations refer. And the existence of this permanence 'must be included in the *determination* of my own existence, constituting with it but a single experience such as would not take place even inwardly if it were not also at the same time, in part, outer'.[42] Despite Kant's determination to link inner and outer experience so that the very possibility of the temporal *cogito*, which is the ground of our experience of the world as representation, depends upon the permanence of objects beyond those representations (whose existence is thus known with certainty and not by faith), his argument remains a fragile one. Kant himself recognizes that 'the representation of something *permanent* in existence is not the same as *permanent representation*', and he does not tell us how we can experience 'the permanent' beyond external representations, or how we can know that it is not – similarly beyond representation – in ourselves.[43]

J. G. Fichte

As interpreter of Kantian thought, Johann Gottlieb Fichte came to the fore during the early years of the last decade of the eighteenth century, and the high point of his influence came in 1794 with his appointment to the chair of philosophy, previously held by Karl Leonhard Reinhold, at Jena.[44] His reputation was secured when his early volume *Attempt at a Critique of All Revelation* (1792) was published under circumstances which led his audience to believe that this was a work by Kant himself, and it was warmly received as such.[45] Fichte also consistently maintained that in his *Science of Knowledge* of 1794 (*Wissenschaftslehre*) he was simply completing Kant's work and that it was 'nothing other than the Kantian philosophy properly understood'.[46] He pointed in particular to the section from Kant's *Critique of Pure Reason* which discussed 'pure' or 'original apperception' as 'the transcendental unity of self-consciousness', and argued 'it is possible to *think of* what has been intuited only on the condition that this is compatible with the possibility of the original unity of apperception'.[47] Fichte's project was an attempt to give a full and dynamic account of the governance of the unity of consciousness over all its manifestations. The idealist project itself therefore, which is defined as the attempt to 'display the basis or foundation of all experience'[48] and to attain to the status of a true science through discovering 'the primordial, absolutely unconditioned first principle of all human knowledge', represents the radicalization of the principle of unity in consciousness as an explanation of the structure of all human knowing.[49]

The belief that it is the task of philosophy to offer an explanation of the whole of experience, thereby overcoming the Kantian dualisms, reflected the sense that philosophy was engaged in a life and death struggle in which the issue of human freedom was radically at stake.[50] In Fichte this manifested in the view that either we must explain human knowledge on the basis of the thing-in-itself, which is 'dogmatism' (i.e. materialism) or on the basis of consciousness itself. Lurking behind the former is the particular understanding of Spinoza, and his 'pantheism', which in this period was understood to offer a wholly deterministic view of reality which left little if any place for human freedom.[51] Fichte is concerned at all costs to lay bare the sphere of otherness, or non-self (*Nicht-Ich*), as being in essence a modality of the self, and not extraneous to it. He distinguishes therefore between the indivisible, infinitely self-positing self, which takes its own infinite activity as object, and the divisible, empirical self, which has as its object the realm of non-self.[52] Both the empirical self and the non-self emerge from the original infinite self-positing of the 'pure' or 'ideal' self, and are to be seen as modalities of it.[53] The problematic for Fichte therefore lies chiefly in the area of the relation between the reflexion of the infinitely self-positing self, which reverts back upon its own pure and infinite activity, and the reflexion of the empirical self, which knows itself on account of its engagement with a determined object, or empirical other. Ultimately, these two activities, which appear to be divided, must be one, for they represent 'the activity of one and the same subject'.[54] Although Fichte concedes that there are no compelling grounds whereby an idealist can persuade a realist of the folly of his or her position, nor indeed the other way round, he points to two distinct ways of overcoming the divide between consciousness of an ideal and an empirical kind.

In the first place, Fichte argues that it is fundamentally a divide in appearance rather than reality, and he advocates a particular mental technique as a means of gaining a glimpse into the priority of the unity of consciousness as a condition of the whole. His method recalls that of Descartes in his Fourth Discourse, whereby body and world are to be thought away, and involves 'abstracting from' or 'thinking away' the object of perception, or indeed all objects of perception, until only the self is left reflexively engaged with its own cognitive activity.[55] This, Fichte suggests, shows the priority of consciousness over the objects of perception; and it is a key strategy for maintaining the freedom of the human spirit in the face of any kind of determinism from outside the self.[56] The second manner of overcoming this divide falls in the area of ethics, and is 'the voice of conscience'. The primal *striving* of the ideal self which leads it to posit itself reflexively in the first place, causes it to absorb or assimilate the non-self through ethical action, configured as communitarian morality and sense of duty. This is to follow the path of action therefore, rather than reflexion, but as in the previous case it is postulated upon the ultimate identity of the 'infinitely self-positing self' and the 'finitely self-positing self', by overcoming and ultimately absorbing the very domain of non-self, which the self likewise has posited.

The idealist destabilizing of being as the medium of relation between self and other leads to an instability also in the application of the language of being. In the first place there is general tendency in the *Science of Knowledge* to link being with determinism, since it belongs to the realm of the non-self and hence represents that which must be overcome in the transcendence of consciousness. Fichte stresses that being is not originary, and it is here that his thought anticipates the later school of phenomenology:

> The essence of transcendental idealism as presented in the *Wissenschafts-lehre*, is that the concept of being is by no means considered to be a *primary* and *original* concept, but is treated purely as a *derivative* one, indeed, as a concept derived through its opposition to activity, and hence, as a merely *negative* concept.[57]

While the empirical intellect may indeed perceive things under the aspect of 'being', the philosopher will see further and will glimpse the pure activity (of the absolute self) which underlies ontological surfaces.[58] This is the theoretical base which grounds Fichte's advocacy of what Husserl will call 'epoché' or the conscious 'bracketing out' of being so that the question as to the real existence or otherwise of objects of perception is no longer posited. Fichte calls this process one of 'abstracting' the intellect from the object and attending only to oneself.[59] It is a strategy which seeks to lay bare the primordial activity of intellect, which remains once the domain of the non-self, or being, has been 'removed', and it is central to his claim that idealism is a programme of action.

But we find another usage of the term 'being' in the *Science of Knowledge*, where Fichte is speaking of the existence of the absolute self or subject. This derives from its own act of self-positing: 'That whose being or essence consists simply in the fact that it posits itself as existing, is the self as absolute subject.'[60] But the pure *activity* of the absolute subject as principle of cognition contrasts with the sense of passivity and limit which otherwise attaches to being in Fichte's work, as the object of cognition. It is only with difficulty therefore that the language of being is applied to the supreme principle itself. But in the later and more popular work *The Vocation of Man* (*Die Bestimmung des Menschen*, 1800) Fichte brings a third and recognizably existentialist ontological register to bear. This time his perspective is that of the empirical self, confronted with an argument for determinism on the one hand and for pure idealism on the other. The first chapter, entitled 'Doubt', in which the former argument is put forward, presents a view of the self as determined within a field of uncompromising causality which leaves no room for freedom. Fichte's narrator rebels against this, declaring 'That I want to be free . . . means: I myself want to make myself be whatever I want to be'.[61] Determinism appears to threaten precisely his ability to act, and thus to exist, so that he can say that if he listens to the argument of this section, then 'I neither exist nor do I act'.[62] But in the second section, entitled 'Knowledge', the self is confronted with its own groundlessness, since the idealist argument with which it is presented establishes the priority of the absolute self, as positing ground of both the empirical self and the realm of non-self. The being of both is derivative, and so the empirical self is forced to proclaim: 'Nowhere do I know of any being, not even of my own. There is no being. I *myself* do not know at all and don't exist. These are only *images* . . . '.[63] The self, which in the first section had expressed its need to act, exist and be free, is in the second section nothing more than 'a certain modification of consciousness'.[64] Its reality is constructed simply of 'images – images which drift by, without there being anything by which they drift; images which hang together through images; images which do not represent anything, without meaning and purpose'. He continues:

> I myself am one of these images. No, I am not even that, but only a distorted image of these images. All reality is transformed into a fabulous dream, without there being any life the dream is about, without there being a mind that dreams; a dream which hangs together in a dream of itself. *Intuition* is the dream; *thought* (the source of all being and all reality which I imagine, of *my* being, my power, my purposes), thought is the dream of this dream.[65]

The third section, entitled 'Faith', seeks to resolve the antinomies of the previous two sections by postulating the role of active moral service, whereby the self attains to its own existence. Its capacity to be is crucially located in the self's own 'real effective power of bringing forth being', which is its real power to act.[66] This seems in some ways to be a return to the argument Fichte put forth in his *Attempt at a Critique of All Revelation*, where he applied the broadly Kantian notion of a final resolution of freedom and necessity in the moral will of human beings, guaranteed by the existence of God. The ethical vision set out in the third part of *The Vocation of Man* similarly sees morality as grounding human existence, but here the emphasis falls on the necessity of the moral order as a way out of the inhospitable landscapes of a radical determinism or idealism (at least in the form the latter was presented by the 'wondrous' or 'malicious spirit' of Part Two). All the being that the self encounters in the realm of the empirical now becomes a ground for the exercise of the moral sense:

> In short, bare pure being that does not concern me and that I would intuit just for the sake of intuition does not exist for me at all; only through its relation to me does anything whatever exist for me. But everywhere only one relation to me is possible, and all others are only subspecies of this one: my vocation to act ethically.

Empirical existence is transformed by being drawn into the moral relation, which is itself the expression of the absolute self and thus of the ultimate unity of all reality. Thus in this and other 'religious' or moral works Fichte has succeeded in changing the cool climes of the *cognitive* and anti-ontological unity of all for an altogether warmer and more human vision of unity as the ethical vocation of the self, which is a self-giving striving of the self towards the other. Guided by conscience and its need to serve through real actions, the self now affirms the real existence of others (that is, as existent for the self through the moral claims they make upon it as autonomous entities[67]) and knows that it too exists '*in life* and *through life*'.[68]

The concluding section of *The Vocation of Man* displays a further shift in Fichte's use of the language of being, which now designates not limitation to action but rather action itself, made possible within a community of free, rational and autonomous agents, who 'recognize' each other's freedoms. This shift in perspective is heralded in the *Grundlage des Naturrechts nach Principien der Wissenschaftslehre* (1796) where Fichte began to stress the role of the social as a community of free agents whose recognition of each other's freedom grounds a sphere of autonomous self-realization through moral freedom and action.[69] In 1798, following the publication of a short article on divine providence, Fichte was accused of atheism, and subsequently lost his chair at Jena.[70] In later works such as *Instruction on the Blessed Life* (*Anweisung zum seeligen Leben*, 1806), we see a further evolution of Fichte's language of being as, in search of a rapprochement with

Christianity, he developed the notion of 'Being' as immutability and simplicity. Our own being can come to participate in the unchanging Being of the principle of unity which manifests in us as love for itself and for others: 'So I live and so I am, and so I am unchangeable, firm and complete for all eternity. For this is no being assumed from without. It is my own, my only true and essential being.'[71] *Instruction on the Blessed Life* represents a reverie on Being, Life and Love, arguing for the identity of the first two on the one hand and, on the other, that Love unites the existent soul with the source of all Being and is itself the revelatory principle of all Life. Here a Christian language of being, of an Augustinian hue, combines with idealism in a distinctly pantheistic mélange of piety and thought.

Friedrich Hegel

With the appearance in 1807 of Hegel's *Phenomenology of Spirit*, idealism appeared to have reached its apogee, and the influence of Hegel on diverse areas of intellectual endeavour would remain a potent force in European intellectual life for decades to come. At the heart of idealism lay a critique of the substantialist philosophy of self as we find it in Descartes and Kant, on the one hand, and of empiricism and determinism on the other. As Walter Davis has argued, rationalism 'covertly models consciousness on a prior conception of the world that it wants to know', whereas empiricism makes it 'the passive product of external relations'.[72] Thus 'the rationalist tradition errs by substantializing mind prior to experience, the empirical tradition by reducing consciousness to a thing among things'.[73] The idealist enterprise on the other hand seeks to radicalize the turn to reflection within experience which is first released by Kant in his First Critique only to be quickly channelled into reflection upon preconceived notions of the categories of experience. Hegel challenges this 'objectification' of mind by drawing out the immediacy of reflection *as experience*. That experience is constituted both by the consciousness of the activity of the self and the consciousness of the other and then by the consciousness of the distinction between the two. The self revealed in this way is not substance but dialectical pulsation or process, which is a constant overcoming of both self and other. This insight by finite spirit into the dynamic of consciousness leads to a further transformation with respect to our apprehension of the external world and to the true nature of the self. In Charles Taylor's words, 'from being knowledge that we as finite spirits have about a world which is other than us it becomes the self-knowledge of universal spirit of which we are the vehicles'.[74] We now no longer understand the external world as a place of stable structures, but come to see in its finitude and passing away (*Aufhebung*) the processes of spirit which constitute the true reality both of the world and of ourselves.

The concept of being is central to Hegel's attempt to show that what appears to be a stable reality, exterior to the self, is in truth a dynamic of self-annihilating processes which are the dialectical life of infinite or absolute spirit. In Section One of the *Phenomenology of Spirit*, being is identified with a primary state of knowledge of the object which is defined as immediacy (*Unmittelbarkeit*) and sense-certainty (*sinnliche Gewissheit*). This is knowledge as apprehension (*Auffassen*), prior to any construction as comprehension (*Begreifen*). The object which is apprehended in this state is a pure 'this', just as the cognizing self is a pure I; as a cognitive state sense-certainty is entirely without reflection: 'all that it says about what it knows is just that it *is*; and its truth contains nothing but the sheer *being* of the thing'.[75] It lacks all mediation, since neither does the object possess the manifold of 'qualities' nor the self the manifold of 'imagining or think-ing'.[76] Here then the way seems barred to the Hegelian dynamic of nega-tion, sublation and mediation. But Hegel develops the notion of a pure and unmediated sense-certainty by pointing firstly to the fact that it is a compound state, requiring the knower and the known: these can thus be said to perform a mediatory function with respect to each other. Secondly, the 'here' and 'now' of immediacy turn out to be categories which are constantly vanishing. The 'now' is fatally conditioned by time, so that the 'being' of immediacy always becomes 'has been', and undermines the adequacy of language as intentional meaning (the 'now' we point to has already become the past). The 'here', on the other hand, is subject to the vagaries of perspectivalism as either our standpoint changes or the subject of perception becomes someone else. According to Hegel's reading of the immediacy of sense-certainty therefore, the 'here' and 'now' which consti-tute that immediacy are themselves 'universals' and thus lack any specific content. Both subject and object are constantly changing within time, and there is no one instant we can point to which stands outside what Hegel elsewhere calls the 'appearance' or 'surface-show' of '*being* that is directly and in its own self a *non-being*'.[77]

The theme of being and non-being, and their interdependence, is more fully developed in the section on being from the *Science of Logic* (1812–16), which was revised in the *Encyclopaedia* of 1830. Here Hegel discusses it together with an analysis of the 'doctrine of essence' and the 'doctrine of the notion'. In his initial discussion of the point of departure for a scientific philosophy, Hegel proposes that philosophy should proceed from 'pure being'. Such a beginning has to be 'an absolute', 'abstract' and without any presuppositions or prior stages.[78] Thus it must be an immediacy which is constituted only by the 'indeterminate immediate' of pure being itself.[79] Only this is 'unanalysable'.[80] The attraction of 'pure being' as the point of departure for philosophy clearly lies for Hegel in the fact that it appears to be a kind of knowledge which is prior to reflection, and thus itself without mediation. As such, it represents the dialectical other of the dynamic of Spirit which is predicated precisely upon reflection and mediation: 'Spirit is the knowledge of oneself in the externalization of oneself; the being that is the movement of retaining its self-identity in its otherness'.[81] The positing of such a beginning for philosophy thus allows Hegel to proceed by assimilating the absence of mediation, as 'pure being', back into its opposite of 'pure knowing', and thus allows him to develop the 'simple rhythm'[82] of his distinctive method, and so 'consciousness on its onward path from the immediacy with which it began is led back to absolute knowledge as its *innermost* truth'.[83] The essential requirement for the science of logic is that 'the whole of the science be within itself a circle in which the first is also the last and the last is also the first'.[84]

Hegel now proceeds to sublate the immediacy of 'pure being' by showing that pure being is an entirely empty notion, in which nothing is either known or intuited, and is thus indistinguishable from the category of nothingness: 'Being, the indeterminate immediate, is in fact *nothing*, and neither more nor less than *nothing*'.[85] But nothing too is 'absence of all determination and content – undifferentiatedness in itself'.[86] There is a difference between intuiting and thinking nothing or something, and so Hegel argues that nothing has a meaning and can be said to exist. As empty intuition and thought, nothing is altogether the same as 'pure being'.[87] The identity of pure being and pure nothing yields a further truth, for the Hegelian dialectic, in that the movement from being into nothingness and from nothingness into being is founded upon the principle of *becoming*, which marks that change of state. Hegel contrasts the thinking of the Eleatics, which took the stasis of being as its starting-point, with 'the deep-thinking Heraclitus', for whom all is becoming.[88] It is only with respect to becoming, as coming-to-be and ceasing-to-be, that indeterminate being and nothing can be distinguished at all, and it is only in the medium of this third term that they can be said to subsist. This third is different from both being and nothingness, and so Hegel can affirm that being and nothing are not finally self-subsistent, and that their ultimate ground is *becoming*. But here Hegel notes a contradiction, for 'becoming is the vanishing of being in nothing, and of nothing in being and the vanishing of being and nothing generally; but at the same time it rests on the distinction between them'.[89] Thus, Hegel argues, becoming is inherently unstable as it unites within itself determinations which are opposed to one another, but this instability, or 'vanishedness of becoming', cannot collapse into nothingness as such, since this has already been transcended, or sublated.[90]

Hegel continues with the argument that becoming, as the unity of being and nothing, emerges as *determinate being* (*Dasein*). In a further cycle of the dialectic, the being of particulars, or determinate being, also contains the elements of both reality and negation, of being and non-being. The being of the entity is its being-for-self (*Sein-für-Sich*), or self-subsisting integrity, while the non-being of the entity is its being-for-other (*Sein-für-Anderes*). This latter term signifies the extent to which any one entity is only thinkable in relation to other entities, which in their otherness to it represent its own negation. Thus the unity of being and nothing which came dialectically into view through the transition of becoming into determinate being, now re-emerges at a further level of the dialectic in the nothingness and being which combine in the determinate being of the concrete entity itself:

> Being and nothing in their unity, which is determinate being, are no longer being and nothing – these are only outside their unity – thus in their unstable unity, in becoming, they are coming-to-be and ceasing-to-be. The being in something is *being-in-itself*. Being, which is self-relation, equality with self, is now no longer immediate, but it is only as the non-being of otherness (as determinate being reflected into itself). Similarly, non-being as a moment of something is, in this unity of being and non-being, not negative determinate being in general, but an other, and more specifically – seeing that being is differentiated from it – at the same time a *relation* to its negative determinate being, a being-for-other.[91]

Hence firstly the self-subsisting resistance of the individual entity (*Sein-für-Sich*) has the otherness outside it, and is opposed to it, while secondly, it contains non-being within itself, since it is dependent on other things for its own existence (*Sein-für-Anderes*).

The determination of the individual entity as being in itself is the realm of what Hegel calls 'essence' and 'the concept', and this again marks a further stage in the dialectical emergence of consciousness that preserves its own self-identity in its manifestation as otherness. The knowledge of that identity is only possible through the successive stages of positing and negating, or sublating, which constitute the forms of consciousness and mark the movement of the Spirit towards its own self-realization. The emergence of essence as the underlying truth of being shows being itself to be illusory, inessential and mere appearance or surface-play. Now the absolute is known no more in the immediacy of being, but in its interiorized and recollected (*erinnert*) manifestation as unified essence. But beyond the self-expression of Spirit as first being (immediacy) and then essence (reflection), the third stage is that of 'the Notion', which is their 'foundation and truth as the identity in which they are submerged and contained'.[92] The Notion is 'the absolutely infinite, unconditioned and free'.[93] If 'being in its transition into essence, has become an *illusory being* or *positedness*', then essence sublates itself by 'restoring itself as a being that is *not posited*, that is *original*,' and the Notion emerges as 'absolute self-identity': it is the universal and self-identical.[94] The perfect adequation between the Notion and objectivity Hegel terms the Idea. The Idea is the unity of reality and the Notion in such a way that it is identical with Truth and with being itself. Only that which is contained within the Idea truly is; all else is appearance. Idea as the unity between the Notion and its own self is the life of the Spirit, the animating principle of the universe, imperfectly realized in some objects and more perfectly in others.[95] Where Idea posits itself as the absolute unity of the Notion with all reality, Hegel calls it the Absolute Idea. By positing itself in this way, it contracts itself into the immediacy of being, but not as a confinement or determination, but rather as a free and sovereign act, accomplished as an ultimate self-liberation in the 'science of spirit'.

Among the idealists it is Hegel who places the greatest emphasis upon the theme of being; indeed, the *Science of Logic* can be read as a grand exposition of the nature and meaning of being itself. But the idealist trends in the understanding of being which we have noted in Fichte are strongly manifest also in Hegel. Although he does not dwell upon the notion of being as a form of determinism, nor indeed as a 'suspension of freedom', he fundamentally shares the perspective of his fellow idealists in that he sets being within a hierarchy which is dominated by the primacy of Spirit, as complex, reflexive knowledge or the knowledge of self-identity maintained in otherness. Being therefore becomes a modality of knowledge, and it is to be transcended in the movement of the Spirit towards the realization of its own free activity. In the case of Hegel specifically this involves the overcoming, or sublating, of his 'pure being' as sheer immediacy, which is resistant to all mediation and reflexion. As the perfect opposite of Spirit, this provides an ideal, indeed the only possible starting-point for his dialectic in its full potency; and being remains in his thought as precisely that form of otherness in which Spirit is called to see and maintain its own self-identity. It is therefore *a stage in the unfolding of the Spirit*, which is re-enacted at different points in the cosmic myth but always in the form of that otherness, the overcoming of which is the dynamic life of the Spirit.

The consequence of Hegel's ontology is precisely that which we have already seen in Fichte: the undermining of the actuality of the self following upon a calling into question of the reality – in its own terms – of the world. But there is no sense of angst at the prospect of such a death of the self as we find in Part Two of Fichte's *The Vocation of Man*. Hegel's work does not represent a philosophy of transition, but rather a consummation of the idealist enterprise. And as we have seen in our discussion of Kierkegaard, the closure and rationalism of the Hegelian system provoked powerful responses. In the case of Kierkegaard, this entailed an appeal to irreducible existence grounded in human subjectivity, confronted with infinite paradox. For Feuerbach and Marx, Hegelianism emasculated the human potential for action, and masked the materialist processes of history. In Nietzsche too, we may feel that the vigorous opposition to reason and embrace of the will, locate him within a distinctively anti-Hegelian tradition, in parallel with the anti-Cartesian motifs which appear the more central target of his polemic.

Conclusion

The principle that the world is subjectively constructed has dominated Western thought since Kant. Where the Idealist tradition breaks away from Kant however, is in the view that mind is not a window upon an extra-mental world – the *Ding an sich* – but that the world is itself a modality of mind. Mind is fundamentally active, according to this view. But we can usefully distinguish between that activity of mind which is also a passivity, as mind engages with objects outside its own parameters and becomes in some sense transparent to them, and that activity of mind in which the mind takes itself as its own object, whereby it becomes transparent to itself. The former is the Kantian position and the latter the Idealist one.

The determination to begin with mind in its active and reflexive mode, tracing consciousness from within itself, is not straightforward however. In our brief excursus above we have seen the development of the reflexive activity of mind in different ways. In the case of Descartes, the *cogito* makes its own existence the object of its cognition by affirming that it does itself exist, and thus grounds a structure of rational belief in a divine creator, in divine causality and in the solidity of finite substance. For Fichte, on the other hand, the act of abstracting the objects of cognition from the mind lays bare the primacy of mind in all human experience as the foundation for a philosophy of reflection which will end in the total reflexive self-identity of the Absolute Self. For Hegel, philosophy begins in a dialectical process of thinking which passes from sheer immediacy to universality, from pure being to nothingness, and from becoming to the dialectical configurations of determinate being. As we have noted, 'pure being', in this sense, is defined as non-reflexive immediacy to thought, which is again abstracted from ordinary empirical experience, and so again qualifies as a manifestation of mind rather than a transparency of mind to an extra-mental other. But as Kierkegaard argued, we begin with reflection through choice and not necessity.

What all these projects have in common is a point of departure in an act of reflection, which is to say in the dynamic actualization that is itself constitutive of mind. But what divides them is that in each case that actualization, as mind takes itself as its own cognitive object, is a subtly different kind of thought, yielding distinct modes of reflexivity. The reflexive affirmation of the existence of the self of Descartes' *Meditations*, is not the thinking away of the external world of Fichte, nor is it the dialectical identification of being and nothingness of Hegel, leading finally to an awareness of self-identity in otherness. Nor indeed is it Schelling's glimpse of the generative ground of both Spirit and Nature in the consciously transcended antinomies of the work of art. While all these thinkers would claim to be dealing with the nature of consciousness *tout court*, in fact the particular point of access to consciousness, even in its reflexive mode, determines the direction of their philosophical trajectory. For all its repeated claims to be linked with the neutrality of natural science, philosophy of consciousness is steeped in narrative strategies which make its account of reality one which is aimed not at description at all, but rather at alerting us to what reality 'is really like' and urging us to see ourselves and the world in a particular way. It operates with a distinction between appearance and reality, and hence belongs to what Strawson has called the 'prescriptive' school of metaphysics.[96]

Throughout the tradition of philosophy of consciousness, there can be discerned a narrative that emphasizes the fragility of the self, to which even Descartes, with his Deceiver and his dreams, is victim. The structure of this instability comes into view most clearly and dramatically in Fichte's *The Vocation of Man* where the author is contemplating his own metaphysical demise in the flux of images born on the surface of thought which is no more than 'the dream of this dream'. At this point Fichte knows that there can be no place for either being or selfhood in the pure activity of consciousness: 'it is absolutely empty'.[97] If knowledge is all that obtains, then the 'I' is no more than 'a certain modification of consciousness'; it is 'necessarily a pure invention, since that capacity and that being itself are merely invented'.[98] By eradicating being, the 'malicious spirit' has also eradicated the self, and has stripped knowledge of subjectivity, of the subject who knows.[99] Thus knowledge, or reality, is redefined not as consciousness (which implies the subject), but as pure event. This is of course simply to replace one form of determinism (that predicated on being) with another (predicated on the event), since the retrieval of freedom by the Idealist project is gained only at the expense of the self who can enjoy that freedom. Although the historical influence of Fichte was slight in comparison with that of Hegel, we can see in the probing and heuristic aspects of his work important indications of a kind of alienation of the self which is set up by Idealism and the kinds of ways in which this can be overcome. Fichte's resolution of the problematic oppositions of materialist determinism ('doubt') and idealist transcendentalism ('knowledge') in the third section ('faith') of his *The Vocation of Man* turns on the surrender of the self to the moral will which alone guarantees the real existence of other minds and preserves the self from falling into the solipsistic annihilation of pure event. Although the postmodern thought of our own day differs from nineteenth-century Idealism in that it is not predicated upon the *cogito*, in many of its forms it does constitute a kind of linguistic idealism, which dismisses the concept of the real. In its rejection of metaphysics, it too can seem to call the reality of the self into question. In the next chapter we shall examine the tensions and transformations that characterize the contemporary, but we shall do so with the memory that, for Fichte, it is an other-orientated love that finally grounds the return of being.

6

The Death of Being?
Deconstruction and Difference

Der Mensch ist etwas, das überwunden werden soll.

Humanity is to be overcome.

Friedrich Nietzsche, *Also Sprach Zarathustra*

Deconstruction, which is the preferred mood of modernity, is by nature parasitical. In the thinkers that follow, we have chosen to focus on those aspects of their work which reflect their protest against, and parody of, traditional models of metaphysics. Nietzsche himself, and those who follow in his footsteps (including Deleuze), established a thorough-going critique of the conventional linkage of self, substance, reason and God, which broadly reflects a Cartesian inheritance, though one moderated by elements deriving both from Kant and Hegel. In the case of Derrida and Levinas, as well as Ricoeur (to be discussed in the following chapter), we can note a protest against the Cartesian tradition particularly in the form it took in the work of Husserl, whose phenomenology worked out towards the beginning of the twentieth century powerfully restated many of the key Cartesian, and to some extent Idealist, positions. What our thinkers have in common however, is a prioritization of language itself as that which fashions the metaphysical and grounds a linguistic cosmology. If being is the medium of relation between self and other, then language is the *sphere of expression* of that relation. The replacing of being with language has the consequence therefore that both self and other become modalities of language itself, which is no longer the sphere of expression of the self–other relation, but rather the ground of their mutuality. This entails the loss of the self as speech agent, and the extinguishing of the possibility of conversation. World, which we have defined as the unfolding of the relation between self and other, now coincides with language itself, and self and other are refigured as verbal inflections that are interior to language itself.

In agreement with Aristotle and Heidegger, we have argued that the very notion of being or presence is persistence of the same across time. It is the identity – and therefore stability – implied in presence which has become the target of modern polemic (even though this is a process which is already to an extent visible in Hegel's dialectical deconstruction of 'being' as 'immediacy'). Such persistence across time has become identified with substance and with stasis, and thus with metaphysical structures which order the world in ways which appear oppressive, open to manipulation by social elites and by the powers of social and intellectual conservatism. Against such notions, contemporary thinkers have elevated process above substance, history above essence, and becoming above being. From an alternative point of view we can call this the triumph of difference over identity, as presence – which is persistence across time – has been dissolved into philosophical perspectives which stress flux, erasure and provisionality.

Friedrich Nietzsche

In Nietzsche's philosophy of paradox and parody substance became metaphor and style took the place of content. At the heart of his critique was a new understanding of language 'as a machine fabricating false identities', whereby identities of the concept and the subject led to 'truths' which are 'illusions about which one has forgotten that this is what they are'.[1] Nietzsche's texts therefore are fundamentally an exercise in subversion and disruption, as he seeks to lay bare the false and life-denying accretions of thought and language which gather round the notions of the concept, the subject, reason, morality and God. His target specifically is Christianity which propagates what he calls 'a hangman's metaphysics' of guilt, sin and judgment.[2] For Nietzsche these illusions are summarized in the traditional concept of *Sein*, or 'being', which is suggestive of stasis and death, to which he seeks to oppose the new values of *Werden*, or 'becoming', which is expressive of 'an overflowing energy' and is 'pregnant with the future'.[3] *Werden* can never become *Sein* and contrasts with the latter as reality to 'appearance' (*Schein*). In typically parodic fashion Nietzsche insists that being manifests as 'the "better" world', 'the "true" world', 'the "other" world', and as the Kantian 'Ding-an-sich', all of which are set in stark opposition to the *reality* of the world.[4]

Nietzsche deploys his critique in particular against philosophical reason. Philosophers are accused of lacking a 'historical sense' and of harbouring 'a hatred even of the idea of becoming'.[5] Their technique is deadening since 'nothing actual has escaped from their hands alive'. They ignore history as process, as 'death, change, age, as well as procreation and growth', which are for them 'objections – refutations even', so that 'what is, does not *become*; what becomes, *is* not'. According to Nietzsche, philosophers

believe, even to the point of despair, in that which is. But since they cannot get hold of it, they look for reasons why it is being withheld from them. 'It must be an illusion, a deception which prevents us from perceiving that which is (*das Seiende*): where is the deceiver to be found?' – 'We've got it', they cry in delight, 'it is the senses! These senses, *which are so immoral as well*, it is they which deceive us about the *real* world. Moral: escape from sense-deception, from becoming, from history, from falsehood'.[6]

Nietzsche insists that it is reason which puts the lie into the senses: 'the lie of unity, the lie of materiality, of substance, of duration … "Reason" is the cause of our falsification of the evidence of the senses'. But in so far as the senses 'show becoming, passing away, change, they do not lie'.[7] It is philosophical thought too which mistakes the last for the first by putting 'the "highest concepts", that is to say the most general, the emptiest concepts, the last fumes of evaporating reality, at the beginning *as* the beginning'.[8] These highest concepts must be free of the constraints of becoming and must be *causa sui*:

> Origin in something else counts as an objection, as casting a doubt on value. All supreme values are of the first rank, all the supreme concepts – that which is (*das Seiende*), the unconditioned, the good, the true, the perfect – all that cannot have become, *must* therefore be *causa sui*. . . . Thus they acquired their stupendous concept 'God'. . . the last, thinnest, emptiest is placed as the first, as cause in itself, as *ens realissimum*.[9]

It is reason and language together which delude us therefore, as *Sprach-Metaphysik*, in that they form our naïve view of subjects and of an ordered and coherent world. Nietzsche continues that 'metaphysics of language – which is to say, of reason' sees the doer behind the deed and

> believes in the ego, in the ego as being, in the ego as substance, and projects its belief in the ego-substance (*die Ich-Substanz*) onto all things – only thus does it *create* the concept 'thing' . . . Being is everywhere thought in, *foisted on*, as cause; it is only from the conception 'ego' that there follows the concept Being.[10]

For Nietzsche, the 'error of Being'[11] is linked with the illusion, borne on language, of the substantiality of the self, and of its existence in a world predicated upon causality and relation: a world which sustains metaphors of a Beyond or of 'the thing in itself', but which is finally a chimera generated by the false and non-natural, non-immediate constructions of reason. And the concept of the divine, in alignment with the Kantian thing-in-itself, stands at the heart of that illusion:

> The thing itself, to say it again, the concept 'thing', is merely a reflection of the belief in the ego as cause . . . And even your atom, *messieurs* mechanists and physicists, how much error, how much rudimentary

psychology, still remains in your atom! – To say nothing of the 'thing in itself', that *horrendum pudendum* of the metaphysicians! The error of spirit as cause mistaken for reality! And the measure of reality! And called *God*![12]

Friedrich Nietzsche is a philosopher of inversions, driven to parody as a method by his commitment to philosophy as an iconoclastic and deconstructive unveiling on the one hand, and to metaphysical religion as a comprehensive account of the self in the context of totality on the other. One of the most brilliant parts of that parody is his concept of the will to power.[13] Ordinarily in the Christian tradition the will is precisely that which in its fallenness grounds our creaturely state and invites us to see beyond the surfaces of event and action into a world of metaphysical entities. But, as he tells us, 'no such substratum exists; there is no "being" behind doing, acting, becoming; "the doer" is merely a fiction imposed on the doing – the doing itself is everything'.[14] By deploying the principle of 'will' as foundation of the world of appearances and becoming, Nietzsche effectively removes it from its matrix in human subjectivity. Freed from the principle of the rational organization of ends, 'will' now denotes the random and conflicting trajectories of pure phenomena, and is thus a cypher for *process* as such: as chance, change, destruction and decay. According to Zarathustra, we are trapped in a fatalistic impotence before the givenness of the past, which condemns the observer self to cycles of resentment and anger, leading to the vengeful desire to inflict pain on others.[15] The problem, as Zarathustra tells the people, is that the will cannot 'will backwards' (*zurückwollen*), but is a victim to the passage of time and to the nihilisms of defeat and purposelessness which it engenders. But at this point 'will', which is the 'metaphysical' principle of flux, process and contingency, and which is altogether exterior to the self, is now retrieved back into the self as the possibility of a vitalistic and 'dionysian' affirmation of existence. The human will can become its own 'redeemer and bringer of joy' when it transforms the 'it was' into 'I willed it thus'.[16] This is to establish the radical freedom of the self in the face of contingency and fate, and is to open the self up to new self-transformations of pure possibility as the Overman. The most extreme form of the 'it was' for Nietzsche is Eternal Return, which implies the loss of the future, and thus of hope and the possibility of liberation. The acceptance of that condition therefore, as *amor fati*, is for Nietzsche 'the highest formula of affirmation that can possibly be attained'.[17] The identification of the subjective human will with the universal will to power is the culmination of Nietzsche's parodic inversion of Christian resignation and is 'the closest *approximation of a world of becoming to a world of being*'.[18]

We find in the extraordinarily rich work of Nietzsche a whole series of philosophical positions which, though at times sketchily drawn, have fed abundantly into later ways of thinking. There is in his work a sense of reality itself as appearance, as surface concealing will to power; we see the role of language as that which determines world; we encounter in his thought the concept of 'event' as signalling the givenness of things; we find the prioritization of perspective over knowledge, and of negotiation over values; we find a contesting of the substantiality of the subject, and of a world bound by predictable causal relations; and we find above all a sense of the heroic which, as Foucault was to write many decades later, is the defining moment of the modern.[19] The language of being, and of his opposition of being and becoming, is central to many of these concerns, but his engagement with ontology is essentially quite different from the tradition before him (although anticipated perhaps in some ways by the Idealists). There is an unmistakable process of alienation and metaphorization at work in Nietzsche's thought which is visible in the detachment of a nexus of concepts from their normal matrix in discursive philosophical analysis. Nietzsche's genealogical method makes terms such as 'the self', 'free will', 'truth' and 'morality' the playthings of a will to power exercised by hierarchical elites. 'Being' too becomes a cultural property in this way, and thus a cypher for the very processes of manipulation and appropriation to which Nietzsche is seeking to draw our attention. Here the language of being has become detached from pure ontology and is now of interest on account of its diverse political and social resonances, in a way that anticipates Adorno's critique of the 'jargon of authenticity'. It is Nietzsche then who first comes to a critical understanding of the narrative character of the language of being, and who alerts us to the rhetorics of manipulation and persuasion which lie concealed in the most formal of ontologies.

Gilles Deleuze

The revaluation of being as becoming has had a pervasive influence in contemporary philosophy, although not always in ways that are consistent with Nietzsche's understanding of becoming as 'innocence' and 'doing', and the non-reflective action of pure living. Implied within this structure is an affirmation of the priority of action, linked with *zurückwollen* or 'willing the past', over being which points forward to Marxian thought, and to philosophers of action such as Hannah Arendt, Simone Weil or even Maurice Blondel. But perhaps on account of the later Heidegger's reading of becoming as the sphere of interpretation, we find a constant tendency to subordinate being to language, which is to develop Nietzsche's idea of *Sprach-Metaphysik*, rather than his revaluation of being as becoming-willing. For Nietzsche the being engendered by language is a chimera of substantialism which veils the processes of reality. In an important essay published in 1966 on 'The Universality of the Hermeneutical Problem', Gadamer argued against Schleiermacher's view that hermeneutics is about clarifying communication, proposing that 'being' is co-terminous with 'world' and both are reducible to language, which 'is the fundamental mode of operation of our being-in-the-world and the all-embracing form of the constitution of the world'.[20] In *Truth and Method* he further developed the notion that world is itself given by, or is a function of, language, arguing that 'In every view of the world the existence of the world-in-itself is implied'.[21] Here too we find the celebrated formula: 'Being that can be understood is language'.[22]

For Gilles Deleuze too, Nietzsche's writings constitute an important source for contemporary thinking on the nature of being and the self.[23] Deleuze is a thinker who is concerned with the nature of philosophy itself and, in particular, with freeing the practice of philosophy from the constraints of the 'image of thought' which since Plato, he argues, has obscured the radical and generative potency of thinking and what he calls 'the art of forming, inventing and fabricating concepts'.[24] Deleuze shares with Nietzsche a deep suspicion of 'being'. In his case however, this is not grounded in a preference for process and 'becoming', but rather in a highlighting of 'difference' as that which both constitutes the authentic possibility of thought and yet constantly escapes the range of thinking. Difference, Deleuze argues, is everywhere present, and, as the '*genitality* of thinking', represents its highest possibilities.[25] Yet there is no concept of difference as such, for it is always contained within kinds of thinking that are predicated upon sameness and the identical. In the same way, there is no true conceptualization of repetition, or of simulacra, which share a single concept and thus, by their multiplicity, make difference manifest.[26] Conventionally philosophy advances through propositions, whereas the true genesis of thought, 'the true philosophical beginning' lies in *problems* which crucially embody difference as a potentiality pointing beyond the terms of reference that are already known to something quite new.[27] Problems are 'the differential elements in thought, the genetic elements in the true'.[28] In terms which Deleuze develops in *What is Philosophy?*, we can say that the 'fabrication' of concepts requires a kind of creative originality which is marked not by its continuity with previously held positions but rather by its disruptive *difference*: that is, by the opening up of a new and unimagined space of thought. The 'dogmatic image of thought' as representation, on the other hand, which is founded upon the consensus of the faculties, recognition and the logical stability of the ground of sufficient reason, denies the possibility of a radical or pure thinking of difference. Deleuze seeks to rethink philosophy therefore as 'a theory of thought without image', in parallel with the turn from representational to abstract art.[29]

Much of *Difference and Repetition* is taken up with an extensive critique of 'the thinking of representation', which constrains difference by enclosing it within 'the four iron collars of representation', which are 'identity in the concept, opposition in the predicate, analogy in judgement and resemblance in perception'.[30] The taming of 'the free oceanic differences' of simulacra is first undertaken by Plato whose system of Forms selected out, on the grounds of purely moral criteria, certain images from free-floating simulacra that were henceforward to function as copies of transcendental models and to be constrained by *identity*. In later tradition the Kantian system similarly emasculated difference by making it that which distinguishes one concept from another: but this is to confuse 'the concept of difference with a merely conceptual difference', which is still mediated by representation.[31] Hegel and Leibniz proposed an orgiastic system by enclosing difference within the infinitely large in the former case, and the infinitely small in the latter. But again difference remained ensnared within representation, with its assumption of identity, opposition or similarity.[32] Nor was it captured in the Hegelian notion of the negative, which is 'the inverted image of difference', since again this presupposes 'the requirements of representation which subordinate it to identity'.[33] In general, then, difference evades thought, since it is cancelled by the very systems which explicate it.

In a typically subversive reading of Kant however, Deleuze suggests that the German philosopher hinted at the possibility of a new kind of thinking of difference when he described the rupture of the consensus of the faculties, specifically imagination and thought, in the perception of the sublime.[34] It is to Kant also that Deleuze attributes the important insight that time functions as the 'inner sense' of the self and so inaugurates the tradition of the 'fractured I', which dissolves the Cartesian subject and begins the tradition of the modern.[35] But the dominant influence for Deleuze at this point is Nietzsche, whose theory of Eternal Return constitutes a turning-point in the history of thought, and represents the summation of a thinking of difference and repetition. The Nietzschean turn of Deleuze's philosophy is evident in his identification of knowing as recognition and representation with the language of being, and specifically with 'the sedentary distributions' of the categories and 'sedentary proportionality' of analogy.[36] Analogy is fundamentally the ontology of representation:

> The analogy of being implies both these two aspects at once: one by which being is distributed in determinable forms which necessarily distinguish and vary the sense; the other by which being so distributed is necessarily repartitioned among well-determined beings, each endowed with a unique sense. What is missed at the two extremities is the collective sense of being (*être*) and the play of individuating difference in being (*étant*). Everything takes place between generic difference and specific difference. The genuine universal is missed no less than the true singular: the only common sense of being is distributive, and the only individual difference is general.[37]

Against analogy therefore Deleuze traces the tradition of ontological univocity, which is the 'one ontological proposition' there has ever been, noting it first in Duns Scotus. A second stage is reached with Spinoza, in whose work 'univocal being ceases to be neutralized and becomes expressive; it becomes a truly expressive and affirmative proposition'.[38] In the ontology of analogy, difference ceases to be thought and 'is dissipated in non-being', while the ontology of univocity preserves the possibility of the thinkability of difference in a radically new way.[39] That possibility only comes to fruition in Nietzsche's 'doctrine' of the Eternal Return, in which the univocity of being is not only thought and affirmed but actually realized.[40] Deleuze sees the Eternal Return as a form of eschatological purification that strips away the Identical with its 'quality and extension', and leaves only repetition and difference, as 'the intensive'.[41] He declares:

> It is because nothing is equal, because everything bathes in its difference, its dissimilarity and its inequality, even with itself, that everything returns – or rather, everything does not return. What does not return is that which denies eternal return, that which does not pass the test. It is quality and extensity that do not return, in so far as within them difference, the condition of eternal return is cancelled. So too the negative, in so far as difference is thereby inverted and cancelled. So too the identical, the similar and the equal, in so far as these constitute the forms of indifference.[42]

The cosmic retrieval of pure difference, as what he calls 'chaosmos', and the eradication of representation as 'the image', outlines the possibility of a new and more creative way of doing philosophy.[43] But Deleuze's Nietzschean inheritance lends this theme a much broader significance in his thought which can be more appropriately described as 'religious' or 'metaphysical', if we take into account the peculiarly Nietzschean inversions of these terms. Representation is error and 'is a site of transcendental illusion'.[44] The four expressions of that illusion, 'thought, sensibility, the Idea and being . . . culminate in the position of an identical thinking subject, which functions as a principle of identity for concepts in general'.[45] Intrinsic to the Eternal Return therefore ('not a doctrine but the simulacrum of every doctrine [the highest irony]'[46]), is the notion that both the self and God are eradicated in the affirmation of pure difference. Like Nietzsche before him, Deleuze preaches the transformation of the self from within a parodic reversal of Christian metaphysics, whereby the openness and therefore *meaning* of history collapses into pure repetition and being is banished in favour of 'dissemblance and disparateness, chance, multiplicity and becoming'.[47] For Deleuze then, as for Nietzsche before him, the Eternal Return represents the triumph of difference, ecstatically realized in the transformed self who has been liberated from all the errors and illusions of representational conventions.[48]

Jacques Derrida

With the work of Derrida we come to a trend in philosophical thinking which is deeply indebted to its reactive engagement with the work of Edmund Husserl, whose phenomenology, developed during the first decades of the twentieth century, offered an influential revitalization of the Cartesian tradition and the philosophy of consciousness.[49] Although Husserl remained dissatisfied with numerous aspects of it, the *Cartesian Meditations* represents the philosopher's most successful attempt to present an outline of his thought in its unity. In the First Meditation, Husserl warmly applauded Descartes' method of exercising extreme scepticism regarding all acquired knowledge in order to establish a new grounding for unprejudiced philosophical inquiry. Even natural sciences will appeal to evidence and experience in a way that prejudges the status of that experience, and so the sciences too must give way before the phenomenologist's interrogation of cognition *as such*.[50] Husserl follows Descartes in advocating that even the existence of the world cannot be taken for granted but must be 'bracketed out' in the primal thought experiment which is the phenomenologist's method of attaining to the apodictic, or what is given. In a series of passages which are crucial for an understanding of his thought, Husserl firstly maintained that 'the world is for us only something that claims being', and that 'not just corporeal Nature but the whole concrete surrounding life-world is for me, from now on, only a phenomenon of being (*Seinsphänomen*), instead of something that is'.[51] But secondly, the act of emptying the world of all its ontological claims (a process that Husserl terms epoché, or 'bracketing out' [*Einklammern*]), does not mean that the world vanishes, but rather that it remains as *appearance* (*Erscheinung*) and specifically as 'appearance to me'. It remains furthermore the object of 'my experience' (*Erfahrung*). The change effected by the epoché is rather that now I take myself as the object of experience and 'apprehend myself purely' in 'my own pure conscious life', as 'the pure ego'. By this act of reductive introspection, I am able to rise above the flow of *cogitationes* or thought-contents, whose existential status is secondary, and can return to 'the realm of transcendental being', which is both presupposed by the former and is prior to it.[52] It is only this new experience of the self through the 'transcendental-phenomenological reduction' which yields a knowledge that is truly apodictic, and thus truly scientific.[53] But crucially the self is itself 'untouched' (*unberührt*) by the epoché in its own existential status. Although the domain of 'internal experience' is de-objectified, as is the external world, the self remains as the *Geltungsgrund*, or 'ground of validity', of the world and its objects.[54]

Husserl powerfully restates the primacy of the *cogito*, whose own self-possession is the sole immediacy, corresponding to a scientifically grounded 'given'. External reality is reduced to the *cogitationes*, or appearances to consciousness, the objective existence of which is suspended by the phenomenologist, through his practice of radical Cartesian doubt.

Only the self as *cogito* survives the epoché, although it too begins – in Idealist fashion – to tip towards a transcendental self-knowing which likewise calls into question the empirical self of everyday consciousness. The consequence of this system, much like that of Descartes himself, was to place the *cogito* at the centre of philosophical discussion, as a privileged sphere of immediacy, untouched by the chaotic processes of culture, language and history, whose serene self-apprehension was rooted in an analysis as rigorous and as detailed as the method of natural science itself.

Amongst students of Husserl's thought we can count Jacques Derrida, who attempted to invert Husserl's metaphysics of presence in his *Speech and Phenomena* (1967), describing his own form of linguistic deconstruction as 'phenomenology of phenomenology'. Derrida's project to dismantle the Western philosophy of presence with respect in particular to Husserl and Heidegger takes the form of an exposition of difference, as both *différance*, which is the unbounded semantic displacement of the sign whereby the consummation of meaning is infinitely deferred, and as the *negativity* which results from the nature of the sign itself, as an opening of absence.[55] This he calls the *trace*, which is:

> in fact the absolute origin of sense in general. Which amounts to saying once again that there is no origin of sense in general. The trace is the difference which opens appearance and signification . . . and no concept of metaphysics can describe it.[56]

His target in *Of Grammatology* is the argument found in Martin Heidegger that perception is governed by a prior, given sense of 'being' as such. In *The Question of Being*, Heidegger argued that every sense of what an entity 'is', 'is preceded by a vista never to be made first by man, of how being "is"'.[57] It is against this notion that a pre-apprehension of being is the opening for the knowledge of any entity that Derrida posits the primacy of the 'trace', as signifying absence, or that to which language points. By prioritizing language, or what he calls *écriture*, Derrida attempts to replace the metaphysics of presence with a strategy of dislocation and difference, since 'the self-identity of the signified conceals itself unceasingly and is always on the move'.[58] He can thus declare famously that 'there is nothing outside or beyond the text' ('il n'y a pas de hors-texte').[59] An essential part of Derrida's critique is the familiar argument that the metaphysics of presence, and of objectivist signification – or 'logocentrism' – entails a complex of mutually supporting entities, which serve to constrain the 'violence' of language or to 'reduce the trace'.[60] These range from belief in deity to belief in reason and the subject, and he declares that his task of 'deconstruction of presence accomplishes itself through the deconstruction of consciousness'.[61]

Derrida's philosophy of the trace is the recognition that 'reality' or 'world' is mediated to us in the first instance by the sign. A sign is by definition not that which it signifies, and so the ground of perception is in fact an absence, a negativity, a pointing beyond itself: it is the approach, or departure, of the other. What we observe in Derrida's work is the new philosophy of linguistics which understands that the sign is filled not with the presence of that which it signifies, but rather with other signs. Signs have their meaning only within the context of signs, and so Derrida's notion of *différance* is born as the fundamental resistance to closure of the sign, affirming the open-ended and provisional character of all human knowing.[62]

But Derrida is aware (more than Deleuze, for instance) that the very negativity which defines his semantic philosophy also offers a potential re-appropriation of his deconstruction back into the reconstructive onto-theologies to which he has declared himself opposed. Having been banished to the very margins of contemporary intellectual life, the *deus absconditus* might redefine that margin as the new epi-centre of a meta-physical/postmetaphysical re-enactment of traditional theism.[63] The text in which Derrida himself most fully explores the relation between decon-struction and negative theology is 'Comment ne pas parler: Dénégations' ('How to Avoid Speaking: Denials').[64] Here he initially acknowledges an apparent symmetry between deconstruction and negative theology to the extent that both develop a 'rhetoric of negative determination'.[65] The two differ however, in that negative theology involves an 'ontological wager of hyperessentiality': it is seeking precisely to argue for the 'existence' of God, as more-being or non-being, as origin of being or surplus of being.[66] Deconstruction, on the other hand, is what John D. Caputo has called 'armed neutrality'.[67] With Pseudo-Dionysius in mind, Derrida points out that this intentionality of negative theology is signalled by the use of a preceding prayer, which is

> not a preamble, an accessory mode of access. It constitutes an essential moment, it adjusts discursive asceticism, the passage through the desert of discourse, the apparent referential vacuity which will only avoid empty deliria and prattling, by addressing itself from the start to the other, to you. But to you as 'hyperessential and more than divine Trinity'.[68]

Negative theology then is a mode of address, accompanied by an encomium or hymn, and bears the distinctive trace of the Other to whom it is uttered. In a deeply engaging passage, in which a fundamentally un-Derridaean view of language as living conversation comes into view, Derrida confronts the possibility that prayer perhaps cannot be written:

> Does one have the right to think that, as pure address, on the edge of silence, alien to every code and to every rite, hence to every repetition, prayer should never be turned away from its present by a notation or by the movement of an apostrophe, by a multiplication of addresses? That each time it takes place only once and should never be recorded?[69]

'Comment ne pas parler: Dénégations' is a deeply personal, even subtly autobiographical work, which is full of contradictions; Derrida himself describes his lecture as 'the most "autobiographical" speech I have ever risked'.[70] Initially, Derrida shows himself to be acutely alert to the danger of 'the becoming-theological of all discourse' so that 'God's name would then be the hyperbolic effect of that negativity or all negativity that is consistent in its discourse'. He knows that 'if there is a work of negativity in discourse and predication, it will produce divinity' and that it is but a small step from saying that divinity is 'produced' to saying that it is 'productive'. The consequence would follow that: 'Not only would atheism not be the truth of negative theology; rather, God would be the truth of all negativity.'[71] This would be precisely the reversal of the parodistic back into the onto-theism which it disputes, redefined as a negative ontology that reinstitutes Creator and creation. But having made his telling points about the difference between deconstruction and negative theology in terms of the hyperessentiality of the latter in the first few pages of his article, which he further develops in his perceptive discussion of the Christian apophatic theologians Pseudo-Dionysius and Meister Eckhart, Derrida concludes his article with a penetrating and detailed reading of Martin Heidegger's distinction between *Offenbarkeit* (primordial openness as being) and *Offenbarung* (divine revelation). This is significant, for it establishes the point that theology has to leave aside the language of being entirely, if *Offenbarung* is not to be assumed into *Offenbarkeit*. This seems implicitly to raise the possibility of just such a theology that is innocent of the language of being, even being 'under erasure'.[72]

Taken together with his extensive and sympathetic engagement with the post-metaphysical theology of Jean-Luc Marion, the powerful and beautiful reverie upon the nature of prayer with which he concludes his article, this final development in his argument invites the reader to consider whether Derrida's ambient exercise in denial and non-speaking may not in fact enclose the possibility of a kind of commitment of 'negative' affirmation of a final non-metaphysical theism. Derrida's own argument that the negativities of deconstruction and apophasis are divided only by *intent* can itself be read as a silent reinstatement of revelation, since it is foundational for the Judaeo-Christian tradition that revelation is given in such a way that it can be either accepted or rejected. The self that is *free* either to accept or reject revelation is already the self of revelation. In addition, within the circuitous ambiguities of this most subtle text, the negativity of *différance* appears to offer itself to be refigured as the negativity of divine *conversation* as the self is dissolved into the pure mutuality of its discourse relation with the divine Creator. This is to trade negation as the condition of semantic replication for negation as a condition of personal-existential communication. And it is with the latter, a most un-Derridaean notion of language which seems quite contrary to the associations of *écriture*, that Derrida concludes, articulating a sense – by hesitant interrogation – that purity of address may, precisely by its deconstructive negations from within *écriture*, be the final journeying of language towards its consummation:

> Does one have the right to think that, as pure address, on the edge of silence, alien to every code and to every rite, hence to every repetition, prayer should never be turned away from its present by a notation or by the movement of an apostrophe, by a multiplication of addresses? That each time it takes place only once and should never be recorded? But perhaps the contrary is the case. Perhaps there would be no prayer, no pure possibility of prayer, without what we glimpse as a menace or as a contamination: writing, the code, repetition, analogy or the – at least apparent – multiplicity of addresses, initiation. If there were a purely pure experience of prayer, would one need religion and affirmative or negative theologies? Would one need a supplement of prayer? But if there were no supplement, if quotation did not bend prayer, if prayer did not bend, if it did not submit to writing, would a theiology be possible? Would a theology be possible?[73]

In 'On the Name' (*Sauf le nom*) Derrida returns to the theme of negative theology, but on this occasion he firmly divorces it from its context in prayer, liturgy and devotion, proclaiming that this aspect, which had been so important in his earlier reading of Pseudo-Dionysius, 'remains structurally exterior to the purely apophatic instance, that is, to *negative* theology as such'.[74] Apophasis is now 'anxious to render itself independent of revelation, of all the literal language of New Testament eventness, of the coming of Christ, of the Passion, of the dogma of the Trinity, etc'.[75] In fact, negative theology is set apart from its original problematic of speaking of the being of God as absolute otherness, and is simply 'the most thinking, the most exacting, the most intractable experience of the "essence" of language: a discourse on language . . . in which language and tongue speak for themselves and record that *die Sprache spricht*'.[76] For Derrida in this article, 'God' simply denotes any other as soon as it becomes 'totally other'.[77] But 'any other is totally other [*tout autre est tout autre*]', and so a 'name of God, in a tongue, a phrase, a prayer, becomes an example of the name and of names of God, then of names in general'.[78] The issue here, as Derrida is reminding us, is not the transcendence of God which is encoded in Christian tradition as 'hyperessentiality' but the question of otherness to language in general, as – in Derrida's view – impossible existence (denoted by 'names'): that placeless place which is 'the other side *of the* world, is that still the world, in the world, the other world or the other *of the* world, everything save the world'?[79] In other words, it is the same issue of the emptiness of *reference* which Derrida addressed in *On Grammatology* and which causes Derrida on the one hand uncompromisingly to attack any simplistic notion of language as referring to some 'world' which is exterior to itself (since language itself is our world) and, on the other, creates in him (or in language, as he would say) a deep longing for the other, the impossible exterior.

Derrida uses negative theology in order to articulate both of these contrasting perspectives. In the first place it is 'a critique . . . of the proposition, of the verb "be" in the third person indicative and of everything that, in the determination of the essence, depends on this mood, this time, and this person: briefly a critique of ontology, of theology and of language'.[80] But at the same time it is also the 'sweet rage against language, this jealous anger of language within itself and against itself'.[81] In this and similar passages we see Derrida's subtle investment of language with the terminology of Christology and Christian asceticism. Not only is it 'this rage' and 'this jealous anger', but also 'this passion that leaves the mark of a scar in that place where the impossible takes place . . . Yes, the wound is there, over there'.[82] Negative theology is 'a wounded writing that bears the stigmata of its own proper inadequation';[83] and 'desert is the other name, if not the proper place of desire' [for existence and the impossible other];[84] and it is 'a *moment* of deprivation, an asceticism, or a provisional kenosis'.[85] With clear Christological associations, Derrida refers to the canon of negative theology as a 'corpus' which 'survives': 'some trace remains right in this corpus, becomes this corpus as *sur-vivance* of apophasis (more than life and more than death), survivance of an internal onto-logico-semantic auto-destruction: there will have been absolute rarefaction, the desert will have taken place, nothing will have taken place but this place. Certainly the "unknowable God", the ignored or unrecognized God that we spoke about says nothing: of him there is nothing said that might hold . . . – Save his name [*Sauf son nom*; "Safe, his name"]... – Save the name that names nothing that might hold, not even a divinity (*Gottheit*), nothing whose withdrawal [*dérobement*] does not carry away every phrase that tries to measure itself against him. "God" "is" the name of this bottomless collapse, of this endless desertification of language.'[86]

For Derrida himself, beyond language there is only 'absence'. Here – as he himself admits – deconstruction seems close to the 'bracketing' of existence we found in the transcendental phenomenology of Husserl.[87] This 'bracketing' destabilizes the human self for Derrida as it did for Husserl, and the careful reader of Derrida's work can note the way in which he constantly invests language itself with the properties of subjectivity: thinking the human subject, with its vulnerability, agency, and longing for otherness solely within language. But Derrida appropriates the objectivity of existent otherness back into language too: it is solely possible, as impossible possibility, within language. And hence the spatial world of the extra-linguistic real becomes *khora*, or no-place, drifting as a non-spatial entity across and over the boundaries of language (world) and world (language).

In other words, existent otherness, to which language in classical tradition 'refers', is now imaged as a non-linguistic imprint (or trace) that can be known, intuited, suspected only within language itself as something that is simultaneously linguistic and other than language, or rather as language itself straining towards something that – as existence – is other to itself. In this context names – as signifiers of entities – take on a particular importance, since they stand for entities, and thus for 'the (impossible) possibility of the impossible'.[88] The name 'God' not only represents every (impossible) naming of otherness, but also stands for the best and 'most impossible' entity of all.[89] Furthermore, to Derrida's understandable delight, gathered around the name of God are a number of texts of negative theology, constituting 'a culture, with its archives and tradition', which subvert the notion of existence precisely in the articulation of the name of one who is beyond all categories, including that of being.[90] This is to name the unnameable. Negative theology, which only functions as negative theology within a realist philosophical framework in order precisely to show that God is not an entity like any other but is different from all, and thus beyond the limits of language, has now become a resource for articulating the limits of language in an entirely new sense, in light of the fact that language has now become totality: language 'is' now all. In other words, the very positing of language as totality means that the limit of language no longer demarcates the boundary between language and world, which is the sphere of reference, nor designates the inability of language adequately to refer to the transcendent and hyperessential God, but now becomes internalized, taken *into* language, as the 'asceticism', 'kenosis', or 'passion' of language itself.

The use of Christological motifs in order to articulate what Derrida calls the 'referential transcendence' of language, kenotically in a self-annihilating *agôn* with itself, flows from Derrida's brilliant inversion of apophatic theology.[91] But its force as parody leads to another problematic. Precisely because all otherness can become total otherness ('tout autre est tout autre'), and because the name of God stands for all names, Derrida once again cannot exclude the possibility of a reversal of the parodic into the very thing that it parodies. Indeed, he appears to move back towards the position he briefly inhabited in 'Comment ne pas parler: Dénégations' when he speaks of the importance of preserving (self-destructing) names, since 'It is a matter of recording the referential transcendence of which the negative way is only one way, one methodic approach, one series of stages. A prayer, too, and a testimony of love, but an "I love you" on the way to prayer and to love, always on the way.'[92] Prayer, we recall, was in the earlier article the complete dissolution of language as reference, or introverted reference, into the mutuality of encounter with the other – the absolute Other – in the pure address of prayer. Having enclosed both self and other, as the possibilities of extra-linguistic existence, within language itself, Derrida now recognizes that the radical otherness of God can at any point emerge as address from within language itself: 'God' can again become 'word'. Through the negations of negative theology (as Derrida defines it), God can speak once again: '[words] name God, speak of him, speak *him*, speak *to him, let him speak in them*'.[93] And this finally is why Derrida so powerfully advocates the preservation of the name (*Sauf le nom* means both 'except the name' and 'safe, the name'), whose self-effacing is simultaneously its 'arrival' in abandonment and *Gelassenheit*, which opens 'the play *of* God (of God and with God, of God with self and with creation)' and, leaving behind the self-annihilating *agôn* of language, now 'opens a passion to the enjoyment *of* God'.[94]

What Derrida offers us therefore, is a view of the universe as reality predicated not on presence, and the logic and substantialities that rest upon it, but on absence as signifying and the indeterminacy of the sign. But his very exploration of these themes leads him to the insight that his detour away from traditional metaphysics can at any stage prove a return to the divine voice which he has sought to reject. This is not an ambivalence of intentionality but rather the recognition that God as presence-absence is already inscribed within language, as trace and memory, and, once thought, cannot easily be set aside.

Emmanuel Levinas

If for Derrida religion is encountered as an ineradicable memory within language, which ever threatens to refigure detour as return, then for Levinas religion in its most radical ethical aspects offers an important resource for reconstruction in an age that has grown weary and suspicious of metaphysical pretensions. It is the convergence of three elements in particular that makes the thought of Emmanuel Levinas such a rich and creative exposition of the self. The first is his prioritization of infinity in a way that shows a debt to Descartes' Third Meditation. This is the governing principle of his thought. But the method of exploration of this theme is that of phenomenology, which proceeds from the 'given' and shows a predilection for the phenomena of the everyday world. The third principle, which is Levinas' own Judaism, mediates between the first two, setting aspects of the ordinary in intimate relation – through ethics – with the infinity (never to be thought) of the self–other relation. It is this that lends a significantly religious dimension to much of his writing. But a further aspect which is essential for an understanding of Levinas' thought is his polemic against Martin Heidegger's philosophy of being in *Totality and Infinity* (1961) and against that of Edmund Husserl in *Otherwise than Being* (1974). In the former text Levinas develops a substantial critique of what we have discussed as the 'cult of being' in Chapter Three, which effaces the self–other relation by prioritizing the *medium* of the relation. Here Levinas maintains that 'ontology' is a kind of totalizing thinking which breeds violence: 'the visage of being that shows itself in war is fixed in the concept of totality, which dominates Western philosophy'.[95] Ontology as such establishes totality by effecting 'a reduction of the other to the same by interposition of a middle and neutral term that ensures the comprehension of being'.⁹⁶ The emphasis is upon *intelligibility* and *knowledge* therefore, which removes from being 'its alterity'.⁹⁷ It is

> to subordinate the relation with *someone*, who is an existent, (the ethical relation) to a relation with the Being of existents, which, impersonal, permits the apprehension, the domination of existents (a relationship of knowing), subordinates justice to freedom.

'Ontology' eradicates the otherness of things in order to establish its own supremacy of knowing: it reduces otherness to the transparency of sameness, and in the social realm institutes a totalizing order of violence and control. 'Metaphysics', on the other hand, is an understanding of the self–other relation which, for Levinas, is predicated upon infinity and relation. Here otherness is not constrained by the self's powers of knowing, but represents a reality which precedes thought and offers meaning which is prior to 'my initiative and my power'.⁹⁸

The self, for Levinas, is the sphere of separateness which serves as a point of departure, 'as entry into the relation', thus grounding the possibility of the other as other. This self, or 'point of departure of relationship' is the 'I'.⁹⁹ Levinas equally sets out to critique what he calls the Hegelian idea that the self is self purely by being set in opposition to the other; this is simply to reduce the other to the same. The relation of the self to the other occurs rather at the empirical level where the self finds itself 'sojourning' in a world. Its relation to that world is one of possessiveness, whereby the assimilation of the other to the same is pursued in terms of the 'at homeness' of the self, who experiences the world as a resource for 'maintaining' itself. Absolute otherness does not offer or refuse itself to be possessed by the self, but contests possessiveness as such by entirely transcending the realm of appropriation and need.¹⁰⁰ The empirical self, which marks the point of entry into the relation with otherness, exists then as 'egoism', as 'self-identification' and as 'at homeness' (being *chez soi*), whose structure manifests in 'body, the home, labor, possession, economy'.¹⁰¹ In a way that anticipates Deleuze, Levinas defines absolute otherness (to which he gives the biblical name of 'the Stranger') as that which stands outside any relation which is reducible to the convertible or the same; he thus contrasts it with empirical otherness, which is always part of a totalizing system of possession and representation.

A proximity to Deleuze can be felt also in Levinas' critique of the Cartesian self, which follows distinctly Kantian lines.¹⁰² Levinas makes creative use of Descartes' argument that the idea of infinity is given a priori to the self, but sharply opposes the grounding of the self in God which Descartes undertakes in the Third Meditation. Levinas argues that the self is constituted in its separateness by interiority, or 'an inner life', which is not reflected in thought but is itself the product of reflection. Thought as the *cogito* is the self's resistance to totalization and is 'the feat of radical separation'. The *cogito*'s own self-possession is the result of a process of remembering, which – Levinas argues – essentially represents an 'inversion of the historical'; and the historical, as he maintains, accomplishes totalization.[103] Thus the self in its very separateness is shown to be only another phenomenon of resistance to the other which is the condition of totalization: 'the being that thinks at first seems to present itself, to a gaze that conceives it, as integrated into a whole. In reality it is so integrated only once it is dead'.[104] But interiority, as the place which is not yet reduced to the totalization of history, secures the possibility of the self's address by the infinite Other, since 'the separation is radical only if each being has its own time, that is, its *interiority*, if each time is not absorbed into the universal time'.[105] Interiority then is the refusal of totalization which is 'necessary for the idea of Infinity, which does not produce this separation by its own force'.[106]

Much of *Totality and Infinity* is taken up with a discussion of the ways in which the self can move from egoism and separateness in relation with the finite other, to a relation with the infinite other, in which the interiority which defines the separateness of the self is entirely emptied out into a relation of pure exteriority. This is the move to what Levinas freely calls 'religion', which is 'the relation between the being here below and the transcendent being that results in no community of concept or totality – a relation without relation'.[107]

There are three mediatory points at which the infinite other is 'revealed', whereby the empirical self is 'called into question' by 'the presence of the Other' as ethics.[108] The first is 'metaphysical desire' itself, or 'desire for the invisible', as Levinas calls it, which 'does not rest upon any prior kinship' and which is not fulfilled but deepened by its object.[109] Desire in this sense disrupts the happiness which is the contentment of the egoistic self.[110] It is precisely the supervention of the infinite other into the 'at homeness' of the self in the world and is, as such, 'desire for a land not of our birth, for a land foreign to every nature' and cannot be accommodated to the conditions of either self or world.[111] Desire in this sense then 'measures the infinity of the infinite'.[112]

The second way in which infinity as a notion which infinitely exceeds any idea of itself becomes concrete for the empirical self is the 'face', for here the (empirical) other appears to us in a way that exceeds *'the idea of the other in me'*.[113] The face is turned to me in nudity, since it is 'by itself and not by reference to a system'.[114] It is the human other in nakedness and vulnerability, who calls into question my possession and enjoyment of the world by his or her 'destituteness' and 'hunger', summoning me to generosity and the giving of gifts.[115] To 'recognize a hunger' is at the same time to recognize the Other in the face and 'to recognize the Other is to give'.[116] But it is 'to give to the master, to the lord, to him whom one approaches as "You" in a dimension of height'.[117] Elsewhere Levinas elegantly captures the way in which the relation with the human other can mediate a new sense of the infinite relation with the wholly Other in the phrase: 'this curvature of the intersubjective spaces inflects distance into elevation; it does not falsify being, but makes its truth first possible'.[118] It is language that plays a crucial role in the thematization of the things of the world and their placing in common, which makes possible the generous giving of the self to the other, since 'to thematise is to offer the world to the Other in speech'.[119]

Language, then, is the third point of mediation in that it is founded by the irreducible face-to-face relation, which, for Levinas, is the most immediate experience. As 'the term of pure experience', it is through the interlocutor that 'the Other enters into relation while remaining καθ' αὐτό, where he expresses himself without our having to disclose him from a "point of view", in a borrowed light'.[120] While language in itself is a system of signs which points to the signified, it also shows the signifier, the one who speaks, since '[T]he Other, the signifier, manifests himself in speech by speaking of the world and not of himself; he manifests himself by proposing the world, by *thematizing* it'.[121] Language and face are intimately related therefore: '[T]he calling in question of the I, coextensive with the manifestation of the Other in the face, we call language'.[122] Indeed, Levinas suggests that 'the "vision" of the face is inseparable from this offering that language is. To see the face is to speak of the world.'[123]

In *Totality and Infinity* Levinas posits a self that is separated ultimately by its condition of knowing, whose subjectivity manifests as interiority on the one hand and a benign, though self-centred, enjoyment of the world on the other. The latter is the self's 'at homeness', in which the other is appropriated possessively in order to serve the interests and needs of the self. The supreme sphere of this 'at homeness' is domesticity itself, which is comprised of 'nourishment', 'habitation' and the intimacy of familial relations. In Jewish terms this is the realm of well-being, contentment, plenitude or *šalōm*. It is into the comfort of this realm that the Other enters – as widow, orphan and stranger – *facing* the self and summoning the self to an entirely new and infinite relation of unmediated desire, in which the interiority of the self, which is the self's own self-positing and resistance, is emptied out into pure externality. At that point enjoyment is overtaken by desire for the invisible, language as the sphere of common signification becomes conversation with the divine and the face of the other becomes the face of God. That externality of infinite relation does not approach as a variation of the self–other relation, which is mapped by system and ontology, but is to be thought as something radically other than it. It is not the negation of being, which would simply be another modality of being, but is itself entirely other, as transcendence and the beyond.

Levinas' second mature work, *Otherwise than Being*, stands almost as a midrash on *Totality and Infinity*, in which he pursues in depth certain elements which are only hinted at in the earlier text and reflects upon some of the parameters which were more or less unproblematically assumed. It is a more vigorously philosophical work which represents a close engagement in particular with the phenomenology of the self developed by Edmund Husserl.[124] The principal theme of *Otherwise than Being* can be summarized as an exploration of the relation between a non-ontological transcendence (or what Levinas calls 'saying') and the realm of consciousness and being (the 'said'). Levinas is aware that the passage from being to transcendence, about which he has written at length in his earlier work, can itself be allocated to the realm of being.[125] There is a stronger focus in this work therefore on what he calls 'illeity', which 'indicates a way of concerning me without entering into conjunction with me' on the part of the Infinite, on the elements within consciousness and the self which anticipate or point towards transcendence, and Levinas shows a far greater concern with how 'saying' and the 'said' are mutually implicating, or how '[B]eing and not-being illuminate one another, and unfold a speculative dialectic which is a determination of being'.[126] *Otherwise than Being* is also a more uncompromisingly dialectical work than *Totality and Infinity*, which lingers less with the points of mediation between self and transcendence (desire, face, language) than with the radical destructuring of the empirical self as a consequence of the imposition of the 'violence' of the good and the disruptive intrusion of the Infinite, 'slipping into me like a thief' (Job 4.12).[127]

Part of the consequence of that dialectic is Levinas' concern with a thorough exposition of 'being', and its associated phenomenological terminology of 'essence', 'manifestation', 'representation', 'consciousness', 'signification' (as 'the said') and 'reduction'. Levinas undertakes this analysis from a perspective that combines Husserlian insights with grammatical exegesis, when he decodes being as a form of 'temporalization'. Consciousness flows from the 'putting of the identical out of phase with itself', which is the 'moderation without change that time operates'.[128] This recuperation of identity across change is the opening that constitutes both consciousness – as thought – and being, since 'the differing of the identical', which takes place through time and reminiscence, 'is also its manifestation'.[129] This manifestation is conveyed, for Levinas, by 'the verb *to be*'.[130] Only the 'verbality' of being preserves the origins of being as the (nominal) said in the pure and constitutive act of (verbal) saying; it makes the 'essence' of being 'vibrate'.[131] Crucially therefore, Levinas follows Husserl in understanding consciousness and the phenomenal to be co-posited, and both to be structured as time. Both the identity retrieved across change (as consciousness) and being itself as the phenomenality of interrelated entities which construct our world are solidifications embedded – as the said – in the past. Inscribed within that past however, are what Levinas terms 'traces' of the Infinite, or the original saying, and which can be glimpsed not only in the 'verbal' character of being which points to its origin in a pure, non-phenomenological saying, but also in a *subjectivity* of the subject that is itself beyond consciousness and the realm of being.

Levinas approaches that subjectivity by developing the notion of 'sensibility' or 'sensation', where he contests the *noema* or Husserlian primacy of thought over sensation: 'the emptiness of hunger is emptier than all curiosity'.[132] This is the domain of 'wounding' and 'enjoyment', of pain and hunger, patience, ageing and death, and it constitutes a pre-cognitive site of originary *passivity*. Levinas is also keen to revalue Kantian *intuition* in terms precisely of this 'immediacy on the surface of the skin', which safeguards the openness of the self to transcendence and the other.[133] Indeed, his prioritization of the realm of sensation with respect to cognition and essence (reflecting Spinoza) is an integral part of his contesting of the domination of consciousness and sameness within the Western tradition. At the level of sensibility, life lives 'from its very life' and 'enjoyment is an enjoying of enjoyment', at a point prior to the emergence of thematization (language as denominator) and thought.[134] The pure passivity and vulnerability of sensation, with its structure of wounding and enjoyment, also marks the inscription of otherness in the self at a point prior to consciousness. It is sensation (or the body, as we might also say) that grounds the possibility of the 'despite-me', which is the overturning of a self-referential enjoyment in the ethical self-dispossession of a 'one-for-the-other'. The trace of the Infinite is inscribed in the self in three primary modalities of alterity: proximity, responsibility and substitution. Proximity is not the awareness of one consciousness of another, but is rather 'an implication, a being caught up in fraternity' which marks a subjectivity that 'is older than knowing or power'.[135] Responsibility, on the other hand, is not only responsibility for the other but is even responsibility for the other's responsibility, thus instituting the uncompromising language of substitution, whereby we suffer for another's fault, even, or specifically, doing so where this is 'meaningless' and thus fully outside the realm of being, essence and its negotiations through logos.[136] This is a responsibility that can never be fulfilled or closed, for there is 'always one response more to give'.[137] Proximity, responsibility and substitution are thus the 'positive form' of the 'negation of the present and representation', and they constitute the very subjectivity of the self, beyond essence and consciousness, in the 'unlimited passivity of an accusative'.[138] Where the self is summoned to an originary and total responsibility for the other as God and neighbour, it ceases to exist within a system of signification and becomes itself pure signifying or saying.

It is primarily where Levinas is reflecting upon the self as the 'point of entry' into the relation with the other that we find superimposed upon the terminology of phenomenology a further assemblage of terms which derive from biblical tradition. These replace the spatial motifs of *Totality and Infinity* which – as 'separation' and 'interiority' – signified the first resistance of the self to the totalization of history and thus served as the ground of the possibility of the wholly exterior relation with the infinite Other. Levinas specifically refers to a 'breathlessness of the spirit' 'in which since Plato what is beyond the essence is conceived and expressed'.[139] This theme of the divine afflatus is maintained also in the terms 'animation', 'inspiration' and 'psyche':

> The one-for-another has the form of sensibility or vulnerability, pure passivity or susceptibility, passive to the point of becoming an inspiration, that is, alterity in the same, the trope of the body animated by the soul, psyche in the form of a hand that gives even the bread taken from its own mouth.[140]

The originary answering to a call is compared with creation *ex nihilo* which 'if it is not a pure nonsense' contains 'the concept of a passivity that does not revert into an assumption', while the act of becoming 'one-for-another' or pure signifying is described as 'witness' and 'prophecy'.[141] Even though Levinas fears that the word 'God' 'subdues the subversion worked by illeity', since in it the 'glory of the Infinite shuts itself up in a word and becomes a being', he does make free use of religious terms such as 'substitution' (cf. 'the Suffering Servant'), martyrdom and 'the inner voice', as well as 'spirit' (and its variants), creation and glory. Indeed, even the great emphasis which Levinas lays upon language as saying and the said may reflect the oral and written traditions of Judaism, or even the tension keenly felt between the Torah as the revelatory deposit of scripture and the living 'presence' of God as an eternal and all-creating 'saying'.

The textual density of *Otherwise than Being* results from an interweaving of the language of phenomenology and of the Bible, showing a far-reaching concern with Husserlian philosophy on the one hand and a deep spirituality on the other. In a final section, the extreme dialectic which stresses the incommensurability of subjectivity and consciousness, saying and the said, is exchanged for a more moderate discussion of the extent to which saying is held in and mediated by the said. Levinas himself acknowledges the paradoxical nature of this project which describes the 'enigma of the Infinite, whose saying in me, a responsibility where no one assists me, becomes a contestation of the Infinite'.[142] The role of religion here, or the word 'God', is to 'break the asymmetry of proximity in which the face is looked at' by establishing a social dimension to illeity, a space of multiple identities gathered around the inscription of saying in the said in the cultural forms of books, law and science.[143] It is above all *justice* which becomes the site of the cultural mediation of the Infinite, and it is justice which is 'the necessary interruption of the Infinite being fixed in structures, community and totality'.[144] The role of philosophy itself is proximate to that of justice since it is the function of philosophy to safeguard the dialectic 'by thematizing the difference and reducing the thematized to difference'.[145] We can understand the intensely rhetorical character of *Otherwise than Being* itself then, in its mixing of terminologies, neologisms and constant repetitions of themes, to be not only a form of midrash, but also proclamation and prophecy, undertaken in a spirit that understands philosophy in specifically 'religious' terms, as 'the wisdom of love at the service of love'.[146]

Conclusion

Contemporary philosophy contains powerfully anti-metaphysical elements in which the persistence of sameness across time is countered by an alternative 'metaphysics' – as a totalization – of difference and otherness. In the case of Nietzsche this is expressed in terms of an opposition between 'becoming' and 'being', the former signalling a prioritization of *history* as flux, change and futurity. For Deleuze, difference is imaged as a primary *concept*, perhaps the originary and most creative concept of all, but which is beyond the range of representational thinking. Difference for Derrida springs from language, offering an infinite deferral of meaning that breaks down the stability of logocentrism on the one hand, and posits the absence or negation which is intrinsic to signifying as the foundational principle on the other. Here it is the nature of the sign, revealed through what Derrida considers to be a radicalization of the phenomenological method, which undermines the continuity and identity of presence. Finally, for Levinas the phenomenal structure of the self, as articulated by Husserl, and the universal comprehensibility of being, as Heidegger saw it, dissolve in the absolute responsibility of the self for the other: an ethical imperative which replaces the intrinsic 'violence' of 'ontology' with the ethical absolute of a radically relational 'metaphysics'.

But to assert the primacy of difference, in whatever guise, is at the same time to elevate the principle of otherness. It is this which aligns aspects of postmodern thinking with the inscriptions of otherness in areas of traditional religious thought, specifically with Christian apophaticism. It is in Derrida, who writes 'everything other is wholly other' ('tout autre est tout autre') that this thematic comes most to the fore, but the tendency for detour to become return is more generally a feature of postmodern thinking. Nietzsche himself was a deeply religious thinker, whose contestation of the person of Jesus can still be viewed as a kind of inner-Christian critique.[147] As we have noted, much in contemporary thought is deeply indebted to Nietzschean problematics and to his genealogical method, to the extent that, in Levinas' ironic aside, 'infidelity to Nietzsche . . . is (despite "the Death of God") taken as blasphemy'.[148] In so far as postmodernity looks back to this inheritance therefore, it appears to be a movement of protest and renewal, which stands in a long European protesting tradition that has repeatedly questioned the prerogatives of power and priestliness. The rebellion against hierarchy and new emphasis upon process recall Luther's call to universal priesthood and affirmation of a non-metaphysical *theologia crucis* against the apparent hubris of medieval substantialisms. The emphasis upon autarchy and individualism is reminiscent of pneumatic awakenings and distributed authority. Post-modernity is in fact perhaps best understood as a movement which is defined not by its practice of deconstruction, nor by its being summoned back to a Christian or para-Christian reconstruction, but rather by its own constructive resistance to the cessation of that conflict, in which tension it finds a home.

In all our thinkers, difference is caught up with the conviction, though in diverse ways, that language constructs world. Language itself presents in the main as text to be deconstructed, as the determinations of culture which we inherit from the past and share with others. Within such a context, which in its more radical forms we have dubbed 'linguistic cosmology', the role of the human subject as speaker is eclipsed by the givenness and governance of such 'texts'. One of the consequences of a revisioned or returning religiosity then, is precisely the restoration or renewal of the possibility of living speech as voice. Again it is in Derrida and Levinas in particular that we see the importance of this theme. For the former, 'living conversation' arises from the margins of philosophy as an unthinkable possibility of speech returning to its source, while for the latter it is the divine self-communication and summons which is so creative and fundamental as to again escape human cognition. But speech, unlike text, presupposes community and agency beyond oneself. It there-fore contests the tendencies towards linguistic idealism and moderated solipsism which afflict many postmodern writings, and, as voice, appears to offer, from the very margins of the postmodern imagination, a new ground for the possibility of presence.

7

Being and Love:
Towards a Christian Ontology of Difference

Paradoxet er Tankens Lidenstab, og den Tænker, som er uden Paradoxet, han er ligesom den Elster der er uden Lidenstab.

The paradox is the passion of thought, and the thinker without the paradox is like a lover without passion.

Søren Kierkegaard, *Philosophical Fragments*

Throughout this work we have maintained the definition of being as the medium of relation between self and other. But being as such remains empty of content and needs to be filled out with a particular conceptuality. We have argued that the language of being, as *the thinking of the relation between self and other*, serves to set down the parameters of self and other, in accordance with its own philosophical colourings. In our historical section we have focused on three paradigms which expound ontology from the perspective of the medium of relation itself, from the self and other in relation and from the self. We have discounted theoretical thinking which subordinates the self to the other, in a materialist philosophy of the self, as not falling within an explicitly ontological model. In Chapter Six we traced the rise of the notion of difference in the modern period, challenging the primacy of being in traditional modes of ontological thought. Presence as the duration of the same within time implies both unity and identity, with which postmodern discourses of fracture and disjunction are in clear conflict. We have acknowledged the problem of a clear 'metaphysical drag' across the centuries, as the content of metaphysical formulations tends to remain static, while much in culture and society undergoes constant change. Metaphysics can easily appear therefore to be an inherently conservative force manipulated by controlling structures of church and state. At the same time we have asserted a traditional Christian commitment to metaphysics, and to a strong account of the self as the one who experiences the alienation of sin and new life of resurrection, and who is called to an *answerability* before God through incarnation and faith. In the present chapter we shall critically survey current responses to the problem of metaphysics and the self from both philosophical and theological standpoints, before seeking to ground a new Christian metaphysics in a theological reduction of compassion, informed by the divine self-dispossession of the incarnation and the eucharistic presence.

Reconstructions

The thinkers discussed in this section can be defined as reconstructive philosopher-theologians who in various ways are attempting to retrieve a sense of the self, while observing a critical distance from traditional metaphysics. Amongst these, the work of Jacques Derrida, which we discussed in Chapter Six, contains the most deconstructive elements, but even here we can note an attempt to reformulate the self within language, as an aspect of text. For Derrida, language itself is invested with the contours of human subjectivity. In the case of Levinas, however, the reconstructive element is more clearly to the fore. Although the Levinasian self virtually disappears under the weight of absolute moral command, the centrality of exteriority in his thought implies a relationality which is inevitably secured in some kind of sense of self. We have argued that this is most clearly apparent in his careful use of Husserl's phenomenology of the self as constructed through interiority across time in *Otherwise than Being*, as a point of departure for his radical ethics. Paul Ricoeur too is in reaction to the work of Husserl, and is committed to the dismantling of the 'self-positing *cogito*' of the philosophy of consciousness tradition. In his latest work, *Oneself as Another*, however, he shows his intense engagement with reconstruction in terms of both the identity and agency of the self through the 'arduous detours' of a careful and multiple hermeneutics of language. Following our discussion of these thinkers, we shall survey a number of philosophical theologians who have been stimulated by their thinking and who have sought, again in various ways, to revisit the problem of the self of Christianity. We shall argue that Mark C. Taylor and John Milbank are indebted to Derrida, while Jean-Luc Marion looks to Levinas and David Ford to both Levinas and Ricoeur. Finally, we shall raise questions concerning the foundations for a contemporary Christian philosophy of the self, seeking to locate these within the divine self-disclosure as self-dispossession and difference, and in the dialectical presence of Christ himself among his people which, for Catholic Christians, finds its consummate expression in the eucharist.

As we have argued, a Christian view of the self requires on the one hand some sense of the self as self-possessing subject who knows its own existence to be imperilled through sin and to be regenerated through faith. On the other hand, Christians profess the continuing personal presence of Christ among his people, which, in Catholic tradition, is entailed in a particular way in belief in the real presence of Christ in the consecrated elements of the eucharistic celebration. Following a postmodern exaltation of 'difference', we have sought to identify the site of being in the self-dispossessing of the self with respect to the other in the phenomenon of

compassion. But for Levinas, the oppositional configuration between self
and other which we have proposed for our metaphysics of compassion is
to be rejected on the grounds that it forms a 'totalizing' system, a unity,
which reabsorbs transcendence, 'destroying the radical alterity of the
other'.[1] The notion of Infinity ruptures any self–other relation:

> The idea of Infinity implies the separation of the same with regard to the
> other, but this separation cannot rest on an opposition to the other which
> would be purely anti-thetical. Thesis and antithesis, in repelling one
> another, call for one another. They appear in opposition to a synoptic
> gaze that encompasses them; they already form a totality which, by
> integrating the metaphysical transcendence expressed by the idea of
> infinity, relativizes it.[2]

Levinas understands what he calls the 'simple' or 'reversible correlation'
between self and other to be grounded in phenomenality, and in the
spatiality which it subtends. Integral to the structure of phenomenality is
the separation of the self constituted by reflective interiority. Through self-
knowledge, which is the self's retrieval of its own identity across time, it
becomes the point of entry into the relation with the other. Subjectivity,
interiority and separation, as the self's resistance to the totalization of
history, thus play an important role for Levinas, but the self survives only
to be overcome by the Infinity of the self–other relation. In the light of this
supervention, the interiority and separation of the self are entirely emptied
out. Here Levinas posits a subjectivity which is not coincident with
consciousness and the realm of the phenomenal, but is constituted as
uniqueness by the singularity of the call of the other to absolute substitutive responsibility. The thought of Levinas, particularly in *Otherwise than
Being*, is marked by the establishing of interiority on the one hand, which is
the closing off or separation of the self from transcendence, and the overcoming of interiority by transcendence on the other. This is expressed in
terms of a transposition of the metaphorics of the self–other relation from
spatiality and distance to ethics and responsibility. Space is the sphere of
the phenomenal and of disclosure, while ethics is structured as Infinity and
originary, inexhaustible desire. This movement from space to ethics is
conveyed in Levinas' repeated formula that the 'difference' between self
and other now becomes the 'non-indifference' of the 'one-for-the-other'.[3]
The same metaphorical play is apparent in Levinas' memorable redescrip-
tion of exteriority as height, or heavenly exaltation.[4]

It is important to understand that the transformation of interiority
into 'pure exteriority', 'subjectivity beyond consciousness' or 'uniqueness'
is expressed at the level of what Ricoeur calls 'hyperbole, to the point of
paroxysm'.[5] Again, particularly in *Otherwise than Being*, Levinas shows a
preference for an extreme register of language as the 'hostage' self suffers
'the violence of alterity' in 'oppression', 'persecution', 'martyrdom' and

'obsession'. Indeed, his own advocacy of 'metaphysics' against the 'total-izations' of 'ontology' can itself be construed as totalizing in its over-whelming of the concrete self and other, and the everyday phenomenal realm which is the site of their encounter. The ground of that rhetoric lies in Levinas' distinction between 'saying' and the 'said', and in his acknowl-edged concern with the (impossible) inscription of the former in the latter. Thus Levinas belongs to a hyperbolic tradition, which could also be said to include thinkers such as Eckhart and Nietzsche, in which a particular understanding of language as ideal and generative communication releases text as potential *kerygma*. United in their respective forms of anti-phenomenality, all three of these *Dichter* (to give them an appropriate German term) look to language, and thus to stylistics, as a way of relativiz-ing and indeed transcending essence.

Ideality weighs heavily in the work of Levinas, which both lends it a formidable rhetorical power and also sets his thinking at an angle to the structure of self and other we have outlined in our kenotic ontology. There we have been at pains to point out that it is the concrete dispossession of self for the sake of a concrete other that is the fulcrum of the dynamic of transcendence, which does not leave being behind but leads precisely to a transformation, or transfiguration, of being, spatiality and the phenomenal. It is this sphere of negotiated alterities that Levinas dismisses as 'calculation, mediation and politics' in which the 'struggle of each against all becomes exchange and commerce'.[6] But only in the sphere of competing entities, as we have argued, are concrete and realized acts of compassion possible. These are not enabled 'through the condition of being hostage', as Levinas suggests, but are themselves the finite and real expressions of the ethical self, which remains bound to the phenomenal.[7] There is no infinite relation beyond the realm of negotiated otherness that is accessible to us as such but only its analogical realizations in the concrete reality of our everyday existence. Central to our encounter with the other in that concrete relation is conversation with others and the recognition that speech discloses an agent of speech like ourselves, but at the end of *Totality and Infinity* Levinas will argue that conversation (*discours*) is conversation 'with God and not with equals'.[8]

Paul Ricoeur stands within the same hermeneutical tradition as Gadamer and Vattimo, and his work can be read as an attempt – in his own words – to depose the 'self-positing *cogito*' of Cartesian–Husserlian tradi-tion. Such an ego, Ricoeur maintains, is 'as abstract and empty as it is in-vincible'.[9] Ricoeur locates himself precisely between the two uninhabitable places of modern thought: the exalted ego of Descartes and the annihilated ego of Nietzsche. Being neither of these, Ricoeur's self is 'atopos', and can be glimpsed only by taking the 'arduous detours' of precise hermeneutical-phenomenological analyses of human life and action.[10] In *Oneself as Another* (1990), he attempts to retrace the self not as self-possessing subjectivity in opposition to its hermeneutical constructions, but rather through its emplotments in the 'objectifying mediations of language, action, narrative, and the ethical and moral predicates of action'.[11] This intention is consonant with Ricoeur's belief in the 'ontological vehemence' of language, or his view that 'language expresses being', which sets him apart in some degree from Gadamer and Vattimo.[12] Ricoeur's interest in ontology, therefore, is explicit. He outrightly rejects ontology of the self in its more traditional guises however, while recognizing that it must be rethought from a kind of residue within tradition:

> an ontology remains possible today inasmuch as the philosophies of the past remain open to reinterpretations and reappropriations, thanks to a meaning potential left unexploited, even repressed, by the very process of systematization and school formation to which we owe the great doctrinal corpora that we ordinarily identify under the name of their authors.[13]

In *Oneself as Another* Ricoeur offers penetrating analyses of the *ipse* and *idem* identities of the self, as agency and responsibility on the one hand and as personal history on the other. These present a subtle and careful contrast to the Levinasian self. Whereas the latter is expressed as the accusative case, which derives from no nominative, Ricoeur argues for a self that stands in the mutuality between self and other which is suggested in the – Aristotelian – theme of friendship. Love or solicitude for the other and love or esteem for the self are now mutually grounding, in the community of a 'living together', in the common pursuit of justice. Otherness is inscribed in the relation of the self and other in such a way that 'solicitude is not something added on to esteem from outside but . . . unfolds the dialogic dimension of self-esteem'.[14] In Aristotle's phrase, a friend is 'another self', and we can only love ourselves appropriately because we love others, and others because we love ourselves. Thus through the thematic of friendship, with its 'search for equality in the midst of inequality', Ricoeur is able constructively to contest the model of the self of both Levinas and Husserl. Friendship is located at a 'midpoint', between the Levinasian 'summons to responsibility, where the initiative comes from the other' and the Schelerian or post-Husserlian 'sympathy for the suffering other, where the initiative comes from the loving self'.[15] Levinasian ethics, as 'violence of alterity', here gives way to an 'ethics of reciprocity', which is a 'search for equality in the midst of inequality'.[16] The mutuality which is constitutive of friendship, whereby we relate to another as if they were ourselves, 'cannot be conceived of in absence of the relation to the good, in the self, in the friend, in friendship, so that the reflexivity of oneself is not abolished but is, as it were, split into two by mutuality'.[17] This concern with the good transcends solicitude, which is the mutuality between friends. As 'plurality', or the recognition of the existence of others with whom one has no face-to-face relation, it becomes an inquiring concern with 'justice' as equality expressed at the level of a societal living-together in and through institutions. Here again Ricoeur distances himself from Levinas precisely in the point that the 'plurality includes third parties who will never be faces'.[18] They remain anonymous, but – as what Ricoeur calls the 'each' – have an important claim upon our reflections on the good.[19] The ethical expression of this relation is a concern through dialogue and reflection with establishing *'equality'* which – as Ricoeur points out – *'is to life in institutions what solicitude is to interpersonal relations'* (original italics). This equality is distributed as a concern with and striving for universal justice, since 'the field of application of equality is all of humanity'.[20] Thus Ricoeur has traded a heavily 'religious' philosophy of substitution for the other, whose axis is the face-to-face, for a more stable, political and social vision of a commitment to mutuality and equality of life under 'just institutions'.

In 'Emmanuel Levinas: Thinker of Testimony', which was published shortly before *Oneself as Another*, Ricoeur developed a less critical evaluation of Levinas' work, exploring themes which are fundamental to Ricoeur's own project.[21] In an analysis which includes readings of Martin Heidegger and Jean Narbert, Ricoeur deploys Levinas as an example of what Ricoeur terms 'the philosophy of testimony'. Philosophies of testimony are to be distinguished from 'those that identify straightaway the self-attestation of the self with reflexive consciousness'.[22] In this article Ricoeur expounds in depth his own rejection of phenomenalism through his reading of Levinas' philosophy of exteriority. The key element in Ricoeur's argument is that 'height' and 'exteriority' are ordered to one another and converge so that 'an increase in superiority' parallels 'an increase in exteriority'.[23] This is to argue that an emphasis upon otherness which is irreducibly extraneous to the self fosters a greater sense of transcendence, or that religion, as a system of transcendence, stands in an inverse proportion to philosophies of consciousness. Levinas' attack upon Heidegger is well-known, but Ricoeur is right to point to the far more extensive and fundamental critique of Husserl, whose phenomenology stands behind Heidegger's temporal self, and whose work was a key early influence upon both Levinas and Ricoeur. Ricoeur discerns 'proximity' in Levinas' thought to break 'with the Husserlian understanding of intentionality, as captive to representation, on the plane of the sensible', and 'testimony' to be opposed 'to the certitude of representation, which encompasses both self-certainty and the manifestation of every being'.[24] That 'certitude of representation' is predicated upon the ambitions of a consciousness which posits itself in principle 'as the beginning of all meaning'. The bid for 'the primacy of consciousness as master of meaning' runs through the claims of ontology as the rhetoric of 'a principle, an *archê*, a beginning, an origin'.[25] Ricoeur holds with Levinas then that representation, consciousness and ontology combine to enthrone the *cogito* as impervious and invulnerable legislator, whose sovereignty is embedded both in primacy of being and primacy of meaning. Whereas for Levinas, neither exteriority nor height show themselves, Ricoeur – who wishes to hold to the empirical self – eludes manifestation through an architecture of attestation, whereby the self is traced as an imprint in the thoughts, actions and words that constitute our reality.

Ricoeur has offered us a magisterial account of the human self in an age suspicious of unmediated self-knowledge but, from the perspective of a Christian account of the self, there is a particular difficulty with respect to two separate trajectories of his thought. In *Oneself as Another*, Ricoeur seeks to reclaim the self through 'attestation', entailing a series of intense reflections upon the analogical self which is present through implication in the multiple structures of linguistic interaction. Here the emphasis lies upon shifters, the speech agent, pragmatic theory and the *spoken word*. But in a series of articles published in *Figuring the Sacred*, which were written during the 1970s, Ricoeur offers intensive reflections upon the nature of the religious text, which proceeds from language as *written text*. Indeed, Ricoeur indicates that he understands faith to be intrinsically linked with textuality, on the grounds of the receptivity implied by 'a word that is addressed to us rather than our speaking it, a word that constitutes us rather than our articulating it'.[26] We are '*instructed* – in the sense of being formed, clarified, and educated' by the '*textuality* of faith', which makes Christian faith distinctively biblical.[27] Faith '*excludes founding oneself*' and presumes 'an antecedent meaning that has always preceded me'.[28] Ricoeur does recognize that there is also a spoken dimension to the textuality of faith, which comes into view through reading and preaching; the latter serves to 'reverse the relation from written to spoken', representing 'a kind of desacralization of the written as such'.[29] It is not the Christian text that is sacred, Ricoeur reminds us, 'but the one about which it is spoken'.[30] Indeed, revelation is 'a historical process' which contrasts perplexingly with the 'anithistorical' character of the sacred text.[31] But nevertheless the question as to who the subject of the speech might be that derives from the written biblical text, and this subject's relation with historical revelation, remain outside the scope of Ricoeur's enquiry. This is strictly limited to philosophical and hermeneutical engagements with texts as the 'articulation' of religious experience and 'the originary expressions of a community of faith'.[32]

The model of revelation at work in Ricoeur's thought is not that of Karl Barth's threefold Word (whereby the Word itself becomes the subject of proclamatory speech), nor is it one which understands the principle of revelation to lie in a transcendentalism that is innate to the reader-listener, or in an historical person who is the referent of the text (despite his gesture to this noted above). The revealing moment is rather that of the 'world of the text', which unfolds before the one who receives it, denoting not the world as given, in a first order reference, but the world as possibility, in second order reference.[33] This is fundamentally the hermeneutical function of poeticity, as developed by Ricoeur, for instance, in an important essay entitled 'Toward a Hermeneutic of the Idea of Revelation'. There Ricoeur sets forth an argument for the 'poetic' text as revelation, which 'alone restores to us that participation-in or belonging-to an order of things which precedes our capacity to oppose ourselves to things taken as objects opposed to a subject'.[34] Poeticity contests the teleological systems which bind language to the world and restores the sentient self to a new and originary engagement with world as an opening of *possibilities*. The distinctively religious character of the opening engendered by biblical texts resides, for Ricoeur, in the circulation of all the different biblical discourses around the name of God: 'narration that recounts the divine acts, prophecy that speaks in the divine name, prescription that designates God as the source of the imperative, wisdom that seeks God as the meaning of meaning, and the hymn that invokes God in the second person'.[35] God remains unknown however, as the 'vanishing point' of the circulating voices that testify to him, and as term of all the extravagant and hyperbolic 'limit-expressions' that are testimony to him.[36]

Derrida, Levinas and Ricoeur offer deeply resonant and creative models of the human self and reality, which constitute an abundant resource for Christian theology. Language stands at the heart of each of our thinkers, and in an age dominated by language theory the particular shade of their linguistic philosophy substantially determines the overall character of their thought.

For Derrida language is equated with 'writing', which brings textuality to the fore. Language does not point to speech and thus to the one who speaks, but rather to itself as a never-ending system of signs: an infinite code predicated upon the priority of absence which is intrinsic to the signifying act. Language does not reveal presence therefore, either of the world or of speech agents. To an extent Derrida mimics Husserl, to whose philosophy Derrida devoted an early work. If for Husserl consciousness is prior and world is that which needs to be bracketed out in the pursuit of an authentically scientific perspective, then for Derrida it is language that is prior, but still the ontological claims of the world fall away. If Husserl effectively replaces presence with mind, then Derrida does so with language.

For Levinas in *Totality and Infinity*, on the other hand, language reveals the speaker. But so central is his concern with the absolute claims of an ethics of responsibility and substitutability for the other that the concrete and contingent other becomes absorbed into the commandments of the infinite Other. Speech between equal agents constructed within the sphere of representation and manifestation is here assimilated into divine commandments that institute pure exteriority, beyond all representational space.

In his later reflections on the self, Paul Ricoeur reclaims the specific other and appeals for a common reflection upon the nature of the good in the search for just institutions by which we live. Language discretely attests to the actuality of persons who speak. But the revelatory is confined to the

sphere of 'the world of the text' that opens up new possibilities of perspective and experience to the one who receives it. Ricoeur himself states that
he does not intend to press his reflections upon speech and the self in *Oneself
as Another* beyond the sphere of the 'philosophical', into the theological
realm of discourse, and so the two aspects of his linguistic philosophy, an
emphasis upon the spoken language and personal agency on the one hand
and a focus upon the text as the site of a liberating revelation on the other,
remain in tension with each other. Christian faith affirms an incarnational
and personal revelation, through which God speaks with us, and understands text to mediate the divine Word of God's address to us. The gulf
between the past, personal revelation of God in Christ (text) and present
selves (speech) is a distinctively theological space which is spanned not
just by the church's witness to the significance of a past event but also by
the continuing presence of Christ among his people, enacted in the liturgical and devotional life of the church.

Three modern theologians

All three of our contemporary philosophers exhibit a deeply religious
sensibility, each in their own distinctive way. The theological assimilation
of the linguistic philosophy of Derrida begins in the English-speaking
world with Mark C. Taylor's *Erring: A Postmodern A/theology* (1981). Taylor
closely follows Derrida's *Of Grammatology*, and argues for the death of
God, 'the disappearance of the self, the end of history and the closure of the
book'.[37] For Taylor the play of difference is inaugurated by the incarnation,
and the eradication of the transcendental signified effected by Derrida's
écriture is already heralded in the passion, or death of God. Incarnation
thus becomes 'inscription': as the incarnate word which 'spells the closure
of all presence that is not at the same time absence and the end of all
identity that is at the same time not difference'.[38] Writing itself, which is the
eternal dissemination and diffusion of difference through the infinite play
of signification and interpretation, functions as the eucharistic dismember-
ment and distribution of bread and wine 'to extend the embodiment of the
word and to expand the fluid play of the divine milieu'.[39] The thrust of
Erring: A Postmodern A/theology remains that of articulating deconstructive
philosophy in Christian language rather than critique of deconstruction
from the perspective of Christian tradition, and in this world of inversions
it is the figure of Nietzsche's Dionysius, the Anti-Christ and '*radically
embodied word*', who ultimately holds sway.[40]

John Milbank

In the case of John Milbank the Derridean inheritance is appropriated in a
quite different, and more richly imaginative, way. Deconstruction and the
play of difference is effectively accepted as a norm, from which base

Milbank seeks to erect his own theological conceptuality. In fact, in *The Word Made Strange* Milbank undertakes a rereading of 'the linguistic turn not as a secular phenomenon, but rather as the delayed achievement of the Christian critique of both the *antique form* of materialism, and the antique metaphysics of substance'.[41] Thus it is in Louth, Vico, Hamann and Herder that we see the 'real achievement of a non-instrumental and metaphorical conception of language' as 'part of an ultimately theological and anti-materialist strategy'.[42] Milbank asserts that Derrida with his depersonal-ized textualism has vanquished the nuanced personalism of Levinas' conception of speech, but Milbank also wishes to intensify Derrida's deconstruction, which remains tied to a residual platonism in his view, since 'only Christian theology, as the conception of a non-violent *semiosis*, is truly "without substance"'.[43] Indeed, although theology and 'sceptical postmodernism' alike have been able 'to think unlimited semiosis', it is only for theology that 'difference remains real difference since it is not subordinate to immanent univocal process or the fate of a necessary sup-pression' but is 'a peaceful affirmation of the other, consummated in a transcendent infinity'.[44]

Milbank's argument then is that deconstruction is fundamentally a Christian phenomenon, and that only Christianity can bring its radicality to perfection. The failure to understand the *sacred* origins of deconstruction leads to nihilism, while the actualization of the trinitarian foundations of deconstruction marks the return of a dynamic and theophanic Christian world-view. By proposing his Christian 'metasemiosis', Milbank succeeds both in contesting the autonomy of contemporary secularism and in creat-ing a strikingly original renarration of the Christian story. But this consid-erable achievement is gained at a cost, for there is a repeated tendency to mould Christian theology around the precepts of a secular philosophy which – for all the rhetorical élan of the argument – remains that of a partic-ular and highly controversial type of postmodern thinking. The influence of a Derridean account of language can be felt throughout Milbank's work.[45] It is present first of all in the shaping of his historical narrative, whereby he uncritically presupposes that there is an irreducible opposi-tion between radicalized semiological difference on the one hand and a stubbornly Aristotelian–Cartesian view of 'substance' on the other. This stark and polemical polarization is already present in Nietzsche, reappear-ing in Derrida and Deleuze. According to this reading, there can be no mediations between 'substance' (Aristotle) and 'relation' (semiosis), and so such a determinedly ontological thinker as Thomas Aquinas is elided into semiosis on account of his theory of participation, which 'would be commensurate with a reality of shifting identities, composed solely of relative figural differences and affinities'.[46] Effectively therefore person-hood is equated with Cartesian transcendentalism by this strategy, and the possibility of a multi-personed universe of speech-agents envisaged, for instance, in dialogism is closed out. The interdependence and mutuality of persons is eclipsed also in his reading of ethics, where Milbank argues for a 'non-reactive creativity'. It is not the suffering other which prompts us to good acts, but the 'pure activity' which issues from the abundant life of the Trinity. A reactive view of virtue 'dethrones Charity, which presupposes nothing, much less evil, before its gratuitous giving . . .'. With distinctly Nietzschean resonances, Milbank argues that passivity towards and responsibility for the suffering other is suggestive of 'a cult of weakness'.[47] In line with this contraction of the personal and interpersonal, for the personhood of Christ Milbank substitutes his function as 'sign'. The death of Christ is precisely the movement from the 'restricted material potency of an unfinished living being' to 'the more universally open, active potency of a finished, definable artefact'.[48] While this figure well captures the evolution of a universal significance in the life of Christ, the *personal* and *embodied* character of the risen Christ surely remains a fundamental though mysterious condition of his universality.

The diminished role of the interlocutor is apparent also in Milbank's notion of the incommensurability of narratives. The question of the 'incommensurability' of conceptual systems is a theme that has engaged a number of critical thinkers, including W. V. Quine and Donald Davidson, who have linked it with problematics to do with 'untranslatability', relativism and truth-criteria.[49] For Alisdair MacIntyre, incommensurability is to a considerable degree a condition of language-constituted traditions, but in *Whose Justice? Which Rationality?* he argues that a hegemonic tradition must have sufficient common ground with others to allow the occurrence of what he calls an 'epistemological crisis' which permits a readjustment or a reaffirmation of the truth claims of that tradition in the light of those of alternative systems.[50] The vitality and hence hegemony of major traditions actually depend upon such a repeated process of correction and revaluation.[51] Milbank dismisses MacIntyre's moderate incommensurability however, on the grounds that it represents the triumph of 'dialectics' over 'narrative' and shows MacIntyre's indebtedness to the Enlightenment tradition. Against the mediations of reason underlying MacIntyre's corrective interactions across traditions, Milbank argues that 'what triumphs is simply the persuasive power of a new narrative'.[52] Here again the absence of the concrete and personal other in Milbank's thought leads to a version of 'radical incommensurability' which is exemplified in the assertion that there can be no place for realism since, for the Christian, there can be no way of viewing the world except as 'an evaluative reading of its signs as *clues to ultimate meanings and causes*': 'thus the Christian grasp of reality *right from the start* is utterly at variance with anything the world supposes to be "realistic"'.[53] But, we might argue, the phenomenon of 'reality' itself is complex, and human experience entails the interweaving of different orders of belief, some personal, some cultural, some imaginative, some religious, and some which – in the modern world – are tied to what Quine calls 'observation sentences' and their ramifications in empirical science.

For all our caution about scientism, we are not at liberty to contest factors such as the speed of light, or the structure of DNA at will. 'Reality' is necessarily constructed from a variety of narrative sources, some of which are scientific, and thus social and shared. Moreover, by revaluing 'truth' as 'persuasiveness', Milbank is seemingly committing himself to a robustly relativist view: 'We should only be convinced by rhetoric where it persuades us of the truth, but on the other hand truth *is* what is persuasive, namely what attracts and does not compel.'[54] This serves also to align Christianity as an exercise in 'persuasiveness' with other rhetorics, which can equally point to their power to persuade which, in Milbank's terms, must be taken as evidence of their 'truth' (indeed, one of the problematics for the Christian community today is precisely the failure of its narrative to 'persuade' so many in contemporary society). How are we to distinguish between gospel and ideology if conversion is the sole or chief criterion? And how are we to judge whether conversion is deeper than the rehearsal of a narrative which in some societies has been a near universal form of cultural practice? Further, rhetoric and persuasion are themselves consummately manifestations of privilege and power. Rhetoric, as advertising and as political campaigning, is about social manipulation and control, in the interests of elite groups.

It is in Milbank's paradigm of the human person as 'fundamentally poetic being' that the subject discretely returns. Poeticity is the human capacity to construct meanings, which as a form of creativity, aligns humanity with the divine *ars* of the *verbum*. To create Christian culture is to return the divine gift, freely and imaginatively, and in a way, as Milbank would argue, that creates vital and new cultural possibilities of Christian life. This is a highly original and gladly provocative way of combining a radically deconstructive view of language with a meaningful philosophy of the self and a dynamically Christian theology of culture. But by reading Christianity through the lens of 'radical incommensurability' and 'writing', Milbank has closed out the dialogical and social character of language and the mutuality of speech agents. His philosophical obligations serve therefore to construct an essentially *monological* and *heroic* view of culture. While this affirms the centrality of language and culture to human identity and action, in a very welcome way, it also understands culture to be a task to which the exceptionally 'poetical' or gifted Christian individual is summoned in the interests of creating Christianity anew as transfiguration and theophany. Deconstructed language, no longer tied to reality or to other speakers, becomes the vehicle for a heroic resacralization of the world carried out on behalf of the community by a solitary individual who possesses exceptional powers of divine poeticity. Both 'radical incommensurability' and 'writing' support creative, monological readings of history which are unhampered by the common space of dialogue with others.[55] Nowhere is this more clear than in Milbank's abbreviated and naïve use of the very term 'narrative'. Where can a narrative be said to begin and end? Are we to take it that Christianity constitutes a single narrative? Or does it not in fact represent a complex interplay of narratives: Catholic and Protestant, Greek and Latin, medieval and modern, conservative and liberal? A discussion, in fact, which itself grounds a community. The de facto assumption then that there is a single Christian narrative again bypasses the essential mutuality of narrative communities, and supports the single voice as solitary herald of unified Christian tradition.

Jean-Luc Marion

Jean-Luc Marion is a philosopher whose work can be seen as a Catholic critique of the phenomenological tradition as we find it developing through the work of Husserl and Heidegger. In his pursuit of a form of revealedness that transcends metaphysics, and his opposition to ontotheology, Marion is significantly indebted to the work of Levinas. His concern in *God without Being* (*Dieu sans l'Être*, 1982) is principally to contest the prioritization of being within Christian tradition itself on the one hand, and the primacy of Heidegger's ontological difference on the other. He begins by drawing a distinction between the 'idol' and the 'icon'. The former serves a human reality and thus 'consigns the divine to the measure of a human gaze', while the latter becomes transparent to divine life, provoking a vision rather than resulting from one.[56] Accordingly, 'in the idol, the gaze of man is frozen in its mirror', while 'in the icon the gaze of man is lost in the invisible gaze that visibly envisages him'.[57] That invisible gaze is the divine self-communicating *agape*, which can only be received transgressively in love. Marion understands being to belong to the sphere of the idol, and so, following Levinas, he opposes to the metaphysical realm, which serves idolatrously to obscure divine activity, the order, logic and claim of a divine dispossessive love. Marion locates two sources for the tradition of ontotheology, which is his chief target. One is what he perceives to be the prioritization of being as a name of God in Thomas Aquinas, which breaks with the Dionysian tradition that privileges the Good.[58] Thomas thus initiates the tradition that will lead to a Cartesian ontotheology, predicated upon the idolatrous *causa sui* of what Marion parenthesizes as 'God', and finally to Nietzsche's proclamation of the 'death of God', which marks the demise of this metaphysical construct. The other is Heidegger's ontological difference, whereby every question concerning God turns out finally to be a question about being.[59] As we noted in our discussion of Derrida in the previous chapter, a Heideggerian metaphysics resolves *Offenbarung* (revelation) into *Offenbarkeit* (the revealedness of being). Marion's concern therefore is with replacing the ontological difference with another kind of difference, which impedes the return of being to being:

> It is necessary that being play according to a rule such that its difference does not refer at all to Being; or even that being be disposed and inter-

preted according to such a difference that it no longer permits Being to recover *itself* in being or permits being to lead *itself* back to Being, so that the play of being can escape Being, which no longer would appear therein – not even under the figure of retreat or of the unthought.[60]

Drawing upon Rom. 4.17 and 1 Cor. 1.28 with their references to an order of grace which commands even the *mê onta*, or 'non-beings', Marion finds his difference which is 'indifferent to ontological difference' in an ontology of creation. It is this creative principle which ensures that 'being and non-being can be divided according to something other than Being', thus 'outwitting' or deflecting beings away from Being, and towards the 'gift'.[61] In an analysis of the use of the term *ousia* in the parable of the prodigal son (Luke 15.12–32), Marion argues that for the father of the parable, the meaning of *ousia* ultimately lies not in its function as property or substance, but in its character as 'gift' or 'exchange', so that '*ousia* is inscribed in the play of donation, abandon, and pardon that make of it the currency of an entirely *other* exchange than of beings'.[62]

Marion's critique of ontotheology is worked out principally in terms both of his rejection of Heideggerian metaphysics and of a Cartesian metaphysics of the idol. In the former perspective, his work approaches that of von Balthasar, who specifically addressed Heidegger's ontological difference and noted Heidegger's refusal to allow being to become transparent to the one who created it.[63] Unlike von Balthasar however, who advocated transcendence as the play of love in a thomistic *analogia entis* of mutuality and symphonic harmony, Marion takes the Levinasian option of essentially opposing to metaphysics the rhetoric of the 'gift' as a non-metaphysical principle, which is expressive of free, divine donation that resists all manipulation, appropriation and contamination by a gaze- or human-centred perspectivalism.

It is here however, that a certain unresolved tension surfaces in Marion's work. In the first place, the inscription of being as 'gift' threatens to return theology to the same metaphysical universe from which Marion had sought to release it. Where there is a gift, there is one who gives. The notion of 'gift' itself is deeply expressive of very human strategies of manipulation and power, and we cannot say that the Deuteronomic tradition understood the divine gift of being to have, as it were, 'no strings attached'.[64] Furthermore, the *ousia* of the parable of the prodigal son is not pure, invisible gift, but is simultaneously 'currency' *and* 'exchange', property *and* generosity. 'Gift' here then has to be contrasted with Levinas' 'otherwise'. His detailed expounding of the 'separateness' and interiority of the self from within a Husserlian paradigm allowed Levinas to establish his non-metaphysical alternative as a contesting of the very spatiality of manifestation and representation. This set up an unbridgeable gulf between his 'ontology' and his 'metaphysics', not to be transcribed as 'distance' (Marion's preferred metaphor), but only as the radical non-spatiality of an absolute ethical command. Levinas' 'otherwise' could simply find no 'place' in the universe of being. But what we in fact find in *God without Being* is an at times acute tension between his commitment to historical revelation on the one hand and his determination to prioritize the Good over Being as a divine name on the other. The logic of the former is incarnation, embodiment and matter, grounding a paradigm of transfiguration, as transformed matter, radiant bodies. The logic of the latter however, is the pure transcendence of the ethical over manifestation and structure. This is the invisible divine, or the 'invisable', which, for Marion, constitutes the icon. However, the *prioritization of the ethical over being strips the ethical of its articulation and its structure*. Entirely pure and detached from the ontic complexities of the created order, the Good now becomes a modality of non-metaphysical transcendence. But the incarnational logic of historical revelation tends in entirely the opposite direction, and communicates a divine involvement precisely in the concrete realities of compromise and negotiation, in which the Christian community is called to realize its ethical ideals. Like Christology itself (of a non-Apollinarian kind), it is thus paramountly a commitment to the *visible* which, for Marion, is coterminous with the idol. An incarnational and ecclesiological ethics will stress the enactment of love precisely within the sphere of being, which is to say between persons in concrete situations, as well as between the soul and God, through the mediation of the incarnate Son. While Marion does acknowledge an ontic or human space, which is 'an interspace, a space undetermined because belonging to the domain neither of the idol nor at the same time of the icon', which in his reflections on the place of prayer in the eucharist is memorably described as 'a struggle between human impotence to receive and the insistent humility of God to fulfil', the thrust of his work lies in an emphasis upon the sovereign independence of revelation from all the idolizing tendencies of human thought and cognition.[65]

Marion makes use of a postmodern anti-foundationalism therefore, to articulate a view of revelation which understands it to recede from the human gaze in pure iconicity, and to be received in faith by the indwelling of the divine Spirit of love in the human mind. The opposition between that love and an idolatrous metaphysics undermines the potentiation of love in his work as dispossession for the sake of the concrete other within the sphere of empirical existence. Thus the overcoming of being raises questions both with regard to the adequacy of Marion's Christian philosophy of the self, as the concrete, embodied person to whom the revelation is addressed, and concerning the consistency of his model of revelation with the historical incarnation in its fullness. This is precisely the entering of the divine into the realm of manifestation, representation and matter in a way that does not *transcend* the material as such but rather *transfigures* it, thus affirming its visibility.

In the later work *Reduction and Givenness* (*Réduction et Donation*, 1989), Marion returns to the theme of givenness, but does so from within the phenomenological tradition as it modulates from Husserl to Heidegger.

Here in a technical discussion he argues for a 'third reduction', following the 'first' or 'transcendental' reduction of Husserl, which is that 'of objects to the consciousness of an *I*', and the 'second' or 'existential' reduction of Heidegger, which was firstly the 'reduction of beings to *Dasein* as the sole ontological being' and then that 'of all beings to Being, which claimed the putting into play of *Dasein*'.[66] The third reduction is the 'call', which is prior to all being and constitutes the 'there' which is 'outside Being'.[67] Remaining strictly within a phenomenological framework, Marion reserves the question as to whether the call is the call of God (though Marion compares it to the call of Moses at the burning bush), and properly focuses upon the self that is called. This is a self which is a respondent or *interloqué* and has 'renounced the autistic autarchy of an absolute subjectivity'.[68] This self is inflected in the accusative (as auditor or one who is called), the locative (as *Dasein*, or 'being-there') and the vocative (as 'convoked', or the *interloqué*), but not in the nominative.[69]

But here again a certain tension appears in Marion's thinking which has resonances also with respect to Christian tradition. He continues by stating that the 'claim poses *me* as the *there* where one might recognise oneself' and so 'the claim does not destroy the irreducible identity-with-self by dismissing any *I* in me, but, inversely, underscores it and provokes it'.[70] Marion confronts the aporetical horizon of a self that is both a self and yet somehow 'beyond being', summoned to an equality of speech with one who calls from a point prior to the emergence of metaphysics. This is moreover a self without mediations, and thus – if ethics is the self-risk of a concrete self for the sake of another – is ethically denuded, since even the call of the other, as the face of the other (in Levinas' sense), 'might dismiss or submerge the first call issued by the claim of Being'.[71] Thus just as Marion has reflected upon the ultimate nature of revelation as standing beyond the sphere of being and the representational, so too the self is here conceived as being called or summoned into a trans-ontological place. The movement then is one which leads away from being, towards a new and radical notion of divine self-communication in a way that transcends its representations and ruptures the ontotheological inheritance. But here Marion is driven not by a theology of the incarnation, which identifies the divine movement as one *into and not away from being,* but rather by his polemical positioning with respect to Husserl and Heidegger, in which metaphysical conviction he shows his indebtedness to the radical anti-ontologism of Emmanuel Levinas.

David Ford

Like John Milbank, David Ford seems entirely at home with a post-Enlightenment analytic in his *Self and Salvation*. He, too, links his work closely with that of radical contemporary thinkers, not however with Derrida and deconstruction but rather the ethical reconstructionism of

Emmanuel Levinas and Paul Ricoeur. With both these philosophers Ford believes in the primacy of ethics and in the need for a fundamental rethinking of the self in the light of a pervasive and constitutive otherness. He also shares their emphasis on a broadly pragmatic view of language, which highlights the place of the speaking and listening other. As with John Milbank, David Ford's method can be seen substantially to reflect his particular understanding of the nature of language, which is not that of the creative and innovative monologue however, but rather a dialogical model of mutual interrogation and learning. The persuasiveness of David Ford's style flows from the integration of 'hospitality' into his theological method specifically by 'hosting dialogues' with thinkers with whom he feels himself to be engaged in conversation, and from his exploration of 'human flourishing . . . in a way which invites intelligent and wholehearted appreciation and even participation' by the reader.[72] Indeed, Ford's text seems to imply a radically dialogical view of the self, whereby human identity can be understood to be in a state of flux, emerging interactively from within spaces opened up by renewed dialogue. And so the dialogical rhythms set up by *Self and Salvation*, between Levinas, Jüngel and Ricoeur, Thérèse of Lisieux and Bonhoeffer, serve finally to establish the text as kerygma: its persuasiveness as an invitation to the 'feasting', which is opposed to the 'totality' that Levinas fears, and which 'allows for his ethical pluralism of being'.[73] This is further linked with 'an eschatology of selfhood' and an ultimate passivity of the self before the other as God, leading to an embodied and glorious transformation (cf. 2 Cor. 3.18).[74]

David Ford seeks to construct his 'post-phenomenological theology of the worshipping self' by setting up a series of interrogative dialogues between Levinas, Jüngel and Ricoeur which form the first half of his book.[75] He believes that Levinas' criticism of 'ontology' as instigating a form of 'totality' would apply also to Jüngel's understanding of love, which through its notions of 'event, unity and dialectic' falls back into the very Hegelianism from which Jüngel had sought to free himself.[76] But he argues, too, that Levinas could learn from Jüngel's account of joy, and asks 'what happens if one introduces a conception of joy as extreme as the conception of responsibility' in Levinas' work?[77] The excess of joy parallels that of responsibility, and Ford wishes to argue that 'responsibility before the other needs to do justice to joy, and may not rule out full worship in faith'.[78] Against the 'extremism' of both Levinas' view of the 'substitutionary responsibility' of the self for all and Jüngel's rejection of this in favour of the sole substitution of Christ, Ford wishes to argue both 'for a substitutionary self, defined by radical responsibility', and for 'Jesus Christ dying for all'.[79] He rereads Jüngel's definition of love ('the unity of life and death for the sake of life') as 'the unity of joy and substitutionary responsibility for the sake of joy', and argues that it is in Ricoeur that we find the kind of theory of the self which supports this definition, opening out into a self of worship, which is otherwise lacking in both Levinas and Jüngel.[80]

In *Oneself as Another* Ricoeur pauses at the threshold of a theological view of the other and of the self. The 'worshipping self' comes into view therefore through Ford's intensifying, dialogical reading of Ricoeur's 'polysemy' of otherness in the direction of the celebratory passivity of the self before God as the Other (a possibility which Ricoeur does not himself develop but which he admits by the pointed ambiguity of his discussion of otherness).[81] It is worship, as an excessive modality of responsibility and joy, that forms 'the celebratory ecology' in which love, as 'the unity of joy and substitutionary responsibility for the sake of joy', can flourish.[82] In the second half of *Self and Salvation*, David Ford gives a developed and extensive analogical format to his model of the worshipping self. This includes reflections on the 'singing self' analysed through the celebratory overflow and harmonies of Ephesians, on the 'eucharistic self' transformed by blessing, abundance and the 'habitus of facing', and the self who 'faces' Jesus Christ as the 'face of God' in whose death we see the ultimate worshipful and therefore anti-idolatrous model of living before God. Additionally, Ford reflects upon Thérèse of Lisieux and Dietrich Bonhoeffer as two saintly individuals whose contrasting and complementary forms of holiness offer 'apprenticeship' in the spiritual transformation of self to us. In his final chapter David Ford argues for 'feasting' as the primary metaphor of an 'eschatological self', one which 'can enact the union of substitutionary joy in the joy of others with substitutionary responsibility'.[83]

Any critical reading of *Self and Salvation* requires a sensitivity to the 'journey of intensification' which the text undertakes, and some acceptance of the dialogical imperatives which are generated by the congruences, complementarities, creative rereadings and critical debates which arise from it.[84] In the case of a reading from the perspective of our own kenotic ontology, this entails a recognition of significant affinities which arise from the common project of delineating a postmodern Christian self on the one hand and a deep-seated complementarity on the other. In the first place, I entirely concur with David Ford's view that the question of the self lies at the heart of current debate and that the reconstruction of the self must reject Christian reductionism on the one hand, while refusing to proceed 'in abstraction from Jesus Christ, as if he did not exist' on the other.[85] I agree too that the theme of dispossession offers a key point of contact between a Christian programme of the self and contemporary experience. In his own view, the analogical and transformed self of worship which he offers retrieves Nietzsche's shattered *cogito*, since it is 'a complex gathering of self in diverse relationships including forms of self-dispossession that require a letting go of control and mastery (often an existential equivalent of shattering) before a God who is trusted as the gatherer of selves in blessing'.[86] Passivity of the self is David Ford's preferred motif, specifically since '[P]assivity before others is first of all before the Lord'.[87] We have argued for a journeying self on the other hand, which comes to itself in and through the other. But both motifs are predicated upon the welcoming of otherness into the very constitution of the self, as a means of retrieving the self between Descartes and Nietzsche while opening the self out towards specifically Christian determinations. Both approaches are also phenomenological, although phenomenology of consciousness as such is clearly alien to David Ford. The use of the Levinasian motif of the 'face', and a desire to concentrate on 'ordinary living', imports significant phenomenological impulses back into David Ford's project however.[88] And the prioritization of the notion of Christ as 'facing' and as 'the face of God' intrinsically critiques Levinas' (and Marion's) eradication of the empirical self, introducing a model of transformation (or transfiguration as we have called it) rather than one of pure transcendence. The analysis of *panim* or 'the face of God' in the Old Testament, leading to the 'facing' of Jesus Christ, parallels my own investigation of *raḥᵉmîm* and *splanghna* ('divine compassion') as christological motifs; and in Isa. 54.8, they even overlap:

> In overflowing wrath for a moment
> I hid my face from you,
> But with everlasting love I will have compassion on you,
> Says the Lord, your Redeemer.[89]

But it is the contrasts between the current volume and *Self and Salvation* that illumine them in the most interesting and perhaps unexpected ways. The differing primacy of joy and compassion in the two works is not in itself of fundamental significance in that Ford's joy is one which is compassionately committed and my own understanding of compassion is that it always presupposes joy. David Ford's 'singing self', 'eucharistic self' and 'worshipping self' are all fundamentally dispossessive, taken up through the multiple passivities that are integral to the nature of the self, into the divine drama. But the radical and conscious act of self-risk for the sake of the other which is compassion, does require a language in which the self can articulate and perform its unity, and in which it can establish its own prior *self-possession* as self-knowing, in a way that the analogical analysis of the self of joy does not.[90] That unity of the self may be fleeting and imperfect, glimpsed only in the self's dispossession (and in its most complete form in the radical decentring of self that is faith), but it fosters an analytical structure that is itself unified and systematic, in which the whole constantly seeks to return to its centre in a single, governing idea. There is a real contrast here then between the slow unwindings of systematic theology and the antiphonal rhythms of the '"essay" genre' of David Ford's repeated dialogues.[91] His is a movement not of 'centring' but of 'intensification', as he calls it, or 'pressing' his sources 'towards a fuller theology', and it is a strategy which, by releasing within its horizontal unfoldings an added movement of depth, contributes to the extraordinary richness of *Self and Salvation*.[92] 'Celebration' and 'feastings' are not only themes held up for discussion in David Ford's book, but they are enacted in the text in a way that brings critique itself to the threshold of worship.

Pierre Rousselot has reminded us that the primary distinction control-ling the classical Christian paradigms of meeting God through cognition and knowing him through love is the question of whether this new percep-tion is to be seen as being essentially disruptive of other cognitions and affections or in continuity with them.[93] The difference between a Christian phenomenology of joy and one of compassion is fundamentally that the former lends itself to a sense of stable transition from delight in the creation to delight in the Creator, while the latter institutes a disruptive model of transition from natural to transformed self. It is therefore the manner, or mood, of the inscriptions of otherness within the self that determines their respective trajectories and finally secures their complementarity.

Creatureliness and the unity of consciousness

The three contemporary theologians we have considered all show a considerable debt to postmodern thinking which they explore in distinct and creative ways. Our metaphysics of compassion, which is predicated upon what we have termed kenotic ontology, differs from all three how-ever, in so far as it seeks specifically to thematize the existence of the self as unity, self-knowledge and self-possession. This is certainly not undertaken as a retrieval of Cartesianism, which has been presented here as a strategic fiction which is rightly rejected by the philosophical currents of modernity, but it does contest the idea that the self-possession of the self must *of necessity* be equated with the Cartesian version of the *cogito* as solitary self-transparency and as principle of ultimate certainty. Our advocacy of a paradigm grounded in the philosophy of consciousness signals rather a return to the function of the *cogito* as developed by Kant in his First Critique. There he stresses that it is the *cogito* which manifests the unity of the self, without which experience cannot be identified as 'my experience', constituting 'my' existence, or 'my' story. Indeed, without that intrinsic, though in some important sense elusive, 'unity of the field of conscious-ness' experience as such, even the experience of fragmentation and disori-entation, would not be possible. We further agree with Kant that the unity of the *cogito* which attends every perception is not to be unproblematically identified with the unity of the self as it constructs itself to itself as repre-sentation through the act of introversion. In other words, the unity of the self manifests only discursively and incompletely, and is more a precondi-tion for experience itself rather than the object of experience. But we have departed from Kant by interpreting the unity of consciousness in the light, in particular, of the principle that unity is one of the properties of being (Aristotle) and that presence is the persistence of the same across time (Heidegger); and have argued that the unity of consciousness finds partic-ular expression in the language of being. The self's affirmation that it *is* constitutes a kind of 'metanarrativity' or 'essential narrativity', which straddles all the contexts and histories which the self inhabits, organizing and centring the diversity of experience. And we have pointed to the importance of the particular colouring of that language of being as a structure of ontological performance. This reflexively acts upon the agent who thinks it and uses it, serving also to map the self–other relation, and with it, the world. It is this same notion of 'metanarrativity' which secures and maintains the capacity of the self to be taken up and discovered yet again within new histories and identities. The central theological expression of such a metanarrativity is the self's capacity to be taken up into and restructured within a divine narrative, whose boundaries we encounter through faith in this world, and whose ultimate depths and resonances shall be made known to us, according to faith, in the beatific vision. Thus the unity of the self is also the sign that we are God's creatures, and corresponds in broad terms to what traditional Christian language terms the 'soul'.

The return to a language of being therefore, is a return to the sense of the self as creature of the Creator God. But we have been at pains to show that the development of a new metaphysical language carries with it certain obligations. In the first place, we have argued for a language of being which is both an acknowledgment of the ontological traditions of the past and an embrace of the present, with its prioritization of radical otherness. It is here that our own project can be set apart from the ontologies of Przawara, Rahner and von Balthasar, as well as those of Bultmann, Tillich and Zizioulas, which, for all their insights and achievements, seem out of place in the vigorously language-centred and deconstructive landscapes of the present day. Amongst these thinkers, it is von Balthasar who in his *Theodramatik* has most vigorously thought through the nature of kenosis, but as a sequel to the Thomist ontology of *harmonia* and *pulchritudo* of his earlier work, rather than a reformation of it.[94] Rahner, for his part, has a powerful sense of the self as the site of an ontological transcendence that resists all reduction to contemporary scientisms. But this is still a Kantian–Heideggerian world, governed by the cognitive faculties of the self, rather than a world that comes into existence only as the self is given over, without remainder, into the alien power of the other. For better or for worse, the intrusion of a radical otherness into the very constitution of the empirical self – through genetics, language, psychoanalysis, social codification, biology – has turned 'substance' into 'process', and has led to the *internalization* of the border between self and other, constructing it as being both everywhere and nowhere. But above all, it is the centrality of language and hermeneutics in modern thinking which has called traditional metaphysics and the theologies which are grounded in it into question. Philosophies of consciousness have been signally resistant to the place of the sign in the construction of human reality, and have frequently been understood to stand in an irreducible opposition to the hermeneutical philosophies of modernity. We have sought to question and address this dichotomy of history by insisting on the narrative character of the 'language of being' itself, and pointing to the intrinsic unity and existence of the self at work within the multiplicity of narratives that constitute our personal, social and historical identities. The fact that the unified existence of the self – albeit incomplete and deferred – is not thematized in contemporary continental philosophical rhetorics does not obviate the problem of the unity of consciousness as grounding the very possibility of experience itself, as set out so usefully by Immanuel Kant.

In our own kenotic ontology, we have sought to accommodate the centrality of language within the formation of the self through the use of dialogism and pragmatics, which stress the role of the speech agent and the nature of language itself as *communication between speakers*. In contrast with the Derridean and other formulations of the language problem, dialogism renders a social account of language and does so from a perspective which predicates conversation between speech agents as the primary or originary site of linguistic expression. Only subsequently does language become text, as the mediated or 'remembered' culture and history which the speech agents differentially inhabit. Dialogism therefore places language at the heart of our understanding of the self, but does so in a way that retains the sociality and interrelatedness of human experience, while also opening out to the textual deposits of culture and history as shared memories, communicated between or among speech situations. Within such a dialogical view of the self, the encounter with the other as interlocutor becomes central to our own self-possession as speaking and reflexive creatures, and becomes, as we have argued, the epiphany of being, as the existential realization of our own dialectical self-transcendence.

A theological reduction of compassion

The very notion of being, as has been argued, is an abstraction and hence a movement of the mind. This is the historical significance of the Parmenidean breakthrough, whereby abstracted existence for the first time replaced the universalization of a material element. But if metaphysics began with Parmenides in one sense, then it began again with Plato, for whom the question of being arose precisely *within* the self–other relation, as a problematic discovered within our world, and not as an abstracted sense of totality, dialectically opposed to the pluriform character of all human experience. During the modern period, as we have seen, the rise of a conceptuality of difference, often – though not exclusively – sustained within an emergent hermeneutical philosophy, has emphasized the sense of otherness at the cost of the sameness which is intrinsic to presence and ontological identity. It is this move which has unbalanced traditional notions of being in which – as in the case of the Thomist paradigm, for instance – difference has always been held in check by sameness. There has come to be a sense in which the 'moderated difference' of various kinds of Christian and para-Christian essentialism is no longer judged to be adequate to the experience of the human self, confronted on all sides by the pressures of what Deleuze has called 'crowned anarchy' and 'nomadic difference'. We have sought to emphasize that difference has now ceased to function as that which delimits the borders that divide the self from the other, of traditional ontology, and has become an internalized border, which – being atopic or without place – constitutes the very condition of the self rather than its circumstance. It has seemed imperative to affirm the principle that ontology is finally a way of speaking about being which, like any other language, is historically contingent. Here therefore we have been on the side of Plato and not Parmenides, whose ontology together with that of his followers, tends towards the hierarchical and the cultic.

The question for us then has been, 'Which historical space should we seek out in order to ground and locate our new language of metaphysics?'. And the answer we have given is that the immeasurable evil of the Holocaust and of the phenomenon of the 'camp' represents the place which is the defining moment of the modern. In some very deep sense it is exemplary of elements that are intrinsic to the modern in that the evil which is in all human communities takes on in the 'camp' a uniquely and monstrously contemporary form. As the site of unsurpassable evil therefore – unsurpassable at least for our age – it is also by necessity the site of the unsurpassable possibility of the good, which is not in fact independent of evil, but reactive to it. Here, too, we have been mindful of the tradition that being is always concealed, and that truth, goodness and being are in some sense intimately connected. With the eclipse of truth and goodness in the Shoah there had equally to be a sense that being itself was shadowed. Following the dialectical logic of tradition concerning the visibility of being, it seemed right to seek being precisely where its concealment was greatest. We then argued that in the phenomenon of compassion, itself born of evil – as resistance to it, we found the outline of the possibility of a new way of speaking about being. In the complex cognitions, affections and volitions of compassion, otherness and difference come into view in an entirely new way. Far from being a Hegelian *Aufhebung*, compassion stands at the heart of empirical reality, and demands to be understood as existence containing thinking and not as a dialectical immediacy of thought. Here we have been aware of our debt to Søren Kierkegaard, whose anti-Hegelian turn to the Infinite Paradox which *could only be communicated within the empirically real*, has been an important guide. Once stripped of its implicit Idealist pretensions, the postmodern exaltation of difference, for all its many deficiencies, is also an invitation to learn to think once again in the presence of the real.

We began the first half of this volume with a phenomenological reduction that drew out the intentional structures of a consciousness compassionately engaged with the world. This led us to a sense of the creatureliness of the self, visible in the unified existence of consciousness in which the self is constituted only in and through the other, and to the dialectical transcendentalism – grounded in the other – which is the self's proper nature. As we draw to the close of the first part of this volume, a second movement is beginning to emerge, which is that of a theological reduction. This is an invitation to reassemble our thinking in the light of specifically Christian belief and experience, and it marks a clear movement away from the philosophical language which has dominated the first half of this text to language that is rooted in traditional Christian sources. In our phenomenological section we argued that the combination of inner and outer transcendence in compassionate affirmation of the other, opens that act to the possibility of an encounter with an infinite, personal other. This should not be understood as being in any sense a necessary consequence, but rather as an unrealized or unfulfilled potentiality within the experience of compassion itself. From the perspective of our theological reduction however, this opening out that inheres within the compassionate act is of the greatest importance. But since it is grounded in the fusion of our affirmation of (infinite) reality as such in inner transcendence and our affirmation of a (finite) other in outer transcendence, the new object which appears on the horizon of our theological reduction is one which is in a sense ordered to the finite object of compassion. In other words, we need to resist at this point any tendency of a theological reduction to renounce the principle of givenness and attention to the human as embodied, speaking reality, which has been characteristic of our phenomenological analysis. We do not wish here to impose a disembodied language of theological nuance and complexity upon the empirical and historical contents of our study of compassion. This would not correspond with the intention to rethink metaphysical and theological systems as far as possible in the presence of the real, as being the sole guarantee of their authenticity. We are acknowledging here then that if our theological reduction is truly to be a reduction of compassion, then it must itself be an historical reflection and its ultimate object – the infinite personal other – must in a sense come to us as a speaking and embodied self, within a specific spatio-temporal location.

The embodied ground of theological reflection takes three forms. In the first place, the individual theologian can only reflect from within his or her own embodied existence, with all the constraints that locality implies. Secondly, the embodied ground of theological reflection must also be the incarnation itself, through which God entered our own contingent and limited historical perspective and our human subjection to the insuperable forces of history and interpretation. But there is a third modality of embodied presence, which combines both the historical situatedness of the theologian and the incarnation. This is the presence of Christ to us within the church, which – for Catholic Christians – finds its supreme expression in the eucharist. Here there is a divine presence which is embodied for us in the here and now. There is, however structured, still a sense of being addressed by and drawn towards the living voice of God in Christ. This is the supreme *actuality* of God, and it is the ground for our theological reduction of compassion. By reflecting upon the presence of God in the complex and disruptive modality of the elements, set within the liturgical matrix, we can retrieve from a theological perspective the same focus upon actual historical embodiment which has served as a basis for a phenomenological reduction of compassion in the first half of this volume. Formal reflection upon the eucharist is reserved for the second volume of this project, where we shall examine the phenomenology of the eucharistic encounter and the structure of the continuing recreation of culture through the incarnation, but the centrality of the eucharistic presence-to-us is presupposed throughout the current work. What we wish to do at this point therefore is to affirm the priority of embodiment for both our phenomenological and our theological reduction, the former turning on actual historical instances of compassion and the latter on the experience of an embodied (and therefore historical) encounter with God in the transformation of the eucharistic elements.

Before proceeding to the theological development of the themes of this book, it is necessary, however, to look back again to the second source of the thinking that underlies kenotic ontology. In addition to the claims of goodness upon the mind which become manifest in readings of outstanding compassionate figures from the Holocaust period, in which we have found the primacy of the principle of difference, we have also identified the divine self-naming at Ex. 3.14 as being of critical significance for the arguments developed here. The textual resonances of the passage suggest that it is a meditation upon divine presence as being simultaneously creativity and compassion. These implications are made explicit in early rabbinic commentaries on the text. We have taken these Jewish readings to be an important alternative to the traditional 'Athenian' gloss of the passage which stresses the association between necessary, eternal being and the nature of God, thus grounding the particular form which ontotheology has taken in the Western tradition. As a corrective reading of this tradition, we have argued for a revisiting of the rabbinic perspective, which understands compassion and creativity to be coterminous with a divine presence which is a being-with God's people. A further element however, is essential to this synthesis. The self-identification of God at Ex. 3.14 is itself an act of naming. It is a speech act. As such, the performance of utterance is intrinsic to what is said, and in the overall context of the linguistic structure of what Christians know as the Old Testament, the self-naming of God represents an intensification, or even culmination of the creative speech of Genesis which calls the world into existence through progressive stages of speech realization.[95] At this point then we see a clear linkage between divine utterance and the very compassion and creativity which are the modalities of God's 'being-with' Israel. God is present where God speaks, and God's saving communication is the modality of God's being with God's people. The rabbis convey something of this primacy of communication in the concept of the *Memra*, signifying God's 'word' or 'utterance'.[96]

From a Christian exegetical perspective however, developed in a respectful attentiveness to the rabbinic commentaries, it is the person of Christ himself who is prefigured in these texts: as the one in whom God speaks, as the one in whom God's compassion is realized and accomplished, and as the one whose presence with us is a shaping of both culture and world, from within the dynamic of a divine creativity.

C.
Fundamental Theology

Introduction:
Word and Silence

Theology begins in silence. All speech is differentiation from silence, since the sounds that are words are carved from silent space. Without silence there can be no sound, and no speech. The silence is of God, for it is the creative bed of all sound, all speech and all world. Nothing spoken can have any other origin, but all is traced back to silence and to the first silence. Theology is a way of speaking which remembers that its words are formed in the silence of God.

God spoke, and his speaking was his Son, who came among us. But the Word was himself both Word and silence: one with the creative speaking and one with the unfathomable silence of God. And his speaking was of two kinds, for as a man he spoke with us and as God he spoke with God, but when he spoke with us, we heard too a divine voice, and when he spoke with God, the Father heard too a human voice. His human speaking, then, was a new way of speaking, at once at home in the human world, but also the speaking of one who is equal to God.

As speaking for God, about God, with God, or in God, Christian speech is grounded in the incarnation, in the speaking of the Word-Silence, which is most fundamentally a speaking-with the Father. In him an entirely new and unheard of kind of speech is inaugurated which, though manifesting in dialogue, is essentially triadic, founded on the multiple, perichoretic dialogue of Persons in relation with Persons. As the speaking of God with God, it is also foundationally *public*, since it is opened up and made manifest to us in the personal interactions of the Trinity's historical narrative, related in scripture and held as the divine voices in the living, historical community of the church. Therefore we can say in the truest sense that this new way of speaking includes us, we who receive this 'speaking word', and offers us participation.[1]

Christian theology is a particular kind of Christian speech in that it is a distinctively *reflexive* form of discourse. Theology's concern with analysis, debate, investigation and clarification is rooted in the desire to make manifest through reflexion what is given to us in the revelation. But it cannot fundamentally be set apart from other kinds of Christian speaking, such as prayer and praise, worship, proclamation and blessing, truth-telling and saying 'what is useful for building up' (Eph. 4.29). For Christian speaking is as such a particular way of being: a faithful and kenotic interacting with

God and the world, which is modelled on and given by the revelation of the Holy Trinity. The theologian then, who is called to participate in this divine speaking-with, is also a Christian whose personal faith includes the call to enact the primal, overflowing and unsurpassable *clarity* of the inner discourse of God. That clarity is known within the tradition as wisdom, to which Thomas Aquinas refers in the inaugural lecture of his first regency in Paris: 'The mountains are the first to catch the sun's rays, and holy teachers likewise are the first to receive radiance in their minds. Like mountains, teachers are the first to be enlightened by the rays of divine wisdom.'[2] That radiance is simultaneously a summoning of the theologian in the whole of his or her being to enact the divine clarity in opening of thought and purity of living.

Placing theology under the sign of a trinitarian mode of speech marks a recognition that Christian theology must always inhabit a sphere of multiple dialogue, dispossession and interpretation, for these are the very conditions of the alterity which is presupposed in the Christian doctrine of the Trinity, in which theological speech is ever called to trace its own originary essence. In the first place then those who are summoned to theology can be said to be drawn ultimately to speak *in* God. Theirs is a speech which is not to be of their own making, but which, radically, is to belong to another. To do theology is therefore in a sense to turn oneself over to another; it is to be dispossessed of self, stripped of one's own meanings. Theologians are summoned to speak in such a way that they themselves become a word spoken in the breath of another. It is in this spirit that Greek patristic theologians used the term *theologia* to denote not only teaching about God but also 'a relationship, above *all* knowledge that human beings can imagine, with a God who is himself above all knowledge'.[3] This same notion is communicated in the metaphor developed by Jean-Luc Marion of a 'divine transgression': the transgressive penetration of the divine Logos into the flux of human speaking.[4] We can say therefore that those who take up this strange new gift of speech choose a kind of pilgrimage, or way of alienation. For, speaking a language which belongs at its root to another, the theologian is like a prophet who puts at risk his or her own speech in the possibility of a new way of speaking-with God, which – transfiguring and overwhelming – transcends the possibilities of the prophet's own utterance. Speaking a language that seems to come from nowhere, the prophet's speech – burdened by an excess of meaning – is made strange.

But secondly, to speak theologically is also to maintain a constant and self-wagering openness to revision and critique. In seeking to participate in trinitarian speech as its first movement, its ground and its end, theology always finds that it falls short. The closer it comes to that divine unity of speech, the more unbridgeable the gulf between theology as 'talk about God' and theology as 'speech in or with God'.[5] It is intrinsic to theology therefore that it should always need to pose questions to itself regarding its own authenticity. Nothing can be taken for granted; rather all is revisable in theology's radical answerability to another. For the Roman Catholic theologian this answerability of theology is also responsibility, exercised within Catholic tradition and the historical community of the church. The single voice of the theologian must find its place in a harmony of many voices, of those who have heard the living speech of God and sought to answer it. Theology's deepest and ineluctable critique then is always critique of self as speech of another, and it is a permanent condition of revisability and openness to deepening insight and correction. It is in this sense that Karl Barth talks about the fragmentary nature of the theological enterprise, its 'gymnastic' character, and of the theologian as one bound to 'a laborious movement from one partial human insight to another with the intention though no guarantee of advance'.[6]

Thirdly, in accordance with its own trinitarian origins, theology must hold open multiple dialogue with other systems of knowledge, including those of a secular kind as well as the sanctioned and sacred discourses of other religions. If the divine revelation of which it is the reflexive participation is itself openly dialogical in character, then it is intrinsic to theology to seek out and to maintain debate and collaboration with alternative rationalities and systems of knowledge. To shirk that responsibility, or to retreat into a supposed citadel of perfection, constructed of the fashionable fundamentalisms of the day, is for theology to fail to realize the potency of its trinitarian determinations. The history of theology shows a consistent and fertile concourse with secular disciplines, particularly with philosophy, as *Fides et Ratio* points out.[7] But conceptualities can be borrowed from other areas of secular culture which cast new light on the subtle contrasts of the gospel message, foregrounding dimensions of the faith which have only been partially seen or, occasionally, not glimpsed at all. Deconstructionist advances in the social sciences, particularly those to do with class or gender, can serve to unmask the human strategies of conquest and power which inevitably surround the institutional and personal appropriation of revelation. Dialogue with other religions can awake in the Christian community a new awareness of spiritual perspectives hidden in our own tradition, thus ensuring that it remains dynamic and alive. And through a common commitment to religious values in society and the mutual respect that arises through collaboration and dialogue with those of other faiths, we can come to a new understanding of ourselves as part of the global community of the religiously committed who stand together in solidarity with the dispossessed against the dehumanizing tyrannies of alienation, materialism and the sectarian pursuit of power.

Fourthly, as reflexivity predicated on trinitarian speech, theology is called to be both rational and communitarian. The ordering and analytical functions which are essential to theology, and which establish clarity and accessibility to the understanding, are not worked out by the individual theologian in isolation from the ecclesial communities to which he or she belongs. Again, the history of theology shows the centrality of a corporate exploration of themes visible in schools of theological thought. Thomas Aquinas reflects a distinctively Dominican tradition, as does Karl Rahner a Jesuit one. The modern theologian, even when not a religious, is also part of a community of scholars working perhaps within a secular university where debate and dialogue and the values of enquiry shared by the scholarly community will contribute fundamentally to his or her work. Nor should we underestimate the role of personal friendship and conversation in the construction of a milieu fertile for the development of new theological ideas as well as that of more formal theological collaboration through colloquia and shared projects. The rationality of theology then is dialogically constructed in a way that reflects something of a distinctively trinitarian mode of thinking, with its semiological perichoresis, where clarity of meaning and depth of understanding are understood to be distilled from fundamentally interactive and interpersonal modes of communication.

But fifthly, theology is a *public* form of discourse; not privately pursued by elitest groups. It seeks out the downtrodden, the dispossessed and the marginalized; it addresses them in their extreme condition, and allows itself to be addressed by them. Only in this way can theology *reflexively* enact Christ's preferential option for the poor and disadvantaged. Theology cannot be the pursuit of a single class or a privileged geographical area, but – like the eucharistic host itself – must be broken open and made available to the people in the particularity of their own lives and circumstances. It must find ways – through images and the mass media, through missions and teaching, through the visual, literary and performing arts – to speak to the people and be spoken to by them. It must learn to listen to the voice of the other, marginalized perhaps by gender, or race, by socio-economic background or by geographical isolation; and, guided by its dialogical instincts, it must constantly be underway towards a comprehensive inclusivism and a universalist perspective. Thus in Nicholas Lash's terms, criticism of his or her own 'group, class, national or cultural consciousness' is one of the theologian's principal tasks, and the gospel message with which the theologian is concerned must be safeguarded in its 'universal accessibility', not in the totalization of its 'universal "agreeability"'.[8]

And finally, theology, as divinely sanctioned speech, must be beautiful. In some way something of the glory which is the inner-trinitarian speech should be reflected in the grace of theological system. Conceptual structure too is harmony of form. Patterns of thought can communicate the attractiveness which is intrinsic to doctrine and which is itself a reflex of the free self-communicating speech of the divine Persons. It is also the task of theology then to challenge the worldly affections of the mind with the sense of a different kind of beauty, which destabilizes and disturbs, even as it opens out to us a new way of living.

8

Fundamental Theology and Poetics

And chiefly thou, O Spirit, that dost prefer
Before all temples th'upright heart and pure,
Instruct me; for thou know'st; thou from the first
Wast present, and with mighty wings outspread
Dove-like sat'st brooding on the vast abyss
And mad'st it pregnant: what in me is dark
Illumine, what is low raise and support;
That to the highth of this great argument
I may assert Eternal Providence,
And justify the ways of God to men.

John Milton, *Paradise Lost*

The primary movement of Christian revelation is one of disclosure: the coming into relation with us of that which was previously concealed. As we have argued, that movement is manifest as a new kind of trinitarian speaking, as God speaking *with* God, in which – through faith – we are called to participate. Theology is that kind of Christian speech which reflects upon this new relation with God, participating, however inadequately, in the originary clarity of the perfect communication between the Persons of the Trinity and the infinite mutual transparency of each to the others. One of the consequences of that movement of disclosure is what we might call a second level of reflexion, which is the communication of what Karl Rahner termed 'the idea of Christianity'.[1] This is to *give an account* of theology not just to Christians themselves, as an act of higher reflection, but crucially to all people, of alternative faith or none, who, according to Christian belief, have nevertheless been addressed in some mysterious sense by God's speaking with us in his Word. But as a kind of theology which gives an account of what theology is both to those outside the Christian tradition and to those who are within, as clarification, fundamental theology has need of material extraneous to itself. The temptation simply to perform theology, and to ask dogmatics to do the work of fundamental theology in a triumph of analyticity, has proved strong over recent decades however, as can be seen from the theological narratives of Karl Barth and Hans Urs von Balthasar.[2] Here fundamental theology becomes 'coextensive de la théologie tout entière'.[3] But this seems in a sense to be the refusal of explanation and of the dialogue which is enjoined in 1 Pet. 3.15:

'Always be ready to make your defence to anyone who demands from you an accounting for the hope that is in you'. The disclosive movement of revelation surely demands expression specifically at the level of *explanation*, however provisional and contingent this may be. Whether as 'foundational theology' for the Christian communities, or as 'apologetics' for non-Christians, self-description, as distinct from self-performance, is vital if theology is to avoid the suspicion of incomprehensibility and incoherence and is to claim its own proper place in the order of things.[4]

But history shows the extent to which the task of fundamental theology, as 'a boundary discipline', has had to be thought anew in different ages, reflecting the changing paradigms of truth and explanation.[5] Among its various guises Francis Schüssler Fiorenza has noted 'apologetics, foundational theology, formal-fundamental theology, basic science of faith, prolegomena to dogmatics, philosophical theology and philosophy of religion'.[6] The origins of fundamental theology lie in the apologetic literature of the early Christian centuries, in which theologians sought to defend Christianity in a political and religious context which had shown and which continued to show considerable animosity towards it.[7] During the Middle Ages, elements of apologetic creep into the debate with Jews and Moslems, and there is a deepening reflection on the relation between *auctoritas* and *ratio*, faith and knowledge, which did lead in the later Middle Ages to discrete, systematic treatments of the foundation of faith.[8] But it is not until the year 1700, still in the aftermath of the Reformation, that we first encounter the term 'fundamental theology.[9] Texts such as *De locis theologicis* (Salamanca, 1563) by the Spanish Dominican Melchior Cano and *Theologicorum dogmatum* (Paris, 1644) by the French Jesuit Denis Pétau were written against the background of a post-Reformation controversy between 'positive' and 'speculative' theology.[10] Positive theology in this context is theology based upon the primary sources of Christian revelation, while speculative theology is scholasticism with its Aristotelian underpinnings. In 1700 the French theologian Pierre Annat published his *Apparatus ad positivam Theologiam methodicus* in which he directly equated 'positive' with 'fundamental' theology (as that which is the foundation or *fundamentum* of all else), marking the first occurrence of the term.[11] In 1593, Pierre Charron published his *Les trois vérités*, in which he advanced the 'threefold proof' of the *demonstratio religiosa*, *demonstratio christiana* and *demonstratio catholica*, which sought to prove first the existence of God, then the supremacy of Christianity and finally the primacy of Roman Catholicism.[12] This was to become the classic form of Catholic apologetics in modern times.[13]

With the rise of rationalism and scientism, especially in the seventeenth century, there was an attempt to link the 'explanation' of Christianity more closely with arguments used in mathematics and natural science. The first instance of the use of a Cartesian *de more geometrico* form of argument has been attributed to Pierre Daniel Huet in his *Demonstratio evangelica* (Paris,

1679).[14] But the theological response to scientific rationalism could also lead to a kind of historical positivism, whereby the prophecies and miracles of the biblical tradition would take on the character of scientific proofs, which commanded conviction. This was the argument of Abbé Houteville's *La religion chrétienne provée par les faits* (1722) and of the Swiss botanist Charles Bonnet in his *Philosophical Reflections on the Proofs of Christianity* (1770). This was to exchange rationalism for verificationism and, optimistically, for the 'empirical' authority of a rigid historical belief. It was in reaction to such ideas that the German thinker Reimarus vigorously attacked the whole concept of a revealed religion, declaring Jesus to be deluded and Christianity to be an entirely fraudulent exercise.

In the late nineteenth century Johannes Nepomuk Ehrlich published his *Fundamentaltheologie* (1859–62), which was the first book to bear this title. Under the influence of the *Critique of Pure Reason*, in which Kant had created a new sense of 'fundamental philosophy' that gave an account of the powers and the limits of reason itself, Ehrlich argued for the basis of theology as a discrete and integrated science. This new emphasis upon *Wissenschaft*, which was so important to the post-Kantian inheritance of Schelling and Fichte, made its mark upon two of the leading Catholic theologians of the period. In his three-volume *Apologetik* (1844–7) Johann Sebastian Drey drew upon the Idealist theme of an a priori ethical sense that is intrinsic to human nature, arguing that it was this which found its fulfilment in the historical notion of the kingdom of God in the Gospel.[15] In a series of penetrating works Anton Günther also developed this anthropological theme along Idealist lines showing a particular debt to J. G. Fichte. Günther sought to establish a symmetry between self-consciousness and divine essence through a transcendental philosophy of the self, and his approach marked a shift away from an extrinsic verificationism and historical positivism towards an evaluation of the intrinsic dimensions of faith. His work, which in some ways paralleled the Protestant theology of Schleiermacher in a Catholic doctrinal context, began the movement towards transcendental anthropology as fundamental theology, but it also met much opposition in the Catholic Church.[16]

From the middle of the nineteenth century, and the emergence of Wilhelm Dilthey's new concept of 'understanding', or *Verstehen*, which assumed the subjectivity of a human observer, there has been a greater realization that the methods of the natural sciences cannot adequately be applied to diffuse and subjective human realities. During the twentieth century this fostered a pronounced emphasis upon the role of anthropology in fundamental theology, which shifted the focus from *proving* the faith to establishing the *meaning* of the Christian revelation in human nature and experience. Maurice Blondel's *L'Action* (1893) and Karl Rahner's transcendental Thomism, as expounded in his *Geist in Welt* (1939), *Hörer des Wortes* (1941), and *Grundkurs des Glaubens* (1976), are outstanding examples of this trend.[17]

In some ways transcendental anthropology does offer an ideal form of fundamental theology. With the scope of reason being curtailed, especially with regard to the data of religion, anthropology can appear to offer a more certain footing in its claim to deal with abstracts and universals: with human nature itself. According to David Tracy, it 'is chiefly concerned, in its phenomenological moment, with our *common* human experience and, in its transcendental or metaphysical moment, with the abstract, general, universal and necessary features of that common experience . . .', thus giving a '"religious dimension" to our ordinary experience'.[18] As fundamental theology, anthropology can show 'how systematic theology is in fact a reasonable, responsible, human risk'.[19] By establishing a prior definition of the human, systematics now becomes the reasonable and justifiable pursuit of a transcendentally constructed self. But in other ways there are good reasons for not wishing to take a transcendental anthropology as fundamental theology.

The first is that it tends towards the view that a specific anthropology has universal validity and fails to grasp the extent to which any transcendentalist anthropology remains committed to its particular, and in general distinctively Western, philosophical sources.[20] The view that anthropology offers a new kind of universalism is one we find expressed, for example, by Pannenberg: 'in the modern age anthropology has become not only in fact but also with objective necessity the terrain on which theologians must base their claim of universal validity for what they say'.[21] But as a *model* or heuristic project of understanding, anthropology cannot be prescriptive and cannot close off alternative models; it is not an argument of the *p* therefore *q* type. Moreover, the particular character of any transcendental anthropology is determined by theological imperatives, and so it is itself indebted to the data of revelation, and is answerable to dogmatics. Thus we can think of theological anthropology as being a self-governing planet in close orbit around a theological sun, which determines its path while recognizing its autonomy. Accordingly, the designation of theological anthropology as fundamental theology runs the risk of obscuring the contingency of the former with respect to what are ultimately theological and systematic constraints.

But secondly, while the delineation of the self of faith, or view of the person which is consistent with the requirements of Christian faith, is certainly necessary today, if we are to recognize the subjective dimension to human experience and belief, the question remains to what extent can we say that this is *to give an account* of Christianity to those who do not share it? Surely Rahner's anthropology is little used to explain Christian faith to those for whom it is alien but serves in the main as a valuable exercise in clarification for Christians themselves who are seeking a new self-understanding in the light of the faith by which they live? And was it not in fact a great strength of the old *demonstrationes* that they used a language of reason to which all could relate, however distant from

Christian faith? In a certain sense then, fundamental theology is poorly served by theological anthropology.

Among the widely diverging approaches to the situating of fundamental theology we have seen in recent years, there have been a number which seek the continuation and development of traditional perspectives, though with new and altogether contemporary emphases.[22] In Germany, Hansjürgen Verweyen's *Gottes letztes Wort: Grundriß der Fundamentaltheologie* (1991) looks back to the *Reflexionsphilosophie* of J. G. Fichte.[23] But there has been a marked trend towards a new emphasis on praxis and interpretation. In his *Glaube in Geschichte und Gesellschaft* (1984) J. B. Metz attacked Rahner's notion of 'transcendental experience' as an inadequate representation of the actual historical experience of suffering humanity, and proposed that transcendentalism be replaced by praxis in order to ground 'a political theology as practical fundamental theology'.[24] Drawing upon the work of Jürgen Habermas, Helmut Peukert further developed this theme in his *Wissenschaftstheorie-Handlungstheorie-Fundamentale Theologie* (1976) by insisting on the necessity of a theological horizon for the very possibility of the maintenance of 'solidarity, inheritance and justice that are so central to communication in periods of emancipatory action'.[25] True justice implies solidarity with the oppressed other in past generations, and this in turn demands an ultimately emancipatory and therefore theological view of history. Hermeneutics has been central to the concern of Eugen Biser in his *Glaubensverständnis: Grundriß einer hermeneutischen Fundamentaltheologie* (1975), as it has for David Tracy and Francis Schüssler Fiorenza in the United States. In *The Analogical Imagination* (1981), in line with his evaluation of theology as a form of 'public discourse', Tracy expounds fundamental theology as that kind of theology which is determined by its audience, which is human kind in general, and is thus universalist and rationalist in appeal. In his *Foundational Theology* (1985) Francis Schüssler Fiorenza argues against theological foundationalism on the grounds of the collapse of philosophical foundationalism in contemporary philosophy and the problematization of the notion of truth. He recommends instead a kind of pragmatism or 'reconstructive hermeneutics' and 'reflective equilibrium', which recognize the provisional character of truth assertions and seek to correct belief in the light of practice.[26]

The turn to hermeneutics both as 'communicative communities' and self-correcting critique constitutes a modern version of the *demonstrationes*, and is fundamentally a variant on the Enlightenment project. While we may admire the honesty of these theologians, who recognize the radically provisional character of reason, we may wonder again in what positive and dynamic sense this kind of fundamental theology can serve as an 'explanation' of Christianity to the broader community, however valuable it may be as a 'clarification' for the Christian community of the provisional nature of theology itself. Indeed, as with transcendental anthropology, what we observe here is a tendency to separate the two functions of

fundamental theology, that of 'clarification' for Christians and 'explanation' for others, and to privilege the former at the expense of the latter. We
are surely under an obligation today to seek for paradigms which can
dynamically project 'the idea of Christianity' into the general experience of
humanity in a way that a particular paradigm of the self, or a rationalism
humbly reflecting upon its own constraints, cannot. We must find new and
positive ways of telling the world what being a Christian 'is like', communicating in any way we can its freedom and its joy.

The model for undertaking this task offered here is that of poetics, or
the science of poetry. The trend towards a prioritization of the sign and
loosening of extra-linguistic reference which is such a dominant aspect of
contemporary intellectual culture can itself be seen to be a kind of universal poeticization of language as such, with deeply significant consequences
for the construction of thought and world. But there are powerful reasons
also for wanting to link fundamental theology with aesthetics and modern
art in general.

Drawing upon Blondel and Ricoeur, as well as von Balthasar, Gerhard
Larcher has recently stressed the extent to which the revelation itself is
communicated *aesthetically*, through the senses (*pulchrum*) and in a way
that offers mediation of the theological (*verum*) and the ethical (*bonum*).[27]
As a sensible modality of communication and attestation, art is thus
protected from the fragmentation of reason which is a condition of the
postmodern, and can continue creatively to mediate the primary elements
of Christian consciousness and tradition within an environment that is
generally hostile to their classical expressions. Where Larcher deviates
from von Balthasar however, is in his view that works of modern art, for all
their 'techniques of negation' and counter-aestheticism, remain 'sense-
events', intimately linked with Ricoeur's 'affirmations originaires', which
open out into mystery, and ultimately into the mystery of God made flesh.
In Larcher's view, the visual dominates contemporary culture, and modern
art – precisely in its confrontation with the 'unrepresentable' and sense of
'the end of art' – offers a place of deep dialogue between church and
culture, faith and 'reason', modernity and tradition.

The outline of a fundamental theology based upon contemporary art
and aesthetics is a development that is at ease both with postmodernity
and tradition, and it promises much for the future. We have preferred
poetry and poetics to the visual arts however, as a consequence of our
prioritization of speech and voice in the systematic theology to follow,
which we understand to be central to any attempt to combine a philosophical perspective after the 'linguistic turn' with a theology of Christian
revelation.[28] There is a risk here however, as with modern art in general,
that poetry might be thought of only as an elitist pursuit for the most
educated in society. But the democratization of art is one of the characteristics of the modern, and the enchantment of the poetic text wholly
transcends the academic context of its systematic study, since in nursery

rhymes, songs and hymns it has widespread popular appeal. We shall argue that one of the key factors which poetry and Christian speech have in common, and which grounds their natural affinity, is the fact that neither the speech of poets nor that of apostles can be said to be ordinary speech, but both are forms of human talking which are powerfully under the sway of some other power, or licence. To that extent therefore, both can be said to have distanced themselves from the conventional speech of human beings, to have undergone some degree of *deviation* from the norm, to be – in Shklovsky's phrase – speech 'made strange'.[29] The analogy of poetics then, and the generative field of the poetic text, is one way in which the Christian community can communicate through reflective understanding something of what it is like to discover in Christ the form of the living Word, and to live by its meanings.

The form of poeticity

Although poetry, in the form of nursery rhymes and popular songs, belongs to the common inheritance of humanity, the science of poetics, which seeks to understand the structure of poeticity, does not. We can make use of a paradigm originally developed by Roman Jakobson in order to draw distinctions between ordinary and poetic speech. According to this model, the shape of the normal speech-act is a triadic combination of addresser, addressee and the message, in which it is the communicative intentionality of the addresser with respect to the addressee that governs the whole.[30] If the communication is to be successful, then the words used must efficiently serve as signs to those things to which they refer. The functionality of language here is fundamentally one of service, requiring the transparency of the signifier with respect to the signified. In the case of poetic language, however, the focus shifts from the intentionality of the addresser within the communicative act to *the message itself*. Now language no longer serves to point beyond itself, or at least no longer does this alone, but rather turns in upon itself and engenders a world not beyond language but contained within it.

The first aspect of poeticity then to align poetic language with theological speech, is the determination on the part of the one who delivers the text that the words are not to be taken straightforwardly in their denotative function, as ordinary reference. In the case of poetry, this is reflected in the use of specific markers such as introductions, titles, the publication of volumes of poetry, the organization of poetry readings, to ensure that such literary or oral texts will be set apart from ordinary speaking. The privacy of the poem, or its non-referential function, is signalled not only by context but also by its recognizable 'poetic form', which is based in one way or another upon simple repetition. Prosodic elements such as stanzas, rhyme, metre, a fixed number of syllables and/or lines, assonance, are all different expressions of the principle of repetition, which immediately marks out poetic discourse to the listener or reader as being in some way speech made strange (after all, too much repetition or non-referential use of speech in other contexts can easily be taken as the sign of madness). In the case of religion, of course, theological speaking is set apart from ordinary speech by its associations with the cult, that is with liturgy, worship and church gatherings, and with a reverential frame of mind. The mixing of Christian speech with ordinary speech is perilous, since the mysterious and invisible realities of which the Christian community speaks cannot be pointed to like objects in the world which are equally perceived by all. Indeed, a blurring of the boundaries between ordinary language and Christian speech which is 'set apart' in this special sense leads either to blasphemy or religious mania. As ways of speaking which are 'set apart' from ordinary usage, both poetry and theology must be protective of their distinctiveness.

But the setting aside of reference to the external world in the poem has the further consequence that poetic language tends inherently towards ambiguity. This is a second point of affinity with theology. In the case of the poem, this ambiguity flows from the prioritization of language itself within the speech-act, in which the communicative function of language is no longer controlled by the addresser's intention to speak to the addressee about the world. Rather, the boundaries of the poem serve to create an inner-linguistic space: a world within the poem. Jakobson has described this as the projection of 'the principle of equivalence from the axis of selection to the axis of combination'.[31] What this means is that when we construct a non-poetic sentence, we *select* a word from a number of broadly equivalent words which we exclude as not suiting our meaning, and then follow it with another word which we have similarly selected out from a range of alternative possibilities. In the poetic function of language however, the choice of a word is determined in no small degree by the other words which surround it and which together construct the body of the poem.[32] The choice of the poetic word then is determined not by its opposition to alternative words from among which it has been selected, but rather by its *combination* with the other words of the poem.[33] Thus 'the succession of similarities and differences are the forces which keep together and enhance poetic constructions'.[34] As Edward Stankiewicz has said, Jakobson's 'message' now becomes 'autotelic', possessing its own goals, and 'the Kantian formula of art as "purposiveness without purpose" epitomizes also the essence of verbal art: poetic language is purposive in terms of the internal organization of the message, and purposeless in terms of the external reference'.[35] This same point was made more succinctly by the critic Northrop Frye when he wrote of the poetic word that it 'does not echo the thing but other words'.[36]

Within the extraordinarily rich context of a fine poem, the individual word becomes ambiguous, or polyvalent, as it takes on a superabundance of meanings. The properties of the poem may involve rhyme and partial rhyme, metrical sequence based on the quantity or quality of vowels, syllabic sequence or accentual sequence. Within the overall texture of the poem, such structures will interact both with the natural expressive tone of the language the poem is written in and with the meanings of the words themselves. Thus the significance of particular words may be heightened through their position in the metrical flow, or alternatively they may be veiled. But in any case, a strong metrical, or prosodic, environment will greatly enhance the interaction of the different elements and make available a whole range of unforeseen and multiple combinations and meanings which are the product both of the normal ostensive functions of the words (made strange of course in the context of the poem), the suggestive associations of the words, and their interaction through the phonological, metrical or accentual systems which together construct the poetic text.

Ambiguity then stands at the heart of poetic meaning, and is essential to it. But for the Christian too, language is rich in its different contextual associations. Christian speaking is deeply indebted to the language of the Bible, with its metaphors, tropes and types. The unseen God is spoken of precisely in terms of the language of the world, which then becomes charged with new and extraordinary significance. Furthermore, the language of Christianity is recontextualized in every age and new cultural world, so that the content of terms sanctioned by Scripture are constantly taking on new meanings. The ambiguity of Christian language then is both a matter of the density and richness of new contextualizations and is the consequence of a divine excess of meaning which revelation commissions language to bear.

A third affinity between poetics and theology lies in the area of origination. The loosening of the referential function of language in the poem leads to the displacement of the self as speaker and, finally, to the problematicization of the authorship of a poem. Of course, in any conventional or legal sense, a poem can rightfully be claimed by the individual who composed it; but there is a deeper issue here to do with the question of the poem's origin. The creative process is notoriously outside the control of the conscious self, relying upon inspiration, creativity and vision, as well as craft, stamina and skill. In earlier traditions, the unfathomability of poetic genesis was expressed as a belief in supernatural agency, in divine or semi-divine beings, who could under certain conditions take over the speech functions of the individual, 'enthusing' them in Plato's sense with or as inspiration. Nor is there any reason to think that the survival of the Muse into the Baroque period was always a purely cosmetic device of strategic anachronism. Modern poets too frankly acknowledge their debt and obligations to some 'energy' which is the incalculable source of their creativity. A twentieth-century poet such as Stefan George can still write of his muse in strongly personalist, pseudo-religious terms, exactly conveying the sense of being at the service, or ambiguously in the power, of another:

Lobgesang

Du bist mein herr! Wenn du auf meinem weg ·
Viel-wechselnder gestalt doch gleich erkennbar
Und schön · erscheinst beug ich vor dir den nacken
. . .
Du reinigst die befleckung · heilst die risse
Und wischst die tränen durch dein süsses wehn.
In fahr und fron · wenn wir nur überdauern ·
Hat jeder tag mit einem sieg sein ende –
So auch dein dienst: erneute huldigung
Vergessnes lächeln ins gestirnte blau.

Hymn of Praise

You are my Lord! When you appear on my path –
In ever changing form but always recognizable
And beautiful – I bow my head before you.
. . .
You cleanse impurity; the wounds you heal
And dry my tears with your sweet sighing.
In following and vassalage – if only we survive –
Each day ends with a victory –
So too your service: renewed homage
Forgotten smile into the blue of stars.[37]

A certain ambiguity concerning authorship of the poem, in whatever
way it may be constructed in different historical periods, is an abiding
feature of poetic discourse, and it is one which invites some comparison
with the experience of the theologian, whose divinely sanctioned speech
we have likewise interpreted as a form of dispossession. But if the poet is
in a sense 'inspired', then why should his or her work not be in a sense
'revealed'. Indeed, there is a pronounced strain in modern poetry, from
Charles Baudelaire to Gottfried Benn, that seems to claim just such a vatic
or visionary function. In the work of Heidegger, looking back to J. G.
Hamann, that disclosure is itself one that is ontological, and poetry itself
becomes 'the establishing of Being by means of the word'.[38] But the 'revelatory' is a function also of the world-creating dimension of the poem, or
what Paul Ricoeur calls the 'world of the text'.[39] This is specifically that
domain of reference which the poem sets up in liberating opposition to
description or teleological reference. Accordingly, for Ricoeur, 'this
suspension or abolition of a referential function of the first degree' releases
'a more primitive, more originary referential function, which may be

called a second order reference only because discourse whose function is descriptive has usurped the first rank in daily life and has been supported in this regard by modern science'.[40] This disclosure is not something that becomes for the reader the object of cognition in her own world, as part of Paul Ricoeur's 'subject–object relation', but rather itself manifests as world in its own indeterminacy and 'pure sensibility'[41], in Hart Crane's phrase, so that the manner of its reception is encounter with and entry into a second world. Thus the poem does not offer itself as experience to us, or at least not that alone, but rather offers itself to us as *the very possibility of experience*, discretely constituted and newly configured. And the reader finds himself or herself restored to 'that participation-in or belonging-to an order of things which precedes our capacity to oppose ourselves to things taken as objects opposed to a subject'.[42]

The central role of the imagination in this revelatory and liberating function of poetry is captured by Wallace Stevens when he describes the poem as a place of imaginings or 'supreme fictions', constituting a counter-realm to the real, freed of the constraints of teleology and functionalism.[43] From this, poetry emerges as the possibility of a human liberation, a place of purification and renewal of the imagining mind, and a place also where, without condition, the mind can touch the tap-root of all experience. For Stevens, poetry represents a bulwark against 'the pressure of reality' which he understands to be not only materialism and commercialism of the modern era, but also an increasing tendency towards violence.[44] It places imagination on equal terms with reality, but 'the imagination gives to everything that it touches a peculiarity, and it seems to me that the peculiarity of the imagination is nobility'.[45] This nobility of the imagination is 'a violence from within that protects us from a violence from without. It is the imagination pressing back against the pressure of reality. It seems, in the last analysis, to have something to do with our self-preservation; and that, no doubt, is why the expression of it, the sounds of its words, helps us to live our lives'.[46]

As reflection upon experience, the poem also offers the reader the experience of itself: its own world as distinct from the 'other' world of which it is an accidental reflex. It is this which leads Robert Frost to speak of 'a better wildness of logic than inconsequence'. For the logic of the poem 'is backward, in retrospect, after the act. It must be felt more than seen ahead in prophecy. It must be a revelation, or a series of revelations, as much for the poet as for the reader'.[47] The special experience of the poem is one akin to love, for it 'begins in delight and ends in wisdom'.[48] Abstracted experience can itself be experience, one akin to our experience of the ordinary world, though freed from it. We grow from it and are increased by it, gaining in wisdom. We can say then that the paths of a poem are for the reader a journeying into his or her own memories and associations, while being confronted with the thoughts, emotions and inner personal reality of another. In reading it, we encounter the interpretative parameters of our own self, structured on the experience of another. And so, like ordinary experience, it takes us in directions we cannot predict, marked with contingency and mortality; as Lorca put it in his *Theory and Function of the Duende*, 'the magical quality of a poem consists in its being always possessed by the *duende* [sense of the presence of death], so that whoever beholds it is baptized with dark water'.[49] But as abstracted experience, removed from the world and set up over against the world, the poet's imagination 'becomes the light in the minds of others' (Wallace Stevens).[50] It changes our experience of the world and thus the nature of the world itself. Indeed, in Bakhtin's phrase, art and life are held together in a relation of mutual *answerability* so that 'inspiration that ignores life and is itself ignored by life is not inspiration but a state of possession'.[51] The imaginative experience which poetry offers is a form of purification, in which the generative powers of the mind are returned to their own source and made available in a new way for the formation of our worlds. This is a process akin to the purification of the blood in the aorta, whereby the old blood is purged of its toxins and, as Paul Celan has it, made 'bright' for the furtherance of life.[52]

The release of the imagination, and resistance to 'the pressure of reality', leads also to a sense of the 'truth' of poetry. But A. E. Housman's remark that 'poetry is not the thing said, but a way of saying it' should serve to remind us that the concept of poetic truth is necessarily a complex one.[53] Something of the same is conveyed by McLeish's adage that a poem should not mean but be.[54] W. H. Auden has criticized this latter phrase, saying: 'This is not quite accurate. In a poem, as distinct from many other kinds of verbal societies, meaning and being are identical. A poem might be called a pseudo-person. Like a person it is unique and addresses the reader personally . . . like a natural being, and unlike a historical person, it cannot lie'.[55] The claim that the poem has its own being is simultaneously the claim that somehow it stands above or beyond the world, and represents a second world, whose truth is both address and *aletheia*, or unrevealedness: the absence of falsehood. The truth of poetry is its own being, as a sovereign hermeneutical space. The attempt to dragoon poets and their work into the functionalities of crudely political, socio-economic (or religious!) ideologies, cuts at the heart of the spontaneity and freedom of the poetic word, and European cultural history is littered with feeble paeons to establishment or ideology, explicitly coerced (as in the case of Mandelstam) or implicitly so (as in the work of some English Poet Laureates). The right precisely to resist accommodation to other kinds of discourse is part of the very essence of poetry as motion, and free generative play. Nor can the poet use the poem to articulate his or her feelings too directly. The creation of a successful poem requires a certain displacement, or even personal *ascesis* on the part of the poet, as he or she seeks for what T. S. Eliot called 'objective correlatives' or 'significant emotion', that is, 'emotion which has its life in the poem and not in the history of the poet'.[56] Precisely because the poem exists as its own world, rather than serving merely as an interpretation of the empirical world, there can be no hegemony in the way that it is read. The poem offers the possibility of a multiplicity of interpretations and appropriations, and its very fecundity, 'the wonder of its unexpected supply' (Robert Frost) subverts any easy closure of interpretation.[57]

In light of modern poetry's claim to be both 'revelation' and 'truth', it is no wonder that poetry has increasingly seemed to take on aspects of self-understanding previously reserved for the distinctively 'religious'. This is already apparent in the work of Mallarmé, who turns from his Christian faith to the new faith of poetry. Hugo Friedrich has remarked on the increasing trend towards a form of religious inwardness and 'transcendentality' in modern poetry, and notes the occurrence of the motif of angels which are however 'angels without God and without a message'.[58] For Hamburger, 'a whole genealogy of such angels could be traced from Rimbaud to Stefan George, Rilke, Wallace Stevens and Rafael Alberti'.[59] Among the religious, pseudo-religious or para-religious elements within modern poetry we could cite the notion of poet as creator and of his work as a *creatio ex nihilo*. This is originally a Romantic idea, and on this theme Gary Giddes quotes Byron's remark ''Tis to create, and in creating live, a being more intense, that we endow with form our fancy, gaining as we give the life we image.'[60] The creative bringing of order within the poem to what is inchoate, fragmented and conflictual is the very essence of the function of the poem as what Bakhtin calls the *consummation* of our life and experience, or what for Rilke is *Auftrag*, that is, our calling or task.[61] This reconciliation or integration of diverse energies within the body of the poem represents in itself a kind of release so that, as Wallace Stevens has it: 'after one has abandoned belief in God, poetry is the essence which takes its place as life's redemption'.[62]

It is, finally, the centrality of language and the supreme excess of language which poetry represents that lends it such a quality of the numinous. The ability to use language is in some sense a defining human quality, and so poetry is 'not an art or branch of art, it's something more. If what distinguishes us from other species is speech, then poetry, which is the supreme linguistic operation, is our anthropological, indeed genetic goal' (Joseph Brodsky).[63] Only in poetry is language used in the fullness of all its possibilities: referential, creative, phonemic. In Bakhtin's words: 'language reveals all of its possibilities only in poetry, since here maximal demands are placed upon it: all its aspects are strained to the extreme, and reach their ultimate limits. Poetry squeezes, as it were, all the juices from language, and language exceeds itself here.'[64] In poetry we encounter in an unparalleled way something essential to our own nature: the ability to govern language – as form – and to master reality – as content given or made available in form. And it also adds something essential to our experience of being alive, namely, the sense of being answerable to and involved in fluid processes of creation and meaning which transcend the parameters of the self and locate us, 'carnivalistically' in Bakhtin's pregnant phrase, in the broader contexts of world and existence.

Towards a theological poetics

As language that is 'set apart', mysterious in its genesis, enchanting in its effects and burdened with an excess of meaning, as language which appears to speak in a revelatory fashion to the heart of things, as a second world, as a way of speaking which defies any appropriation by imperatives other than its own, poetry appears to offer a real analogy to the language of Christians and, above all, to the wisdom-speech that is theology. But for all these striking affinities, which are so valuable for a fundamental theology that seeks to give an account of faith for those outside it, the distinctions between poetry and theology need also to be pointed out. Otherwise there is a risk that theology itself will simply become a matter of language alone: a kind of poetry. We can see real differences with respect to inspiration, for instance, since although the poet may be said to experience a degree of dispossession through inspiration, the dispossession of the theologian is emphatically a coming into possession by another, by God as Spirit or illumining grace. And although readers of the poem are called to give themselves over to the aesthetic encounter with a world that is fundamentally shaped by the experience and feelings of another, the theologian is an individual who is summoned in the whole of his or her personal existence to participate fully in the trinitarian ground from which that sacred speech emerges. The theologian is to become part of the 'poem' he or she delivers. For the poet, on the other hand, there is no new dispensation, nor can there be, for the deity served by the poet is no more than a cypher – however graphic – for the mystery of the provenance of poetry.

We must be careful in applying the term 'revelation' too for the linguistic disclosure which is at the heart of the poetic text. Although both poetic and religious disclosure can be said to be not so much phenomenal as grounding the possibility of appearance (*phainesthai*) as such, as constituting a second world and thus allowing the emergence of a realm of new possibilities of experience and existence, revelation as a religious term in its highest manifestations implies some kind of transcendent communicative act, founded upon a divine communicative intentionality.[65] Such a communicative agency is alien to poetry except in its most abruptly oracular forms. And if the reception of a poem by a sensitive reader can indeed have something of the force of a revelation, if we are opened up by poetry, confronted with new imaginings, associations and semantic possibilities, then we should remember that poetry in the final analysis is 'a revelation in words by means of the words' (Wallace Stevens).[66] What is 'revealed' as such then in good poetry is the generative function of language itself: the infinite play of its own free possibilities.

If both poetry and theology is language 'made strange', then the measure of the deviation is, arguably, the extent to which the language of poets is answerable to the mystery of its own genesis (as muse) and to the very particular discipline of the poetic art (as *technê*), while the deviation of theology is the extent to which theological language is answerable to God and to understandings that are illumined by processes of grace. This same distinction manifests also with regard to the respective types of meta-phoricity which they embody. In the case of theology, metaphoricity disrupts normal referencing with respect to the world in order to speak of what is given to us *from beyond* the world. Theological language is human speech that is configured and refigured in response to a divine advent; and its expressivity is one which is ordered to that advent. Poetic metaphoricity on the other hand functions entirely *within* the world, since language refer-ring to language, revelation 'in words by means of the words', never leaves the realm of the created, for all its generative fecundity and gifting of new possibilities of perceiving. Indeed, given the different relation between language and world that operates in theology and poetry, we can say that poetic metaphoricity determines the relation between poetry and world as one which is *aesthetic*, predicated upon irony and a horizontal perspective. Theological metaphoricity on the other hand determines the relation between theology and world as one which is *critical*, predicated upon judg-ment and a vertical perspective. If then with respect to inspiration we can say that poetry suffers a dispossession without coming into the possession of another, so too we can say that poetry delivers a revelation, but it is revelation without content.

In the light of these distinctions, we should examine also the poet's claim to create. For W. H. Auden, poetic creativity is only 'analogous' to divine creation and 'is not an imitation, for were it so, the poet would be able to create like God *ex nihilo*; instead, he requires pre-existing occasions of feel-ing and a pre-existing language out of which to create'.[67] A necessary part of creation is the establishing of order, and it is of creative ordering that W. H. Auden prefers to speak in an extended metaphor of the poem as a 'verbal society' (perhaps making skilful use of motifs from Augustine's *City of God*). The poem itself stands for the 'form' of the church constructed via a process of election by the ecclesial-poetic integration of the raw elements of life or humanity:

> The nature of the final poetic order is the outcome of a dialectical struggle between the recollected occasions of feeling and the verbal system. As a society the verbal system is actively coercive upon the occasions it is attempting to embody; what it cannot embody truthfully it excludes . . . In a successful poem, society and community are in one order and the system may love itself because the feelings which it embodies are all members of the same community, loving each other and it. A poem may fail in two ways; it may exclude too much (banality), or attempt to embody more than one community at once (disorder).[68]

Indeed, Auden warns against the explicit appropriation of Christian language at this point: 'Every beautiful poem presents an analogy to the forgiveness of sins; an analogy, not an imitation, because it is not evil intentions which are repented of and pardoned but contradictory feelings which the poet surrenders to the poem in which they are reconciled.'[69] And he points too to the danger that poetic beauty will be confused for goodness:

> The effect of [poetic] beauty, therefore, is good to the degree that through its analogies, the goodness of created existence, the historical fall into unfreedom and disorder, and the possibility of regaining paradise through repentance and forgiveness are recognized. Its effect is evil to the degree that beauty is taken, not as analogous to, but identical with goodness, so that the artist regards himself or is regarded by others as God, the pleasure of beauty taken for the joy of Paradise, and the conclusion drawn that, since all is well in the work of art, all is well in history. But all is not well there.[70]

This abrupt conclusion to the Augustinian metaphor of the poem as Augustine's transhistorical 'other city', is not a contesting of the poetic as idolatry (as we do find at times in the Christian tradition), but is rather a warning against a Nietzschean appropriation of poems as 'saving fictions', which sing the conscience to sleep and persuade us against an active and ethical involvement with the world. What we can discern here, then, once again is the difference between poetry and religion worked out in terms of a distance that is for the former aesthetic and for the latter critique.

It is in terms of the ethical and the personal that we must seek the locus of the radical distinction between poetry and theology, for all their symmetries. The position which we have outlined in the opening chapters of this volume is clear: Christianity has a fundamental concern with the ethical, understood as a self-dispossessing ethics, which requires a metaphysics. Kenosis needs a language of existential self-knowledge and self-possession if the compassionate self is to know itself to be put at risk for the sake of the other. Although the openness of reading, which Cixous refers to as 'a relentless process of de-selfing, de-egoization', has a kenotic structure in some degree, it is finally something other than a Christian ethics of enacted dispossession for the sake of a concrete other.[71] While we endorse the need to think language most radically and at the heart of Christianity, we would point out that language is fundamentally a social and inter-personal exchange. It is a sign system that is used by speech-agents, who thereby relate with other speech-agents in the construction (or destruction) of a common social reality. While language can in itself be generative, in accordance for instance with Ricoeur's view of the text as a form of 'generative poetics', and thus serve to refigure our world, it remains a phenomenon – albeit displaced through text – which presupposes a human speaker. We cannot unthink the one who speaks, the one who is performed in speech relations, whose self-possessing existence is the precondition for any self-dispossessing ethical act. For theology to retreat into language *per se* is to risk that ethical subject, and to risk also the divine self-communication to us through the self-dispossession of God for our sake in Jesus Christ. To take Jesus as 'essentially a linguistic and poetic reality' (John Milbank) then is to risk trading Jesus as the divine-human person in whom God speaks, for Jesus as a figure of speech.[72]

This focus upon the singularity of *personal* as distinct from *textual* or *linguistic* revelation is apparent also in the significant difference between the seemingly unending play of interpretation of literary texts and the canonization of texts and closure of interpretation which we find in Christian tradition. Although the cultural expressions of Christianity show precisely this unending character, the credal texts of Christianity command a consensus of response and understanding. The *credimus* contrasts fundamentally with the free flowing diversity of meanings and form which characterize the reception of most if not all cultural artefacts. Within the Christian economy resistance to closure manifests not as a multiplication of meanings at the level of the horizontal, but rather as a vanishing into depth at the level of the vertical. The divine-human object of our understanding escapes what Levinas calls 'the hegemony of comprehension' not by a rapid Ovidian series of metamorphoses, but because the surface of that revelation – what David Ford, adapting Levinas, calls 'the face of God' – constantly dissolves into ever greater depth.[73] In Christian hermeneutics, we remain grasped by the personal mystery that underlies the text, of whom the text speaks, who speaks with us from within the text, and we do so within a relatively stable unity of interpretation which is enriched but not fragmented by its diversity.

This brings us finally to an assessment of how poetics leads us to the threshold of theology but not beyond; and the issue is that of history. The poem does at some subtle level remain tied to the empirical realm; that is the foundation of its metaphoricity.[74] But in general, the poem is a semiotic system, or 'world', which is set up against the realm of ordinary perception and existence. Abstracted from the 'real' world, it is in an important sense other than it. Theology, on the other hand, if it is not to become a purely rhetorical, demythologized space, has deep obligations to history and to historical belief. This again is to reinstitute agency, without which we shall lose sight of that divine-human agency which was exercised by Jesus in his self-giving for us and the commensurate divine-human agency which is the condition of faith. The otherness of theology as metaphor is not given by a stratum of residual reference to ordinary objects in our world therefore, as with poetry, but rather by a point at which metaphor and empirical experience converge. This occurs in our recognition of who Christ is which, for all the complexities of the resurrection narratives and the nature of faith, entails belief which is historical at its core. For as

Kierkegaard noted, it is only historical belief that can become truly dialectical, allowing us to glimpse the coming into existence of the Infinite Paradox in history. And only by undergoing what Kierkegaard called the 'passion of thought' can our own existence become truly 'historical' in turn, as we are conformed to God's revelation to us in Christ. It is not that a theological poetics lacks historicity therefore, but rather that historicity in the sense developed above is *the very condition of the poeticity of a theological poetics*. The radical and dialectical antitheses of Christian faith, of incarnation and Trinity, personally made manifest to us in the hypostatic union, are the consummation, overflow and 'passion' of human existence itself, accomplished in every form of human feeling, thinking and speaking.

9

The Structure of Revelation as Communication

ὅτι ἐγὼ ἐξ ἐμαυτοῦ οὐκ ἐλάλησα, ἀλλ᾽ ὁ πέμψας
με πατὴρ αὐτός μοι ἐντολὴν δέδωκεν τί εἴπω καὶ
τί λαλήσω. καὶ οἶδα ὅτι ἡ ἐντολὴ αὐτοῦ ζωὴ αἰώνιός
ἐστιν. ἃ οὖν ἐγὼ λαλῶ, καθὼς εἴρηκέν μοι ὁ
πατήρ, οὕτως λαλῶ.

... for I have not spoken on my own, but the Father who sent me has himself given me a commandment about what to say and what to speak. And I know that his commandment is eternal life. What I speak, therefore, I speak just as the Father has told me.

John 12.49–50 (NRSV)

The word begins in silence. The uttering of the word is both God's creation and God's speaking with us in his Son, through whom all things were made.[1] Both the speaking of the creation and the speech of the Son are divine forms of disclosure: God's words uttered differentially from within the silence that is God's self. Both the creation and the incarnation are for us the setting of a task of relation: a coming to terms with the excess of meaning in the divine words by which we ourselves were created, and by which we are summoned into new creation in a relationship of participatory speaking-with.

The first undertaking of a theology of revelation then is to distinguish between the two different kinds of disclosure, between the revelation of a world in a general sense and that kind of revelation which is understood to convey *ultimate* meaning or to embody ultimate value as specifically 'religious' or 'particular' revelation.[2] The appeal to ultimate value often leads to a characterization of the one who reveals in terms that are analogically related to human personhood, so that the concept of the self-disclosure or self-communication of an ineffable sublime implies a mechanism of divine intentionality and design, grounded in a personal structure of cognition and will.[3] General revelation, on the other hand, as 'revelation of the truth of the world', which is virtually coterminous with the revealedness of what is, focuses more upon the astonishing or even miraculous character of the world.[4] Revelation in this sense is the unveiling of what Paul Ricoeur calls 'this primordial ground of our existence, of the originary horizon of our being-there',[5] and it is a contesting of 'the pretension of consciousness to constitute itself'.[6] But for a monotheistic, creationist religion such as Christianity, the distinction between general and partic-ular revelation is not always easily maintained. The surplus within the trinitarian relations which Christian faith affirms envisages a God who spontaneously gives of herself, repeatedly and in innumerable ways, through inwardness, the apprehension of beauty or design in the natural environment, the experience of human relationship or the subtleties and refinements of art, through movements of the imagination, or the intellect, through dance, song or even physical sensation.[7] Indeed, there is no aspect of human experience which cannot become a point of revelation of the divine being to us, precisely because all created form and life betrays the mark of God's authorship and can – at God's willing – become transparent to him. And yet, from a Christian perspective, all such disclosures have to be seen as being contained and transcended within the supreme revelatory form of an individual person, Jesus Christ. This is not an affirmation of a spiritual triumphalist kind however, but rather the recognition that *knowledge comes to us most truly and profoundly in the mode of personal knowing*. Only a personal revelation can embrace such communicative elements as knowledge, speech, action, relation, existence, trust and love (even in some specific ways, touch). Only a personal revelation, and the personal encounter which follows from it, can convey the sense of revela-tion as disclosure of *presence* with all the resonances of that term as a dis-closure event of *ultimate* value or meaning.[8]

The personalist theistic religions (Judaism, Christianity and Islam) tend to prefer what George Mavrodes calls 'the communication model of reve-lation', which draws upon the paradigm of ordinary linguistic communi-cation, echoing communication between persons.[9] For Keith Ward, the general concept of religious revelation, as we find it in the theistic religions, implies 'the communication of information which is received, not so much by investigation as by obedient response'; further, the content of revelation 'must be beyond normal human cognitive capacity, and it must be inten-tionally communicated'.[10] This gives revelation as communication an essentially threefold structure, implying one who reveals, the revealed and one to whom something is revealed. In the terminology of Roman Jakobson's model of communication, which we have already used for an explanation of the formal structure of poeticity, there is an addresser, a message and an addressee.[11] To these three principles, a reading of com-munication informed by modern pragmatic theory adds the situation in which the event of communication occurs and the effect which it brings about, or what linguists call the 'perlocutionary force'.[12] The principle of communication and therefore of revelation is dependent upon the presence of all three of Jakobson's terms. Thus, the intentionality of the addresser, which is expressed as the message, must take into consideration the nature of the one addressed if the words uttered are to become a 'message' rather than a monologue delivered into an empty space.[13] Similarly, the one spoken to must understand the middle term to be the communication of the other, if it is to become 'message' and thus address. Additionally, the act of communication as a whole is necessarily bound into specific spatio-temporal contexts and narratives which make possible that particular communication in that particular time and place. Furthermore, in the case of *universal* revelation, which reaches out to times and places remote from the original locus of revelation, we must also consider the role of the text, understood both as written and as social (or ritual) textuality, in the embodiment and transmission of the revelation through diverse histories and cultures.

But the specifically Christian model of revelation subverts Jakobson's paradigm in one fundamental way, since his addressor, message and addressee are unmistakably and irreducibly different from each other, although they exhibit some degree of congruence. The first and the third must be 'on the same wave-length', and the message itself must be meaningful for both (though not necessarily in the same way), otherwise we cannot say that a communicative act has taken place. In the case of Christian revelation however, that signifying congruence is heightened to such an extent that *added to the affirmation of difference between the three terms is the assertion of their identity*. So perfect is the communication implied in the Christian revelation that there is a complete collapse of cognitive distance. In the hypostatic union interpretative space becomes identity of person: hermeneutics yielding to ontology. Retaining Jakobson's terminology therefore, we can now state that God (the addresser) and creation as humanity (the addressee) both become identical with each other – as well as remaining wholly distinct – in the message (the God-Man). The identity of the Father and the incarnate Word is expressed in the Nicene *homoousios*, while Chalcedon affirms the identity of the creation with the Word through his hypostatic assumption of human nature. It is this superimposition of identity upon a structure of difference, thus yielding a dialectic of identity and difference, which draws forth the distinctive form of Christian revelation, setting it apart from the concept of the 'revealedness of the world' (general revelation) or poetic 'word-world'. These latter concepts affirm the radical prioritization of the middle term of the three-fold structure of communication, preserving the role of the addressee but leading to the disappearance of the addresser so that the message, or middle term, no longer communicates an intentionality. In Bakhtinian terms, the 'voice' is no longer that of the addresser speaking in or through the message but is now transposed to the message itself. It is the poem itself that speaks, it is the 'world' itself that communicates. This disappearance of the addresser as such contrasts with the identification of both addresser and addressee in the message, while preserving their difference, which forms the dialectical structure of Christian revelation.

Revelation as divine communication differs from human communication therefore to the extent that it is a perfect communication, entailing the personal union of addressor and addressee, collapsing hermeneutics into the *homoousios*. But it differs also in that the divine movement towards and into the recipient is necessarily a *kenotic* one, since the Word can only enter our own condition of contingency and mortality by emptying himself and 'taking the form of a slave, being born in human likeness'.[14] Divinity must become something other to itself, while remaining itself, in the communicative process, if revelation is to be complete. In its most primary and originary form, that revelation is the revelation of God as the Word to the human nature of Christ, who is for us 'spiritualis doctrinae et fidei primus und principalis Doctor'.[15] If the perfect knowing which is expressed in the hypostatic union of the divine and human natures in Christ entails a form of divine kenosis, then it is matched by a parallel act of human kenosis. This is visible in the submission of the human will of Christ to his divine will.[16] In his obedient reception of the fullness of divine revelation, the human nature of Christ becomes transformed, and itself radiates the glory of the revelation to all humankind and to all that is.

But the divine communication that is revelation differs from human communication in a further vital respect. The created order cannot become the recipient of the divine Word by its own power, for that would be to hear its own word rather than that of the Creator. We have already stressed that a communicative act, which can only take place where a message is truly given and received, is tied to a spatio-temporal context. There has to be an historical situation for the revelation therefore, which is not purely imposed from without, but which also emerges as a possibility from within the created order. This *consent* of the creation to the incarnation is something that we must attribute to the action of the Holy Spirit, who goes before by speaking through the prophets and by acting to purify, guide and sanctify the created order. The Spirit is in attendance at the formation of the world, and is theophanically present within the world.[17] Above all, it is the agency of the Spirit that brings about the virgin birth.[18] The Spirit inhabits the created order in such a way as to establish the ground of the revelation by moving the creation to receive it from within. It represents the principle of *communicability* which still remains within the divine initiative but is understood to be God at work within the creation. It is the Spirit too that will guide the reception and transmission of the incarnate Word, empowering and illumining the faithful, and pointing to the final fulfilment of the creation in the parousia.

Speaking to and speaking with

The concept of the Word stands at the heart of the Christian model of God revealed. But in professing that God *speaks*, theology is committed to reflection upon divine speech as speech, while also recognizing that God's self-giving to us always constitutes a surplus above and beyond the parameters of what we can grasp of him in the divine revelation.[19] The analysis of divine speech as speech then represents an attempt to clarify that aspect of human reality with which tradition has modelled the divine disclosure, while recognizing that such aspects are transformed in and through the hypostatic union, and become part of the divine life. But to fail to carry out such an analysis is to risk falling victim to unreflected presuppositions about the nature of speech as such and thus to foreclose on certain pathways of meaning given in the self-donation of God in Jesus Christ and, in consequence, on certain ways of receiving his revelation to us in the Word.[20]

We have argued above that the primary characteristic of Christian revelation lies in its structure of identity and difference, whereby the addresser and addressee become one 'without confusion' in the message. This certainly supports a hermeneutical ontology of address; and indeed the notion of revelation as divine address runs throughout the scriptures and is a foundational part of the Christian model of revelation. The great emphasis upon a theology of address which is exemplified in both Catholic and Protestant tradition is not based upon scriptural texts alone however, but also shows the influence of particular models of language found in classical linguistics. We can follow Wittgenstein in taking the image of language proposed by St Augustine in the *Confessions* (I, 8) as an example of these. For Augustine, the primary constituent of language is the 'word', primarily the 'noun', which 'refers' so that 'the individual words in language name objects – sentences are combinations of such names . . . Every word has a meaning. This meaning is correlated with the word. It is the object for which the word stands.'[21] In *The Trinity* Augustine develops the role of intentionality in his notion of the 'word' as the *verbum cordis*, which is an internal form of knowledge, presupposing both external cognition and a degree of judgment.[22] Language as 'word' is bound up with human experience, and with the faculty of judgment, which is innate to the human mind, reflecting our access to authentic knowledge. But it is linked also with human intentionality, which grounds the distinction between ethical and unethical actions. Crucially, therefore, Augustine understands language to be fundamentally nominal and to be suspended between the world of objects, the human mind and the divine reality which alone can guarantee its truth. This is an adequationist view of word and language, or more properly a linguistics of mediation. Only by intimate and internal movements of the will, refusing to enjoy things *non propter se sed propter aliud*, can human language as a system of cognition, action and communication attain authenticity as a reflection of the divine reality. In other words, Augustine's view of language returns us to the *frui-uti* opposition of Book One of *De doctrina christiana*, against the background of a linguistic structure that focuses upon a transcendental logic of reference and address. He understands language to be a concatenation of free-standing words, mirroring a universe constructed of substantial units, and stresses its functionality with respect to the intentional ends of the mind that applies the word in communication with another. The truth of the word is measured according to the extent that it embodies the true intentions and judgments of the one who speaks. Not all post-classical theories of language are predicated upon a divinely instituted created order, of course, but correspondence and reference between the word and the object signified have proved of long-lasting influence.

Pragmatics, the dominant linguistic theory of today, sees in language a very different animal. Here the emphasis is upon the dialogical sociality of utterance, and the fact that speech is generated within specific contexts.[23] This is to emphasize 'contextual meaning' or 'meaning in interaction'.[24] The view that language is embedded in social contexts, involving a common intent to communicate and presupposed shared knowledge (which the linguist H. Paul Grice called the 'co-operation principle' and 'conversational implicature' respectively), has led pragmatics to develop into a highly interdisciplinary field of study which may focus either upon language itself as the 'grammaticalization' of communication, or upon human communication more generally of which language is only a part.[25] Whether broadly or narrowly conceived, pragmatic linguists study human interaction and relating through speech, which Edna Roger has memorably likened to 'the metaphor of the dance … movement, rhythm, coming close, moving away…', and the aspects of speech upon which they focus are those which incorporate the social and dialogical dimensions of communication such as 'deixis, implicature, presupposition, speech acts, conversational interaction'.[26] This is a linguistic philosophy of embodiment therefore, which understands language to be used by speakers who are themselves located in specific spatio-temporal contexts (hence the term 'deixis', which refers to those words such as 'here' and 'now', 'this' and 'that', whose meaning is dependent upon the speaker's embodied position in time and space) and which sees language as part of human relationship in general: 'we do not relate and then talk, but relate in talk'.[27] Pragmatics contests the tendency of classical linguistics to break language into fragments, preferring to see it as process and conversation. As talk is interactive and processive, discourse and conversation analysis have shown the way in which the meaning of a word or phrase can only be analysed within the sentence, and the sentence within the broader structure of conversation, in which speech is based upon shared knowledge and a speaker's implicit desire to collaborate with his or her interlocutors.

A pragmatic reading of Christian revelation of the Word as communicative act not only sets that act in a specific spatio-temporal context (what we have referred to above as the 'perlocutionary' dimension), but also, crucially, points out that the divine Word which is spoken cannot be seen as a single, atomic unit, self-sustaining and complete in itself, but rather must be thought of as a dynamic process: that is, as the communication of a *conversation*. This does not replace the language of address, but understands that address to be itself a form of divine–human conversation. It is to redefine a hermeneutical ontology of address therefore as a hermeneutical ontology of speech-in-relation, by which we are addressed. If, as we have argued, Jakobson's addresser and addressee become one in the message, then the 'voices' of both are reduplicated in the message in a structure of identity and difference. Thus the Father can speak with the Son and the Son with the Father, and the Son, in whom the Father dwells, can speak with us, through the Spirit of the Father and the Son who dwells in us. This is to place 'conversation', and therefore social, and interpersonal, relation at the heart of our formula of revelation. And this mutual indwelling of two voices, one divine and one human, in Christ, who is the Word-as-speech, creates a common ground, a place of speech and hence of relation, between God and his people.

Divine conversations

Old Testament

The Hebrew Scriptures are constructed of different forms of discourse which give witness through doxology and praise, prophecy and remembrance to Israel's encounter with Yahweh. A number of the oldest texts, such as 'the Song of the Sea' (Ex. 15.1–19), are liturgical in origin and are communal recollections of God's saving action for his people. The historical narratives speak of divine election and covenant, while the prophets are 'mandated' individuals whose voices have been overwhelmed by the divine voice, warning Israel and summoning her back to fidelity to God. The voice of the psalmist speaks intimately to God, praising him, calling out to him or lamenting Israel's failings before his face. Language itself, both divine and human, is a significant theme in the Old Testament, which 'does not accent thought or concept or idea, but characteristically *speech*', and is extensively governed by the divine *fiat* of the Genesis creation narrative.[28] Gen. 1.1–2.4 establishes the generative power of God's word, which later tradition called 'creation out of nothing', signifying that this was neither emanation nor a 'mythically understood manifestation of the divine nature and its power'.[29] Here the word does not perform a signifying function, pointing to something beyond itself, but itself embodies action, so that 'God's act is understood as God's word, which is only possible since God's word is an efficacious word (*wirksames Wort*), that is, act'.[30] This *acte linguistique institutif d'existence* is rapidly followed and accentuated by a further *acte linguistique de dénomination*, in which God names those things which he has called into being, thus giving order to existence, or rather drawing out from existence its intrinsic knowable structure.[31] Among all of creation, humankind is to an extent set apart by the fact that we are created in God's 'likeness'. The human act of naming animals reported in Genesis shows that human speech participates to a degree in the originary power of divine speech.[32] Indeed, we are told that human language is a divine gift, and that it has something of the effective power of action of divine speech, since 'death and life are in the power of the tongue'.[33] So central is the linguistic function to human existence, that the word can be viewed as 'an effective "extension" of the personality', with binding power; once Isaac has blessed Jacob, the blessing cannot be withdrawn (Gen. 27.33–40).[34] The priority of the linguistic sign over its referent is shown also in the pronouncing of the name of God, either in blessing or in cultic acts of 'calling upon' God's name; and it is this too which underlies the divine prohibition against taking the Lord's name in vain.[35] Additionally, for a name to be forgotten or expunged is synonymous with death, while to have the name preserved for ever is to enjoy life everlasting.[36] Numerous etymologies in the Old Testament concerning personal names and the names of places constitute a kind of 'symbolic recharging', or the reintegration of places and people into the divine narrative, which is the cycle of linguistically founded existence.[37]

In the Exodus account of the divine theophany on Mt Sinai, and giving of the Decalogue to humanity however, we see a shift from a theology of creation to a covenantal theology of ethical action, in which the world God has created is 'to be transformed'.[38] But still the word of God remains one of the primary continuities between these two dimensions, since it is still creative and efficacious in the covenantal context of prophecy and address:

> For as the rain and the snow come down from heaven, and do not return there until they have watered the earth, making it bring forth and sprout, giving seed to the sower and bread to the eater, so shall my word be that goes out from my mouth; it shall not return to me empty, but it shall accomplish that which I purpose, and succeed in the thing for which I sent it. (Isa. 55.11)[39]

Among all the diverse kinds of speech that attest to God's covenantal action in the world, it is prophecy which represents the intersection of human and divine speech, and, as with the occurrence of a vision at the commissioning of Isaiah and Ezekiel, it is often announced by a point of transition from one to the other. For Jeremiah, on the other hand, there is no initial vision and his commissioning takes place in the form of an address by God, leading to an exchange in which, in Peter Neumann's phrase, 'the event of the word' (*Wortereignis*) has become 'dialogue' (*Zwiegespräch*), in which the prophet protests his inadequacy to fulfil the task appointed him.[40] The brief and fragmentary 'conversation' which occurs between the prophet and God stands outside the usual genres of prophetic speech, such as imprecation, accounts, exhortation and lament.[41] And the prophet appears himself to be sufficiently empowered by God's word to sustain a dialogue with God, who addresses him directly by name.[42] Something of this exceptional agency may also be reflected in the fact that it is Jeremiah and not God who is the subject of the verbs which describe the exercise of power 'over nations'.[43]

The specific interactive character of the calling of Jeremiah looks back to the primary model of Moses' own commissioning; indeed, the Jeremiah text is likely to recall the Mosaic tradition.[44] It is Moses to whom God reveals his covenant on Mount. Sinai in the central theophany of the Old Testament, and the role of Moses as receiver of God's covenantal revelation gives him a key position in the narrative of the people of God, which anticipates the revelation of God to his creation in the person of Jesus Christ. The theophany begins with God calling Moses twice by name, eliciting the response: 'Here am I'.[45] God then tells Moses that he must not come near and must take off his shoes as he is standing on 'holy ground'. This is the first occurrence of the word 'holy' (*qadeš*) in the Old Testament, and it brings Moses to a new understanding of the world in which he lives. God then names himself for the first time to Moses as 'the God of your father, the God of Abraham, the God of Isaac, and the God of Jacob', thereby bringing Moses to a new understanding of who he himself is. At this point Moses is overcome and hides his face, 'for he was afraid to look at God'. God's response is to speak of his own compassion for Moses' people, and to tell Moses that he has heard their cry, knows their sufferings and has come to deliver them from their taskmasters.[46] God then commissions him 'to bring my people, the Israelites, out of Egypt', but Moses responds with protestations of self-doubt so that God assures him that he will be with him.[47] When Moses asks him what he should say if the people ask the name of God, the second act of naming takes place, when God says: 'I am who I am. . . Say this to the people: "I am has sent me to you"', followed quickly by the third: 'Say this to the people of Israel, "The Lord [YHVH], the God of your fathers, the God of Abraham, the God of Isaac, and the God of Jacob, has sent me to you": this is my name for ever, and thus I am to be remembered throughout all generations'.[48] Despite God's graphic description of the despoiling of the Egyptians, Moses remains uncertain that he will be believed so that God gives him the miraculous powers of the three signs of transformation.[49] When Moses then objects that he lacks eloquence, and encourages God to send someone else, God becomes angry and tells him that his brother Aaron 'shall be a mouth' for him, thus adding yet another dimension to the historical process of divine envoicing or 'speaking-in'.[50]

In this Exodus passage which narrates Moses' struggle for submission to the creative will of God, we can note the emergence of a second paradigm of speech to complement the primary model of address, which is that of God's utterances to Israel, summoning his prophets and people to listen to him. The commissioning narrative of Moses is rich with the kind of autonomous dialogue of which we have a fragmentary glimpse in the commissioning of Jeremiah, and which can properly be designated as 'conversation'. This implies a linguistic exchange between two speakers, who, whatever their differing social standing, have an acknowledged equality of speech agency. The content of the speech event is thus determined by the interchange between them. This is no longer the addressor, message, addressee formula of Jakobson therefore but rather the 'meaning in interaction' of conversation analysis, where the semiotics of speech is not determined by the communicative intentionality of a speaker to a listener but is rather arrived at by a dialogical mechanism which is processive and negotiated, drawing the addressor and addressee into a dynamic relationship. Moses' resistance to his commissioning, like that of Jeremiah, opens up a conversational moment in the speech interaction of commissioner and commissioned, since once the commission is accepted, the prophet's speech will be assumed into God's own word. It is appropriate to note here however, that Moses and God do not speak as equals: God commands and Moses briefly resists. The invitation to both Moses (and Jeremiah) to 'converse' with God leads to Jeremiah's recognition of the subversion of his own speech ('I do not know how to speak. . .') and Moses' statement that he is 'not eloquent' but 'slow of speech'.[51] Both are brought to the limits of their own human speech by this summons to 'conversation' with God. And so this is not conversation in the fullest sense, which implies mutuality and a free indeterminacy of communication, enriched with mutual delight. But it stands nevertheless between the sacred genres of prophetic discourse, where the human is absorbed into the divine voice, and the full mutuality of Son, Spirit and Father that is to come.

The theophany on Mount Sinai is Moses' second 'conversation' with the God of his fathers, and here we can note the use of the particular verbal form *dabar 'im*, or 'speaking with', to designate this exceptional form of divine–human speaking. This phrase needs to be distinguished from the more common *dabar 'el* and *dabar l*ᵉ ('speaking to'), which is the language of address. On each of the eight occasions when the verbal phrase *dabar 'im* is used of Moses, the context is the granting of the Decalogue on Mount Sinai.[52] But at the same time, God's self-revelation to Moses as a 'speaking with' is firmly set within the communal context of God's address to the Israelites, whom he has called to be 'a priestly kingdom and a holy nation'.[53] Though dialogical therefore, this is not a closed form of speech. God's declaration to Moses marks the first occurrence of the term: '"I am going to come to you in a dense cloud, in order that the people may hear when I speak with you (*dabar 'im*) and so trust you ever after"'.[54] Moses leads the people to the mountain, where there is 'thunder and lightning' and 'thick cloud'. As the blast of the trumpet grew louder, we are told that 'Moses would speak and God would answer him in thunder'.[55] Here the ambiguity in the Masoretic text of *qōl* as both 'thunder' and 'voice' conveys the quite exceptional character of God's 'speaking with' Moses.[56] Following the imparting of the Decalogue, the people, who have witnessed the 'conversation' between Moses and God with all its dramatic and cosmic accompaniments, tell Moses that they do not wish to be drawn into this same experience: '"you speak to us (*dabar 'im*), and we will listen; but do not let God speak to us (*dabar 'im*), or we will die"'.[57] Such an equality of speech with God, or immediacy of revelation, would indeed be death.[58] In Deut. 5.4–5 and 9.10, where Moses reminds the people that God spoke with them (*dabar 'im*) face to face, with himself standing between them and God, we can see that 'speaking with' specifically refers to Moses' mediatory role.[59]

The 'conversation' between God and Moses, which was first initiated by a process of divine naming at the burning bush, stands at the very centre of the covenantal theology of the Old Testament. It marks the historical moment when God gave the Decalogue, which is 'the law of a redeemed people', granted within the narrative context of exile and liberation.[60] That God chooses to locate his people within the moral order is a sign of election, covenant and promise. But that the covenant was given through one man, who was himself drawn into an exceptional and gracious 'speaking with' God, shows the centrality not just of language, but of speech itself as a medium of *social relation*, in the continuing drama of God's faithfulness to his people.

New Testament

The life of Jesus has been described as a life of prayer.[61] Formal Jewish prayer at the time of Jesus included morning and evening prayer, as well as the *Schemone Ezre* (the '18 Prayer') with its many blessings of God, which was prayed in the afternoon.[62] Eating and drinking were also attended by a short prayer, and additional prayers were said or sung at festivals. Many natural events were greeted with a short act of praise, as were significant social occasions such as circumcision, marriage and death. In addition, the cult of the temple and the synagogue involved many frequent acts of prayer, especially on feast days, and each day closed with a night prayer.[63] The New Testament records that Jesus followed the different kinds of prayer which defined the Jewish life of godliness in his own daily life, and in his life together with his disciples.[64] In addition, there are numerous Gospel accounts of Jesus' free or spontaneous prayer, before and after miracles, on the occasion of significant events, such as his baptism, and when confronted with temptation. These prayers are either of an intercessory kind or they express Jesus' gratitude to the Father, and they are generally preceded by the appellation 'abba'. From the perspective of trinitarian 'conversation', it is these passages which shall be of most interest to us.

The New Testament account shows that Jesus speaks in a multiplicity of ways, engaging differently with the Pharisees, the crowds and his disciples. One of these ways of speaking is with the Father himself, where the outline of a divine 'conversation' can be discerned, which is the speaking of God with God. In the following analysis we shall argue that these occasions come at crucial moments in the narrative of the unfolding drama of the Trinity, and they mark the nodal points of the inner relations of the Trinity, worked out in time and space and human history. This speech of God with God in the Gospels, which is the construction of 'a common social reality' attended by shared knowledge and deixic points of reference, can only offer a glimpse of the full, perfect and eternal communion of the divine Persons. That multiple dialogue always remains in itself unheard, but fragments come to our ears in the historical realizations narrated in the Gospel record.

'You are my Son, the Beloved; with you I am well pleased'

There are three occasions in the New Testament when the Father speaks with the Son: at the baptism of Jesus, at the transfiguration and when Jesus is troubled by the thought of his own imminent death. In the Synoptic tradition, the baptism of Jesus marks the beginning of his ministry, when John recognizes in him the successor who is to baptize in the Holy Spirit.[65] It represents a significant stage in the transition from the old dispensation to the new. The consummation of the ministry of John is perhaps indicated in the fact that the baptism of Jesus takes place after the people have been baptized (more directly in Luke, but still implicitly so in Matthew and Mark).[66] Although Jesus offers himself for baptism by John in Matt. 3.15, there is no suggestion that John himself is in any sense agent of the descent of the Spirit upon Jesus as he emerges from the water.[67] But the descent of the Spirit underlines that while John baptizes with water, Jesus will baptize with the Holy Spirit and with fire.[68] The 'opening' of the heavens which accompanied the descent of the Spirit is an apocalyptic sign and is 'conventional language in visions and epiphanies for the divine origin of what (who) is then to make its (his) appearance as God's representative'.[69] The descent of the dove has no typically apocalyptic associations however, although it may recall the return of the dove to Noah after the flood (Gen. 8), or alternatively may simply be a reference to the way that a dove descends to earth.[70] The Lucan narrative has the Spirit descending 'bodily in the form of a dove', which may suggest that the Spirit has somehow been drawn sympathetically into the process of incarnation, and can be read perhaps as a type of indirect *communicatio idiomatum*.[71]

A central theme for all three Synoptic writers is the occurrence of the divine voice accompanying the anointing with the Spirit.[72] In Luke and Mark, the voice says 'You are my Son, the Beloved; with you I am well pleased', while Matthew turns this second person address into a proclamation: 'This is my Son, the Beloved, with whom I am well pleased'.[73] Two Old Testament passages which highlight adoption into a filial relationship with God on the one hand (Ps. 2.7) and the 'servant of God' theme on the other (Isa. 42.1), form the background to this declaration.[74] But it is the latter which is more important, since it is closer to the wording of the

Synoptics (and shares the third person form of Matthew).[75] The theme is one of intense and intimate affirmation in a moment of divine election, expressed in the bestowing of the spirit upon God's servant.[76] But neither Ps. 2.7 nor Isa. 42.1 can account fully for the Synoptic view of the baptism of Jesus, which transcends both the notion of adoption into filial relationship with God and the motif of the servant of God who is acceptable to him. Within the dynamic of direct divine address, we can see here an entirely new departure in the Father's recognition and affirmation of the sonship of Jesus. In the Septuagint, the phrase *eudokêsa en* often has the sense of 'to take pleasure or delight in', translating the Hebrew verb *rāṣāh*.[77] The Greek term also has a volitional and social force however, and can mean 'consent' as well as conveying the sense of 'election'.[78] In the Synoptic passages narrating the baptism of Jesus, these elements richly combine. It is precisely the Father's *spoken* affirmation of his Son, enacting his relational and affective 'delighting in', which begins the construction of an historical and social reality between Father and Son based upon election and consensus.[79]

'This is my Son, my Chosen'

The transfiguration of Jesus also occurs in the Synoptic Gospels, but not in John, where it may not have been judged to sit well with the emphasis upon glory which characterizes the later sections of that Gospel. The transfiguration accounts look back not only to the baptism of Jesus but also to the theophany to Moses on Mount Sinai. The glory of the Lord rested on Sinai for six days, and then the voice spoke to Moses on the seventh day.[80] This typology may underlie the opening of the transfiguration accounts in Mark and Matthew, which states that it occurred after six days (although Luke prefers eight days).[81] Similarly, Jesus' three companions on Mount Tabor – Peter, James and John – may match Aaron, Nadab and Abihu, who were Moses' three companions on Mount Sinai. The recapitulation of Ex. 24 is maintained in Matthew's statement that Jesus' 'face shone like the sun', recalling Moses' shining face when he descended to the people from Sinai.[82] However, according to Luke 9.31, Moses himself speaks with Jesus about his forthcoming 'departure' from Jerusalem, together with Elijah, suggesting that Jesus fulfils both the Law and the Prophets.[83] If the voice that speaks from the cloud recalls Sinai, then the words the Father speaks to the Son evoke the baptism of Jesus. Matthew and Mark at this point have 'This is my Son, the Beloved', to which Matthew further adds 'with him I am well pleased', while Luke has 'This is my Son, my Chosen'.[84] Luke's preferred word *eklelegmenos* (chosen, elected) recalls the use of *eklektos* in the Septuagint to describe Moses, David and the suffering servant.[85] The final admonition to 'listen to him', recorded by all three Synoptic writers, also recalls Moses' warning to the people that they should heed the words of the new prophet.[86]

The transfiguration occurs at a crucial point in the development of the Gospel narrative in that it immediately follows Peter's confession of the messiahship of Jesus, eliciting Jesus' foretelling of his own death and resurrection and the consequences of discipleship in his name.[87] The revealing of the glory of Jesus by his Father in the presence of the disciples points back to the divine theophany at the baptism of Jesus but it is a fore-taste too of the supreme affirmation that is to come in Jerusalem when the Father will raise the Son from the dead. The proleptic character of this peri-cope is highlighted by the disciples' confusion and Peter's inappropriate advice that they should build booths or tents for the heavenly three. It is only after the resurrection and the glorification of Jesus that they will understand the significance of the Father's repeated affirmation of the Son.

'Father, I thank you for having heard me'

The raising of Lazarus occurs in the Fourth Gospel and not in the Synoptic tradition, although both Mark and Luke record other instances in which Jesus brings the dead to life.[88] The Lazarus pericope narrates the last of Jesus' miraculous signs and contains elements which seem in some degree to anticipate the passion of Christ; on being informed by Mary and Martha of the illness of their brother Lazarus, Jesus says to them: 'This illness does not lead to death; rather it is for God's glory, so that the Son of God may be glorified through it'.[89] Within the semantics of the Fourth Gospel, the term 'glorified' is specifically suggestive of Jesus' death and resurrection, and he continues by declaring that he is 'the resurrection and the life' and that 'Those who believe in me, even though they die, will live, and everyone who lives and believes in me will never die'.[90]

The narrative relates that when Jesus arrived at the tomb, from where the stone had been removed, he looked upward and said: 'Father, I thank you for having heard me. I knew that you always hear me, but I have said this for the sake of the crowd standing here, so that they may believe that you sent me' (John 11.41–42). At this point, petitionary prayer, which is the most common form of Jesus' prayer, becomes a prayer of thanks, since the Father has 'heard' the Son before the Son has actually spoken.[91] Jesus' statement to the Father that he has spoken only for the sake of the people underlines both the public character of the trinitarian speech, as revelation, and the fact that it is only an historical representation or enactment of the 'silent' and ideal speech between the Persons to which Jesus at this point refers.[92] The raising to life of Lazarus, still bound in cloth, at the prompting of Jesus' call to him concludes the pericope and again underlines the extent to which the resurrection of Jesus himself is proleptically present in this narrative of a return to life. Jesus' final words: 'Unbind him, and let him go' anticipate Jesus' own freeing from the 'linen clothes' which are left in his own tomb when he is risen into glory.[93]

'Father, glorify your name'

The account of the raising of Lazarus needs to be taken with the Johannine passage in which Jesus is troubled by the thought of his imminent death, which comes in the following chapter.[94] This pericope also appears to parallel in some degree the Synoptic accounts of the transfiguration of Jesus in that it is placed after Jesus' triumphal entry into Jerusalem, at a point when he is experiencing distress at the thought of the events to come in Jerusalem, and when the significance of his life and death is being both proclaimed and challenged. Echoing the Lazarus passage, this pericope also begins with Jesus' troubled state. But on this occasion, Jesus shows a certain indecisiveness as to what he should say to the Father. This lack of certainty is itself indicative of the potential of his imminent suffering and death to disturb his relationship with the Father. But Jesus immediately continues: 'And what should I say? Father, save me from this hour? No, it is for this reason that I have come to this hour. Father, glorify your name.'[95] Following this struggle and prayer, a voice comes from heaven, which some hear as thunder and others as an angelic voice, saying 'I have glorified it, and I will glorify it again.'[96] The reference to thunder recalls again the Mosaic inheritance, as does the cloud that will finally descend upon them.[97] The first reference to glorification here must be taken in the sense of Jesus' life up to the present point. He has lived a life of service to the Father, and has worked his will through his many signs and teachings. Glorification in this sense can be taken together with passages such as John 17.4, for instance, where Jesus clearly understands his ministry to be precisely for the glorification of God, and of his name: 'I glorified you on earth by finishing the work that you gave me to do.'[98] The second reference to glorification then becomes a promise of Jesus' death and resurrection. This is drawn out in the continuation of this passage, when Jesus tells the people, 'Now is the judgment of this world; now the ruler of this world will be driven out. And I, when I am lifted up from the earth, will draw all people to myself.'[99] The Greek words for 'lifted up' and for 'glorify' also occur in a line which is crucial for our understanding of the suffering servant at LXX Isa. 52.13, where we read: 'See, my servant shall prosper; he shall be exalted and lifted up, and shall be very high'.[100]

The exchange between the Father and the Son at this point sums up the highly complex theme in the Fourth Gospel between the Father's glory, the glory of the Son and their relation. We can identify three senses of the glory of the Son in play throughout the Gospel. In the first place, the Son has possessed glory from the beginning, as the Logos who 'was with God' and who 'was God' (John 1.1), as we see in John 17.5: 'So now, Father, glorify me in your own presence with the glory I had in your presence before the world existed'.[101] This is the glory of God with God prior to the incarnation. But secondly, the incarnate Son manifests glory through his works, such as the miracle of Cana: 'Jesus did this, the first of his signs, in Cana of Galilee, and revealed his glory'.[102] Jesus is at pains to attribute the glory of his works to God however, as when he says 'if I glorify myself, my glory is nothing. It is my Father who glorifies me' and 'those who speak on their own seek their own glory; but the one who seeks the glory of him who sent him is true and there is nothing false in him'.[103] Here Jesus is unequivocally locating the agency of glorification in the Father.[104] From the raising of Lazarus onwards however, we begin to see more clearly the distinction between our second glory, which is the glory of the incarnate Christ through his works, and our third glory, which is the glorification of Christ through his death and resurrection. We see this not only proleptically in the reference to the glorification of Jesus in the Lazarus narrative, and in the association of 'glorified' and 'lifted up' of John 12.31–32, but it is apparent also in passages such as 'when Jesus was glorified, they remembered that these things had been written of him and had been done to him' and 'as yet there was no Spirit, because Jesus was not yet glorified'.[105] This third sense of glory is the making present, or revealing, of our first type, which was the glory Jesus had in the presence of God 'before the world existed'.[106] Both the Lazarus narrative and the account of Jesus' concern at his own death mark a crucial stage then in the *making public* of Jesus' first glory, from his pre-existence, which has been only glimpsed in the miracle stories but which, with his death and resurrection, will become more fully manifest. Following the voice from heaven, which some heard as thunder and others took to be the voice of an angel, Jesus says to the people, 'This voice has come for your sake, not for mine'.[107] He thus repeats the statement he made in the Lazarus story where he was referring not to the Father's words but to his own words to the Father. But in both cases there is an attempt to underline the dynamic of revelation that is at work in the occurrence of the divine speech, in which firstly the Son speaks with the Father and, secondly, both Father and Son speak with one another.

As the hour of the Son of man's glorification draws nearer, we can see a subtle shift in agency. Now Jesus refers to his miraculous works in terms not of his glorification through God, but of his own glorification of the Father: 'I glorified you on earth by finishing the work that you gave me to do . . . '.[108] His equality with the Father comes more clearly to the fore: 'Father, the hour has come; glorify your Son so that your Son may glorify you'.[109] At the same time, Jesus assumes a greater agency with respect to the church, stating, 'I will do whatever you ask in my name, so that the Father may be glorified in the Son' and 'The glory that you have given me I have given them, so that they may be one as we are one'.[110] The profound reciprocity of Son and Father, one in the unity of glory but two in the bestowal of glory, is captured in the lines preceding the giving of the new commandment: 'Now the Son of Man has been glorified, and God has revealed his glory in him. If God has revealed his glory in him, God will also glorify him in himself and will glorify him at once.'[111]

'My Father, if it is possible, let this cup pass from me; yet not what I want but what you want'

In all three Synoptic Gospels, the account of Jesus' prayer in the garden of Gethsemane follows the last supper and Jesus' prophecy that Peter shall deny him three times. The events in the garden show the clear gulf between Jesus and his disciples, reinforcing the uniqueness of Jesus' destiny and what will come to be seen as the total dependence of the church upon him.[112] In Mark and Matthew the accompanying disciples are named as Peter, James and John, all of whom have protested that they would suffer with their Lord.[113] Peter had protested at Jesus' prophecy that all would desert him, proclaiming: 'Even though all become deserters, I shall not' and 'Even though I must die with you, I will not deny you'.[114] James and John, the sons of Zebedee, also pronounced themselves able to share 'the cup' that Jesus was to drink.[115] When Jesus breaks off his prayer on three occasions to chide his sleeping disciples, Peter's threefold denial of Jesus is foreshadowed which Jesus himself has predicted in the preceding passage.[116] The slumber of the disciples recalls the need for an eschatological vigilance, which Jesus preached at Mark 13.32–37, and it is this which may underlie the note of great urgency in his admonishing of Peter, James and John.

The language used to convey Jesus' troubled state is unusually emphatic, and it recalls Ps. 116.2: 'The snares of death encompassed me; the pangs of Sheol laid hold on me; I suffered distress and anguish.'[117] The symbolism of the passage shows that his distress is caused not by his fear of physical suffering as such but by the weight of the coming alienation from God. From the point at which Jesus accepted baptism from John, it was clear that he would take upon himself the burden of human sin as alienation from God. It is this that is implied in the word 'cup' (*potêrion*) which is the Old Testament 'cup of staggering' or 'cup of wrath' that God in his anger gives his errant people to drink.[118] The prayer of Jesus in the garden of Gethsemane represents a point of emotional and physical intensity, when for Jesus 'the full meaning of his submission to the Father confronted him with its immediacy'.[119] The bond with his disciples seems unsustainable, and all his attention is focused upon the Father, from whom he first petitions release from his destiny, and to whose will he then accedes.

'My God, my God, why have you forsaken me?'

The cry of dereliction on the cross appears in a sense to follow on from Jesus' prayer in Gethsemane. Once again it represents an extreme condition, not this time fear of what is to come, but a lament as to the loss of God which is now complete. If in the former prayer Jesus was weighed down with a sense of the alienation from God that he was to undergo, then in the

cry of dereliction we hear his grief at the cessation of 'conversation' and the
present absence of God to his soul. These last words of Jesus on the cross,
followed by a 'loud cry', are common to the Matthean and Marcan traditions (Mark 15.34–37; Matt. 27.46–50), but are replaced in Luke by the
words: 'Father, into your hands I commend my spirit' (23.46). The former
is a quotation from Ps. 22.1 and the latter from Ps. 31.5. Mark and Matthew
cite what they believed to be the actual words of Jesus, before giving a
Greek translation. In Matthew the address to God is in Hebrew, while the
difficult question 'Why have you forsaken me?' is in the more homely
Aramaic. Mark renders the Hebrew 'Eli' as the Aramaic 'Eloi'. The appellation 'Eli' and its Aramaic variant may refer to the merciful rather than the
strict God. This is its sense at Num. 12.13 and Ps. 118.27.[120] The passage
quoted from Ps. 31.5 in Luke was used as a form of night prayer, in which
the speaker 'delivered himself to the divine mercy'.[121]

If, as we have seen, the points at which Jesus addresses the Father
directly and most personally have been at his greatest times of trial, not
when confronted with the need to perform a miracle but rather with the
struggle within himself, then the Marcan and Matthean cry of dereliction
represents the supreme culmination of their discourse. The issue in each
case is the relationship between the Son and the Father, and the Son's total
acceptance of the Father's will. In the Johannine passage (John 12.27–28),
Jesus' conflicting feelings never attain actual expression; his final words
are 'Father, glorify your name'. It is within this environment of anticipated
glory that his words are answered by a voice from heaven, saying 'I have
glorified it, and I will glorify it again'. In the Gethsemane pericope, there is
some ambiguity as to whether Jesus is answered or not, for the angel can
be construed as a divine response in the variant passage included by Luke.
But the cry of dereliction emphatically receives no such answer. It is Jesus'
first address to the Father without the intimate 'abba', and his dying
words, spoken as God with God, are overheard and misinterpreted by the
men at the foot of the cross, who think that he is calling upon Elijah. Here
then Jesus' human speaking is annihilated, and his 'conversation' with the
Father is at its end.

The cry of dereliction can be said both to signal the silence of God and to
be its cause, since Jesus' last words remain unanswered. God's silence is
richly significant in the Old Testament and takes different forms.[122] In
Isaiah, for instance, God's silence is identified with his wrath towards
Israel: 'Why do you keep silent and punish us so severely?'.[123] The Psalmist
pleads with God not to 'remain silent' and far away, for if God is silent,
then he may die.[124] Death itself is imaged as silence.[125] The silence of the
Father in the context of the cross suggests therefore that Christ's experience of abandonment is an extension of the 'cup of wrath' metaphor of
Gethsemane. But we find a further semiotics of divine silence in the distinction between God 'falling silent', as an expression of his anger and
removal of his favour within a specific situation, and the possibility that

God will withdraw his speech altogether, thus annulling his original creative act. Such a silence, as Job knows, would mean cosmic annihilation: 'If he should take back his spirit to himself, and gather to himself his breath, all flesh would perish together, and all mortals return to dust'.[126] The threat that God's silence as passing wrath might become cosmic silence, and thus the wholesale destruction of all that is, is intrinsic to the eschatological terror of the later prophets, who form such an important element in the apocalyptic background to the story of Jesus. In the context of Jesus' speaking relation with God, we must say then that the Son experiences in his abandonment both the divine silence which signals personal death and the silence which speaks cosmic annihilation.[127] As a withdrawal of his Spirit, the silence of God is further to be thought of in pneumatological terms. The Spirit is the animating presence of God on earth, and in humanity, and it is the circulation of the divine life between Father and Son.[128] The breaking of the conscious flow between Father and Son is therefore an interiorization of their mutual loss within the Spirit, refigured now as divine silence. The silence of God, which is the kenosis of the Spirit, is God's own loving embrace of the otherness that he willed in the creation, and which he now takes within himself. By assuming difference from himself into himself as Spirit-silence, the Father overwhelms and transforms the human speaking of his Son, who is the Word through whom all things were made, and so renews and redeems the order of creation.[129]

'Abba! Father!'

As the principle of a human speech that is reordered as a speaking with God in God, the Spirit is communicated to the world from within the trinitarian silence that is the abandonment of the Cross. In the Gospel of John the coming of the Spirit is linked with the 'glorification' or resurrection of Jesus.[130] It is only because Jesus shall leave the world that the Spirit can come.[131] The role of the Spirit-Paraclete who is to come is to 'testify' to Jesus as the 'Spirit of Truth'.[132] The Holy Spirit will teach the disciples everything and will remind them of all that Jesus has said.[133] The Spirit-Paraclete will guide them 'into all the truth':

> for he will not speak on his own, but will speak whatever he hears, and he will declare to you the things that are to come. He will glorify me, because he will take what is mine and declare it to you. All that the Father has is mine. For this reason I said that he will take what is mine and declare it to you.[134]

Passages such as these establish the Spirit as a movement of fullness and as agent of a new kind of speech, testifying to Jesus, teaching the truth about him, declaring what is his and glorifying him. This is a speech agency which is exercised perichoretically in relation with the other Persons of the

Trinity ('he will not speak on his own, but will speak whatever he hears'). Just as it fails to recognize the Son, the world cannot receive the Spirit-Paraclete, 'because it neither sees nor knows him', but he will abide with the followers of Jesus, and he will be in them.[135] The Spirit is indeed like the breath that forms another's voice, which Jesus breathes upon his disciples.[136] By virtue of its indwelling in the other Persons of the Trinity on the one hand and in the church on the other, the Spirit represents the integration of human life into the fullness of the divine life, and the kinds of speaking of and to God which it prompts are the mark of our participation in the Sonship of Christ and our sharing in the divine speech.

Paul's discussion of life in the Spirit at Rom. 8.9–17 begins with the statement that the church lives 'in the Spirit', who gives 'life and peace', and not in the flesh.[137] It does so because the Spirit himself dwells in the church. This deeply trinitarian notion of mutual indwelling is supported by Paul's reference to the Holy Spirit as simultaneously the 'Spirit of Christ' and 'the Spirit of him who raised Jesus from the dead',[138] and it parallels the description of our baptism in the Spirit (1 Cor. 12.13) which is baptism into the burial and death of Christ, who 'was raised from the dead by the glory of the Father'.[139] The new life in the Spirit is one which puts to death 'the deeds of the body', manifesting also as a new distinctive kind of Christian speech which is 'bearing witness' when we cry 'Abba! Father!'.[140] This may be a reference to the Lord's prayer, but, importantly, it is not we who are the agents of speech at this point but the indwelling Spirit himself who bears witness 'with our spirit that we are children of God'.[141] In an extension of the theme of adoption, Gal. 4.4–7 states that since we have become the children of God, 'God has sent the Spirit of his Son into our hearts, crying, "Abba! Father!"'. So you are no longer a slave but a child, and if a child then also an heir, through God'. It is the Spirit that supports us in our weakness, when we do not 'know how to pray as we ought', since it intercedes for us 'with sighs too deep for words'. And in a figure that repeats the proclamations of Jesus that speech between himself and the Father is not actually necessary, Paul continues that the Father 'knows what is the mind of the Spirit', because the will of the Spirit and the Father are one.[142] Through the action of the Spirit therefore, the faithful too are drawn into a relation with the Father which transcends the need for words.

The Holy Spirit prompts us to speak to the Father with the Son in the words of a child of God, as heirs of God through and in the Son. In the Letter to the Ephesians the role of the Holy Spirit is richly explored in terms of both speech and understanding that is ordered to the divine. The Holy Spirit is linked with the praise of God's glory that follows upon the new life of redemption (1.12–14), the unifying Spirit gives both Jew and gentile access to the Father (2.18), the Spirit reveals the mystery of Christ to the holy apostles and prophets (3.5), the Spirit grounds the love and peace which is the unity of the church (4.2–4). The Spirit is grieved by dissension and evil talk and Christians are urged to say only 'what is useful for building up' (4.29–30), 'obscene, silly and vulgar talk' must be replaced with 'thanksgiving' (5.4), the 'empty words' of those who wish to deceive are to be eschewed (5.6), and the saints of Ephesus are to 'pray in the Spirit at all times in every prayer and supplication', and especially for the author himself so that a message may be given to him 'to make known with boldness the mystery of the gospel' (6.18–19). The theme of the new kind of pneumatic speech which extends through these verses reaches a climax in the motif of being 'filled with the Spirit' (in contrast with the inebriation of wine) as the Christians of Ephesus 'sing psalms and hymns and spiritual songs' amongst themselves, 'singing and making melody to the Lord' in their hearts, 'giving thanks to God the Father at all times and for everything in the name of our Lord Jesus Christ' (5.18–20). Here the envoicing of the Spirit finds expression as the overflow in song of love, praise and gratitude, which is the divinely given excess of what David Ford calls 'the singing self'. This is the 'logic of superabundance in the everyday life of a community', and as the voices of 'singing husbands and wives, singing parents and children, singing masters and slaves' harmonize together in the Spirit, they create 'a new vocal social space of community in song'.[143]

In the account of Pentecost from Acts, we find yet another aspect of pneumatic speech, or envoicing by the Spirit. The 'sound like the rush of a violent wind' that invades the room where the disciples are gathered, and the 'divided tongues, as of fire' are both suggestive of the presence of the Holy Spirit.[144] The disciples, who are filled with the Spirit, begin to speak in other languages, 'as the Spirit gave them ability', so that the 'devout Jews' who are present with them, who come from 'from every nation under heaven living in Jerusalem', are each able to understand their native tongue.[145] This glossolalia contrasts therefore with that described in 1 Cor. 12.3–14.2, where the understanding of what is being said equally requires a gift of the Spirit.[146] Immediately following the descent of the Spirit, Peter preaches to the crowd, reminding them of God's promise to pour out his Spirit 'upon all flesh'.[147]

The experience of Pentecost suggests therefore that just as the Spirit indwells the Christian, bringing the gift of prayer in the Son to the Father, as dialogue with the Trinity, so too the Spirit prompts that particular kind of Christian speech which is preaching, as dialogue with the world. To proclaim the Gospel is to speak in a way that allows the voice of Christ to emerge in our own voice, and to engage the listener in a divine dialogue. The 'voice' of the Spirit is the extension of the perichoretic speaking of the Trinity, as it is shared out and distributed among those who are caught up into the divine speech. It is the resonance of the multiple dialogue of the Trinity amongst those whom the Spirit unites in praise and thanksgiving through the harmonies of shared vocal spaces, and who, partaking in his body in unity with one another, know Jesus as their 'Lord'.[148]

Conclusion

We have argued throughout for the principle of the *personal* revelation of God to us in Jesus Christ, which is therefore, in David Cunningham's words, 'marked by all the beauty and the ambiguity inherent in any knowledge that we gain from another human being'.[149] As the deepest and most fundamental kind of knowing within our experience, personal knowing bears within it all the communicative elements of trust, affectivity, dependence and love, as well as speech and cognition.[150] To speak of Christ as personal revelation is also to acknowledge the narratives, and thus the historical particularities, in which the personhood of Christ is embedded. These were bound up with the failure of prophecy, the consolidation of the Roman Empire in the eastern Mediterranean regions, and the dramatic quickening of an apocalyptic expectation. In that unique environment the life of Jesus Christ emerged as a 'precise, historical pattern . . . which manifests God', as a life which 'becomes for ever the image of God, as a historically purposing and redemptive power and value'.[151] But the pragmatic linguists' emphasis upon *situation* as the unique placing in which any particular act of communication can take place must be paralleled with the pragmatic understanding of the word as part of a sentence, and the sentence as part of a discourse. The discourse that is the most originary form of language is *conversation*, or living and open-ended speech in which, while much is taken for granted as being already known and shared, the participants exercise a significant openness to one another: a listening that is not the mere imposition of one text upon another, but rather a participative learning and an acknowledgment. It is this that constitutes the imaging of the other within the dialogical character of language as such, entailing the act of recognition which, as we have argued, is fundamental to the possibility of kenotic affirmation.

This emphasis upon the divine word communicated to us in Jesus of Nazareth as living, trinitarian speech posits a deep problematic that underlies the Christian experience of revelation. Jesus belongs to past, present and future, all in a certain sense. The church's proclamation that the revelation is for the whole of humankind entails the recognition that the living Word has to become present again, and be heard again, by communities far removed in time and space from first-century Palestine. One of the key ways in which the voice of Christ is mediated is through the reading of the Bible, within the worshipping communities who profess his name, and the many para-scriptural kinds of Christian texts, from hagiography to homilies and modern films, which inform the Christian life. The chief setting for the transposition of the written word back into the spoken word which, for Paul Ricoeur, governs the sacred textualities of the Judaeo-Christian tradition, is the liturgical re-presentation of God-for-us in the eucharist.[152] Through the *epiklesis*, the Spirit plays a fundamental part in the eucharistic celebration, integrating the human voice into the ecstatic rhythms of divine speech: as witness, proclamation, prophecy, prayer and praise. There the Spirit serves not only as the principle of the full communication between Father and Son, as the breath that passes between them, shining forth as total exchange, transparency and love, but also as the principle of our own participation in the divine speaking, in the actuality of its historical manifestation.[153] The presence of the Spirit is the enabling power that unites the speaking of the faithful today with the speaking of Father and Son in the incarnation, and beyond that with the originary speech of God at the creation, by whose trinitarian Word all things were made and by whose silence and speaking all things have been redeemed.

The Phenomenology of Faith as Cognition

Denn auch das gehört zum wahren Wesen des Wortes: Nachfolge nur als einen von jedem Nachfolgenden selbst zu gehenden Gang möglich werden zu lassen. Ein wahres Wort lehrt und ermöglicht stets, den fremden Weg als unseren eigenen Gang zu gehen.

This too belongs to the true nature of the word: to allow the act of following after to become possible only as a process which each follower must go through himself. A true word teaches and will always enable us to proceed along a foreign way as our own pathway.

Eberhard Jüngel, *Gott als Geheimnis der Welt*

Faith begins with the awareness that we are being addressed in our own natural speech situation by the speaking of God with God which is revelation. The triadic speech of the Persons brings our ordinary ways of speaking to silence, and thus to a new kind of attentiveness or listening which can in turn become sacred speech, inspired by the Spirit and enlivened by the rhythms of the divine Word. Listening and speaking are the two pulsations of the Christian response to revelation. The one dictates the other, for speaking without listening is to fail to speak *with* the other, and listening without speaking is a failure to be drawn into the conversation that is the life of faith. In this section we shall argue that faith is to be understood as that kind of movement between silence and speaking, between attentiveness and affirmation, which marks our own responsivity to the revelation of God.

The structure of Christian revelation is formed around the divine initiative: a process in which God both speaks to us as 'the living Word' and listens, as the one who emptied himself for our sake. The contours of Christian faith follow the structure, form and content of the Christian revelation, and are ordered to its expression. Since the revelation is personal, the form of the cognition which is faith is likewise personal. Since the structure of revelation is dialectical, dialectic plays throughout this personal knowing, in its linguistic, cognitive and existential aspects. But the subjective and experiential dimension of faith will also be seen to be distinctly kenotic, finding its content and substance in the kenosis of radical discipleship, as a reflection of the divine and human decentring of self in the hypostatic union. Doctrine as the expression of Christian revelation both communicates the personhood of Christ to the understanding, although marked by dialectic, and, by regulating Christian faith as personal knowing, registers its authenticity.

The patterning of dialectical and kenotic cognition, which is personal in form and doctrinal in expression, yields an understanding of faith as *dialectical responsivity*. This is the outworking of faith as personal knowing through all the dimensions of the human person which are transformed by the new relationship with Christ which faith brings. This entails a dialectical refiguring of all the elements of our relatedness: intellectual cognition, emotional or feeling life, and the sense and experience of the body. We are changed by those whom we know, and to enter into faith, where the term of our knowing is the infinite Person of Christ, is to open ourselves to unforeseeable change and to the radical journeying which is the inner structure of discipleship. But a second and equally primary function of faith is exercised not in the first place with respect to Jesus as prior object of our faith but is expressed rather in terms of the new relation with others that faith engenders. If incarnation is structured around the twofold movement of self-dispossession, divine and human, then it calls forth an equivalent dispossession within us which is expressed as a compassionate movement towards others. The kenosis that opens between ourselves and Jesus, who is himself infinite kenosis, lays a claim to all our relations and to all possible relations. Indeed, it opens up a habitable space for all the innumerable others who are to be welcomed and loved. Here we can speak of a kind of 'deflected love', which opens out from within the dispossession of faith and our loving knowledge of Jesus, towards the host of unknown other selves for whom Jesus speaks and in whom we can discern his voice.[1] There is thus a two-way flow within faith: a transformative dynamic of ourselves in relation, which we have called dialectical responsivity, whereby our ordinary interpersonal cognitions are made strange in our relation with Christ, and an opening up of ourselves towards others where the transformation effected in us through our relation with Christ yields a new decentring and risking of self for the sake of the other.

In the sections which follow, we seek to identify the structure of faith as personal knowing in the light of the phenomenological paradigm of encounter which we outlined in Chapter Two. On the one hand, this allows us to set up significant continuities between our knowledge of Christ in faith and our encounter with other persons. At every point however, we have to recognize the way in which the language and categories of interpersonal relations are radicalized and transcended by the infinity of Christ's personhood. That divine excess is marked by the identity of recognition and affirmation which characterizes faith (which in ordinary knowing are held apart), by the universality of Christ's world-centredness (which is otherwise limited and contingent), by the inexhaustible character of the kenotic attractiveness of Christ as goodness, and by the continuity of his presence through history in tradition. Whereas in Chapter Two our intention was to outline the phenomenological ground of the intentionality of consciousness which is compassion, in this chapter we are not concerned with the compassionate engagement of the self with Christ as such. Although this is a legitimate aspect of the life of faith which, in certain historical periods – principally the thirteenth and fourteenth centuries – has come into cultural prominence, faith is characterized more generally as recognition–affirmation of who Christ is for us and for the world. In our present discussion we emphasize compassion towards others as a primary *expression* of faith, through which – by the transformation which is integral to all human relating – we participate in and are conformed to the trinitarian self-communication.

Faith as personal knowing

The paradigm case for the emergence of faith as personal knowing and its expression as the following of discipleship is the pericope of 'Peter's declaration', recorded in its fullest form in the Matt. 16.13–20.[2] This passage occurs at the end of Jesus' mission in Galilee and marks an intensification of his relationship with his disciples before his entry into Jerusalem, where he will undergo his Passion. For all three evangelists, the passage is immediately followed by an account of the nature of discipleship with its commitments to a public and self-risking ministry of witness, and then by an account of the transfiguration, whereby the divine sonship of Christ is reaffirmed by the Father and made publicly accessible to Peter, James and John.

It is Jesus himself who initiates the exchange, and when he asks the disciples 'Who do people say that the Son of Man is?',[3] they reply: 'Some say John the Baptist, but others Elijah, and still others Jeremiah, or one of the prophets'.[4] These suggestions reflect alternative readings of his identity within the religious framework of the day, contrasting with the secularist view that Jesus was merely 'the carpenter's son' on the one hand and the new dramatic possibility that he was the Son of God on the other.[5] Jesus seems dissatisfied with these answers and asks them directly, 'But who do you say that I am?', where the emphatic form of 'you' used here (Gr: Ὑμεῖς) sets up an opposition between 'the people' (Gr: οἱ ἄνθρωποι; cf. Luke 9.18: οἱ ὄχλοι) and Jesus' disciples, who are themselves to be set apart by their response to his question.[6] Simon Peter answers, '"You are the Messiah, the Son of the living God"', which delights Jesus, for he continues: '"Blessed are you, Simon son of Jonah! For flesh and blood has not revealed this to you, but my Father in heaven"'.[7] This statement represents a thematic crux in the dialogue, based on the word 'blessed' (μακάριος). This is not the μακάριος of the Beatitudes however, where its significance is eschatological and suggestive of a religious joy founded upon an objective certainty of salvation. Rather this use of 'blessed' echoes Luke 1.45: 'And blessed is she who believed that there would be a fulfilment of what was spoken to her by the Lord'.[8] Here Mary's blessedness also reflects the action in her of a divine grace, prompting her subjective faith in the promise and fulfilment of God.[9] Jesus continues by saying that he will build his church upon Peter, the Rock, giving to him the keys of the kingdom of Heaven, and he urges the disciples not to tell anyone that he is the Messiah.[10] Jesus now tells his disciples what it means to be the 'Son of the living God' in that he will go to Jerusalem where he will 'undergo great suffering at the hands of the elders and chief priests and scribes', he will 'be killed' and 'on the third day be raised'.[11] The implications for his disciples are clear: 'If any want to become my followers, let them deny themselves and take up their cross and follow me. For those who want to save their life shall lose it, and those who lose their life for my sake will find it'.[12]

The character of this pericope, which is sustained almost entirely by Jesus' initiative, located between the Galilean ministry and Jesus' entry into Jerusalem, offers us a glimpse into the meaning of discipleship, and thus of faith. It represents the point at which Jesus solidifies his relation-ship with his disciples, who are called both to recognize his messiahship through faith and to understand that Christian discipleship will be configured to Jesus' own suffering and death, with the promise of new life. Much is still only proleptically present here; there is no mention of the Spirit, for instance, who will dominate Christian thinking on and experi-ence of the graciousness of faith. Peter, having been declared the 'Rock' upon which Jesus will build his church, promptly seeks to persuade Jesus not to fulfil his ministry at all and earns the rebuke of being called 'Satan' by Jesus.[13] But although the Passion has not yet taken place, and the new life of Easter and of Pentecost is not yet known, the events at Jerusalem fill the horizon.

Despite its extraordinary character, the kind of knowledge to which Jesus prompts Peter is still a personal one; and involves all the elements of personal knowing which we explored in Chapter Two, including that of recognition. We may assume that Peter is there by his own free will, and so can say that he chooses to maintain a horizon of interpretation within which Jesus can inscribe himself into Peter's world. Rather than closing that horizon down, and declaring Jesus to be no more than 'the carpenter's son' (cf. John 6.42), Peter remains open to the field of possibility of how Jesus might choose to speak to him: of who Jesus might be. The fact that the people believe Jesus to be John the Baptist, Elijah or Jeremiah shows the pervasive influence of the categories of Peter's own world in its estimation of who Jesus is, a factor which must have exercised an influence upon him too. It is Jesus himself who prompts Peter to the recognition of who he truly is, not only in terms of his own use of the phrase 'Son of Man', which may have messianic connotations here, but also by virtue of the fact that the conversation is taking place at all, which is at Jesus' own instigation.[14] But while there is a clear continuum between the structure of the personal knowing of Jesus as Messiah embodied in this passage and personal knowing as such, we must note also crucial differences. In our analysis of personal relations in Chapter Two we argued that *affirmation*, which is a positive nourishing of the existence of the other, necessarily looks back to and is dependent upon a prior act of *recognition* of the other in his or her distinction from us. While acknowledging that recognition itself requires a degree of positive will to allow the emergence of the other in their world-centredness, which is to say according to the logic and meanings of their own world rather than our own, we made a fundamental distinction between recognition as a primarily cognitive process and affirmation as a volitional one. It emerges from the pericope given above however, that in the case of Jesus himself, these two dimensions do not diverge but rather come together. The recognition which is faith presupposes a radical and open-ended act of affirmation, entailing discipleship, which sets this kind of personal knowledge apart from any other.

The second question which arises at this point concerns the form of that affirmation. Jesus' comment to Peter that he is 'blessed' signals the exceptional character of Peter's insight, which goes beyond any purely cognitive understanding and becomes also *an act*, that is, Peter's affirmation of Jesus. It is this act which can only have been caused by a divine intervention in the mind and heart of Peter, which Jesus attributes to the agency of the Father. The recognition of the divine nature of Christ, who thus represents a singularity in the eyes of his contemporaries, demands a leap beyond normal cognitive structures and a preparedness to think the unthinkable. The inscription of Jesus in his true identity as Messiah in Peter's world marks a point of radical affirmation of Jesus for the disciple. It not only permits Jesus to emerge in his own world-centredness, as the centre of creation, which is so exceptional as to require direct divine assistance, but it is also Peter's discovery of the true nature of discipleship, entailing commitment to a particular life-form which is based upon an imitation of Jesus, in his relation with the Father, and a quite literal following of him. Peter's commitment to Jesus in recognition of who he is will lead him to witness the arrest of Jesus when he denies three times 'that he knows the man' (when once again acknowledgment of who Jesus is is shown to be more than an issue of pure cognition).[15] It will also lead him to a life of evangelical service, and finally to his own martyrdom. Thus the personal recognition which is faith fundamentally includes within itself processes of affirmation which turn out, in this pericope, to be embedded within a dynamic of *divine* affirmation and will. Here then we encounter for the first time the problematic that to know Jesus truly, to 'recognize' him, is given by being already in a certain relationship with him which itself presupposes the knowledge of who he is. Although a form of personal knowing like any other, faith is the recognition of Jesus as God which is simultaneously our affirmation of him as God: an affirmation which transcends our own will and embeds us within an inner-trinitarian mutuality of both knowing and affirming.

Universal world-centredness

The pericope from Matt. 16.13–20 shows that faith entails the coincidence of recognition, as we come to see who Jesus is, with the affirmation of his mission, in a fusion of understanding and will. This too has to be seen as a consequence of the infinite Personhood of Christ, which transforms and radicalizes the normal structure of interpersonal relations. But that Personhood is also importantly expressed at the level of the world-centredness of Christ, the understanding of which is intrinsic to the act of recognition–affirmation. We have already argued that the recognition of the world-centredness of the other is a condition of all authentic personal knowing, for affirmation of the other requires an understanding of the other precisely and specifically in terms of their own world. Affirmation of the personal other is always affirmation of them as *centre* of their own world. To fail to do this is to compress the other into the teleologies of our own world and thus to reduce or even eradicate the horizon within which they can emerge to us in their distinctive otherness from ourselves.

But the biblical narratives convey the sense that in the case of Jesus the simultaneous recognition and affirmation of who he is encloses the realization of who we most truly are and that our own innermost salvation is effectively bound up with him. We can say then that the recognition and affirmation of Jesus' alterity as centre of his own world is at the same time *the discovery that his world-centredness is the centre of our own world*. This does not undermine or compromise our own world-centredness however, but rather fulfils it. In encountering him, we have the eschatological sense that somehow who we are and who we shall ultimately be is inextricably bound up with who he is. Indeed, through faith we are drawn to the understanding that he, through whom 'all things were made', is not only the centre of our own world but also the centre of all possible worlds.[16] And with this there comes also the recognition of the *authority* of Jesus, as one who speaks not only from the centre of his own world, but as world-centredness itself, in a way that decisively draws in the centre of our own world.

The biblical framework conveys this universal world-centredness of Christ in diverse ways. The first concerns his speaking since, for the Fourth Evangelist, his voice is simultaneously the voice of the Father. We have already seen in the previous chapter how the mutual 'envoicing' of the different persons of the Trinity sets up a speech rhythm which invites our own participation, as those who are incorporated into the body of Christ. This manifests as prayer and praise, which is the intimate speech of God with God in which we participate through faith. It finds expression also as witness and proclamation, which is the opening up of the possibility of that trinitarian speech to the world by the faithful, who are 'envoiced' by the Spirit of Pentecost. The speaking, or the Father's 'envoicing' of the Son, which is of such concern to the Fourth Evangelist, shows affinities in particular with the latter, since it is a way of divine speaking which is direct address to the world. This is not the human kerygma of Pentecost in which people are envoiced by the Spirit, but is rather divine kerygma, in which the word spoken by Jesus to the world is the Father's own word. Here the call to the church is not to participate in the intimacy of divine speech as prayer and praise, speaking to God in the Spirit as 'abba', but rather to *receive* the meaning of Jesus' words in loving affirmation of who he is, since the word that he speaks is not his own but comes rather 'from the Father' who sent him.[17]

The connection between Jesus' words of authority, the voice of the Father in him, the action of the Spirit and their life-giving reception by the world, is brought out in John the Baptist's proclamation about Jesus that

> He whom God has sent speaks the words of God, for he gives the Spirit without measure. The Father loves the Son and has placed all things in his hands. Whoever believes in the Son has eternal life; whoever disobeys the Son will not see life, but must endure God's wrath.[18]

Indeed, it is Jesus' authoritative word that shall raise the dead from their graves, and, at the end of time, shall stand as judge over those who have rejected him.[19] Jesus' word is so efficacious because he speaks to the world those things he has received from the Father, whose presence in him is evident both in his words and his works.[20] The full eschatological intensity of the Son's transparency to the Father becomes evident at John 12.48–50, where we read

> The one who rejects me and does not receive my word has a judge; on the last day the word that I have spoken will serve as judge, for I have not spoken on my own, but the Father who sent me has himself given me a commandment about what to say and what to speak. And I know that this commandment is eternal life. What I speak therefore, I speak just as the Father has told me.

A second biblical tradition chiefly represented in the Letter to the Hebrews appeals more overtly to the kenoticism of the incarnation. What we have called the infinite personhood of Christ is expressed in terms of his eternal priesthood. Whereas the 'former priests . . . were prevented by death from continuing in office', Christ 'holds his priesthood permanently, because he continues for ever'.[21] He has no need to make a daily offering but has done so 'once for all when he offered himself'.[22] He 'has been made perfect for ever' and the temple he enters as a priest is not one 'made by human hands' but is heaven itself.[23] Christ's priesthood is a realization of the unbounded solidarity with the people which grounds his atoning sacrifice, by which 'he became the source of eternal salvation for all who obey him'.[24] In the Letter to the Romans the universality of Christ is manifest in terms of his identification as the second Adam: 'just as one man's trespass led to condemnation for all, so one man's act of righteousness leads to justification and life for all'.[25] If the whole of humanity fell with Adam, then the whole of humanity is drawn into the personal story of Jesus as the saving Son of God. Irenaeus will call this sense of Christ as standing at the centre of human history as *anakephalaiôsis* or 'recapitulation'. The Chalcedonian formula whereby the full humanity of Jesus is expressed in his 'human nature', which he holds in common with ourselves, and by which we too are drawn into the mystery of his death and resurrection, once again affirms the centrality of Jesus' narrative for all human existence. The patristic principle *quod non assumptum non salvatum* expresses precisely this recognition of Jesus as the centre of our own and of all possible worlds, which is the heart of human salvation. In an early homily for Easter Saturday, Jesus declares:

> Arise, O man, work of my hands, arise, you who were fashioned in my image. Rise, let us go hence; for you in me and I in you, together we are one undivided person. For you, I your God became your son; for you, I the Master took on your form, that of slave; for you, I who am above the heavens came on earth and under the earth; for you, man, I became as a man without help, free among the dead; for you, who left a garden, I was handed over . . . from a garden and crucified in a garden.[26]

According to a third biblical tradition, the universal world-centredness of Jesus is expressed not in terms of Christology or the world-historical significance of the incarnation, but rather as a distinctively Christian ethical world-view. As the centre of all possible worlds, Jesus can legitimately claim to be in some special sense present in others, most specifically in those who are poor and marginalized. In an intensification of the divine solidarity with 'widows and orphans' which is enshrined in many Deuteronomic texts, Jesus affirms his identity with the suffering and oppressed in Matt. 25.31–46, when the eschatological judgment of the nations will depend on whether they have fed the hungry, given drink to the thirsty, welcomed the stranger, clothed the naked, and visited those in prison. When questioned by the 'righteous' as to when it was that they did these things, the king will reply 'Truly I tell you, just as you did it to one of the least of these who are members of my family, you did it to me'.[27] This universalist ethic, which has the character of 'deflected love', is based upon the universal world-centredness of Jesus Christ, and issues in the further command to 'love your enemies and pray for those who persecute you, so that you may be children of your Father in heaven'.[28] In his infinite personhood, Jesus Christ is both the one through whom God created all things, and who can say 'before Abraham was, I am', and is to be identified with each and every human individual.[29]

Infinite kenosis

In our phenomenology of personal encounter outlined in Chapter Two, we further argued that attractiveness is one of the functions of the kenosis exercised by one person with respect to another. The self-displacement of compassion sets up a flow of enriched existence which draws others towards those who act in this way, as if by the attraction of being itself. Indeed, the kenotic discrepancy between ourselves and others opened out by their acts of compassion constitutes a space which calls to be filled, and to be filled precisely by ourselves undertaking risk, or self-emptying on behalf of another. In our own ontological emptiness, we are moved and drawn by that space, as by the gravity of existence. This grounds the infectious character of love, the 'loving mercy' that unites the church, and explains the special attractiveness of the holy or self-dispossessed individual.[30]

In the case of Jesus Christ then, that personhood, and kenosis, is exercised not just with regard to other human beings, but also perichoretically with regard to the other divine Persons. The kenosis that comes into view in the passion and resurrection of Jesus Christ is thus an infinite one, in which we glimpse that the being and love which in us are divided are entirely one in him. In consequence, that divine kenosis constitutes a centre of attraction, or loveliness, the influence of which extends to all sentient things. As Paul reminds us, the whole of the creation 'waits with eager longing for the revealing of the children of God'.[31] The essential attractiveness of Christ and of Christianity resides in the same 'loving mercy' or *splanghna* which binds the church together, in the Pauline theology of the 'heart' and 'mutual love'.[32] Whereas for the church this is a conscious participation in the compassionate love of Christ which serves as the ground of its unity, outside the ecclesial community it is inchoately perceived as an attractiveness or deepening which is made present in so far as the members of the church with whom non-Christians come into contact themselves perform the compassion of Christ towards others. The iconic beauty of the authentic Christian life is itself founded on the prior movement of a divine kenosis, opening up new depths of existence, in which the individual Christian participates and which he or she is called upon to manifest and perform.

A second important consequence of the infinite kenosis of Jesus, which is a condition of his infinite personhood, is that the relationship with Christ which is faith can be said to include its own cessation. The infinity of Christ's personhood flows from the inner-trinitarian relations which are shown in the resurrection of Christ to transcend death. In terms of the passion narrative itself, the divine Father–Son relation which appears to be extinguished in the Father's silence as the Son dies on the cross, is regenerated in the glorification of the Son in the resurrection and in the new speaking of the trinitarian Spirit which fills the earth. Thus, while every ordinary human relation must face its own end, not least on account of the contingency of life, the experience of alienation, or loss of relation, is itself discovered to constitute a moment *within* the relation that is faith. It can therefore be embraced as an aspect of the new way of relating which faith brings. This is an interplay of light and dark therefore, whereby the boundary that marks the limit of the relation is discovered to be internal to it. In this we can ourselves come to inhabit the silence of God, which is the complete loss of relation, or annihilation, that Jesus experienced on the cross, and thereby come into the transformed reality of a new and Spirit-filled existence.

Tradition as presence in memory

The church's encounter with the infinite personhood of Christ is centred in the celebratory *anamnesis* of Christ's presence for us and among us which, in Catholic tradition, finds its highest expression in the transformation of the eucharistic elements into his body and blood. It is this sacramental mystery which stands at the heart of the church's remembrance, as the remembering of one who is simultaneously a figure from the past and an eschatological promise of the coming of the kingdom at the end of time. The *presence* of Jesus is rendered infinite and eternal, but yet still remains presence, with all the spatio–temporal connotations which that word has for us in the phenomenological analysis of encounter with other persons which we have applied so far. The mystery of Christ's sacramental embodiment is of central significance therefore to the structure and expression of Christian faith.

Sacraments are signs, and it is in the nature of a sign not to be that which it signifies. Thus the signifier points to the presence of that which it signifies, but its own presence, as material sign, simultaneously signals the *absence* of the signified in a way which, most notably for Derrida, is prior to any sense of presence.[33] The semiotics of the Catholic understanding of sacraments is distinct from this however to the extent that – since the twelfth century – they have been said to be 'efficacious signs' which engender in the participants the same supernatural grace that they signify. This dynamic understanding of the sign which is integral to the Catholic understanding of the sacraments, whereby the sign (which is not the signified, and thus stands for the *absence* of the signified) actually begins to make the signified *present*, attains a further and consummate degree of intensification in the doctrine of the real presence. Here the dynamic semiotics of Catholic sacramentality is expressed in the ultimate identity of the bread and wine with the body and blood, whereby Christ becomes truly embodied but in the elements of bread and wine. At this point the extent to which the bread and wine, by signalling the body and blood as sign, also mark its *absence*, is overtaken by the material *presence* of that for which it stands. As Denys Turner has written, the semiotics of the eucharist at this point is 'affirmation interpenetrated by negation, presence interpenetrated by absence'.[34] The overwhelming of the natural function of the sign as absence by the simultaneous presence of that which it signifies in the eucharist is the result not of human interpretative mechanisms but rather of the divine pleroma itself and the divine self-bestowal which is the foundation and content of the Christian revelation. The resulting aporia of the real presence re-enacts the aporetic structure of the Nicene and Chalcedonian formulae, and again calls for the embrace of faith. Once again, moreover, a primary expression of that faith is the mutuality of compassionate love as the unity of the church community, which is manifested both in the kiss of peace, which from earliest times has formed part of the eucharistic celebration, and in the intercession on behalf of the church and the world.

The embodied presence of Christ which is the eucharistic mystery, but which is performed and mediated also by the body of the church, is the ground for our phenomenology of faith. In his eucharistic presence Jesus therefore goes before us, and faith is not so much the advent of something new but rather the discovery of something which is prior to us. The modern Christian finds himself or herself in a situation not so dissimilar from Peter in the pericope from Matthew analysed above. Jesus already addresses us, from within the midst of his people, and asks us: 'Who do you say that I am?'. The indexical interrogative which the church puts to Christ – Bonhoeffer's 'who are you?' – is the opening of the conversation of faith, and contrasts with the question 'who was he?', which represents the secular engagement with Jesus. Ordinarily conversation as verbal interaction between people presupposes in its fullness a high degree of mutual recognition in which each person summons the other into the enactment and realization of personhood in mutual relation and interaction. In the case of our 'conversation' with Christ however, whose personhood is infinite, it is not we who summon him to personhood but he who summons us. Our speaking with Christ – the question 'who are you?' – is only possible because of his prior presence to us within the community of those who profess his name. We do not address him *ex nihilo* then, but he already speaks with us, though at first seemingly distantly and inchoately, summoning us in the Spirit to speech with him.

Conclusion

The presence of Jesus goes before us. But it is a dialectical presence, of infinite personhood, which both fills the horizon of our knowledge and transcends it. Christ's embodiment encloses a further dialectical resonance for it is simultaneously his body and not his body, since Christ's body is accomplished in forms of otherness: in the transformation of the eucharist, in the multiple enactments of the liturgy, in the voicings of Scripture, and is distributed performatively through the bodies of the faithful. This absence in presence and presence in absence of the body of Christ sets up an irreducible tension of mystical longing, an eros of faith, which lies at the heart of Christian existence. But the embodied presence of Christ, for all its dialectical complexity, secures the view that our knowledge of God in Jesus Christ is first and foremost a personal knowing, and thus a knowledge in relation. The character of the relational as a mode of knowing is that it involves a reciprocal interaction: we are changed by those whom we know. The process of coming to know Jesus Christ is a mode of responding to him, whereby the constitution of our own being, as body, feelings and mind, is itself made subject to that relation, and so dialectically transformed.

In the previous chapter we argued that in the hypostatic union the distance between Creator and creature, which was bridged on Sinai by theophany and the divine 'speaking with', has in Christ been entirely overcome by divine initiative, and that in the New Testament hermeneutics has thus been replaced by an ontology of revelation. The fullest self-communication of God must be understood not to be 'a speaking with' but rather to be 'a becoming one with' the created. Instead of a 'conversation' between God and Moses, sustained by divine grace and initiative, we now find a mutual 'envoicing', an indwelling of the Father's voice in the Son and an opening out of the trinitarian speech to the world in a process that is specifically linked with the divine speech agency of the Holy Spirit dwelling within us. In this context, our phenomenology of faith, drawing out the particular ways in which personal knowing is made strange in faith, points to learning a new way of speaking, which is fully interpersonal and founded not upon human propensities but upon divine grace. God speaks to us first in the Person of Jesus Christ, but his speaking is also a multiple speech: language itself as a world of infinite love and relation within the Trinity. To speak with Jesus in this way, to hear his calling to us, is to make an affirmation about who he is which has profound consequences for who we are, in that faith is a kind of knowledge that can only be lived out in a life under Christ's authority, as dispossessive discipleship. This is neither a propositional nor a practical knowledge (although it contains elements of both), but is a personal knowledge whose structure is a particular way of being with Christ, which is outlined by Jesus himself to Peter and the apostles in the pericope from Matt. 16.13–20. We cannot affirm him in his world-centredness, which is also our own world-centredness, without already standing in a certain relation with him, touched by or even enfolded in the Spirit, but we can only enter that ground by affirming him. This is the miracle of faith, which is never attained, but only ever *understood* or discovered as already given.

The outcome of faith is that our own existence itself becomes 'incarnational'. Jesus is the kenosis of God, given to us as love, whom we receive in a parallel motion of kenotic love as recognition–affirmation and obedient following, or discipleship. The existential reformation we receive in faith then is essentially an opening out of the closed self as excess in prayer, song and proclamation on the one hand and as compassionate affirmation on the other. In the deflection of love, the kenotic space that opens up between ourselves and Christ is inhabited by the presences of innumerable others, who lie before us as forms of world-centredness that demand in turn our recognition in speech and affirmation in compassion. This self-risking opening to others is itself a condition of faith as a coming into relation with the self-risking opening of God to his creation. To this extent therefore compassion, like joy, is a participation of the self in the incarnation, and the becoming visible in us of God's love for the world.

D.
Systematic Theology of Compassion

Introduction:
Doctrine as Christian Knowledge

πάντα δι᾽ αὐτοῦ ἐγένετο, καὶ χωρὶς αὐτοῦ ἐγένετο οὐδὲ ἕν.

Through him all things came into being, and without him not one thing came into being.

John 1.3

Personal knowing as the knowing of persons is necessarily subjective; we each know each other in individual ways and within a relation that is constructed between self and self. Objective elements obtain within such a relation, of course, to the extent that we possess information *about* the other. Indeed, the acquisition of such information either from the other directly or from alternative sources is integral to the process of coming to know another human being. In this way we can come to know someone as centre of their own respective world, as distinct from a feature of our own. As we have argued previously, the process of allowing the other to inscribe themselves as centre of their own world within our world is the precondition for our affirmation of them. In the case of Jesus Christ however, that world-centredness is a universal world-centredness, which means that by faith he is discovered to be simultaneously the centre of my world and of all possible worlds. Within this context, information about Jesus Christ takes on a different status from information we possess about another human being. Since our relation with him is in the context of a universal world-centredness, information *about* him also takes on a universal significance, and becomes proclamation. If Christian revelation is dialectical in *structure*, personal in *form* and kenotic in *content* therefore, then we must also argue that it is doctrinal in *expression*, as the making public of who Jesus Christ is. And so, despite its character as the embodiment of inward faith, Christian doctrine is both communitarian and public, being proclaimed through the worship of the church and, by the diverse artistic representations of doctrine which are produced in every generation, made available for all.

All personal knowledge entails implications for more objective knowledge, that is, for the way we understand the world. If we are defined in our personhood by our relation to other persons, then included within that

personhood is a bundle of values to inform judgments, and presuppositions to inform experience. In other words, the kind and quality of our
personal relations are bound in some degree to influence the way that we
understand and experience the world in which we live. In the case of faith,
or the personal knowledge of Jesus Christ, of course, this tendency is
advanced to a quite different level, since we identify in him an infinite
world-centredness. In relating to him through faith, we are relating to the
one through whom all things were made and whose infinite Personhood
constitutes the centre of the world. It is inevitable therefore that our
personal knowledge of Jesus Christ will have profound implications for
our knowledge and understanding of the world, of which, according to
faith, he is the centre.

The commitment to Christology as exegesis of the world has taken
various forms at different times in Christian history. For the Greek fathers,
the concept of the Logos played a key role in their understanding of the
metaphysics of the world, which was composed, for Maximus the Confes-
sor for instance, of many *logoi*: the essences of things ordered to the divine
reality.[1] In the Western tradition it was the exegetical canons, as laid down
by Eucharius of Lyon, which united both scripture and the world in functional systems of symbolic meaning, with Christ at their centre.[2] With the
advent of the natural sciences in the sixteenth and seventeenth centuries
however, which introduced the model of efficient causality, the scriptural
and the scientific accounts of the world appeared increasingly to diverge
so that finally the two systems seemed fundamentally incompatible.[3]

And yet, despite this history of retreat in the face of natural science with
its experimental verification, the Christian remains committed to the view
that Jesus Christ is of an importance which transcends the subjectivity of
either the individual or the community who gather in his name. Somehow
and against all the odds, Christians must seek to lay claim to the world.
The fact that Christ constitutes an *infinite* personhood, and is the centre of
all possible worlds, obliges the Christian to grapple with a subjectivity
whose excess dictates that it will also be recognized to be objectivity, visible
not only in the community of shared faith but also beyond that, in the
inclusion finally of all that is. This recognition entails a number of problematics. The first is the relation between the knowledge that is faith and
scientific knowledge of the world. The recent rapprochement between
science and religion in the modern age seems more the reflection of a
contemporary desire to show the reasonable character of religious belief
by stressing its affinities with scientific method and data than an attempt to
understand the nature of the world from the perspective of Christian
revelation. This is fundamentally an apologetic process that looks back to
the Enlightenment rather than the objectification of Christ which was
characteristic of pre-modern cosmologies. The persuasive power of
Christian doctrine lies not in its power as an *explanatory* model of the
world, but rather in its mediation of a relationship with Christ, which is

experienced and valued by the subject as giving the ultimate *meaning* of existence.[4] Meaning here is eschatological, and implies a prior acceptance of the ultimate authority of the revelation (despite any counter-indicators, and despite all – legitimate – discussion as to the nature and content of that revelation), whereas explanations are functional, of the moment and are to be revised in the light of new evidence. This distinction between explanation and meaning is foundational for the relation between science and religion, and it reflects the differences between knowledge of arguments and facts, and knowledge of persons, specifically of an infinite Person.

The second problematic is that of the relation between the different world religions with their seemingly mutually exclusive faith positions. The universality of Christ as centre of the world renders any sectarian reading of salvation, founded upon historical and cultural contingency, deeply unsatisfying. This remains the case even for those who would wish to stress the particularity of the Christian revelation. The tendency here is to think of universality as implying the continuous replication of what is already present (all the peoples of the earth confessing Christ in a single church), whereas a universality which is founded upon the *infinite* world-centredness of Christ, will lie outside our calculations in its realizations. The objectification of Christology in terms both of cosmology and the otherness of world religions remains a task to which the Christian is always called, but which is to be pursued humbly and heuristically, in the knowledge that the infinity of Christ, and of the relation he posits with us, can never be accommodated to the categories of our finite existence.

Thirdly, we can point to the emergence of a universal objectivity from the subjectivity of our personal encounter with Christ in the kind of relation we enjoy with the earth itself and with the world as such. The Christian prioritization of God's address to us in the person of Christ, together with the infinite world-centredness of Christ, means that the Christian is called to relate to the world in terms of her relation with Christ. We cannot simply bracket the world as if it were untouched by the incarnation, which is God's way of speaking with us, or indeed regard our own relation with the world as being untransformed by the new relation with God which has been established for us in Jesus Christ. In other words, the world is not purely utilitarian but is now the place of God's presence for us. We are called to hear God speak to us in and through his creation, reverencing the earth and understanding it to be part of our essential relation with God in Christ. This too is a kind of objectification of Christology, and is the recognition that all our relating is changed by the one, infinite relation with him.

That kind of Christian thinking which we call systematic theology begins precisely in the tension between subjectivity and objectivity which is rooted in the infinity of Christ's personhood. As person, Christ addresses us in our own subjectivity, but as infinite person, he does so in a manner which includes the world of which, in faith, we hold him to be the centre.

Systematic theology then reflects the drive to transcend the subjectivity of the purely interpersonal relation of faith in the recognition that knowledge of Christ lays claim also to the extra-subjective realm: to the human community at large and ultimately to the world. There are many modes of articulation of the objectifying perspective which we call systematic theology, one of which is apologetics which we have allocated to a further level of theological reflexivity as fundamental theology. Another mode is that of a piecemeal rational analysis which Dietrich Ritschl has called 'the *loci* method' which reflects a 'concern for classification, sub-division and networking of individual theological themes'.[5] But the kind of systematic theology we are pursuing here is of Ritschl's second type, or 'monothematic theology', which centres in a single organizing principle. Although this can indeed lead to 'fossilization' and the encouragement of closed systems, as Ritschl argues, there is an important sense in which such systems can function well as mediating between the subjectivity of faith and its objective horizon.[6] If unity is integral to the nature of personhood as such, then the unity of monothematic systems makes visible something of the unity that is central to the personhood of Christ, yet which always escapes us in its infinite particularity. The dynamic coherence of such a unified system can effectively convey something of the subjective reality of interpersonal faith within an objective matrix through the communicative and creative power of such inclusive concepts. While the partial, problem-solving approach of Ritschl's '*loci* method' certainly has its place, the *communicative* potentialities of a monothematic system seem greater in that unified, dynamic concepts can more easily open up new imaginative horizons of insight and meaning. Most specifically, such systems, where they successfully avoid the dangers of the closure to which Ritschl also refers, become a means whereby the theological community can speak *with* the world, and thus ground their discourse in the linguistic structures of the revelation itself.

The systematic and unifying principle we have chosen here is compassion.[7] In Chapter One, we argued that compassion is the foundational social virtue, which occupies a place of priority in the moral order. We also argued that as a virtue which exercises an internal dispossession, it is peculiarly appropriate in the modern world which has experienced such radical forms of dispossessive violence. We believe that compassion can also be shown to enjoy a priority among the names of God, and to be central to Christology, as well as having a significant place in the history of secular ethics.[8] In the analysis given in Chapters One and Two, we aimed to show the kenotic structure of compassion, as decentring of the self for the sake of the other, which also lends it priority as a site for the emergence of being. This is to add a further dimension to compassion as the locus of an ontological epiphany. The kenotic structure of compassionate consciousness, which we have laid bare in terms of a phenomenological reduction, opens out into a second stage however, which we have termed a theological reduction of compassion. In Chapter Two we gave a detailed argument that the inner and outer forms of transcendence which are intrinsic to compassion combine in the expectation of an encounter with a subject who is both infinite and particular. This we have identified with the infinite Personhood of Christ. The opening out of compassion to Christology can be expressed in purely ontological terms also in that the infinite kenosis of God in Jesus Christ establishes him as the supreme epiphany of being itself. All acts of kenotic existence therefore intrinsically stand in a dynamic relation to the supreme and infinite act of divine kenosis in Jesus Christ, whose world-centredness is infinite and universal. In terms of language, the transition from a phenomenological to a theological reduction entails a parallel move from language as conversation, exercised in equality by two speakers, which is the sphere of human compassion, to the principle of 'envoicing' or mutual indwelling, which is the sphere of trinitarian life. The communication of the Word, who is indwelt both by the voice of the Father and by human speech, represents the mediation and meeting point of the divine and human order.

In the systematic theology of compassion that follows, we begin by tracing the different vocabularies that have been used over the centuries to convey the notion of what we mean today by compassion. Secondly, we offer an overview of the language of compassion in the Old and New Testaments, as it is used of God especially by the rabbis, and of Christ. This is followed by a section which discusses the place of compassion in the Christian life, again as we find it in scriptural sources. Finally we develop the notion of compassion as the potentiation of the *imago dei* in us.

In Chapter Twelve we shall return to the theme of language, and to Bakhtinian dialogism, as a way of elucidating the Trinity, the creation, and the incarnation. Our point of departure is again the structure of divine speech, as multiple envoicings, and the spatiality conceived through it, or which it subtends. The space that is creation we shall read as manifesting a structure of hierarchy and power, and the incarnation, at the centre of the created world, is the compassionate self-dispossession of God who spans the distance between self and other, reanimating and regenerating the created order with the divine breath. In the final chapter we shall return to the theme of being, and to the ancient principle of the transcendentals, seeking to show the way in which the life of the church as enhanced existence is simultaneously recognizable as a life lived in goodness and in truth. We shall stress in particular the character of ecclesial speech, which is simultaneously animated by divine speech and formed in the recognition that it always falls short of the divine envoicing, and shall point to compassion and solidarity as the modes of ecclesial speaking-for-the-other which mark the coming into visibility of the body of Christ as church. In the conclusion to the volume we shall argue for a renewed cosmology, reimaged in the light of the structure of the eucharistic transformation, and hospitable again to the language of presence.

11

Compassion: Human and Divine

זָרַח בַּחֹשֶׁךְ אוֹר לַיְשָׁרִים חַנּוּן וְרַחוּם וְצַדִּיק:

They rise in the darkness as a light for the upright;
they are gracious, compassionate and righteous

Ps. 112.4

In Chapter One we developed the argument that compassion is a human condition which is constituted by the simultaneous interplay of cognitive, affective and volitional dimensions. Cognition is involved to the extent that we reconstruct, or recognize, the other in their need; it is affective to the extent that we share in the suffering of the other, and it is volitional to the extent that our recognition and our feeling prompt us to act in a way that will be in the other's best interests. Naturally, the stage of action will involve calculations regarding the best interests of the other, with reference both to our own preconceived notions of the good and the good of the other, as we are able to reconstruct them. This process is both rational and dialogical. The intention to act for the sake of the other is fundamental to compassion, but this is not disabled, as we have argued, by our inability to alleviate the other's suffering. The failure to carry out a compassionate act may result from the absence of practical means and opportunities rather than a lack of will on our part. Cruelty also presupposes a facility for entering into the condition of the other cognitively, though it emphatically does not presuppose a shared affectivity. It is the role of affectivity too which sets compassion apart from mercy, which – according to Seneca's definition – is a 'tendency towards leniency in matters of exacting punishment'.[1] This implies a value-laden volitional act for the sake of the other but not a compassionate sharing in the suffering of the other. Similarly, someone who engages compassionately with another may judge mercy in that instance not to be for the greater good.

In Chapter Two we read the cognitive and affective dimensions of compassion as the process whereby the self – through *Einfühlung* – enters the subjectivity of the other. This is to allow one's own feelings to be moulded by perspective of the other. These feelings remain our own but are now, through the sympathetic imagination, ordered to the world-centredness of another person. Thus in compassion we can say that the self re-enacts the alienation and dispossession of the one who suffers through a voluntary act of displacement and dispossession. The dispossession of oppression, on the one hand, and the dispossession of compassion on the other, are ordered one to the other therefore. But within the context of our phenomenology of consciousness, we added a further dimension to cognition, affectivity and volition, which was that of ontology. The realignment of our feelings according to the world-centredness of the other entails the ontological emergence of the other. To quote Edith Stein again, in compassion we know the suffering of the other secondarily (it does not as such become our suffering; rather ours is a 'suffering with'), but we know the subjectivity (or world-centredness) of the suffering other primordially. Within the dialectical structure of consciousness, as the mutually grounding relation of self and non-self, the other does not emerge as an object to be known in the world but rather as an epiphany, and an encounter with the dialectical structure of consciousness itself. The epiphany of the other is simultaneously the opening of a new horizon as enhanced or enriched existence, which we have called being. In so far as we have compassion then, we experience the alienation of our feelings which no longer reflect our own world-centredness but the constructed subjectivity of another. This entails an epiphany of the other, who is encountered not as an object of knowledge but *primordially*, as the mutuality or sociality of consciousness itself. The alienation of our feelings according to the subjectivity of the other is pity, and the further volitional act to embrace the suffering of the other and to intervene on their behalf is compassion. It is this act, entailing self-risk for the sake of the other, which yields the possibility of enhanced existence or being.

In the next section we shall survey the history of the concept of compassion, concluding with some recent debates. In the following section we shall trace the biblical evidence for the view that the presence of YHWH with his people is revealed in and as God's compassionate actions for Israel and that Jesus is to be understood as the incarnate compassion of God. Finally, we shall assess the debate as to whether God suffers in Christ, and seek to argue that, where the self is compassionate, the image of God is formed in us.

The concept of compassion

The history of the concept of compassion in philosophical tradition is marked by a deep division between those who have argued that compassion is essentially a matter of feeling, and is in consequence irrational, and those who have argued that it contains a cognitive dimension and is thus a form of reason. The complexity of this argument follows from the fact that there are two classes of the words which have been used over the centuries to denote what we mean by compassion, which is to say the recognition of another's condition, entailing a degree of participation in the suffering of the other, an embrace of that fellow-suffering, and a preparedness to act on their behalf. The first are terms which, like the English word 'compassion' itself, intrinsically convey the sense of 'fellow-suffering' or 'suffering with'. Among these we can cite the Latin word *commiseratio*, as well as *compassio*, the Greek words συμπάθεια (συμπαθεῖν) and συμπάσχειν and the German *Mitleid*. Where these words are used, we can be sure that the notion of 'fellow-suffering' is implied. The other family, often more influential than the former, do not however implicitly express the notion of 'suffering with' in their morphology, but have at times been used with this meaning. These include the Latin *clementia*, *misericordia*, *humanitas* and sometimes *pietas*, the Greek ἔλεος and οἶκτος, the English 'mercy' and 'pity', and the French *pitié*. Of course, these terms have also been used in ways which do not include the notion of 'fellow-feeling', and so their precise significance in this respect is always contingent upon their context.[2] Furthermore, it is generally only context which allows us to discern the extent to which the phenomenon described includes a volitional dimension whereby we positively embrace our own fellow-suffering and determine at our own risk to intervene for the sake of the other.

The theme of pity is of some considerable importance in classical art and aesthetics. In characters such as Oedipus, Electra and Philoctetes, the Greek tragedies confronted their audiences with powerful images of cruel and undeserved suffering. For Plato the feelings of pity which such scenes aroused seemed to be in conflict with justice and reason, and thus to be undesirable. Indeed, in the *Republic* the arousal of pity was the reason Plato gives for his disapproval of the work of Homer and the tragedians: 'pleasure and pain will be lords of your city instead of law and that which shall from time to time have approved itself to the general reason as the best'.[3] In the *Apology* Socrates speaks against those who beg and plea for mercy on the grounds that 'the judge is not here to grant favours in matters of justice'.[4] For Aristotle however, pity has a cognitive as well as an affective dimension, and the capacity of the tragedian to inspire it is an intrinsic part of the value of art. In the *Poetics* pity is closely linked with fear, and both together are 'purged' or 'released' in a pleasurable process of 'catharsis'.[5] It is the tragedian's task to construct a plot which will inspire these powerful emotions in us, as when one member of a family seriously transgresses against another without knowing it, only to recognize the crime later in fullness of horror so that 'the recognition astounds us'.[6] In *On Rhetoric* Aristotle treats pity (ἔλεος) under the emotions which aid the persuasive powers of a speaker. It is defined as 'a certain pain at an apparently destructive or painful evil happening to one who does not deserve it and which a person might expect himself or one of his own to suffer'.[7] Additionally, it may be the memory of the same evil having befallen us which forms the basis of pity. In both cases however, there is an element of cognition, or recognition, at work, and it is this process which dictates that those most like ourselves 'in age, in character, in habits, in rank, in birth' are the ones whom we most easily pity. This is the case, Aristotle insists, since 'people pity things happening to others in so far as they fear for themselves'.[8] It may be that the discussion in *On Rhetoric* reflects Aristotle's engagement with pity from the perspective of an aesthetic and purgative response, since nowhere does he raise the possibility of acting upon pity to alleviate the suffering of those whose misfortune is undeserved.[9] Nevertheless, as Martha Nussbaum has observed, Greek tragedy presented the well-born young man with numerous insights into the experiences of the less fortunate, including foreigners and women disadvantaged by their social position, and it is undoubtedly the case that tragic art 'provides a powerful vision of social justice'.[10]

The attitude of the Stoics to compassion was markedly different from that of Aristotle, and recalls Plato's suspicion of compassion as an irrational feeling or passion. The Stoic position is forcefully articulated by Seneca in his *On Mercy*. He defines mercy (*clementia*) as 'the inclination of the mind towards leniency in the exacting of punishment', and advocates it warmly, declaring that it is particularly fitting in a ruler.[11] Despite the fact that many think it a virtue, pity (*misericordia*), on the other hand, is 'a weakness of the mind'.[12] It is 'the failing of a weak nature' that succumbs at the sight of another's ills.[13] Seneca's disregard for pity or compassion centres crucially upon its disassociation from reason, in which it contrasts with mercy: 'pity regards the plight, not the cause of it; mercy is combined with reason'.[14]

One of the first critics of the 'Stoic' view of compassion, which was to enjoy a long history, was the Christian poet Lactantius, who lived from the third to the fourth century. For all its faults, the *Divine Institutes* was the first attempt in the Latin world to compose a Christian *summa*.[15] In this work Lactantius launches a vigorous defence of compassion, which he calls *misericordia* or *humanitas*, against Seneca.[16] It is the first demand of religion and 'a proper virtue of the just and of those who worship God, because it alone gives the structure (*ratio*) of common life'.[17] Lactantius' argument is principally that God gave animals natural strength with which to protect themselves, while to human beings he gave the corporate strength of compassion (*hunc pietatis adfectum*) 'in order that man might show kindness to others, love them and cherish them, protecting them from all dangers and coming to their aid'.[18] This is 'the bond of human society',[19] and it is '*contra naturam*' for us to harm other human beings.[20] *Humanitas* is to be displayed to those who are 'suitable' and 'unsuitable' alike, and 'this is done humanely (*humane*) when it is done without hope of reward'.[21] Lactantius' view of the role of compassion as the fundamental principle of human society is summed up in the line: 'since God is kind, he wished us to be a social animal: and so we should think ourselves in other people'.[22]

The role of empathy and compassion as a social virtue came influentially to the fore in a number of political and moral thinkers of the eighteenth century, who were themselves rediscovering and readapting elements in ancient ethics and politics. One of the classical discussions of 'sympathy' from this period is that given by Adam Smith at the beginning of his *Theory of Moral Sentiments* (1759). Stoic influence can be felt in Smith's thought, which manifests in particular in his view of the importance of 'self-command' which 'is not only itself a great virtue, but from it all the other virtues seem to derive their principal lustre'.[23] Adam Smith's notion of 'sympathy' as the social bond between people may also be a reflection at the moral level of the Stoic principle of cosmic 'sympathy' as the organic harmony of the world-order. Sympathy is ubiquitous within human life, and is felt no less by the 'greatest ruffian' and 'most hardened violator of the laws of society' as it is by 'the virtuous and humane'.[24] Smith's reflections include a detailed and penetrating analysis of the role of the imagination in the phenomenon of sympathy, since the suffering we feel on account of another results from our own imaginative reconstruction of what 'we ourselves should feel in the like situation'.[25] It is not our 'senses' which inform us of what the other suffers, but our imagination which follows 'the impressions of our own senses only, not those of his'.[26] As a consequence of this, 'we enter as it were into his body, and become in some measure the same person with him, and thence form some idea of his sensations, and even feel something which, though weaker in degree, is not altogether unlike them'.[27] It is not uncommon even to experience sensations in our own bodies which correspond to the suffering parts of the other.[28] But on the other hand, Smith can point to an entirely spontaneous response to another's state of mind, since 'a smiling face is, to every body that sees it, a cheerful object; as a sorrowful countenance, on the other hand, is a melancholy one'.[29] At the root of Adam Smith's discussion of sympathy is a tension between a Christian inheritance, which privileges fellow-feeling as 'pity and compassion' for those who suffer, and a Stoic tradition which understands sympathy as a universal social bond which is to 'be made use of to denote our fellow-feeling with any passion whatever'.[30] And in the final analysis, it is the extent to which the 'affections' of others agree or disagree with our own which determines the basis of our moral judgment.[31]

If Adam Smith was more concerned with the social effects of sympathy as a form of cognition of others' states of mind than in the volitional aspects of compassion which might form the basis of a moral or political programme, then Jean-Jacques Rousseau, also writing in the mid eighteenth century, was drawn by the educational effects of pity from the perspective of the wholesome development of the individual. In *Emile or On Education*, he advocated the encouragement of the imagination in a young person as a first step on the route to empathizing with others and coming to the self-understanding that he is the member of a species. By seeing others in their weakness, and by realizing that the same fate could befall ourselves, we form bonds of dependence: 'it is man's weakness which makes him sociable'.[32] We identify with others in their suffering and feel compassion for them, so that 'if our common needs unite us by interest, our common miseries unite us by affection'.[33] In the education of our young, we should eschew images of pomp and luxury, since these will prove an illusion; 'men are not naturally kings, or lords, or courtiers, or rich men. All are born naked and poor; all are subject to the miseries of life, to sorrows, ills, needs, and pains of every kind. Finally all are condemned to death.'[34] It is the sympathy stirred by the understanding of the sufferings of others which brings about in the souls of the young the development of 'tenderness' and 'sensitivity'; and it is this which sets them on the course of a truly civil identity. In his analysis of empathy, Rousseau points out that it is easier for the mind to enter into the sorrows of another than into their joy, for in the former case we feel relieved that the misery has not befallen us, and in the latter we may well feel the stirrings of envy and resentment that another has fared better in life than we have ourselves.[35] We can only empathize with those who suffer if we can truly identify with them, so that if we believe that such a fate could never under any circumstances happen to us, we will not be able to feel pity for them. For Rousseau, pity plays a crucial role in the development of the moral base of personhood, and in the preservation of the self from the undesirably self-centred attitudes of *amour-propre*.

The discussion of *Mitleid* that we find in Immanuel Kant returns in certain ways to the perspectives of the Stoics. A privileging of rationality over affectivity in the compassionate moment is apparent in his *Ethische Elementarlehre*, where Kant makes a distinction between *humanitas practica* and *humanitas aesthetica*. The former is a sharing of each other's feelings which is rooted in a free choice of the will, while the latter is 'a sensitivity towards common feelings, whether of pleasure or pain, which comes from nature itself'.[36] The former is a free act which Kant calls *teilnehmend* ('participatory' or 'a sharing in'), while the latter is *ansteckend* ('infectious') and thus evocative of illness or disease; it also goes by the name of *Mitleidenschaft* (literally 'compassion'), where *-leidenschaft* is strongly suggestive also of the passions in a more general, affective sense. Accordingly, Kant is able to apply the Stoic adage that he should strive to save a friend unless nothing can be done, in which case he should eschew feeling, since this is no longer orientated towards practical ends.[37] Against the view that compassionate action is predicated upon *Mitleid* or feeling, rather than *Pflicht* or 'duty', Kant powerfully maintains that to act from feeling, or 'mercy' (*Barmherzigkeit*) is 'an offensive kind of benevolence' which 'should not occur among men'. He points out also, following the Stoic view, that it cannot be right for us to multiply the amount of suffering in the world unnecessarily, which we do when we allow ourselves to suffer together with another. In such a case the suffering of one becomes the suffering of two.[38] The cultivation of *Mitleid* remains indirectly a duty however, since without such painful compassionate feeling, we will not be prompted to the caritative action in which alone our duty is fulfilled.[39]

Kant's questioning of the value of compassion following Stoic principles elicited two lines of critical attack. The first was that of Schopenhauer who read compassion as the breaking down of individuality in favour of universalism, in *On the Basis of Morality*. In terms of Kant's Transcendental Aesthetic, he allocated pluralism to the sphere of the phenomenal, in opposition to a noumenal realm of universalist non-differentiation which he believes to be the spiritual basis of vedic philosophy. Thus all plurality is only 'appearance'.[40] Where we are compassionate therefore, the difference between individuals is eliminated 'to a certain extent at least', and so 'is no longer absolute'.[41] As such, compassion as *Mitleid* serves as the very foundation of ethics: 'Only in so far as an action has sprung from it [compassion] does it have moral value; and every action which results from any other motive has none'.[42] Within the context of Schopenhauer's metaphysical system, with its basis in a kind of vedic monism, the good is refigured as that which transcends the individual self, the latter being fatally rooted in illusion, self-delusion and self-will. Where 'the non-self has to a certain extent become the self', as in compassionate feeling, the process of overcoming phenomenal individualism is begun.[43] The philosopher accordingly skirts the issues to do with rationality and feeling which are central to Kant's discussion of the topic, and which fall outside the chief area of his concern.

The second came from the pen of Hermann Cohen who was in many ways 'Kant's severest opponent'.[44] In his late work *The Religion of Reason out of the Sources of Judaism* (1919), he proposed the primacy of community before the individual. Using the language of I–Thou which was to prove such an influence on his students Franz Rosenzweig and Martin Buber, Cohen argued that Kant had failed to acknowledge the primary role of the *Mitmensch* in the formation of the self. Deploying traditional Jewish precepts of community and *Nächstenliebe*, Cohen argued for a new emphasis on the immediacy of ethics as praxis, grounded in *Mitleid*, against the abstractions of Kantian rationalist universalism.

Friedrich Nietzsche's reflections upon the nature of compassion echo some of the suspicions evident in Kant's treatment of this theme; he too refers to it as *eine Ansteckung*, or 'infection', and laments the fact that 'suffering is spread through compassion'.[45] But Nietzsche's Stoic critique of compassion is embedded in a more general attack upon Christian morality, and it shares the inversion of the language of Christianity which is so typical of his method. Thus compassion is 'a sin', and the overcoming of compassion is to be counted 'among the higher virtues'.[46] Christianity is 'the religion of compassion' and, as such, compassion shares its decadent and life-denying qualities: 'Compassion stands in contrast to the tonic effects which heighten the energy of life: it has a depressive effect. We lose strength when we feel compassion'.[47] Indeed, the greatest example of the unnecessary spread of suffering through compassion is the death of Christ himself.[48] There is nothing 'more unwholesome in all our unwholesome modernity than Christian compassion', which is a form of 'self-indulgence', and represents merely the 'praxis of nihilism'.[49]

With the rise of the phenomenological movement, under the influence of Edmund Husserl, during the first two decades of the twentieth century, the question of empathy again came to prominence, but this time in connection with an acute form of the Cartesian problem of 'other minds'. Amongst Husserl's followers, it was Max Scheler and Edith Stein who particularly engaged with the theme of intersubjectivity. In 1913 Scheler published *Zur Phänomenologie und Theorie der Sympathiegefühle und von Liebe und Hass* (second edition as *Wesen und Formen der Sympathie*, 1922), while Edith Stein published her doctoral thesis of 1916 as *Zum Problem der Einfühlung* (1917). In both cases the authors offered a critique of earlier work by T. Lipps and others who understood empathy to be the retrieval of our own past experience at the occasion of another's present feeling. This seemed to be predicated on the Cartesian assumption that it is the self which is the primordially given, and (in Husserl's version) that the other, and the experiences of the other, need to be laboriously reconstructed from our own immediate experience of alien bodies. As part of his advocacy of an ethical personalism against such atomistic and individualistic thinking, Scheler drew useful distinctions between *Miteinanderfühlen* (whereby for instance a father and mother share grief at the loss of their child), *Mitgefühl* (empathy-compassion), *Gefühlsansteckung* (the raising of our spirits as we join a merry party), *Nachfühlung* (the imaginative reconstruction of another's experience) and *Einsfühlung* (the identification with another). He argued that *Einsfühlung* grounds *Nachfühlung* while the latter enables *Mitgefühl*. *Mitgefühl*, in turn, grounds *Menschenliebe* or *humanitas*, whereby we love our fellow human beings, and leads to the highest state of a universal love of God and of all his creatures. Both Scheler and Stein offered detailed and acute analyses of empathy which represented a significant advance on previous thinkers. Their interest however, lay chiefly in establishing the primordiality of the other to the self, within the empathetic act, against the Cartesian–Husserlian philosophy of the isolated self, rather than in the phenomenon of dispossessive compassion as such.

In our own period discussion of compassion has reflected either psychological or juridical interest, rather than the more philosophical engagement with the rationality or otherwise of compassion as a state of mind. A significant exception to this has been the work of Martha Nussbaum. In a seminal article Nussbaum has mounted a powerful defence of compassion as 'the basic social emotion', arguing that the opponents of pity have seen a false opposition between reason and emotion.[50] Compassion is in fact 'a certain kind of reasoning', 'a certain kind of thought about the well-being of others'.[51] Against pity's – generally Stoic – detractors, she argues that it is not a demeaning emotion at all and can include admiration for the heroic fortitude of one who suffers; the compassionate person can reasonably distinguish between insignificant and serious reversals in fortune and does not necessarily fetishize wealth and material goods; the partiality of pity is a necessary condition of it, since 'the good of others' only becomes meaningful for us 'when it is brought into relation with that which we already understand'.[52] Nussbaum further argues that pity need not open the door to rancour and retribution since the compassionate person can discriminate in matters of revenge as much as those of pity. Moreover, the inclusivity of compassion can appropriately moderate retribution in that it can also envisage the suffering of its victim.[53] Although Nussbaum sometimes seems to conflate compassion (cognitive, affective and volitional) with empathy (cognitive and affective) in her discussion of the political, juridical and economic ramifications of pity, her contribution to the debate, founded upon precise historical readings, philosophical critique and humane liberal values, has been considerable.

The compassion of God

Old Testament

The thinking of the philosophers on compassion reflects a classical inheritance which engaged with the problem of the relation of cognition and affectivity in compassionate acts. In the case of the Judaeo-Christian tradition, however, compassion takes on a new priority since it is intimately linked with the action of God for his people, with his own self-naming and with the life of the saints who follow God's ways. There is accordingly a rich diversity in the terminology and conceptualization of compassion in the Old Testament, which requires careful linguistic analysis. The theme is substantially governed by passages from Exodus (especially Ex. 3, 6.1–13, 33.12–23) which combine reference to the compassionate acts of God, who liberates his people from slavery in Egypt, with divine theophany of the Name. At Ex. 3.1–22 God first calls to Moses by name, naming himself as 'the God of your father, the God of Abraham, the God of Isaac and the God of Jacob'.[54] He tells Moses that he has heard the cry of his people and knows their sufferings, and that he will deliver them from the Egyptians into the promised land. God then commissions Moses to lead the Israelites out of Egypt. Moses hesitates and requests of God some way of proving to the people that God does indeed go with him: 'But Moses said to God: "If I come to the Israelites and say to them, 'The God of your ancestors has sent me to you,' and they ask me, 'What is his name?' what shall I say to them?"'.[55] God's answer is to proclaim his name to Moses: *ehyeh ašer ehyeh* ('I am that I am', or 'I will be who I will be').[56] Moses is to tell the Israelites: 'I AM [*ehyeh*] has sent me to you'. At Ex. 6.1–13 God declares himself again as YHWH and tells Moses that although he 'appeared to Abraham, Isaac and Jacob as God Almighty [i.e. El Shaddai]', he did not make himself known to them by his 'name, the Lord [YHWH]'. Moses is to take the name of the Lord with him: 'Say therefore to the Israelites, "I am the LORD, and I will free you from the burdens of the Egyptians and deliver you from slavery to them"'. The same theme of theophanic self-naming as YHWH, in combination with the liberating and compassionate actions of God, appears in the passage at Ex. 33.12–23 where Moses asks God to show him his glory in order that he may know God so that both he and the people of Israel may be marked out as having found favour with God. God agrees to his request, promising to allow his goodness to pass before him and to proclaim before him the name 'the Lord [YHWH]'. He adds: 'and I will be gracious (*ḥānan*) to whom I will be gracious, and will show mercy (*rāḥam*) on whom I will show mercy'.[57]

Much commentary and debate, both Christian and Jewish, has been occasioned by the passage at Ex. 3.14 which establishes the link between the name YHWH and *hāyāh*, which is the verb 'to be', even if the precise nature of that link remains obscure. Whether the name YHWH is to be linked with the present tense of *hāyāh* ('he is'), or the causative ('he causes to be'), the passage of divine self-naming points back to the uses of *hāyāh* in the opening verses of Genesis, where God's Word summoned the world into being. Indeed, the act of God's self-naming to Moses, can be viewed as the culmination of the divine institution of existence, as the Creator God sets himself in most intimate relation with human kind.[58] At Ex. 3.14 the divine name of YHWH is expanded by the phrase *ehyeh ašer ehyeh*, where *ehyeh* is the indefinite form of *hāyāh*. Here *ehyeh* takes on an enigmatic and indeterminate sense, suggesting 'I will be who I will be', as well as the present tense, or indeed, a temporal indeterminacy which flows from the refusal of specific tense.[59] The suggestion of the future tense further yields the possibility that the significance of God's name will only be revealed gradually, through his unfolding actions.[60] Patristic tradition, based upon Septuagint and Vulgate readings, generally understood this phrase to be a free-standing, ontological statement about the nature of God's being, which transcends any act of naming.[61] The glossing of Ex. 3.14 as being a statement of God's necessary and eternal existence, freed from any contingency and constraint, became the basis of traditional Western metaphysics. In its classical forms it framed divine presence as much in terms of ontology as of naming, and at times saw a kind of continuity – albeit one that was forever marked with dissimilarity – between the existence of entities in the world and divine existence.

Rabbinic readings of the Exodus passages however, struck out in a very different direction.[62] The first stage of this exegesis is found in the Targumim, or interpretative Aramaic paraphrases of the Hebrew text, which date from the first centuries of the Common Era. One of the primary characteristics of these readings is the association that is made between the *Memra* and God's self-naming. The *Memra* is a theological motif found only in the Targumim which means the 'word' or 'utterance' of God and looks back to earlier forms of God's 'word' (*dabar*). Robert Hayward has described the *Memra* as 'a *personalising substitutive attribute* of the Deity like Wisdom, Holy Spirit and Name'.[63] In the earliest strata of the texts it is particularly associated with the verb 'to be', *hāyāh*, and only later, and secondarily, becomes subject of other types of verbs, primarily verbs of 'saying'.[64] *Memra* itself derives from the Aramaic root *'mr*, meaning 'to say' and thus in its most frequent form 'the *Memra* of YHWH . . .' combines the principles of speech and existence.[65] Close examination of the Targumim of the kind that Robert Hayward and others have undertaken shows that the use of the *Memra* by the rabbis, specifically but not exclusively in texts from Exodus, draws together the notion of divine utterance as theophany, divine creativity, divine compassion manifest in saving acts, and the theme of divine presence with and for Israel. Within this complex network of relations, this very presence-with is itself glossed as utterance, as the linguistic self-presencing of God for and with his people. The *Memra* as such represents a higher, exegetical level of phrases such as 'the Lord said . . .', combining and emphasizing the creative and compassionate dimensions of the divine utterance. Two marginal glosses on Ex. 3.14 from Codex Neofiti exemplify the connection between divine speech, presence-with, creativity and compassion:

> First Gloss:
> the Memra of the Lord (said) to Moses: He who said to the world: 'Be', and it came into being, and who again will say to it: 'Be', and it will be. And he said: Thus shall you say to the children of Israel: ('WHO I AM ('hyh) has sent me).'

> Second Gloss:
> I have existed before the world was created and have existed after the world has been created. I am he who has been at your aid in the Egyptian exile, and I am he who will (again) be at your aid in every generation. And he said: Thus shall you say to the children of Israel: 'I AM ('HYH) sent me to you.'[66]

Indeed, according to another early tradition which linked the *Memra* specifically with the root *'tgly*, meaning 'to reveal', the *Memra* itself is 'revealed' in order to save and redeem Israel.[67] Both Targum Neofiti and Pseudo-Jonathan interpret God's words at Ex. 3.8, 'I have come down to deliver them from the power of the Egyptians', as a revelation of the *Memra*: 'I have been revealed in my *Memra*' (Neofiti) and 'I have been revealed to you today because of my *Memra*' (Pseudo-Jonathan). The Targumim regularly translate God's 'I will be with you' (cf. *ehyeh*) as 'My *Memra* will be for your support', thus extending the fusion of divine speech and compassionate presence.[68] Later midrashic tradition continues this theological position, although no longer with explicit use of the term *Memra*. Mekilta Kaspa repeats the idea found in Targum Pseudo-Jonathan that 'the world was created by mercy, and by mercy it is sustained', and in Mekilta Nezikin Rabbi Ishmael states: 'Come and see the mercies of Him who said, and the world was there . . .'.[69] It is in a number of midrashic texts also that we find the identification of the name YHWH with God's quality of compassion, as in the passage from the Rabbah on Exodus (3.14):

> Rabbi Abba bar Mammel said: God said to Moses: I am called according to my acts. At times I am called El Shaddai, Seba'ot, Elohim and Yahweh. When I judge creatures, I am called Elohim; when I forgive sins, I am called El Shaddai; when I wage war against the wicked, I am called Seba'ot, and when I show compassion for my world, I am called Yahweh.[70]

For the rabbis therefore the compassion and creativity of God were modalities of the divine presence in the world, which was an active and historical presence *with* and *for* Israel, serving in the formation of a holy people who would be mindful of the Covenant and reverently honour his holy name.

The Exodus passages stand as key moments in the history of Israel and in the evolution of Israel as a people called to holiness. The couplet *raḥūm* and *ḥannūn* which is used at Ex. 33.19 frequently reoccurs in the Old Testament with specific reference to God.[71] The adjective *ḥannūn* itself is used of God alone, except on one occasion where it designates the qualities of one who fears God, where it is again coupled with *raḥūm*.[72] It derives from the noun *ḥēn*, meaning 'grace' or 'favour' (*ḥānan*: 'to show grace or favour') and is associated with monarchical privilege.[73] Its twin *rāḥum* shows more analogues. The verb *rāḥam* (pi) can indicate the compassion of a king, but in two metaphors applied to God's love for Israel it can also signify the familial compassion of a father for his children or that of a mother: 'Can a woman forget her nursing child, or show no compassion for the child of her womb?'.[74] It marks the compassion shown to orphans, and that of the husband to his wife, where it is opposed to the anger which the husband might otherwise feel.[75] *Raḥūm* and *rāḥam* are cognate with *reḥem*, meaning 'womb', and together they suggest the fellow-feeling of a sibling group born of the same mother, which in a polygynous and patrilineal society is likely to be an important sub-unit of social solidarity and bonding.

As the signifier of a divine quality which can apply also to human relationships, the root *rḥm* has much in common with the noun *ḥesed*, which denotes the fundamental orientation of God towards his people that grounds his compassionate action. As 'loving-kindness', which is 'active, social and enduring', *ḥesed* is Israel's assurance of God's unfailing benevolence.[76] Although not itself a legal term, it is the content of the Covenant. Human analogues to the divine *ḥesed* include *ḥesed* as the social bond between husband and wife as we find between Abraham and Sarah, familial relations between Laban, Bethuel and Isaac, Israel and his son Joseph, and the friends David and Jonathan.[77] Like *rhm* therefore, *hesed* is a term of social bonding which originated in the sphere of family relations.

Other terms that are used, such as *hāmal* and *hūs*, reflect a juridical rather than familial origin.[78] The sense of both is 'to pity', 'to take pity on' or 'to spare'. Further, both imply a differential in the relation of power between the one who administers mercy and the one who receives it. As noted above, although mercy implies a kind of rationality informed by principles and values, it does not denote of itself the affective aspect of compassion, which underlies our reading of compassion as dispossession and displacement. In line with their legal origins, both *hāmal* and *hūs* are primarily used in a negative, or punitive, sense, where God is the subject. *Hāmal* is favoured in the prophetic writings, especially by Ezekiel and Zechariah.[79] *Hūs* is likewise used by the prophets, but its juridical origins are more clearly shown by its five occurrences in Deuteronomy. Again the emphasis in its use is upon withholding pity; although we can note, as with *hāmal*, some positive usages.[80] Unlike *hāmal*, *hūs* can convey a particular physical dimension of pity by its evocation of tears in its repeated association with the word *'ayin* (cf. 'the pity of your eye'). Not all the Old Testament terms for pity can appropriately be rendered as 'compassion' therefore, since most incline more towards the sense of 'sparing' or 'showing mercy' which, as we have seen, fails to convey the same sense of a shared affectivity which is suggested by the complex of words around the root *rhm*.

New Testament

The concept of compassion as we find it in the New Testament is dominated by the terminology of σπλάγχνα and σπλαγχνίζομαι, which translate *rahᵉmîm* and *rāham* respectively.[81] The original sense in classical Greek of σπλάγχνα is that of 'innards' or 'entrails' (cf. σπλαγχνεύω, 'to eat the inwards of a victim after a sacrifice'[82]), which lends the word something of the physical immediacy and powerful affectivity of *rahᵉmîm* and *rāham* (cf. *rehem*, meaning 'womb'). Although most developments in Christian vocabulary can be traced already in the Greek translation of the Hebrew Scriptures, it is notable that the LXX generally renders *rahᵉmîm* with the noun οἰκτιρμοί and *rāham* with the verbs οἰκτίρω and ἐλεέω. Only in the later parts of the LXX do we find the occurrence of σπλάγχνα as 'viscera', where it is a sacrificial term, although at Prov. 12.10 it translates *rahᵉmîm* in a metaphorical application.[83] Other occurrences suggest the 'natural love' of a parent for the child.[84] The verbal form occurs only at Prov. 17.5, where it does clearly mean 'to take pity on'.

The terminology of σπλάγχνα and σπλαγχνίζομαι plays a markedly messianic role in the late Jewish apocryphal text known as the *Testaments of the Twelve Patriarchs*, which narrates the final utterances of the twelve sons of Jacob (cf. Gen. 49), and contains substantial eschatological elements. The dating of this text is however unclear. It may belong to the second century BCE.[85] Alternatively it has been dated to between c. 190 CE and c. 225 CE.[86] Whatever the history of its composition, it shows strong parallels with the terminology of compassion as we find it in the New Testament, which may reflect a shift in terminology for the translation of *raḥᵉmîm*, taking place already in the later Second Temple period, or may be the result of extensive Christian interpolation in the text. In the *Testaments of the Twelve Patriarchs* the word σπλάγχνα no longer has the sense of 'inner parts' or the centre of feeling, but is specifically 'the seat of mercy'.[87] This leads on to the transferred sense of 'loving mercy' or compassion itself.[88] Compassion is extended to God, who manifests his compassion in the eschaton: 'In the last days God will send his compassion on the earth, and whenever he finds compassionate mercy, in that person he will dwell'.[89] In another section, the Messiah himself is called 'the compassion of the Lord': 'and the Lord will disperse them over the face of the whole earth until the compassion of the Lord (τὰ σπλάγχνα τοῦ κυρίου) comes, a man who effects righteousness, and he will have compassion on all who are far and near'.[90] Furthermore, if compassion is the quality that God displays at the end of time, then the righteous too are called to universal compassion: 'Now, my children. I tell you to keep the Lord's commands; show mercy to your neighbour, have compassion on all (εὐσπλαγχνία), not only human beings but to dumb animals.'[91] The exercise of compassion is the sure promise of the crown of glory: 'See then, my children, what is the goal of the good man. Be imitators of him in his goodness because of his compassion, in order that you may wear crowns of glory.'[92]

In the New Testament writings themselves the word σπλαγχνίζομαι is generally reserved for Jesus alone, although it is also attributed to figures who represent divine forgiveness and mercy in three parables of Jesus.[93] In the parable of the wicked servant (Matt. 18.23–35), God's σπλαγχνίζομαι is contrasted with the μακροθυμία of the servant (v. 26) and the ἐλεέω of v. 33, but it is contrasted also with God's anger at his servant's own failure to take pity on a debtor.[94] Again, something of the messianic connotations of the term as used of Jesus can be seen from his response to the father's request to have pity on his little boy, who is possessed by a spirit. Jesus is asked: 'if you are able to do anything, have pity on us (σπλαγχνίζομαι) and help us'.[95] This apparent ambivalence about Jesus' powers, and perhaps implied contradiction in the use of σπλαγχνίζομαι, is addressed in Jesus' reply: 'If you are able! – All things can be done for the one who believes'.[96] In each case that Jesus 'takes pity' upon someone, he performs a miracle to alleviate their suffering. Jesus pities the grieving widow at Nain and raises her son, he pities the two blind men and gives them sight, he has pity on a leper and cures him of his disease.[97] In particular Jesus takes pity on the crowds gathered to hear him, and so he feeds and heals them: an image which sums up his ministry of teaching and caring for humanity.[98] The notion of Jesus himself as the compassion of God is evoked in the Song of

Zechariah cited in the Gospel of Luke, where we read: 'By the tender mercy of our God, the dawn from on high will break upon us.'[99] This is the only occurrence of splanghna in the Synoptic tradition, and it has here the eschatological meaning that we noted in the *Testaments of the Twelve Patriarchs*.

The compassion of his people

We have noted the extent to which the language of love and mercy, as used of God, has its origins in the close familial relations denoted by *ḥesed* and *rḥm*. Human love and compassion therefore provide the analogical language for divine love and mercy, which, in the image of a parental *rāḥam*, tend at times towards an affectivity which is analogically evocative of a divine compassion. But if *ḥesed* and *rāḥam* are primary qualities of God's righteousness, then those who serve God as his righteous people are called to display love and mercy to those around them. They who fear the Lord are themselves 'gracious (*ḥannūn*), compassionate (*raḥūm*) and righteous'.[100] It is of course not possible to legislate for compassion, as a form of existential displacement, empathy or altruistic affectivity; but in the Deuteronomic legal texts, we find clear obligations to care for the dispossessed of society. These are the 'widows and orphans' and 'resident aliens', who are disadvantaged by their lack of kinship ties and familial supports: 'the Levites, because they have no allotment or inheritance with you, as well as the resident aliens, the orphans, and the widows in your towns, may come and eat their fill so that the Lord your God may bless you in all the work that you undertake'.[101] They are to be included in the rejoicing of the Festival of Weeks and the Festival of Booths, and they are to receive the sacred portion of the first fruits offered to God in memory of his deliverance of the people of Israel from Egypt to the Promised Land.[102] The failure to care for widows and orphans is cited by Eliphaz in his tirade against Job, as a reason for God's displeasure.[103] God warns his people that if they abuse the resident alien, widow or orphan, then he shall heed their cries and shall turn his anger upon Israel; for he is 'compassionate' (*ḥannūn*).[104] For Zechariah, the failure to 'show kindness (*ḥesed*) and compassion (*raḥᵉmîm*) to one another' and not to 'oppress the widow, the orphan, the alien, or the poor' is the reason for God's wrath so that he 'scattered them with a whirlwind among all the nations that they had not known' and 'the land they left was desolate'.[105]

The development of the terminology of σπλαγχνίζομαι and σπλάγχνα in the New Testament, lends a different resonance to the language of mercy and caritative altruism and adds a more positively affective dimension. 'Compassion' must be preferred as a translation of these particular terms therefore rather than the more juridical 'mercy'. We have already noted the use of the verb for the active and efficacious compassion of Jesus in the Synoptics (and for the representation of the active compassion of

God in parables), and the phrase 'the tender mercy of our God' at Luke 1.78 (literally: 'the compassion of the mercy of our God') in an eschatological and christological setting.[106] While the verbal form σπλαγχνίζομαι does not occur in the Pauline texts at all, the noun σπλάγχνα is used and has a considerable importance both from the perspective of a Christian anthropology and the relation with Christ through faith that grounds it.

The original meaning of σπλάγχνα as 'entrails' or 'bowels' occurs at Acts 1.18.[107] Its meaning at Wis. 10.5 is that of Abraham's deep and natural affection for his son.[108] Pauline usage differs from both these, in that it combines ecclesiological and at times christological resonances with the anthropological significance of the term. Although we should regard Pauline usage as forming a unity, it is striking that three Pauline texts, 2 Corinthians, Philemon and Philippians, each develop the idea in a subtly different way. It is taken together with the word 'heart' (καρδία), for instance, in our first text, and forms part of his appeal to the church at Corinth, to whom he says that he has opened his heart ('Our heart [καρδία] is wide open to you'), and whose response he seeks: 'There is no restriction in our affections, but only in yours'.[109] The word 'affections' translates σπλάγχνα here, which can be interpreted as marking our affectivity *in relation with others*. Paul has declared that his 'heart' (καρδία) has been opened to the Corinthians, and his complaint is that his 'affections' (σπλάγχνα) are not being reciprocated by them. If the 'heart' denotes the centre of affectivity at this point, then it may be that σπλάγχνα denotes something more akin to unitive love as the basic Christian disposition. It is καρδία enriched by the mutual and self-dispossessing love which is most deeply characteristic of the Pauline church. The subtle distinction between καρδία and σπλάγχνα may in fact conceal a suppressed christological dimension, which we shall discuss below. The word σπλάγχνα underlies the NRSV translation of 'heart' at a later point in the same letter, where it refers to Titus' visit to the church at Corinth. Paul writes: 'And his heart (τὰ σπλάγχνα αὐτοῦ) goes out all the more to you, as he remembers the obedience of all of you, and how you welcomed him with fear and trembling.'[110] This again points to the warmth of Christian mutual love, highlighted at the point of its inception through mission.

In the Letter to Philemon, Paul again uses the word σπλάγχνα in the sense of the emotional centre of 'the saints', which is refreshed (ἀναπαύω) through the love of Philemon, their brother.[111] Paul uses the same phrase when he appeals to Philemon on behalf of Onesimus: 'Yes, brother, let me have this benefit from you in the Lord! Refresh my heart in Christ.'[112] The σπλάγχνα which is again to be refreshed by the mutual love of the church seems to be a distinctively ecclesial centre of feeling. When Paul refers to his 'child' Onesimus as 'my own heart' (τὰ ἐμὰ σπλάγχνα), whom he is now sending back into the care of Philemon, to whom he previously belonged as slave, the intense feelings of relation conveyed by σπλάγχνα have become hypostasized in the person of the individual concerned.[113]

In the Letter to the Philippians the ecclesiological character of this terminology is supplemented with more explicitly christological dimensions.
Following the salutation, the letter continues with Paul's prayer for the
church at Philippi in which he expresses his strong affection and bond of
unity with them and states: 'For God is my witness, how I long for all of
you with the compassion of Christ Jesus (ἐν σπλάγχνοις Χριστοῦ Ἰησοῦ)'.[114]
The Greek phrase literally means 'in the bowels/compassion of Christ',
and it suggests that the σπλάγχνα which Paul feels for his 'saints in Christ
Jesus who are in Philippi', which we have elsewhere seen to be powerfully
expressive of the mutuality of Christian love, can in fact be defined as a
compassionate love not *felt* by Christ but rather *given* by him.[115] It is 'of
Christ Jesus' in the sense that it is the condition which marks the change
from ordinary human relations to the ecclesial mutuality which takes place
in Christ. But the subject of the compassion here remains Paul himself, who
is appealing to the Philippians, as he did to the Corinthians, to respond to
the σπλάγχνα which defines his ecclesial love for them. The same principle
holds in the second occurrence in this letter, where Paul urges the full
unity of the Christian life upon them: 'If then there is any encouragement in Christ, any consolation from love, any sharing in the Spirit, any
compassion and sympathy (εἴ τις σπλάγχνα καὶ οἰκτιρμοί), make my joy
complete: be of the same mind, having the same love, being in full accord
and of one mind.'[116] The qualities of church unity exhibited here, which are
primarily those of the Spirit expressed as a loving unity of mind, include
'compassion and sympathy' in which 'sympathy' is a more general and
less intense term.[117] Once again however, the subject is not Christ himself,
but rather those who practise these virtues through their participation in
Christ in the church which is his body. The members of the church, who
have been adopted into sonship and made 'heirs' of God, are called to
show splanghna to one another and, as God's chosen ones, holy and
beloved, are to 'clothe' themselves 'with compassionate mercy' (σπλάγχνα
οἰκτιρμοῦ).[118] Indeed, for the author of the First Letter of John, the failure to
act upon compassionate feeling (τὰ σπλάγχνα αὐτου) means that God's
love does not abide in us.[119]

The word σπλάγχνα then, is part of the vocabulary of the unity of
the Christian church, together with gifts of the Spirit, the metaphor of the
'body' and the socio-political connotations of *koinonia*. But it differs from
these to the extent that it focuses upon the realm of feeling, of intense
compassionate affection, which is experienced in some important sense
within Christ, who is himself 'the merciful compassion of our God'
(σπλάγχνα ἐλέους θεοῦ ἡμῶν).[120] We can therefore say that if God's *raḥᵉmîm*
owed something to human feeling within close relations, such as the feeling of a parent for their child, then in σπλάγχνα natural human affection is
refigured by divine self-giving and becomes the foundation of the new life
that is the spirit of the church. Compassion in this sense then represents the
transformation of humanity by the supremely compassionate act of God in

the incarnation. God is πολύσπλαγχνος, and by *becoming* compassion in the flesh, God has summoned his people likewise to become compassion within the community of the church, whose mutuality re-enacts, through participation, the original mutuality of Father, Son and Spirit.[121]

The image of God

Discovering new ways of speaking about God and reflecting upon old ones are central to the theological project. In Christian tradition the act of naming, and a theology of divine names, have often played a key part in this, and it is here that revelation, doctrine of God and natural theology sometimes merge. Although classical theologians of the names of God such as Pseudo-Denys and Thomas Aquinas believed that their discussion of the names of God, including the transcendentals, was entirely rooted in biblical theology, both were inclined to prioritize those names which are most universal and, in their immateriality, most detached from specific spatio-temporal contexts.[122] The use of what Thomas calls the 'proper' names of God (such as 'good', 'wise', 'life', 'being' etc.[123]) can appear to engage with the problematic of how we are to *understand* God, rather than how we are to relate with him, but the determination of Pseudo-Denys to begin his discussion of the divine name 'good' with 'an invocation of the Trinity' reminds us that speaking *about* God in classical theology, both patristic and medieval, is generally intimately related with speaking *with* God, in accordance with God's address to us in Jesus Christ: 'we must begin with a prayer before everything we do, but especially when we are about to talk of God'.[124] The metaphorical names of God, whose content, unlike that of the 'proper' names, derives from material contexts, function more clearly as the language of relational access and address.[125] Janet Soskice has pointed out that the 'separation of referring and defining is at the very heart of metaphysical speaking', which is why we can speak of the transcendent God at all.[126] The question arises therefore, 'What kind of language we are using when we speak of the compassion of God?'

As a complex and what Thomas calls 'concrete' notion, linked with materiality and even with bodiliness in the associations both of *raḥᵉmîm* and σπλάγχνα, to speak of compassion as a divine attribute and name clearly belongs to metaphor and not to the 'proper' names of God. Metaphors for God derive in the main from prophetic and priestly speech in the Scriptures where the language of kingship and kinship is revalued in terms of Israel's attestation of God's presence and action. But according to our arguments in the exegesis of Ex. 3.1–22, 6.1–13 and 33.12–23, to speak of God as compassionate is based not just on this level of inspired, prophetic discourse, but is grounded ultimately in God's own self-description. This is to lend it a certain priority therefore. And yet, as Denys Turner has reminded us, we should be wary of saying that any way of speaking about God can be prioritized, since the hierarchical language of the divine names sets up measures of similarity and dissimilarity between the different ranks of naming.[127] This is the ladder we climb towards heaven. But if God is infinitely different from his creatures, then he must also be infinitely distant from each rung on the ladder, and so the hierarchy of measurement which constitutes the ladder cannot map out the distance between God and his creatures. In other words, the distance between God and ourselves escapes incremental measurement. This is the divine logic which tempers all speaking about God, and which Pseudo-Denys recognizes in his prioritization of the way of negation, as Thomas does by stressing repeatedly that the divine names never capture God's essence.[128]

But we would wish to argue that the language of compassion stands apart from the reasoning of the divine names on two grounds. In the first place, it actually belongs to the self-naming of God, and is implied in the threefold naming: 'I am the God of your father, the God of Abraham, the God of Isaac and the God of Jacob', 'I am that I am' and 'Yahweh'. Therefore, although it is subject to the same divine, disruptive logic as all language about God, the Jew and the Christian have a direct warrant for the prioritization of the language of compassion which results not from the nature of language itself, or from our subjective experience of God, but rather from divine self-revelation. God, who has revealed himself as the Creator, has also said: speak of me as one who is compassionate. Secondly, the Old Testament theology of compassion, which is intimately bound in with God's self-naming, anticipates God's Immanuel in the person of Christ, as 'God with us'. The incarnation of the compassionate and liberating essence of God in Christ, which is foundational for all Christian knowledge of God, points us back to the Exodus passages in which – assisted by rabbinic readings – an ultimate unity of compassion, presence and creativity can be discerned. For Christians it is Jesus who embodies the compassionate and liberating action of Yahweh, and he is with God one God. The name of God as compassionate belongs not only to God's self-description, therefore, but also to his hypostatic self-communication; and thus can be said to be revealed.

But even with its source in God's self-naming, to speak of God as 'compassion' or 'compassionate' is neither a proper name of God, on the grounds of its materiality, nor is it particularly remarkable as a metaphorical way of speaking about God. Its significance lies however, in another dimension of naming God which has little to do with cognition as such, and more to do with the prioritization of particular human values. For the early monks of the deserts, the impassibility of God grounded their cultivation of *apatheia*, or freedom from the passions. Similarly, the silence of God was the source or inspiration for Hesychasm. Modern theologians have criticized the traditional names of God as being in the service of established social elites, fostering indifference to injustice and strengthening structures of control.[129] Feminist theologians in particular have pointed to the way in which a preference for divine names that convey male power replicate gender privilege, and serve to legitimate and solidify a lack of equality between the sexes.[130] What we can discern here then is an *ethics of naming*, which acknowledges the intimate relation between the way in which we speak of God and our own highest ideals and values. After all, if God declares himself to be 'gracious and compassionate' in the Exodus narratives, then Deuteronomy repeatedly urges the Jewish people to show compassion towards 'widows and orphans' and to the 'stranger', just as Paul exhorts Christians to exercise the 'compassion of Christ'. The ways in which we choose to speak of God will legitimate or prioritize particular principles of action in the world.

It is in the tradition of reflection upon what constitutes the image of God in us, with its intimate link to the theology of sanctity, that the most radical form of this 'ethics of naming' can be found. The self of kenotic ontology outlined in the introduction to this volume springs in no small part from the recognition that a Christian enquiry into the self is marked with aporia, as the self comes into view to itself as that which is most intimately and constitutively in relation with God. This is in the spirit of Augustine's 'noverim me, noverim te' of the *Soliloquies*.[131] This Augustinian trajectory is maintained also in the place that we have given to the structure of consciousness in our argument concerning the phenomenology of both compassion and faith. In a way that parallels Augustine's analysis of memory, understanding and will in the *De trinitate*, we have argued here that the mutual grounding of self and other, which is the foundation of consciousness, can be appropriated as the image of the triune God in us. It is in the epiphany of the personal other to ourselves in the phenomenon of compassion that we discover the trinitarian character of consciousness, in which self and other encounter each other through the medium of a third, which is the mutually possessed life of consciousness itself. The logic of the image precipitates the further possibility of an embrace of the other, and the fulfilment or realization of the dialectical structure of consciousness through the kenotic dispossession of self for the sake of the other. We have argued that this leads to heightened existence, or being, and can now add that this corresponds to the *similitudo* or 'likeness' to God which tradition affirms to be the activation of the image.

The critique of the traditional names of God generally presupposes a human freedom to choose among them in accordance with ethical and political imperatives. We have not argued here however, that compassion is to be prioritized as a way of speaking about God out of a desire explicitly to see a more compassionate world. Rather our argument has been that this language is given with the hypostatic self-communication of God himself, and is therefore part of the process of revelation: with the slow unfolding of the meaning of the *ehyeh ašer ehyeh*. Although not cognitive as such, compassion then becomes a way of receiving and appropriating the revelation. It is a way of aligning ourselves with the divine revelation, and thus of receiving it. The language of compassion does not itself belong to the *speaking with* Christ which we have taken to be the formal structure of faith, but is rather the *expression* of faith in terms of dispossessive disciple-ship and reminds us that faith is not a knowledge known but a relationship performed. To speak of God as compassion is to accept his injunction that we ourselves should be compassionate, and it is to understand that under-going the dispossession of self entailed by compassion is to align our own 'being' with God's 'being', and thus, performatively, to participate in the ecstatic ground of the Holy Trinity itself. It is to activate God's image in us in accordance with Lev. 11.44: 'be holy, for I am holy'. Compassion there-fore is the unified, existential expression of the transformed person of faith. In accordance with the Pauline theology of σπλάγχνα, it is the foundation of the mutuality of the church, and is itself constitutive of the new creation.

Conclusion

We have argued above that the word *hesed* and the root *rhm* are an essen-tial part of the self-disclosure of God to his people, and that both originally signified the bonding relation within close kinship groups, *rhm* itself being cognate with *rehem* or 'womb'. It was *rhm* too, with its verbal, nominal and adjectival forms of *rāham*, *rahᵉmîm* and *rahūm*, which came to be translated in the later period by the Greek terms σπλαγχνίζομαι, σπλάγχνα and -σπλαγχνός, with their connotations of 'entrails' and of emotional feeling so intense that it demanded expression in the visceral language of physical inwardness (cf. 'moved in his bowels', 'moved with compassion'). In the New Testament these Greek terms took on explicitly messianic, eschato-logical and ecclesiological significance. But despite the enormous impor-tance of the concept of compassion in both Testaments, and the rich resonances around the Hebrew and Greek terms which convey it, compas-sion is not one of the virtues which is singled out in earlier periods as being the primary mark of God with us. The reasons for this are certainly to be found in the tendency to reformulate σπλάγχνα and σπλαγχνίζομαι as the 'works of mercy' based upon passages such as Matt. 25.34–46 and Tob. 1.7. In the former we read: 'Come, you that are blessed by my Father, inherit the kingdom prepared for you from the foundation of the world; for I was hungry and you gave me food, I was thirsty and you gave me something to drink, I was a stranger and you welcomed me, I was naked and you gave me clothing, I was sick and you took care of me, I was in prison and you visited me'. Further contributing to the diffusion of compassion in the works of mercy was the lack of a single and established term in the Latin language, where *clementia*, *misericordia*, *humanitas* and even *pietas* might be used. The late Latin word *compassio* does not occur at all in the Vulgate Bible. Indeed, as we have seen, there is a sense in which 'compassion' as a unified concept, unequivocally implying 'suffering with', is more modern in kind – though it is arguably present in the Hebrew *rhm*, and it is inter-esting to note in this respect that the original King James translation has forty-one occurrences of 'compassion' and 'compassionate', whereas the RSV has seventy-five.

But in whatever linguistic form, compassion stands at the heart of the Christian response to God. This is not to undervalue the role of Christian joy. Indeed, we have argued that compassion and joy are ordered one to the other, and have understood discipleship to be a fundamentally joyful process of self-dispossession and excess.[132] Nor is it to deny that there are a multitude of other dimensions to faith, each with its own importance. What we have argued here rather is that the presence of God with us is known to us through his acts of liberating compassion and that this insight is given by God himself and is therefore of fundamental importance in our thinking about him. We have also suggested that the theological language of compassion serves in the main not as a 'proper' or as a metaphorical name of God, but rather to remind us that we can only think about God in depth, and draw near to him in understanding where we re-enact within ourselves the conditions of his own being, which is to say dispossession of the self for the sake of the other. This is to begin to realize the symmetry that exists between his trinitarian nature and the structure of our own consciousness, as the dialectical and mutually grounding relation of self and other. And it is the enlivening of the divine image in us, when our natural human affections become σπλάγχνα in Christ, and our existence with and towards others is a full, lived and personal expression of the divine *raḥᵉmîm*.

12

Divine Pragmatics:
Speech, Space and Power

Самообъективация (в лирике, в исповеди и.т.п.) как
самоутверждение и – в какой мере – преодоление.
Объективируя себя (т.е. вынося себя вовне), я
получаю возможность подлинно диалогического
отношения к себе самому.

Self-objectification (in the lyric, in the confession, and so forth) is a kind of self-
alienation and, to some degree, an overcoming of the self. By objectifying myself
(i.e. by placing myself outside) I gain the opportunity to have an authentically
dialogical relation with myself.

Mikhail Bakhtin, 1961 год заметки (Notes from the Year 1961)

The twin themes of our study are kenosis and speech, compassion and
conversation, which we have sought to unite in the pragmatic principles of
language which affirm speech as social interaction between multiple
agents in dialogue with one another. If speech is the medium of that interaction, then the personal character of speaking with others is the site of a
potential dispossession of self for the sake of the other as kenosis. In this
way we hope to hold together the primacy of language and its generative
possibilities with the notion of persons who know themselves to exist and
who can, and indeed must, make use of the language of being, with its
indices of the decentring of self, transfiguration and, ultimately, the
reception of eternal life. This, we have argued, allows the reformulation of
tradition, with its crucial commitments to metaphysics, within the
specifically language-centred environment of modernity. For the purposes
of a systematic theology however, something more will be required. Here
we shall need to think the nexus of person and speech away from a subjective axis, from the individual as such, towards the objectivity of a theological account of the world in which such kenotic performance can take
place. This accords with the movement towards objectivity which we
described in an earlier section as the primary systematic impulse, grounded
in the universal world-centredness of Christ proclaimed by faith. Here we
shall begin with a further reflection upon silence and the word, before
considering a dialogical model for a new appropriation of the doctrines of
Trinity, creation and incarnation.

The Judaeo-Christian tradition affirms the unity of the word and the world. God said: 'Let there be light, and there was light'.[1] We must begin again with silence, since the sound that is speech is differentially produced from within silence. Like the black character on the white page, the spoken word is carved from silence and only sounds in differentiation from it. In addition to our assertion that in the beginning was the word, in the beginning was the divine *fiat*, we shall have to add the further affirmation then that in the beginning was the silence that allowed the word to be formed and heard. That silence moreover must be of God, and must be the primordial and generative ground of all that is.

The speech that breaks the silence is revelation as creation. It is not simply noise, nor is it pure disclosure, but in some important sense it is a distinctly personal revelation, since from words we can infer the speakers who use them. Words, even divine words, are creative performance of the self in relation to others. Language intrinsically implies the indexicality of reference and address, and thus of speech agency, in terms of the one who speaks, of those who are spoken to and that which is spoken about. Speech as sound, then, presupposes a differentiation from silence which is the result of a personal act of will. And so, if the first sound is the uttering of the word, we have to reckon with a Creator God who speaks and who therefore chooses to speak. The emergence of word and world is not accidental but is the fertile consequence of a motion of the divine person and will; and is revelation. But if the transcendent, unoriginated and infinite God who is one with the silence, who is the silence, chooses to break that silence by speaking, then God's creative speaking is in some sense identical with himself. It is a self-reproduction through a creative act of the will: language mediating the power and presence of God as God's word goes forth. Therefore God is both in the silence and in the speech, somehow present both in the sameness and in the differentiation. But his presence in speech is not the same as that in silence, for in speech he is creatively present both to himself and to us and the world. And so we can argue that if silence is God in himself, then in the divine speech, the *fiat*, God sets himself in a creatively differential relation with himself, as silence, and in a generative relation with the world.

In the divine *fiat* God reveals himself to us as one who speaks. But we must think of God too as one who speaks, prior to the words of creation, when the divine silence was still unbroken, since God did not become something other when he chose to break the silence. What is distinctive about the creative speech is not that God should speak, but that he chose to speak *of* and *to* the world, and subsequently to us as particular creatures made in his image within it. Before he broke that silence, with words which were as much himself as the silence was himself, God spoke, but spoke in a way which *was not yet distinct* from silence. We have to think here of a kind of speaking which is paradoxically one with silence and not differentiated from it. This divine speech, which underlies God's creative and world-summoning utterance, is the true ground of creation. In Christian terms, it is the speech of God with God, in the immanent Trinity, which is disclosed to us historically and narratively in the incarnation. That historical disclosure impels us to reflect upon the Trinity in itself, prior to any historical process, but in doing so we must be acutely aware that we are reflecting upon something which, for all its intimate connection with the creation, actually transcends the space–time parameters of the created world and thus can only be approached conceptually through the use of heuristic metaphors and analogies which necessarily conceal as much as they reveal. In the following two sections we seek to reflect figuratively upon the immanent Trinity and its silent speech, and upon the processes whereby the differential speaking of the Creator God brought forth the world, summoning ourselves, and all things, into existence.

Trinity

The *Troitsa*, or icon of the Trinity, painted sometime in the first quarter of the fourteenth century by Andrei Rublev, stands as one of the great achievements of Russian religious art.[2] The visit of the three angels to Abraham and Sarah at the grove of Mamre was read as a prototype both of the Christian Trinity and the Christian eucharist in the early church.[3] It lent itself well therefore to representations of the Trinity in Byzantine iconographic tradition. It is in this tradition that Rublev's icon can be located, who, as a monk of the Adronikov monastery in Moscow, would have had access to earlier Byzantine works. Rublev's own 'Trinity' does not fit seamlessly with that tradition however, and there are aspects of his 'Trinity' which reflect his own artistic imagination. In the first place, the historical or narrative element which was usual in representations of the three angels has been almost entirely stripped away. In place of an account of the sacrifice of the calf, the ornate meal with different foods, the prophecy that Sarah will give birth to a child, we find only three angelic figures, a meal, the chalice, the Mamre oak, a building and a rock. Even Abraham and Sarah are absent. As V. N. Lazarev has remarked, action and history are removed to be replaced by symbolic meanings.[4] For N. A. Demina, the oak of Mamre has become the 'tree of life', the palace represents 'the sphere of joyful or inspired knowledge' (perhaps linked also with the notion of home-building as spiritual life) and the mountain signifies 'sublimity'.[5] Above all, the meal prepared for the angels by Abraham and Sarah has now become the Christian eucharist, with a chalice at the centre of the icon, around which the three figures are gathered.

There is widespread agreement in both Russian and non-Russian commentaries on the symbolic character of the icon, and its principal meanings. Where opinions differ however, is in the identification of the three angels with the individual Persons of the Trinity and the extent to which Rublev can be seen either to be reproducing tradition or innovating within it: whether he is 'a pious monk' or 'an inspired artist'.[6] The history of modern interpretation of the icon began in 1904, with the restoration work of V. P. Gurianov, who removed the italianized layer which covered the original masterpiece.[7] In 1928 N. Malitskii proposed that the central figure is Christ, arguing from other ancient icons in which the central figure is shown to be Christ by the addition of a halo marked with a cross.[8] He pointed also to the *laticlavium*, or stripe, which distinguished the clothing of the central figure. For D. Ainalov, on the other hand, it was equally evident that the central figure was God the Father, with Christ on his right-hand side (the observer's left); after all, was this not shown to be the case by an inscription on the 'zyrianskoi' icon, which was placed in the Vologodskii Cathedral by Stephan Permskii, another follower of Sergii Radonezhskii, in 1395?[9] This deep disagreement running through the Russian commentary tradition is apparent also in the work of Lazarev and Demina, the former supporting the view that Christ is the central angel and the latter that it is God the Father.[10] Alpatov himself, in his survey of this discussion, confesses that he first espoused Ainalov's view and then followed Malitskii. He now brings strong historical arguments to bear against both positions and concludes that the solution to this problem is not decisive for an understanding of the icon.[11] Not only is there a diversity of traditions on this matter in Byzantine iconography, but the Bible itself gives us no hint as to which figure is which, and we are finally in the same situation of ignorance about who is represented in them as were Abraham and Sarah when they received the prophecy.[12] Indeed, Alpatov insists that Rublev's intention was not to show each figure in its distinctiveness, but rather all three figures in their unity.[13]

Alpatov's view at this point is interesting, and receives support from the composition of the icon itself. The work itself is indeed multi-dimensional, and not only at the level of exegetical meanings. The icon is formed also by the interplay between the surface or exteriority, or what the Russian commentators call *svetlost'* which is the distinctively Rublevian 'lightness or translucency', and what they term *grust'*, which is a powerful, dark and interior sense of 'grief, sorrow, pain'. The geometry of the picture is constructed by interacting circles and rectangular planes. The latter form an unclosed triangle at the centre foreground, opening out, seemingly to an unseen observer, who is thus afforded a glimpse within the triangle. The angularity of these oblique planes is complemented by a primary circle which encloses all three figures; its movement begins from the left foot of the right-hand figure and, following the bowed heads of this and the central figure, returns back to the foreground through the answering gaze of the left-hand figure and the symmetrical positioning of his feet. The symmetry of the shoulders and heads of the right-hand and central figure coalesce with the posture of the left-hand figure in such a way as to create a sense of a three-dimensional circularity, into which again the observer is drawn. The rising right leg of the left-hand figure seems to accelerate the emphatic rhythms that pulse through the triad, countering the descending line of the central figure's inclined gaze. The figuration of the icon creates a circle that is at once self-contained and opened out; the point of access into the unclosed triangle is paralleled by the outflow of the three faces, and in particular the face of the right-hand figure, who appears not to look at either the central or left-hand figure but rather to gaze both within and beyond the circle, communicating outwards the inner rhythms of the divine unity and difference.

The attenuation of the narrative in Rublev's icon releases its doctrinal structure, and the observer is confronted with the problematic of identity and distinction which is already adumbrated in the coincidence of the singular and triadic subject in the opening lines of the biblical passage: '[t]he Lord appeared to Abraham by the oaks of Mamre . . . [h]e looked up and saw three men standing near him'.[14] Alpatov's second point of disagreement, as to whether Rublev was 'a pious monk' or 'an inspired artist', is a false one however. The difference between his icon and other representations of the Trinity is not a question of the extent to which he has adhered to or deviated from Orthodox tradition, but is a matter of depth. By representing the trinitarian *perichoresis*, which is the defining movement of the Christian Trinity, Rublev has penetrated to the highest and most purely doctrinal dimension in his exegesis of Gen. 18.1–15. This is artistic innovation therefore, but under the guidance of a new and radically perichoretic theology. What the history of interpretation of this particular icon shows however, is that the human mind is ill at ease with the indeterminacy of the figures as we have read them, without specific identification, maintained in unity through mutual interpenetration and the shared rhythms of their gaze. The human mind, which instinctively manufactures meaning in the form of narratives, has imposed and re-imposed upon this material an identification of the figures in their individuality, and thus their narrative relations. It is not the figures in their individuality which Rublev offers the observer however, but – to borrow a felicitous concept from Gilles Deleuze – the Persons in their *particularity*.[15] Particularity, in this sense, is pure *hypostasis*: individuality stripped of its narrative contents.

The Threeness and Oneness of the Christian Trinity is a triunity which cannot be thought. Human thinking itself is representational, being predicated on a space–time continuum, and is thus intrinsically narrativist. The Trinity in itself however, must be thought outside the space–time continuum. The radical mystery of the Christian Trinity comes into view in a particular way when we set beside it the primary ontological formula that we applied in the first half of this volume. Being as the medium of relation between self and other both preserves the distinctness of self and other and guarantees their relation. But in so far as the Three and the One are identical, there can be no medium of relation between them, as being or space–time.[16] Trinitarian theology is constrained by the need to find onto-logical language then in which to express their identity while also finding ontological language in which to preserve their distinctness. This sets up a peculiar tension which is manifest in the formula *mia ousia – treis hypostaseis* in which *ousia* and *hypostasis* as ontological terms are set apart from their ordinary usages and are newly defined *by being set in opposition to each other*, within the unity of the Godhead.[17] This a-logical structure commands a kind of thinking that circles a single divine aporia manifest-ing in three distinct forms. That aporia is simultaneous unity and distinc-tion, which appears firstly in the relation between God in himself and God made visible to us in the world. We are obliged to attempt to think the Trinity in its immanence, through and beyond the *oikonomia*, by virtue of the claim that the divine narrative in history is distinctively a revelation of the uncreated God; otherwise, as Rahner has observed, the revelatory structure of trinitarian belief becomes myth.[18] Once that commitment is made, then we are obliged to confront the second and third manifestation of the same aporia, in terms on the one hand of the relation between the three *hypostaseis* and the *ousia* and, on the other, of the immanent relation between one *hypostasis* and another.

The attempt to think the Trinity in its immanence from within the terms of the economic Trinity sets thought at odds with language. In the first place, Father and Son filter ungendered trinitarian relations through gendered metaphors.[19] But it is also the case that since a man becomes a father only with the birth of his first child, he pre-exists the point at which he becomes a father, whereas his son does not. Thus there is a subtle prior-itization of the Father with respect to the Son, since the former is sugges-tive of pre-existence.[20] The metaphors of Father and Son carry with them also the notion of embodiment, and indeed of warm familial relation, unlike the Spirit, to whom they are therefore subtly opposed and implicitly prioritized. Most significantly, Father and Son command a reciprocal relationality which is entirely lost in the case of the Spirit, inevitably lend-ing thinking on the relations that obtain in the immanent Trinity a persist-ent tendency towards bipolarism. Conceiving the immanent Trinity from the *oikonomia* turns out then to be a necessary but impossible task, in which language – as representation – is constantly rebuffed and trinitarian theo-logy forced to acknowledge its own inadequacy. While we must affirm the identity of the Trinity in both immanence and *oikonomia*, we can only do so aporetically, in the knowledge of their simultaneous difference.

The principle *mia ousia – treis hypostaseis* critiques the domestication of divine revelation by a human thinking that too easily accommodates it to the narratives of a spatio-temporal framework. We should not think of the Triunity as a positive theological statement therefore, but rather as a nega-tive one, in the particular sense which the term 'negative' takes on in the tradition of Christian negative theology.[21] Although the *mia ousia – treis hypostaseis* does not have a negative structure as such, it does function as a

negation or contradiction which is a concealed affirmation, since to affirm
the transcendent Godhead in positive language restricts and 'contains' the
Uncreated in categories that derive from the created order. Paradoxically,
to speak of God – worshipfully – in negations can affirm him in his
transcendence in a way that the affirmations intrinsic to positive language
cannot.[22] These 'negative affirmations' of the Christian apophatic tradition
allow the use of language 'under erasure' (as Derrida would say), thus
harnessing the expressivity of language in our speaking with, to and about
God, while marking 'theological' language off from ordinary language
use. Negative theology critiques the many positive ways in which we are
able to speak with, to and about God that are given through Scripture and
liturgical tradition, reminding us of the provisional character of all theological language and preserving the essential mystery of God-with-us.
Similarly, the aporetic character of the terms *ousia* and *hypostasis* as they are
coposited in the articulation of divine identity and difference serves to
place the immanent Trinity at the centre of the economic Trinity, thus preserving the transcendence of God. Although this seems to be more an
apophasis of concept than that of speech which characterizes negative
theology, the *mia ousia – treis hypostaseis* is not merely an elaboration of
thought or a divine riddle, but is rather performative and existential, and
its expressive centre lies at the very heart of Christian experience and belief
in the credal and liturgical affirmations of the worshipping church.

The Triune formula is set in opposition to the narrativization of the
revelation of God in himself which is innate to all human thinking, and it
thus points us beyond the economic Trinity to the divine life 'outside' the
creation, without which again – as Rahner has observed – the economic
Trinity itself can be no more than a spatio-temporal construct, or myth.[23]
Despite its austerity however, the *mia ousia – treis hypostaseis* does not
prohibit trinitarian theology, but rather creates its authentic possibility.
The Triunity *demands* to be thought positively, not only on account of its
centrality in the performance of Christian ritual and belief, but also
because it preserves the ontological language of substance, relation and
individual identity. These are terms in which we, as existent and substantial persons (or whatever language we may choose to use of ourselves), are
deeply implicated, and which accordingly lay some incontrovertible claim
upon us. The Christian community is always obliged to think the *mia ousia
– treis hypostaseis* through anew in *positive* terms, as faith seeks understanding. But in the filling out of the contents of *ousia* and *hypostasis* narrativity necessarily reasserts itself. In attempting to gain purchase on the
aporia, we inevitably prioritize either Oneness with respect to Threeness,
or Threeness to Oneness. Both terms lend themselves to empirical thought;
it is only in their copositing that they become aporetic and transcendental.
Thinking that we recognize unity, we reflect on how the One can be simultaneously Three, or recognizing distinction, we ask how the Three can also
be One. The crucial question at this point is where we locate the centre of

divine subjectivity and agency. The tendency in Western trinitarian theology has been to link subjectivity with the *ousia* which, as Colin Gunton and Catherine Lacugna have argued with respect to Augustine, has served to mythologize the Trinity as dominant unity and self-possession.[24] It is notable in fact that redefined as 'identity', which is given by the attribution of subjectivity, the concept of the 'one' tends to lose the radical unfathomability which it has in the thinking of Plotinus or Eckhart (where it is free of any association with subjectivity), and takes on instead something of the character of what Kant called the 'unitary field of consciousness' and 'transcendental apperception'. So pervasive is the unitary power of human consciousness that a trinitarian theology which links subjectivity with unity in the Trinity will inevitably fall into a subtle kind of anthropomorphism and will be irretrievably slanted in the direction of a prioritization of the One at the cost of the Three. It is too easy to forget that this is not a Oneness like any other, but rather a divine unity posited only by a simultaneous divine Threeness. On the other hand, the identification of each *hypostasis* as the centre of its own subjectivity and agency fails to take account of the fact that subjectivity *individuates* and that the positing of a subjectivity which does not individuate (in the sense that the three *hypostaseis* are also simultaneously one) is a contradiction in terms and thus close to nonsense. And yet the attribution of subjectivity to God in some way is an essential step if God in himself is to be understood to be in some sense personal.

The recognition of the aporetic character of the one *ousia* and three *hypostaseis*, which are defined only within the mystery of their simultaneity, justifies the view that the history of Christian trinitarian thinking – whether centred in identity or distinction – is in some important sense a history of error. Much writing on the Trinity, especially in the modern period, is principally critique of the positions of others which are held to account for much misunderstanding and misery.[25] The recognition of the aporetical character of the *mia ousia – treis hypostaseis* frees the tradition from a true–false dichotomy however, allowing us to revalue the diversity of perspectives as *generous fecundity*. The very variety of the models testifies to the capacity of the immanent Trinity always to exceed its economic formulations: escaping broader definition, but constantly imaging itself in new ways in the human mind and imagination. But even if all trinitarian theology is a priori analytically inadequate to the challenge posited by Triunity, this does not mean to say that all trinitarian models are equally valid. The revelation after all is not the Triune formula itself but the God-with-us in Jesus Christ to which the formula points. In place of a language of description, we must invoke the language of participation therefore, and measure this against our encounter with God in Christ. We should seek models of the Trinity, provisional ways of 'filling out' the content of the one *ousia* and three *hypostaseis*, which enlarge the theological imagination on the one hand, while fostering and deepening the experience of faith on the other.[26] We must ask whether and in what way any particular model offers modes of appropriation and understanding which can be said authentically to *conform* us to the divine revelation of the trinitarian nature of God in Christ. The particular model of trinitarian theology that we shall attempt here therefore knows its own origin in refracted light, and that it is itself no more than a flawed representation of that which transcends the narratives of space and time. But it knows also that the object of its reflection is infinitely fertile, and productive of a rich fecundity, offering itself to be taken up into new forms of conceptualization and representation which are always alien to it. That movement itself is incarnational, and, as such, conforms our own existence to the divine pulsation of unity and distinction.

Triadic speech

Evdokimov has pointed out that the three angels of Rublev's icon who are seated at the table are conversing.[27] We have already considered the conversation of the divine persons in their historical relation, as speech between Father and Son, and as the voice of the Holy Spirit speaking in and for others. We have seen that it is in their speaking together that the mutual relation between Father and Son is historically developed and maintained. The visible role of the Holy Spirit is in part to enable that conversation but principally to insert the Christian faithful into the multiple divine dialogue so that the church prays 'Abba! Father!' in the Spirit and with the Son. We argued that all these instances of divine speech can be interpreted as fragments of a divine, inner-trinitarian conversation: a silent speaking between the Persons which is non-historical and un-spoken, and which is glimpsed partially, but still powerfully, at critical points in the Gospel narrative, where mutual relation is being negotiated as affirmation, delight, glorification, petition, obedience and self-giving. At these points, we have suggested, language as conversation becomes expressive and constitutive of the very relationship that exists between the Persons in their historical manifestations. This is not a radicalized divine speech therefore which points to a Transcendental Signified through excess of signification, favoured by some kinds of contemporary de-construction, but is rather a way of speaking between (divine) agents which points to and itself accomplishes the invisible depths of love and self-giving between them.

In the image of this speech presented to us by the missions of the Persons, Father and Son speak together, while the Holy Spirit – as the breath that passes between them – is both the possibility of that communi-cation and the point of access for the church into the divine conversation. But the equality of the Persons in their immanence demands that we should think divine speech at its origin yet more radically. Human conversation for instance has its natural focus in a relationship of two speakers. Dialogue between two human beings presupposes the existence of other speakers and indeed of the world itself, as that concerning which they talk. The sphere of reference both as other speakers who are implied in the conversation and the world which unfolds from it stand in a particular relation to the speakers, so that together they form what Bakhtin termed 'a living triunity'.[28] The form of that unity is externality, since other speakers and the referent, or world, of which they speak stand outside both themselves and their relation. But in God nothing is external. The voicings of the trinitarian Persons have no external point of reference, for all is contained in the Trinity without residue. The relations between the Persons are infinite and all-encompassing; there is no externality. We must think of that to which the trinitarian dialogues refer then as being itself a Person, specifically the Holy Spirit, who is contained within the trinitarian conversation, and not excluded from it. That to which speech refers, the world to which it is answerable, is itself Person and itself speaks with the other Persons in equality and mutual inhabiting of voice. There is no outside to contain this speech; rather it contains all. There is no referent outside itself, and yet the reference of the divine conversation is infinite and is to all things, not as externality without but constructed rather as content within.

Thinking the sphere of reference as a Person collapses exteriority and interiority alike, and trades spatiality for infinity of relation. This leads to a further significant distinction between human and divine speech. When the gaze of each partner meets the other in human dialogue, communication can become introverted, cut off from the world and from other relations within the world. The I–Thou can set up a closed and narcissistic structure of communication, as the self in each case is reflected back via the other in a face-to-face relation of mutuality. The dynamic of the Holy Spirit as a third and equal participant in the conversation between Father and Son breaks this fascination. No longer does one gaze meet the other face on, but now the eyes are turned to a third. The object of relation is now not the other in relation to the self, in which the self can all too easily discern its own reflection, but is rather the other in relation to a third. Thus the gaze is not reflected back but in a sense circulates, becoming pure movement, pure relationality, opening out into the possibility of infinite encounters. This is the nature of an infinite relationality, in which engagement with a particular other dissolves into engagement with the universal, which crystallizes again as engagement with the particular, in a continuing cycle of gaze and movement.

Furthermore, in light of the infinity of relation that obtains between them, and the fact that their speech must be fully coincident both with personhood and relation, there must be a sense also in which the Father, Son and Holy Spirit inhabit each other's speech. It is axiomatic for us that in every speech occasion our voice is our own. Indeed, the power of mimicry trades on this fact. But because the three Persons are of one essence, we must be able to say that they can inhabit each other's voices. There must be here some kind of *perichoresis* of utterance, or *communicatio idiomatum* of the voice. In some way, perhaps unimaginable to us, the Father and the Spirit speak in the voice of the Son, the Son and the Spirit in the voice of the Father, and the Father and the Son in the voice of the Spirit. Perhaps we can see some glimpse of this in New Testament accounts of the Holy Spirit, where we read for instance that the Spirit will guide the disciples 'into all the truth', 'for he will not speak on his own, but will speak whatever he hears, and he will declare to you the things that are to come. He will glorify me, because he will take what is mine and declare it to you'.[29] Here we have a sense of the Spirit as agent of speech, but whose speech agency exists in a perichoretic relation with the other Persons of the Trinity, as he testifies to Jesus and glorifies him. In the same way, it is the Spirit who cries out 'Abba! Father!' in us, and who prays in us 'with sighs too deep for words', as a voice inserted into or superimposed upon our own.[30] The mission of the Spirit is precisely the extension of the trinitarian indwelling of voice into the created world, just as the mission of the Son is to speak to us the words which the Father has spoken to him.

Human speech in its most intimate aspects provides some analogue, however remote, to the structure of the divine conversations in their originary form, since it is always dialogical, and intrinsically tends towards what Mikhail Bakhtin calls 'utterance' and 'addressivity'.[31] That is, it gathers itself into units which presuppose an addressee, and thus invites response. Human speech seeks out an interlocutor, through whom it can come into fuller self-realization. Conversation, which is the kind of speaking that takes place between free agents in full mutual recognition, is the highest form of dialogue, and the most complete realization of the nature of language itself as communication and exchange. When we speak freely and openly with another, as a sovereign agent who is the centre of our own world, we invite the other to speak to us in the same way, from their own world-centredness, and thus a programme of equality and mutual recognition is implied. It is only in the modalities of concealment and deception, of denigration and destructive criticism, that we close down the dialogical implications of our speaking. Otherwise, conversation should lead to mutual interest, understanding, exchange and delight. It is enrichment and delight precisely because we encounter the other as the centre of their own world, and thus conversation with them becomes a disclosure of other worlds and other possibilities. In the case of compassion, which – as we have argued – is the most radical form of the encounter with difference, we enter into the experience of the other: we inhabit the one who suffers. Here the mutuality of conversation can become a new kind of 'compassionate speech', which is marked by care and concerned address to the other. But it is characterized also by lending our own voice to them, by *speaking on the other's behalf*, as a voicing of their own reality. We may make the case for them, pleading on their behalf, and call the community to address their need. This is an important way in which otherness enters kenotically into our own speaking. We may also turn to God for their sake, calling upon him in intercessory prayer. Praying for others in our church community, who are bereaved, sick, poor or marginalized, is also in an important sense to allow ourselves to be 'envoiced' by the other.

Perichoresis as envoicing is a way of conceptualizing the Trinity in itself which is as inadequate as any other. But the theme of compassionate speech does offer a new and distinctive model of the nature of the trinitarian Persons, in accordance with the phenomenology of the compassionate self outlined in Chapter Two. The aporia of divine identity and distinction is at play not only in the relation between the economic and immanent Trinity, and between *hypostasis* and *ousia*, but also in the relation between the three *hypostaseis*. Here the Christian revelation disrupts the logic that if A = D, B = D and C = D, then A = B = C. If the *hypostaseis* are both identical with the *ousia* and different from it, then we must affirm both A = B = C and A ≠ B ≠ C. Much modern trinitarian theology uses the contemporary concept of the 'person' as a way of understanding the sense of *hypostasis*. The classical Thomist concept of the *hypostaseis* as subsistent relations was overtaken by the ontological terminology of Barth and Rahner, who insisted upon *Seinsweise* and *Subsistenzweise* respectively, before this ontologism was in turn critiqued by those who wished to argue – with different nuances – for *hypostasis* as person-in-relation. This is to counter an emphasis upon what Rowan Williams has called the 'self-expressive' character of divine communication with a more dynamic and participatory model, and has been welcomed as marking a return to Cappadocian thinking.[32] At times the person-*hypostasis* is seen as being constituted by relation, and at times it is understood intrinsically to exercise relation, showing various degrees of emphasis upon the person as autonomous centre, or agent of relation.[33] In some more recent studies, we can discern the distinctive influence of postmodernism with its suspicion of an autonomous or self-positing subjectivity.[34] Not all developments of the social Trinity take adequate account of the problematics of person and relation however, which have been so thoroughly explored by thinkers such as Levinas and Ricoeur. In the first place, to argue for person-in-relation against a static *hypostasis* is not to argue for an *ethical* view of the person as such: relations may be exploitative, destructive or oppressive. Secondly, the self must transcend relationality in one important sense if the subject is not to be fragmented in the multiplicity of relations which fall to persons (both human and divine). In other words, to be a self is to possess an openness towards new narrative relations in which it will recognize itself and be recognized by others, as constituting the same subjectivity. There must be something in the self that resists the closure of narrative therefore, as Levinas has argued, which, as we have seen, is the potential site of self-knowing, self-risking ethical activity, predicated upon a prior degree of self-possession.[35] In thinking the divine *hypostasis* from the perspective of human personhood therefore, we advocate the model of personhood which emerges from our analytic of kenotic ontology, in which subject and relation are held together in the self-dispossessing movement of compassion. In the self-risking affirmation of the other we are recreated in a new unity of self and other which we have described as heightened existence or being. Here personhood is neither to be identified as a centre of subjectivity and action, exercising relation, nor with subsistent relation as such. It is rather glimpsed in the self-risking movement of the self-possessing self towards and for the sake of the other which, as we have proposed, is the kenotic embrace of our own absence within the self–other relation of consciousness. This is a stepping into emptiness and darkness on behalf of the other, as the realization of the dialectic of the self. As such, it can be identified with neither the self as subject nor with the self as relation, but rather *with the transition between the two*: that is, the movement from the centred self into pure relation through the self-dispossession of compassion, which is radically ordered to the other.[36] The constitution of personhood through the dialectical embrace of the other is for us a fleeting and partial reality, though one which grants a new union of self and other in the transformation of being. But it does offer us some glimpse, however inchoate, of what the pulsation between unity and distinction which constitutes the personal life of the Trinity might mean.

Creation

In the linguistic model of God's action that we have outlined above, the point of creation is marked by the extension of reference into an external sphere as a free act of the divine will. This represents the linguistic generation of the world from within the inner-trinitarian sphere of encounter and communication, as a domain which God addresses, in blessing and command, and with which – through the action of his Spirit – he shows that he is intimately concerned. The Genesis narrative itself images the creation in terms of the power of divine language, and its governance of the ontological order. God's first words include the jussive form of the verb 'to be': *yᵉhî* ('let there be light'), as expressive of the creative and divine will.[37] Originary reference is inevitably in the jussive, since God must first call the world into being before he can speak of it. By summoning the world into existence, first as light, the divine speech posits exteriority. From this point on there is a realm which is characterized by a fertile and free otherness to the Trinity in its exteriority to it. Concealed within the jussives of the divine command is sovereignty on the one hand and care for the world on the other. By proclaiming the *yᵉhî* ('let there be'), God creates the world and commits himself to it in a covenant of grace. The world that is created is in the most intimate way possible God's world: structured according to his words and animated by his spirit-breath. In a sequence of eleven jussives (six of which are jussives of the verb 'to be'), God summons the light, the dome to separate 'the waters from the waters', the gathered waters, the dry land, vegetation, lights in the dome 'for signs and for seasons' and 'to give light upon the earth', 'swarms of living creatures' in the waters and birds that 'fly above the earth'.[38] Each occurrence of the $y^eh\hat{\imath}$ ('let there be') is matched by $w^ey^eh\hat{\imath}$ ('and there was'), underlining the rule of language over existence. Once the essential structure of the visible universe has been established in this way, God blesses the world and all the creatures, thus completing his primary creative act by affirming the result of his creation. If the jussives summoned the created world into existence, then the divine act of blessing establishes the world as the forum of divine action on the one hand and as the object of God's action on the other.

The third and final stage in the linguistic construction of the creation occurs with the use of a series of imperatives that immediately follow the act of blessing: 'Be fruitful and multiply and fill the waters in the seas, and let birds multiply on the earth'.[39] The verb in the imperative form belongs not to reference, nor to action, but to the language of address. By speaking to his creation in this way, God grounds the priority of divine command and establishes the possibility of reciprocal address. But it is only with the creation of humankind, who are able to exercise power over the world, that this possibility is realized: 'God blessed them, and God said to them, "Be fruitful and multiply, and fill the earth and subdue it; and have dominion over the fish of the sea and over the birds of the air and over every living thing that moves upon the earth"'.[40] In this case however, God speaks to humankind with full indexicality, presupposing the power to see and to understand, and showing the use of 'shifters', or personal pronouns ('I' and 'you'), which may be used of any speaking subject and are thus held in common: 'See, I have given you every plant yielding seed that is upon the face of all the earth . . .'.[41] The stage is now set for the reality of a reciprocal human speaking to God. As beings who are called into existence by the divine speech act through address, the parameters of our existence are determined by our own speech relation with God. This is an answering relation of speech, which is a creative human response to the originary speech of God as creation and commandment: in praise, affirmation, prayer, witness, song, poetry and theology.

The creation of the world as a domain exterior to God, but in which he is deeply implicated and with which he is profoundly concerned, posits also God's exteriority to himself, which is a kind of divine alienation. The world thus becomes God's sphere of action *ad extra*, in the missions of Father, Son and Holy Spirit, who are now narratively refigured within the parameters of temporality and space which constitute exteriority. The theme of the creation involves the missions of all three Persons, as we shall see, but it shows a special relation with the mission of the Holy Spirit. Unlike the First and Second Persons of the Trinity, who are imaged as speech-agents, the metaphoricity of the Spirit reaches back into the natural order, in a richly associative matrix of meanings around the word *rūaḥ*. The *rūaḥ* plays a critical role in the account of the creation analysed above since – as the *rūaḥ ᵉlohîm* – it 'swept over the face of the waters' (Gen. 1.2). As 'wind' ('the wind of God', or 'a mighty wind'), *rūaḥ ᵉlohîm* points to the polarity of wind and water that is a characteristic of ancient eastern creation myths, whereby the wind dries land from the sea.[42] As 'the Spirit of God' however, it is suggestive of God's dynamic creative action. But whether as 'wind' or 'Spirit', the verbal noun *rūaḥ*, which is itself dynamic, conveys the power and agency of God with respect to the creation. In addition, although its original meaning is likely to have been the movement of air, *rūaḥ* derives from an earlier root *rwḥ*, which also underlies the verbal form *rāwaḥ* meaning 'to be wide' or 'spacious'. It thus has a secondary historical association with spatiality, or 'ce qui est aéré, donc spacieux'.[43] From this perspective therefore, *rūaḥ* suggests the very structure of the cosmos as 'atmosphere' and 'space': extension which is 'breathed out' by divine words.

The diverse meanings of the word *rūaḥ* in the Old Testament, which include 'wind', 'breath', 'life', 'courage', 'anger', 'mind', as well as human and divine 'spirit', find their unity in the concept of divine action. The wind that withers the 'flower of the field' may represent the vanity of human life and ambition, but the 'strong east wind' that divided the waters for the escaping Israelites, and the wind that 'lifted the locusts and drove them into the Red Sea', served as the instrument of God's intervention in the world.[44] Hovering between the status of a metaphor for the indwelling of the divine in the natural order on the one hand and the metaphorization of divine action in the world on the other, the wind can become the site of a theophany, as in Isaiah's proclamation that 'the Lord will come in fire, and his chariots like the whirlwind', or indeed in the mysterious *dᵉmāmāh*, frequently translated as 'breeze' or 'breath of wind', in which Eliphaz and Elijah encountered God.[45] Most powerfully and consistently, it is the wind that represents God judgment, eradicating Israel's enemies with a 'fierce blast' or scattering Israel 'like chaff'.[46] As Hosea says of Israel: 'Although he [Ephraim] may flourish among rushes, the east wind shall come, a blast from the Lord, rising from the wilderness'.[47]

But the 'breath of God' that brings judgment, also brings life, making living creatures of humans and animals.[48] The word *rūaḥ* in the sense of 'spirit' is intimately bound in with a complex of anthropological terms that denote the foci of human cognition and action. It has been identified as the principle of 'vitality' or 'process of breathing in which the dynamic vitality of the self is expressed'.[49] But *rūaḥ* differs from words such as *ḥayîm* ('life'), *nepheš* ('soul'), *lēb* ('heart') by virtue of the fact that it is only said to *indwell* the self; it does not represent the human person as such. It is significant in this respect that the *rūaḥ* not only derives from God in the most intimate fashion but is also said to return to God after death.[50] Although *rūaḥ* does show some features that are purely vitalistic (such as 'courage' and 'anger'), its primary sense as a term of theo-anthropology is to express the profound relation that exists between God and his human creatures.[51]

The ambiguity of *rūaḥ* as an anthropological term is heightened by the many occasions where *rūaḥ* marks the intervention of God in history through the agency of his spirit. In the Book of Judges, the 'spirit of the Lord' descended upon Samson, giving him exceptional strength, as it came also upon Gideon, Jephthah and Othniel.[52] In 1 Samuel this tradition of the descent of the spirit upon individuals continues, albeit in a royal context, with the anointing of Saul and David.[53] Ezra tells that God instructed his people through his 'good spirit' and he proclaims to God: 'Many years you were patient with them, and warned them by your spirit through your prophets; yet they would not listen'.[54] And it is the prophets, chiefly, who become divine agents through the advent of the divine spirit-breath. The true prophet is known by his or her ability to tell the future.[55] In the prophet a divine knowledge is given of time itself, and of the meaning of history. Thus it is the prophets who warn Israel of the impending 'day of the Lord', when all shall be called to account. And it is the prophets too who constantly call the powerful to account for their abuse of power and for their failure to care for the weakest and most marginalized in society: 'Wash yourselves; make yourselves clean; remove the evil of your doings from before my eyes; cease to do evil, learn to do good; seek justice, rescue the oppressed, defend the orphan, plead for the widow'.[56] Most frequently it is the most powerful groups in society, such as the ruling powers and the priesthood, who are the target of prophetic condemnation.

It is the spirit then who is the presence of God within his creation which, exterior to God and free with respect to him, is also formed of his spirit-breath and animated by his word-wind.[57] It is the spirit at work within the creation and humankind who draws the created order towards its natural end in God, and it is the spirit who descends upon the gifted persons who guide Israel and who – in the spirit of holiness – teach Israel the ways of righteousness and compassion. From a Christian perspective however, the action of the Spirit in the world is itself a trinitarian event, since it points in turn to the Second Person of the Trinity, 'through whom all things were made' and who is therefore another face of God's implication in and concern with his creation. Isaiah proclaims that 'the Spirit of the Lord' shall rest upon the messiah, who shall possess 'the spirit of wisdom and under-standing, the spirit of counsel and might, the spirit of knowledge and the fear of the Lord'.[58] The Suffering Servant too shall be the ultimate putting into question of the abuse of power which is the corruption of divinely granted freedom. The servant, upon whom God puts his spirit, 'will not grow faint or be crushed until he has established justice in the earth'.[59]

Incarnation

The creative utterances of God with which the Book of Genesis opens summons the world into being by reference, command and address. The spatial, social and dialogical dimensions of divine speech created a space inhabited first by creatures and then by human beings, who represent the whole of the creation in their capacity to answer God in prayer, worship and assent. By virtue of our moral consciousness, we human beings can freely accept God's commands and can become interlocutors with God, celebrating his works and testifying to his greatness. The affirmation of God's order, through a life of holiness founded upon the love of God and of our neighbour, is the recognition that the creation is other to God and free, and yet is at the same time fundamentally contained within him. Holiness is the recognition that in every attachment to, desire for, or use we make of the world, and of all the persons, creatures and things in it, we are actually setting ourselves in relation with God, who is the Creator of the world and immanent within it. By God's creative speech-act, we are summoned then to the understanding that all we think, say and do is a manner of relating with God and of responding to him. When we speak of the world, we are called to remember that it is of God's world that we speak, who through his creation has set himself definitively in relation with us. And when we speak of God, we should understand that our speaking *of* him is rooted in our speaking *with* him, as a response to his prior speaking with us. The doctrine of God as Creator is not an invitation to wrestle with the aporia of a creative act performed outside the space–time continuum (since it is held precisely to inaugurate the space–time continuum), but rather to understand that God and the world are simultaneously different and one. In Christian tradition this simultaneity of distinction and identity is expressed in the immanence and transcendence of God and is signalled also by linking the creation 'in' time with the generation of the Word from eternity. The distinction and unity of the Son with respect to the Father forms the ground of the distinction and unity of the creation with respect to the Trinity as a whole.

In the Old Testament narratives, it is the prophets who receive the Word of God and for whom the Word becomes an indwelling power; it is they therefore who are summoned into a conscious awareness of the divine speech relation. In the actualization of that relation, they are called to allow the divine voice to insert itself within their own voice: a struggle which typifies many of the 'commissioning' passages. For many of the prophets, the commissioning is marked by the 'occurrence' of the Word to them, where the Hebrew *hāyāh* (to occur, to happen, to be), which also appears repeatedly in the opening verses of Genesis ('and it came to be'), evokes the generative speech of the creation narrative. God speaks 'in' the prophet, and his words admonish Israel for her corruption, urging the people of God to return to the ways of righteousness and justice.[60] As we have seen in the discussion of revelation in Chapter Nine, the calling of a prophet such as Jeremiah goes beyond the formulaic and begins to take on the character of a conversation. It is Moses however, who is exemplar of the prophetic calling, and he speaks to God 'face to face'.[61] God speaks *with* Moses, thus elevating him to a representative role, and God's speaking *with* him is at the same time God's speaking *through* him to all his people. To the extent that God speaks 'in' Moses, and in other of the prophets, and to the extent that Moses compassionately intervenes for his people by interceding with God on their behalf, allowing their voices to speak through him, we can identify the beginnings of a trinitarian 'envoicing'. God speaks with Moses and through him, to the people of God, while Moses beseeches Yahweh's help on behalf of Israel, who are suffering persecution and exile.

It is in the person of Christ that this two-way flow of speech agency takes on a new and more radical form. God speaks with the world through Jesus, not through the mediations of theophany as with Moses, but directly, so that those who have seen the Son have seen the Father.[62] Jesus speaks 'with authority', and his own words – spoken for instance to Lazarus – have the generative power of God himself. But when Jesus speaks, his followers hear a human voice, and Jesus too can pray to God, speaking with him not only as God with God but also in the fullness of his humanity. What is revealed to us in him therefore is on the one hand a divine, trinitarian conversation, which is a loving and infinite mutuality of relation, and on the other, a new kind of human speech: one that is filled with the presence of God, who has called us to sonship and to a new possibility of speaking *with* God. But there is a further dimension to the multiple 'envoicings' of Jesus. As we noted in our discussion of the phenomenology of faith in Chapter Ten, faith entails the recognition that Jesus is not only the centre of his own world but also the centre of our world and of all possible worlds. Thus the voice of Christ speaks in a sense from within ourselves, and we find ourselves in him. In more traditional language, the Son has assumed human nature as such, and so he contains us in our contingency and finitude. Thus Christ comes to represent us, through his humanity, and it is he who gives voice to our deepest needs before God, as he 'intercedes' with the Father on our behalf.[63] Our own voice enters his, just as his voice enters us, in the recognition of his universal humanity. As the voice of God however, Christ summons us with absolute authority to the truth of our own existential condition, in ethical suspension between the rejection and acceptance of God and the affirmation or occlusion of our human other.

There are a multiplicity of conversations in Jesus: of God with God, God with us, the humanity of Christ – and thus the creation – with God, the humanity of Christ with ourselves. Alternatively we can say that there are a multiplicity of 'envoicings' in Jesus: the Father speaks in the Son, humanity speaks in Christ with the Father, and Christ gives voice to humanity compassionately when he intercedes with the Father on our behalf. It is the Holy Spirit who as the spirit, breath, air of God makes these conversations and envoicings possible. It is she who – as divine breath and spirit – represents the very possibility of relational speech in the Trinity, and – as the breath and wind of God – grounds the powerful generative utterance of God in the creation. Moreover, as the principle of the divine life within creation, the Spirit is associated in a most particular way with the incarnation. She attends Mary at the Annunciation, and descends upon the Son at the proclamation of the Father's affirmation of him. Unlike John, Jesus baptizes in the Spirit. Most importantly, in the words of the Niceno-Constantinopolitan Creed, Jesus himself was 'born of the Holy Spirit and the Virgin Mary', affirming the most intimate connection possible. It is the Spirit then that stands at the heart of the revelation which, as we have seen, requires the appropriate reception of the divine communication if it is to be revelation and not a heteronomous monologue. That capacity to receive the revelation must itself be given by divine initiative, which we have understood to be the action of the Spirit as God's presence within the creation, 'speaking through the prophets' and preparing for the coming of the messiah. In particular we must associate the Spirit with the formation of the human nature of Christ, to whom the revelation is primordially given, since it is by him alone that it is perfectly received.

But the Spirit is active too in a further and critical way at the very centre of the dramatic unfolding which is the incarnation. According to the Lucan narrative Jesus experiences the loss of God in the silence of the Father, when he cries out the unanswered question: 'Lord, Lord, why have you forsaken me?'. That silence between Father and Son marks the point at which all the errors, deceptions and denials of the created order, all the refusals to speak, to praise and to listen, all the lies, corruptions and misunderstandings are taken up into the trinitarian speech and are redeemed. The rupture of relation itself becomes in that moment a new possibility of relation, as the silence of the world, which is bleak emptiness, is refigured by the divine breath as fullness of silence from which the speaking Spirit will break forth in new abundance. In the silence of God on the cross, the semantics of alienation becomes the fecund expressivity of speech redeemed.

Conclusion

The model of revelation outlined in Chapter Nine stressed the extent to which the divine initiative must include the human recipient, and shape human history and responsibility. The failure to achieve this would be the failure of revelation itself, which would no longer be a message given and received but rather a heteronomous communication: a monologue from heaven. We identified the human nature of Christ as the first and fullest recipient, through whose union with the Word the revelation is accomplished. But the movement of God into the hypostatic union is necessarily a kenotic one, and our study of Jesus as *splanghna theou* shows that the content of that kenosis is compassion: the compassion of God for his creation. To be compassionate entails a specific structure of cognition, affirmation and volition, whereby we recognize the other in their world-centredness, at the nodal point of their own interweaving narratives, and actively affirm and nourish their existence, even at our own self-risk. The incarnation marks the point at which God freely entered human history, empathetically *recognizing* who we are, in our emptiness and fallenness, and *affirming* us compassionately in the fullness of who we might become. But by our previous argument, this infinite divine act of compassion must also be seen as the epiphany of infinite being, since the self-emptying of God in Christ is the performance in history of the infinite loss and regaining which constitutes the trinitarian relations. The divine compassion enacted and fulfilled in the person of Christ holds a central position for the whole of humanity therefore, and for the whole of creation. In Jesus the possibilities of our own becoming are made manifest. The Christian community are those who receive that manifestation in Jesus in such a way that they perceive him to be simultaneously their own personal way and end. But as an epiphany of infinite being, the compassion of God that is accomplished in Jesus Christ points also to the divine creativity that is at work within human nature itself and at the centre of the formation of the world.

13

The Christian Church:
Truth as Transgression

Truth is an ideal expressive of the Universe, at once coherent and comprehensive.
It must not conflict with itself, and there must be no suggestion which fails to fall
inside it. Perfect truth in short must realize the idea of a systematic whole.

F. H. Bradley, *Essays on Truth and Reality*

In the person of Christ God has entered the heart of human speaking. He
has taken possession of our language and so of all the possible worlds that
language engenders. Above all, he has resituated the relation between one
speech agent and another within the primal inner-trinitarian ground of
triadic speech, in which self and other combine in a dispossessive excess of
love and affirmation. Jesus inaugurated a new possibility of speaking, in
equality with God, which has forever changed the parameters of human
conversing and human relating. The invitation to speak with God, in a
conversation of equals, is grounded in a prior act of God shaping history
through the Spirit and preparing human kind to receive the triadic speech
of God with understanding. The people of God are those who have come
to hear the living voice of Jesus Christ, who speaks with us in the scriptures, in worship and in the communities who gather in his name. The
Christian church is the making manifest of the faith relation and is
grounded specifically in the new community that obtains between those
who are called to speak with God in this way, and who enter the triadic
speech rhythms of the Trinity.

In our discussion of the Trinity as triadic speech, we argued that the
sphere of reference – the world, or that which speech agents speak together
about – is in the Trinity itself a Person and agent of speech: the Holy Spirit.
Thus in the Trinity as it exists in itself there is no externality, but all is
contained within the divine Persons and their relations. It is only with the
act of creation that God wills a world that is exterior to himself as a sphere
of divine reference, in which his presence remains active however, through
the operations of the Holy Spirit. It is the Spirit who prepares the way for
the speaking of God's word in history as the making manifest of triadic
speech. For that to be possible, human history had to be shaped and
prepared to receive the new speech with understanding. The structure of
that speech as given in history pivoted on the speaking relation of Father

and Son, with the Spirit glimpsed in the main as the divine *preceding* which allows human speakers to receive the speech of the Trinity and to participate in it. From the silence of the cross the creative Spirit was regenerated, releasing a new abundance of speaking in and with God: as public witness, praise, prophecy and preaching. In these new, distinctively ecclesial forms of speaking, the Spirit shapes the world to receive ever more deeply the divine self-communication as triadic speech.

Within the pragmatic understanding of language that we have applied here, speech remains for us fundamentally a way of *relating*. To talk of triadic speaking then, is to say something about the manner of our existence with and before the other. In our analysis of Rublev's icon of the Trinity, we have stressed the extent to which the presence of the Third Person disrupts any tendency there might be for the gaze between Father and Son to become enclosed or narcissistic. The Third Person opens out their relation, defining it as one which is simultaneously personal and universal. This same dynamic is re-enacted at the level of the incarnation and of faith. Here the universal and the personal overlap firstly in the universal world-centredness of Jesus which communicates that he is both centre of his own world and of all possible worlds. But it comes into view also in the fact that our self-emptying affirmation of Jesus, which we call faith, delivers not Jesus himself as object of our compassion but rather the external other who we discover anew *within* the relationship with Christ. In other words, faith, in which Christ is the object of our affirmation, is expressed in discipleship, where the suffering other becomes the object of our compassionate affirmation. In a sense our relation with Christ deepens and draws life to the extent that we 'hear' the triadic voice in the suffering other and discover there the epiphany of a new and trinitarian existence.

The turn to the other which arises from the structure of faith comes into view first and foremost as the *splanghna*, or compassionate love, which for Paul in his Letter to the Philippians is the ground of the church. It is those who share our faith who first arise within the relation with Christ as the object of our compassionate love. This is not to proclaim favouritism and exclusivity but rather is to acknowledge the bond with those whose own existence is transfigured in and through the incarnation. Self-emptying love creates a shared realm of transfigured existence as mutual indwelling. What remains distinctive to this love, despite all the inadequacies and failures of human communities, is the naming of it as Jesus among his people: 'where two or three are gathered in my name, I am there among them'.[1] The dispossessive mutuality of self and other is the membership of the 'body of Christ' and the formation of the ecclesial reality; as such it sets up a trinitarian rhythm of universal and personal love which was communicated first in the historical narrative of Father, Son and Spirit.[2]

Triadic speech, in which the people of God are called to participate, is the sharing out of the trinitarian dynamic which is the unity of being and love. Springing from the divine self-disclosure, the Christian church is the extension and deepening of the revelation in history and, as such, is the making visible of the inner-trinitarian movement which is communicated to us in the person of Jesus Christ as the speaking Word of God. It is this movement into visibility which constitutes the *bodiliness* of the church, whose members are baptized 'into one body'.[3] Just as the human, embodied nature of Christ 'serves the divine Word as a living organ of salvation', so too the church unified as the 'body of Christ' enacts the transformational, triadic speech of the revelation.[4] The faithful who constitute the church are those whose own speaking has been overtaken by the divine speech, and whose own existence has been claimed by the new trinitarian existence made manifest in history. Caught between human and divine speaking, the people of God are called to witness to the truth of the revelation not only in what they say, as representation, but also in what they do, as the deepening visibility through embodiment of what has been revealed.

Christian truth

The concept of Christian truth sits uneasily between conventional uses of the term and the claim that God has made himself known, has become *visible* in an unparalleled way in the person of Christ and the community who confess his name. On the grounds of the world-centredness of Christ, the Christian thinker is compelled to seek to show that Christianity is more than a subjective and personal conviction on the one hand, while repelling the notion that faith is reducible to truth–falsity claims on the other. Faith is predicated upon a belief in revelation not simply as the disclosure of a truth within the world but rather as the coming into visibility of the truth which is the root of the world. And yet there is something within Christian self-understanding which pushes towards an empirical and therefore universal dimension to its truth claims. For centuries apologetics was dominated by the belief that scriptural evidence constituted empirical proof for Christian claims, supported by the truths of natural theology which were evident to reason. Following the rise of philosophical empiricism, apologetics increasingly stressed the meaningfulness of Christian belief, in a move which marked a drift from an objectivist correspondence view of the truth of Christianity to one rooted in coherence and subjectivity. But some residue of the empirical must remain in Christian truth claims if these are to be consistent with the principle that Christian revelation is cosmic and incarnational, manifest within the world.

The empirical truth claim to which we would point is not that of miracles, which are easily susceptible to a variety of explanations, or that of the resurrection itself, since biblical scholarship has shown the extent to which the resurrection appearances only occur within the context of the proto-community of faith. Rather, it is the claim of the empty tomb which marks the empirical and universal character of Christian belief. Implied within the affirmation that Christ rose from the dead is the affirmation that his body did not decay. The empty tomb then is intrinsic to, though distinct from, belief in the resurrection. Those who believe in the resurrection explain the empty tomb on the grounds that Christ rose from the dead. But it follows from this that – according to Christian belief – those who do not believe in the resurrection are still confronted with the aporia of the empty tomb. Christianity has never proposed a cognitive dichotomy at this level of seeing, such that those with faith saw an empty tomb and those without faith saw the dead body of Christ. Rather the claim is that anyone could have seen that the tomb was empty. While it is the case that the issue of whether the tomb was empty or not, and the causes of its emptiness, are no longer in any sense verifiable, these are issues on which it would in principle have been possible to make authoritative and binding judgments at the time. Thus while the resurrection of Christ, which constitutes the heart of Christian believing, belongs to distinctively ecclesial cognition, the *absence* of the body of Christ in the empty tomb could have been registered by anyone, even though observers who were outside the cycle of faith would presumably have found some alternative explanation or simply noted it as an inexplicable event.

In general however, Christian claims exhibit features which are more consonant with coherence and pragmatic theories of truth. In line with other world religions, Christianity offers a totalizing understanding of the meaning of existence. Where religious beliefs differ from a philosophical account of reality is that they are often embedded within social and ritual practices which characterize religion as a totalizing life-orientation. It is surely not the case that most Christians in modern secular society choose their beliefs on account of their intrinsic persuasiveness and then pursue a series of practices in accordance with those beliefs. Rather, a distinctive set of beliefs are seen to be operative within a particular community whose identity is grounded in the practice of praise and worship. Christian identity begins with the desire to be part of that community who hear the voice of Christ and stand in a dynamic and living relation with God made flesh for us. The recognition of Christian truth is in its most primary sense therefore prior to any set of beliefs, and is to be identified with a personal summons and an assent as we enter into an ever deeper relation with God who speaks with us in his Son in a practising community of faith. The truth of Christian doctrine, as we have argued previously, resides in the capacity of its propositions to communicate and express the personhood of Christ, in whom God has chosen to set himself definitively in relation with the world. The deepest truth of the incarnation itself therefore is precisely God's coming into visibility, which is communicated to us not primarily in a set of beliefs or doctrines, for all the importance of these, but most foundationally in God's personal coming into relation with us through Jesus Christ, who still speaks in and with his community – the people of God, the body of Christ – today.

While Christianity exhibits elements of what contemporary theories know as the correspondence, coherence, and pragmatic functions of truth, we need also to define Christian truth as being in some fundamental sense *aletheia*: the disclosure or becoming visible of God to and among his people. But the transcendental character of Christian truth suggests that it is better communicated in terms not so much of its content as its effects. The nature of triadic speech, which we have used as our primary image of the Trinity, is that possessiveness is continuously broken open even as it is formed. The mutual gaze of the self–other relation, in which narcissistic forces can rebound and aggregate, is constantly intercepted by the presence of the third, who dissolves the sense of self into a universal rhythm of openness and emptying out. Christian truth then, which is given to us, is best defined and known by virtue of this opening out, as a visible life of discipleship and service, acted out within the world. The reception of Christian truth as faith is always transgressive in this sense, taking us beyond the boundaries of what we perceive to be specifically our own possession; and is always dispossessive as we come under the power of another.

In an earlier discussion we made a plea for poeticity as a model for fundamental theology. In the phenomenon of inspiration the poet's own voice is taken over by another way of speaking. In the reception or reading of a poem, we enter a new sphere of non-teleological language which constructs a world to us that is a transformational alternative to the empirical world of ordinary reference. In the same way, the man or woman of faith is overtaken by a new way of seeing and speaking, which constitutes a new mode of human existence, grounded in the divine self-disclosure of triadic speech. This truth cannot ever be adequately grasped and made our own but – as excess – must rather be visibly *performed* within the world.

Richard Schechner has defined the concept of performance as differing from that of ritual to the extent that the former implies an activity 'which is done by an individual or group in the presence of and for another individual or group', while the activity of the latter is for the sake of the participants.[5] All human activity is in a sense performative, in that we publicly interact with our fellow human beings through a system of shared verbal and corporal codes. When we speak or act, we do so for the sake of the other, in order that they should understand what we mean and intend. Indeed, performance in an important sense can be identified with culture, as that shared system of signs and codes whereby we communicate with one another and construct a common social reality.

But we can use the notion of performance in a special and enhanced sense in the case of the church, which as the 'body of Christ' is conformed in its very existence to the incarnational movement of divine self-communication to the world. This making visible is in itself a kind of bodily performance before the eyes of the world. But what is performed publicly is a compassionate and dispossessive truth which can itself only be authentically communicated through compassionate and dispossessive existence. This is the performance of a kind of text therefore which stands over and against the empirical world. The recitation of the Christian poem is akin to taking part in a theatrical performance, in which the stage props are real objects, the scene settings are real places, but the script shared among the actors is the unfolding and realization of a divine narrative. In the performance of that script, each and every actor plays both themselves and Another, speaks both with their own voice and with the voice of Another. And each Christian dramatically represents both who he or she is now and who, in the light of the incarnation, they are called to be.

Thus the church in this aspect is itself a field of performance, a bodily acting out of the truth of the revelation, in a kind of theatre of dispossession. Those who are outside the poem are thus confronted with its mystery. By seeing the poem performed, they are invited to empathize with the characters within it, and to develop a sense of what life might be like, within the poem and not outside its enchantment. They are further confronted with the possibility of another way of being society, at times radically at odds with the world. In the spirit of Brecht's 'alienation effect', the church as the 'theatre of dispossession' can challenge and unsettle its audience simply by displaying an alternative manner of existence, inviting them to reflect critically upon the character of their own lives and experience. Dispossessive compassion, as we argued in our phenomenological reduction of compassion, is infectious and self-communicating for it is finally grounded in the gravity of existence, manifest in those whose life is transfigured, drawing us towards them by the weight of our own emptiness.

The Marian church

Speaking and listening are both necessary conditions for the possibility of authentic conversation, which is patterned on and grounded in the divine conversations revealed to us in the person of Christ. But we have noted also the intensification of this dynamic, as the distinctively trinitarian and christological phenomenon of 'envoicing', in which the church is drawn in its own way to participate. This movement traditionally finds expression in the church's understanding of the role of Mary as Mother and model of the church. It is she who first received the speaking Word, in the proclamation of the angel at the annunciation and in the overshadowing of the Holy Spirit who is the presence of God in his creation, forming and preparing the world for the divine self-communication of the Word. Her reception of the Word is marked by her own consenting response: 'Here am I, the servant of the Lord: let it be with me according to your word', in which the first Mosaic phrase locates Mary in the tradition of the listening prophets while belonging also to the new dispensation.[6] The moment when Mary, in the words of *Lumen Gentium*, 'received the Word of God in her heart and in her body and gave Life to the world', was the most intense engagement of the Spirit within history.[7] That engagement manifested first not as speech but as listening: a listening in 'obedience' (a word which derives from the Latin form *oboedire*, which also has the meaning 'to hear or to listen'). Mary's listening to the speech of God is a listening in the Spirit, and when she speaks her assent, her voice is Spirit-filled. Thus the assent of Mary to the divine Word belongs in itself to the communicative movement which is the incarnation. In that moment her voice was filled with the presence of Another, and she spoke in a way that implicated all the faithful who were to come after. Mary's was a human speaking that became conformed to the rhythms of receiving and giving at the heart of the Word of God, and is the primal speech of the Christian church. The church remembers Mary's presence with the twelve at Pentecost in the inauguration of the new ecclesial way of speaking as prophecy, praise and preaching, as the public and visible fulfilment of her most intimate relation with the Spirit of God.

Mary's listening to the divine speech finally yielded a new way of speaking which comes into view for the first time in the account of the marriage feast at Cana.[8] Jesus had not yet begun his public ministry, and at first chooses not to intervene when the supply of wine is exhausted. But Mary says to the servants, 'Do whatever he tells you'. As the 'first of his signs' which reveal his glory, Jesus then asks the servants to fill the six empty jars with water, which miraculously become filled with wine. Mary's words at this point represent a kind of intercession therefore. Mary has in church tradition frequently been linked with intercession, and she is seen as the one who 'intercedes before her Son in the fellowship of the saints'.[9] If the Lucan birth narratives present her as the site of primary Christian speech therefore, her intercessory function represents a deepening and intensification of that speaking, whereby the process of envoicing begins to become explicit with the initiation of Jesus' public ministry.

The Marian church, which is the whole of the church in its listening aspect, is expressed in particular as an intercessory mode of speech, whereby the church speaks on behalf of others. That distinctively ecclesial speaking is expressed in the *oratio fidelium* of the early church which since Vatican II has returned to the heart of the eucharist. In the bidding prayers, the people 'exercise their priestly function by interceding for all mankind'.[10] This is a form of what we have called envoicing, and it suggests a compassionate engagement with others which leads in turn to an empathetic entering into the perspective of the poor, the sick and the marginalized.

The Marian church is called to become a place of truth where the marginalized can speak to society at large, and where their case is put. At all points the Marian church questions the complacency of society and its indifference to the sufferings of others, as through the Marian church those who do not conform in some way to the dominant norms of society find a voice. If society privileges men above women, then the Marian church speaks for the experiences of women, and allows women who are marginalized in their social access to speak through the church. The Marian church speaks for the developing world in the developed world. It speaks to those who are healthy and strong for the handicapped and the socially disadvantaged. It speaks for those who face persecution on account of their ethnic background or prejudice on account of their sexual orientation. It speaks for those without power, for children or the unborn. It speaks for the living environment, and for compassion towards animals in medical research and farming. Such intercessory, Marian speaking represents the solidarity of the church with the oppressed. As the *eleemosynaria trinitatis* ('almsgiver of the Trinity'), as Jakobus a Voragine called her, Mary is the model of the church's active support for the poor.[11] In the Third General Conference of Latin American Bishops held at Puebla in 1979, Mary was identified as the 'active co-worker' in the redemption, who 'shows quite clearly that Christ does not annul the creativity of those who follow him'.[12] In the vision which befell the Indian Juan Diego in 1531 at Guadalupe, Mary became a powerful healing presence in Latin American history. It is she who 'will listen to the silenced poor', since through her the evils of colonialization suffered by the Indians and the division between Spaniard and Indian were drawn in a liberating way into the light of the redemption:

> In the presence of Juan Diego their crushed dignity is restored and from their imposed worthlessness, [the Indians] are called upon to be the chosen servants and messengers. The Empire would condemn them to a perpetual status as minors – not even allowing them into sacred orders and certainly not listening to their ideas or opinions. Yet the Mother of God would listen to them, constitute them as her trusted messengers, and be ever present to protect and defend them.[13]

Virgil Elizondo continues:

> It is only when the silenced, ignored and ridiculed Indians, Mulattos and Mestizzos, began to speak freely about the inner meaning of their faith experience that the full theological implications of Marian devotions could be known by the rest of the Christian world.[14]

In what may seem a paradoxical formulation, the Marian church speaks even for and with those who are excluded from the church itself, such as divorced and remarried couples. The trinitarian character of the church, manifested in the incarnation, calls into question the stable limits of the church's visibility, which becomes a dynamic boundary across which conversations are maintained in the church's openness to ever greater and more visible unity. The visibility of the church is such that it always exceeds our expectations and lies beyond our reckoning. The experience of those who fall outside the limits and norms of the Catholic Church always remains integral to the destiny of the church therefore since the very unity of the church is a participation in the incarnation as the body of Christ. If Mary stands in the 'Magnificat' tradition of Hannah, Deborah, Miriam and Judith, calling for justice for the oppressed, then she is herself also an outsider and is 'the last and most crucial link in a long genealogical chain, wherein four foreign and/or sinful women – Tamor, Rahab, Ruth, the wife of Uriah – had entered into the history of the messianic line'.[15] In another contemporary context, David Flusser, a modern Jewish scholar, has referred to her as 'a sorrowful Jewish mother' who must be seen in terms of the specific history of Jewish suffering.[16] As the church allows the voices of those outside its own limits to be heard within it, in its Marian aspect, the church also recognizes that its own speech is grounded in the radical openness of trinitarian relations, which exceed final human calculation, and thus remains true to its own destiny.

Christian speech was born in the silence of the cross, where the triadic speech of the Trinity entered the cosmic silence of the Father which was the annihilation and withdrawal of all that is. From that end of speech, the new speech of the Spirit emerged: from emptiness there came the new breath of regeneration. The listening silence of Mary then, in fear and awe, was already a participation in trinitarian life, without which the Spirit could not have filled her voice, nor our voices sound in her words.

The Petrine church

The truth of the church is intimately bound up with the coming into visibility which is the *bodiliness* of the Christian church. This incarnational truth attains a particular density of expression in the bishops and ordained ministers of the church. As the sacred minister of the eucharist, the bishop expresses the visible unity of the church in a particularly intensive way, with respect to the people of God in his own diocese, to the church as the universal body and even beyond the visible boundaries of the church with people of good will.[17] That unity is also exercised in the bishop's commitment to conversation or open-hearted dialogue, both within the college of bishops and with the laity and with the human community at large. The character of the dialogue is both pastoral and educational since the bishops are entrusted with safeguarding the deposit of revelation for the whole church. It is to them that the primary responsibility falls for preaching the gospel and for maintaining the continuity of the church's teaching.

Since the truth of the revelation that is preserved within the community of the church is itself one which is dialogical and dispossessive, the bishops and those responsible for overseeing the teaching office of the church are called to exercise their teaching and regulative functions in a pastorally sensitive way, so that no dissonance appears between the nature of whatis being taught and the manner of the teaching of it. The exceptional visibility of the hierarchy lays exceptional demands upon them to be seen to perform Christian truth in the very proclamation of that truth. *Lumen Gentium* calls upon the bishop to treat his priests 'as sons and friends', and to 'exercise a powerful influence for good on those over whom they are placed, by abstaining from all wrong doing in their conduct' and to be 'compassionate to those who are ignorant and erring'.[18] The task of the bishops is that of 'schooling the faithful in a love of the whole Mystical Body of Christ and, in a special way, of the poor, the suffering, and those who are undergoing persecution for the sake of the church'.[19] As exposition of doctrine, the teaching of the bishops and those who exercise the magisterium of the church is grounded in the divine revelation itself, whose communicative structure, as we have seen, is such as to take account of the one who receives the revelation. That communicative movement in itself entails a degree of self-emptying or kenosis, and so the inner coherence of Catholic teaching calls for expression in the self-risking identification of the teacher with those with whom he is in dialogue. Failing to enter empathetically into the world of the other is to occlude the other and is to limit teaching to the heteronomous pronouncement of principles against the other, without adequate provision for the personal reception of such teaching. Christian teaching, on the other hand, is an interactive process, a conversation in 'the Spirit of truth', in the words of *Lumen Gentium*, so that 'the People of God, guided by the sacred teaching authority, and obeying it, receives not the mere word of men, but truly the word of God'.[20]

Those who bear responsibility for the doctrinal regulation of faith and for church order are themselves members of the body whose own faith is measured by the extent to which their own existence and relating has been overtaken by the divine self-communication of triadic speech. The Catholic Church is a pilgrim church of individuals who have been called into a radical unity of trinitarian relation as the visible Body of Christ. Christian teaching is a kind of speaking which knows that it too is born of the difference between the speaking of God with God, made accessible to us through the incarnation, and ordinary human speaking and relating. It is summoned therefore to be self-aware and to be radically ordered to the other, without whom such speech can become empty self-aggrandizement. This marks the great importance in our time of Pope John Paul II's penitent acknowledgment of the errors and mistakes of the Catholic Church, which shows precisely the awareness in the Roman Pontiff, who holds supreme authority for the teaching of the Church, of the distinction between human and divine speaking. In those penitential remarks, the whole church can come to the renewed understanding of its own location between the divine self-communication and the expressive acts of a purely human speaking. Instructed in this way, the church can realize its own nature more intensely as human speech that is illumined and transfigured by the speech of Another.

Mission

Christian faith occurs precisely where our own speaking and relating is overtaken by the divine dynamic of triadic speech. It thus entails two kinds of affirmation. The first is that we truly encounter God in Christ and – through the Spirit – hear in the Son the voice of the Father. The second affirmation is that this new kind of speech-relation can never become our own property but always remains gifted by the divine disclosure. Our own new speaking, as an attitude of faith, is grounded in the relation into which we enter through listening to the voice of Christ, in scripture, liturgy and the body of those who celebrate his name. The speaking of the Petrine church as teaching and of the Marian church as intercession is neither ordinary speaking nor is it divine speaking but rather is a human speaking that has been overtaken by the trinitarian self-disclosure and has been conceived in the domain between the two which is marked by excess, risk and penitence. Christian truth too is of this kind, and is affirmed between a human reality and the disclosure of a divine reality which transcends any capacity we have to render an adequate account of it. Christian truth is therefore both a coming into possession and a form of dispossession. It fills us with a pervasive trust and knowing even as it robs us of the security of stable self-knowledge which dissolves in the dynamic of our own deepening relation with the divine being-in-relation, who is the trinitarian Word. The witness to Christian truth before the world is thus simultaneously the confession of our own individual and corporate inadequacy before the transcendent reality of the divine speaking that has come upon us. The affirmation of that truth and the penitence that we discover at the heart of our embrace of it necessarily belong to each other, and they find existential expression in the life of self-emptying risk for the sake of the other which is discipleship. It is the Christian form of life as compassionate self-exceeding before the other which is the true communication of Christian truth as the dispossessive, overflowing eruption of being and love from within the Godhead.

In the exercise of its missionary function therefore, which is intrinsic to its trinitarian origins, the church is called both to witness effectively to the truth by which it has been possessed and to acknowledge its own inadequacy and sinfulness in the presence of that truth. Only in this way can the risk be avoided that the church will mistakenly take its own speaking to be either ordinary human speech or indeed divine speech, and fail to understand that ecclesial speaking is human speaking that knows itself to be under the sway or power of the triadic, revealed speech of the Trinity. That space, which itself guarantees the possibility of transfigured speech, is secured only by a penitential awareness on the part of the body of Christ of the extent to which our ordinary speaking and relating has been claimed by another speaking and relating which shines through it. Ecclesial speaking occurs therefore in an intermediate realm, of penance and transfiguration, and is, by its very nature and calling, a journeying speech which knows itself to be under the command of the revealed speech of God.

Conversation with other religions

Christians live in the power of a truth whose dimensions reflect both truth as subjective personal and social meaning and truth as universal reference, as well as truth as pragmatic expression of personal ideals and values. The religious character of that truth however, resides in its claim to ultimate meaning and value, which sets it apart from other kinds of truth claims. We have argued that truth in this sense never comes into the possession of those who receive it, but is gifted within a dynamic and continuing relation of the church with the incarnate Christ, the living voice of God. Such is the excess and transcendence of divine truth that its reception and communication is expressed both as explicit witness to doctrine and faith as *fides quae* but also and crucially as *fides qua* in the performance of a life-style of dispossession for the sake of the other. It is in the latter that the deep communication of the truth occurs, as the absolute and total claim of the truth laid upon us as concrete individuals living in the real world. Christian truth, in its fullness, cannot be definitively known or understood, and so cannot as such be communicated as knowledge or information, but only lived out and made manifest in believing, discipleship and compassion.

The greatest task of reflection for those who live in the power of Christian truth comes not in confrontation with secular modes of living and believing, which in general make no parallel claim to ultimate value and meaning, but in the encounter with other world religions. The dialogue between religions has deepened and intensified as globalization and modern mass communication have made a wide range of religious traditions available across the world. It is naïve to think that such religious traditions are not themselves changed by their advance into the West, but in many cases they are also supported by substantial ethnic groups whose practice of Buddhism, Hinduism or Islam, for example, is close or identical with that in countries where these religions have flourished for centuries. Religious pluralism is a condition of modern life, and a significant engagement with other religious identities has become intrinsic to the theological vocation as it has become part of the experience of countless Christians in their ordinary walk of life.

But the problematics posed by inter-faith dialogue touch the heart of Christian believing. The conceptuality of a world religion inevitably tends to be universalist and totalizing; that is perhaps a precondition for the propagation of a unified religious system across diverse times and cultures. For a world religion to dismantle its claim to universal significance would be for it to undermine the parallel claim to be concerned with ultimate meanings and value.[21] In its dialogue with other religions,

Christianity – in step with its partners – is confronted with a multiplicity of choices, each of which reflects in some fundamental way the nature of Christian self-understanding.

It is possible simply to dismiss other religions as error, choosing not to take note of what they appear to have in common with Christianity in terms both of ways of constructing the world and the ethical values which they enact within the world. This approach is more likely to occur where religions have no natural contact with each other, but in a world in which contact is frequent and diverse, such triumphalism undermines the very claim that Christians make both to the goodness of God and to the moral integrity of Christian life. Furthermore, it reflects the human judgment that God has not revealed himself outside the Christian dispensation. It is one thing to claim on the basis of revelation the fullness of God's self-disclosure to the world in Jesus Christ, which properly transcends our understanding, and it is another to proclaim the understanding that God has not revealed himself to any other community in any other way. The latter is a statement that reflects an all too familiar kind of human thinking and, as we have argued, it is the function of the church in its Marian aspect, to open itself to conversation and relations which extend beyond the visible limits of the church, thus contesting the very human tendency to reify what are – according to trinitarian logic – more properly dynamic boundaries. But if such an exclusivist position sets up an irreducible tension between faith in terms of traditional belief and faith as an ethical life form, then these two aspects of Christian existence come into conflict again when we simply affirm the equality of all the world religions despite their diversity. This reduces the importance of the *fides quae* of Christian doctrine to the extent that Christian ethical life is no longer distinctive to Christianity but is part of a generalized religious commitment. This also ruptures the link between knowing Christ through scripture and the sacraments, and the expression and communication of that personal knowing through the propositions of credal faith.

Compromise has been sought either in the development of a philosophical paradigm of 'ultimate reality' which describes all the world religions as 'metaphor', or in the evolution of inter-faith theology from within the respective traditions which, in the case of Christianity, entails the recognition that specific other religions authentically represent degrees of divine disclosure. The 'metaphorical' reading of religion is easily seen to be itself a colonizing and totalizing hermeneutic in that it disregards the non-metaphorical claims of traditional religious belief in all the world religions in favour of a reading of reality which is itself finally a kind of intellectualist subjectivity current in a particular academic and Western social class.[22] Although attended at every stage by interpretative difficulties, it is the theology of compromise, or what Jacques Dupuis calls an 'inductive method' which proceeds from 'the reality as experienced today with the problems it raises' without seeking to 'offer a definitive solution', which –

with the realism of a *modus vivendi* – creatively finds a place for other religions within the Christian scheme and begins to establish a new range of meaning in inter-faith encounter.[23] Most importantly, it allows the possibility of conversation and dialogue, leading in the judgment of some to enrichment of the Christian tradition through the addition of new insights from other religions, or, as others have maintained, to the discovery of hidden elements within the Christian tradition itself, newly envisioned through contact with other religions.[24]

A commitment to serious inter-faith discussions entails a deep reflection upon the nature of the truth which each religion proclaims to be divine and seeks to affirm in dialogue with its partners. In the case of Christianity this entails the knowledge that Christian truth is centred in Jesus Christ, who is God's self-communication with us in personhood. But, as we have argued, that truth is not to be seen, as at times in the past, in terms of some definitively understood content of revelation. Christian revelation is not a divine monologue, but rather the disclosure of inner-trinitarian relations imaged as triadic speech. It is personal communication as process and exchange. The conviction of the church that God is definitively present with us in the person of Christ, who indwells the church, the eucharist and scripture, is matched by the knowledge that to be fully present as a person is not to be definitively known, as some code or collection of facts. Indeed, the very character of personhood is that it transcends any capacity we have to catalogue it. The presence of divine personhood to us and among us is then *a fortiori* the laying claim to us by a divine relation which transcends any capacity we might have to harness it to purely human ways of acting and thinking. To live in faith is to live in the presence of fullness, which we can only receive, in a total responsivity of obedience and love, without commanding or controlling or in any way seeking to *possess* the divine dynamic which has come among us. Indeed, the authentic ecclesial consciousness is that there is always an excess, a going before which subverts our natural humanization of the divine speaking, and draws us back to the primal abundance which is the dynamic of the revelation itself.

The encounter with other religions demands then that we should approach them in openness of heart and mind, and in a spirit of dialogue. As David Lockhead has reminded us, 'an invitation to dialogue that demands conversion to anything but dialogue itself . . . must be an invitation to monologue in disguise'.[25] The Christian community must approach such conversations in the knowledge that a commitment to dialogue is not a subversion of a high Christology but rather its enactment as 'we see the church called into the same intimate dialogue with the world that is represented by the divine-human dialogue in Jesus'.[26] The benefits can also be rich and manifold, not least in so far as there may be dimensions of divine self-communication which we have received in the incarnation and not seen or not understood aright. It is possible through dialogue that we may discover insights about ourselves, via the other, which deepen our own reception of Christian revelation. It is possible too that we may discover a new solidarity, a new ecclesiality even, which extends beyond the visible borders of the church. This is difficult territory, in particular for Christians for whom the visibility of the church is central to self-definition. But if we profess that God through the incarnation has already taken the whole of creation and human history back into the trinitarian reality, then Christian time is in some important sense already eschatological time. We live in the period between the first and second coming when what has already been fulfilled awaits its fullest manifestation at the level of the concrete and the visible. As the people of God then we set up borders and limits in accordance with human and divine law, but can only do so in the knowledge that they have already been subverted by the trinitarian reality which knows nothing other or external to itself. From a truly Christian perspective then, the secure borders and limits of autonomous ecclesial institutions constantly dissolve in the disruptive and ecstatic play of trinitarian difference. The instantiation of this is the Christian encounter with others, from non-Christian religious traditions and at times without the explicit influence of a world religion, whose own lives are informed and animated by the radical self-dispossession of compassion, in which we see the face of Christian truth, and the trace of the God who goes before.

Conclusion

The claim to truth is implicitly or explicitly an appeal to consensus and to the maximal recognition of the validity of a point of view. In Christianity, truth claims are bound up with the unity of the person of Christ who is God's self-communication with us. The very concept of personality is based upon a unified field of experience which, in the case of Christ, attains an eternal expression and thus an infinite depth of realization. The truth on which Christianity is founded is therefore one that is unified and divine. As we have stressed throughout however, precisely because that truth is the self-communication of God, its reception necessitates the recognition of its power of excess with respect to any human capacity to integrate that truth into ordinary forms of human thinking and living. Its reception manifests not as conviction as to the unchanging certainty of the propositional statements which derive from it, but rather our conviction that God is truly and definitively present with us in the person of Christ, and that it is on this presence that the church in its destiny is founded. What the communication of divine truth does not give is an ordinary human conviction regarding the propositional domains which derive from the personal encounter with Truth as Jesus Christ. The unity of propositional truth, which includes our understanding of where the limits of the church lie, and the proper ordering in significant detail of the Christian life, is authentically truth and is authentically participation in the unity of the divine truth which is revealed to us in Jesus Christ. But it is of necessity no more than this.

Intrinsic to the 'possession' of truth divinely revealed is the dispossession of self which is our accommodation of its excess and which is the yielding of the self into the creative flow of trinitarian speech. The fertility of our integration into the dynamic trinitarian rhythms of understanding and relating must always act upon the stability of our conceptual understandings, so that the latter are themselves always revisited in deepening reflection and understanding in the context of the relations of conversation with others, both within and outside the church, to which we are summoned through our reception of the very divine revelation which we seek to communicate, in which God-in-relation, God-as-relation, has set himself in relation with us. It is for this reason that the borders and limits of the church, which fall naturally into place as a necessary condition of human seeing and knowing, must in themselves always be re-envisioned as *difference*, according to a trinitarian logic, in which the self becomes envoiced by the other and empties itself out for the sake of the other. This is not to be identified with the recommendation of any one or any set of adaptations of the norms that currently obtain in the Catholic Church but is rather an argument concerning the fundamental character of Christian truth itself, which – as divinely revealed – cannot simply be held as an exaggerated form of human truth, but must constantly be re-enacted, reappropriated and performed in the light of the unfolding experience of the church as it broadens and deepens in love's visibility.

Afterword
Towards a Eucharistic Cosmology

οὐκ ἄλλον ἦν τὸ φθαρτὸν εἰς ἀφθαρσίαν μεταβάλειν, εἰ μὴ αὐτοῦ τοῦ Σωτῆρος τοῦ καὶ τὴν ἀρχὴν ἐξ οὐκ ὄντων πεποιήκοντος τὰ ὅλα

It was in the power only of the Saviour himself to turn the corruptible to incorruption, since it was he who had at the beginning also made all things out of nothingness.

Athanasius, *De Incarnatione Verbi*

A Theology of Compassion has been governed by two distinct trajectories of thinking. The first of these has been an attempt to explicate the meaning of goodness as it unfolds from within my own – compassionate – engagement with texts which relate compassionate actions from the past. The second was a reflection, in the manner of a Christian midrash, or interpretative commentary, upon the divine name revealed at Ex. 3.14, in which God declares Godself as YHWH and explicates this as the continuing presence of God with Israel in and through God's saving and compassionate acts. The former trajectory led to a 'transcendental analytic of compassion' based on a phenomenological analysis of the structure of compassionately engaged consciousness in which the dialectical structure of consciousness (as 'I' and 'Not-I' or 'Other-I') grounded a new metaphysical language of 'being'. In 'kenotic ontology', 'being' is a cypher for the condition of intensified or enriched existence which follows from the putting at risk of the self for the sake of the other, with whom the self stands in a dialectical relation of mutual grounding. The first chapters of the book are governed by the method of phenomenology in the service of a transcendental philosophy which portrays the self as dialogically constituted and ecstatically ethical, in which self-realization is a dialectical journeying through and with the other. As philosophy of existence, this stands within what Peter Ochs has called the tradition of 'redemptive knowledge', which is a corrective rereading of the Cartesian–Kantian school from Jewish sources through a new emphasis upon the place of the concrete other, made visible in compassion (Hermann Cohen), as mediated through the linguistic relation of the 'I–Thou' (Rosenzweig, Buber).[1] The corrective rereading of the transcendental tradition in the opening chapters of

A Theology of Compassion from the perspective of a prioritization of compassion can itself be seen to be an attempt to repair the metaphysical tradition of the West through a new attentiveness to the deep logic of our post-Holocaust histories on the one hand and to our scriptural source texts on the other.

The second trajectory, a Christian midrash on Ex. 3.14 and related texts, led us to a new understanding of Jesus Christ as representing not only the saving face (in David Ford's terms) – or compassion – of God, and thus in some deep sense the creativity of God, but also as being the 'Word' of God. We have not understood this as a conventional piety of jaded biblical language, as archaic messianic tag, but rather – under the guidance of the rabbis and their explorations of the *Memra* – as a dynamic, world-generating performance of divine speech. In the case of God, presence *is* speech, and the fullness of presence is a divine speaking-with. Against such a background therefore we are invited to conceive of the Trinity itself as a form of divine 'conversation' and of the creation as an institutive linguistic act. Adapting elements from Bakhtin's theory of language, we argued in Chapter Twelve that creation itself occurs when the trinitarian Persons will to refer to an external world, and that this is reflected in the use of the originary jussive $y^ehî$ ('let there be') in the opening verses of Genesis. That act of creation is shown to be a process as God's speech proceeds from impersonal jussives, through blessings, to personal imperatives, which mark the first beginnings of the covenant with Israel. The divine self-naming at Ex. 3.14 is the final stage in the Hebrew articulation of the divine creation through language, when God 'knows Moses by name' and names Godself before Moses. This sets God and Israel within an intimate relation of naming and of the knowing which is intrinsic to naming. It is this moment that provides the matrix for a Christology which understands Jesus to be the compassionate presence of God with the creation. But by the same account Jesus is also in some very deep sense the utterance or speech of God: the divine speaking *with* creation.

It is here that the mediatorship of Christ becomes visible in a new way. For in his divine nature as the Word, Jesus belongs to and participates in the divine conversation which is prior to the creation. This is the speech which is one with the primordial silence. This is the speech of God with God in which nothing is exterior, but the sphere of reference is itself construed as a third speaking Person. Creation comes about when the Trinity wills external reference. At that point, space–time precipitates as text, crystallizing out of, falling from the originary divine conversation. This text, the primary text of creation, is our Ur-Text, to which we referred in the introduction as 'primal bestowal'. It is the 'pure presence' which is the basis of all reality. The life of the senses and the dynamic of language, which together interact in the formation of the real, are potentiations, or participations, in the foundational presence-with of the primal bestowal: that which makes the 'is' possible. But in his human nature, Jesus Christ is

at the same time part of the human potentiations of that Ur-Text. He is one
with us as creatures who live within the precarious and contingent domain
of interpretation. What truth and stability we have is fleeting and always
prone to decay. We are surrounded by ambiguity and displacements of
meaning, and our cultures, and philosophies, are conjectural. Our speech,
even our most intimate speech, is always liable to misappropriation and
misinterpretation. If, as God, Jesus Christ is part of the divine conversation, from which the Ur-Text of existence precipitates as ground and
possibility of the myriad human potentiations of the richness of its meanings, then, as a human being, he is himself a recipient and inhabitor
of these secondary texts, which are as much erroneous as true, as much
illusory as real. As one who speaks in the divine conversation which is an
infinite and divine purity of presence, and as one whose human existence
is at the level of construction, conjecture and risk, we discover in the
person of Christ a unity of presence which brings the divine conversation
to the heart of human culture and experience. In him, the trinitarian
conversation becomes real for us: opened out and distributed at the heart
of the precarious human texts in and by which we live.

But precisely because the primal bestowal is itself figured as 'text', in
accordance with the divine originary speech of our scriptural sources, the
human texts, for all their inadequacies, are also true participations in the
divine movement of creation. Human semiosis mediates as well as
obscures. The different ways in which human communities construct
meanings and live within the semiotic formations of society, as both
language and material culture, can themselves participate in the divine
movement of signification which underlies the real as such. They create
and constitute our worlds and, in so far as they body forth the primal
bestowal which originates at a point infinitely beyond our constructions,
they can themselves partially, though truly, mediate the elemental divine
self-giving which is the foundation of a reality which encompasses the
human self within a broader framework of otherness, realism, truth,
presence and answerability.

It is the Ur-Text too as primal ground which allows the many different
kinds of texts which inform human living to interact with each other:
scripture with world, speech with culture, consciousness with writing,
phenomenology with hermeneutics, Judaism with Christianity. Each can
correctively act upon the other, each can repair the other, each can enrich
the other. And all texts, as participative reproductions of the Ur-Text, are
subject to the same ethical law of attention to the suffering other which is
the trinitarian life from which the Ur-Text springs. It is the texts of compassion, whether as speech or writing, words or artefacts, that creatively
hold at their centre the sense of the other which stand in a privileged
relation with the Ur-Text of kenotic triadic speech. As Spirit-filled communications of remembrance and creative self-correction, it is scriptural texts
which most specifically approximate to the trinitarian presencing through

primal speech, communicating the dynamic of the divine reality. But other forms of cultural textualization, whether linguistic or material, can also be compassionately centred in the other in such a way that we come to feel in them the brightness of the Trinity, speaking, presencing, blessing. Society and culture, as well as art, philosophy, technology and science, can all serve to mediate the other-centred dynamic of trinitarian life. For Christians in the Catholic tradition however, there is no place where the originary, creative and redeeming triadic speech of the Trinity is more to be found than the eucharist, in which – as we shall see in the following volume – the nature of reality itself is figured, and with it the structure of wisdom, which is the formation of a learning self in tune with its own creatureliness and with the createdness of the world. There, at the heart of the church, in its communal acts of sacred remembering, Jesus is discovered to be the divine voice that speaks with us again. The world finds itself again in the presence of the God who speaks. And the people hear again the voice of the Creator God who summons us to existence, who generates and blesses, who commands and calls.

Select Bibliography

Adorno, Theodor, *Jargon der Eigentlichkeit*, Frankfurt am Main: Suhrkamp Verlag 1964.

Agamben, Giorgio, *Homo Sacer: Sovereign Power and Bare Life*, trans. Daniel Heller-Roazen, Stanford, CA: Stanford University Press 1998.

Allen, D. J., *The Philosophy of Aristotle*, Oxford: Oxford University Press 1970.

Alpatov, M. V., 'O Znachenii "Troitsy" Rubleva', *Etyudy po istorii russkogo iskusstva*, vol. I., Moskva: Izdatelstvo Iskusstvo 1967, pp. 119–26.

Ariew, Roger, Cottingham, John and Sorell, Tom (eds), *'Meditations': Background Source Materials*, Cambridge: Cambridge University Press 1998.

Aristotle, *Metaphysics*, ed. W. D. Ross, Oxford: Clarendon Press 1924.

——, *Poetics*, trans. James Hutton, London and New York: Norton 1982.

——, *On Rhetoric*, trans. George A. Kennedy, Oxford: Oxford University Press 1991.

Ashton, John, *Understanding the Fourth Gospel*, Oxford: Clarendon Press 1991.

Athanasius, *De incarnatione*, ed. R. W. Thompson, Oxford: Oxford University Press 1971.

Auden, W. H., 'The Virgin and the Dynamo', *The Dyer's Hand*, New York: Random House 1948, pp. 61–71.

Augustine, *Confessions*, ed. James J. O'Donnell, Oxford: Clarendon Press 1992.

Bakhtin, Mikhail, *The Problem of Speech Genres*, in *Mikhail Bakhtin: Speech Genres and Other Late Essays*, ed. Caryl Emerson and Michael Holquist, Austin: University of Texas Press 1986, pp. 60–102.

——, 'Art and Answerability', *Art and Answerability: Early Philosophical Essays by M. M. Bakhtin*, ed. M. Holquist and V. Liapunov, Austin: University of Texas Press 1990, pp. 1–3.

——, *1961 god zametki*, *Sobranie Sochinenii*, vol. 5, Moscow: Russkie Slovari 1996.

Balthasar, Hans Urs von, *Herrlichkeit: eine theologische Ästhetik*, Einsiedeln: Johannes Verlag 1961–69.

Barnes, Jonathan, *Early Greek Philosophy*, Harmondsworth: Penguin 1987.

—— (ed.), *The Cambridge Companion to Aristotle*, Cambridge: Cambridge University Press 1995.

Barth, Karl, *Church Dogmatics*, Edinburgh: T&T Clark 1936–69.

Bauman, Zygmunt, *Modernity and the Holocaust*, Cambridge: Polity Press 1989.

Baumgartner, Hans Michael, 'Transcendentales Denken und Atheismus: der Atheismusstreit um Fichte', *Hochland* 56, 1963/4, pp. 40–8.

Bayer, Oswald, *Gott als Autor: zu einer poietologischen Theologie*, Tübingen: Mohr Siebeck 1999.

Beierwaltes, Werner, *Denken des Einen: Studien zur neuplatonischen Philosophie und ihrer Wirkungsgeschichte*, Frankfurt am Main: Vittorio Klostermann 1985.

Beiser, Frederick C., *The Fate of Reason: German Philosophy from Kant to Fichte*, Cambridge, MA: Harvard University Press 1987.

Berkeley, George, *Philosophical Works*, ed. Michael R. Ayers, London: Dent 1975.

Biser, Eugen, 'Das Wahrheitsproblem der Glaubensbegründung: Erwägungen zu einer aktuellen Frage der Fundamentaltheologie', *Hochland* 61, 1969, pp. 1–12.

Blondel, Maurice, *Action (1893): Essay on a Critique of Life and a Science of Practice*, trans. Oliva Blanchette, University of Notre Dame Press 1984.

Bouillard, Henri, 'La tâche actuelle de la théologie fondamentale', *Vérité du Christianisme*, Paris: Desclée 1989, pp. 149–79.

Boyle, Nicholas, *Who Are We Now?*, Edinburgh: T&T Clark 1998.

Brenner, Rachel Feldhay, *Writing as Resistance: Four Women Confronting the Holocaust*, Pennsylvania: Pennsylvania State University Press 1997.

Brentano, Franz, *On the Several Senses of Being in Aristotle*, ed. and trans. Rolf George, Berkeley: University of California Press 1975.

Brown, Lesley, 'The Verb "To Be" in Greek Philosophy: Some Remarks', *Language: Companions to Ancient Thought 3*, ed. Stephen Everson, Cambridge: Cambridge University Press 1994, pp. 212–36.

Brown, Peter, *Augustine of Hippo: A Biography*, London: Faber & Faber 1969.

Brueggemann, Walter, *Theology of the Old Testament: Testimony, Dispute, Advocacy*, Minneapolis: Augsburg Fortress 1997.

Bryant, Joseph M., *Moral Codes and Social Structure in Ancient Greece*, New York: SUNY Press 1996.

Burkert, W., 'Das Proömium des Parmenides und die Katabasis des Pythagoras', *Phronesis* 15, 1969, pp. 1–30.

Bury, R. G., *The Symposium of Plato*, Cambridge: Heffer 1932.

Bussanich, John, *The One in Relation to Intellect in Plotinus*, Leiden: E. J. Brill 1988.

Caird, G. B., 'The Glory of God in the Fourth Gospel: An Exercise in Biblical Semantics', *New Testament Studies* 15, 1968–9, pp. 265–77.

Cantwell Smith, W., *Towards a World Theology*, London: Macmillan 1981.

Caputo, John D., 'Mysticism and Transgression: Derrida and Meister Eckhart', *Derrida and Deconstruction*, ed. Hugh J. Silverman, London: Routledge 1989, pp. 24–39.

Cargas, Harry James (ed.), *The Unnecessary Problem of Edith Stein*, Studies in the Shoah, vol. IV, Maryland: University Press of America 1994.

Certeau, Michel de, *Heterologies: Discourse on the Other*, trans. Brian Massumi, Minneapolis: University of Minnesota Press 1986.

Charlesworth, James H. (ed.), *The Old Testament Pseudepigrapha*, I, London: Darton, Longman & Todd 1983.

Childs, Brevard S., *Exodus: A Commentary*, Old Testament Library, London: SCM Press 1974.

Cixous, Hélène, *Coming to Writing and Other Essays*, ed. Deborah Jenson, trans. Sarach Cornell, Cambridge, MA: Harvard University Press 1991.

Cohen, Hermann, *Religion der Vernunft aus den Quellen des Judentums*, ed. Bruno Strauss, Frankfurt: J. Kaufmann 1929.

Coxon, A. H., *The Fragments of Parmenides*, Assen: Van Gorcum 1986.

Cunningham, David S., *These Three Are One: The Practice of Trinitarian Theology*, Oxford: Blackwell 1998.

Curd, Patricia, *The Legacy of Parmenides*, Princeton: Princeton University Press 1998.

Davidson, Donald, 'On the Very Idea of a Conceptual System', *Inquiries into Truth and Interpretation*, Oxford: Oxford University Press 1984, pp. 183–98.

Davies, Oliver, *Meister Eckhart: Mystical Theologian*, London: SPCK 1991.

——, *Meister Eckhart: Selected Writings*, Harmondsworth: Penguin 1994.

——, 'Von Balthasar and the Problem of Being', *New Blackfriars* 79, no. 923, January 1998, pp. 11–17.

——, 'Thinking Difference: A Comparative Study of Gilles Deleuze, Plotinus and Meister Eckhart', *Deleuze and Theology*, ed. Mary Bryden, London: Routledge 2001, pp. 76–86.

——, 'Soundings: Towards a Theological Poetics of Silence', *Silence and the Word*, ed. Oliver Davies and Denys Turner, Cambridge: Cambridge University Press 2002, forthcoming.

Davis, Walter A., *Inwardness and Existence: Subjectivity in/and Hegel, Heidegger, Marx and Freud*, Wisconsin: University of Wisconsin Press 1989.

d'Costa, Gavin, *Theology and Religious Pluralism*, Oxford: Blackwell 1986.

Deleuze, Gilles, *Nietzsche*, Paris: Presses Universitaires de France 1965.

——, *Nietzsche et la Philosophie*, Paris: Presses Universitaires de France 1970.

——, *Kant's Critical Philosophy: The Doctrine of the Faculties*, trans. Hugh Tomlinson and Barbara Habberjam, Minneapolis: University of Minnesota Press 1984.

——, and Guattari, Félix, *What Is Philosophy?*, trans. Graham Burchell and Hugh Tomlinson, London and New York: Verso 1994.

——, *Difference and Repetition*, trans. Paul Patton, London: Athlone Press 1994.

——, 'Immanence: A Life...', *Theory, Culture and Society* 14.2, May 1997, pp. 3–7.

Demina, N. A., 'Troitsa Andreya Rubleva', *Andrei Rublev i Khudozhniki ego Kruga*, Moscow: Izdatelstvo Nauka 1972, pp. 45–81.

Derrida, Jacques, *Speech and Phenomena*, trans. David Allison, Evanston, IL: Northwestern University Press 1973.

——, *Of Grammatology*, London and Baltimore: Johns Hopkins University Press 1976.

——, '"Genesis and Structure" and Phenomenology', *Writing and Difference*, trans. Alan Bass, London: Routledge 1978, pp. 154–68.

——, 'Différance', *Margins of Philosophy*, trans. Alan Bass, Chicago: University of Chicago Press 1982, pp. 1–27.

——, 'How to Avoid Speaking: Denials', *Languages of the Unsayable: The Play of*

Negativity in Literature and Literary Theory, ed. Sanford Budick and Wolfgang Iser, New York: Columbia University Press 1989, 3–70.

——, 'Sauf le Nom', *On the Name*, trans. David Wood, John P. Leavey, Jr. and Ian McLeod, Stanford, CA: Stanford University Press 1995, pp. 34–85.

Descartes, René, *Oeuvres*, ed. Charles Adam and Paul Tannery, Paris: Librairies Philosophique J. Vrin, 1964–76.

——, *Philosophical Writings*, ed. and trans. Elizabeth Anscombe and Peter Thomas Geach, London: Nelson 1954.

Dickey, Laurence, *Hegel: Religion, Economics and Politics of the Spirit, 1770–1807*, Cambridge: Cambridge University Press 1987.

——, 'Hegel on Religion and Philosophy', *The Cambridge Companion to Hegel*, ed. Frederick C. Beiser, Cambridge: Cambridge University Press 1993, pp. 301–47.

Diehls, H. and Kranz, W., *Die Fragmente der Vorsokratiker*, vol. I, Berlin: Weidmannsche Verlagsbuchhandlung 1954.

Doig, James, *Aquinas on Metaphysics: A Historico-Doctrinal Study of the Commentary on the Metaphysics*, The Hague: Martinus Nijhoff 1972.

Dulles, Avery, *A History of Apologetics*, London: Hutchinson 1971.

——, *Models of Revelation*, 2nd edn., Dublin: Gill & Macmillan 1992.

Dupuis, Jacques, *Toward a Christian Theology of Religious Pluralism*, Maryknoll, NY: Orbis 1997.

Ebeling, Gerhard, *Einführung in Theologische Sprachlehre*, Tübingen: J. C. B. Mohr 1971.

Eckhart, Meister, *Deutsche und Lateinische Werke*, Stuttgart: Kohlhammer Verlag 1936–.

Ehrlich, Victor, *Russian Formalism*, 3rd edn., New Haven: Yale University Press 1981.

Elders, Leo J., *The Metaphysics of Being in St. Thomas Aquinas in a Historical Perspective*, Leiden: E. J. Brill 1993.

Elizondo, Virgil, 'Our Lady of Guadalupe as a Cultural Symbol: "The Power of the Powerless"', *Concilium* 102, 1977, pp. 25–33.

——, 'Mary and the Poor: A Model of Evangelising Ecumenism', *Concilium* 168, 1983, pp. 59–65.

Evdokimov, Paul, *L'art de l'icône*, Paris: Desclée de Brouwer 1972.

Fackre, Gabriel, *The Doctrine of Revelation: A Narrative Interpretation*, Edinburgh: Edinburgh University Press 1997.

Farley, Edward, *Divine Empathy*, Minneapolis: Fortress Press 1996.

Farness, Jay, *Missing Socrates*, Pennsylvania: Pennsylvania State University Press 1991.

Fichte, J. G., *Fichtes Werke*, ed. I. H. Fichte, repr. Berlin: de Gruyter 1971.

——, *Johann Gottlieb Fichte: Attempt at a Critique of All Revelation*, ed. and trans. Garrett Green, Cambridge: Cambridge University Press 1978.

——, *The Science of Knowledge*: *J. G. Fichte*, ed. and trans. Peter Heath and John Lachs, Cambridge: Cambridge University Press 1982.

——, *Johann Fichte: The Vocation of Man*, ed. and trans. Peter Preuss, Indianapolis and Cambridge: Hackett 1987.

——, *Introductions to the Wissenschaftslehre and other Writings*, ed. and trans. Daniel Breazeale, Indianapolis and Cambridge: Hackett 1994.

Fiddes, Paul S., *The Creative Suffering of God*, Oxford: Clarendon Press 1988.

——, *Freedom and Limit: A Dialogue between Literature and Christian Doctrine*, London: Macmillan 1991.

——, *Participating in God: A Pastoral Doctrine of the Trinity*, London: Darton, Longman & Todd 2000.

Fides et Ratio, Encyclical Letter of Pope John Paul II, London: Catholic Truth Society 1998.

Fisher, B. Aubrey and Adams, Katherine L., *Interpersonal Communication: Pragmatics of Human Relationships*, 2nd edn., New York: McGraw-Hill 1994.

Fisichella, Rino, *La rivilazione: evento e credibilitá*, Bologna: Edizioni Dehoniane Bologna 1985.

Ford, David F., *Self and Salvation*, Cambridge: Cambridge University Press 1999.

Foucault, Michel, *What Is Enlightenment?*, in *The Foucault Reader*, ed. Paul Rabinow, Harmondsworth: Penguin 1984, pp. 32–50.

Freiberg, Dietrich von, *Opera Omnia*, vol. 1, *Schriften zur Intellekttheorie*, ed. Bernard Mojsisch, Hamburg: F. Meiner 1977.

Freydberg, Bernard, *The Play of Platonic Dialogues*, New York: Peter Lang 1997.

Fries, H. and Schweiger, G. (eds), *Katholische Theologen Deutschlands im 19. Jahrhundert*, I, Munich: Kösel-Verlag 1975.

Funkenstein, Amos, *Theology and the Scientific Imagination: From the Middle Ages to the Seventeenth Century*, Princeton: Princeton University Press 1986.

Gadamer, Hans-Georg, 'The Universality of the Hermeneutical Problem', *Philosophical Hermeneutics*, trans. David E. Linge, California: University of California Press 1976, pp. 3–17.

——, *Truth and Method*, 2nd English edn., London: Sheed & Ward 1979.

Galilei Galilei, *Opere*, vol. 1, ed. Ferdinando Flora, Milan and Naples: Riccardo Ricciardi Editore 1953.

Gerson, Lloyd, *Plotinus*, London and New York: Routledge 1994.

——(ed.), *The Cambridge Companion to Plotinus*, Cambridge: Cambridge University Press 1996.

Geuss, Raymond, *Morality, Culture, and History*, Cambridge: Cambridge University Press 1999.

Giddens, Anthony, *The Consequences of Modernity*, Cambridge: Polity Press 1990.

Giddes, Gary (ed.), *Twentieth Century Poetry and Poetics*, 4th edn., Toronto: Oxford University Press 1996.

Gilson, Etienne, *Being and Some Philosophers*, 2nd edn., Toronto: Pontifical Institute of Medieval Studies 1952.

Girard, René, *Resurrection from the Underground: Feodor Dostoevsky*, New York: Crossroad 1997.

Green, Garrett, *Imagining God: Theology and the Religious Imagination*, Grand Rapids, MI: Eerdmans 1989.

Guardini, Romano, *Religion und Offenbarung*, Würzburg: Werkbund Verlag 1958.

Gunton, Colin E., *The Promise of Trinitarian Theology*, Edinburgh: T&T Clark 1991.

——, *A Brief Theology of Revelation*, Edinburgh: T&T Clark 1995.

Guthrie, W. K. C., *A History of Greek Philosophy, Vol. IV, Plato: The Man and His Dialogues: Early Period*, Cambridge: Cambridge University Press 1975.

Haar, Michel, 'Nietzsche and Metaphysical Language', *The New Nietzsche*, ed. David B. Allison, Cambridge, MA: MIT Press 1985, pp. 5–36.

Haas, Alois, 'Seinsspekulation und Geschöpflichkeit in der Mystik Meister Eckharts', *Gott Leiden Gott Lieben*, Frankfurt am Main: Insel Verlag 1989, pp. 172–88.

Habermas, Jürgen, 'The Entwinement of Myth and Enlightenment', *New German Critique* 26, 1982, pp. 13–20.

——, *On the Logic of the Social Sciences*, trans. Shierry Weber Nicholsen and Jerry A. Stark, Cambridge: Polity Press 1988.

——, *Postmetaphysical Thinking: Philosophical Essays*, trans. William Mark Hohengarten, Cambridge: Polity Press 1992.

Hadot, Pierre, *Plotinus or the Simplicity of Vision*, trans. Michael Chase, Chicago: University of Chicago Press 1993.

Halper, Edward C., *One and Many in Aristotle's Metaphysics: The Central Books*, Columbus: Ohio State University Press 1989.

Hamburger, Michael, *The Truth of Poetry*, London: Anvil Press 1982.

Haraway, Donna, *Simians, Cyborgs and Women: The Reinvention of Nature*, London: Free Association 1991.

Harl, Marguerite, 'Citations et commentaires d'Exode 3, 14 chez les Pères grecs des quatre premiers siècles', *Dieu et l'Être: Exégèses d'Exode 3, 14 et de Coran 20, 11–24*, Paris: Études Augustiniennes 1978, pp. 87–108.

Harvey, David, *The Condition of Postmodernity*, Oxford: Blackwell 1990.

Hauerwas, Stanley H., *Wilderness Wanderings*, Colorado: Westview Press 1997.

Hayward, Robert, *Divine Name and Presence: The Memra*, Totowa, NJ: Allanheld, Osmun 1981.

Hegel, G. W. F., *Werke*, Frankfurt am Main: Suhrkramp Verlag, 1968–.

——, *Hegel's Science of Logic*, trans. A. V. Miller, London: Routledge 1969.

——, *Hegel's Phenomenology of Spirit*, trans. A. V. Miller, Oxford: Oxford University Press 1977.

Heidegger, Martin, *Gesamtausgabe*, Frankfurt am Main: Vittorio Klostermann 1975–.

——, *Einführung in die Metaphysik*, Tübingen: Max Niehmeyer Verlag 1953.

——, *An Introduction to Metaphysics*, trans. Ralph Manheim, New Haven and London: Yale University Press 1959, pp. 93–206.

——, *Parmenides*, trans. André Schuwer and Richard Rojcewicz, Bloomington and Indiana: Indiana University Press 1992.

——, 'Introduction to "What is Metaphysics?"', *Pathmarks*, ed. William McNeill, Cambridge: Cambridge University Press 1998, pp. 277–90.

——, 'On the Question of Being', *Pathmarks*, pp. 291–322.

——, 'Letter on Humanism', *Pathmarks*, pp. 239–76.

——, 'Postscript to "What is Metaphysics?"', *Pathmarks*, pp. 231–8.

Heiser, John H., *Logos and Language in the Philosophy of Plotinus*, Lampeter: Edwin Mellen Press 1991.

Henry, P. and Schwyzer, H. R. (eds), *Plotini Opera*, 3 vols. Oxford: Clarendon Press 1964–82.

Herbstrich, Waltraud, *Edith Stein: A Biography*, trans. Bernard Bonowitz OCSO, San Francisco: Ignatius Press 1985.

Hilberg, Raul, *The Destruction of the European Jews*, New York: Holmes & Meier 1983.

Hillesum, Etty, *Etty: A Diary 1941–43*, trans. Arnold J. Pomerans, London: Grafton Books 1985.

Hintikka, Jaako, '*Cogito, Ergo Sum*: Inference or Performance', *Descartes: A Collection of Critical Essays*, ed. Wallis Doney, Notre Dame: University of Notre Dame Press 1968, pp. 108–39.

Hollander, H. W. and Jonge, M. de, *The Testaments of the Twelve Patriarchs: A Commentary*, Leiden: E. J. Brill 1985.

Housman, A. E., *The Name and Nature of Poetry*, Cambridge: Cambridge University Press 1933.

Husserl, Edmund, *Cartesianische Meditationen*, ed. Elisabeth Ströker, Hamburg: Felix Meiner Verlag 1977.

——, *Cartesian Meditations*, trans. Dorion Cairns, Dordrecht: Kluwer 1995.

Jakobson, Roman, 'Linguistics and Poetics', *Selected Writings*, III, The Hague: Mouton 1981, pp. 18–51.

Jaspers, Karl, *Nietzsche und das Christentum*, Hameln: Verlag der Bücherstube Fritz Seifert 1938.

Jeremias, Joachim, 'Das Gebetsleben Jesu', *Zeitschrift für die neutestamentliche Wissenschaft* 25, 1926, pp. 123–40.

——, *New Testament Theology*, trans. J. Bowden, London: SCM Press 1971.

Johnson, Aubrey R., *The One and the Many in the Israelite Conception of God*, Cardiff: University of Wales Press 1942.

——, *The Vitality of the Individual in the Thought of Ancient Israel*, 2nd edn., Cardiff: University of Wales Press 1964.

Johnson, Elizabeth A., 'Mary in Praxis-Oriented Theology', *Kecharitômenê: Mélanges René Laurentin*, Paris: Desclée 1990, pp. 467–82.

Jonge, M. de, *The Testaments of the Twelve Patriarchs*, 2nd edn., Assen: Van Gorcum 1975.

Jüngel, Eberhard, *God as the Mystery of the World*, trans. Darrell L. Guder, Edinburgh: T&T Clark 1983.

Kahn, Charles, 'The Verb "Be" in Ancient Greek', *The Verb "Be" and Its Synonyms*, VI, ed. J. W. M. Verhaar, Dordrecht: D. Reidel 1973.

——, 'Why Existence Does Not Emerge as a Distinct Concept in Greek Philosophy', *Philosophies of Existence Ancient and Medieval*, ed. Parviz Morewedge, New York: Fordham University Press 1982, pp. 7–17.

——, *Plato and the Socratic Dialogue*, Cambridge: Cambridge University Press 1996.

Kant, Immanuel, *Critique of Pure Reason*, trans. Norman Kemp Smith, London: Macmillan, 2nd impr. 1933.

——, *Die Metaphysik der Sitten*, in *Werke*, hg. Benzion Kellermann, Bd VII, Hildesheim: Verlag Dr H. A. Gerstenberg 1973.

Kearney, Richard, *Poetics of Imagining*, Edinburgh: Edinburgh University Press 1998.

Kee, Alistair, *Nietzsche against the Crucified*, London: SCM Press 1999.

Keller, Pierre, *Kant and the Demands of Self-Consciousness*, Cambridge: Cambridge University Press 1998.

Kierkegaard, Søren, *Samlede Værker*, ed. P. P. Rohde, Copenhagen: Gyldendal, 1962–64.

——, *Fear and Trembling*, ed. and trans. Walter Lowrie, Princeton: Princeton University Press 1968.

——, *Philosophical Fragments*, ed. and trans. Howard V. Hong and Edna H. Hong, Princeton: Princeton University Press 1985.

——, *Works of Love*, ed. and trans. Howard V. Hong and Edna H. Hong, New York: Harper & Row 1962.

——, *Concluding Unscientific Postscript to Philosophical Fragments*, vol. 1, ed. and trans. Howard V. Hong and Edna H. Hong, Princeton: Princeton University Press 1992.

Kirk, G. S. and Raven, J. E., *The Presocratic Philosophers*, Cambridge: Cambridge University Press 1957.

Kirwan, Christopher, 'Augustine on the Nature of Speech', *Language: Companions to Ancient Thought 3*, ed. Stephen Everson, Cambridge: Cambridge University Press 1994, pp. 188–211.

Kluback, William, *The Legacy of Hermann Cohen*, Atlanta, GA: Scholars Press 1989.

Kouloughli, Djamel-Eddine, 'La thématique du langage dans la Bible', *Histoires des idées linguistiques, I, La naissance des métalangages en Orient et en Occident*, ed. Sylvain Auroux, Liège-Bruxelles: Pierre Mordaga 1989, pp. 65–78.

Kuzmina, V. D., 'Drevnorusskie pismennye istochniki ob Andree Rubleva', *Andrei Rublev i ego Epokha*, ed. M. V. Alpatov, Moscow: Izdatelstvo Iskusstvo 1971, pp. 103–124.

Lacoue-Labarthe, Philippe, *La fiction du politique*, Strasbourg: Association des Publications près les universités de Strasbourg 1987.

Lactantius, *Opera Omnia*, CSEL 19 and 27, 1890–7.

Lacugna, Catherine Mowbray, *God for Us*, New York: HarperCollins 1973.

Larcher, Gerhard, Müller, Klaus, and Pröpper, Thomas (eds), *Hoffnung, die Gründe nennt. Zu Hansjürgen Verweyens Projekt einer erstphilosophischen Glaubensverantwortung*, Regensburg: Verlag Friedrich Pustet 1996.

Larcher, Gerhard, 'Subjekt – Kunst – Geschichte: Chancen einer Annäherung von Fundamentaltheologie und Ästhetik', *Fundamentaltheologie – Fluchtlinien und gegenwärtige Herausforderungen*, ed. Klaus Müller, Regensburg: Verlag Friedrich Pustet 1998, pp. 299–321.

Largier, Niklaus, '"Intellectus in deum ascensus". Intellekttheoretische Auseinandersetzungen in Texten der deutschen Mystik', *Deutsche Vierteljahrsschrift für Literaturwissenschaft und Geistesgeschichte* 69, H. 3, September 1995, pp. 423–71.

Lash, Nicholas, *Theology on the Way to Emmaus*, London: SCM Press 1986.

Latourelle, René, 'A New Image of Fundamental Theology', *Problems and Perspectives of Fundamental Theology*, ed. René Latourelle and Gerald O'Collins, New York/Ramsey: Paulist Press 1982, pp. 37–58.

Lazarev, V. N., *Andrei Rublev i ego Shkola*, Moscow: Izdatelstvo Iskusstvo 1966, pp. 33–6.

Les sources de Plotin: Entretiens Hardt V, Vandoeuvres-Genève: Fondation Hardt 1960.

Lessing, G. E., *Theological Writings*, ed. and trans. Henry Chadwick, Stanford, CA: Stanford University Press 1957.

Levinas, Emmanuel, *Otherwise than Being*, trans. Alphonso Lingis, Pittsburg: Duquesne University Press 1981.

——, *Totality and Infinity*, trans. Alphonso Lingis, Dordrecht: Kluwer 1991.

Levinson, Stephen C., *Pragmatics*, Cambridge: Cambridge University Press 1983.

Libera, Alain de, *Introduction à la Mystique Rhénane*, Paris: O.E.I.L. 1984.

Lloyd, Genevieve, *Spinoza and the Ethics*, London and New York: Routledge 1996.

Lockhead, David, *The Dialogical Imperative: A Christian Reflection on Interfaith Encounter*. London: SCM Press 1988.

Lorca, Federico Garcia, *Obras Completas*, I, Madrid: Aguilar 1980.

Lossky, Vladimir, *Théologie négative et connaissance de Dieu chez Maître Eckhart*, Paris: J. Vrin 1960.

Louth, Andrew, *The Origins of the Christian Mystical Tradition*, Oxford: Clarendon Press, 1981.

Lyotard, Jean-François, *The Postmodern Condition: A Report on Knowledge*, trans. Geoffrey Bennington and Brian Massumi, Manchester: Manchester University Press 1984.

MacIntyre, Alisdair, *Whose Justice? Which Rationality?*, London: Duckworth 1988.

MacKenna, Stephen, *Plotinus: Enneads*, Harmondsworth: Penguin 1991.

Margerie, Bertrand de, SJ, 'Mary in Latin American Liberation Theologies', *Kecharitômenê: Mélanges René Laurentin*, Paris: Desclée 1990, pp. 365–76.

Marion, Jean-Luc, *Sur l'ontologie grise de Descartes*, Paris: Librairie Philosophique J. Vrin 1981.

——, *Sur la théologie blanche de Descartes*, Paris: Presses Universitaires de France 1981.

——, 'The Essential Incoherence of Descartes' Definition of Divinity', *Essays on Descartes' Meditations*, ed. Amélie Oksenberg Rorty, Berkeley: University of California Press 1986, pp. 297–338.

——, *God without Being*, trans. Thomas A. Carlson, Chicago: University of Chicago Press 1991.

——, 'Cartesian Metaphysics: The Simple Natures', *The Cambridge Companion to Descartes*, ed. John Cottingham, Cambridge: Cambridge University Press 1992, pp. 115–39.

——, *Reduction and Givenness*, trans. Thomas A. Carlson, Evanston, IL: Northwestern University Press 1998.

Maritain, Jacques, *A Preface to Metaphysics*, London: Sheed & Ward 1939.

Marshall, I. Howard, *The Gospel of Luke*, NIGTC, Exeter: Paternoster Press 1978.

Marx, Werner, *Introduction to Aristotle's Theory of Being as Being*, The Hague: Martinus Nijhoff 1977.

Maurer, A., *Master Eckhart: Parisian Questions and Prologues*, Toronto: Pontifical Institute of Medieval Studies 1974.

Mavrodes, George I., *Revelation in Religious Belief*, Philadelphia: Temple University Press 1988.

May, Gerhard, *Creatio ex Nihilo*, trans. A. S. Worrall, Edinburgh: T&T Clark 1994.

McFadyen, Alistair, *The Call to Personhood: A Christian Theory of the Individual in Social Relationships*, Cambridge: Cambridge University Press 1990.

McFague, Sallie, *Models of God*, Philadelphia: Fortress Press 1988.

McGinn, Bernard, 'Meister Eckhart's Condemnation Reconsidered', *The Thomist* 44, 1980, pp. 390–414.

McInerny, Ralph M., *The Logic of Analogy*, The Hague: Martinus Nijhoff 1961.

McIntosh, Mark, *Mystical Theology*, Oxford: Blackwell 1998.

Meijer, P. A., *Plotinus on the Good or the One*, Amsterdam: J. C. Gieben 1992.

Merleau-Ponty, Maurice, *The Visible and the Invisible*, trans. Alphonso Lingis, Evanston, IL: Northwestern University Press 1968.

——, 'Dialogue and the Perception of the Other', *The Prose of the World*, trans. John O'Neill, London: Heinemann 1974, pp. 131–46.

Mey, Jacob L., *Pragmatics: An Introduction*, Oxford: Blackwell 1993.

Midrash Rabbah III, trans. S. M. Lehrman, London: Soncino 1961.

Milbank, John, *Theology and Social Theory: Beyond Secular Reason*, Oxford: Blackwell 1990.

——, *The Word Made Strange: Theology, Language, Culture*, Oxford: Blackwell 1997.

Moltmann, Jürgen, *Der gekreuzigte Gott*, Munich: Ch. Kaiser Verlag 1972.

——, *The Trinity and the Kingdom of God*, trans. Margaret Kohl, London: SCM Press 1981.

Moran, Gabriel, *Theology of Revelation*, London: Burns & Oates 1967.

Murphy, Nancey and Ellis, George, *On the Moral Nature of the Universe: Theology, Cosmology and Ethics*, Minneapolis: Fortress Press 1996.

Neumann, Peter K. D., 'Das Wort, das geschehen ist . . . Zum Problem der Wortempfangsterminologie in Jer. I–XXV', *Vetus Testamentum* 23, 1973, pp. 171–217.

Nicholson, Ernest W., *God and His People*, Oxford: Oxford University Press 1986.

Nietzsche, Friedrich, *Sämtliche Werke: Kritische Studienausgabe in 15 Bänden*, ed. G. Colli and M. Montinari, Berlin: de Gruyter 1980.

——, *Twilight of the Idols*, trans. R. J. Hollingdale, Harmondsworth: Penguin 1968.

——, *Thus spoke Zarathustra*, trans. R. J. Hollingdale, Harmondsworth: Penguin 1969.

——, *Ecce Homo*, *Also sprach Zarathustra*; *Ecce Homo*, trans. R. J. Hollingdale, Harmondsworth: Penguin 1979.

——, *On the Genealogy of Morals*, trans. Douglas Smith, Oxford: Oxford University Press 1996.

Nussbaum, Martha, 'Compassion: The Basic Social Emotion', *Social Philosophy and Policy* 13.1, Winter 1996, pp. 27–58.

Ochs, Peter, *Peirce, Pragmatism and the Logic of Scripture*, Cambridge: Cambridge University Press 1998.

O'Collins, Gerald, *Fundamental Theology*, London: Darton, Longman & Todd 1981.

——, *Retrieving Fundamental Theology*, London: Geoffrey Chapman 1993.

O'Daly, Gerard J. P., *Plotinus' Philosophy of the Self*, Shannon: Irish University Press 1973.

Ogilvie, R. M., *The Library of Lactantius*, Oxford: Clarendon Press 1978.

O'Loughlin, Thomas, 'The Symbol Gives Life: Eucharius of Lyon's Formula for Exegesis', *Scriptural Interpretation in the Fathers: Letter and Spirit*, ed. T. Finan and V. Toomey, Dublin: Four Courts Press 1995, pp. 221–52.

O'Meara, Dominic, *Plotinus: An Introduction to the Enneads*, Oxford: Clarendon Press 1993.

Onians, R. B., *The Origins of European Thought*, Cambridge: Cambridge University Press 1951.

Osborne, Catherine, *Eros Unveiled: Plato and the God of Love*, Oxford: Clarendon Press 1994.

Owens, Joseph, *The Doctrine of Being in the Aristotelian Metaphysics*, Toronto: Pontifical Institute of Medieval Studies 1951.

Pannenberg, Wolfhart, *Anthropology in Theological Perspective*, Edinburgh: T&T Clark 1985.

Pears, D. F., 'Is Existence a Predicate?', *Philosophical Logic*, ed. P. F. Strawson, Oxford: Oxford University Press 1967, pp. 97–102.

Persson, Per Erik, *Sacra Doctrina: Reason and Revelation in Aquinas*, trans. J. A. R. Mackenzie, Oxford: Blackwell 1970.

Peukert, Helmut, *Science, Action, and Fundamental Theology: Toward a Theology of Communicative Action*, Cambridge, MA and London: MIT Press 1984.

Pickstock, Catherine, *After Writing: On the Liturgical Consummation of Philosophy*, Oxford: Blackwell 1998.

Plato, *The Collected Dialogues*, ed. E. Hamilton and H. Cairns, Princeton: Princeton University Press 1961.

Posselt, Teresia Renata, *Edith Stein: Eine grosse Frau unseres Jahrhunderts*, Freiburg: Herder 1957.

Price, A. W., *Love and Friendship in Plato and Aristotle*, Oxford: Clarendon Press, 1989.

Prudhomme, Jeff Owen, *God and Being: Heidegger's Relation to Theology*, New Jersey: Humanities Press 1997.

Pseudo-Dionysius: The Complete Works, ed. and trans. Colm Luibheid, New York: Paulist Press 1987.

Quine, W. V., *Pursuit of Truth*, Cambridge, MA: Harvard University Press 1990.

Rad, Gerhard von, *Old Testament Theology, I, The Theology of Israel's Historical Traditions,* Edinburgh: Oliver & Boyd 1962.

Rahner, Karl, *The Trinity,* trans. J. Donceel, Tunbridge Wells: Burns & Oates 1970.

——, *Foundations of Christian Faith: An Introduction to the Idea of Christianity,* trans. William V. Dych, London: Darton, Longman & Todd 1978.

Randles, W. G. L., *The Unmaking of the Medieval Christian Cosmos, 1500–1760,* Aldershot and Vermont: Ashgate 1999.

Reif, Stefan C., *Judaism and Hebrew Prayer,* Cambridge: Cambridge University Press 1993.

Ricoeur, Paul, 'Towards a Hermeneutic of the Idea of Revelation', *Essays on Biblical Interpretation,* ed. Lewis S. Mudge, London: SPCK 1981, pp. 73–118.

——, *The Rule of Metaphor,* trans. Robert Czerny, London: Routledge 1986.

——, *From Text to Action,* Evanston, IL: Northwestern University Press 1991.

——, *Oneself as Another,* trans. Kathleen Blamey, Chicago: University of Chicago Press 1992.

——, *Figuring the Sacred: Religion, Narrative and Imagination,* trans. David Pellauer, ed. Mark I. Wallace, Minneapolis: Fortress Press 1995.

Rist, J. M., *Eros and Psyche: Studies in Plato, Plotinus and Origen,* Toronto: University of Toronto Press 1964.

Ritschl, Dietrich, *The Logic of Theology,* trans. John Bowden, London: SCM Press 1986.

Rorty, Richard, 'Is Derrida a Transcendental Philosopher?', *Derrida: A Critical Reader,* ed. David Wood, Oxford: Blackwell 1992, pp. 235–46.

Rousseau, Jean-Jacques, *Emile or On Education,* trans. Allan Bloom, Harmondsworth: Penguin 1991.

Rousselot, Pierre, 'Pour l'histoire du problème de l'amour au moyen age', *Beiträge zur Geshichte der Philosophie des Mittelalters,* B. 6, H. 6, Münster 1908, pp. 1–102.

Russell, Bertrand, 'Logic as the Essence of Philosophy', *Readings in Logic,* ed. I. M. Copi and J. A. Gould, New York: Macmillan 1964, pp. 42–69.

Rutherford, R. B., *The Art of Plato,* London: Duckworth 1995.

Sallis, John, *Being and Logos,* 3rd edn., Bloomington: Indiana University Press 1996.

Schechner, Richard, *Performance Theory,* rev. edn., London: Routledge 1988.

Schenk, Wolfgang, 'Altisraelitische Sprachauffassungen in der Hebräischen Bibel', *Geschichte der Sprachtheorie, II, Sprachtheorien der abendländischen Antike,* ed. Peter Schmitter, Tübingen: Gunter Narr Verlag 1991, pp. 3–25.

Schmitz, J., 'La Théologie Fondamentale', *Bilan de la Théologie,* ed. R. Vander Gucht and H. Vorgrimler, Tournai-Paris: Casterman 1970, pp. 9–51.

Scholder, Klaus, *The Birth of Modern Critical Theology,* trans. John Bowden, London: SCM Press 1990.

Schopenhauer, Arthur, *Grundlage der Moral,* in *Sämtliche Werke,* III, Munich: Piper 1912.

Schüssler Fiorenza, Francis, *Foundational Theology: Jesus and the Church,* New York: Crossroad 1985.

Schwöbel Christoph, *God: Action and Revelation*, Kampen: Kok Pharos 1992.

Scully, James, *Modern Poetics*, New York: McGraw-Hill 1965.

Secada, Jorge, *Cartesian Metaphysics*, Cambridge: Cambridge University Press 2000.

Sells, Michael A., *Mystical Languages of Unsaying*, Chicago and London: University of Chicago Press 1994.

Smith, Adam, *The Theory of Moral Sentiments*, ed. D. D. Raphael and A. L. Macfie, Oxford: Clarendon Press 1976.

Soskice, Janet Martin, *Metaphor and Religious Language*, Oxford: Oxford University Press 1985.

——, 'The Gift of the Name: Moses and the Burning Bush', *Gregorianum* 79.2, 1998, pp. 231–46.

Spinoza, Benedict de, *Opera*, ed. C. Gebhardt, Heidelberg: Carl Winters 1924–6.

——, *Ethics*, ed. and trans. Edwin Curley, Harmondsworth: Penguin 1996.

Edith Stein, *Selbstbildnis in Briefen II, Teil 1934–1942*, *Werke*, XI, Druten: De Maas & Waler; Freiburg–Basel–Vienna: Herder 1977.

——, *On the Problem of Empathy*, trans. Waltraut Stein, The Collected Works of Edith Stein, III, Washington, DC: ICS Publications 1989.

Stirnimann, Heinrich, '"Fundamentaltheologie" im frühen 18 Jahrhundert?', *Freiburger Zeitschrift für Theologie und Philosophie* 24, 1977, pp. 460–76.

Stevens, Wallace, 'The Noble Rider and the Sound of Words', *The Necessary Angel*, New York: Knopf 1951, pp. 3–36.

Stock, Alex, *Poetische Dogmatik*, 3 vols., Paderborn: Schöningh 1995–98.

Strawson, P. F., *Individuals*, London: Methuen 1959.

——, *The Bounds of Sense*, London: Methuen 1966.

——, 'Is Existence Never a Predicate?', *Freedom and Resentment*, London: Methuen 1974, pp. 189–97.

Studer, Basil, *Trinity and Incarnation*, Edinburgh: T&T Clark 1993.

Sturlese, Loris, 'Mystik und Philosophie in der Bildlehre Meister Eckhart', *Festschrift für Walter Haug und Burghart Wachinger*, Tübingen: Max Niemeyer Verlag 1992, pp. 349–61.

Tanay, Emanuel, 'A Catholic Jew', *Edith Stein*, ed. Cargas, pp. 27–31.

Targum Neofiti 1: Exodus, trans. with Introduction and Apparatus by Martin McNamara, MSC, The Aramaic Bible 2, Edinburgh: T&T Clark 1994.

Taylor, Charles, *Hegel*, Cambridge: Cambridge University Press 1975.

Taylor, Mark C., *Erring: A Postmodern A/theology*, Chicago: Chicago University Press 1981.

Tec, Nechama, *When Light Pierced the Darkness*, Oxford: Oxford University Press 1986.

Teichman, Jenny, 'Deconstruction and Aerodynamics', *Philosophy* 68 no. 263, January 1993, pp. 53–62.

Thibault, Herve J., *Creation and Metaphysics*, The Hague: Martinus Nijhoff 1970.

Third General Conference of Latin American Bishops: Puebla. Slough: St Paul Publications and London: CIIR 1980.

Thomas Aquinas, *Commentary on the Metaphysics of Aristotle*, vol. I, trans. John P. Rowan, Chicago: Henry Regnery 1961.

——, *On Being and Essence*, trans. Armand Maurer, Toronto: The Pontifical Institute of Medieval Studies, 1968.

Thomas, Jenny, *Meaning in Interaction*, London: Longman 1995.

Thunberg, Lars, *Microcosm and Mediator*, Chicago and La Salle, IL: Open Court 1995.

Torrell, Jean-Pierre, *Saint Thomas Aquinas, Vol. I, The Person and His Work*, trans. R. Royal, Washington, DC: Catholic University of America Press 1996.

Touati, Charles, 'Ehye ašer ehye (*Exode* 3, 14) comme "l'Être-avec"', *Dieu et l'Être: Exégèses d'Exode 3, 14 et de Coran 20, 11–24*, Paris: Études Augustiniennes 1978, pp. 75–84.

Tracy, David, *The Analogical Imagination*, London: SCM Press 1981.

Tshibangu, Tharcisse, *Théologie positive et théologie spéculative*, Louvain: Publications Université de Louvain 1965.

Turner, Denys, *The Darkness of God*, Cambridge: Cambridge University Press 1995.

——, 'The Darkness of God and the Light of Christ: Negative Theology and Eucharistic Presence', *Modern Theology* 15.2, April 1999, pp. 143–58.

Vajda, Georges, 'Bref aperçu sur l'exégèse d'Exode 3, 14 dans la littérature rabbinique et en théologie juive du Moyen Age', *Dieu et l'Être: Exégèses d'Exode 3, 14 et de Coran 20, 11–24*, Paris: Études Augustiniennes 1978, pp. 67–74.

Valadier, Paul, *Nietzsche et la critique du christianisme*, Paris: Editions du Cerf 1974.

van den Brom, Luco, 'Models of Revelation and Language', *Revelation and Experience. Proceedings of the 11th Biennial European Conference on the Philosophy of Religion, Soesterberg 1996*, ed. Vincent Brümmer and Marcel Sarot, Utrecht: Universiteit Utrecht 1996, pp. 56–71.

Vattimo, Gianni, *The Adventure of Difference*, trans. Cyprian Blamires, Cambridge: Polity Press 1993.

Vaux, Roland de, 'The Revelation of the Divine Name YHWH', *Proclamation and Presence* ed. John I. Durham and J. R. Porter, London: SCM Press 1970, pp. 48–75.

Verweyen, Hansjürgen, *Gottes letztes Wort: Grundriß der Fundamentaltheologie*, Düsseldorf: Patmos Verlag 1991.

Volf, Miroslav, *After Our Likeness: The Church as the Image of the Trinity*, Grand Rapids, MI: Eerdmans 1998.

Wagner, Andreas, *Sprechakte und Sprechaktanalyse im Alten Testament*, Berlin: de Gruyter 1997.

Ward, Graham, *Barth, Derrida and the Language of Theology*, Cambridge: Cambridge University Press 1995.

——, 'Kenosis and Naming: Beyond Analogy and Towards *Allegoria Amoris*', *Religion, Modernity and Postmodernity*, ed. Paul Heelas, Oxford: Blackwell 1998, pp. 233–257.

Ward, Keith, *Religion and Revelation*, Oxford: Oxford University Press 1994.

Weinberg, Werner, 'Language Consciousness in the Old Testament', *Zeitschrift für die alttestamentliche Wissenschaft* 92, 1980, pp. 185–204.

Westermann, Claus, *Basic Forms of Prophetic Speech*, trans. Hugh Clayton White, London: Lutterworth Press 1967.

White, Nicholas P., *Plato on Knowledge and Reality*, Indianapolis: Hackett 1976.

——, 'Plato's Metaphysical Epistemology', *The Cambridge Companion to Plato*, ed. Richard Kraut, Cambridge: Cambridge University Press 1992, pp. 277–310.

Williams, Catrin H., *I Am He: The Interpretation of 'Anî Hû' in Jewish and Early Christian Literature*, Tübingen: J. C. B. Mohr 2000.

Williams, Jane, 'The Fatherhood of God', *The Forgotten Trinity*, London: BCC/CCBI 1991, pp. 91–101.

Williams, Robert R., *Recognition: Fichte and Hegel on the Other*, New York: State University of New York Press 1992.

Williams, Rowan, 'Barth and the Triune God', *Karl Barth: Studies of His Theological Method*, ed. Stephen Sykes, Oxford: Clarendon Press 1979, pp. 147–93.

——, 'Trinity and Revelation', *Modern Theology* 2.3, 1986, pp. 197–212.

——, 'Between Politics and Metaphysics: Reflections in the Wake of Gillian Rose', *Modern Theology* 11.1, 1995, pp. 3–22.

Wippel, John F., *Metaphysical Themes in Thomas Aquinas*, Washington: Catholic University of America Press 1984.

Witt, Charlotte, *Substance and Essence in Aristotle: An Interpretation of Metaphysics VII–IX*, Ithaca: Cornell University Press 1989.

Wittgenstein, Ludwig, *Philosophical Investigations*, 3rd edn., trans. G. E. M. Anscombe, Oxford: Blackwell 1968.

Wright, M. R., *Cosmology in Antiquity*, London and New York: Routledge 1995.

Wyschogrod, Edith, *Saints and Postmodernism*, Chicago and London: University of Chicago Press 1990.

Yule, George, *Pragmatics*, Oxford: Oxford University Press 1996.

Zak, William F., *The Polis and the Divine Order*, London: Associated University Presses 1995.

Zizioulas, John D., *Being as Communion*, New York: St Vladimir's Seminary Press 1985.

zum Brunn, Emilie, *St Augustine: Being and Nothingness*, New York: Paragon House 1988.

Notes

Introduction

1. Walter A. Davis, *Inwardness and Existence: Subjectivity in/and Hegel, Heidegger, Marx and Freud*, Wisconsin: University of Wisconsin Press 1989, p. 24.
2. See, for instance, the 1998 papal encyclical *Fides et Ratio*, Prooemium, §5 and passim.
3. Key thinkers of difference, against ontology, variously construed, include not only Levinas, Foucault, Lyotard, Habermas and Ricoeur but also Rorty, Deleuze, Vattimo and Derrida.
4. See below, pp. 10–12.
5. Paul Ricoeur, *Oneself as Another*, trans. Kathleen Blamey, Chicago: University of ChicagoPress 1992, p. 298.
6. Jürgen Habermas, *Postmetaphysical Thinking: Philosophical Essays*, trans. William Mark Hohengarten, Cambridge: Polity Press 1992, p. 9.
7. Although I have in general not followed the practice, all the references to being in this book are in fact to 'being' as a way of speaking about the primary bestowal of existence.
8. For Edith Wyschogrod's detailed and imaginative exploration of the place of narrative as hagiography in the formulation of a postmodern ethics, see her *Saints and Postmodernism*, Chicago: University of Chicago Press 1990.
9. I have chosen to use the impersonal form for the subject and the self in the main. This is far from ideal, and may unhelpfully suggest an overly abstract register in which I speak of gendered selves. But it does seem preferable to the alternatives, which are either the exclusive use of feminine pronouns, masculine pronouns or some arbitrary combination.

Chapter 1

1. Cf. Immanuel Kant, *Critique of Pure Reason*, trans. Norman Kemp Smith, London: Macmillan, 2nd impr. 1933, p. 8.
2. Jürgen Habermas, *Postmetaphysical Thinking: Philosophical Essays*, trans. William Mark Hohengarten, Cambridge: Polity Press 1992, p. 13. On the theme of the 'grand narratives', see Jean-François Lyotard, *The Postmodern Condition: A Report on Knowledge*, trans. Geoffrey Bennington and Brian Massumi, Manchester: Manchester University Press 1984.
3. Quoted in David Harvey, *The Condition of Postmodernity*, Oxford: Blackwell 1990, p. 44.

4. Paul Ricoeur, *The Rule of Metaphor,* trans. Robert Czerny, London: Routledge 1986, p. 239.

5. Habermas, *Postmetaphysical Thinking*, p. 6.

6. Michel de Certeau, *Heterologies: Discourse on the Other*, trans. Brian Massumi, Minneapolis: University of Minnesota Press 1986, p. 179. On the theme of reflection about reflection as a condition of the 'postmodern', see also Anthony Giddens, *The Consequences of Modernity*, Cambridge: Polity Press 1990, pp. 36–45.

7. Habermas describes Nietzsche's view of truth as being driven by 'taste' (Jürgen Habermas, 'Die Verschlingung von Mythos und Aufklärung', *Mythos und Moderne*, ed. K.-H. Bohrer, Suhrkamp: Frankfurt am Main 1983, p. 422 (quoted in Raymond Geuss, *Morality, Culture, and History*, Cambridge: Cambridge University Press 1999, p. 8).

8. Nicholas Boyle, *Who Are We Now?*, Edinburgh: T&T Clark 1998, p. 318; Rowan Williams, 'Between Politics and Metaphysics: Reflections in the Wake of Gillian Rose', *Modern Theology* 11.1, 1995, pp. 3–22 (here p. 4).

9. Jacques Derrida, 'Sauf le Nom (Post-Scriptum)', *On the Name*, trans. David Wood, John P. Leavey, Jr. and Ian McLeod, Stanford, CA: Stanford University Press 1995, pp. 34–85 (here pp. 54 and 58).

10. I am not intending to argue the case for this understanding of Christian apophaticism here. See Denys Turner, *The Darkness of God*, Cambridge: Cambridge University Press 1995; Mark McIntosh, *Mystical Theology*, Oxford: Blackwell 1998; Andrew Louth, *The Origins of the Christian Mystical Tradition*, Oxford: Clarendon Press 1981; Michael A. Sells, *Mystical Languages of Unsaying*, Chicago and London: University of Chicago Press 1994; Oliver Davies and Denys Turner (eds), *Silence and the Word*, Cambridge: Cambridge University Press 2002, forthcoming.

11. See pp. 260–1 below.

12. We live in the age of the 'cyborg', and our popular culture persistently explores the dissolution of the borders of the self in images of creatures who are part human and part machine. See Donna Haraway, *Simians, Cyborgs and Women: The Reinvention of Nature*, London: Free Association 1991 and David M. Rorvik, *As Man Becomes Machine*, London: Sphere 1979.

13. Giddens, *The Consequences of Modernity*, especially pp. 1–54.

14. E.g. Jürgen Moltmann, *The Trinity and the Kingdom of God*, trans. Margaret Kohl, London: SCM Press 1981, pp. 21–5. See also the discussion in Janet Martin Soskice, 'The Gift of the Name: Moses and the Burning Bush', *Gregorianum* 79.2, 1998, pp. 231–46.

15 Gianni Vattimo, *The Adventure of Difference*, trans. Cyprian Blamires, Cambridge: Polity Press 1993 (Italian original, 1980), pp. 31–2. See also Jürgen Habermas, *On the Logic of the Social Sciences*, trans. Shierry Weber Nicholsen and Jerry A. Stark, Cambridge: Polity Press 1988, especially pp. 162–70.

16. Giorgio Agamben, *Homo Sacer: Sovereign Power and Bare Life*, trans. Daniel Heller-Roazen, Stanford, CA: Stanford University Press 1998, p. 166.

17. Agamben insists on the authentically scientific nature of these experiments, pointing to the distinguished scientific reputations of some of the experimenters, thus implicating European civilization more in the atrocities of the camp (Agamben, *Homo Sacer*, p. 156).

18. Matt. 27.25.

19. 'Dans l'apocalypse d'Auschwitz ce n'est ni plus ni moins que l'Occident, en son essence, qui s'est révélé – et qui ne cesse, depuis, de se révéler' (Philippe Lacoue-Labarthe, *La fiction du politique*, Strasbourg: Association des Publications près les universités de Strasbourg 1987, pp. 36–8). In his magisterial study *The Destruction of the European Jews* (New York: Holmes & Meier 1983, vol. 3, p. 994), Raul Hilberg wrote: 'The machinery of destruction, then, was structurally no different from organized German society as a whole. The machinery of destruction *was* the organized community in one of its special roles' (quoted in Zygmunt Bauman, *Modernity and the Holocaust*, Cambridge: Polity Press 1989, p. 9).

20. His argument is reinforced by the juridical basis of the camp, in the Weimar Republic at least, as an exceptional entity under the law of *Schutzhaft* or 'protective custody' (cf. internment), itself standing outside the normal operation of the law. Pointing to the *Verordnung zum Schutz von Volk und Staat* of 1933, which declared the state of exception without recognizing it to be a temporary measure, Agamben maintains that under the National Socialists the camp, the state of exception, itself became the norm (Agamben, *Homo Sacer*, pp. 166–80).

21. Quoted in Rachel Feldhay Brenner, *Writing as Resistance: Four Women Confronting the Holocaust*, Pennsylvania: Pennsylvania State University Press 1997, p. 77.

22. For the following, see Etty Hillesum, *Etty: A Diary 1941–43*, trans. Arnold J. Pomerans, London: Grafton Books 1985, pp. 9–14.

23. Edith Stein, *Life in a Jewish Family*. For the biography of Edith Stein, see Waltraud Herbstrich, *Edith Stein: A Biography*, trans. Bernard Bonowitz OCSO, San Francisco: Ignatius Press 1985.

24. *Etty: A Diary*, p. 25.

25. *Etty: A Diary*, pp. 228–9.

26. *Life in a Jewish Family* (quoted on p. 78).

27. On *Life in a Jewish Family* as an exercise in practical empathy, see Brenner, *Writing as Resistance*, pp. 77–8.

28. Quoted in Brenner, *Writing as Resistance*, p. 60.

29. Edith Stein, *Selbstbildnis in Briefen II, Teil 1934–1942*, *Werke*, XI, Druten: De Maas & Waler; Freiburg–Basel–Vienna: Herder 1977, Letter 287, p. 124.

30. Stein, *Selbstbildnis in Briefen II*, Letter 296, p. 133 (quoted in Herbstrich, *Edith Stein*, p. 168).

31. Opposing views on her canonization can be found in Harry James Cargas (ed.), *The Unnecessary Problem of Edith Stein*, Studies in the Shoah, vol. IV, Maryland: University Press of America 1994.

32. Specifically, Edith Stein was killed because she was a Jew, but was not spared as a Catholic Jew because of the pastoral letter read out in Dutch Catholic Churches (and those of the Gereformerde Kerk) on 26 July 1942. This included the strongly worded condemnation of the deportations contained in a telegram to the Reichskommissar of 11 July, to which the National Socialist authorities objected. For a detailing of these events and their influence upon the case of Edith Stein, see Teresia Renata Posselt, *Edith Stein: Eine grosse Frau unseres Jahrhunderts*, Freiburg: Herder 1957, pp. 179–87.

33. Emanuel Tanay has also welcomed the beatification of Stein as serving to 'enshrine the Holocaust family in Christian consciousness' ('A Catholic Jew', *Edith Stein*, ed. Cargas, pp. 27–31 [here p. 31].

34. Paul Ricoeur, *Oneself as Another,* trans. Kathleen Blamey, Chicago: University of Chicago Press 1992, pp. 193.

35. Paul Ricoeur, *Figuring the Sacred: Religion, Narrative and Imagination*, trans. David Pellauer and ed. Mark I. Wallace, Minneapolis: Fortress Press 1995, p. 315.

36. Catherine Osborne has recently explored the interaction of *eros* and *agape* in classical and early Christian texts, contesting their opposition in Nygren (Catherine Osborne, *Eros Unveiled: Plato and the God of Love*, Oxford: Clarendon Press 1994, pp. 52–85). I am also indebted to conversations with Julius Lipner concerning distinctions between 'the two loves'.

37. Martha Nussbaum, 'Compassion: The Basic Social Emotion', *Social Philosophy and Policy* 13.1, Winter 1996, pp. 27–58.

38. Ricoeur, *Oneself as Another*, p. 191.

39. It is notable that the phenomenological tradition has in general eschewed the terminology of both love and the specific virtues, preferring that of empathy (although this too includes the ambiguity that it may or may not include volitional and dispossessive elements).

40. Edmund Husserl defined phenomenology in the following terms: 'Every type of originary intuition forms a legitimate source of knowledge; whatever presents itself to us by intuition at first hand, in its authentic reality, as it were, is to be accepted simply for the thing as which it presents itself, yet merely within the limits within which it presents itself' (*Ideen I*, §24; *Husserliana* III/I, 51).

41. Kant's attack on the 'substantiality', 'simplicity', 'personality' and 'ideality' of the Cartesian and Idealist self is set out in his analysis of the 'paralogisms of pure reason' (*Critique of Pure Reason*, A341–A405, B399–B432). The Kantian view of the self – as the transcendental ground of all experience – is certainly more formal than the one we are entertaining here, but in our argument a full self-possessing knowledge of the self as uncompromised and substantial object is in no sense a necessary condition for the powerful, performative enactment of the self as self-possessing agent, within the multiple narratives of experience. Our 'essential narrativity' of the self is proximate to Kant's unknowable 'transcendental unity of apperception', but a modern understanding of language as performance and expressivity allows the articulation of that ground in the language of ontology without reification of the self as unified and substantial object. For a further discussion of Kant's 'unity of apperception', see below, pp. 40–1 and 157–9.

42. Aristotle, *Metaphysics*, X, 1.

43. 'But for us *einai* and *ousia* as *par-* and *apousia* means this in the first instance: in presencing there prevails, in an unthought and concealed manner, presence and duration – there prevails time' (Martin Heidegger, 'Introduction to "What is Metaphysics?"', *Pathmarks*, ed. William McNeill, Cambridge: Cambridge University Press 1998, pp. 277–90 [here p. 286]).

44. 'Here the question really is *who* will be the heir, the only son of the dead God. The idealist philosophers believe that it is enough to respond in terms of the self or subject to resolve the problem. But the Self is not an *object* alongside other selves, for it is constituted by its relation to the Other and cannot be considered outside of this relation. It is this relation which the effort to substitute oneself for the God of the Bible always corrupts. Divinity cannot be

identified either with the Self or with the Other; it is perpetually part of the struggle *between* the Self and Other' (René Girard, *Resurrection from the Underground: Feodor Dostoevsky*, New York: Crossroad 1997, pp. 93–4).

45. Nussbaum, 'Compassion: The Basic Social Emotion', p. 49.
46. In her study *When Light Pierced the Darkness*, Oxford: Oxford University Press 1986, Nechama Tec undertook a study of individuals who reacted positively and at their own risk to the victims of the Holocaust and concluded both that they did not come from any one socio-economic group and that they regarded such altruistic behaviour as 'natural' (pp. 184–93).
47. In the concept of *karuṇā*, for instance, which plays a fundamental role in the ethical formation of the Buddhist (Peter Harvey, *An Introduction to Buddhism*, Cambridge: Cambridge University Press 1990, pp. 209–12). On the place of *ren* as 'humaneness' in the Confucian tradition, see Xinzhong Yao, *An Introduction to Confucianism*, Cambridge: Cambridge University Press 2000. For *raḥmah* in Islam, see Kenneth Cragg, *The Mind of the Qur'an*, London: Allen & Unwin 1973, pp. 110–28.
48. See the studies by Donald W. Winnicott in the field of child development, especially regarding the growing child's experience of maternal empathy: 'The Theory of the Parent–Infant Relationship', 'Development of the Capacity for Concern' and 'From Dependence towards Independence in the Development of the Individual', *The Maturational Processes and the Facilitating Environment*, London: Hogarth Press 1965, pp. 37–55, 73–82, 83–92.

Chapter 2

1. This is close to Berkeley's axiom *esse est percipi*, although of course we are not advocating here Berkeley's philosophy of theological idealism. See his *Principles of Human Knowledge*, Part One, § 3 (George Berkeley, *Philosophical Works*, ed. Michael R. Ayers, London: Dent 1975, p. 90).
2. Edmund Husserl, *Cartesianische Meditationen*, ed. Elisabeth Ströker, Hamburg: Felix Meiner Verlag 1977, § 8 (Edmund Husserl, *Cartesian Meditations*, trans. Dorion Cairns, Dordrecht: Kluwer 1995 [originally The Hague: Martinus Nijhoff 1950], pp. 18–19).
3. See Benedict de Spinoza, *Ethics*, IIP49S3Bii, where he opposes the notion that the will discerns which of our perceptions it will affirm, and argues, for instance, that a child believes a winged horse to exist unless other perceptions contradict this conclusion.
4. See in particular the *First Introduction to the Wissenschaftslehre* (*Fichtes Werke*, I, p. 426).
5. For a fuller discussion of Derrida's critique of traditional metaphysics, see below, pp. 122–9.
6. This emphasis upon the role of language in the recognition of the other is not intended to exclude animals, particularly higher primates, from the cycle of human ethical responsibility. Language as we know it is the product of a distinctively human evolution, but it is arguable that elements of identity which underlie the use of the indexical 'I' may also obtain in some form in the semiological interactions of higher primate societies, which can at times attain a high degree of complexity.

7. P. F. Strawson, *Individuals*, London: Methuen 1959, pp. 99–116.
8. Maurice Merleau-Ponty, *The Visible and the Invisible*, trans. Alphonso Lingis, Evanston, IL: Northwestern University Press 1968, p. 218. On language in particular, see also his 'Dialogue and the Perception of the Other', *The Prose of the World*, trans. John O'Neill, London: Heinemann 1974, pp. 131–46.
9. Paul Ricoeur, *Oneself as Another*, trans. Kathleen Blamey, Chicago: University of Chicago Press 1992.
10. Paul Ricoeur, 'Towards a Hermeneutic of the Idea of Revelation', *Essays on Biblical Interpretation*, ed. Lewis S. Mudge, London: SPCK 1981, pp. 73–118 (here p. 106).
11. Ricoeur, *Oneself as Another*, p. 302.
12. Ricoeur, *Oneself as Another*, pp. 20–1.
13. Ricoeur, *Oneself as Another*, pp. 19 and 22.
14. Ricoeur, *Oneself as Another*, p. 317.
15. Ricoeur, *Oneself as Another*, p. 3.
16. Ricoeur, *Oneself as Another*, p. 318.
17. Immanuel Kant, *Critique of Pure Reason*, trans. Norman Kemp Smith, London: Macmillan, second impr. 1933, pp. 152–3.
18. *Critique of Pure Reason*, B 134; Norman Kemp Smith, p. 154.
19. Norman Kemp Smith, p. 153.
20. Norman Kemp Smith, p. 169. See below, pp. 157–9.
21. P. F. Strawson, *The Bounds of Sense*, London: Methuen 1966, p. 98.
22. Edith Stein, *On the Problem of Empathy*, trans. Waltraut Stein, The Collected Works of Edith Stein, III, Washington, DC: ICS Publications 1989, p. 11.
23. Stein, *On the Problem of Empathy*, p. 10.
24. Stein, *On the Problem of Empathy*, p. 17.
25. In an earlier period, the work of Hermann Cohen represented an ethical intensification of the self–other relation as implied in the transcendental analytic of Immanual Kant. Cohen critiqued Kant's idealist and universalist concept of ethics with the development of his own ethical philosophy of experience. In compassion, the other is transformed from a 'He' to a 'Thou', from 'Nebenmensch' to 'Mitmensch', which sets the self in a position of 'correlation' with the divine creativity and compassion. See Hermann Cohen, *Religion der Vernunft aus den Quellen des Judentums*, ed. Bruno Strauss, Frankfurt: J. Kaufmann 1929, repr. Cologne: J. Melzer 1959, p. 170.
26. In his work *Gottes letztes Wort: Grundriß einer Fundamentaltheologie* (Düsseldorf: Patmos Verlag 1991), Hansjürgen Verweyen has constructed a fundamental theology on the basis of Fichte's *Reflexionsphilosophie*. Verweyen seeks to ground the 'ultimate validity' of the gospel on the transcendental unity of consciousness which finds its expression in the recognition of the freedom of the other implicit in the moral imperatives of interpersonal relationships. As the transparent image of unconditioned freedom, summoning us to an unconditional obedience, the person of Christ represents the revelation of this ultimate validity, or final unity of meaning, in history. Verweyen's project shows the extent to which philosophy of consciousness can contribute to current debates. Verweyen's concern is with the embedding of 'reason' as 'meaning' within the structures of consciousness itself in interaction with other selves, and with the person of Christ, as part of an attempt to revalue the demonstrations of traditional fundamental theology. For discussion of

themes raised by Verweyen's project, see Gerhard Larcher, Klaus Müller and Thomas Pröpper (eds), *Hoffnung, die Gründe nennt: Zu Hansjürgen Verweyens Projekt einer erstphilosophischen Glaubensverantwortung*, Regensburg: Verlag Friedrich Pustet 1996.

27. J. G. Fichte, *Fichtes Werke*, ed. I. H. Fichte, repr. Berlin: de Gruyter 1971, III, p. 36.
28. *Fichtes Werke*, III, pp. 39–40.
29. Maurice Blondel, *Action (1893): Essay on a Critique of Life and a Science of Practice*, trans. Oliva Blanchette, University of Notre Dame Press 1984, p. 128.
30. Blondel, *Action (1893)*, p. 124.
31. 'The interior life, which earlier seemed to absorb all that nourished its knowledge, finds itself incomplete and dead if it does not spend itself and spread itself; surpassing the universe of facts, it is surpassed by an unknown into which action alone enables it to penetrate' (Blondel, *Action (1893)*, p. 149).
32. Blondel, *Action (1893)*, p. 141.
33. Blondel, *Action (1893)*, p. 306.
34. Blondel, *Action (1893)*, pp. 263 and 274.
35. Blondel, *Action (1893)*, pp. 425 and 404.
36. Blondel, *Action (1893)*, p. 342.
37. For the following, see Karl Rahner, *Foundations of Christian Faith: An Introduction to the Idea of Christianity*, trans. William V. Dych, London: Darton, Longman & Todd 1978, pp. 17–23.
38. Ricoeur, *Oneself as Another*, p. 192.
39. Ricoeur, *Oneself as Another*, p. 189.

B. Introduction

1. Theodor Adorno, *Jargon der Eigentlichkeit*, Frankfurt am Main: Suhrkamp Verlag 1964.
2. Jacques Maritain, *A Preface to Metaphysics*, London: Sheed & Ward 1939, p. 8; D. F. Pears, 'Is Existence a Predicate?', *Philosophical Logic*, ed. P. F. Strawson, Oxford: Oxford University Press 1967, pp. 97–102 (here p. 98). Strawson himself however, has argued for the meaningfulness of existence as a logical predicate in his paper 'Is Existence Never a Predicate?', *Freedom and Resentment*, London: Methuen 1974, pp. 189–97.
3. Thomas Aquinas, *De veritate*, q. 1, a. 1: *Illud autem quod primo intellectus concipit quasi notissimum, et in quo omnes conceptiones resolvit, est ens* ('that which the intellect first conceives as, in a way, the most evident and to which it reduces all its concepts, is being'); Duns Scotus, *Op. Ox.*, I, d. 39, q. 1., n. 13 (ed. Viv. X, 625a): *Ens habet conceptum simpliciter simplicem, et ideo non potest esse definitio; Op. Ox.*, I, d. 2, q. 2, n. 31 (ed. Viv. VIII, 478b): *Ens autem per nihil notius explicatur.*
4. G. W. Leibniz, *Principles of Nature and Grace, Founded on Reason*, § 7; Martin Heidegger, *Einführung in die Metaphysik*, Tübingen: Max Niehmeyer Verlag 1953, especially pp. 1–39.
5. Charles Kahn, 'Why Existence Does Not Emerge as a Distinct Concept in Greek Philosophy', *Philosophies of Existence Ancient and Medieval*, ed. Parviz Morewedge, New York: Fordham University Press 1982, pp. 7–17 (here p. 8); see also his study 'The Verb "Be" in Ancient Greek', *The Verb "Be" and Its Synonyms*, VI, , ed. J. W. M. Verhaar, Dordrecht: D. Reidel 1973. A more recent

discussion, by Lesley Brown, concludes that the same Greek verb *esti* could be used in a complete and incomplete sense, implicitly supporting Kahn's point that the Greeks lacked a concept of being which might have prompted them to distinguish the two meanings ('The Verb "To Be" in Greek Philosophy: Some Remarks', *Language: Companions to Ancient Thought 3*, ed. Stephen Everson, Cambridge: Cambridge University Press 1994, pp. 212–36).

6. Kahn, 'Existence', p. 7.
7. Kant's famous discussion of the nature of existence comes in the *Critique of Pure Reason*, A598.
8. See, for instance, the arguments for a moral – or kenotic – paradigm of the universe, grounded in the natural and social sciences, Nancey Murphy and George Ellis, *On the Moral Nature of the Universe: Theology, Cosmology and Ethics*, Minneapolis: Fortress Press 1996.
9. See Colin Gunton's useful discussion of Faraday and trinitarian thought in his 'Relation and Relativity', *The Promise of Trinitarian Theology*, Edinburgh: T&T Clark 1991, pp. 142–61, for instance, where he points to 'some conceptual parallels between the concepts in which the being of God is expressed and the ways in which we may conceive the world' (p. 146).
10. Martin Heidegger, 'Introduction to "What is Metaphysics?"', *Pathmarks*, ed. William McNeill, Cambridge: Cambridge University Press 1998, pp. 277–90 (here p. 286).
11. Aristotle, *Metaphysics*, VI, 2; X, 1.
12. Bertrand Russell was right to point to the way in which the forms of language determine how we conceive of entities in the world ('Our Knowledge of the External World', repr. as 'Logic as the Essence of Philosophy', *Readings in Logic*, ed. I. M. Copi and J. A. Gould, New York: Macmillan 1964, pp. 42–69). However, rather than being misled by the grammar of existence, embedded within ordinary language usage, we can argue that language itself embodies the existence of the self and the multiple presences which it encounters as given in the world.
13. Karl Rahner, *Foundations of Christian Faith: An Introduction to the Idea of Christianity*, trans. William V. Dych, London: Darton, Longman & Todd 1978, p. 15 (translation slightly adapted).
14. Anthony Giddens, *The Consequences of Modernity*, Cambridge: Polity Press 1990, pp. 36–45.
15. For rabbinical readings of Ex. 3.14, in both targum and midrash, see below, pp. 241–3.

Chapter 3

1. Aristotle, *Metaphysics*, I, 3.
2. M. R. Wright, *Cosmology in Antiquity*, London and New York: Routledge 1995, p. 95.
3. H. Diehls and W. Kranz, *Die Fragmente der Vorsokratiker*, vol. I, Berlin: Weidmannsche Verlagsbuchhandlung 1954, p. 231. G. S. Kirk and J. E. Raven, *The Presocratic Philosophers*, Cambridge: Cambridge University Press 1957, p. 269. See also M. R. Wright, *The Presocratics*, Bristol: Bristol Classical Press 1985, pp. xxi and 79. Etienne Gilson reads Parmenides from a subtly

Heideggerian position as instituting the distinction between the finite existence of entities and infinite being (*Being and Some Philosophers*, 2nd edn., Toronto: Pontifical Institute of Medieval Studies 1952, pp. 6–10), whereas Charles Kahn sees in Parmenides the beginnings of a veridical notion of being so that Parmenides' conjunction of thought and being is an investigation of the conditions of truth ('Why Existence Does Not Emerge as a Distinct Concept in Greek Philosophy', *Philosophies of Existence Ancient and Medieval*, ed. Parviz Morewedge, New York: Fordham University Press 1982, pp. 7–17, especially pp. 11–14).

4. Diehls and Kranz, vol. I, pp. 235–6; Jonathan Barnes, *Early Greek Philosophy*, Harmondsworth: Penguin 1987, p. 134.

5. Augustine, *De libero arbitrio*, II, 8, 22.

6 Diehls and Kranz, vol. I, pp. 228–30; Barnes, *Early Greek Philosophy*, p. 131.

7. On the possible Pythagorean influence, see A. H. Coxon's commentary, *The Fragments of Parmenides*, Assen: Van Gorcum 1986, pp. 15–17). In his article 'Das Proömium des Parmenides und die Katabasis des Pythagoras' (*Phronesis* 15, 1969, pp. 1–30) W. Burkert urges the reader to strip away the motifs of a journey upwards and into light, 'diese platonisch-christliche Symbole' (p. 15), and points to the possible influence of Hesiod (p. 16), Epimedes of Crete (pp. 16–17) and the theogony of Orpheus (p. 17), as well as Pythagoras. Patricia Curd questions the possibility of identifying any particular influences at all (*The Legacy of Parmenides*, Princeton: Princeton University Press 1998, pp. 19–20).

8. In Patricia Curd's terminology, both being and the beautiful are 'self-predicating' in Plato's thought, and thus show a debt to Eleatic ontology (*The Legacy of Parmenides*, pp. 228–41).

9. Lloyd Gerson (ed.), *The Cambridge Companion to Plotinus*, Cambridge: Cambridge University Press 1996, pp. 2–3.

10. See the Index Fontium of P. Henry and H. R. Schwyzer (eds), *Plotini Opera*, 3 volumes (*editio minor*), vol. 3, Oxford: Clarendon Press 1982, pp. 348–65. On the sources of Plotinus, see also *Les sources de Plotin: Entretiens Hardt V*, Vandoeuvres-Genève: Fondation Hardt 1960.

11. Plato, *Republic*, 509a, 518c.

12. Plotinus, *Enneads*, II, 9, 1. But P. A. Meijer argues that the particular name for the One used by Plotinus is often not arbitrary but context-dependent (*Plotinus on the Good or the One*, Amsterdam: J. C. Gieben 1992, pp. 58–64).

13. *Enneads*, V, 2, 2. In the case of the One or Good as ultimate source, Plotinus uses an interesting analogy of light from the sun to explain how the Good exercises causation, without itself being subject to change: 'It must be a circumradiation – produced from the Supreme but from the Supreme unaltering – and may be compared to the brilliant light encircling the sun and ceaselessly generated from that unchanging substance' (*Enneads*, V, 1, 6). Quotations from Plotinus are taken from Stephen MacKenna's translation (Harmondsworth: Penguin 1991) with occasional slight adaptations.

14. 'There is in everything the Act of the Essence and the Act going out from the Essence: the first Act is the thing itself in its realized identity, the second Act is an inevitably following outgo from the first, an emanation distinct from the thing itself'(*Enneads*, V, 4, 2).

15. *Enneads*, II, 9, 8.

16. *Enneads*, III, 6, 6.
17. *Enneads*, V, 1, 4.
18. 'Intellect by its intellective act establishes being, which in turn, as the object of intellection, becomes the cause of intellection and of existence to the Intellect' (*Enneads*, V, 1, 4).
19. *Enneads*, VI, 7, 38.
20. Though dialectic, as Plotinus understands it, is the 'precious part of philosophy' (*Enneads*, I, 3, 5), we do not find in Plotinus much sense of the 'living word' of the *Phaedrus*, though Porphyry records his use of the 'diatribe' or lecture form. See also John H. Heiser, *Logos and Language in the Philosophy of Plotinus*, Lampeter: Edwin Mellen Press 1991, pp. 1–2. Heiser develops the thesis that language, or 'the giving of logos', plays a central role for Plotinus in the determination of the self.
21. *Enneads*, V, 2, 1.
22. *Enneads*, VI, 8, 16 and VI, 9, 4.
23. *Enneads*, V, 3, 13.
24. *Enneads*, V, 3, 13.
25. *Enneads*, V, 5, 13.
26. *Enneads*, VI, 7, 38.
27. *Enneads*, VI, 9, 3.
28. *Enneads*, V, 3, 14.
29. 'A knowing principle must handle distinct items: its object must, at the moment of cognition, contain diversity; otherwise the thing remains unknown . . . similarly the knowing principle cannot remain simplex . . . it is dual to itself' (*Enneads*, V, 3, 10).
30. *Enneads*, VI, 9, 3. For a discussion of the relevant texts on the One and Intellect, with respect particularly to the different phases of intellection involved, see John Bussanich, *The One in Relation to Intellect in Plotinus*, Leiden: E. J. Brill 1988. See also Werner Beierwaltes, *Denken des Einen: Studien zur neuplatonischen Philosophie und ihrer Wirkungsgeschichte*, Frankfurt am Main: Vittorio Klostermann 1985, especially pp. 123–47.
31. J. M. Rist, *Eros and Psyche: Studies in Plato, Plotinus and Origen*, Toronto: University of Toronto Press 1964, pp. 190–1.
32. E.g. 'the one who seeks . . . is lifted and sees, never knowing how; the vision floods the eyes with light, but it is not a light showing some other object, the light is itself the vision. No longer is there thing seen and light to show it' (*Enneads*, VI, 7, 36); *Enneads*, VI, 9, 3–4.
33. *Enneads*, III, 8, 9.
34. Pierre Hadot, *Plotinus or the Simplicity of Vision*, trans. Michael Chase, Chicago: University of Chicago Press 1993, p. 32. See also Gerard J. P. O'Daly, *Plotinus' Philosophy of the Self*, Shannon: Irish University Press 1973, pp. 82–94.
35. Plotinus, *Enneads*, V, 2, 1; see also V, 1, 6: 'The offspring must seek and love the begetter . . . when in addition the begetter is the highest Good, the offspring (inevitably seeking its good) is attached by a bond of sheer necessity, separated only in being distinct'. On beauty, see IV, 8, 6; V, 8, 9 and VI, 7, 32: 'It cannot be beauty since it is not a thing among things. It is lovable and the author of beauty; as the power to all beautiful shape, it will be the ultimate of beauty, that which brings all loveliness to be'.
36. See Dominic O'Meara, *Plotinus: An Introduction to the Enneads*, Oxford:

Clarendon Press 1993, pp. 88–99, and Lloyd Gerson, *Plotinus*, London and New York: Routledge 1994, pp. 212–18.

37. Plotinus, *Enneads*, III, 5, 7. See Catherine Osborne's discussion of the differences between platonic and plotinian love in her *Eros Unveiled: Plato and the God of Love*, Oxford: Clarendon Press 1994, pp. 114–16 (here p. 114).

38. Hadot, *Plotinus*, p. 34.

39. While Plotinus aims at 'union' with the divine, Plato's desire is for 'likeness' to the divine (Rist, *Eros and Psyche*, pp. 190–1).

40. Plotinus, *Enneads*, VI, 9, 11.

41. On the influence of the *Liber de causis* and Avicenna's highly platonizing way of reading Aristotle's *De anima*, see Alain de Libera, *Introduction à la Mystique Rhénane*, Paris: O.E.I.L. 1984, pp. 25–72.

42. Dietrich's text *De intellectu et intelligibili*, which presented a fully developed theory of intellect, was particularly influential (Dietrich von Freiberg, *Opera Omnia*, vol. 1, *Schriften zur Intellekttheorie*, ed. Bernard Mojsisch, Hamburg: F. Meiner 1977, pp. 125–210. It is summarized by Bernard Mojsisch, in his *Die Theorie des Intellekts bei Dietrich von Freiberg*, Beiheft I, *Corpus philosophorum teutonicorum medii aevi*, Hamburg: F. Meiner 1977. See also de Libera, *Introduction*, pp. 163–229). Niklaus Largier has pointed out, however, that there is a greater range of images of passivity in Eckhart's work, which may reflect the more existential character of Eckhart's philosophy (Niklaus Largier, '"Intellectus in deum ascensus". Intellekttheoretische Auseinandersetzungen in Texten der deutschen Mystik', *Deutsche Vierteljahrsschrift für Literaturwissenschaft und Geistesgeschichte* 69, H. 3, September 1995, pp. 423–71).

43. On the background to *In agro dominico*, see my 'Why were Meister Eckhart's Propositions Condemned?', *New Blackfriars* 71, October 1990, pp. 433–45 (summarized in *Meister Eckhart: Mystical Theologian*, London: SPCK 1991, pp. 22–50). See also Winfried Trusen, *Der Prozess gegen Meister Eckhart*, Paderborn: Schöningh 1988.

44. *Meister Eckhart: Lateinische Werke* (= LW), III, Stuttgart: Kohlhammer 1994, pp. 4, 5f.

45. LW II, p. 282.

46. Joseph Koch, *Kleine Schriften*, I, Rome 1973, p. 385. V. Lossky has well summed up the difference between Eckhart and Thomas on analogy when he says that analogy, for the latter, was a way of speaking about God and creatures *non secundam puram aequivocationem* while, for the former, it is a way of speaking of the First Cause and its effects *non omnino univoce* (Vladimir Lossky, *Théologie négative et connaissance de Dieu chez Maître Eckhart*, Paris: J. Vrin 1960, p. 322).

47. German Sermon 9; *Meister Eckhart: Deutsche Werke* (= DW), I, Stuttgart: Kohlhammer 1958, p. 157; ET M. O'C. Walshe, vol. 2, London: Element Books 1987, p. 155.

48. Latin Sermon 29 (LW IV, pp. 269f; ET O. Davies, *Meister Eckhart: Selected Writings*, Harmondsworth: Penguin 1994, pp. 258–62; here p. 260).

49. In the first of the *Parisian Questions*, which can be dated to 1302–3, Eckhart maintained that 'understanding is superior to existence and belongs to a different order' (LW V, p. 42; ET A. Maurer, *Master Eckhart: Parisian Questions and Prologues*, Toronto: Pontifical Institute of Medieval Studies 1974, p. 46); that God himself is 'an intellect and understanding' (LW V, p. 40; Maurer, p. 45), and that being, as for Proclus, is 'the first of created things' (LW V, p. 41;

Maurer, p. 45). Eckhart is prepared to accept Thomas' concept of God as 'purity of existence' (*puritas essendi*), but only in the sense outlined in the *Commentary on Genesis*: *sibi esse est intelligere* ('the nature of God is intellect, and for him to be is to know': LW I, pp. 194f.).

50. Latin Sermon 29 (LW IV, pp. 269f.; Davies, p. 262).
51. German Sermon 69 (DW III, pp.169–80; Davies, pp. 209–14).
52. Cf. German Sermon 16a (DW I, p. 259; M.O'C Walshe, *Meister Eckhart. Sermons and Treatises*, Dorset: Element Books 1979, vol. 1, p. 121): 'Thus too I say of the image of the soul: . . . [t]his image is the Son of the Father, and I myself am this image, and this image is wisdom'. On this important though fragmentary sermon, see Loris Sturlese, 'Mystik und Philosophie in der Bildlehre Meister Eckhart', in *Festschrift für Walter Haug und Burghart Wachinger*, Tübingen: Max Niemeyer Verlag 1992, pp. 349–61.
53. German Sermon 16a (DW I, p. 259; Walshe, vol. 1, p. 121).
54. German Sermon 69 (DW III, pp. 178–80; Walshe, vol. 1, pp. 298–9).
55. It is also this structure which leads to what Alois Haas has called the 'analogical and dialectical' impulses of his work, undermining any stasis in the language that is used of God, since language, by its nature, reflects finite existence or what Duns Scotus called 'denominated being' (Alois Haas, 'Seinsspekulation und Geschöpflichkeit in der Mystik Meister Eckharts', *Gott Leiden Gott Lieben*, Frankfurt am Main: Insel Verlag 1989, pp. 172–88; here p. 172).
56. It is important to note that Eckhart never suggests that we can become entirely deified, or 'intellectualized' in his terms. He rigorously applies the 'inquantum' principle, which recognizes the extent to which we remain embodied and finite creatures on earth. On the role of the *inquantum* principle as safeguarding the distinction between God and creature, see Bernard McGinn, 'Meister Eckhart's Condemnation Reconsidered', *The Thomist* 44, 1980, pp. 390–414 (especially pp. 406–7).
57. Spinoza, *Ethics*, IP8 and IP12–13.
58. *Ethics*, ID6.
59. *Ethics*, ID3 (translations from the *Ethics* are taken from Benedict de Spinoza, *Ethics*, ed. and trans. Edwin Curley, Harmondsworth: Penguin 1996).
60. *Ethics*, ID4 and ID5.
61. *Ethics*, IIP40S1.
62. *Ethics*, IIP40S2III.
63. *Ethics*, IP15S5.
64. *Ethics*, IIP44dem.
65. *Ethics*, IIP41S2IV and IIP42.
66. *Ethics*, IIP49S3B(ii).
67. Genevieve Lloyd, *Spinoza and the Ethics*, London and New York: Routledge 1996, p. 69.
68. Spinoza, *Ethics*, IIP13.
69. *Ethics*, IIIP4–7.
70. *Ethics*, IIIP9S.
71. *Ethics*, IIIP12–13.
72. *Ethics*, III General Definition of the Affects.
73. *Ethics*, IIP15.
74. *Ethics*, IIPost5; IIP16.
75. *Ethics*, IIP28.
76. *Ethics*, IIIP1.

77. *Ethics*, IVD8.
78. *Ethics*, IVP18.
79. *Ethics*, IVP35.
80. *Ethics*, IVApp. XXXII (Curley, *Ethics*, p. 160).
81. *Ethics*, VPreface (Curley, *Ethics*, p. 160).
82. *Ethics*, VP3Cor (Curley, *Ethics*, p. 163).
83. *Ethics*, IIP45.
84. *Ethics*, VP17–18.
85. *Ethics*, VP29.
86. *Ethics*, VP32Cor.
87. *Ethics*, I Appendix.
88. Martin Heidegger, *Parmenides*, trans. André Schuwer and Richard Rojcewicz, Bloomington and Indiana: Indiana University Press 1992, p. 7.
89. Martin Heidegger, 'Introduction to "What is Metaphysics?"', *Pathmarks*, ed. William McNeill, Cambridge: Cambridge University Press 1998, pp. 277–90 (here p. 285). See also Martin Heidegger, *An Introduction to Metaphysics*, trans. Ralph Manheim, New Haven and London: Yale University Press 1959, pp. 93–206.
90. Martin Heidegger, 'On the Question of Being', *Pathmarks*, pp. 291–322 (here p. 309).
91. Heidegger, *Being and Time*, Part One, I, § 9.
92. Heidegger, 'Introduction to "What is Metaphysics?"', *Pathmarks*, p. 289.
93. Heidegger, *Being and Time*, Part One, I, § 9.
94. Heidegger, 'Letter on Humanism', *Pathmarks*, pp. 239–76 (here pp. 248–9).
95. Heidegger, 'Letter on Humanism', *Pathmarks*, p. 247.
96. Heidegger, 'Letter on Humanism', *Pathmarks*, p. 266.
97. Heidegger, 'Postscript to "What is Metaphysics?"', *Pathmarks*, pp. 231–8 (here p. 234).
98. Heidegger, 'Introduction to "What is Metaphysics?"', *Pathmarks*, p. 278.
99. Heidegger, 'Postscript to "What is Metaphysics?"', *Pathmarks*, p. 233.
100. Heidegger, 'What is Metaphysics?', *Pathmarks*, pp. 82–96 (here p. 88).
101. *Pathmarks*, p. 91.
102. Heidegger, 'Introduction to "What is Metaphysics?"', *Pathmarks*, p. 282.
103. Heidegger, 'On the Question of Being', *Pathmarks*, p. 308.
104. Heidegger, 'On the Question of Being', *Pathmarks*, p. 300.
105. Heidegger, *An Introduction to Metaphysics*, p. 4.
106. Heidegger, *An Introduction to Metaphysics*, p. 5.
107. Heidegger, *An Introduction to Metaphysics*, p. 8.
108. Heidegger, *An Introduction to Metaphysics*, p. 10.
109. Heidegger, *An Introduction to Metaphysics*, p. 37.
110. Heidegger, *An Introduction to Metaphysics*, p. 38.
111. Heidegger, *An Introduction to Metaphysics*, p. 44.
112. Heidegger, *An Introduction to Metaphysics*, pp. 45, 51.
113. Heidegger, *An Introduction to Metaphysics*, p. 12.
114. The existential character of 'oneness' is drawn out by Plotinus in his comment that 'Existence is a trace of the One – our word for entity may probably be connected with that for unity' (*Enneads*, V, 5, 5), and in Eckhart's statement that 'the One and being are convertible. What falls from the One, falls from existence' (Comm. Ex., § 134; LW II, p. 123).

115. The exception here is again Eckhart, for whom the incarnation guarantees a universalism which powerfully moderates the elitist tendencies of a Greek noeticism.

Chapter 4

1. Jeff Owen Prudhomme offers a useful survey of Heidegger's thinking on the relation between theology and ontology in his *God and Being: Heidegger's Relation to Theology*, New Jersey: Humanities Press 1997, and argues that the one remains ordered towards the other within the Heideggerian framework.
2. Karl Barth, *Church Dogmatics*, III/1, Edinburgh: T&T Clark 1958, p. 32.
3. Athanasius, *De incarnatione*, § 4–5.
4. Jerome, *Comm. On the Epistle to the Romans* (quoted in R. Klibansky, *The Continuity of the Platonic Tradition*, London: Warburg Institute 1939, p. 21).
5. In *The Polis and the Divine Order* (London: Associated University Presses 1995) William F. Zak has traced the destructive interaction of human agency, divine sovereignty and the polis in Greek tragedy, stressing the disruption of community by the individualistic needs of the hero in the face of divinely ordained fate.
6. Joseph M. Bryant, *Moral Codes and Social Structure in Ancient Greece*, New York: SUNY Press 1996, pp. 261–99.
7. Bernard Freydberg, *The Play of Platonic Dialogues*, New York: Peter Lang 1997, p. 24.
8. According to John Sallis, myth has 'a bond to something intrinsically opaque, a bond to an element of darkness in contrast to that which is capable of being taken up into the light of *logos*' (*Being and Logos*, 3rd edn., Bloomington: Indiana University Press 1996, p. 16).
9. For Freydberg, this allegory offers a guiding discussion of the relation between *logos* and *mythos*, and he asks 'why is the doctrine of intellectualism, which proclaims the intelligibility of all being, presented by Plato in *images*?' (*The Play of Platonic Dialogues*, pp. 26–9, 40). For Sallis too, it is the playful exchange and rich layering of myth and reasoned argument, character and debate, within the organic and demonstrative body of the dialogue which constitutes what he calls 'the way of dialogue' and it is in this dramatic 'mirror-play' that we must attempt the exegesis of platonic being (Sallis, *Being and Logos*, pp. 13 and 18).
10. Friedländer's term is quoted in W. K. C. Guthrie, *A History of Greek Philosophy, Vol. IV, Plato: The Man and His Dialogues: Early Period*, Cambridge: Cambridge University Press 1975, p. 189. On the place of the *Phaedo* in the evolution of Plato's epistemology, see Nicholas P. White, *Plato on Knowledge and Reality*, Indianapolis: Hackett 1976, pp. 63–87.
11. 'If beauty and goodness and all such reality, which we are always talking about, really exist, if it is to them, as we rediscover our own former knowledge of them, that we refer, as copies to their patterns, all the objects of our physical perception – if these realities exist, does it not follow that our souls must exist too even before our birth, whereas if they do not exist, our discussion would seem to be a waste of time?' (Plato, *Phaedo*, 76d–e).

All the translations from Plato's dialogues are taken from Plato, *The Collected Dialogues*, ed. E. Hamilton and H. Cairns, Princeton: Princeton University Press 1961, with some slight modifications, unless otherwise stated.

12. *Phaedo*, 78e.
13. *Republic*, 479c–d.
14. Nicholas P. White, 'Plato's Metaphysical Epistemology', *The Cambridge Companion to Plato*, ed. Richard Kraut, Cambridge: Cambridge University Press 1992, pp. 277–310.
15. Here we also note the privileging of the sense of sight and the knowledge which comes through vision, which is to remain a deeply influential leitmotif of the platonic tradition:

    'But beauty, as I said before, shone in brilliance among those visions; and since we came to earth we have found it shining most clearly through the clearest of the senses; for sight is the sharpest of the physical senses, though wisdom is not seen by it, for wisdom would arouse terrible love, if such a clear image of it were granted as would come through sight, and the same is true of the other lovely realities; but beauty alone has this privilege, and therefore it is most clearly seen and loveliest' (Plato, *Phaedrus*, 250d).

    The *Phaedrus* translations with some minor changes are by H. N. Fowler in the Loeb edition (*Plato I: Euthyphro, Apology, Crito, Phaedo, Phaedrus*, London: Heinemann 1971).
16. *Phaedrus*, 250d–251b.
17. *Symposium*, 207a.
18. *Symposium*, 206, b–e.
19. This may be why Plato often seems to prefer homosexual relationships, since heterosexual relationships appear to exhaust the principle of self-propagation, which is the essence of civilization, in purely physical generation.
20. *Symposium*, 208e.
21. *Symposium*, 209a.
22. A. W. Price, *Love and Friendship in Plato and Aristotle*, Oxford: Clarendon Press 1989, pp. 28–35.
23. *Symposium*, 211d. Catherine Osborne has powerfully attacked the notion found in Nygren and Vlastos that platonic *erôs* is purely selfish or self-referential love. She offers a wide-ranging discussion of this theme in her *Eros Unveiled: Plato and the God of Love*, Oxford: Clarendon Press 1994, but see especially pp. 74–9 and 222–6. See also J. M. Rist, *Eros and Psyche: Studies in Plato, Plotinus and Origen*, Toronto: University of Toronto Press 1964, pp. 204–7.
24. *Symposium*, 209c. As Price has noted, these lines contain three occurrences of the root koino-, thus powerfully reinforcing the notion of communality (Price, *Love and Friendship*, p. 28).
25. In the *Symposium* Socrates himself appears to be a mix of historical and textual elements, so that he embodies the description of *erôs* given by Alcibiades. R. G. Bury offers a detailed analysis of the textual symmetries between *erôs* and Socrates (*The Symposium of Plato*, Cambridge: Heffer 1932, pp. lx–lxiv). In *Missing Socrates*, Pennsylvania: Pennsylvania State University Press 1991, Jay Farness offers an interesting study of the interrelation of the historical and textual Socrates in the name of 'literary protocols' (p. 9) and relates the 'reproduction of Socrates' (p. 138) to Greek portraiture (pp. 135–69). See also R. B. Rutherford, *The Art of Plato*, London: Duckworth 1995, pp. 199–204, and the

substantial study on this theme by Charles Kahn, *Plato and the Socratic Dialogue*, Cambridge: Cambridge University Press 1996.

26. *Symposium*, 208b.
27. Augustine, *Confessions*, VII, 9, 13. On the vexed question of which particular texts Augustine may be referring to, see Augustine, *Confessions*, ed. James J. O'Donnell, vol. 2, Oxford: Clarendon Press 1992, pp. 413–18. Peter Brown agrees with Hadot 'in placing Plotinus, not Porphyry, at the centre of Augustine's reading in 386' (Peter Brown, *Augustine of Hippo: A Biography*, London: Faber & Faber 1969, p. 94).
28. *Confessions*, VII, 11, 17.
29. *De Trinitate*, V, 2, 3. Augustine in fact identifies all the transcendentals with God, affirming that 'God is Truth itself' (*De lib. Arb.*, II, 15, 39) and that 'the Supreme Good beyond all others is God. It is thereby unchangeable good, truly eternal, truly immortal' (*De Nat. Bon.*, 1). He urges us to consider 'what his beauty is. He made all those beautiful things which you see and you love. If these are beautiful, then what is he himself?' (*En. in Ps.*, 85, 6).
30. Emilie zum Brunn, *St Augustine: Being and Nothingness*, New York: Paragon House 1988, p. 15.
31. Ps. 101.27–28. See Augustine, *En. in Ps.*, 102, 27–30.
32. *De beat. Vita*, 2, 8. I have translated *frugalitas* as 'fruitfulness' here. *Frugalitas* was proposed by Cicero as one translation for *sôphrosunê*, with the general sense of 'moderation' or 'virtue' (Charlton Lewis and Charles Short, *A Latin Dictionary*, sv. II), but another of its possible meanings is 'fruitfulness' (I. B.), which would seem to be the translation required here on account of the consonance with *frux* and *fructus*, as a complement to the sense of 'temperance'.
33. 'The soul loses strength when it consents to evil, and begins to be less, and for this reason to have less vigour than when, not consenting to any evil, it remained steadfast in virtue. It is even worse when it turns away from what is to the highest degree in order to tend towards what is less, in such a way that it itself is less. Now the less it is, the closer it comes to nothingness. For all things whose being diminishes tend towards absolute nothingness' (*Contra Sec.*, 15).
34. Zum Brunn, *St Augustine*, pp. 38–42. The question that arises at this point is why it is that the evil soul does not cease to exist altogether. Augustine answers that the soul possesses a certain form which maintains it in being, and that no soul can be utterly deprived of this 'form element' in such a way as to fall into nothingness (*De Imm. An.*, 7, 12 and 8, 13). Emilie zum Brunn has a useful discussion of these texts (zum Brunn, *St Augustine*, pp. 21 and 36).
35. *De lib. Arb.*, 3, 7, 21.
36. *En. in Ps.*, 31, 2.
37. 'Hold fast rather to the love of God, so that just as God exists for ever and ever, so you too may remain eternally: because such is each one as is his love. Do you love earth? Then you shall be earth. Do you love God? What shall I say? You shall be God? I dare not say it of myself, let us hear the scriptures: "I have said, you are gods, and all of you, sons of the Most High"'. (*In Io Ep.*, 2, 14; the scriptural quotation is from Ps. 82.6).
38. *De Mor.*, 26, 50.
39. *De Mor.*, 26, 51.
40. *De ver. Rel.*, 46, 89.
41. 'Let a man love his neighbour as himself. No one is his own father or son or

kinsman or anything of the kind, but is simply a human being. Whoever loves another as himself ought to love that in him which is his real self. Our real selves are not bodies. So we are not to desire and set great store by a man's body. Here too the precept is valid: You shall not covet your neighbour's property. Whoever then loves in his neighbour anything but his real self does not love him as himself. Human nature is to be loved whether it be perfect or in process of becoming perfect, but without any condition of carnal relationship' (*De ver. Rel.*, 47, 90).

Note also 'Nor should our love for others differ from one person to another' (*De ver. Rel.*, 47, 91).

42. *De ver. Rel.*, 47, 91.
43. *De Doc. Chr.*, I, 4, 4. On the parallel with *caritas* and *cupiditas*, see *De Doc. Chr.*, III, 10, 16.
44. *De Doc. Chr.*, I, 5, 5.
45. *De Doc. Chr.*, I, 22, 20.
46. 'It is not the case that all things which are to be used are to be loved; but only those which exist in some kind of association with us and are related to God, like a man or an angel, or which, being related to us, stand in need of the kindness of God as received through us, like the body' (*De Doc. Chr.*, I, 23, 22).
47. It dates from the same period as *In Io Eu.*, which also contains some valuable material on love (especially chapter 13, 34–35), much in line with *In Io Ep.*
48. *In Io Ep.*, 7, 8.
49. 'Let love be fervent to correct, to amend: but if there are good habits, then you should delight in them; if there are evil ones, they should be amended and corrected. Do not love the error in the man, but the man himself: for God made the man, while man made the error' (*In Io Ep.*, 7, 11).
50. *In Io Ep.*, 8, 5: 'Wish your neighbour your equal, that you may both be under the one Lord, on whom nothing can be bestowed'.
51. *In Io Ep.*, 8, 10.
52. *In Io Ep.*, 9, 9.
53. *In Io Ep.*, 6, 13.
54. 'He loved us when we were ungodly, to make us godly; he loved us when we were unrighteous, to make us righteous; he loved us when we were sick, to make us whole' (*In Io Ep.*, 9, 10).
55. 'Our soul, brothers and sisters, is ugly by reason of wickedness: by loving God it becomes lovely. But God is always lovely, never ugly, never changeable. He who is always lovely first loved us; and what were we when he loved us but foul and ugly. Not to leave us foul, no, but to change us and to turn our ugliness into beauty. And how shall we become lovely? By loving him, who is always beautiful. As the love increases in you, so too does your loveliness increase: for love is itself the beauty of the soul' (*In Io Ep.*, 9, 9).
56. *In Io Ep.*, 9, 10.
57. *In Io Ep.*, 7, 4. The ambiguity of the Latin (*Deus dilectio est*) allows this reading, whereas it is clear that the Greek original means: 'God is love' (ὁ θεὸς ἀγάπη ἐστίν).
58. Jean-Pierre Torrell, *Saint Thomas Aquinas, Vol. I: The Person and His Work*, trans. R. Royal, Washington, DC: Catholic University of America Press 1996, pp. 232–3.
59. This work may belong to the period following 360 BCE, when Eudoxus of

Cnidos, whose thought is scrutinized in *On Ideas*, visited the Academy. See D. J. Allen, *The Philosophy of Aristotle*, Oxford: Oxford University Press 1970, p. 14. For Aristotle's rejection of platonic forms in the *Metaphysics*, see in particular Zeta, 13, 1038b8–12.

60. Jonathan Barnes (ed.), *The Cambridge Companion to Aristotle*, Cambridge: Cambridge University Press 1995, p. 67.

61. On the structure of the work, see Aristotle, *Metaphysics*, ed. W. D. Ross, vol. I, Oxford: Clarendon Press 1924, pp. xiii–xxxiii.

62. Aristotle, *Metaphysics*, ed. Ross, vol. I, p. lxxvii.

63. Barnes, *Cambridge Companion to Aristotle*, p. 69.

64. On the problematics of rendering Aristotle's metaphysical terminology into Latin and English, especially the limitations of translating *ousia* as 'substance', which 'fails to express the direct relation with Being', see Joseph Owens, *The Doctrine of Being in the Aristotelian Metaphysics*, Toronto: Pontifical Institute of Medieval Studies 1951, pp. 68–9. Owen prefers the term 'entity' (pp. 72–5). Charlotte Witt has an interesting discussion of Aristotle's attempt to overcome the problem of universality and particularity with the argument that we know individual entities by actual knowledge and universals by potential knowledge (Charlotte Witt, *Substance and Essence in Aristotle: An Interpretation of Metaphysics VII–IX*, Ithaca: Cornell University Press 1989, pp. 143–79).

65. Aristotle, *Metaphysics*, Alpha, 982b, 9–11.

66. *Metaphysics*, Gamma, 1003a, 1–32.

67. *Metaphysics*, Gamma, 1003a 34–1003b 19. The parallel here is not an exact one, of course, since *ousia* constitutes the *archê* of being, whereas 'health' is neither a substance nor a nature. Similarly oneness is a property of *ousia* in a way that it is not of 'health', and hence functions differently as a *terminus* or *pros hên* of the manifold senses of being. For a discussion of these points, see Franz Brentano, *On the Several Senses of Being in Aristotle*, ed. and trans. Rolf George, Berkeley: University of California Press 1975, pp. 58–66.

68. *Metaphysics*, Lambda, 1069a 30–1069b 2

69. *Metaphysics*, Epsilon, 1026a 10–22.

70. *Metaphysics*, Epsilon, 1026a 27–33

71. *Physics* II, 3, 194b 23–35.

72. This is the theme of *Metaphysics*, Book Theta.

73. *Metaphysics*, Theta, 1051b 25–30.

74. *Metaphysics*, Lambda, 1072a 19–20.

75. With respect to 'indivisibility', Edward C. Halper argues that the One and the Many is the central theme of the *Metaphysics* (*One and Many in Aristotle's Metaphysics: The Central Books*, Columbus: Ohio State University Press 1989, especially pp. 227–55).

76. Aristotle, *Metaphysics*, Lambda, 1072b 25–30. See also *Physics*, VIII, 10, 267b 15–25.

77. *Metaphysics*, Lambda, 1072a 26–27.

78. *Metaphysics*, Lambda, 1072b 3–4.

79. Thomas Aquinas, ST I, q. 45, a. 1.

80. ST I, q. 45, a. 2.

81. ST I, q. 45, a. 5. In Books II and IV of the *Scriptum super libros Sententiarum* Thomas admits the possibility that angels serve ministerially in creation, since

they are 'immaterial' or 'pure acts'; but by the time of writing *Contra Gentiles*, II, 21, and *De potentia*, 3, 4, he had come to the view that creation was a property only of a being who was 'pure act of existence' (Herve J. Thibault, *Creation and Metaphysics*, The Hague: Martinus Nijhoff 1970, pp. 54–6).

82. Thomas specifically excludes God himself from *ens commune* however, in order to safeguard the divine transcendence. See *Expositio in librum Dionysii De divinis nominibus*, c. 5, lectio 2, n. 660 and Leo J. Elders' discussion of this in his *The Metaphysics of Being in St. Thomas Aquinas in a Historical Perspective*, Leiden: E. J. Brill 1993, pp. 20–32.

83. Thomas Aquinas, *Commentary on the Metaphysics of Aristotle*, vol. I, trans. John P. Rowan, Chicago: Henry Regnery 1961, p. 2. Here God is included within the object of metaphysical inquiry but only as being's cause.

84. This distinction first appears in Al-farabi and again in Avicenna, although in the latter *esse* is seen as an accident or 'something added' to essence. Thomas criticizes Avicenna on this point at *In IV Metaphysicam*, 2, 556 and 558; 3, 1982 *Commentary on the Metaphysics of Aristotle*, vol. I, pp. 223–4; vol. II, p. 723).

85. Aristotle, *Metaphysics*, Delta, 2, 1003b 27–30.

86. Thomas Aquinas, *De ente et essentia*, 1, 2 (*On Being and Essence*, trans. Armand Maurer, The Pontifical Institute of Medieval Studies, Toronto 1968, pp. 29–30); 1, 4 (Maurer, p. 32).

87. Gerald B. Phelan, 'The Existentialism of St. Thomas', *G. B. Phelan: Selected Papers*, ed. A. G. Kirn, Toronto 1967, p. 81. Quoted in Maurer, *On Being and Essence*, p. 16.

88. Thomas Aquinas, *In Boeth. de Trin.*, 5, 3. On this theme, see John F. Wippel, *Metaphysical Themes in Thomas Aquinas*, Washington: Catholic University of America Press 1984, pp. 69–104.

89. Thomas wrote *De ente et essentia* sometime between 1252 and 1256, when he was still a student at Saint-Jacques in Paris and prior to his inception as a master. Tolomeo records that Thomas wrote it 'for his brothers and companions when he was not yet a master'. See Torrell, *Saint Thomas Aquinas*, p. 47.

90. Thomas Aquinas, *De veritate*, 2, 11: *finiti ad infinitum nulla est proportio* (for this account of the history of proportion in Thomas, see Thibault, *Creation*, p. x).

91. *In Boeth. de Trin.* 1, 2, c: *est proportio creaturae ad deum ut causati ad causam* (Thibault, *Creation*, p. x).

92. ST I, q. 4, a. 2.

93. ST I, q. 44, a. 1.

94. ST I, q. 3, a. 4.

95. ST I, q. 4, a. 1.

96. ST I, q. 4, a. 2.

97. ST I, q. 4, a. 3.

98. ST I, q. 3, a. 7.

99. ST I, q. 3, a. 4.

100. ST I, q. 3, a. 1–8.

101. ST I, q. 3, a. 4.

102. James Doig, *Aquinas on Metaphysics: A Historico-Doctrinal Study of the Commentary on the Metaphysics*, The Hague: Martinus Nijhoff 1972, pp. 59–64.

103. It is important in this respect that Thomas prefers the analogy based upon *unius ad alterum* to that based on *multorum ad unum*; see ST I, q. 13, a. 5; see also

Ralph M. McInerny, *The Logic of Analogy*, The Hague: Martinus Nijhoff 1961, pp. 80–125.

104. *De veritate*, 1. The commentary on Aristotle's *Metaphysics* contains a fuller typology of the *differentiae*, including negations and privations, generation, corruption and change, quantities, qualities and the properties of substance, as well as substance itself (M IV, I. 540–543).

105. *De veritate*, 1.

106. Price, *Love and Friendship*, p. 160; cf. p. 11.

107. Aristotle, *Nicomachean Ethics*, IX, 1168b 5.

108. *Nicomachean Ethics*, VIII, 1156b 10–11.

109. Thomas Aquinas, ST 2–2, q. 23, a. 1; cf. Aristotle, *Nicomachean Ethics*, 1158b 24–39 and 1159b 2: 'Equality and similarity, and above all the similarity of those who are similar in being virtuous, is friendship'. But Catherine Osborne makes the point that there was a tendency for Christian commentators to misunderstand Aristotle's texts on *philia*, which in fact dealt with an 'ethics of co-operation among well-bred classical citizens' (*Eros Unveiled*, p. 162).

110. ST 2a2ae, q. 23, a. 2.

111. ST 2a2ae, q. 25, a. 1.

112. In the following chapter we offer a fuller discussion of the Hegelian system, as part of a survey of Idealism.

113. According to Laurence Dickey, Hegel embraced Protestantism and *Sittlichkeit* more or less at the same time, during the 1790s ('Hegel on Religion and Philosophy', *The Cambridge Companion to Hegel*, ed. Frederick C. Beiser, Cambridge: Cambridge University Press 1993, pp. 301–47, here p. 332).

114. Laurence Dickey's *Hegel: Religion, Economics and Politics of the Spirit, 1770–1807*, Cambridge: Cambridge University Press 1987, offers a systematic overview of the ways in which Hegel's thinking on religion and politics combine, especially in the development of the notion of 'Sittlichkeit'.

115. Søren Kierkegaard, *Fear and Trembling*, ed. and trans. Walter Lowrie, Princeton: Princeton University Press 1968, p. 121.

116. Kierkegaard, *Fear and Trembling*, p. 122, 128.

117. Kierkegaard, *Fear and Trembling*, p. 122. Cf. pp. 70–1:
'Abraham cannot be mediated, and the same thing can be expressed also by saying that he cannot talk. So soon as I talk, I express the universal, and if I do not do so, no one can understand me. Therefore if Abraham would express himself in terms of the universal, he must say that his situation is a temptation (*Anfechtung*), for he has no higher expression for that universal which stands above the universal which he transgresses.'

118. Kierkegaard, *Fear and Trembling*, p. 72.

119. Kierkegaard, *Fear and Trembling*, p. 80.

120. Kierkegaard, *Fear and Trembling*, pp. 131, 37.

121. Kierkegaard, *Fear and Trembling*, p. 57.

122. Kierkegaard, *Fear and Trembling*, p. 47.

123. Kierkegaard, *Fear and Trembling*, pp. 57, 51.

124. Kierkegaard, *Fear and Trembling*, pp. 121, 79.

125. G. E. Lessing, 'On the Proof of Spirit and of Power', *Theological Writings*, ed. and trans. Henry Chadwick, Stanford, CA: Stanford University Press 1957, pp. 51–6 (here p. 55).

126. Søren Kierkegaard, *Philosophical Fragments*, ed. and trans. Howard V. Hong and Edna H. Hong, Princeton: Princeton University Press 1985, pp. 55–71.

127. Søren Kierkegaard, *Concluding Unscientific Postscript to Philosophical Fragments*, ed. and trans. Howard V. Hong and Edna H. Hong, vol. 1, Princeton: Princeton University Press 1992, p. 209.

128. Kierkegaard, *Concluding Unscientific Postscript*, p. 209.

129. Kierkegaard, *Concluding Unscientific Postscript*, p. 354.

130. Kierkegaard, *Concluding Unscientific Postscript*, p. 310.

131. Kierkegaard, *Concluding Unscientific Postscript*, p. 123.

132. Kierkegaard, *Concluding Unscientific Postscript*, p. 112. Original italics.

133. Kierkegaard, *Concluding Unscientific Postscript*, p. 114.

134. Kierkegaard, *Concluding Unscientific Postscript*, pp. 115–16.

135. Kierkegaard, *Concluding Unscientific Postscript*, p. 326.

136. Kierkegaard, *Concluding Unscientific Postscript*, pp. 356–60.

137. Søren Kierkegaard, *Works of Love*, ed. and trans. Howard V. and Edna H. Hong, New York: Harper & Row 1962, pp. 26, 132 and 159.

138. Kierkegaard, *Works of Love*, p. 170.

139. Kierkegaard, *Works of Love*, p. 47.

140. LXX: καὶ ἡ ὑπόστασίς μου ὡσεὶ οὐθὲν ἐνώπιον σοῦ. The NRSV (39.5), which follows the Hebrew at this point, has: 'You have made my days a few handbreadths, and my lifetime is as nothing in your sight. Surely everyone stands as a mere breath.'

141. Plato, *Phaedo*, 61e.

142. Augustine, *In Io Ep.*, 10, 7.

Chapter 5

1. Amos Funkenstein, *Theology and the Scientific Imagination: From the Middle Ages to the Seventeenth Century*, Princeton: Princeton University Press 1986, pp. 50–70.

2. Michel Foucault, *Les mots et les choses*, Paris: Gallimard 1966, p. 67 (quoted in Funkenstein, *Theology*, p. 28).

3. Funkenstein, *Theology*, p. 50.

4. *Il saggiatore*, § 6, in Galileo Galilei, *Opere*, vol. 1, ed. Ferdinando Flora, Milan and Naples: Riccardo Ricciardi Editore 1953, p. 121.

5. Funkenstein, *Theology*, pp. 12, 290–327.

6. For a valuable overview of the transitions from the medieval to the modern period, in terms of optics and astronomy as well as conceptuality, see W. G. L. Randles, *The Unmaking of the Medieval Christian Cosmos, 1500–1760*, Aldershot and Vermont: Ashgate 1999.

7. See L. Blanchet, *Les antécédents du "Je pense, donc je suis"*, Paris: Presses Universitaires de France 1920; and more recently Roger Ariew, John Cottingham and Tom Sorell (eds), *'Meditations': Background Source Materials*, Cambridge: Cambridge University Press 1998; and Jorge Secada, *Cartesian Metaphysics*, Cambridge: Cambridge University Press 2000. See also Augustine's *Si fallor, sum*, which can be found in *De civitate dei*, XI, 26, and Thomas Aquinas' version in *De veritate*, X, 12, ad 7.

8. That is, 'une ontologie par dénégation' (Jean-Luc Marion, *Sur l'ontologie grise de Descartes*, Paris: Librairie Philosophique J. Vrin 1981, p. 185).

9. Marion, *Sur l'ontologie grise de Descartes*, p. 186.
10. Marion, *Sur l'ontologie grise de Descartes*, p. 186 (my italics). The notion of 'thing' here contains values and commands our attention as something with which we can 'be concerned'.
11. Werner Marx, *Introduction to Aristotle's Theory of Being as Being*, The Hague: Martinus Nijhoff 1977, p. 22.
12. The question of the univocity or otherwise of substantia in Descartes' thought is a complex one, and it may be that he has a debt to Suarez on this point, who may have tended towards a univocity of substance, despite his protestations to the contrary (see for instance his *Disputationes* 32, sec. 1., n 6 and 9; quoted in Jean-Luc Marion, 'The Essential Incoherence of Descartes' Definition of Divinity', *Essays on Descartes' Meditations*, ed. Amélie Oksenberg Rorty, Berkeley: University of California Press 1986, pp. 297–338; here p. 332). But a comparison between God as 'infinite substance' and the creature as 'finite substance' in Descartes with Duns Scotus' finite and infinite *ens* is instructive as the latter enjoys a purely formal commonality.
13. Descartes, *Discourse on the Method*, I (*Descartes: Philosophical Writings*, ed. and trans. Elizabeth Anscombe and Peter Thomas Geach, London: Nelson 1954, p. 13).
14. *Discourse*, III (*Descartes: Philosophical Writings*, p. 24). He also takes as his maxims philosophical consistency, resignation and commitment.
15. *Discourse*, II (*Descartes: Philosophical Writings*, p. 21). The Discourse was originally published together with the Dioptrics, the Meteorics and the Geometry.
16. *Discourse*, IV (*Descartes: Philosophical Writings*, pp. 31–2).
17. *Discourse*, IV (*Descartes: Philosophical Writings*, pp. 32–3).
18. For the scholastic sources for this text, see Ariew, Cottingham and Sorell (eds), *'Meditations': Background Source Materials*. Suarez proposed knowing God through our own imperfection, for example, (pp. 29–50), while Pierre Charron argued for the exercise of a thorough-going scepticism as a prelude to wisdom (pp. 52–67).
19. *Meditations on First Philosophy*, I (*Descartes: Philosophical Writings*, pp. 62–5).
20. Jean-Luc Marion, 'Cartesian Metaphysics: the Simple Natures', *The Cambridge Companion to Descartes*, ed. John Cottingham, Cambridge: Cambridge University Press 1992, pp. 115–39 (here p. 123).
21. 'Haud dubie igitur ego etiam sum, si me fallit; et fallat quantum potest, nunquam tamen efficiet, ut nihil sim quamdiu me aliquid esse cogitabo. Adeo ut, omnibus satis superque pensitatis, denique statuendum sit hoc pronuntiatum, Ego sum, ego existo, quoties a me profertur, vel mente concipitur, necessario esse verum' (Charles Adam and Paul Tannery (eds), Réne Descartes, *Oeuvres*, VII, Paris: Librairies Philosophique J. Vrin 1964, p. 25, l. 7–13; *Meditations*, II, *Descartes: Philosophical Writings*, p. 67).
22. 'Et ayant remarqué qu'il n'y a rien du tout en ceci: je pense, donc je suis, qui m'assure que je dis la vérité, sinon que je vois très clairement que, pour penser, il fait être' (René Descartes, *Discours de la Méthode*, ed. Étienne Gilson, Bibliothéque des Textes Philosophiques, Paris: Librairies Philosophique J. Vrin 1976, p. 33, l. 16–19 (*Discourse*, IV, *Descartes: Philosophical Writings*, p. 32).
23. It is interesting in this respect that whereas Thomas states that the intellect cannot know itself directly but only by its engagement with an object that is other than itself (ST I, q. 87, art. 1), Descartes denies that 'a thinking being needs

any object other than itself in order to exercise its activity' (Adam and Tannery, IX, p. 206; *The Philosophical Works of Descartes*, trans. Elisabeth S. Haldane and G. R. T. Ross, II, London: Constable 1955, p. 128).

24. Jaako Hintikka, '*Cogito, Ergo Sum*: Inference or Performance', *Descartes: A Collection of Critical Essays*, ed. Wallis Doney, Notre Dame: University of Notre Dame Press 1968, pp. 108–39 (here pp. 113–14).

25. Hintikka, '*Cogito, Ergo Sum*: Inference or Performance', p. 122.

26. This is what Marion calls 'la théologie blanche', which breaks with the past but rejects the answers of modernity; see his *Sur la théologie blanche de Descartes*, Paris: Presses Universitaires de France 1981.

27. Martin Heidegger, *Einführung in die Phänomenologische Forschung*, *Gesamtausgabe*, Bd. 17, Frankfurt am Main: Vittorio Klostermann 1994, pp. 247–53.

28. 'I recognised that I was a substance whose whole essence or nature is to be conscious and whose being requires no place and depends on no material thing' (*Discourse*, IV; *Descartes: Philosophical Writings*, p. 32).

29. David Hume, *A Treatise of Human Nature*, Book I, Part IV, Section VI.

30. Immanuel Kant, *Critique of Pure Reason*, trans. Norman Kemp Smith, London: Macmillan, 2nd impr. 1933, pp. 504–5.

31. Kant, *Critique of Pure Reason*, pp. 152–3.

32. Kant, *Critique of Pure Reason*, p. 154.

33. Kant, *Critique of Pure Reason*, p. 153.

34. Kant, *Critique of Pure Reason*, p. 155.

35. Kant, *Critique of Pure Reason*, p. 153.

36. Kant, *Critique of Pure Reason*, p. 334.

37. Kant, *Critique of Pure Reason*, p. 169. Cf. 'we have no knowledge of the subject in itself, which as substratum underlies this "I", as it does all thoughts' (p. 334). Gilles Deleuze notes that Kant inaugurates here a disjunction in the self which is more radical than that of Rimbaud's famous formula 'I is another' (Gilles Deleuze, *Kant's Critical Philosophy: The Doctrine of the Faculties*, trans. Hugh Tomlinson and Barbara Habberjam, Minneapolis: University of Minnesota Press 1984, p. ix).

38. P. F. Strawson, *The Bounds of Sense*, London: Methuen 1966, p. 162.

39. This has most recently been explored in a highly imaginative way by Pierre Keller who in his study *Kant and the Demands of Self-Consciousness* (Cambridge: Cambridge University Press 1998) has argued for what he terms 'abstractive consciousness' (p. 238) or 'impersonal consciousness of self' (p. 237), which abstracts from the self's own self-awareness, grounding the numerical identity of the self, the corrigibility of our judgments and the 'communicability of beliefs' which 'presupposes the possibility of a consciousness from which we may distinguish ourselves' (p. 239). This is to combine a heightened sense of the transcendentality of the unity of apperception with a new and welcome emphasis on intersubjectivity.

40. Kant, *Critique of Pure Reason*, p. 245.

41. Kant, *Critique of Pure Reason*, Preface to 2nd impr., p. 34, note a.

42. Kant, *Critique of Pure Reason*, Preface to 2nd impr., p. 36, note a.

43. Kant, *Critique of Pure Reason*, Preface to 2nd impr., p. 36, note a.

44. On Reinhold, and his relation to Fichte, see Frederick C. Beiser, *The Fate of Reason: German Philosophy from Kant to Fichte*, Cambridge, MA: Harvard University Press 1987, pp. 226–65.

45. The circumstances are described by Garrett Green in the introduction to his translation of the text: *Johann Gottlieb Fichte: Attempt at a Critique of All Revelation*, Cambridge: Cambridge University Press 1978, pp. 4–7.

46. J. G. Fichte, *Second Introduction to the Wissenschaftslehre*, ed. I. H. Fichte, *Fichtes Werke*, repr. Berlin: de Gruyter 1971, I, p. 469; J. G. Fichte, *Introductions to the Wissenschaftslehre and other Writings*, ed. and trans. Daniel Breazeale, Indianapolis and Cambridge: Hackett 1994, p. 52).

47. *Fichtes Werke*, I, p. 475; Breazeale, p. 59.

48. *First Introduction to the Wissenschaftslehre* (*Fichtes Werke*, I, p. 423; Breazeale, p. 8).

49. *The Science of Knowledge*: *J. G. Fichte*, ed. and trans. Peter Heath and John Lachs, Cambridge: Cambridge University Press 1982, p. 93 (*Fichtes Werke*, I, p. 91).

50. This position is articulated most forcefully in the *First Introduction to the Wissenschaftslehre*, where Fichte specifically precludes the possibility of any other philosophy: 'As one will surely become convinced by the present account, these two philosophical systems are the only ones possible' (*Fichtes Werke*, I, p. 426; Breazeale, p. 11).

51. See the remarks on Spinozism as opposed to the 'critical' philosophy in the *Wissenschaftslehre* (*Fichtes Werke*, I, p. 101; Heath and Lachs, p. 102). The first part of the *Vocation of Man* is a brilliant exposition of scientific determinism postulated on the principle of sufficient reason. On Spinozism in Germany in this period, see Beiser, *The Fate of Reason*, pp. 44–108, 158–63.

52. *Fichtes Werke*, I, pp. 255–7; Heath and Lachs, pp. 225–7.

53. 'Both self and not-self are alike products of original acts of the self, and consciousness itself is similarly a product of the self's first original act, its own positing of itself' (*Fichtes Werke*, I, p. 107; Heath and Lachs, p. 107).

54. *Fichtes Werke*, I, p. 257; Heath and Lachs, p. 227.

55. *Discourse*, IV; *Descartes: Philosophical Writings*, p. 32. On this theme in Fichte, see *First Introduction to the Wissenschaftslehre* (*Fichtes Werke*, I, pp. 425–30; Breazeale, pp. 10–15).

56. Although clearly linked with the phenomenology of consciousness as we find it later in Husserl, and with his technique of epoché, the Fichtean abstraction does not serve as an attempt to lay bare the conditions under which representations arise, or Reinhold's *Vorstellungsvermögen*. It is not, again in Reinhold's phrase, a philosophy of the conditions of consciousness, but rather a strategy for breaking through to a different and ideal kind of knowledge.

57. *Second Introduction to the Wissenschaftslehre* (*Fichtes Werke*, I, pp. 498–9; Breazeale, p. 84).

58. *Second Introduction to the Wissenschaftslehre* (*Fichtes Werke*, I, pp. 498–9; Breazeale, p. 84).

59. *First Introduction to the Wissenschaftslehre* (*Fichtes Werke*, I, p. 427; Breazeale, p. 12).

60. *Fichtes Werke*, I, p. 97; Heath and Lachs, p. 98.

61. *Die Bestimmung des Menschen* (*Fichtes Werke*, II, p. 193; *Johann Fichte: The Vocation of Man*, ed. and trans. Peter Preuss, Indianapolis and Cambridge: Hackett 1987, p. 22, but this is my own translation).

62. *Fichtes Werke*, II, p. 196; Preuss, p. 24.

63. *Fichtes Werke*, II, p. 245; Preuss, p. 63.

64. *Fichtes Werke*, II, p. 244; Preuss, p. 63.

65. *Fichtes Werke*, II, p. 245; Preuss, pp. 63–4.

66. *Fichtes Werke*, II, p. 250; Preuss, p. 69.

67. 'But the voice of my conscience calls to me: whatever these beings may be in and for themselves, you ought to treat them as self-subsistent, free, autonomous beings completely independent of you' (*Fichtes Werke*, II, p. 259; Preuss, p. 76).

68. *Fichtes Werke*, II, p. 278; Preuss, p. 91.

69. Robert R. Williams sees the trend in the *Grundlage des Naturrechts* to *Aufforderung* and to action as fundamentally moderating the 'metaphysical idealism' of the *Wissenschaftslehre* (Robert R. Williams, *Recognition: Fichte and Hegel on the Other*, New York: State University of New York Press 1992, pp. 49–70). The preferred word in this text for the ontological shift is not *Sein* but the more positive *Realität*.

70. 'Über den Grund unseres Glaubens an eine göttliche Weltregierung', *Fichtes Werke*, V, pp. 175–89. On the *Atheismusstreit* in general, see Hans Michael Baumgartner, 'Transcendentales Denken und Atheismus: der Atheismusstreit um Fichte', *Hochland* 56, 1963/4, pp. 40–8.

71. *Fichtes Werke*, II, p. 319; Preuss, p. 123.

72. Walter A. Davis, *Inwardness and Existence: Subjectivity in/and Hegel, Heidegger, Marx and Freud*, Wisconsin: University of Wisconsin Press 1989, pp. 13 and 10.

73. Davis, *Inwardness and Existence*, p. 10.

74. Charles Taylor, *Hegel*, Cambridge: Cambridge University Press 1975, p. 91.

75. *Phänomenologie des Geistes*, G. W. F. Hegel, *Werke*, III, Frankfurt am Main: Suhrkamp 1970, pp. 82–3; *Hegel's Phenomenology of Spirit*, trans. A. V. Miller, Oxford: Oxford University Press 1977, p. 58.

76. *Phänomenologie des Geistes*, pp. 82–3.

77. *Phänomenologie des Geistes*, p. 116; *Hegel's Phenomenology of Spirit*, p. 87.

78. *Wissenschaft der Logik*, I; G. W. F. Hegel, *Werke*, V, Frankfurt am Main: Suhrkamp 1979, pp. 68–9; *Hegel's Science of Logic*, trans. A. V. Miller, London: Routledge 1969, pp. 69–70. It is for this same reason that Hegel rejects the possibility that God might serve as the point of departure, thus locating himself in the tradition inaugurated by Avicenna's reading of Aristotle (*Werke*, V, p. 79; *Hegel's Science of Logic*, p. 78)

79. *Werke*, V, p. 82; *Hegel's Science of Logic*, p. 81.

80. *Werke*, V, p. 75; *Hegel's Science of Logic*, p. 75.

81. *Phänomenologie des Geistes*, p. 552; *Hegel's Phenomenology of Spirit*, p. 459.

82. *Werke*, V, p. 50; *Hegel's Science of Logic*, p. 54.

83. *Werke*, V, p. 70; *Hegel's Science of Logic*, p. 71.

84. *Werke*, V, p. 70; *Hegel's Science of Logic*, p. 71.

85. *Werke*, V, p. 83; *Hegel's Science of Logic*, p. 82.

86. *Werke*, V, p. 83; *Hegel's Science of Logic*, p. 82.

87. *Werke*, V, p. 83; *Hegel's Science of Logic*, p. 82.

88. *Werke*, V, p. 84; *Hegel's Science of Logic*, p. 85.

89. *Werke*, V, p. 113; *Hegel's Science of Logic*, p. 106.

90. *Werke*, V, p. 113; *Hegel's Science of Logic*, p. 106. On the term 'sublate' or *aufheben*, see Hegel's own discussion, *Werke*, V, pp.113–15; *Hegel's Science of Logic*, pp. 106–8.

91. *Werke*, V, p.128; *Hegel's Science of Logic*, p. 119.

92. *Wissenschaft der Logik*, II, *Werke*, VI, Frankfurt am Main: Suhrkamp 1978, p. 245; *Hegel's Science of Logic*, p. 577.

93. *Werke*, VI, p. 274; *Hegel's Science of Logic*, p. 601.
94. *Werke*, VI, p. 274; *Hegel's Science of Logic*, p. 601.
95. *Werke*, VI, pp. 462–9; *Hegel's Science of Logic*, pp. 755–60.
96. P. F. Strawson, *Individuals*, London: Methuen 1959, pp. 9–11.
97. *Fichtes Werke*, II, p. 247; Preuss, p. 65.
98. *Fichtes Werke*, II, p. 244; Preuss, p. 63.
99. *Fichtes Werke*, II, p. 241; Preuss, p. 60: 'But according to the above I myself disappear no less than it (viz. the external world), I become a mere presenting without sense and without purpose.'

Chapter 6

1. Michel Haar, 'Nietzsche and Metaphysical Language', *The New Nietzsche*, ed. David B. Allison, Cambridge, MA: MIT Press 1985, pp. 5–36 (here p. 6) and *Über Wahrheit und Lüge*, § 1. Unless otherwise noted, all references are to Friedrich Nietzsche, *Sämtliche Werke: Kritische Studienausgabe in 15 Bänden*, ed. G. Colli and M. Montinari, Berlin: de Gruyter 1980.
2. Friedrich Nietzsche, *Götzen-Dämmerung*, 'Die Vier Grossen Irrtümer', § 7.
3. *Die fröhliche Wissenschaft*, § 370.
4. Karl Schlechta (ed.), *Friedrich Nietzsche: Werke*, Frankfurt am Main: Ullstein Verlag 1969, IV, p. 276.
5. *Götzen-Dämmerung*, 'Die "Vernunft" in der Philosophie', § 1. Translation in *Twilight of the Idols*, trans. R. J. Hollingdale, Harmondsworth: Penguin 1968, p. 35.
6. 'Die "Vernunft" in der Philosophie', § 1; Hollingdale, p. 35.
7. 'Die "Vernunft" in der Philosophie', § 2; Hollingdale, p. 36.
8. 'Die "Vernunft" in der Philosophie', § 4; Hollingdale, p. 37.
9. 'Die "Vernunft" in der Philosophie', § 4; Hollingdale, p. 37.
10. 'Die "Vernunft" in der Philosophie', § 4; Hollingdale, p. 37.
11. 'Die "Vernunft" in der Philosophie', § 4; Hollingdale, p. 37.
12. *Götzen-Dämmerung*, 'Die Vier Grossen Irrtümer', § 3; Hollingdale, 50.
13. Michel Haar remarks that the theory of the Will to Power as a way of '"identifying" things in their totality' appears to re-enact 'the traditional move of metaphysics' (Haar, 'Nietzsche and Metaphysical Language', pp. 7–8).
14. *Zur Genealogie der Moral*, I, § 13; *On the Genealogy of Morals*, trans. Douglas Smith, Oxford: Oxford University Press 1996, p. 29. We should exercise a certain scepticism regarding Nietzsche's apparent dismissal of some of the key terms of traditional metaphysics. Nietzsche himself clearly presupposes the existence of the self and of other selves in his own work (otherwise who is he writing for?), the affirmation of Eternal Return is predicated upon freedom of the will, truth is implied in the unveiling of either truth as illusion or truth as unpalatable reality, and the dismissal of Christian 'morality' as life-denying on the principle of life's affirmation is itself the application of an implicit morality (see Raymond Geuss, 'Nietzsche and Morality', *Morality, Culture, and History*, Cambridge: Cambridge University Press 1999, pp. 167–97).
15. *Also sprach Zarathustra*, II, 'Von der Erlösung'; *Thus Spoke Zarathustra*, trans. R. J. Hollingdale, Harmondsworth: Penguin 1969, p. 161.
16. *Also sprach Zarathustra*, II, 'Von der Erlösung'; J. Hollingdale, p. 161.
17. *Ecce Homo, Also sprach Zarathustra*; *Ecce Homo*, trans. R. J. Hollingdale, Harmondsworth: Penguin 1979, p. 99.

18. *Der Wille zur Macht*, § 617 (Schlechta, IV, 487). For the 'innocence of becoming', see also *Der Wille zur Macht*, § 552 and 787, and *Götzen-Dämmerung*, 'Die Vier Grossen Irrtümer', § 8. For the 'eternal joy of becoming', see *Ecce Homo*, 'Die Geburt der Tragödie', § 3.

19. Michel Foucault, *What Is Enlightenment?*, in *The Foucault Reader*, ed. Paul Rabinow, Harmondsworth: Penguin 1984, pp. 32–50 (here p. 40).

20. Hans-Georg Gadamer, 'The Universality of the Hermeneutical Problem', *Philosophical Hermeneutics*, trans. David E. Linge, California: University of California Press 1976, pp. 3–17 (here p. 3).

21. Hans-Georg Gadamer, *Truth and Method*, 2nd English edn., London: Sheed & Ward 1979, p. 406.

22. Gadamer, *Truth and Method*, p. 432.

23. Gilles Deleuze made a significant contribution to the extensive influence of Nietzsche in contemporary French thinking with his early studies: *Nietzsche*, Paris: Presses Universitaires de France 1965, and *Nietzsche et la Philosophie*, Paris: Presses Universitaires de France 1970.

24. Gilles Deleuze and Félix Guattari, *What is Philosophy?*, trans. Graham Burchell and Hugh Tomlinson, London and New York: Verso 1994, p. 2.

25. Gilles Deleuze, *Difference and Repetition*, trans. Paul Patton, London: Athlone Press 1994, p. 266.

26. 'Repetition is difference without a concept' (Deleuze, *Difference and Repetition*, p. 23).

27. Deleuze, *Difference and Repetition*, p. 129.

28. Deleuze, *Difference and Repetition*, p. 162.

29. Deleuze, *Difference and Repetition*, p. 276.

30. Deleuze, *Difference and Repetition*, p. 262.

31. Deleuze, *Difference and Repetition*, p. 27.

32. Deleuze, *Difference and Repetition*, pp. 45–9.

33. Deleuze, *Difference and Repetition*, p. 235.

34. Deleuze, *Difference and Repetition*, p. 146.

35. Deleuze, *Difference and Repetition*, p. 86.

36. Deleuze, *Difference and Repetition*, pp. 284–5.

37. Deleuze, *Difference and Repetition*, p. 303.

38. Deleuze, *Difference and Repetition*, p. 40.

39. Deleuze, *Difference and Repetition*, p. 262.

40. Deleuze, *Difference and Repetition*, pp. 41–2.

41. Deleuze, *Difference and Repetition*, p. 243; cf. p. 299.

42. Deleuze, *Difference and Repetition*, p. 243.

43. Deleuze, *Difference and Repetition*, p. 299.

44. Deleuze, *Difference and Repetition*, p. 301 ('The history of the long error is the history of representation, the history of the icons'), p. 265.

45. Deleuze, *Difference and Repetition*, p. 265.

46. Deleuze, *Difference and Repetition*, p. 95.

47. Deleuze, *Difference and Repetition*, p. 300.

48. For a comparison of Deleuze, Eckhart and Plotinus, see Oliver Davies, 'Thinking Difference: A Comparative Study of Gilles Deleuze, Plotinus and Meister Eckhart', *Deleuze and Theology*, ed. Mary Bryden, London: Routledge 2001, pp. 76–86.

49. In his important *Cartesian Meditations*, first published in 1931 in French,

Husserl specifically claimed Descartes as a forerunner, and even described his own transcendental phenomenology as a kind of 'neo-Cartesianism', albeit one in which the content was substantially changed; see Edmund Husserl, *Cartesianische Meditationen*, ed. Elisabeth Ströker, Hamburg: Felix Meiner Verlag 1977, § 1; Edmund Husserl, *Cartesian Meditations*, trans. Dorion Cairns, Dordrecht: Kluwer 1995 (originally The Hague: Martinus Nijhoff 1950), p. 1. The work only appeared in German in 1950.

50. *Cartesianische Meditationen*, § 4–6; *Cartesian Meditations*, pp. 9–16.

51. *Cartesianische Meditationen*, § 8; *Cartesian Meditations*, pp. 18–19.

52. *Cartesianische Meditationen*, § 8 ; *Cartesian Meditations*, p. 21.

53. Husserl is harsh in his criticism of Descartes for having allowed pure 'intuition or evidence' to be translated into the *substantia cogitans* and thus into the 'absurd position' of transcendental realism (*Cartesianische Meditationen*, § 10; *Cartesian Meditations*, p. 24).

54. *Cartesianische Meditationen*, § 11; *Cartesian Meditations*, pp. 25–6. This is not the self as an internalized relation, but rather as the 'realm of *transcendental-phenomenological self-experience*', in Husserl's phrase, thus marking a profound affinity of thought between Husserlian phenomenology and idealism.

55. This project is already apparent in Derrida's early study of Husserlian metaphysics in *Speech and Phenomena*, trans. David Allison, Evanston, IL: Northwestern University Press 1973. See also '"Genesis and Structure" and Phenomenology', *Writing and Difference*, trans. Alan Bass, London: Routledge 1978, pp. 154–68, where Derrida notes concerning Husserl that 'in criticizing classical metaphysics, phenomenology accomplishes the most profound project of metaphysics' (p. 166). In *Of Grammatology*, Husserl's system is described as 'the most radical and most critical restoration of the metaphysics of presence' (J. Derrida, *Of Grammatology*, London and Baltimore: Johns Hopkins University Press 1976, p. 49).

56. Derrida, *Of Grammatology*, p. 23.

57. M. Heidegger, *The Question of Being*, London: Vision Press 1956, p. 43 (translation slightly amended).

58. Derrida, *Of Grammatology*, p. 49.

59. Derrida, *Of Grammatology*, p. 158.

60. With respect to his critique of 'logocentrism', Derrida has been accused of applying the same rational tools which he repudiates. See, for instance, Jenny Teichman, 'Deconstruction and Aerodynamics', *Philosophy* 68 no. 263, January 1993, pp. 53–62.

61. Derrida, *Of Grammatology*, p. 70. There is a continuing debate between Culler, Norris and Gasché as to whether Derrida's *différance* is to be seen as 'play' or 'philosophy', whether it is purely a critique of language or has wider consequences and hence belongs to general philosophy (see the useful summary by Richard Rorty in his 'Is Derrida a Transcendental Philosopher?', *Derrida: A Critical Reader*, ed. David Wood, Oxford: Blackwell 1992, pp. 235–46).

62. For Derrida's own summary of *différance*, see his article 'Différance', *Margins of Philosophy*, trans. Alan Bass, Chicago: University of Chicago Press 1982, pp. 1–27.

63. Recent attempts to use Derridean negativity as the basis for fundamental theology appear to confirm this trend. See, for instance, Joachim Valentin,

Atheismus in der Spur Gottes: Theologie nach Jacques Derrida, Mainz: Matthias-Grünewald 1997.

64. Originally published in Jacques Derrida, *Psyché: Inventions de l'autre*, Paris: Galilée 1987, pp. 535–95. The English translation, from which we are quoting here, is published in Sanford Budick and Wolfgang Iser (eds), *Languages of the Unsayable: The Play of Negativity in Literature and Literary Theory*, New York: Columbia University Press 1989, pp. 3–70.
65. Derrida, 'Denials'; Budick and Iser, *Languages of the Unsayable*, p. 4.
66. Derrida, 'Denials'; Budick and Iser, *Languages of the Unsayable*, p. 8.
67. John D. Caputo, 'Mysticism and Transgression: Derrida and Meister Eckhart', *Derrida and Deconstruction*, ed. Hugh J. Silverman, London: Routledge 1989, pp. 24–39 (here p. 24).
68. Derrida, 'Denials'; Budick and Iser, *Languages of the Unsayable*, p. 41.
69. Derrida, 'Denials'; Budick and Iser, *Languages of the Unsayable*, p. 62. But intriguingly Derrida continues: 'But perhaps the contrary is the case. Perhaps there would be no prayer, no pure possibility of prayer, without what we glimpse as a menace or as a contamination: writing, the code, repetition, analogy or the – at least apparent – multiplicity of addresses, initiation.'
70. Derrida, 'Denials'; Budick and Iser, *Languages of the Unsayable*, p. 66, n. 13.
71. Derrida, 'Denials'; Budick and Iser, *Languages of the Unsayable*, p. 6.
72. 'If he [Heidegger] were to write a theology, the word *being* would not be under erasure; it wouldn't even appear there' (Derrida, 'Denials'; Budick and Iser, *Languages of the Unsayable*, p. 58).
73. Derrida, 'Denials'; Budick and Iser, *Languages of the Unsayable*, p. 62.
74. Jacques Derrida, 'Sauf le Nom (Post-Scriptum)', in *On the Name*, trans. David Wood, John P. Leavey, Jr. and Ian McLeod, Stanford, CA: Stanford University Press 1995, pp. 34–85 (here p. 51).
75. Derrida, 'Sauf le Nom', p. 71. Derrida perhaps means that *he* is anxious to render apophasis independent of revelation.
76. Derrida, 'Sauf le Nom', pp. 59, 54.
77. Derrida, 'Sauf le Nom', p. 74.
78. Derrida, 'Sauf le Nom', p. 76.
79. Derrida, 'Sauf le Nom', p. 60.
80. Derrida, 'Sauf le Nom', pp. 49–50.
81. Derrida, 'Sauf le Nom', p. 59.
82. Derrida, 'Sauf le Nom', p. 59.
83. Derrida, 'Sauf le Nom', p. 61.
84. Derrida, 'Sauf le Nom', p. 80.
85. Derrida, 'Sauf le Nom', p. 74. Cf. 'the statement of negative theology empties itself by definition, by vocation, of all intuitive plenitude. *Kenosis* of discourse.' (p. 50).
86. Derrida, 'Sauf le Nom', pp. 55–6.
87. Derrida, 'Sauf le Nom', p. 67.
88. Derrida, 'Sauf le Nom', p. 43.
89. Derrida, 'Sauf le Nom', p. 76.
90. Derrida, 'Sauf le Nom', p. 54.
91. Derrida, 'Sauf le Nom', p. 69.
92. Derrida, 'Sauf le Nom', p. 68.
93. Derrida, 'Sauf le Nom', p. 58.

94. Derrida, 'Sauf le Nom', p. 79.
95. Emmanuel Levinas, *Totality and Infinity*, trans. Alphonso Lingis, Dordrecht: Kluwer 1991, p. 21.
96. Levinas, *Totality and Infinity*, p. 43.
97. Levinas, *Totality and Infinity*, p. 44.
98. Levinas, *Totality and Infinity*, p. 51.
99. Levinas, *Totality and Infinity*, p. 36.
100. Levinas, *Totality and Infinity*, pp. 37–8.
101. Levinas, *Totality and Infinity*, p. 38.
102. Deleuze's *La philosophie critique de Kant: Doctrine des facultés* (Paris: Presses Universitaires de France) was published in 1963.
103. 'Totalization is accomplished only in history' (Levinas, *Totality and Infinity*, p. 55).
104. Levinas, *Totality and Infinity*, p. 55.
105. Levinas, *Totality and Infinity*, p. 57.
106. Levinas, *Totality and Infinity*, p. 57.
107. Levinas, *Totality and Infinity*, p. 80.
108. Levinas, *Totality and Infinity*, p. 43; cf. p. 50.
109. Levinas, *Totality and Infinity*, pp. 33–4.
110. Levinas, *Totality and Infinity*, p. 62.
111. Levinas, *Totality and Infinity*, pp. 33–4.
112. Levinas, *Totality and Infinity*, pp. 49, 62.
113. Levinas, *Totality and Infinity*, p. 50 (original italics).
114. Levinas, *Totality and Infinity*, p. 75.
115. Levinas, *Totality and Infinity*, pp. 75, 50.
116. Levinas, *Totality and Infinity*, p. 75.
117. Levinas, *Totality and Infinity*, p. 75. Alphonso Lingis points out in a footnote on this passage that 'You' here is 'the "you" of majesty, in contrast with the "thou" of intimacy'.
118. Levinas, *Totality and Infinity*, p. 291.
119. Levinas, *Totality and Infinity*, p. 209; cf. p. 174.
120. Levinas, *Totality and Infinity*, p. 67.
121. Levinas, *Totality and Infinity*, p. 96 (italics in original).
122. Levinas, *Totality and Infinity*, p. 171.
123. Levinas, *Totality and Infinity*, p. 174.
124. The important text here is *Zur Phänomenologie des inneren Zeitbewusstseins, Husserliana*, vol. 10, The Hague: Nijhoff 1966 (*On the Phenomenology of the Consciousness of Internal Time*, trans. J. B. Brough, Dordrecht: Kluwer 1991).
125. Emmanuel Levinas, *Otherwise than Being*, trans. Alphonso Lingis, Pittsburg: Duquesne University Press 1981, p. 3.
126. Levinas, *Otherwise than Being*, pp. 12, 3.
127. Levinas, *Otherwise than Being*, pp. 43, 150.
128. Levinas, *Otherwise than Being*, p. 34.
129. Levinas, *Otherwise than Being*, p. 9.
130. Levinas, *Otherwise than Being*, p. 34.
131. Levinas, *Otherwise than Being*, p. 35.
132. Levinas, *Otherwise than Being*, p. 72.
133. Levinas, *Otherwise than Being*, p. 64.
134. Levinas, *Otherwise than Being*, p. 73.

135. Levinas, *Otherwise than Being*, pp. 82–3.
136. Levinas, *Otherwise than Being*, pp. 112–18.
137. Levinas, *Otherwise than Being*, p. 84.
138. Levinas, *Otherwise than Being*, pp. 151, 112.
139. Levinas, *Otherwise than Being*, p. 5.
140. Levinas, *Otherwise than Being*, p. 67.
141. Levinas, *Otherwise than Being*, pp. 113, 149–53.
142. Levinas, *Otherwise than Being*, p. 154.
143. Levinas, *Otherwise than Being*, p. 158.
144. Levinas, *Otherwise than Being*, p. 160.
145. Levinas, *Otherwise than Being*, p. 165.
146. Levinas, *Otherwise than Being*, p. 162.
147. Karl Jaspers was one of the first commentators on Nietzsche to note the extent to which his critique of Christianity sprang from the tension between Christian reality and Christian ideals (Karl Jaspers, *Nietzsche und das Christentum*, Hameln: Verlag der Bücherstube Fritz Seifert 1938, p. 9: 'Nietzsches *Feindschaft* gegen das Christentum als Wirklichkeit ist untrennbar von seiner tatsächlichen *Bindung* an das Christentum als Anspruch'. For a modern survey of the question of Nietzsche and Christianity, see also Paul Valadier, *Nietzsche et la critique du christianisme*, Paris: Editions du Cerf 1974; and Alistair Kee, *Nietzsche against the Crucified*, London: SCM Press 1999.
148. Levinas, *Otherwise than Being*, p. 177.

Chapter 7

1. Emmanuel Levinas, *Totality and Infinity*, trans. Alphonso Lingis, Dordrecht: Kluwer 1991, pp. 35–6.
2. Levinas, *Totality and Infinity*, p. 53.
3. Emmanuel Levinas, *Otherwise than Being*, trans. Alphonso Lingis, Pittsburg: Duquesne University Press 1981, p. 178.
4. Levinas, *Otherwise than Being*, p. 183.
5. Paul Ricoeur, *Oneself as Another*, trans. Kathleen Blamey, Chicago: University of Chicago Press 1992, p. 338.
6. Levinas, *Otherwise than Being*, p. 4.
7. Levinas, *Otherwise than Being*, p. 117.
8. Levinas, *Totality and Infinity*, p. 297.
9. Paul Ricoeur, 'Towards a Hermeneutic of the Idea of Revelation', *Essays on Biblical Interpretation*, ed. Lewis S. Mudge, London: SPCK 1981, pp. 73–118 (here p. 106).
10. Ricoeur, *Oneself as Another*, pp. 16, 19.
11. Ricoeur, *Oneself as Another*, p. 302.
12. The recognition that hermeneutics must somehow remain in dialogue with ontology is one of Ricoeur's most fundamental convictions: there must be *un être à dire* (Paul Ricoeur, *From Text to Action*, Evanston, IL: Northwestern University Press 1991, p. 19).
13. Ricoeur, *Oneself as Another*, pp. 298–9.
14. Ricoeur, *Oneself as Another*, p. 180.

15. Ricoeur, *Oneself as Another*, p. 192.
16. Ricoeur, *Oneself as Another*, pp. 192–3.
17. Ricoeur, *Oneself as Another*, p. 183.
18. Ricoeur, *Oneself as Another*, p. 195.
19. Ricoeur, *Oneself as Another*, p. 202.
20. Ricoeur, *Oneself as Another*, p. 202.
21. Paul Ricoeur, 'Emmanuel Levinas: Thinker of Testimony', *Figuring the Sacred: Religion, Narrative and Imagination*, trans. David Pellauer, ed. Mark I. Wallace, Minneapolis: Fortress Press 1995, pp. 108–26.
22. Ricoeur, 'Emmanuel Levinas: Thinker of Testimony', p. 109.
23. Ricoeur, 'Emmanuel Levinas: Thinker of Testimony', p. 109
24. Ricoeur, 'Emmanuel Levinas: Thinker of Testimony', pp. 119, 123.
25. Ricoeur, 'Emmanuel Levinas: Thinker of Testimony', pp. 120–1.
26. Paul Ricoeur, 'Manifestation and Proclamation', *Figuring the Sacred*, pp. 48–67 (here p. 65).
27. Paul Ricoeur, 'Naming God', *Figuring the Sacred*, pp. 217–35 (here p. 218). Original italics.
28. Ricoeur, 'Naming God', p. 224. Original italics.
29. Paul Ricoeur, 'The "Sacred" Text and the Community', *Figuring the Sacred*, pp. 68–72 (here p. 71).
30. Ricoeur, 'The "Sacred" Text and the Community', p. 68.
31. Ricoeur, 'The "Sacred" Text and the Community', p. 72.
32. Paul Ricoeur, 'Philosophy and Religious Language', *Figuring the Sacred*, pp. 35–47 (here pp. 35–7).
33   Ricoeur, 'Philosophy and Religious Language', p. 43.
34. Ricoeur, 'Towards a Hermeneutic of the Idea of Revelation', *Essays on Biblical Interpretation*, p. 101.
35. Ricoeur, 'Naming God', *Figuring the Sacred*, pp. 216–235 (here p. 227).
36. Ricoeur, 'Naming God', pp. 228–30.
37. Mark C. Taylor, *Erring: A Postmodern A/theology*, Chicago: University of Chicago Press 1981, p. 8.
38. Taylor, *Erring*, p. 118.
39. Taylor, *Erring*, p. 120.
40. Taylor, *Erring*, p. 145. Taylor shows a proximity to Vattimo on this and other points.
41. John Milbank, *The Word Made Strange: Theology, Language, Culture*, Oxford: Blackwell 1997, p. 97.
42. Milbank, *The Word Made Strange*, p. 106.
43. Milbank, *The Word Made Strange*, pp. 178, 61, 85.
44. Milbank, *The Word Made Strange*, p. 113.
45. Graham Ward, in his *Barth, Derrida and the Language of Theology*, Cambridge: Cambridge University Press 1995, and Catherine Pickstock, in her *After Writing: On the Liturgical Consummation of Philosophy*, Oxford: Blackwell 1998, also base their respective theologies of the Word extensively on the Derridean analysis of the nature of language.
46. Milbank, *The Word Made Strange*, p. 111.
47. Milbank, *The Word Made Strange*, p. 208.
48. Milbank, *The Word Made Strange*, p. 138.
49. W. V. Quine summarizes his influential idea of 'radical translation', showing

the 'indeterminacy of translation' and 'indeterminacy of reference' in his *Pursuit of Truth*, Cambridge, MA: Harvard University Press 1990, especially pp. 37–59. In his 'On the Very Idea of a Conceptual System', *Inquiries into Truth and Interpretation*, Oxford: Oxford University Press 1984, pp. 183–98, Donald Davidson develops Quine's position in order to attack the notion both of relativism and 'the concept of an uninterpreted reality', since 'if we cannot intelligibly say that schemes are different, neither can we intelligibly say that they are one' (p. 198).

50. Alisdair MacIntyre, *Whose Justice? Which Rationality?*, London: Duckworth 1988, pp. 361–9.

51. 'Only those whose tradition allows for the possibility of its hegemony being put in question have rational warrant for asserting such a hegemony' (MacIntyre, *Whose Justice? Which Rationality?*, p. 388).

52. John Milbank, *Theology and Social Theory: Beyond Secular Reason*, Oxford: Blackwell 1990, pp. 339–47.

53. Milbank, *The Word Made Strange*, p. 244.

54. Milbank, *The Word Made Strange*, p. 250.

55. Does not a monological rendering of an 'ontology of peace' itself entail the risk of a certain kind of violence – towards the interlocutor and the speech community of which the theologian as *poeta theologicus* is a part?

56. Jean-Luc Marion, *God without Being*, trans. Thomas A. Carlson, Chicago: University of Chicago Press 1991, p. 14; cf. p. 17. In Marion's definition of the idol as that which subjects the divine to the 'measure' of the human gaze, we can feel the Cartesian *mensura*, and *l'ontologie grise*, of which Marion has written at length elsewhere. See pp. 98–100 above.

57. Marion, *God without Being*, p. 20.

58. Marion, *God without Being*, pp. 73–107.

59. For references in Heidegger's work to this problematic, see Marion, *God without Being*, p. 40, n. 23.

60. Marion, *God without Being*, p. 85.

61. Marion, *God without Being*, p. 95.

62. Marion, *God without Being*, p. 100.

63. See note 94 below.

64. There is a considerable anthropological literature on the social significance of gifts and the exchange of goods of which Marcel Mauss, *The Gift: Forms and Functions of Exchange in Archaic Societies*, trans. Ian Cunnison, London: Cohen & West 1970, is perhaps the best known.

65. Marion, *God without Being*, pp. 110, 182.

66. Jean-Luc Marion, *Reduction and Givenness*, trans. Thomas A. Carlson, Evanston, IL: Northwestern University Press 1998, p. 197.

67. Marion, *Reduction and Givenness*, p. 198.

68. Marion, *Reduction and Givenness*, p. 200.

69. Marion, *Reduction and Givenness*, pp. 199, 201.

70. Marion, *Reduction and Givenness*, p. 201.

71. Marion, *Reduction and Givenness*, p. 197.

72. David Ford, *Self and Salvation*, Cambridge: Cambridge University Press 1999, p. 107.

73. Ford, *Self and Salvation*, p. 271.

74. Ford, *Self and Salvation*, pp. 267, 103.

75. Ford, *Self and Salvation*, p. 32.
76. Ford, *Self and Salvation*, pp. 64–5.
77. Ford, *Self and Salvation*, p. 74.
78. Ford, *Self and Salvation*, p. 81.
79. Ford, *Self and Salvation*, p. 68.
80. Ford, *Self and Salvation*, pp. 80, 92, 73. See Eberhard Jüngel, *God as Mystery of the World*, trans. Darrell L. Guder, Edinburgh: T&T Clark 1983, p. 317.
81. Ford, *Self and Salvation*, p. 95. See Ricoeur, *Oneself as Another*, p. 355.
82. Ford, *Self and Salvation*, p. 99.
83. Ford, *Self and Salvation*, p. 271.
84. Ford, *Self and Salvation*, p. 167.
85. Ford, *Self and Salvation*, p. 167.
86. Ford, *Self and Salvation*, p. 99.
87. Ford, *Self and Salvation*, p. 103.
88. Ford, *Self and Salvation*, pp. 33, 45. The residual phenomenology in Levinas is discussed on pp. 32–3.
89. See below, pp. 159–63.
90. The language of being, as developed along the lines of our kenotic ontology, does enact the unity of the *idem* and *ipse* identities proposed by Paul Ricoeur, the *ipse* identity being grounded in the ethical imperative of the other as mediated through the dialectic of consciousness and the *idem* identity residing within the self-thematization of the self precisely within the multiple conversations with Other–I as other selves. The former broadly corresponds to our 'affirmation' of the other, while the latter is 'recognition'.
91. Ford, *Self and Salvation*, p. 167.
92. Ford, *Self and Salvation*, p. 9.
93. Pierre Rousselot, 'Pour l'histoire du problème de l'amour au moyen age', *Beiträge zur Geschichte der Philosophie des Mittelalters*, B. 6, H. 6, Münster 1908, pp. 1–102 (here p. 1).
94. See in particular Volumes I and III, 1, 2 of *Herrlichkeit*, and the first volume of *Theologik*. For some observations on von Balthasar's ontology, see O. Davies, 'Von Balthasar and the Problem of Being', *New Blackfriars* 79 no. 923, January 1998, pp. 11–17.
95. See below, pp. 266–7, for a development of this theme.
96. Again, see below, pp. 241–3.

C. Introduction

1. See below, pp. 189–95.
2. Simon Tugwell OP (ed. and trans.), *Albert and Thomas*, Classics of Western Spirituality, New York: Paulist Press 1988, p. 357.
3. Lars Thunberg, *Microcosm and Mediator*, Chicago and Lasalle, IL: Open Court 1995, p. 357.
4. Jean-Luc Marion, *God without Being*, trans. Thomas A. Carlson, Chicago: University of Chicago Press 1991, pp. 1–4.
5. Lateran Council, Cap. 2: 'inter creatorem et creaturam non potest tanta similitudo notari, quin inter eos maior sit dissimilitudo notanda' (Denzinger, § 432, p. 202).

6. Karl Barth, *Church Dogmatics*, I/1, The Doctrine of the Word of God, trans. G. W. Bromiley, ed. G. W. Bromiley and T. F. Torrance, 2nd edn., Edinburgh: T&T Clark 1975, p. 14.

7. *Fides et Ratio*, London: Catholic Truth Society 1998, passim.

8. Nicholas Lash, *Theology on the Way to Emmaus*, London: SCM Press 1986, pp. 32, 25.

Chapter 8

1. Karl Rahner, *Foundations of Christian Faith: An Introduction to the Idea of Christianity*, trans. William V. Dych, London: Darton, Longman & Todd 1978. For Rahner, of course, this is the 'first level of reflexion' (pp. 1–23), a term which we prefer for theology itself as a reflexive mode of Christian speech.

2. In the spirit of von Balthasar, Rino Fisichella (*La rivilazione: evento e credibilitá*, Bologna: Edizioni Dehoniane Bologna 1985) sees fundamental theology as based on the Trinitarian mystery as revealed in Christ and the church.

3. Henri Bouillard, 'La tâche actuelle de la théologie fondamentale', *Vérité du Christianisme*, Paris: Desclée 1989, pp. 149–79 (here p. 178).

4. On the different presuppositions of apologetics and fundamental theology, see Gerald O'Collins, *Fundamental Theology*, London: Darton, Longman & Todd 1981, p. 23. But although these two differ by virtue of their respective contexts, they both draw upon a process of reflexion.

5. René Latourelle, 'A New Image of Fundamental Theology', *Problems and Perspectives of Fundamental Theology*, ed. René Latourelle and Gerald O'Collins, New York/Ramsey: Paulist Press 1982, pp. 37–58 (here p. 37).

6. Francis Schüssler Fiorenza, *Foundational Theology: Jesus and the Church*, New York: Crossroad 1985, p. 249.

7. We can divide this literature into two types: 'soft' explanation which took the form of an appeal for tolerance by representing Christianity as an organic and legitimate part of the culture and the age, and 'hard' explanation which sought to evangelize by projecting Christianity competitively into the society of the day (e.g. the distinction between Justin Martyr's *Apologia* and his *Dialogue with Trypho*). See also Avery Dulles, *A History of Apologetics*, London: Hutchinson 1971, p. 23.

8. A. Lang, *Die Entfaltung des apologetischen Problems in der Scholastik des Mittelalters*, Freiburg: Herder 1962, pp. 11–13. See also Gerhard Larcher, 'Modelle fundamentaltheologischer Problematik im Mittelalter', in *Handbuch der Fundamentaltheologie*, IV, Freiburg: Herder 1988, pp. 334–6.

9. For the following, I am indebted to the historical schemes given by both Francis Schüssler Fiorenza (*Foundational Theology*, pp. 251–64) and Hansjürgen Verweyen (*Gottes letztes Wort: Grundriß der Fundamentaltheologie*, Düsseldorf: Patmos Verlag 1991, pp. 13–35).

10. On the contribution of Melchior Cano as leading representative of reflexive theology between the Reformation and Descartes, see Tharcisse Tshibangu, *Théologie positive et théologie spéculative*, Louvain: Publications Université de Louvain 1965, pp. 186–210.

11. It is notable however, that he understands it in a way that is directly contrary to its subsequent and classical usage. On Annat, see Heinrich Stirnimann,

'"Fundamentaltheologie" im frühen 18 Jahrhundert?', *Freiburger Zeitschrift für Theologie und Philosophie* 24, 1977, pp. 460–76.

12. J. B. Sabrié, *De l'humanisme au rationalisme: Pierre Charron*, F. Alcan: Paris 1913.

13. It also influenced the Protestant humanist Hugo Grotius in his *De veritate religionis christianae* of 1627, where he attempted to establish the superiority of Christianity against all other religions, while arguing also that it was founded upon natural religion.

14. Franz-Josef Niemann, 'Fundamentaltheologie im 17. Jahrhundert', *Zeitschrift für katholische Theologie* 103, 1981, pp. 178–85 (here pp. 184–5). Eugen Biser also notes the importance of the *de more geometrico* for Christian apologetics, and contrasts this with biblical and existential truth in his 'Das Wahrheitsproblem der Glaubensbegründung: Erwägungen zu einer aktuellen Frage der Fundamentaltheologie', *Hochland* 61, 1969, pp. 1–12 (here pp. 4–6).

15. Initially, he was also influenced in part by Schleiermacher. See Abraham Peter Kustermann, *Die Apologetik Johann Sebastian Dreys (1777–1853)*, Beiträge zur Geschichte der Eberhard-Karls-Universität Tübingen 36, Tübingen: J. C. B. Mohr (Paul Siebeck) 1988, pp. 180–8.

16. Günther's firm criticism of the limitations of neoscholasticism made him powerful enemies, and his works were placed on the Index in 1857. J. Pritz gives a useful evaluation of Günther's life and work, and of his condemnation, in H. Fries and G. Schweiger (eds), *Katholische Theologen Deutschlands im 19. Jahrhundert*, I, Munich: Kösel-Verlag 1975, pp. 348–75.

17. ET *Spirit in the World*, London: Sheed & Ward 1968; *Hearer of the Word*, New York: Continuum 1994; and *Foundations of Christian Faith*.

18. David Tracy, *The Analogical Imagination*, London: SCM Press 1981, p. 160.

19. Tracy, *The Analogical Imagination*, p. 163.

20. Schüssler Fiorenza, *Foundational Theology*, p. 284. He refers to Rorty's refutation of the ahistoricity of transcendentalism on this point ('Verificationism and Transcendental Arguments', *Nous* 5, 1971, pp. 3–13 and 'Transcendental Arguments, Self-Reference and Pragmatism', *Transcendental Arguments and Science*, ed. Peter Bieri, Dordrecht: Reidel 1979, pp. 77–104).

21. Wolfhart Pannenberg, *Anthropology in Theological Perspective*, Edinburgh: T&T Clark 1985, p. 16.

22. In his study 'New Trends in Fundamental Theology: Trends in the Postconciliar Period' (*Problems and Perspectives of Fundamental Theology*, ed. Latourelle and O'Collins, p. 13), Jean-Pierre Torrell refers to the significant lack of consensus as to the meaning of the subject area in two important collaborative studies: 'La théologie fondamentale á la recherche de son identité' (*Gregorianum* 50, 1969, pp. 757–76) and 'Fundamental Theology' (*Concilium* 6 no. 5, 1969). For overviews of fundamental theology in the twentieth century, see J. Schmitz, 'La Théologie Fondamentale', *Bilan de la Théologie*, ed. R. Vander Gucht and H. Vorgrimler, Tournai–Paris: Casterman 1970, pp. 9–51; H. Stirnimann, 'Erwägungen zur Fundamental-theologie. Problematik, Grundfragen, Konzept', *Freiburger Zeitschrift für Theologie und Philosophie* 24, 1977, pp. 291–365; J. Flury, *Um die Redlichkeit des Glauben: Studien zur deutschen katholischen Fundamentaltheologie*, Freiburg, Switzerland: Universitätsverlag 1979; J-P. Torrell, 'New Trends', pp. 11–22, and Gerald O'Collins, *Retrieving Fundamental Theology*, London: Geoffrey Chapman 1993, pp. 40–7.

23. See further comments on Verweyen's project above, p. 42 n. 26, in the context of philosophy of consciousness and fundamental theology.

24. ET *Faith in History and Society*, New York: Crossroad 1980.

25. ET *Science, Action, and Fundamental Theology: Toward a Theology of Communicative Action*, Cambridge, MA and London: MIT Press 1984, p. xx.

26. Schüssler Fiorenza, *Foundational Theology*. See also T. Guarino, 'Revelation and Foundationalism: Towards Hermeneutical and Ontological Appropriateness', *Modern Theology* 6, 1990, pp. 221–35.

27. Gerhard Larcher, 'Subjekt – Kunst – Geschichte: Chancen einer Annäherung von Fundamentaltheologie und Ästhetik', *Fundamentaltheologie – Fluchtlinien und gegenwärtige Herausforderungen*, ed. Klaus Müller, Regensburg: Verlag Friedrich Pustet 1998, pp. 299–321.

28. In his *Gott als Autor: zu einer poietologischen Theologie* (Tübingen: Mohr Siebeck 1999), Oswald Bayer develops a theology of God's creative language as a 'Poesie des Versprechens', combining speech act theory with Hamann's identification of poetry with prophecy. In his *Poetische Dogmatik* (Paderborn: Schöningh, vol. 1 1995; vol. 2 1996; vol. 3 1998), Alex Stock sets out a range of liturgical and paraliturgical sources for a cultural Christology which evades the limitations of a narrowly metaphysical engagement with hypostasis.

29. Viktor Shklovsky first discusses his concept of the 'priëm ostranenia', or 'strategy of alienation', as poetological principle in his articles 'Potebnia' (1916) and 'Iskusstvo kak priëm' (1917), published in *Poetika*, Petrograd 1919, pp. 3–6 and 101–14 (discussed in Victor Ehrlich, *Russian Formalism*, 3rd edn., New Haven: Yale University Press 1981, pp. 76–8). John Milbank similarly takes poeticity as a creatively alienating force as a key notion for theology today in his work *The Word Made Strange: Theology, Language, Culture*, Oxford: Blackwell 1997. See in particular pp. 24–32.

30. Roman Jakobson, 'Linguistics and Poetics', *Selected Writings*, III, The Hague: Mouton 1981, pp. 18–51 (here pp. 21–2).

31. Jakobson, 'Linguistics and Poetics', p. 27.

32. What this means concretely is that where the poetic function does not apply, we might say of a sleeping child: 'the child/ infant/ boy/ girl/ son/ daughter snoozes/ sleeps/ dozes/ slumbers'. Whichever one of these options we choose will depend on what seems most appropriate at the time (do we know the sex of the child?), and the chief criterion will be efficiency of communication within a specific speech context. Where the poetic function does apply however, then we shall have to take into account the semantics and phonology of what precedes and follows this statement within the overall unit of utterance. If it is followed by the words 'and the father snores', for instance, then we may opt for 'son' and 'snoozes' ('the son snoozes and the father snores'). 'Son' picks up 'father' in a way that 'boy' does not, and 'snoozes' seems to be appropriate for an infant in the way that 'snores' is for a full grown man. Thus perhaps we see the future man in the sleeping child (and the child in the man?).

33. Poetic effects are not confined to such texts however, and can be found in ordinary language; see Deborah Tannen, *Talking Voices: Repetition, Dialogue, and Imagery in Conversational Discourse*, Cambridge: Cambridge University Press 1989, especially pp. 36–97. An argument for the interdependence of poetics and semiotics can be found in L. Dolezel and K. Hausenblas, 'Poetika i

Stilistika', *Poetics, Polish, Russian*, ed. D. Davie *et al.*, Gravenhage: Mouton 1961, pp. 39–52.

34. Edward Stankiewicz, 'Poetic and non-Poetic Language in their Interrelation', *Poetics*, ed. Davie *et al.*, pp. 11–23 (here p. 15).

35. Stankiewicz, 'Poetic and non-Poetic Language in their Interrelation', p. 15.

36. Northrop Frye, *Anatomy of Criticism*, Princeton: Princeton University Press 1957, p. 81.

37. Stefan George, *Gedichte*, Stuttgart: Ernst Klett 1983, p. 64 (my translation).

38. 'Dichtung ist worthafte Stiftung des Seins' (Martin Heidegger, 'Hölderlin und das Wesen der Dichtung', *Erläuterungen zu Hölderlins Dichtung*, *Gesamtausgabe*, IV, Frankfurt: Klostermann 1981, pp. 33–48; here p. 41).

39. Paul Ricoeur, 'Towards a Hermeneutic of the Idea of Revelation', *Essays on Biblical Interpretation*, ed. Lewis S. Mudge, London: SPCK 1981, pp. 73–118 (here p. 100).

40. Ricoeur, 'Towards a Hermeneutic of the Idea of Revelation', p. 101.

41. '[I]n poetry the rationale of metaphor belongs to another order of experience than science . . . the logic of metaphor is so organically entrenched in pure sensibility . . .' Quoted in James Scully, *Modern Poetics*, New York: McGraw-Hill 1965, pp. 161–2.

42. Ricoeur, 'Towards a Hermeneutic of the Idea of Revelation', p. 101.

43. Wallace Stevens, 'The Noble Rider and the Sound of Words', *The Necessary Angel*, New York: Knopf 1951, pp. 3–36 (here p. 31).

44. Stevens, 'The Noble Rider', pp. 19–20.

45. Stevens, 'The Noble Rider', p. 33.

46. Stevens, 'The Noble Rider', p. 36.

47. Robert Frost, 'The Figure a Poem Makes', *Complete Poems*, London: Cape 1967, pp. 17–20 (here p. 19).

48. Frost, 'The Figure a Poem Makes', p. 18.

49. Federico García Lorca, *Obras Completas*, I, Madrid: Aguilar 1980, p. 1106: 'La virtud mágica del poema consiste en estar siempre enduandado para bautizar con agua oscura a todos los que lo miran'.

50. Stevens, 'The Noble Rider', 29.

51. Mikhail Bakhtin, 'Art and Answerability', *Art and Answerability: Early Philosophical Essays by M. M. Bakhtin*, ed. M. Holquist and V. Liapunov, Austin: University of Texas Press 1990, pp. 1–3 (here p. 2).

52. See the poem *Nah, im Aortenbogen*, in Paul Celan, *Gedichte*, II, Frankfurt am Main: Suhrkamp Verlag 1975, p. 202: Nah, im Aortenbogen,/ im Hellblut:/ das Hellwort.// ('Near, in the bend of the aorta, in the bright blood: the bright word.').

53. A. E. Housman, *The Name and Nature of Poetry*, Cambridge: Cambridge University Press 1933, p. 37.

54. Quoted in Michael Hamburger, *The Truth of Poetry*, London: Anvil Press 1982, p. 34.

55. W. H. Auden, 'The Virgin and the Dynamo', *The Dyer's Hand*, New York: Random House 1948, pp. 61–71 (here p. 68).

56. T. S. Eliot, 'Tradition and the Individual Talent', *Selected Essays*, London: Faber & Faber 1932, pp. 13–22.

57. Frost, 'The Figure a Poem Makes', p. 18.

58. Quoted in Hamburger, *The Truth of Poetry*, p. 28.

59. Quoted in Hamburger, *The Truth of Poetry*, p. 28.

60. Gary Giddes (ed.), *Twentieth Century Poetry and Poetics* 4th edn., Toronto: Oxford University Press, 1996, p. xvi.

61. Rainer Maria Rilke, *Werke in drei Bänden*, I, Frankfurt am Main: Insel Verlag 1966, p. 442.

62. Wallace Stevens, 'Adagia', *Opus Posthumous*, London: Faber & Faber 1957, pp. 157–80 (here p. 158).

63. Joseph Brodsky, quoted in Geddes (ed.), *Twentieth Century Poetry and Poetics*, pp. xv–xvi.

64. Mikhail Bakhtin, 'Content, Material and Form in Verbal Art', *Art and Answerability*, ed. Holquist and Liapunov, p. 294.

65. See below, pp. 189–90.

66. Stevens, 'The Noble Rider', p. 33.

67. Auden, 'The Virgin and the Dynamo', p. 70.

68. Auden, 'The Virgin and the Dynamo', pp. 68–9.

69. Auden, 'The Virgin and the Dynamo', p. 71.

70. Auden, 'The Virgin and the Dynamo', p. 71.

71. Hélène Cixous, *Coming to Writing and Other Essays*, ed. Deborah Jenson, trans. Sarach Cornell, Cambridge, MA: Harvard University Press 1991, p. 156 (quoted in Graham Ward, 'Kenosis and Naming: Beyond Analogy and Towards *Allegoria Amoris*', *Religion, Modernity and Postmodernity*, ed. Paul Heelas, Oxford: Blackwell 1998, p. 235).

72. Milbank, *The Word Made Strange*, p. 3.

73. See above, pp. 153–7.

74. In 'The Poet as Fool and Priest' (*Journal of English Literary History* 25 no. 4, Dec. 1956, pp. 279–98), Sigurd Burckhardt argues that since words can never be totally severed from their meanings '[t]here can be no non-representational poetry; the very medium forbids it' (p. 280).

Chapter 9

1. John 1.3.

2. Although reflection upon revelation shares the critical reflexivity of fundamental theology, and also its answerability to the givenness of particular revelation, it must be concerned not with giving an account of Christianity, but with clarifying the revelation upon which it is based, establishing the relation between the categories of general and particular revelation, and examining the nature of revelation as *communication*. Theology of revelation therefore will necessarily engage with the alignment between revelation as communication and the cognition which is faith.

3. It is questionable whether the category of 'religious' revelation can also be applied to 'primal disclosures' therefore, where there is no unified or personalized concept of deity, and where there is often a seamless continuity between the visible and invisible world. There is a marked tendency in writing on primal religion to make use of religious categories originally generated by reflection on theistic religions, and it has to be recognized that such categories, whether deriving from Christianity or Islam, may also have penetrated deep into the consciousness of most small-scale communities in the modern period.

See Wendy James, *The Listening Ebony*, Oxford: Oxford University Press 1988. For a different view, see Keith Ward, *Religion and Revelation*, Oxford: Oxford University Press 1994, pp. 50–110.

4. Colin E. Gunton, *A Brief Theology of Revelation*, Edinburgh: T&T Clark 1995, p. 34. Here, too, the miraculous character of the congruence between subject and object, mind and world, comes into view.

5. Paul Ricoeur, 'Towards a Hermeneutic of the Idea of Revelation', *Essays on Biblical Interpretation*, ed. Lewis S. Mudge, SPCK 1981, pp. 73–118 (here p. 102).

6. Ricoeur, 'Towards a Hermeneutic of the Idea of Revelation', p. 109. Rowan Williams quotes both these passages and comments on them in his article 'Trinity and Revelation', *Modern Theology* 2.3, 1986, pp. 197–212.

7. On the theme of revelation and the imagination, see Paul S. Fiddes, *Freedom and Limit: A Dialogue between Literature and Christian Doctrine* (London: Macmillan 1991), pp. 3–26. General typologies of revelation include George I. Mavrodes, *Revelation in Religious Belief*, Philadelphia: Temple University Press 1988 and Avery Dulles, *Models of Revelation*, 2nd edn., Dublin: Gill & Macmillan 1992. On the role of the imagination in revelation, see Garrett Green, *Imagining God: Theology and the Religious Imagination*, Grand Rapids, MI: Eerdmans 1989, and on the revelatory properties of the imagination, Richard Kearney, *Poetics of Imagining*, Edinburgh: Edinburgh University Press 1998.

8. It is necessary to reject any tendency to use a general theology of revelation to 'contain' or contextualize a positivist, confessional view of revelation in the hope of being able thereby to persuade others of what they appear otherwise to be unable to see. The entanglements of revelation under the species *De revelatione* with the threefold demonstrations of classical apologetics can seem unfortunate in this respect (see Gabriel Moran, *Theology of Revelation*, London: Burns & Oates 1967, p. 25). As Romano Guardini has pointed out, 'only revelation can tell us what revelation is' (Romano Guardini, *Religion und Offenbarung*, Würzburg: Werkbund Verlag 1958, pp. 118–19).

9. Rather than his 'causality' or 'manifestation' model (Mavrodes, *Revelation*, pp. 111–12). For a critique of Mavrodes, on the grounds of the narrowness of his conception of revelation, see Luco van den Brom, 'Models of Revelation and Language', *Revelation and Experience: Proceedings of the 11th Biennial European Conference on the Philosophy of Religion, Soesterberg 1996*, ed. Vincent Brümmer and Marcel Sarot, Utrecht: Universiteit Utrecht 1996, pp. 56–71.

10. Ward, *Religion and Revelation*, pp. 57, 16.

11. See Roman Jakobson, 'Linguistics and Poetics', *Selected Writings*, III, The Hague: Mouton 1981, pp. 18–51 for this model of communication theory, and the discussion at pp. 177–8 above.

12. Drawing upon the work of Eilert Herms, Christoph Schwöbel employs five principles of communication so that 'A discloses in the situation B the content C for the recipient D with the result E' (*God: Action And Revelation*, Kampen: Kok Pharos 1992, pp. 86–7). On the 'perlocutionary force', see Jacob L. Mey, *Pragmatics: An Introduction*, Oxford: Blackwell 1993, pp. 112–13.

13. For Thomas Aquinas, for instance, the occurrence of revelation requires the presence in the mind of the recipient of a supernaturally derived *iudicium* so that 'revelation occurs when the seeing of a thing is accompanied by the understanding of it' (*In 2 ad Cor.* 12, 1; cf. *De Ver.* 12, 7, quoted in Per Erik

Persson, *Sacra Doctrina: Reason and Revelation in Aquinas*, trans. J. A. R. Mackenzie, Oxford: Blackwell 1970, pp. 24–5.

14. Phil. 2.7.
15. ST 3a, 7, 7. According to V. White, revelation for Thomas is 'a vision . . . in the inspired mind of the apostle and the Evangelist, a vision indeed and above all in the prophetic and human mind of Jesus Christ himself' (*L'année théologique* 11, 1950, p. 129; quoted in Persson, *Sacra Doctrina*, p. 25. On the theme of revelation in Thomas Aquinas, see Persson, especially pp. 19–40).
16. The revelation of the divine nature to the human nature is therefore one which is itself received over time, and becomes manifest through the life and sacrifice of Christ.
17. See below, pp. 207–9.
18. Luke 1.35.
19. Gerhard Ebeling, in his *Einführung in Theologische Sprachlehre* (Tübingen: J. C. B. Mohr 1971) is one of the first modern theologians to begin to explore critically the relation between developments in language theory and the theological expressions of faith.
20. There is a parallel here in biblical exegesis: 'Die Sprechaktanalyse als neue grammatische Reflexion eröffnet also sehr vielfältige neue exegetische Reflexionen' (Andreas Wagner, *Sprechakte und Sprechaktanalyse im Alten Testament*, Berlin: de Gruyter 1997, p. 327).
21. Ludwig Wittgenstein, *Philosophical Investigations*, 3rd edn., trans. G. E. M. Anscombe, Oxford: Blackwell 1968, pp. 2–3.
22. The relevant texts can be found in *De trinitate*, IX, 12–15; XV, 19–20. Christopher Kirwan does not give an adequate account of the axiological and trinitarian dimensions in Augustine's model of language in his 'Augustine on the Nature of Speech', *Language: Companions to Ancient Thought 3*, ed. Stephen Everson, Cambridge: Cambridge University Press 1994, pp. 188–211.
23. In his study *Foundations of the Theory of Signs* (1938), Charles Morris, who was influenced by the American school of philosophical pragmatism, defined pragmatics as 'the study of the relation of signs to their interpreters' (Jef Verschueren *et al.* (eds), *Handbook of Pragmatics Manual*, Amsterdam/ Philadelphia: John Benjamins 1995, pp. 2–3).
24. George Yule, *Pragmatics*, Oxford: Oxford University Press 1996, p. 3. See also Jenny Thomas, *Meaning in Interaction*, London: Longman 1995, and Mey, *Pragmatics*. The origins of pragmatics can be traced back to linguistic anthropology on the one hand, specifically the work of Malinowski and J. R. Firth, which set out the social contexts of speech, and to semiotics on the other (J. R. Firth, *The Tongues of Men* 1937). In addition to foundational work by the American anthropologists Sapir and Whorff, and by the philosophers Charles Peirce and Ludwig Wittgenstein, all of whom stressed the centrality of language in the construction of social and cognitive realities, speech-act theory as developed by J. L. Austin in his *How to Do Things with Words* (1962) and later by John Searle in his *Speech Acts* (1969) also drew out the social and contextual aspects of language. This new movement was in reaction to Bertrand Russell's view of ordinary language use as debased communication from the perspective of a strict logical coherence, and it stressed the effective communication between speakers in their social environments and the extent to which speech is not tied to reference but is commensurate with action. In 1967, Paul

Watzlawick, Janet Beavin and Don Jackson published their *Pragmatics of Human Communication: A Study of Interactional Patterns, Pathologies, and Paradoxes*, lending added popularity to the term (see B. Aubrey Fisher and Katherine L. Adams, *Interpersonal Communication: Pragmatics of Human Relationships*, 2nd edn., New York: McGraw-Hill 1994, p. 4).

25. Stephen C. Levinson, *Pragmatics*, Cambridge: Cambridge University Press 1983, p. 9; Mey, *Pragmatics*, p. 37.

26. Fisher and Adams, *Interpersonal Communication*, pp. 1–2; Verschueren *et al.*, *Handbook*, p. 9.

27. Fisher and Adams, *Interpersonal Communication*, p. 1.

28. Walter Brueggemann, *Theology of the Old Testament: Testimony, Dispute, Advocacy*, Minneapolis: Augsburg Fortress 1997, p. 117.

29. Gerhard von Rad, *Old Testament Theology, I, The Theology of Israel's Historical Traditions*, Edinburgh: Oliver & Boyd 1962, p. 142. The theme of *creatio ex nihilo* first appears in explicit form in 2 Macc. 7.28, but see Gerhard May's cautionary comments on too literal a reading of this passage in his *Creatio ex Nihilo*, trans. A. S. Worrall, Edinburgh: T&T Clark 1994, pp. 6–8.

30. Werner H. Schmidt, *Die Schöpfungsgeschichte der Priesterschaft*, Neukirchen-Vluyn: Neukirchner Verlag 1964, p. 171.

31. Djamel-Eddine Kouloughli, 'La thématique du langage dans la Bible', *Histoires des idées linguistiques, I, La naissance des métalangages en Orient et en Occident*, ed. Sylvain Auroux, Liège-Bruxelles: Pierre Mordaga 1989, pp. 65–78 (here p. 66). On language in the Old Testament, see also Wolfgang Schenk, 'Altisraelitische Sprachauffassungen in der Hebräischen Bibel', *Geschichte der Sprachtheorie, II, Sprachtheorien der abendländischen Antike*, ed. Peter Schmitter, Tübingen: Gunter Narr Verlag 1991, pp. 3–25; and Werner Weinberg, 'Language Consciousness in the Old Testament', *Zeitschrift für die alttestamentliche Wissenschaft* 92, 1980, pp.185–204.

32. Gen. 2.19: 'whatever the man called every living creature, that was its name'.

33. Ex. 4.11: 'Who gives speech to mortals? Who makes them mute or deaf, seeing or blind? Is it not I, the Lord?'; cf. Prov. 18.21.

34. Aubrey R. Johnson, *The One and the Many in the Israelite Conception of God*, Cardiff: University of Wales Press 1942, p. 6.

35. Ps. 20; Num. 6.22–27; Ex. 20.7.

36. Jer. 11.19; Isa. 48.19; 56.5.

37. Kouloughli, 'La thématique', p. 74.

38. Ernest W. Nicholson, *God and His People*, Oxford: Oxford University Press 1986, p. 208. Nicholson has an excellent discussion of the evolution of a covenant theology and its likely links with the early prophets in the final chapter 'The Distinctiveness of Israel's Faith', pp. 191–217.

39. The equation of word and action is particularly drawn out here by the homonym *dabar* meaning both 'word' and 'thing' in the above passage.

40. Peter K. D. Neumann, 'Das Wort, das geschehen ist . . . Zum Problem der Wortempfangsterminologie in Jer. I–XXV', *Vetus Testamentum* 23, 1973, pp. 171–217 (here p. 183).

41. Claus Westermann, *Basic Forms of Prophetic Speech*, trans. Hugh Clayton White, London: Lutterworth Press 1967, p. 90.

42. Jer. 1.11.

43. In all other occurrences of these motifs Yahweh is the agent (Robert P. Carroll,

Jeremiah, London: SCM Press 1986, p. 94). It may also be significant that this is one of the few first-person accounts of commissioning (the LXX emends 'the word of the Lord came to me' to *pros auton*, or 'to him': Carroll, p. 94).

44. Alternatively, both may depend upon an earlier, programmatic source for commissioning (William L. Holladay, *Jeremiah I*, Philadelphia: Fortress Press 1986, p. 27).

45. Ex. 3.1–6. For a fuller discussion of the dynamic of this passage, see below, pp. 241–4.

46. Ex. 3.7–9.

47. Ex. 3.10–12.

48. Ex. 3.14–15.

49. Ex. 4.1–9.

50. Ex. 3.16–4.17.

51. Jer. 1.6; Ex. 4.10.

52. For every usage of *dabar 'im* in the Old Testament, see F. Brown, S. R. Driver and C. A. Briggs (eds), *A Hebrew and English Lexicon of the Old Testament*, sv. 3. e. It is also used once to refer to God speaking with Balaam (Num. 22.19), but the use of 'speaking with' is generally reserved for Moses' relation with God. The occurrence at Josh. 24.27 (NRSV: 'all the words of the Lord that he spoke to us'; LXX: *pros hēmas*) is in the context of remembrance of the covenant, as is Ezra's reference to 'speaking with' in his National Confession (Neh. 9.13). Gideon also uses 'speaking with' in his conversation with the angel, but his purpose is to establish whether he is conversing with God or not: 'If now I have found favour with you, then show me a sign that it is you who speak with (*dabar 'im*) me' (Judg. 6.17). The occurrence in Hos. 12.4 comes in a passage that is notoriously unclear: 'He strove with the angel and prevailed, he wept and sought his favour; he met him at Bethel, and there he spoke with him'. The LXX correction of 'with him' to 'with us' shows the confusion over the subject of the verbs in 4b. According to James L. Mays, the subject must be God (*Hosea*, London: SCM Press 1969, p. 164), but see also Hans Walter Wolff, *Hosea*, trans. G. Stansell, Philadelphia: Fortress Press 1974, pp. 212–13, and James M. Ward, *Hosea: A Theological Commentary*, New York: Harper & Row 1966, p. 210.

53. Ex. 19.6.

54. Ex. 19.9.

55. Ex. 19.16–19.

56. God speaks *b⁶qōl* where *qōl* can mean either 'voice' or 'thunder'. Ex. 19.16 has the plural form *qōlōt* for 'thunder', which has led most translators to take *qōl* at Ex. 19.19 also as 'thunder'. For parallels, see Ps. 18.13 and 29.3 (Brevard S. Childs, *Exodus: A Commentary*, Old Testament Library, London: SCM Press 1974, p. 343).

57. Ex. 20.19. God has already given the Decalogue at this point. For the view that Ex. 20.18–21 must originally have preceded Ex. 20.1–17, see Walter Beyerlin, *Origins and History of the Oldest Sinaitic Tradition*, trans. S. Rudman, Oxford: Blackwell 1965, pp. 4–6, 12–14.

58. Cf. Ex. 33.20.

59. There may well be a combination of two traditions here, one (a Deuteronomic tradition) which stressed Moses' role as mediator for his people in the giving of the Decalogue. On this, see Childs, *Exodus*, pp. 351–60, 607–9. Cf. also Ex. 33.9,

where we are told that whenever Moses entered the tent of meeting, 'the pillar of cloud would descend and stand at the entrance of the tent, and the Lord would speak with (*dabar 'im*) Moses', Ex. 33.11: the Lord 'would speak to (*dabar 'el*) Moses face to face, as one speaks to a friend', and Deut 10.4, where an almost exact parallel is given, the verbal phrase 'speak to' (*dabar 'el*) being used, though with none of the intimacy of Ex. 33.11. Finally, at Num. 11.17, God tells Moses to gather the elders of Israel: 'I will come down and talk with you (*dabar 'im*) there; and I will take some of the spirit that is on you and put it on them; and they shall bear the burden of the people along with you so that you will not bear it all by yourself'.

60. Ricoeur, 'Towards a Hermeneutics of the Idea of Revelation', p. 83.

61. Joachim Jeremias, 'Das Gebetsleben Jesu', *Zeitschrift für die neutestamentliche Wissenschaft* 25, 1926, pp. 123–40. I have used this article extensively for the following.

62. Cf. Dan. 6.11 and Ps. 55.17. The version of this prayer which was contemporary with Jesus shows many affinities with the Lord's Prayer.

63. Later rabbinic tradition (cf. b. Berakhot 5a; Tanhuma B ps2 §23 (73a)) gives Ps. 31.6 (31.5) as an example (Hermann L. Strack and Paul Billerbeck, *Kommentar zum Neuen Testament aus Talmud und Midrash*, vol. II, Munich 1924, p. 269).

64. For references to the relevant passages, see Joachim Jeremias, *Gebetsleben*, especially pp. 127–31. See also Stefan C. Reif, *Judaism and Hebrew Prayer*, Cambridge: Cambridge University Press 1993, pp. 53–87 for a reconstruction of early Jewish prayer in the period before the destruction of the Temple.

65. In the account of the descent of the Spirit given in the Gospel of John (1.32–34), the motif of the baptism has disappeared, as has the sounding of the voice of God.

66. I. Howard Marshall, *The Gospel of Luke,* NIGTC, Exeter: Paternoster Press 1978, p. 152.

67. Matt. 3.16; Mark 1.10; Luke 3.21 states simply 'when Jesus also had been baptised'.

68. Mark 1.8; Luke 3.16 and Matt. 3.11.

69. C. F. Evans, *Saint Luke*, London: SCM Press 1990, p. 247. Matt. 3.16 (καὶ ἰδοὺ ἠνεῴχθησαν οἱ οὐρανοί and Luke 3.21 (καὶ προσευχομένου ἀνεῳχθῆναι τὸν οὐρανὸν) refer to the 'opening of the heavens', while Mark 1.10 refers to their being 'torn apart' (καὶ εὐθὺς ἀναβαίνων ἐκ τοῦ ὕδατος εἶδεν σχιζομένους τοὺς οὐρανοὺς). Matthew and Luke both have *ep' auton* against Mark's *eis auton*, but Evans, *Saint Luke*, p. 245 contests the existence of a Q tradition here. For this apocalyptic motif, cf. Ezek. 1.1; 3 Macc. 6.18; John 1.51; Acts 7.56; 10.11; Rev. 19.11.

70. Joachim Jeremias, *New Testament Theology*, trans. John Bowden, London: SCM Press 1971, p. 52; see also L. E. Keck, 'The Spirit and the Dove', *New Testament Studies* 17, 1970–71, pp. 41–67.

71. It is also in accord with a Lucan tendency to 'objectivize the supernatural' (Evans, *Saint Luke*, p. 247).

72. This again may be the *baṭ qol*, or 'echo' of God's voice, which is characteristic of the end of the age of the prophets in rabbinic Judaism, but O. Betz takes the view that the *baṭ qol* is a later tradition (*Theological Dictionary of the New Testament*, X, ed. Gerhard Kittel, Grand Rapids, MI: Eerdmans 1964–, pp. 288–90, 298f.)

73. In Luke and Mark the syntax allows the alternative reading: 'You are my beloved Son . . .', which may be preferable (Marshall, *Luke*, p. 156 and John Nolland, *Luke 1–9.20*, Word Biblical Commentary 35A, Dallas, Texas: Word Books 1989, p. 164). The text also supports the sense 'You are my only Son . . .', a common construction in the Septuagint.

74. Ps. 2.7: 'I will tell of the decree of the Lord: He said to me, "You are my son; today I have begotten you."' (LXX: διαγγέλλων τὸ πρόσταγμα κυρίου, Κύριος εἶπεν πρός με υἱός μου εἶ σύ, ἐγὼ σήμερον γεγέννηκά σε). This clearly underlies the early variant reading for Luke 3.22: 'You are my Son, today I have begotten you'), which cannot however be preferred as it is attested in only one Greek manuscript 'and that an erratic one' (Marshall, *Luke*, p. 155).

75. 'Here is my servant, whom I uphold, my chosen, in whom my soul delights; I have put my spirit upon him' (cf. LXX Isa. 42.1, following the punctuation of the Rahlfs' edition: Ιακωβ ὁ παῖς μου, ἀντιλήμψομαι αὐτοῦ· Ισραηλ ὁ ἐκλεκτός μου, προσεδέξατο αὐτὸν ἡ ψυχή μου· ἔδωκα τὸ πνεῦμά μου ἐπ' αὐτόν, κρίσιν τοῖς ἔθνεσιν ἐξοίσει).

76. Isa. 42.1 differs from the baptism of Jesus however, in that the word *pais* ('servant') is used and not *huios* ('son'), and we do not find *eudokēsa* for 'delights in' (as in the three Synoptic accounts) but the weaker *prosedeksato* ('welcome' or 'accept'). The quotation of this same passage from Isaiah in Matt. 12.18 substitutes *eudokēsa* for *prosedeksato*, by assimilation perhaps to Matt. 3.17.

77. Gottlob Schrenk, εὐδοκέω, *Theological Dictionary of the New Testament*, II, p. 738.

78. *Theological Dictionary of the New Testament*, II, pp. 739–40.

79. The use of the aorist here may be 'equivalent to a Hebrew stative perfect, expressing God's continuing delight in his Son' (see Matthew Black, *An Aramaic Approach to the Gospels and Acts*, 3rd edn., Oxford: Oxford University Press 1967, pp. 128f.). For a more general discussion of the background to the baptism of Jesus, see A. Feuillet, 'Le Baptême de Jésus', *Revue Biblique* 71, 1964, pp. 321–51.

80. Ex. 24.16.

81. Marshall believes that Luke may have abandoned the OT type at this point, which is weak (Marshall, *Luke*, p. 382).

82. Ex. 34.29–35.

83. On the senses of the word exodus as 'departure' and 'death', as well as its resonances with the historical Exodus, see Marshall, *Luke*, pp. 384–5.

84. Matt. 17.5: ἔτι αὐτοῦ λαλοῦντος ἰδοὺ νεφέλη φωτεινὴ ἐπεσκίασεν αὐτούς, καὶ ἰδοὺ φωνὴ ἐκ τῆς νεφέλης λέγουσα, Οὗτός ἐστιν ὁ υἱός μου ὁ ἀγαπητός, ἐν ᾧ εὐδόκησα· ἀκούετε αὐτοῦ (as in the baptism, the meaning may be 'This is my beloved Son'); Mark 9.7: καὶ ἐγένετο νεφέλη ἐπισκιάζουσα αὐτοῖς, καὶ ἐγένετο φωνὴ ἐκ τῆς νεφέλης, Οὗτός ἐστιν ὁ υἱός μου ὁ ἀγαπητός, ἀκούετε αὐτοῦ; Luke 9.35: καὶ φωνὴ ἐγένετο ἐκ τῆς νεφέλης λέγουσα, Οὗτός ἐστιν ὁ υἱός μου ὁ ἐκλελεγμένος, αὐτοῦ ἀκούετε.

85. Ps. 106.23; 89.19–20; Isa. 42.1.

86. Deut. 18.15.

87. Catrin Williams makes the point that 'the true meaning of his messiahship cannot be understood in isolation from his suffering, death and resurrection' (Catrin H. Williams, 'Interpretations of the Identity and Role of Jesus', *The Biblical World*, ed. John Barton, London: Routledge 2002, forthcoming).

88. Mark 5.21–43; Luke 7.11–17.
89. John 11.4.
90. John 11.24–26.
91. But Jesus seems to treat his thanking of the Father as a petition when he says that he has only spoken for the sake of the people since he knows that the Father will always hear him.
92. On this theme, see below, pp. 262–6.
93. John 11.44; 20.5.
94. John 12.27–36.
95. John 12.27–28.
96. John 12.28–29.
97. Cf. Ex. 19.19; 19.16.
98. See also John 2.11; 11.4.
99. John 12.31–32.
100. LXX Isa. 52.13: ἰδοὺ συνήσει ὁ παῖς μου καὶ ὑψωθήσεται καὶ δοξασθήσεται σφόδρα. John Ashton attacks Bultmann's view that 'lifted up' is paradoxically the humiliation of the cross. But inevitably the crucifixion will come to mind, which is simultaneously the lowest point of Jesus' kenosis and descent and the highest point of his exaltation (John Ashton, *Understanding the Fourth Gospel*, Oxford: Clarendon Press 1991, pp. 495–6).
101. See also John 1.14; 2.11.
102. John 2.11. Cf. 11.4: 'This illness does not lead to death; rather it is for God's glory, so that the Son of God may be glorified through it'. But given the degree to which the Lazarus narrative, as the last of Jesus' signs on earth, anticipates the death and resurrection of Jesus himself, the word 'glorified' here may anticipate Jesus' own hour of glorification.
103. John 8.54; 7.18. Cf. 5.41; 8.50; 12.43.
104. But see John 17.1, 4, which are discussed below.
105. John 12.16; 7.39. Cf. also 12.23.
106. John 17.4.
107. John 12.30.
108. John 17.4. Cf. 'It is my Father who glorifies me' (8.54).
109. John 17.1.
110. John 14.13; 17.22.
111. John 13.31–32. I have followed G. B. Caird's translation of the second ἐδοξάσθη as the intransitive passive 'has revealed his glory' (see G. B. Caird, 'The Glory of God in the Fourth Gospel: An Exercise in Biblical Semantics', *New Testament Studies* 15, 1968–69, pp. 265–77).
112. William Lane, *The Gospel according to Mark*, New London Commentary on the New Testament, London: Marshall, Morgan & Scott 1974, pp. 515–21.
113. Luke simply refers to 'the disciples' (Luke 22.39, 45).
114. Mark 14.29; cf. 26.33; cf. Luke 22.33; Mark 14.31; Matt. 26.35.
115. Mark 10.35–40; cf. Matt. 20.20–23.
116. Luke omits Jesus' threefold interruption of his prayer.
117. Luke, which is milder on this point, contains the variant addition however, concerning the sweat of Christ, which 'became like great drops of blood falling on the ground' (Luke 22.44). See the discussion of this in Marshall, *Luke*, pp. 832–3.
118. Ps. 60.3; Isa. 51.17, 22. See *potērion* in TDNT. See also R. Le Déaut, 'Gouter le

calice de la mort', *Biblica* 43, 1962, pp. 82–6 and H. A. Brongers, 'Der Zornsbecher', *Oudtestamentische Studiën* 15, 1969, pp. 177–92.

119. Lane, *Mark*, p. 516.
120. Strack and Billerbeck, *Kommentar zum Neuen Testament aus Talmud und Midrash*, vol. I, Munich 1924, p. 1042.
121. Strack and Billerbeck, vol. II, p. 269.
122. For a discussion of the specific terminology of silence in the Old Testament *hārēš, ḥāšāh, damam*) see my 'Soundings: Towards a Theological Poetics of Silence', *Silence and the Word*, ed. Oliver Davies and Denys Turner, Cambridge: Cambridge University Press 2002, forthcoming.
123. Isa. 64.12. In Ps. 83.1 it is seen as a divine refusal to destroy the enemies of Israel.
124. Pss. 35.22; 28.1.
125. Ps. 115.17: 'The dead do not praise the Lord, nor do any that go down into silence'.
126. Job 34.14–15. Speech is linked with life and the holy spirit in Job at 27.3–4 and 33.3–4 (cf. Gen. 2.7).
127. Matthew may be drawing out this apocalyptic motif in his account of the earthquakes and rending of the Temple veil (27.51). I am grateful to Catrin Williams for this observation.
128. See below, pp. 267–9.
129. Here we are presenting an argument which approximates to that put forward by Jürgen Moltmann in *Der gekreuzigte Gott*, Munich: Ch. Kaiser Verlag 1972, pp. 222–36; Eberhard Jüngel, *God as the Mystery of the World*, trans. Darrell L. Guder, Edinburgh: T&T Clark 1983, pp. 368–74; and Paul Fiddes, *The Creative Suffering of God*, Oxford: Clarendon Press 1988, whereby non-being is assumed into the Trinity through the Passion of the Son and, in Fiddes' phrase, 'resurrection happens, overcoming death, *because* death has entered into the being of God' (p. 267). See the chapter on Christology below for a fuller account of this theology of silence (pp. 269–72).
130. John 7.39, although 3.34 and 6.63 speak of the spirit as an actual presence. This ambivalence may reflect the sense of the interim glory of the pre-resurrection Jesus which we have noted above.
131. John 16.7.
132. John 15.26.
133. John 14.26.
134. John 16.13–15.
135. John 14.17.
136. John 20.22.
137. Rom. 8.9, 6.
138. Rom. 8.9, 11.
139. Rom. 6.4.
140. Rom 8.13, 15.
141. The reference may also be to free charismatic prayer (cf. 1 Cor. 14.15). Barrett makes the point that the distinction between the Lord's Prayer and charismatic prayer may not have been as sharp in early Christianity as it appears today (C. K. Barrett, *The Epistle to the Romans*, London: A&C Black, 2nd edn. 1991, p. 153).
142. Rom. 8.26–27.

143. David Ford, *Self and Salvation*, Cambridge: Cambridge University Press 1999, pp. 120–2.

144. Acts 2.1–3. For the image of the wind, cf. Ezek. 37.9–14 and John 3.8. For the image of fire, cf. Ex. 3.2–12. Matthew and Luke both report the prophecy of John the Baptist that one will come who baptizes 'in the Holy Spirit and in fire' (Matt. 3.11; Luke 3.16).

145. Acts 2.4, 5–13.

146. 1 Cor 12.3–14.2 (here 12.10).

147. Joel 2.28. This parallels the way in which, according to Luke, Jesus preaches in the synagogue soon after the Spirit descended upon him at his baptism (Luke 4.16–30).

148. 1 Cor 12.3.

149. David Cunningham, *These Three Are One*: *The Practice of Trinitarian Theology*, Oxford: Blackwell 1998, p. 83.

150. In his *The Doctrine of Revelation: A Narrative Interpretation* (Edinburgh: Edinburgh University Press 1997), Gabriel Fackre places personal action at the centre of revelation. But such aspects of the incarnation should not be removed from their context within the personhood of Christ, since the notion of personhood in its fullness demands that actions be resolved into personal agency and be seen as a constitutive part of human identity, manifesting personality. To separate the actions of Christ from his personhood is to remove them from the sole context in which they can have personal meaning and be expressive of personal agency. Thus they are made free-floating fragments which we come to receive as saving 'items of information' through the divine illumination of faith in a cognitive process which lacks any personal and hence also any kenotic dimension.

151. Ward, *Religion and Revelation*, p. 195.

152. Paul Ricoeur, 'The "Sacred" Text and the Community', *Figuring the Sacred: Religion, Narrative and Imagination*, trans. David Pellauer, ed. Mark I. Wallace, Minneapolis: Augsburg Fortress 1995, pp. 68–72 (here p. 71).

153. At Luke 10.21–23, we are told that Jesus 'rejoiced in the Holy Spirit' before thanking the Father for having revealed to infants things hidden from the wise, continuing: 'All things have been handed over to me by my Father; and no one knows who the Son is except the Father, or who the Father is except the Son and anyone to whom the Son chooses to reveal him' (cf. Matt. 11.25–27).

Chapter 10

1. I am borrowing this term from an essay by Rowan Williams on 'deflected love' in St John of the Cross, where St John is showing that Christian love refuses the closure of a mutual, bipolar love through deflection to a third (R. D. Williams, 'St John of the Cross and the Trinity', *Silence and the Word: Negative Theology and Incarnation*, ed. O. Davies and D. Turner, Cambridge: Cambridge University Press 2002, forthcoming. The scholastic origins of the concept that the perfection of love requires a shared, triadic structure lie in the development of this theme by Richard of St Victor in Book Three of his *On the Trinity*.

2. Cf. Mark 8.27–30 and Luke 9.18–21.

3. Matt. 16.13–14. The Matthean text substitutes 'Son of Man', with its possible messianic connotations, for Mark's 'I' (Mark 8.27: 'Who do men say I am?'). The use of the pronoun is repeated by Luke at Luke 9.18.

4. Matthew adds Jeremiah to the list which we otherwise find in Mark and Luke, perhaps because Jeremiah had predicted the coming of the Messiah in his own experience of rejection and suffering (R. E. Brown, J. A. Fitzmyer and R. E. Murphy (eds), *The New Jerome Biblical Commentary*, London: Geoffrey Chapman 1989, p. 659).

5. Matt. 13.55.

6. Matt. 16.15.

7. Matt. 16.17. The phrase 'Son of the living God' embellishes and strengthens Mark's 'You are the Messiah' (Mark 8.29) and Luke's 'the Messiah of God' (Luke 9.20), in which Matthew may have discerned uncomfortable political connotations (*The New Jerome Biblical Commentary*, p. 659); Matt. 16.18.

8. Greek: καὶ μακαρία ἡ πιστεύσασα ὅτι ἔσται τελείωσις τοῖς λελαλημένοις αὐτῇ παρὰ κυρίου. *Exegetical Dictionary of the New Testament*, 2, 378, s.v. μακάριος.

9. The word *hoti* can be taken to mean either that Mary is blessed because what she believes will come true, or 'it may give the content of what she believed'. The latter is more likely (I. Howard Marshall, *The Gospel of Luke*, NIGTC, Exeter: Paternoster Press 1978, p. 82).

10. Matt. 16.18–20.

11. Matt. 16.21.

12. Matt. 16.25.

13. Matt. 16.22–23.

14. Joachim Jeremias, *New Testament Theology*, trans. John Bowden, London: SCM Press 1971, pp. 272–6.

15. Matt. 26.69–75.

16. John 1.3.

17. John 14.24.

18. John 3.34–36.

19. John 5.25–29; 12.48.

20. John 8.28; 14.10.

21. Heb. 7.23–24.

22. Heb. 7.27.

23. Heb. 9.24.

24. Heb. 5.9.

25. Rom. 5.18.

26. Divine Office, Easter, reading for Holy Saturday.

27. Matt. 25.40.

28. Matt. 25.40; 5.44–45.

29. John 8.58.

30. See above, pp. 35–6.

31. Rom. 8.19.

32. See below, pp. 246–9.

33. Here I am drawing on Denys Turner's important study of the semiotics of the Eucharist in his 'The Darkness of God and the Light of Christ: Negative Theology and Eucharistic Presence', *Modern Theology* 15.2, April 1999, pp. 143–58.

34. Turner, 'The Darkness of God and the Light of Christ', p. 157.

D. Introduction

1. For a discussion of Maximus' texts on this theme, see Lars Thunberg, *Microcosm and Mediator*, Chicago and La Salle, IL: Open Court 1995, pp. 72–9.
2. Thomas O'Loughlin, 'The Symbol Gives Life: Eucharius of Lyon's Formula for Exegesis', *Scriptural Interpretation in the Fathers: Letter and Spirit*, ed. T. Finan and V. Toomey, Dublin: Four Courts Press 1995, pp. 221–52.
3. See Klaus Scholder, *The Birth of Modern Critical Theology*, trans. John Bowden, London: SCM Press 1990.
4. The distinction between these two terms is significant. The Christian theologian, who already accepts the surplus of meaning in Christ, proceeds heuristically to develop the consequences of that meaning in terms of understandings which will always remain provisional in the light of the ultimate meaning of Christ. The natural scientist on the other hand is concerned with understandings as such, and where an explanatory model fails, another will be applied. For all the attractions of large-scale and 'canonized' models of explanation, there can, or should, be no appeal to an authoritative, though as yet undisclosed, source of understanding in the natural sciences.
5. Dietrich Ritschl, *The Logic of Theology*, trans. John Bowden, London: SCM Press 1986, pp. 112–13.
6. Ritschl, *The Logic of Theology*, pp. 111–12.
7. Edward Farley, in his *Divine Empathy* (Minneapolis: Fortress Press 1996, pp. 300–15), understands the 'efficacious empathy' in Jesus Christ to be 'the expression of divine creativity'.
8. See Chapter One, n. 46.

Chapter 11

1. Seneca, *De clementia*, II, 3, 1.
2. The term *misericordia* is a special case. It has been widely used in Christian tradition for 'mercy' or 'kindness', as well as 'compassion'. It is a word that occurs frequently in the Vulgate where it is used both in the sense of actions (*misericordiam facere*) and feelings.
3. Plato, *Republic* 607a (*Plato the Republic*, trans. Paul Shorey, vol. 2, Loeb, London: Heinemann 1935, p. 465).
4. Socrates, *Apol.* 34c.
5. Aristotle, *Poetics*, c.6, 1449b (*Poetics*, trans. James Hutton, London and New York: Norton 1982, p. 50).
6. *Poetics*, c.14, 1454a (Hutton, p. 59).
7. Aristotle, *On Rhetoric*, II, c.8, 1385b (*On Rhetoric*, trans. George A. Kennedy, Oxford: Oxford University Press 1991, p. 152).
8. *On Rhetoric*, II, c.8, 1386a (Kennedy, p. 154). Intense fear, or dread, for ourselves drives out pity however (1385b).
9. Although good people are most pitiable (*On Rhetoric*, II, c.8, 1386b).
10. Martha Nussbaum, 'Compassion: The Basic Social Emotion', *Social Philosophy and Policy* 13.1, Winter 1996, pp. 27–58 (here p. 40).
11. Seneca, *De clementia*, II, 3, 1 and I, 5, 2.
12. *De clementia*, II, 4, 4: 'Et haec vitium animae est'.
13. *De clementia*, II, 5, 1: 'est enim vitium pusilli animi'.

14. *De clementia*, II, 5, 1.
15. Johannes Quasten, *Patrology*, II, Utrecht–Antwerp: Spectrum 1975, pp. 393–410.
16. In his book *The Library of Lactantius* (Oxford: Clarendon Press 1978, p. 73) R. M. Ogilvie points out it is by no means clear that Lactantius knew Seneca's *De clementia*. But it is evident that it is the Stoic dismissal of compassion as 'a disease of the soul' that is Lactantius' target at this point (*L. Caeli Firmiani Lactanti Opera Omnia*, CSEL 19, p. 534).
17. Lactantius, *Divinae Institutiones*, VI, 10; *Opera Omnia*, 19, p. 514.
18. *Divinae Institutiones*, VI, 10; *Opera Omnia*, 19, p. 514.
19. *Divinae Institutiones*, VI, 11; *Opera Omnia*, p. 518.
20. *Divinae Institutiones*, VI, 11; *Opera Omnia*, p. 519.
21. *Divine Institutions*, VI, 11; *Opera Omnia*, p. 521.
22. *Divinae Institutiones*, VI, 10; *Opera Omnia*, p. 515: 'deus enim quoniam pius est, animal nos voluit esse sociale: itaque in aliis hominibus nos ipsos cogitare debemus'.
23. Adam Smith, *The Theory of Moral Sentiments*, VI, iii, 11 (*The Theory of Moral Sentiments*, ed. D. D. Raphael and A. L. Macfie, Oxford: Clarendon Press 1976, p. 241).
24. Smith, *The Theory of Moral Sentiments*, I, i, I, 1 (Raphael and Macfie, p. 9).
25. Smith, *The Theory of Moral Sentiments*, I, i, I, 2 (Raphael and Macfie, p. 9).
26. Smith, *The Theory of Moral Sentiments*, I, i, I, 2 (Raphael and Macfie, p. 9).
27. Smith, *The Theory of Moral Sentiments*, I, i, I, 2 (Raphael and Macfie, p. 9).
28. Smith, *The Theory of Moral Sentiments*, I, i, I, 3 (Raphael and Macfie, p. 10).
29. Smith, *The Theory of Moral Sentiments*, I, i, I, 6 (Raphael and Macfie, p. 11).
30. Smith, *The Theory of Moral Sentiments*, I, i, I, 5 (Raphael and Macfie, p. 10).
31. Smith, *The Theory of Moral Sentiments*, I, i, 3, 1–10 (Raphael and Macfie, pp. 16–19).
32. Jean-Jacques Rousseau, *Emile or On Education*, trans. Allan Bloom, Harmondsworth: Penguin 1991, p. 221.
33. Rousseau, *Emile*, p. 221.
34. Rousseau, *Emile*, p. 222.
35. Rousseau, *Emile*, p. 223.
36. Immanuel Kant, *Die Metaphysik der Sitten*, 2 Teil, *Ethische Elementarlehre*, ch. 34; *Werke*, hg. Benzion Kellermann, Bd VII, Hildesheim: Verlag Dr H. A. Gerstenberg 1973, p. 270.
37. Kant, *Die Metaphysik der Sitten*, ch. 34; Kellermann, Bd VII, p. 270.
38. Kant, *Die Metaphysik der Sitten*, ch. 34; Kellermann, Bd VII, p. 271.
39. Kant, *Die Metaphysik der Sitten*, ch. 34; Kellermann, Bd VII, p. 271.
40. Arthur Schopenhauer, *Grundlage der Moral*, § 22; *Sämtliche Werke*, III, Munich: Piper 1912, pp. 737–8.
41. Schopenhauer, *Grundlage*, § 16; *Sämtliche Werke*, III, pp. 678–9.
42. Schopenhauer, *Grundlage*, § 16; *Sämtliche Werke*, III, pp. 678–9.
43. Schopenhauer, *Grundlage*, § 16; *Sämtliche Werke*, III, p. 679.
44. William Kluback, *The Legacy of Hermann Cohen*, Atlanta, GA: Scholars Press 1989, p. 111.
45. Friedrich Nietzsche, *Der Antichrist*, § 7.
46. Friedrich Nietzsche, *Ecce Homo*, Warum ich so weise bin, § 4.
47. Nietzsche, *Der Antichrist*, § 7.
48. Nietzsche, *Der Antichrist*, § 7.

49. Nietzsche, *Der Antichrist*, § 7.
50. Nussbaum, 'Compassion', pp. 27–58. I am indebted to this work for the basic structure of the overview of historical debate on compassion which I have used here.
51. Nussbaum, 'Compassion', p. 28.
52. Nussbaum, 'Compassion', pp. 45–8.
53. Nussbaum, 'Compassion', pp. 49–50.
54. Ex. 3.6.
55. Ex. 3.13.
56. Ex. 3.14.
57. Ex. 33.19.
58. See the following chapter, pp. 262–9.
59. For a valuable overview of the philological issues surrounding this text, and possible meanings which range from 'I am that I am', to 'I shall be who I shall be' and 'I am He who is' (de Vaux's preferred option), see Roland de Vaux, 'The Revelation of the Divine Name YHWH' in John I. Durham and J. R. Porter, eds., *Proclamation and Presence*, London: SCM Press 1970, pp. 48–75.
60. Brevard S. Childs, *Exodus: A Commentary*, Old Testament Library, London: SCM Press 1974, p. 76.
61. Ontological discussion in patristic exegesis is generally confined to apocalyptic and typological texts, with the exception of Origen, who sought to build on the 'I am' a cosmic and participatory cosmology. See Marguerite Harl, 'Citations et commentaires d'Exode 3, 14 chez les Pères grecs des quatre premiers siècles', *Dieu et l'Être: Exégèses d'Exode 3, 14 et de Coran 20, 11–24*, Paris: Études Augustiniennes 1978, pp. 87–108. In the West it was primarily the commentaries on Ex. 3.14 by Augustine, which are scattered throughout his work, which proved the decisive influence.
62. See Charles Touati, 'Ehye ašer ehye (*Exode* 3, 14) comme "l'Être-avec"', *Dieu et l'Être*, pp. 75–84 and Georges Vajda, 'Bref aperçu sur l'exégèse d'Exode 3, 14 dans la littérature rabbinique et en théologie juive du Moyen Age', *Dieu et l'Être*, pp. 67–74.
63. Robert Hayward, *Divine Name and Presence: the Memra*, Totowa, NJ: Allanheld, Osmun 1981, p. 6 (original italics).
64. Hayward, *Divine Name and Presence*, pp. 6–10.
65. Robert Hayward points to the extensive use of the *Memra* in Targum Neofiti's paraphrase of Genesis, where the associations between the *Memra* and creation are clearly established (p. 5).
66. *Targum Neofiti I: Exodus*, translated, with Introduction and Apparatus by Martin McNamara, The Aramaic Bible 2, Edinburgh: T&T Clark 1994, p. 19 (translation slightly adapted).
67. Hayward, *Divine Name and Presence*, pp. 9–10.
68. Hayward, *Divine Name and Presence*, p. 19.
69. Hayward, *Divine Name and Presence*, pp. 51–2.
70. *Midrash Rabbah III*, trans. S. M. Lehrman, London: Soncino 1961, p. 64.
71. E.g. 2 Chron. 30.9; Neh. 9.17, 31; Pss. 103.8; 111.4; 145.8; Joel 2.13; Jonah 4.2.
72. They who fear the Lord are themselves 'gracious, merciful and righteous' (Ps. 112.4).
73. Cf. Esth. 5.2.
74. 1 Kings 8.50; Ps. 103.13; Isa. 49.15.
75. Hos. 14.3; Isa. 54.8.

76. H.-J. Zobel, *Ḥesed, Theological Dictionary of the Old Testament* 5, ed. G. J. Botterweek and H. Ringgren, trans. J. T. Willis, Grand Rapids, MI: Eerdmans 1974, pp. 44–64 (here p. 51).

77. Gen. 20.13; 24.49; 47.29; 1 Sam. 20.8, 14.

78. For a thorough discussion of these two terms, which form the basis of the following, see M. Tsevat, *Ḥāmal, Theological Dictionary of the Old Testament* 4, pp. 470–2 and S. Wagner, *Ḥūs, Theological Dictionary of the Old Testament* 4, pp. 271–7.

79. Cf. Zech. 11.6: 'For I will no longer have pity on the inhabitants of the earth, says the Lord'. It is also used in a positive sense however: Pharoah's daughter takes pity (*ḥāmal*) on the baby Moses (Ex. 2.6).

80. E.g. Ps. 72.13, where its meaning is soteriological: 'He has pity on the weak and the needy, and saves the lives of the needy'.

81. On these two words, see Helmut Köster, Σπλάγχνον κτλ, *Theological Dictionary of the New Testament*, VII, ed. Gerhard Kittel, Grand Rapids, MI: Eerdmans 1964–, pp. 548–59.

82. H. G. Liddell and R. Scott, *A Greek–English Lexicon*, rev. edn., Oxford: Clarendon Press 1996, p. 1628, sv.

83. Prov. 26.22; 2 Macc. 6.8. Cf. Prov. 12.10: 'The righteous know the needs of their animals, but the mercy of the wicked is cruel' (LXX: δίκαιος οἰκτίρει ψυχὰς κτηνῶν αὐτοῦ τὰ δὲ σπλάγχνα τῶν ἀσεβῶν ἀνελεήμονα; MT: יוֹדֵעַ צַדִּיק נֶפֶשׁ בְּהֶמְתּוֹ וְרַחֲמֵי רְשָׁעִים אַכְזָרִי).

84. E.g. 4 Macc. 14.13 (cf. 15.29): 'Observe how complex is a mother's love for her children, which draws everything toward an emotion felt in her inmost parts (σπλάγχνα)'. Cf. also Wis. 10.5.

85. For a discussion of the content and background to the *Testaments of the Twelve Patriarchs*, see James H. Charlesworth, *The Old Testament Pseudepigrapha*, London: Darton, Longman & Todd 1983, I, pp. 775–81.

86. M. de Jonge, *The Testaments of the Twelve Patriarchs*, 2nd edn., Assen: Van Gorcum 1975, pp. 121–8. For an overview of the vexed questions concerning the dating of this text, and the original language of its composition, see H. W. Hollander and M. de Jonge, *The Testaments of the Twelve Patriarchs: A Commentary*, Leiden: E. J. Brill 1985, pp. 1–29.

87. *Test. Zebulun* 2.4; 5.3, 4.

88. *Test. Zebulun* 7.3; 8.2, 6.

89. *Test. Zebulun* 8.2 (Charlesworth, p. 807).

90. *Test. Naphtali* 4.5. H. C. Kee's translation actually has 'mercy' at this point, but the meaning is clearly 'compassion' (Charlesworth, p. 812). Cf. *Test. Levi* 4.4: 'Blessing shall be given to you and to all your posterity until through his son's compassion the Lord shall visit all the nations forever' (Charlesworth, p. 789).

91. *Test. Zebulun* 5.1; cf. 8.1 (Charlesworth, p. 806).

92. *Test. Benjamin* 4.1 (Charlesworth, p. 826).

93. The parable of the unforgiving servant (Matt. 18.23–35), the good Samaritan (Luke 25–37) and the prodigal son (Luke 15.11–32).

94. Matt. 18.34: ὀργισθεὶς ὁ κύριος.

95. Mark 9.22.

96. Mark 9.23.

97. Mark 1.41; Luke 7.11–17; Matt. 20.29–34. The alternative reading of the Marcan passage is 'Jesus grew angry'. If this is a later emendation, then it shows part of

a tradition to describe Jesus increasingly in messianic terms (*Theological Dictionary of the New Testament*, VII, p. 554).

98. Matt. 9.36; 14.14; 15.32; Mark 6.34; 8.2.
99. Luke 1.78: διὰ σπλάγχνα ἐλέους θεοῦ ἡμῶν, ἐν οἷς ἐπισκέψεται ἡμᾶς ἀνατολὴ ἐξ ὕψους.
100. Ps. 112.4: זָרַח בַּחֹשֶׁךְ אוֹר לַיְשָׁרִים חַנּוּן וְרַחוּם וְצַדִּיק The NRSV again has 'merciful' here.
101. Deut. 14.29.
102. Deut. 16.11, 14; 26.12–13.
103. Job 22.9.
104. Ex. 22.21–24, 27.
105. Zech. 7.8–14.
106. See note 99 above.
107. For the classical Greeks, the seat of the feelings however was not the σπλάγχνα but rather the heart and lungs (R. B. Onians, *The Origins of European Thought*, Cambridge: Cambridge University Press 1951, pp. 32–5).
108. Wis. 10.5: αὕτη καὶ ἐν ὁμονοίᾳ πονηρίας ἐθνῶν συγχυθέντων ἔγνω τὸν δίκαιον καὶ ἐτήρησεν αὐτὸν ἄμεμπτον θεῷ καὶ ἐπὶ τέκνου σπλάγχνοις ἰσχυρὸν ἐφύλαξεν.
109. 2 Cor. 6.12: οὐ στενοχωρεῖσθε ἐν ἡμῖν, στενοχωρεῖσθε δὲ ἐν τοῖς σπλάγχνοις ὑμῶν.
110. 2 Cor. 7.15.
111. Philemon 7: χαρὰν γὰρ πολλὴν ἔσχον καὶ παράκλησιν ἐπὶ τῇ ἀγάπῃ σου, ὅτι τὰ σπλάγχνα τῶν ἁγίων ἀναπέπαυται διὰ σοῦ, ἀδελφέ.
112. Philemon 20.
113. Philemon 12.
114. Phil. 1.8.
115. Phil. 1.1.
116. Phil. 2.1–2: Εἴ τις οὖν παράκλησις ἐν Χριστῷ, εἴ τι παραμύθιον ἀγάπης, εἴ τις κοιν-ωνία πνεύματος, εἴ τις σπλάγχνα καὶ οἰκτιρμοί, 2.2 πληρώσατέ μου τὴν χαρὰν ἵνα τὸ αὐτὸ φρονῆτε, τὴν αὐτὴν ἀγάπην ἔχοντες, σύμψυχοι, τὸ ἓν φρονοῦντες.
117. See the contrast between εὔσπλαγχνοι and συμπαθεῖς at 1 Pet. 3.8 discussed below.
118. Col. 3.12.
119. 1 John 3.17. See also Eph. 4.32: 'and be kind to one another, tenderhearted (εὔσπλαγχνοι), forgiving one another, as God in Christ has forgiven you', and 1 Pet. 3.8: 'Finally, all of you, have unity of spirit, sympathy, love for one another, a tender heart (εὔσπλαγχνοι), and a humble mind'.
120. Luke 1.78: 'the tender mercy of our God' (NRSV).
121. James 5.11: ἰδοὺ μακαρίζομεν τοὺς ὑπομείναντας· τὴν ὑπομονὴν Ἰὼβ ἠκούσατε καὶ τὸ τέλος κυρίου εἴδετε, ὅτι πολύσπλαγχνός ἐστιν ὁ κύριος καὶ οἰκτίρμων. This translates the Hebrew phrase חַנּוּן וְרַחוּם,: though differently from the LXX.
122. Pseudo-Dionysius, *The Divine Names*, 588C, 589B and 592B (ed. and trans. Colm Luibheid, *Pseudo-Dionysius: The Complete Works*, New York: Paulist Press 1987, pp. 50–2); Aquinas, ST I, q. 13, a. 3. See also the remarks on the priority of the name 'He Who Is' at ST I, q. 13, a. 11, and the discussion on the function of metaphor in communicating 'spiritual truths' to 'the simple, who are unable by themselves to grasp intellectual things' at ST, q. 1, a. 9.
123. ST I, q. 13, a. 3.
124. *The Divine Names*, 680B and 680D (Luibheid, *Pseudo-Dionysius*, p. 68).
125. ST I, q. 13, a. 3.
126. Janet Martin Soskice, *Metaphor and Religious Language*, Oxford: Oxford University Press 1985, p. 140.

127. Denys Turner, *The Darkness of God*, Cambridge: Cambridge University Press 1995, especially pp. 19–49.

128. *The Divine Names*, 593C (Luibheid, *Pseudo-Dionysius*, p. 54), *The Mystical Theology*, 1033C (Luibheid, *Pseudo-Dionysius*, p. 139); Aquinas, ST I, q. 13, a. 1 and 2.

129. E.g. Jürgen Moltmann, *The Trinity and the Kingdom of God*, trans. Margaret Kohl, London: SCM Press 1981, pp. 21–5. See the discussion of these critiques in Janet Martin Soskice, 'The Gift of the Name: Moses and the Burning Bush', *Gregorianum* 79.2, 1998, pp. 231–46.

130. Sallie McFague, *Models of God*, Philadelphia: Fortress Press 1988, pp. 63–9.

131. Augustine, *Soliloquia*, II, 1 ('May I know myself, may I know you').

132. See above, pp. 155–7.

Chapter 12

1. Gen. 1.3.

2. Rublev himself was born around the year 1360, and died in 1430. It is impossible to date the icon of the Trinity precisely, but it evidently belongs to the last quarter of his life. An early tradition records that it was commissioned by Nikon to celebrate the memory of Sergii Radonezhskii, who had died in 1391 or 1392 (V. N. Lazarev, *Andrei Rublev i ego Shkola*, Moscow: Izdatelstvo Iskusstvo 1966, pp. 33–6 and N. A. Demina, 'Troitsa Andreya Rubleva', *Andrei Rublev i Khudozhniki ego Kruga*, Moscow: Izdatelstvo Nauka 1972, pp. 45–81 [originally published Moscow: Izdatelstvo Iskusstvo 1963]). Sergii was a mediatory figure who played a crucial role in the reconciliation and unification of the Moscow princes against the Tartar threat, at a time when the freedom and even existence of Russia was under immediate threat. Such was his influence at this critical time that he was soon honoured as a saint after his death. He had been Nikon's teacher at the monastery of the Trinity which he himself had founded near Radonezh, and Nikon succeeded him as igumen there. It is possible that Nikon commissioned the Trinity icon from Rublev at the same time that the foundations for the new Cathedral, also dedicated to the Trinity, were laid in the year 1422 (Demina, 'Troitsa', p. 47; Lazarev, *Andrei Rublev*, pp. 35–6). For a useful survey of the Old Russian sources for Rublev's life, including contemporary manuscript collections from Moscow and hagiographical material, see also V. D. Kuzmina, 'Drevnorusskie pismennye istochniki ob Andree Rubleva', *Andrei Rublev i ego Epokha*, ed. M. V. Alpatov, Moscow: Izdatelstvo Iskusstvo 1971, pp. 103–24.

3. Gen. 18.1–15.

4. Lazarev, *Andrei Rublev*, pp. 35–6.

5. Demina, 'Troitsa', pp. 63–4.

6. M. V. Alpatov, 'O Znachenii "Troitsy" Rubleva', *Etyudy po istorii russkogo iskusstva*, vol. I., Moskva: Izdatelstvo Iskusstvo 1967, pp. 119–26 (here p. 122).

7. Demina, 'Troitsa', pp. 55–6.

8. 'K istolkovaniyu kompozitsi "Troitsy"', *Seminarium Kondakovianum* 1928, p. 30 (quoted in Alpatov, 'O Znachenii', p. 120).

9. D. Ainalov, *Geschichte der russischen Monumentalkunst zur Zeit des Grossfürstentums Moskau*, Berlin and Leipzig 1933, p. 94 (quoted in Alpatov, 'O Znachenii', p. 120).

10. Lazarev points out that in all the Cappadocian frescoes of the Trinity, the central figure is Christ and that fifteenth-century copies of Rublev's icon place a halo solely around the head of the central angel, who is therefore to be understood as Christ. Lazarev believes that a cross in the halo around Rublev's Christ has been obliterated, and he holds that the 'zyrianskoi' icon is archaic and is an exception (Lazarev, *Andrei Rublev*, p. 61). Demina on the other hand finds the contemporary parallel of the 'zyrianskoi' icon to be conclusive (Demina, 'Troitsa', pp. 62–3). A few years previously A. Wenger had argued that the central figure is God the Father but that Christ is the figure to the observer's *right* ('Bulletin de spiritualité et de théologie byzantines', *Revue des Etudes Byzantines* 13, 1955, pp. 183–4 quoted in Lazarev, *Andrei Rublev*, p. 61.

11. Alpatov, 'O Znachenii', p. 120. With respect to the *laticlavium* in the garment of the central angel, Alpatov points out that we cannot tell whether the other angels lack this feature. Against Lazarev's view that a cross has been obliterated from the halo around the central angel's head, he points out that such speculation is 'fruitless' (p. 121).

12. Alpatov, 'O Znachenii', p. 121.

13. Alpatov, 'O Znachenii', p. 121.

14. Gen. 18.1–2.

15. Gilles Deleuze, 'Immanence. A Life…', *Theory, Culture and Society* 14.2, May 1997, pp. 3–7.

16. This is not the dialectic of the One and the Many of platonic tradition, however, where the subordination of the latter to the former dictates an account of the genesis of the Many from the One which naturally tends towards the narrative structures of an account of causality as origination or emanation, as *proodos* and *epistrophê*. In the Christian Trinity, there can be no such prioritization of one term with respect to the other: the Threeness and the Oneness are co-posited, and are equal.

17. In the anathema attached to the Creed pronounced at Nicaea, the two terms were still equivalents, in the sense that *mia hypostasis* was as acceptable as *mia ousia* (cf. Athanasius, *Tom. ad Ant.* 6 and *Ep. ad Afr.* 4). Only at the Synod of Alexandria (362) were the terms officially separated in their application. The formula *mia ousia – treis hypostaseis* belongs to the Council of Constantinople (381). It represented the triumph of Cappadocian theology, which sought throughout to maintain the ontological weight of the determinations of the Three against terms such as *prosôpon*. On the history of the formula, see Basil Studer, *Trinity and Incarnation*, trans. Matthias Westerhoff, ed. Andrew Louth, Edinburgh: T&T Clark 1993, pp. 139–46. For the history of *ousia* and *hypostasis* as philosophical terms, see the bibliography in *Handbuch theologischer Grundbegriffe*, II, ed. Heinrich Fries, Munich: Kösel Verlag 1963, sv. Substanz.

18. Karl Rahner, *The Trinity*, trans. J. Donceel, Tunbridge Wells: Burns & Oates 1970, pp. 31–3; Lacugna takes a different view (Catherine Mowbray Lacugna, *God for Us*, New York: HarperCollins 1973, pp. 221–4).

19. For a feminist critique of the traditional language of the Trinity, see Jane Williams, 'The Fatherhood of God', *The Forgotten Trinity*, London: BCC/CCBI 1991, pp. 91–101.

20. Although Zizioulas is right to stress the value of grounding the being of God not in the *ousia* but in the person of the Father, there may be some echo of the pre-existence of the Father in his monarchical view of the Father within the

Trinity (John D. Zizioulas, *Being as Communion*, New York: St Vladimir's
Seminary Press 1985, pp. 41, 88–9). See also Miroslav Volf's critique of this in
his *After Our Likeness: The Church as the Image of the Trinity*, Grand Rapids, MI:
Eerdmans 1998, pp. 76–81.

21. Studer, *Trinity and Incarnation*, p. 152: '[a]ll dogmatic statements remain
essentially negative. They do not intend to penetrate the mystery itself; they
rather determine the framework within which the mystery, as proclaimed in
the apostolic tradition, may be safeguarded.'

22. It is important in this respect always to remember the extent to which Christian
apophasis functions at a performative level of language use, specifically linked
with the language of liturgy.

23. See note 18 above.

24. Colin E. Gunton, *The Promise of Trinitarian Theology*, Edinburgh: T&T Clark
1991, pp. 43–8 and Lacugna, *God for Us*, pp. 81–104.

25. Also, as David Cunningham has argued, the setting up of such genealogies of
error (or what he calls 'historical scapegoating'), whether associated with
Augustinianism or Thomism or any other school, often fail to take account of
the rhetorical contexts of their original articulation and of the performative
nature of the language that we use about the Trinity in general (David
S. Cunningham, *These Three Are One: The Practice of Trinitarian Theology*, Oxford:
Blackwell 1998, pp. 31–5).

26. Paul Fiddes also presents a strong argument for participation rather than
description in his recent *Participating in God: A Pastoral Doctrine of the Trinity*,
London: Darton, Longman & Todd 2000.

27. Paul Evdokimov, *L'art de l'icône*, Paris: Desclée de Brouwer 1972, p. 208.

28. Mikhail Bakhtin *1961 god zametki*, *Sobranie Sochinenii*, vol. 5, Moscow: Russkie
Slovari 1996, p. 333).

29. John 16.13–14.

30. Gal. 4.4–7; Rom. 8.26.

31. *The Problem of Speech Genres*, in *Mikhail Bakhtin: Speech Genres and Other Late
Essays*, ed. Caryl Emerson and Michael Holquist, Austin: University of Texas
Press 1986, pp. 60–102 (here pp. 95–9).

32. Rowan Williams, 'Barth and the Triune God', *Karl Barth: Studies of
His Theological Method*, ed. Stephen Sykes, Oxford: Clarendon Press 1979,
pp. 147–93 (here p. 186).

33. This distinction is not always clearly maintained. In his *These Three Are One*,
David Cunningham states 'God is not (first) three independent entities who
(then) decide to come into relation with one another; God is, rather, "relation
without remainder"' (pp. 165–6), but he also makes use of the language of
'indwelling' (begging the question who is indwelling who?). Miroslav Volf, on
the other hand, specifically uses the language of indwelling in order to
preserve the distinctness of the self in the interests of a Free Church
ecclesiology (*After Our Likeness*, pp. 181–9).

34. In his *The Call to Personhood: A Christian Theory of the Individual in Social
Relationships*, Cambridge: Cambridge University Press 1990, Alistair
McFadyen presents a view of the self which 'is both dialogical (formed through
social interaction, through address and response) and dialectical (never
coming to rest in a final unity, if only because one is never removed from
relation)' (p. 9) and concludes: 'Conceiving of persons in this dialogical and

dialectical way makes it impossible to think of us as having a clearly defined "centre" or "foundation"' (p. 10).

35. See above, pp. 130–1.
36. I think this is implicitly Paul Fiddes' own position since, while arguing for divine Persons as dynamic and subsistent relations, he acknowledges the starting point for the human appropriation of those relations within the empirical self (pp. 62–112).
37. Gen. 1.3–26.
38. Gen. 1.3–20.
39. Gen. 1.22.
40. Gen. 1.28–29.
41. Gen. 1.29.
42. For much that follows, I am obliged to the article on *rūaḥ* in the *Theologisches Wörterbuch zum Alten Testament* VII, Stuttgart: Kohlhammer 1993, cols. 386–425.
43. D. Lys, 'Rûach: Le souffle dans l'Ancien Testament', *Études d'Histoire et de Philosophie Religieuses* 56, 1962, p. 19. Opinion is divided on whether the motif of spaciality preceded that of breathing, or came after it.
44. Ps. 103.15–16; Ex. 14.21; 10.19.
45. Isa. 66.15; Job 4.16; 1 Kings 19.11–12.
46. Isa. 27.8; Jer. 13.24.
47. Hos. 13.15.
48. Gen. 2.7; cf. Ezek. 37:1–14, where there is again an interplay between *rūaḥ* as 'spirit' and 'wind'.
49. A. R. Johnson, *The Vitality of the Individual in the Thought of Ancient Israel*, 2nd edn., Cardiff: University of Wales Press 1964, p. 36.
50. Eccl. (Koh.) 12.7.
51. Johnson, *The Vitality of the Individual*, pp. 23–37.
52. Judges 13.25; 14.6; 6.34; 11.29; 3.10.
53. 1 Sam. 10.6; 16.13.
54. Neh. 9.20, 30.
55. Deut. 18.15–22.
56. Isa. 1.16–17.
57. Cf. Pss. 147.18; 148.8.
58. Isa. 11.2.
59. Isa. 42.1–4.
60. The phrase *dabar b*e is used for instance at Num. 12.2, 2 Sam. 23.2 and 1 Kings 22.28.
61. E.g., Ex. 33.11. See also Num. 12.6–8, where Moses speaking with God 'face to face' is contrasted with the prophets.
62. Cf. John 14.7.
63. Rom. 8.34.

Chapter 13

1. Matt. 18.20.
2. Cf. 1 Cor. 12.27 and Rom. 12.4.
3. 1 Cor. 12.13.
4. *Lumen Gentium*, §8.

5. Richard Schechner, *Performance Theory*, rev. edn., London: Routledge 1988, p. 30.

6. Luke 1.38.

7. *Lumen Gentium*, §53.

8. John 2.1–11.

9. *Lumen Gentium*, §69.

10. General Instruction for the Roman Missal, xxix.

11. *Marienlexikon*, II, St Ottilien: EOS Verlag 1989, p. 553.

12. *Third General Conference of Latin American Bishops: Puebla*. Slough: St Paul Publications and London: CIIR 1980, 2.3 (§ 281). See also Bertrand de Margerie SJ, 'Mary in Latin American Liberation Theologies', *Kecharitômenê: Mélanges René Laurentin*, Paris: Desclée 1990, pp. 365–76.

13. Virgil Elizondo, 'Mary and the Poor: A Model of Evangelising Ecumenism', *Concilium* 168, 1983, pp. 59–65 (here p. 63).

14. Elizondo, 'Mary and the Poor', p. 64. See also her 'Our Lady of Guadalupe as a Cultural Symbol: "The Power of the Powerless"', *Concilium* 102, 1977, pp. 25–33.

15. Elizabeth A. Johnson, 'Mary in Praxis-Oriented Theology', *Kecharitômenê: Mélanges René Laurentin*, pp. 467–82 (here p. 478).

16. Quoted in Johnson, 'Mary in Praxis-Oriented Theology', p. 479.

17. *Lumen Gentium*, §23.

18. *Lumen Gentium*, §§28, 26, 27.

19. *Lumen Gentium*, §23.

20. *Lumen Gentium*, §12.

21. For Gavin d'Costa, it is the 'fruitful tension' between 'those two most important Christian axioms: that salvation comes through God in Christ alone, and that God's salvific will is truly universal' which grounds the kind of open inclusivism of which he is a passionate advocate (Gavin d'Costa, *Theology and Religious Pluralism*, Oxford: Blackwell 1986, p. 136).

22. For a penetrating critique of John Hick, see d'Costa, *Theology and Religious Pluralism*, pp. 29–46.

23. Jacques Dupuis, *Toward a Christian Theology of Religious Pluralism*, Maryknoll, NY: Orbis 1997, p. 14.

24. Dupuis, *Toward a Christian Theology of Religious Pluralism*, pp. 80–121, offers an overview of the different comparative strategies employed in the theology of religions. W. Cantwell Smith advocates a compound theology but acknowledges his own indebtedness in this to a language which expresses a distinctly Christian conceptualization (W. Cantwell Smith, *Towards a World Theology*, London: Macmillan 1981).

25. David Lockhead, *The Dialogical Imperative: A Christian Reflection on Interfaith Encounter*, London: SCM Press 1988, p. 4.

26. Lockhead, *The Dialogical Imperative*, pp. 96–7.

Afterword

1. Peter Ochs, *Peirce, Pragmatism and the Logic of Scripture*, Cambridge: Cambridge University Press 1998, p. 290.

Index of Names

Index of Subjects